Year of the Rabbit

Tian Veasna

Translation by Helge Dascher

Drawn & Quarterly

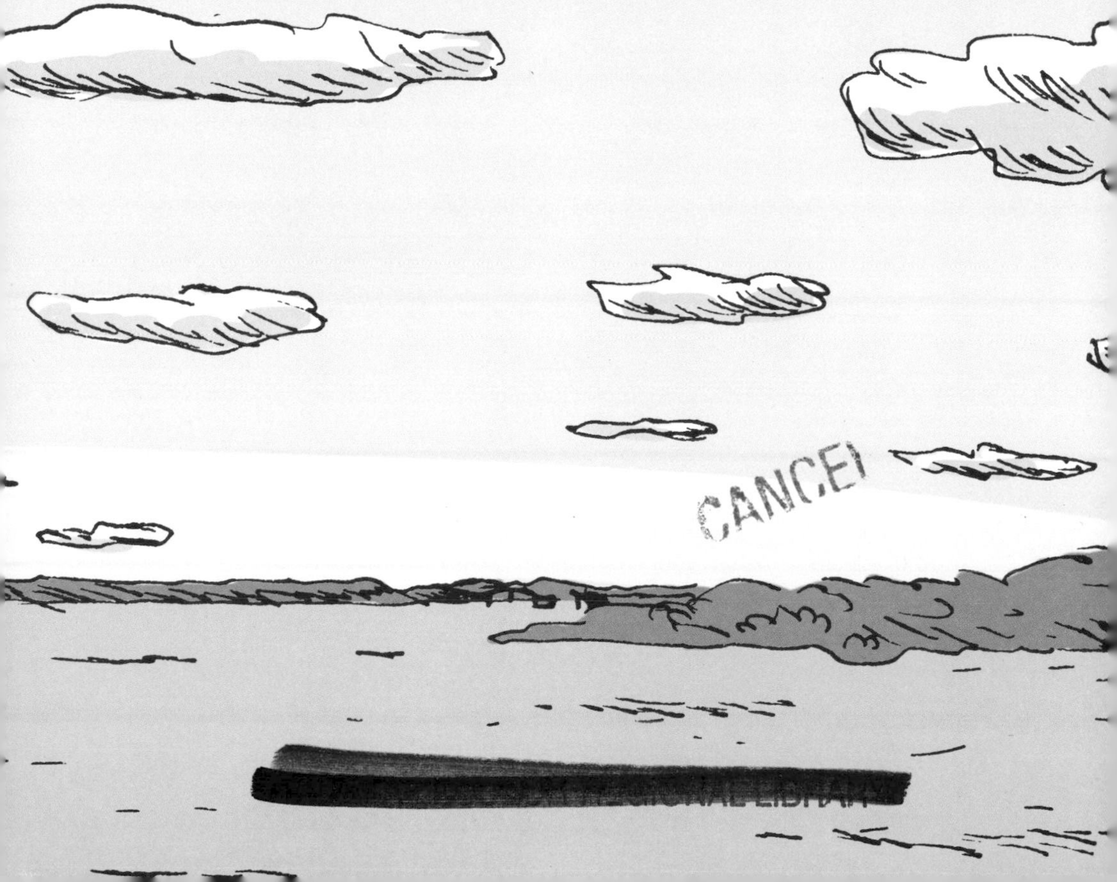

Originally published in French by Gallimard as *L'Année du Lièvre* (2011, 2013, 2016).

drawnandquarterly.com

978-1-77046-376-9 | First edition: January 2020 | Printed in China | 10 9 8 7 6 5 4 3 2 1

Cataloguing data available from Library and Archives Canada

Published in the USA by Drawn & Quarterly, a client publisher of Farrar, Straus and Giroux
Published in Canada by Drawn & Quarterly, a client publisher of Raincoast Books
Published in the United Kingdom by Drawn & Quarterly, a client publisher of Publishers Group UK

Drawn & Quarterly acknowledges the support of the Government of Canada and the Canada Council for the Arts for our publishing program, and the National Translation Program for Book Publishing, an initiative of the Roadmap for Canada's Official Languages 2013–2019: Education, Immigration, Communities, for our translation activities.

Drawn & Quarterly reconnaît l'aide financière du gouvernement du Québec par l'entremise de la Société de développement des entreprises culturelles (SODEC) pour nos activités d'édition. Gouvernement du Québec—Programme de crédit d'impôt pour l'édition de livres—Gestion SODEC.

Cet ouvrage a bénéficié du soutien des Programmes d'aide à la publication de l'Institut français.

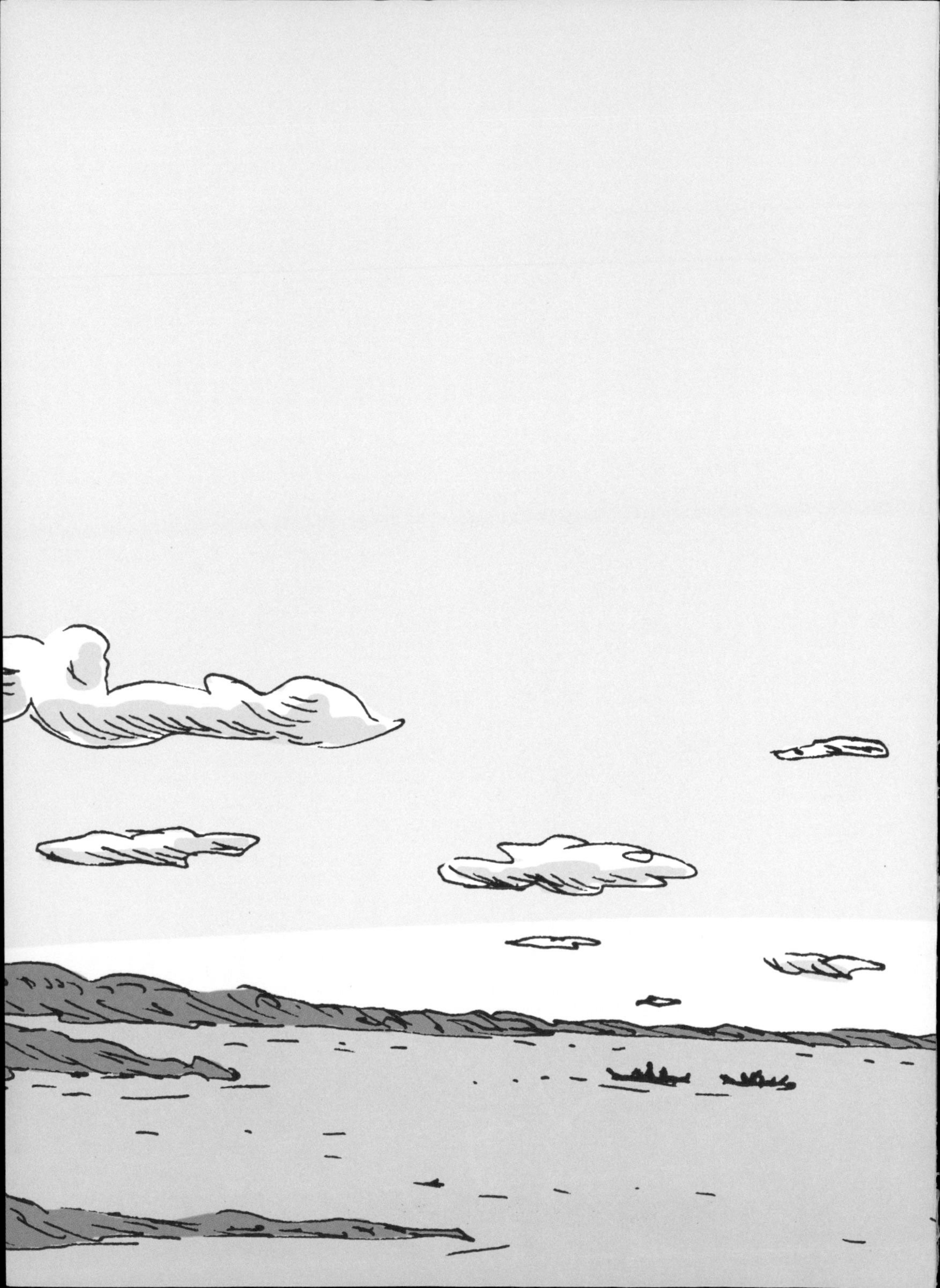

To my parents, my brother, and my family.
To Jean, who would have been happy to see this book.

Thanks to Lewis Trondheim and Thierry Laroche for their advice,
to Delphine Perret, Lucie Albon, and Geneviève Villard for
their support, and to Rithy Panh.

Tian

Preface
By Rithy Panh

It is the mark of a talented artist to be able to give the illusion of simplicity to an account of the unthinkable. This story is so painful that for years, survivors were unable to tell it to their children. The experience of chaos eats away at our insides and leaves us helpless, torn between wanting to live again and the fear of not having the strength. It's like standing in front of a bridge that lies in ruins and looking at the other riverbank, where our souls might find peace and ease...

Conceived by radical ideologues and implemented by zealous leaders, the murderous utopia of the Khmer Rouge regime could only be achieved through the unleashing of a reign of terror, one that isolated individuals and destroyed every vestige of traditional society. Family ties, solidarity, respect, faith, compassion... All moral foundations were annihilated, just as the people who believed in them were exterminated. It was not only a matter of killing, but of erasing us and denying our dignity. How can one understand what those black-clad men inflicted on others?

But humans are not easily eradicated, and that is their strength. In Tian's description of his family's desperate escape, disaster is repeatedly averted through minor miracles. Like the Khmer Rouge chief who lets the young doctor get away, the old peasant who intervenes to save the family from execution, and the villager who offers his hut so the young woman can give birth. As long as humans resist, it seems as if nothing truly irreparable could happen, even when everything is collapsing and fear is destroying society. But how long can a person hold out against the spread of a totalitarian terror that only gradually reveals its true face? Where can a person find refuge when every door is locked? Who can be trusted when every movement is watched? When divulging a name can result in death?

I first encountered Tian's work in *The Year of the Rabbit*. His talent speaks for itself. I noted the documentary precision—the maps, definitions, proverbs, and slogans. I admired the tight structure of the narrative, the fluid drawing, the movement, the various perspectives, the abundance and accuracy of the details—like so many points of reference mapped in our memories. It is these points of reference that connect us to our dead.

More than anything, though, I was moved. His book touched me to the core because it is accurate, because it is true, because it is essential. Many readers will find in it the strength to get through their long nights of grief... Their impossible mourning.

Rithy Panh is a filmmaker.
His works include the influential
S21: The Khmer Rouge Killing Machine
and *The Missing Picture*

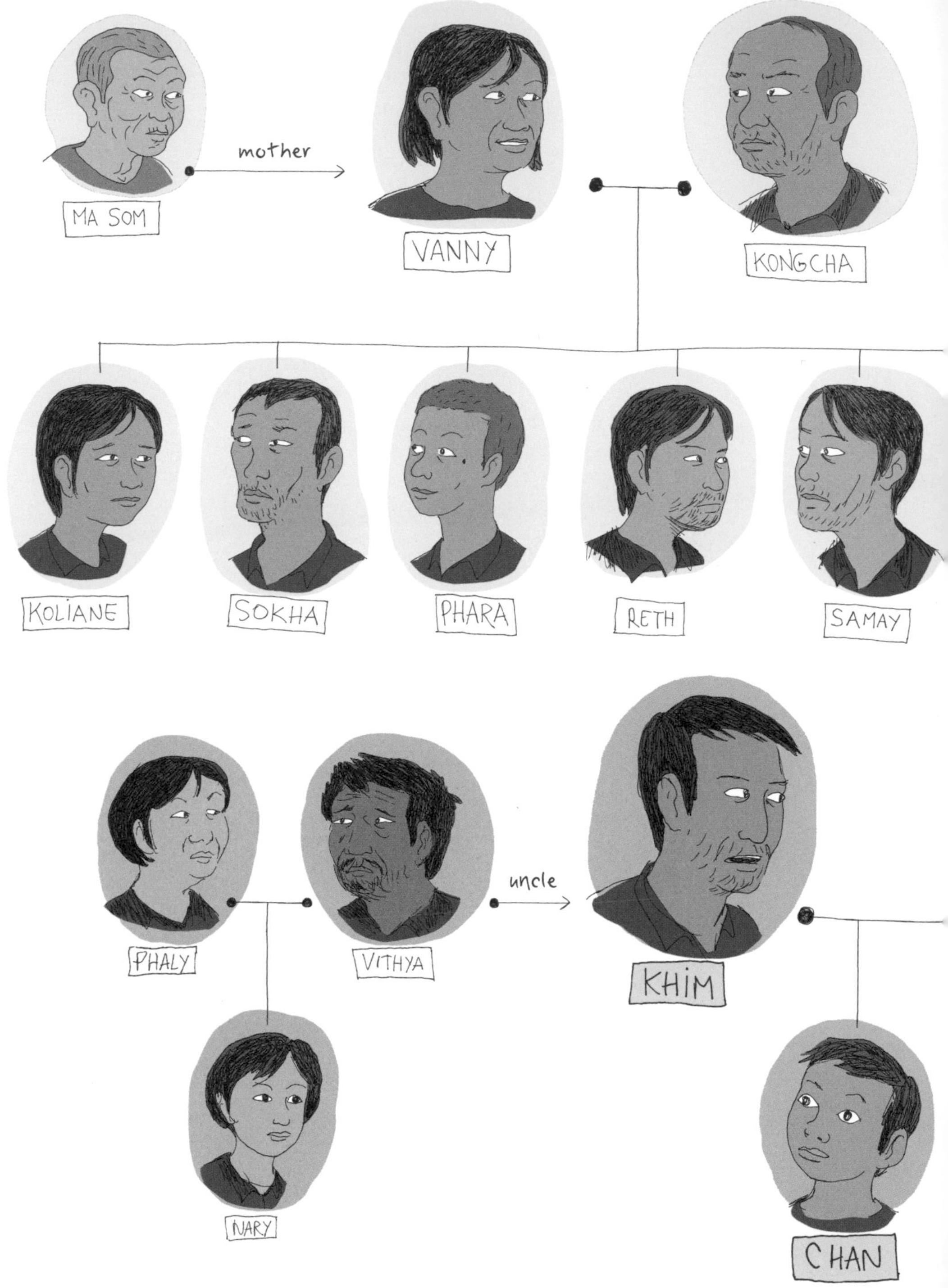
MA SOM
mother
VANNY
KONGCHA
KOLiANE
SOKHA
PHARA
RETH
SAMAY
PHALY
VITHYA
uncle
KHiM
NARY
CHAN

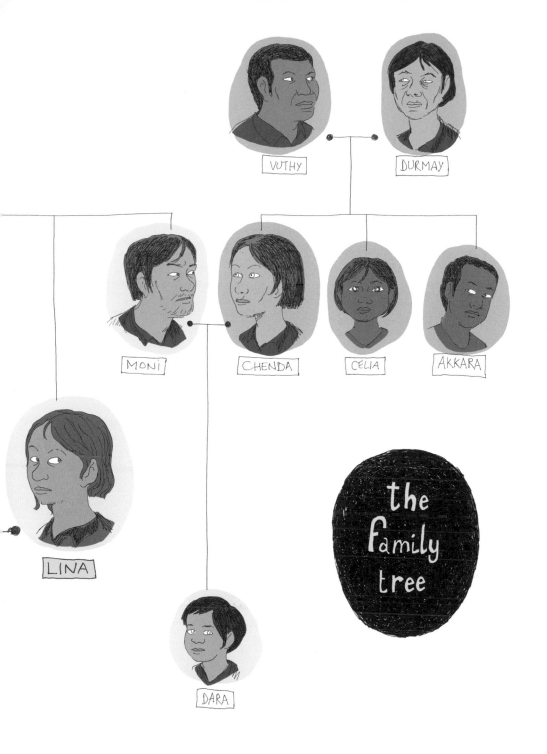

Crows will fill the sky. The towns and houses will be emptied of people [...] Blood will flow as high as the elephant's chest. The alienated and the ignorant will seize power and enslave the learned. It will be a time without religion, without Buddhism. The thmil [atheist barbarians] will have absolute power and will persecute the believers [...]. Only the deaf and mute will survive.

Put Tumneay
Eighteenth-century prophecy

part one

GOODBYE, PHNOM PENH

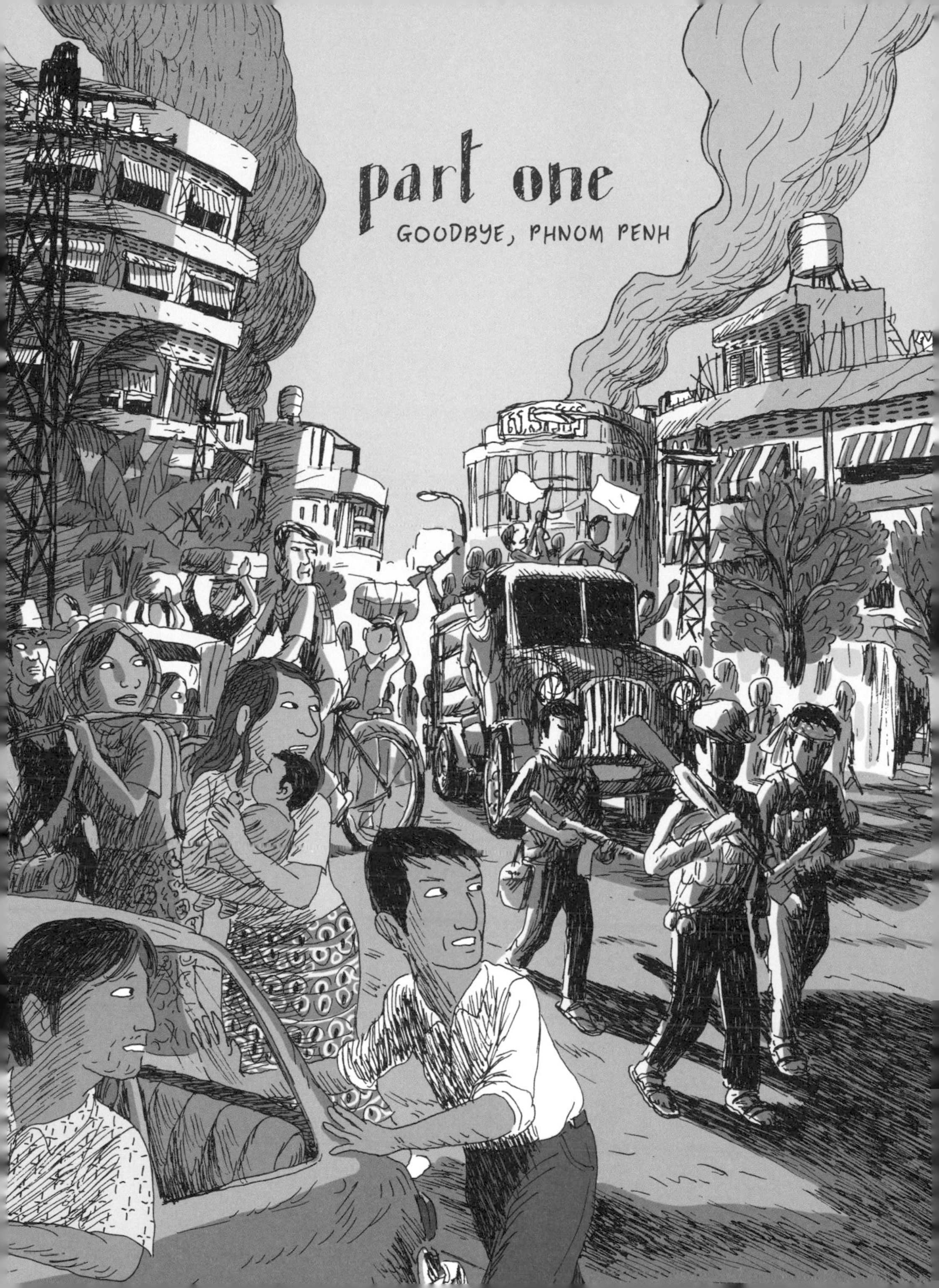

chapter 1

GLORIOUS APRIL 17, 1975!

China
China
Hanoi
Mekong
Gulf
of
Tonkin
Vientiane
Thailand
Laos
South
China
Sea
Bangkok
Cambodia
Battambang
Mekong
Phnom Penh
Vietnam
Gulf
of
Thailand
Capital
Border
0 50 100 km
River

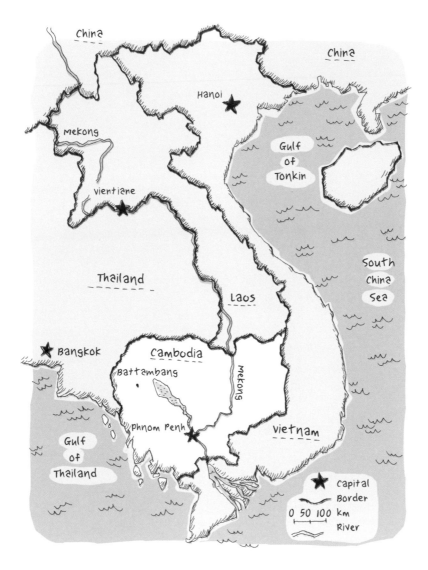

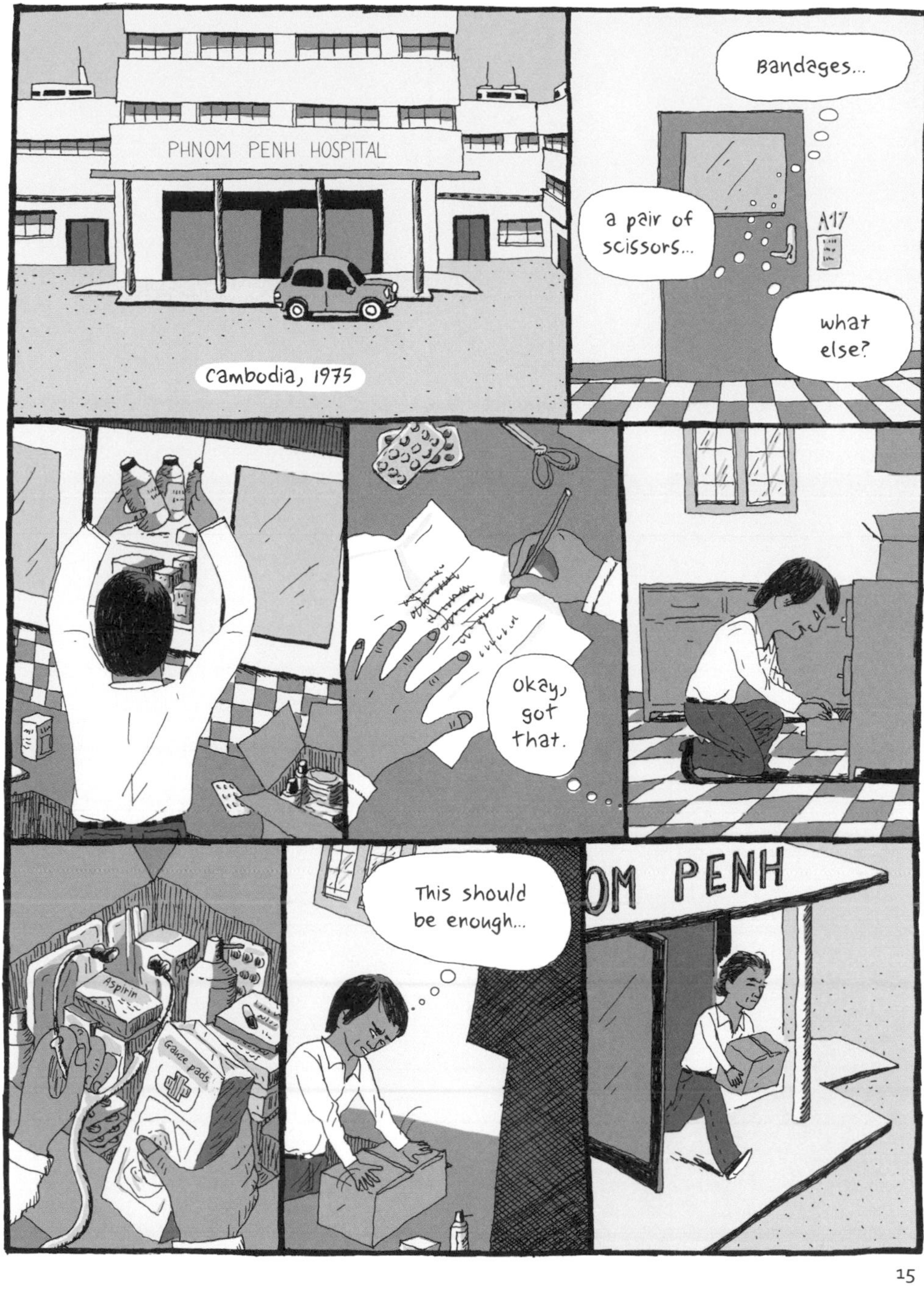
PHNOM PENH HOSPITAL
Cambodia, 1975
Bandages...
a pair of scissors...
A17
what else?
Okay, got that.
Aspirin
Gauze pads
This should be enough...
OM PENH

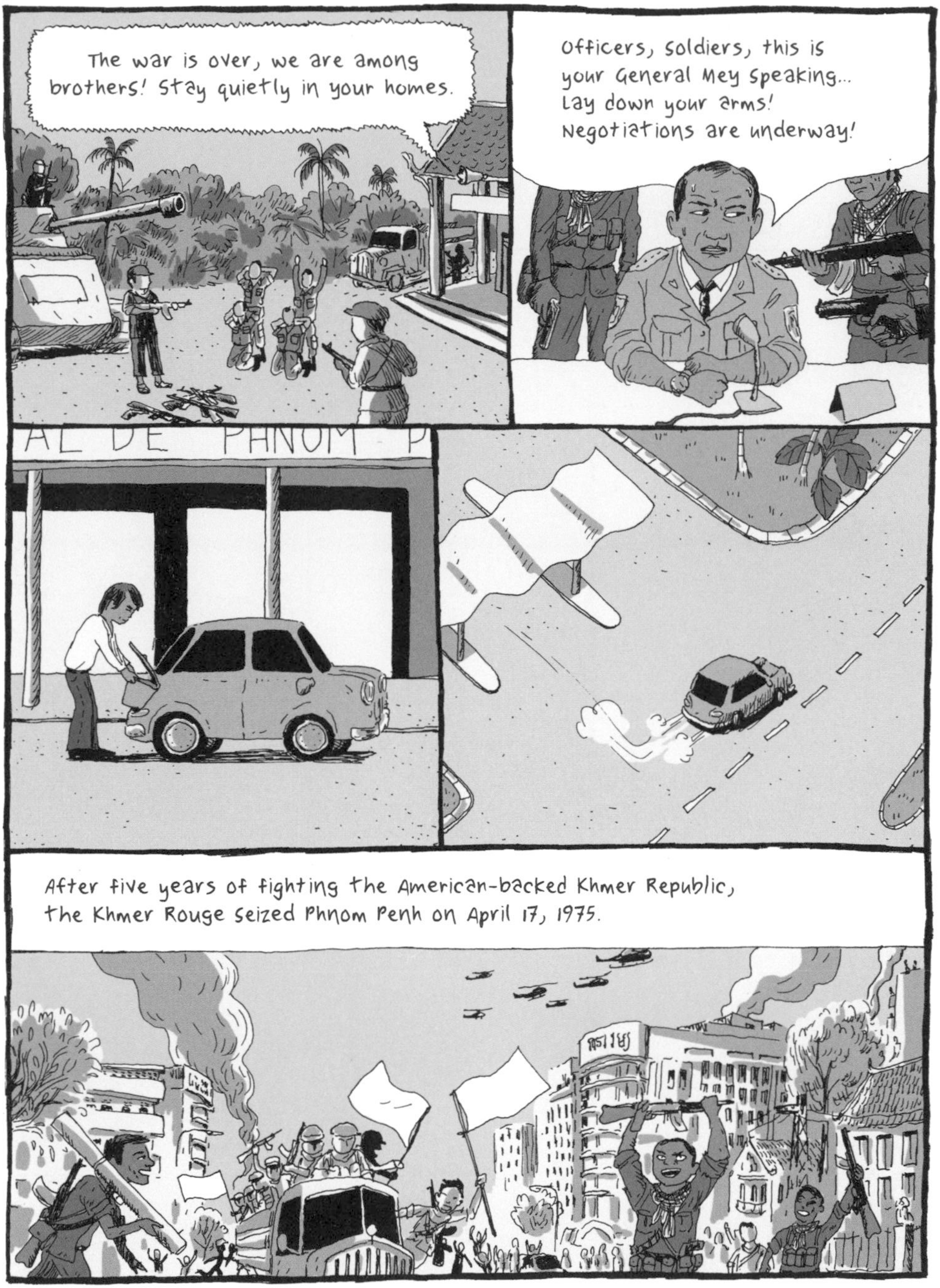
The war is over, we are among brothers! Stay quietly in your homes.
Officers, soldiers, this is your General Mey speaking... Lay down your arms! Negotiations are underway!
AL DE PHNOM P
After five years of fighting the American-backed Khmer Republic, the Khmer Rouge seized Phnom Penh on April 17, 1975.

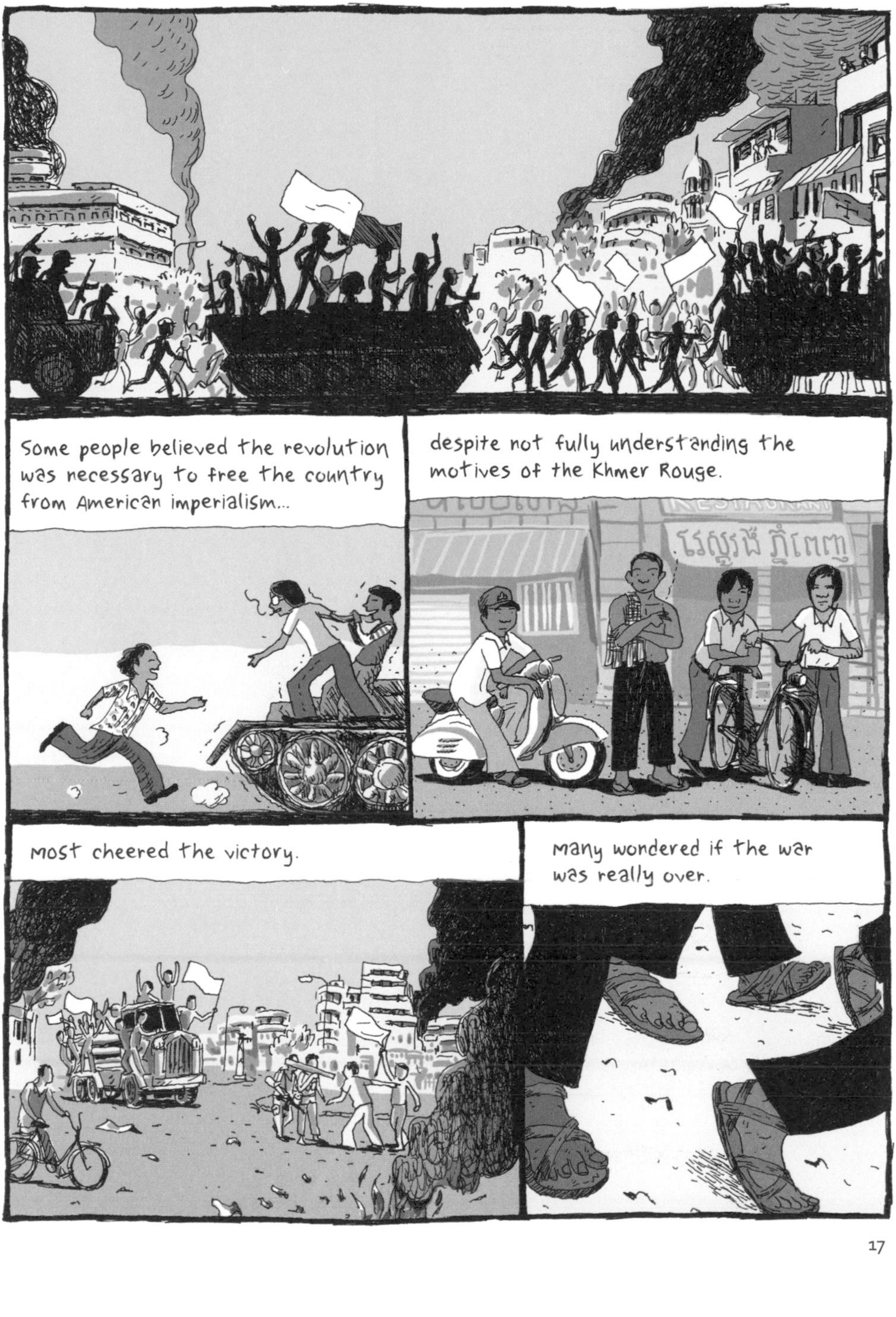
Some people believed the revolution was necessary to free the country from American imperialism...
despite not fully understanding the motives of the Khmer Rouge.
Most cheered the victory.
Many wondered if the war was really over.

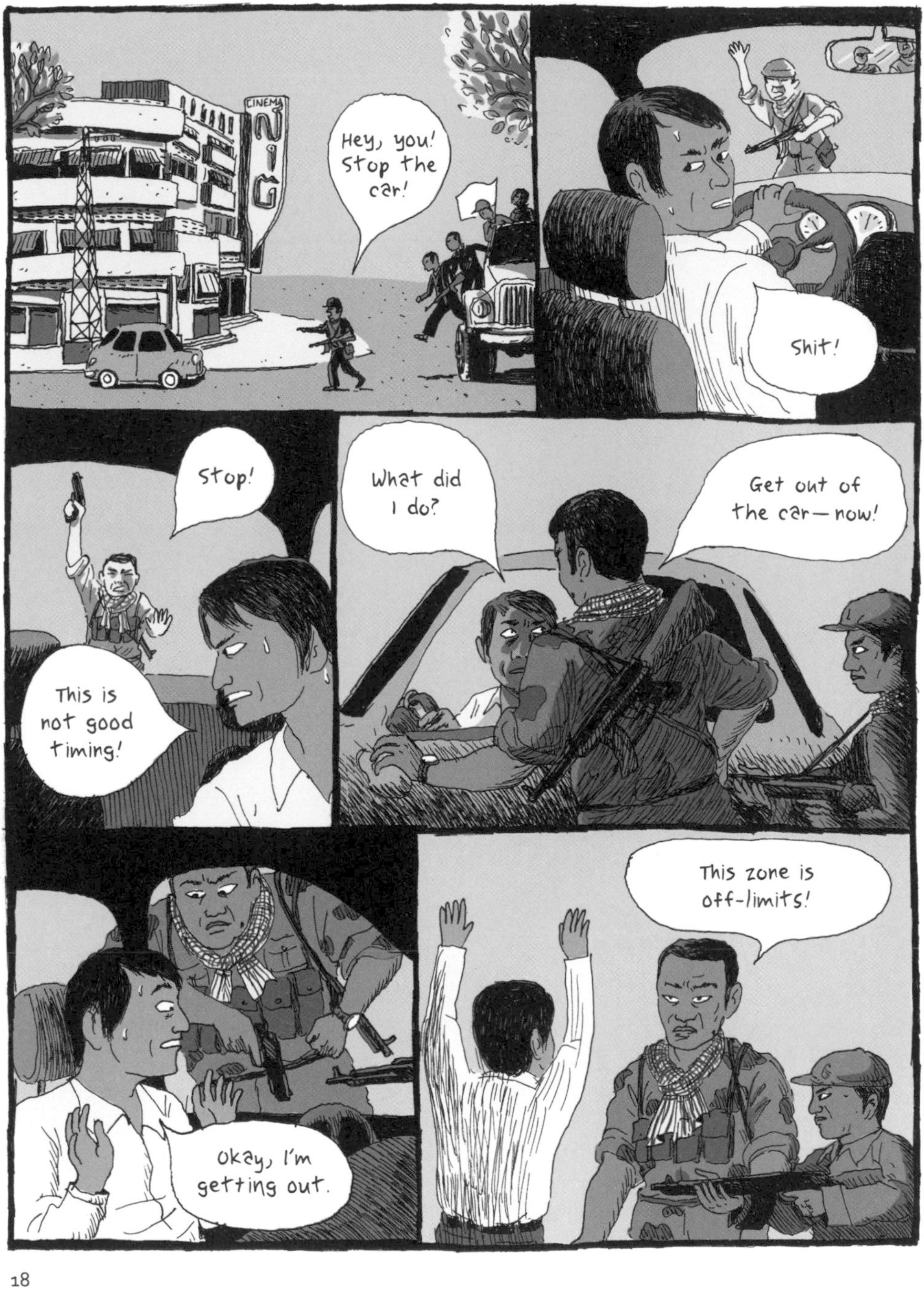
CINEMA
Hey, you! Stop the car!
Shit!
Stop!
This is not good timing!
What did I do?
Get out of the car—now!
Okay, I'm getting out.
This zone is off-limits!

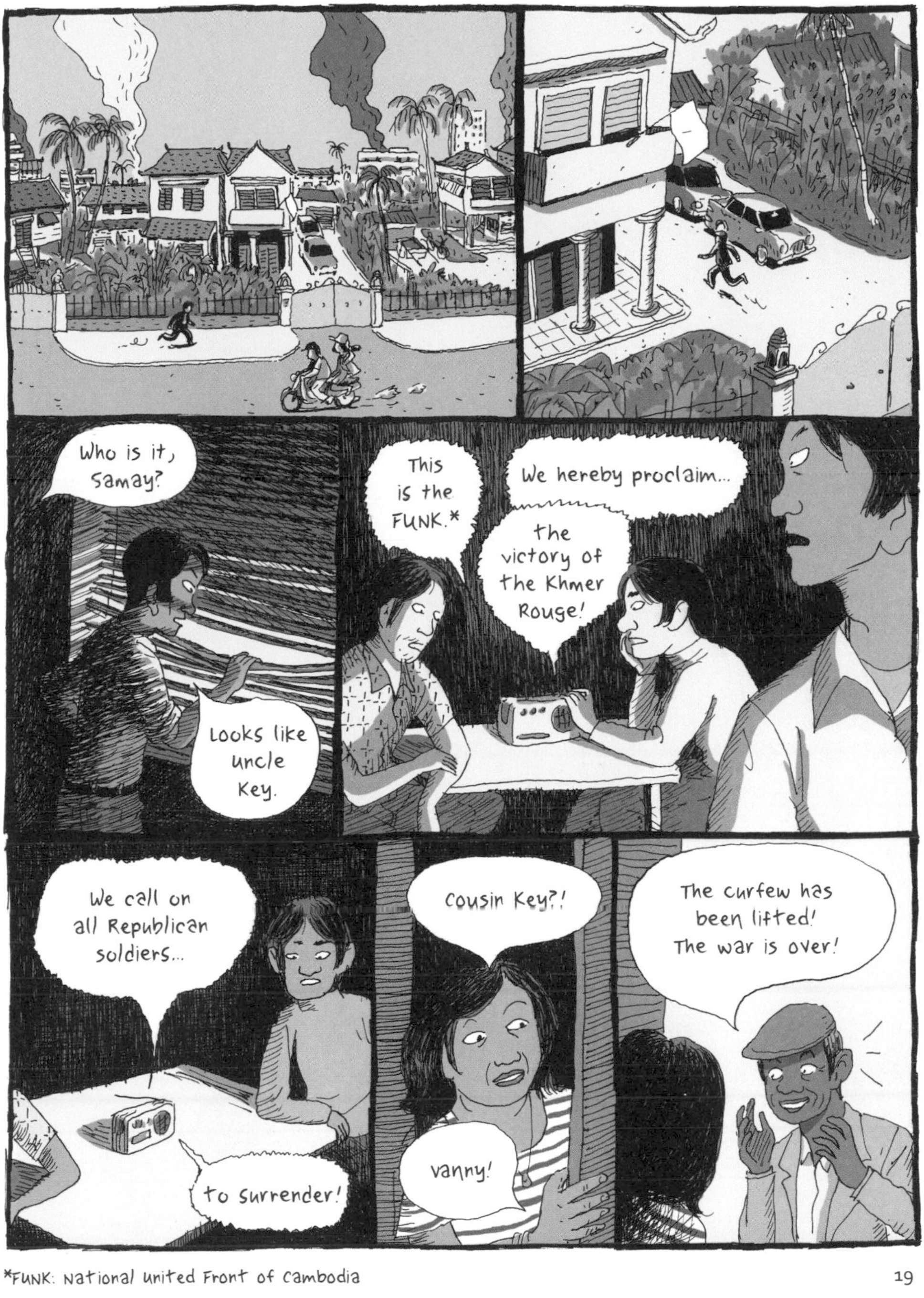
Who is it, Samay?
Looks like uncle Key.
This is the FUNK.*
We hereby proclaim...
the victory of the Khmer Rouge!
We call on all Republican soldiers...
to surrender!
Cousin Key?!
Vanny!
The curfew has been lifted! The war is over!

*FUNK: National United Front of Cambodia

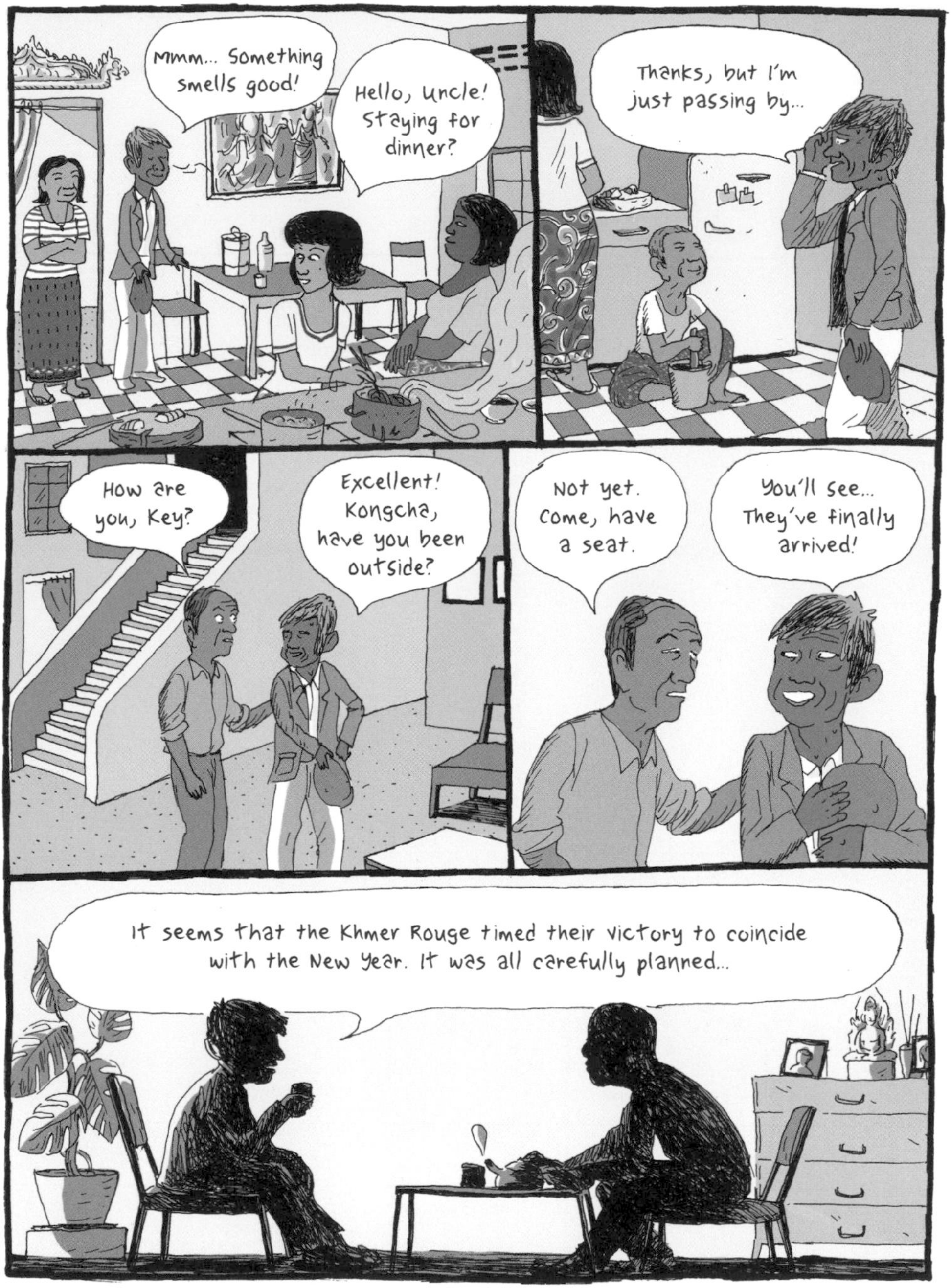
Mmm... Something smells good!
Hello, Uncle! Staying for dinner?
Thanks, but I'm just passing by...
How are you, Key?
Excellent! Kongcha, have you been outside?
Not yet. Come, have a seat.
You'll see... They've finally arrived!
It seems that the Khmer Rouge timed their victory to coincide with the New Year. It was all carefully planned...

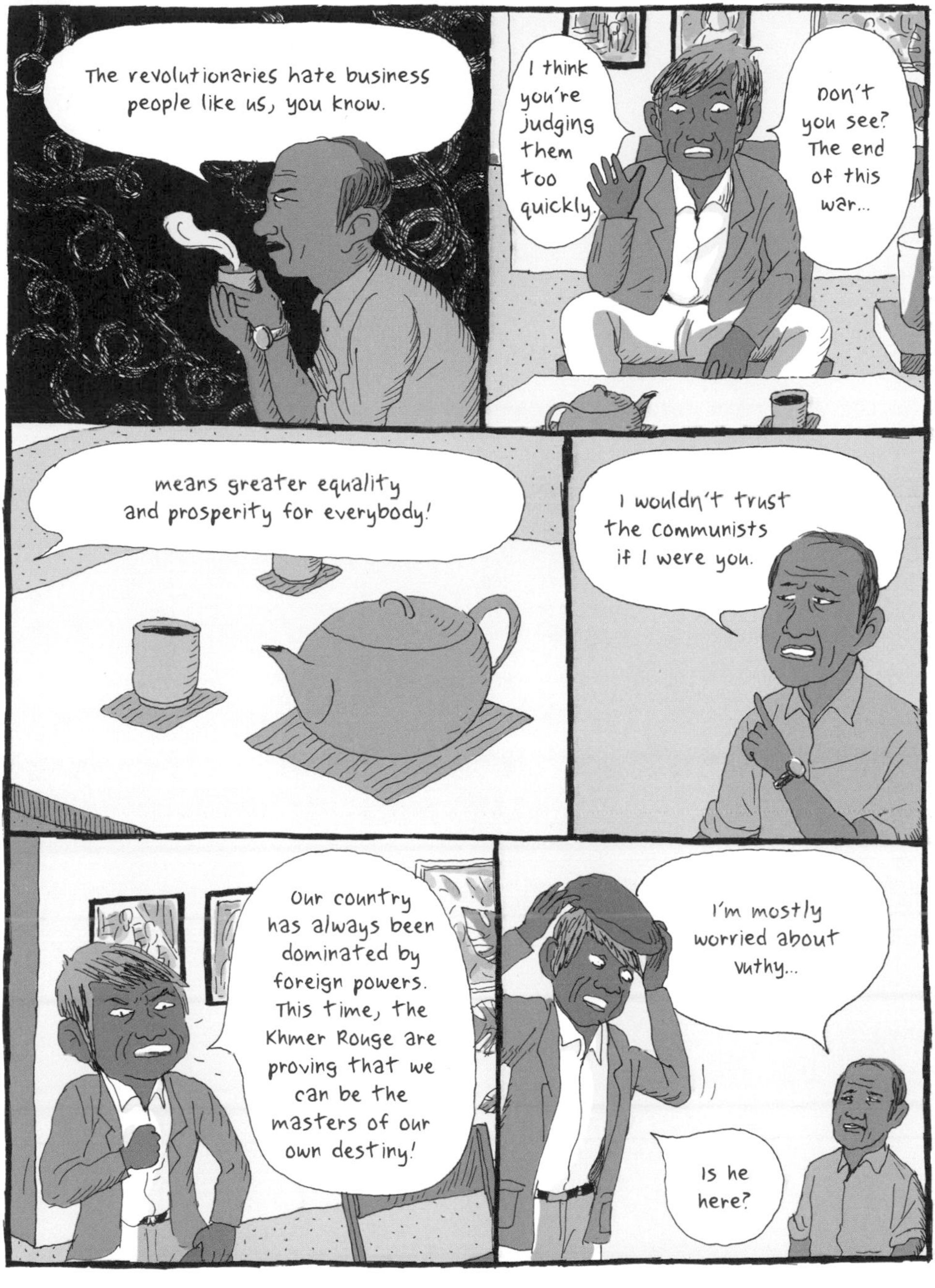
The revolutionaries hate business people like us, you know.
I think you're judging them too quickly.
Don't you see? The end of this war...
means greater equality and prosperity for everybody!
I wouldn't trust the communists if I were you.
Our country has always been dominated by foreign powers. This time, the Khmer Rouge are proving that we can be the masters of our own destiny!
I'm mostly worried about Vuthy...
Is he here?

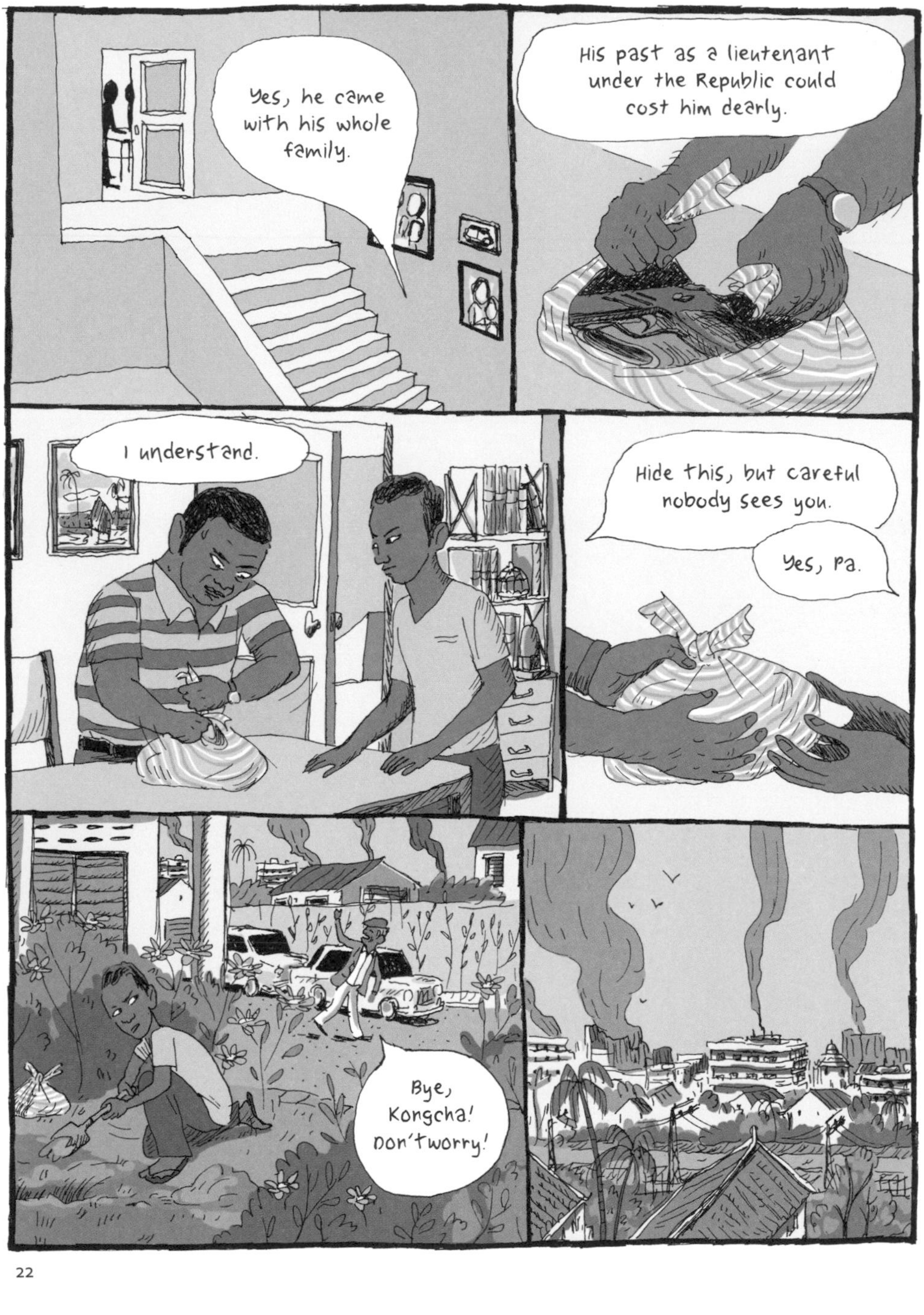
Yes, he came with his whole family.
His past as a lieutenant under the Republic could cost him dearly.
I understand.
Hide this, but careful nobody sees you.
Yes, Pa.
Bye, Kongcha! Don't worry!

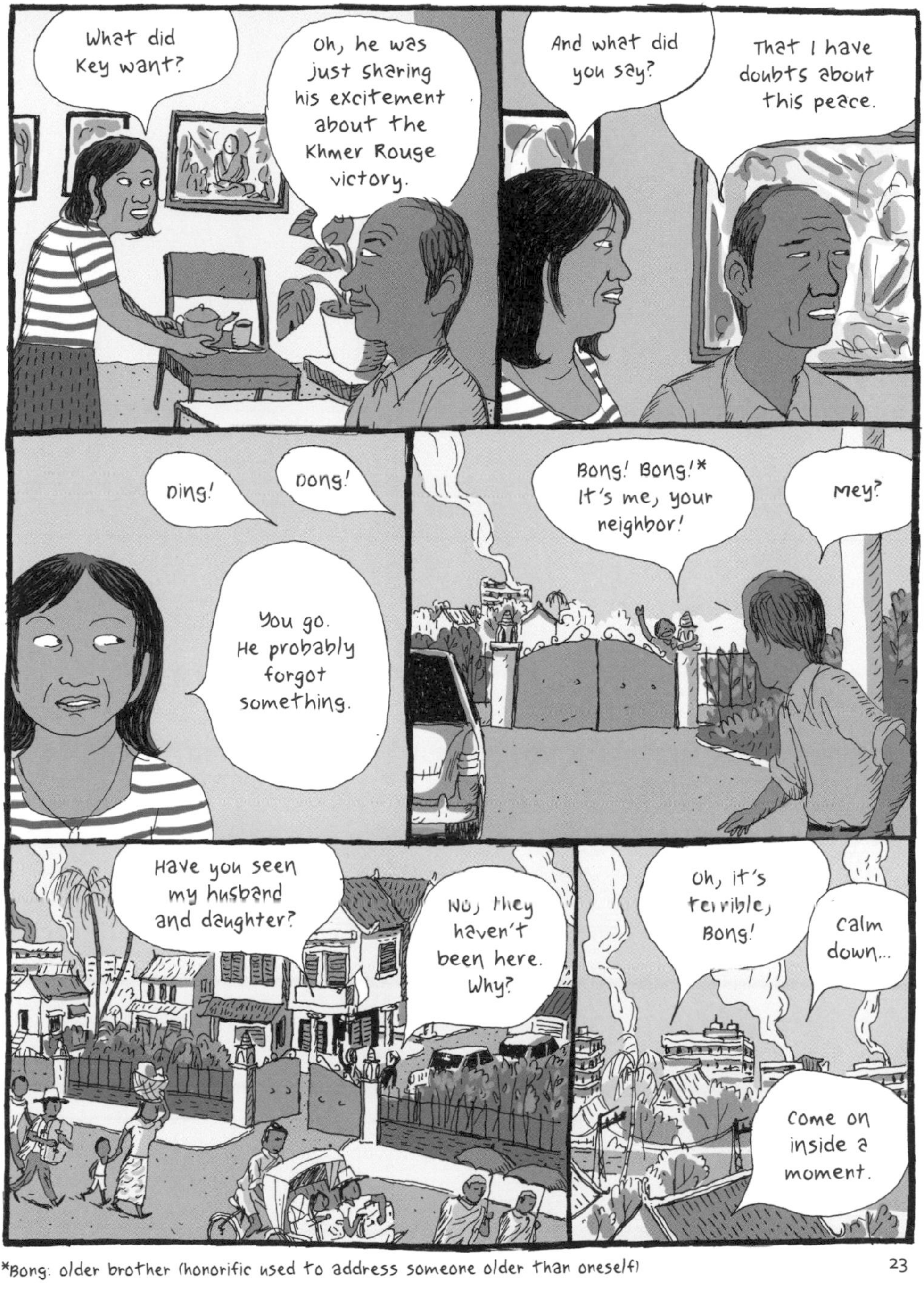
What did Key want?
Oh, he was just sharing his excitement about the Khmer Rouge victory.
And what did you say?
That I have doubts about this peace.
Ding!
Dong!
You go. He probably forgot something.
Bong! Bong!* It's me, your neighbor!
Mey?
Have you seen my husband and daughter?
No, they haven't been here. Why?
Oh, it's terrible, Bong!
Calm down...
Come on inside a moment.

*Bong: older brother (honorific used to address someone older than oneself)

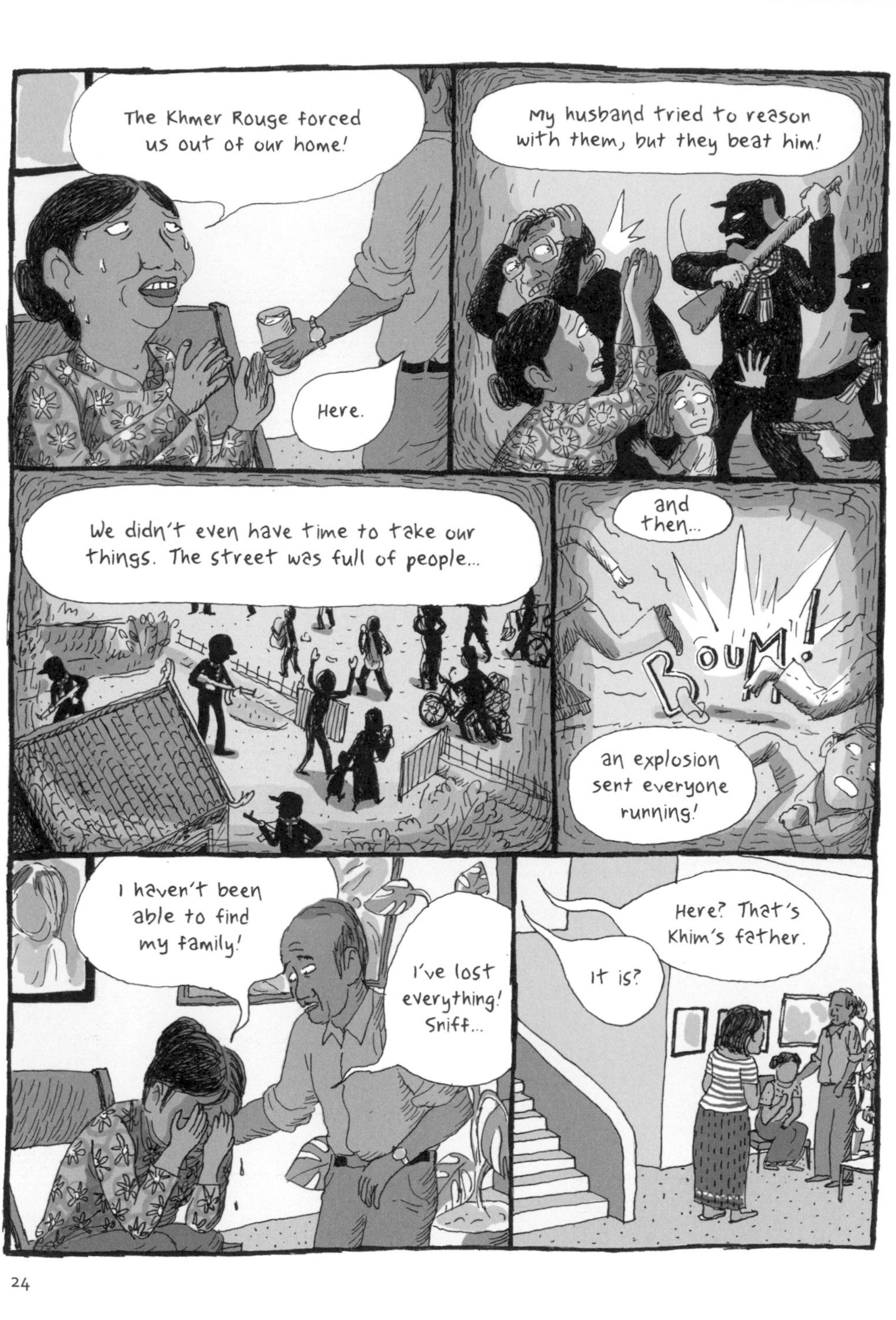
The Khmer Rouge forced us out of our home!
Here.
My husband tried to reason with them, but they beat him!
We didn't even have time to take our things. The street was full of people...
and then...
BOUM!
an explosion sent everyone running!
I haven't been able to find my family!
I've lost everything! Sniff...
Here? That's Khim's father.
It is?

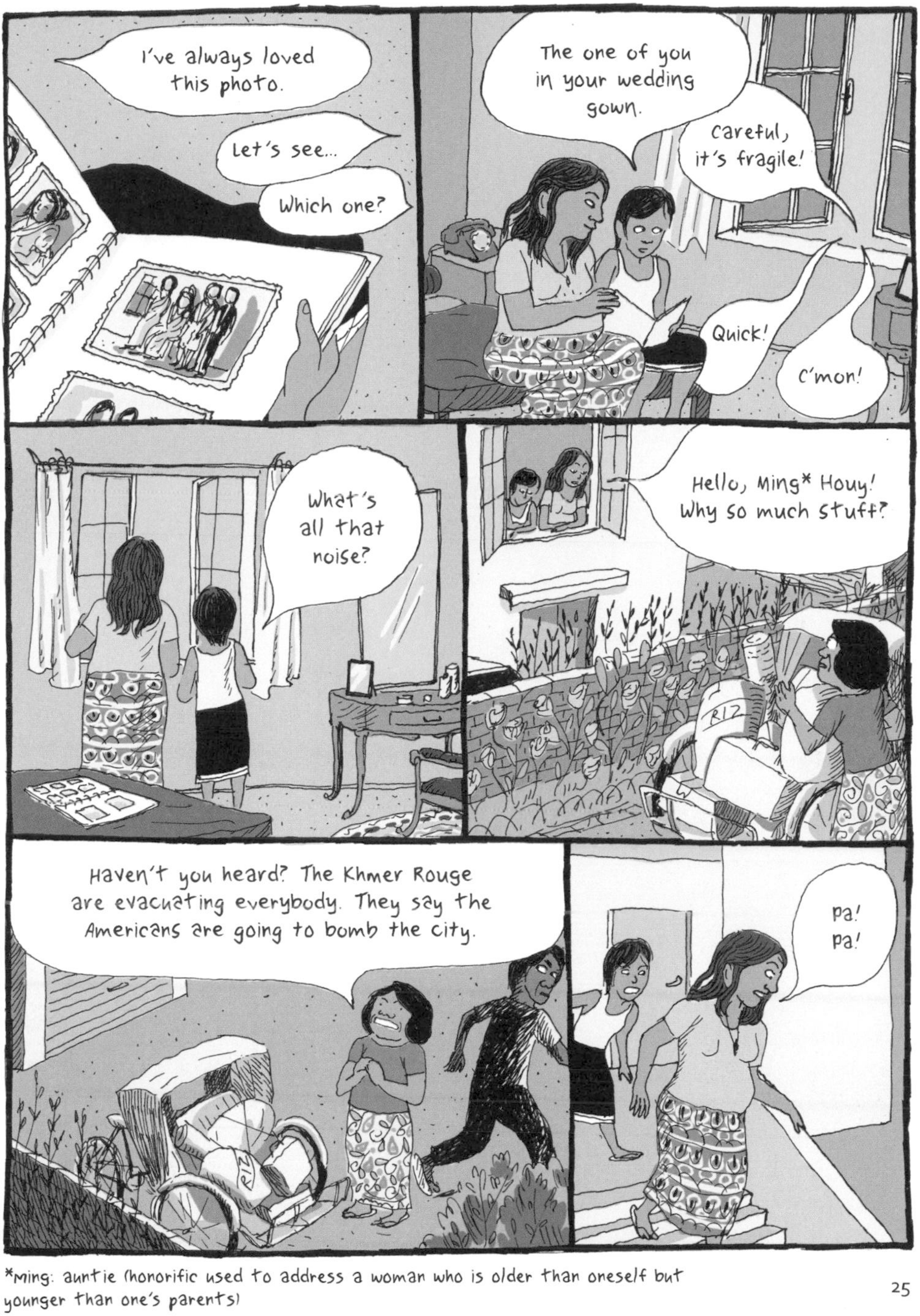
I've always loved this photo.
Let's see...
Which one?
The one of you in your wedding gown.
Careful, it's fragile!
Quick!
C'mon!
What's all that noise?
Hello, Ming* Houy! Why so much stuff?
RIZ
Haven't you heard? The Khmer Rouge are evacuating everybody. They say the Americans are going to bomb the city.
RIZ
Pa! Pa!

*Ming: auntie (honorific used to address a woman who is older than oneself but younger than one's parents)

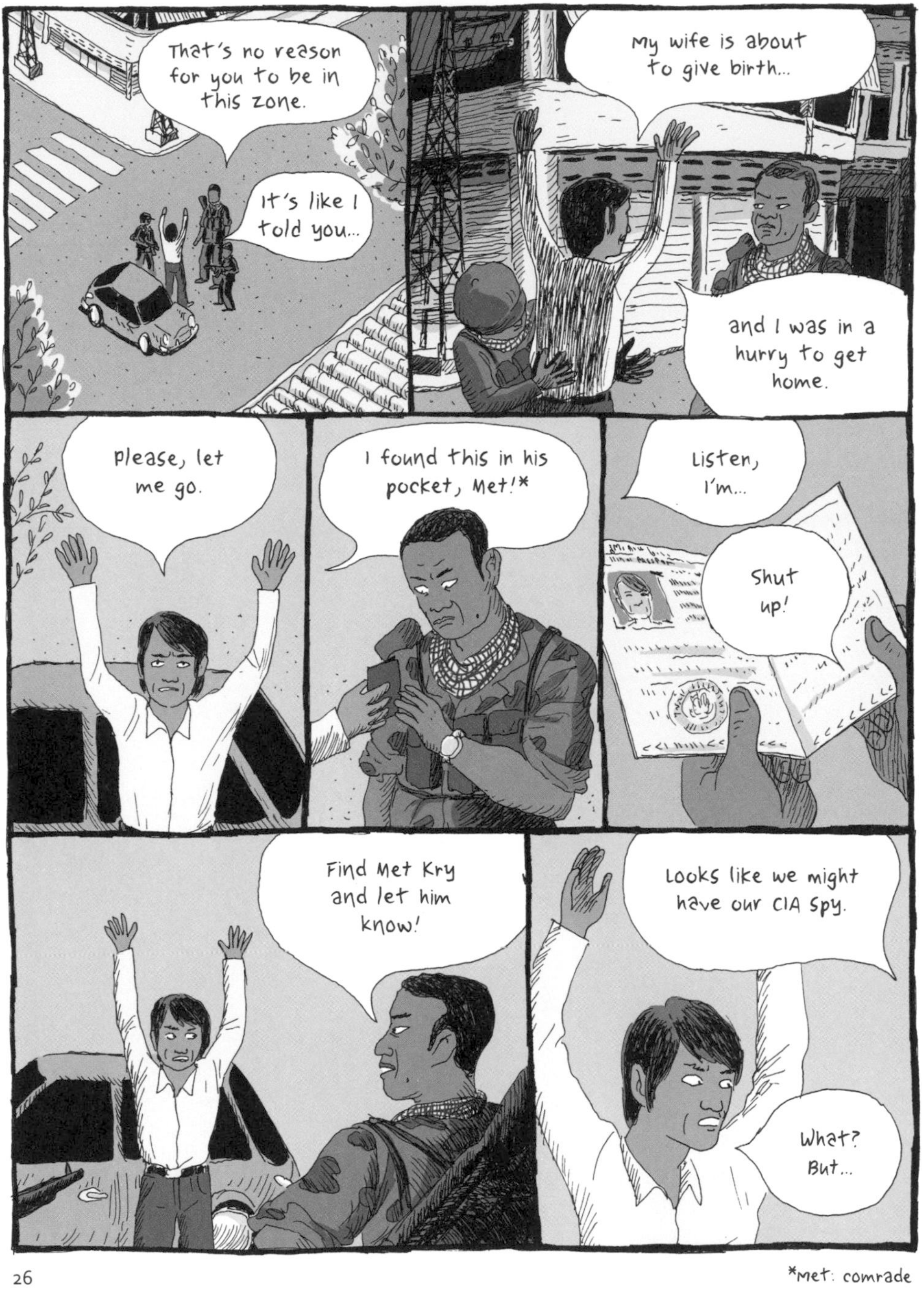
That's no reason for you to be in this zone.
It's like I told you...
My wife is about to give birth...
and I was in a hurry to get home.
Please, let me go.
I found this in his pocket, Met!*
Listen, I'm...
Shut up!
Find Met Kry and let him know!
Looks like we might have our CIA Spy.
What? But...

*Met: comrade

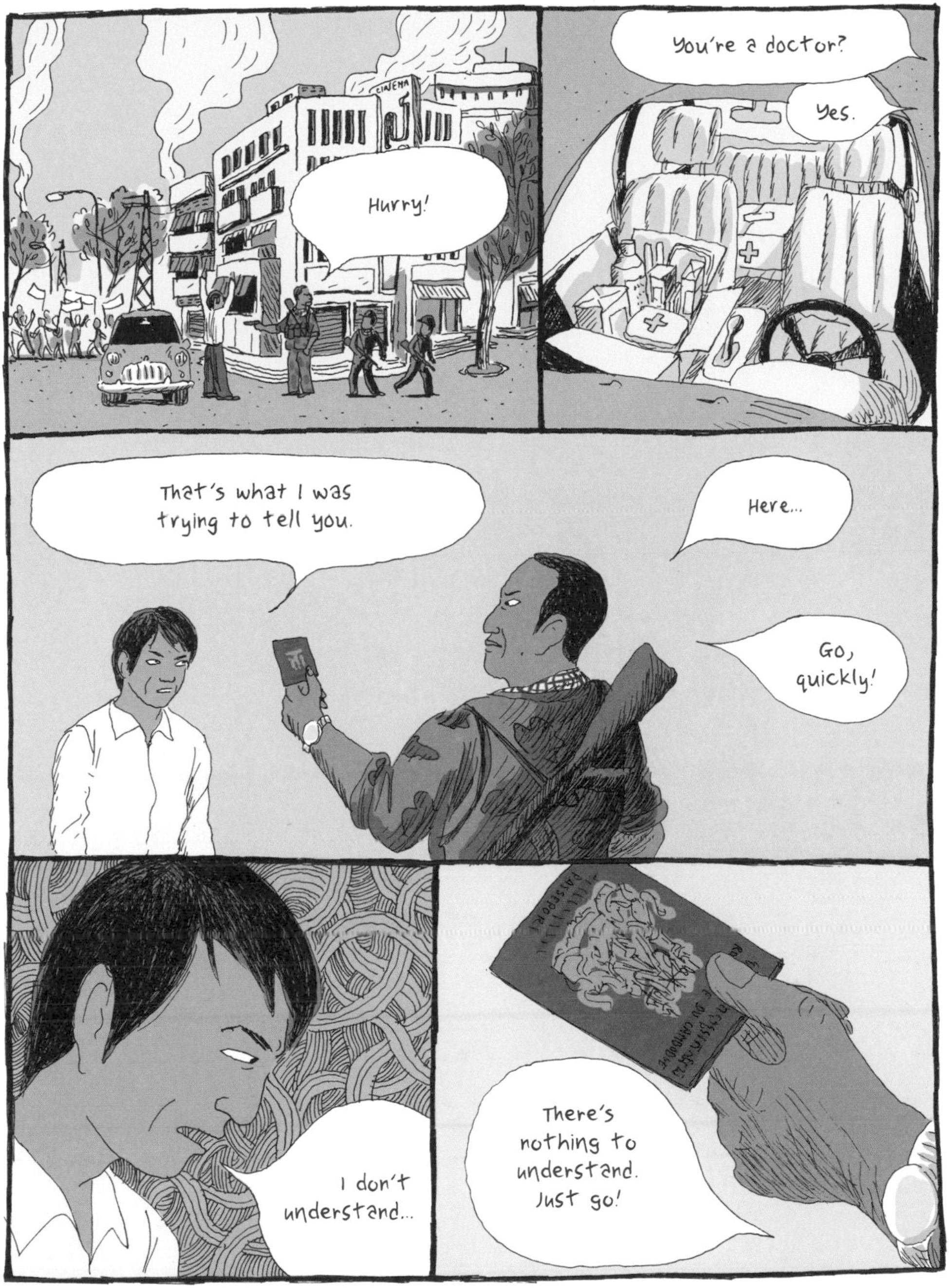
CINEMA
Hurry!
You're a doctor?
Yes.
That's what I was trying to tell you.
Here...
Go, quickly!
I don't understand...
There's nothing to understand. Just go!

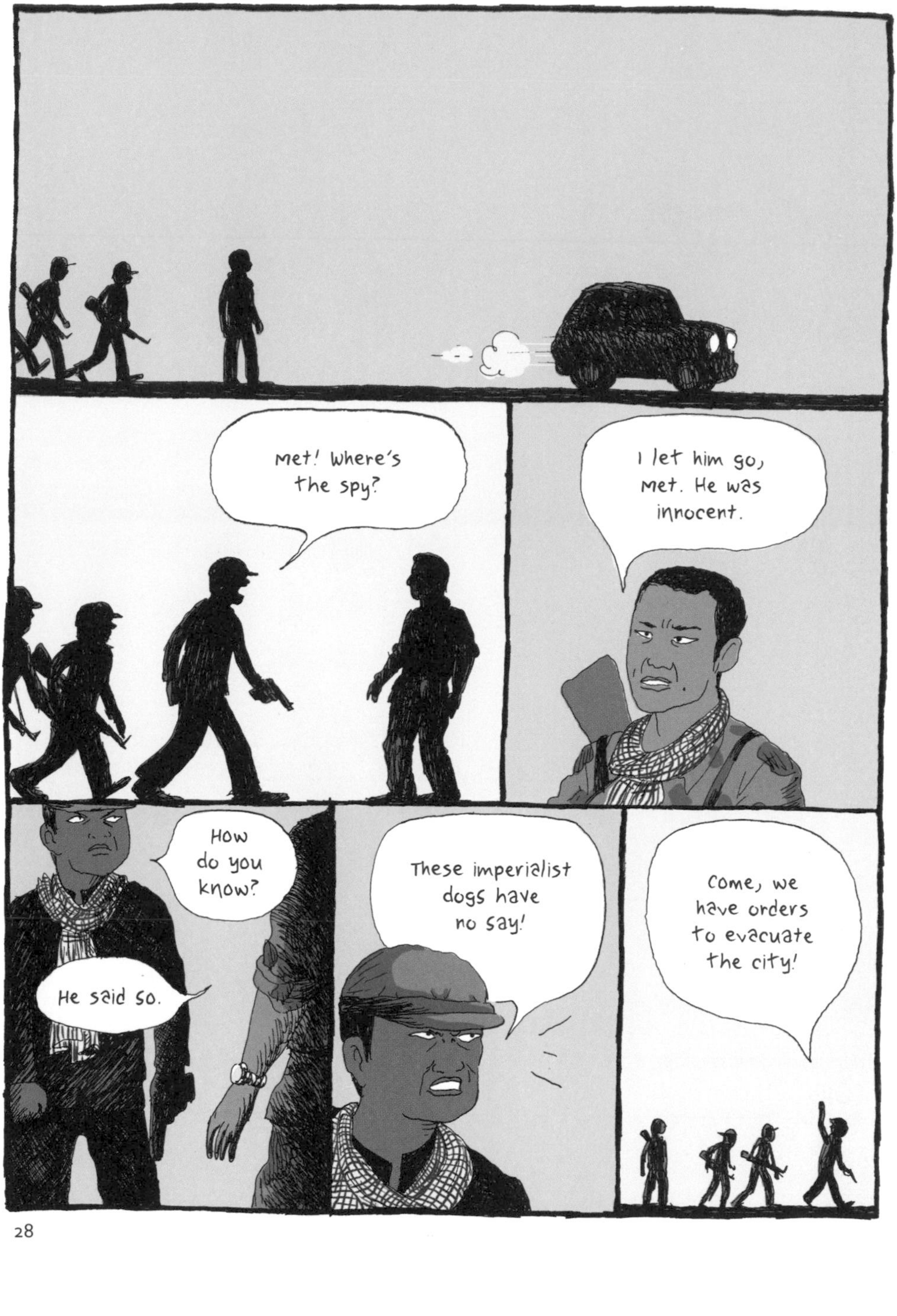
Met! Where's the spy?
I let him go, Met. He was innocent.
How do you know?
He said so.
These imperialist dogs have no say!
Come, we have orders to evacuate the city!

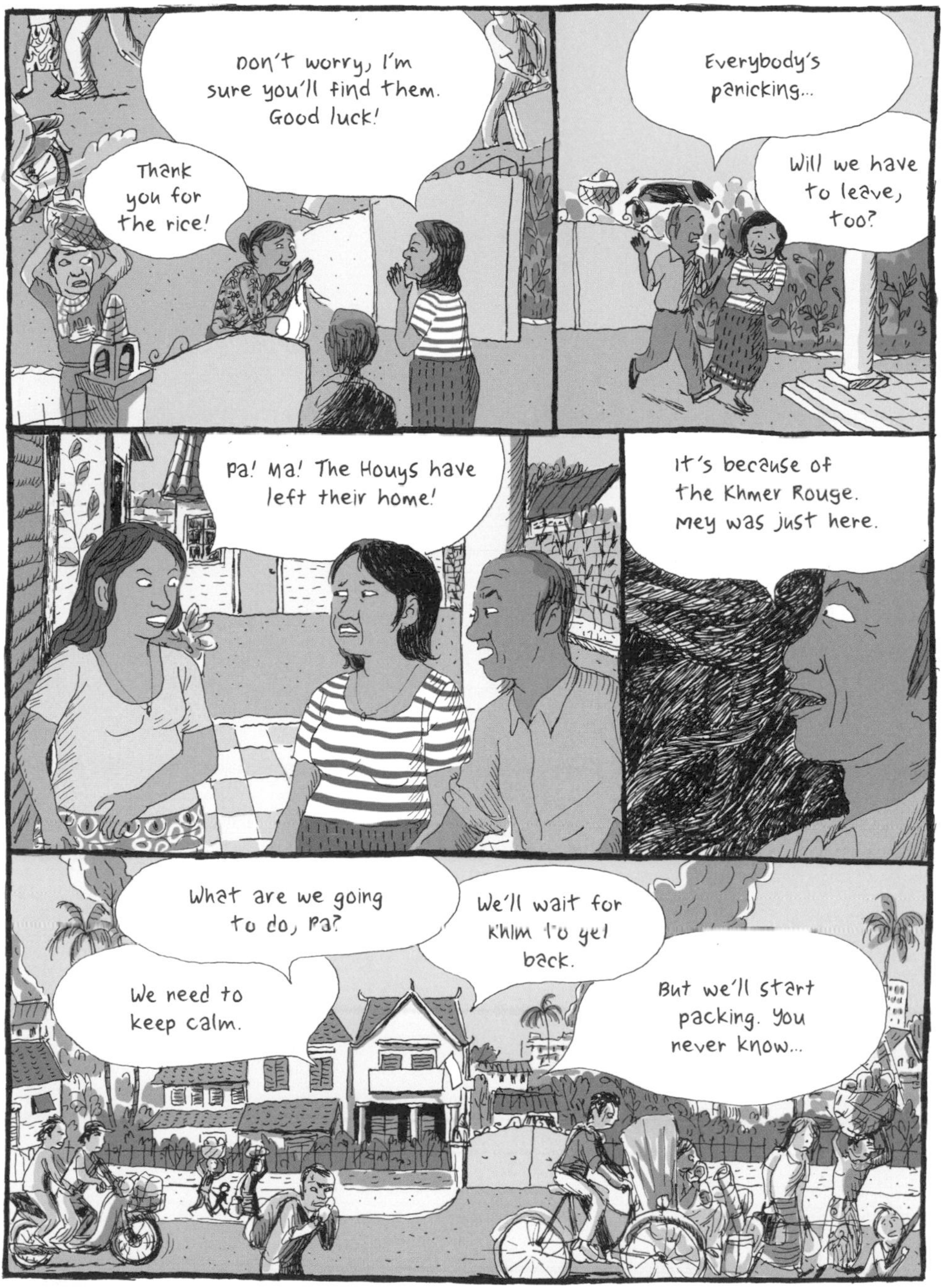
Don't worry, I'm sure you'll find them. Good luck!
Thank you for the rice!
Everybody's panicking...
Will we have to leave, too?
Pa! Ma! The Houys have left their home!
It's because of the Khmer Rouge. Mey was just here.
What are we going to do, Pa?
We need to keep calm.
We'll wait for Khim to get back.
But we'll start packing. You never know...

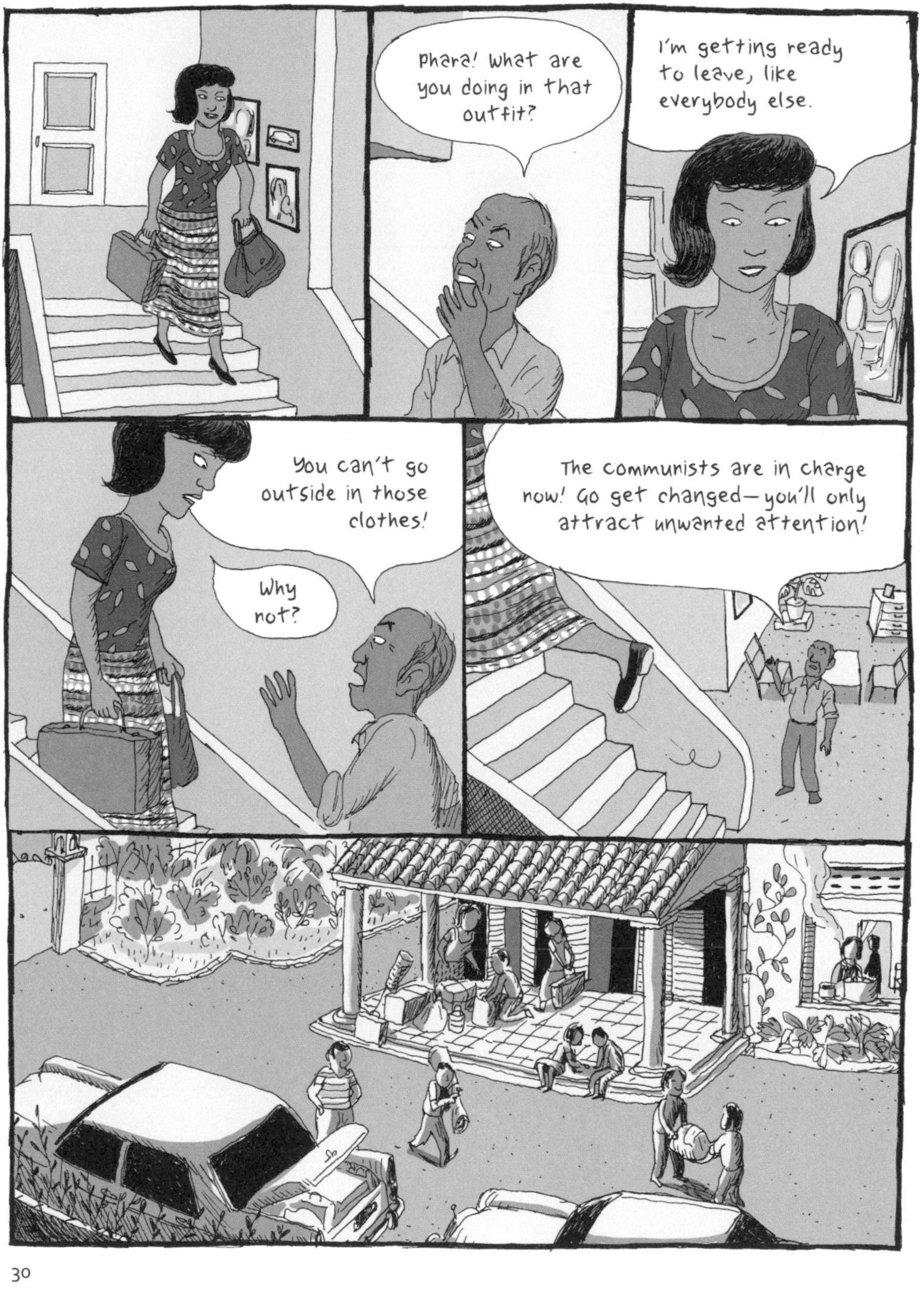
Phara! What are you doing in that outfit?
I'm getting ready to leave, like everybody else.
You can't go outside in those clothes!
Why not?
The communists are in charge now! Go get changed—you'll only attract unwanted attention!

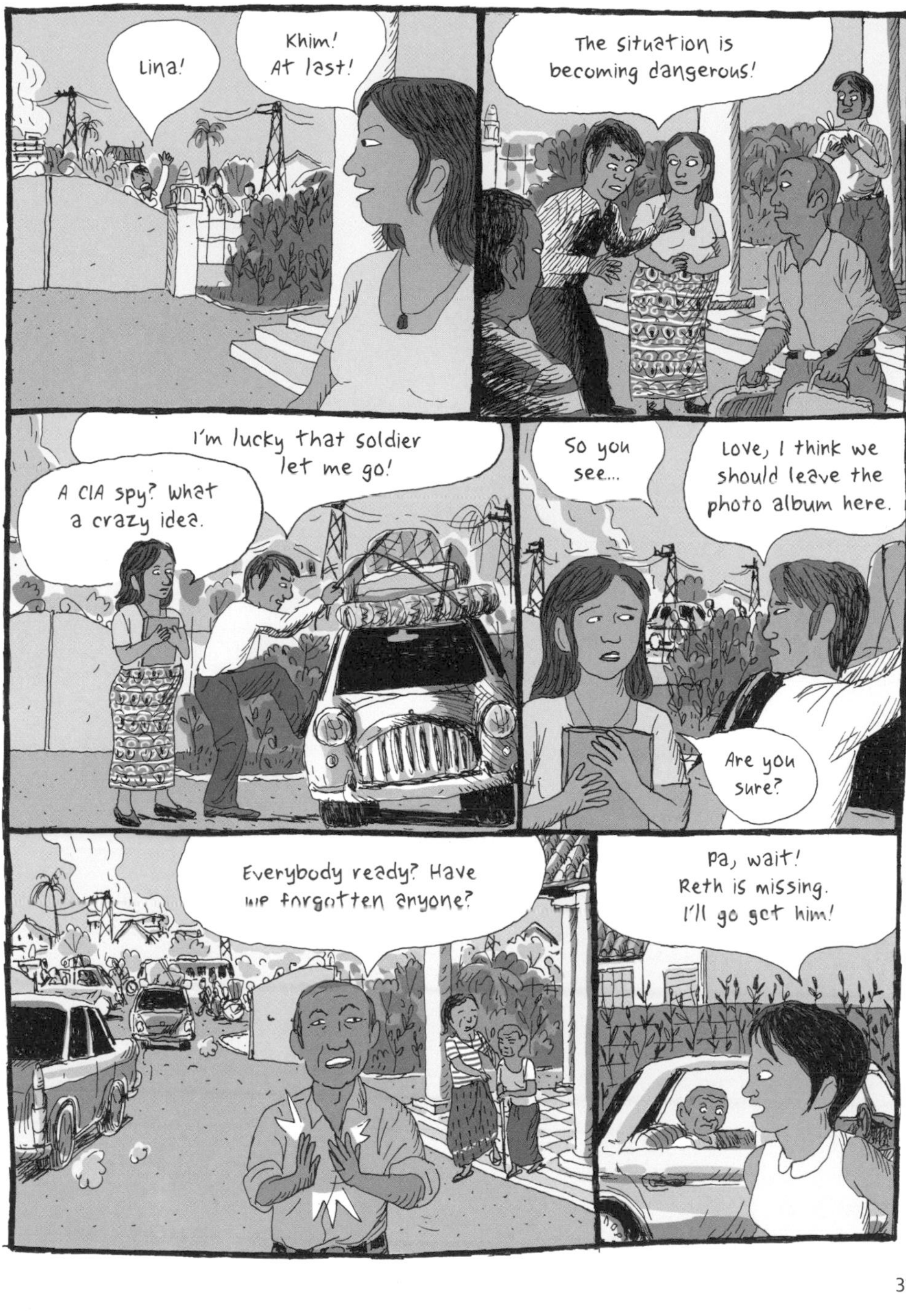
Lina!
Khim! At last!
The situation is becoming dangerous!
I'm lucky that soldier let me go!
A CIA spy? What a crazy idea.
So you see...
Love, I think we should leave the photo album here.
Are you sure?
Everybody ready? Have we forgotten anyone?
Pa, wait! Reth is missing. I'll go get him!

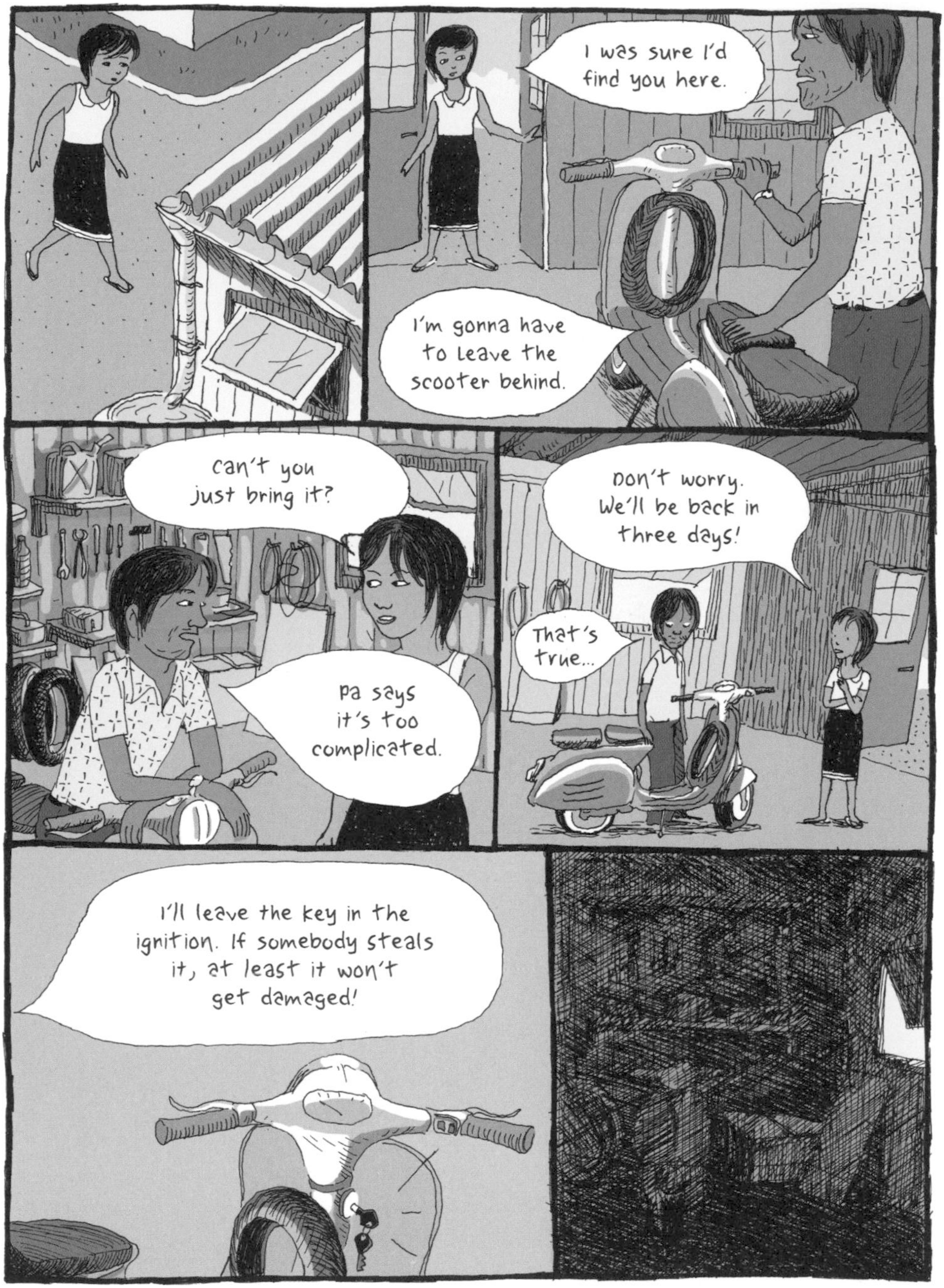
I was sure I'd find you here.
I'm gonna have to leave the scooter behind.
Can't you just bring it?
Pa says it's too complicated.
Don't worry. We'll be back in three days!
That's true...
I'll leave the key in the ignition. If somebody steals it, at least it won't get damaged!

chapter 2

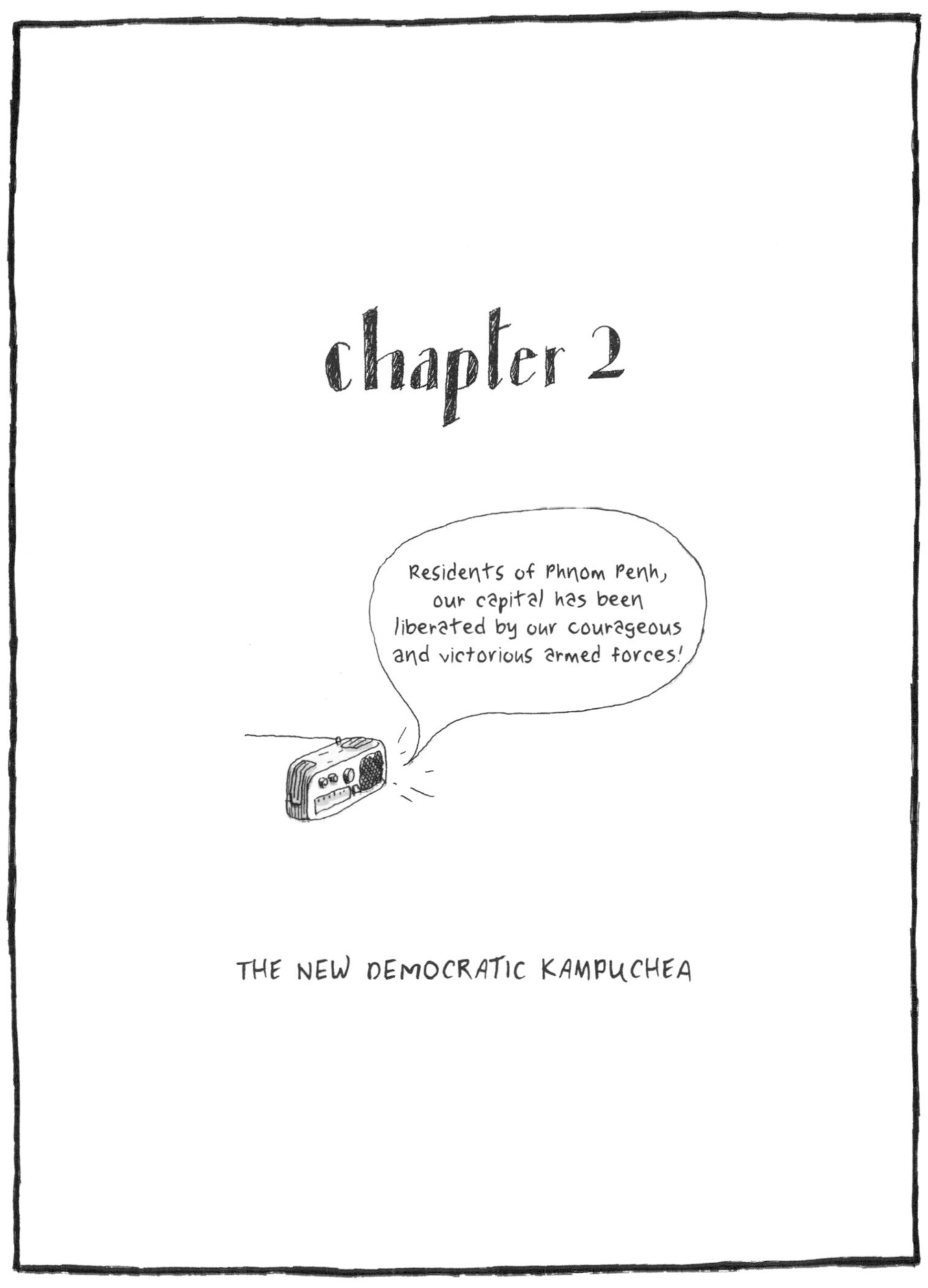
Residents of Phnom Penh, our capital has been liberated by our courageous and victorious armed forces!

THE NEW DEMOCRATIC KAMPUCHEA

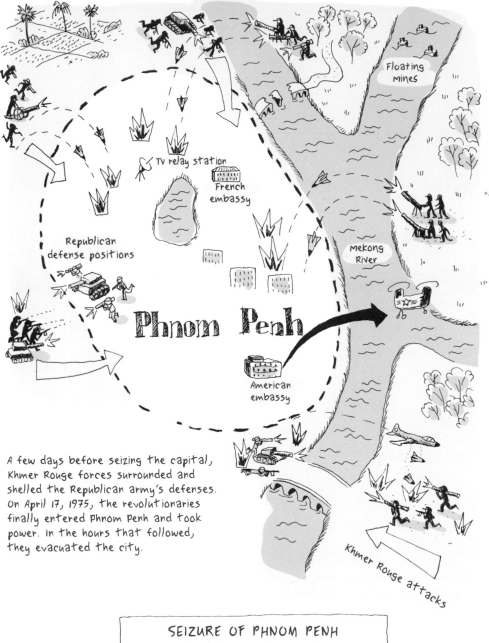

Floating mines

TV relay station

French embassy

Republican defense positions

Phnom Penh

Mekong River

American embassy

A few days before seizing the capital, Khmer Rouge forces surrounded and shelled the Republican army's defenses. On April 17, 1975, the revolutionaries finally entered Phnom Penh and took power. In the hours that followed, they evacuated the city.

Khmer Rouge attacks

SEIZURE OF PHNOM PENH
BY THE KHMER ROUGE

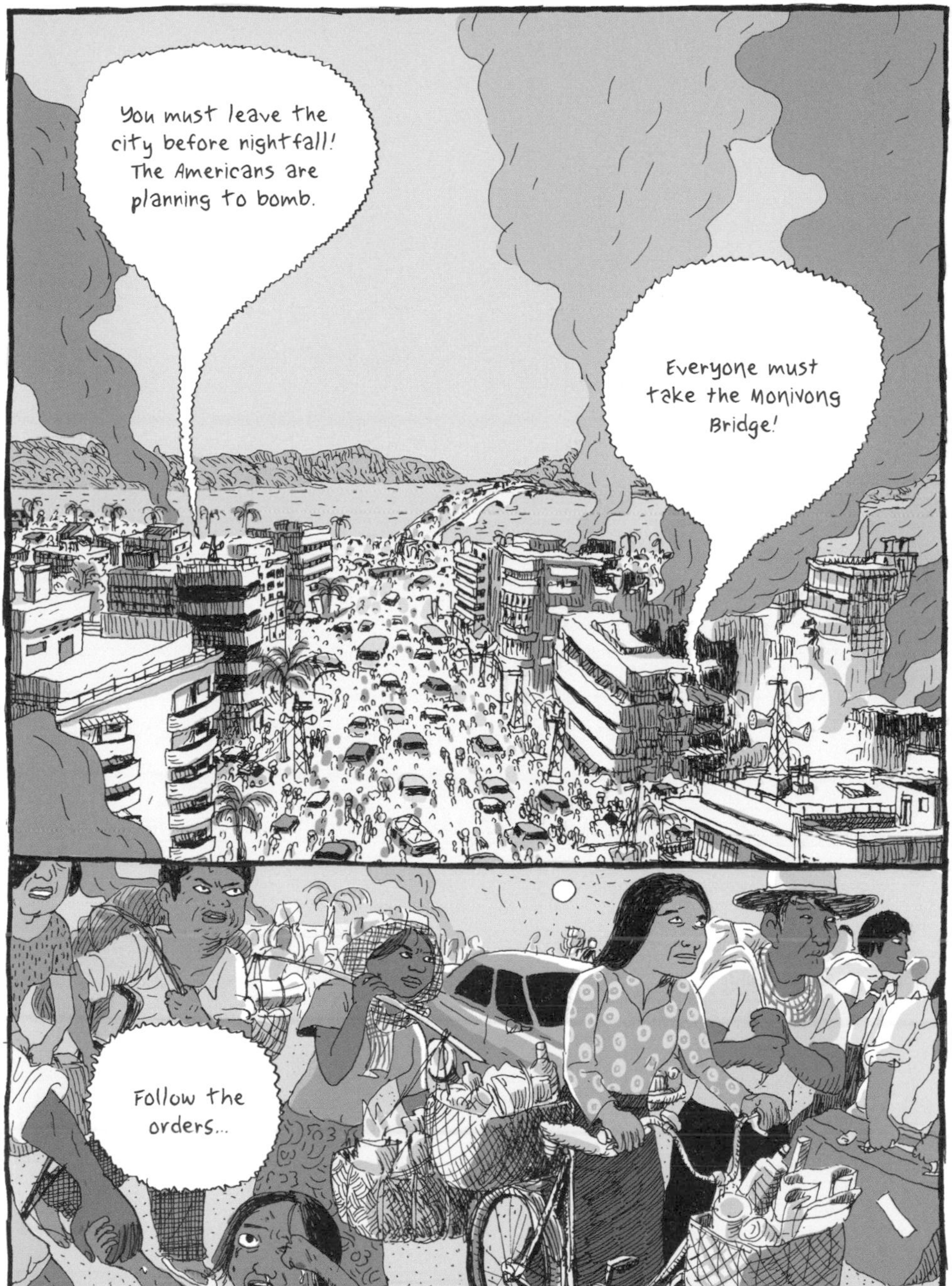
You must leave the city before nightfall! The Americans are planning to bomb.
Everyone must take the Monivong Bridge!
Follow the orders...

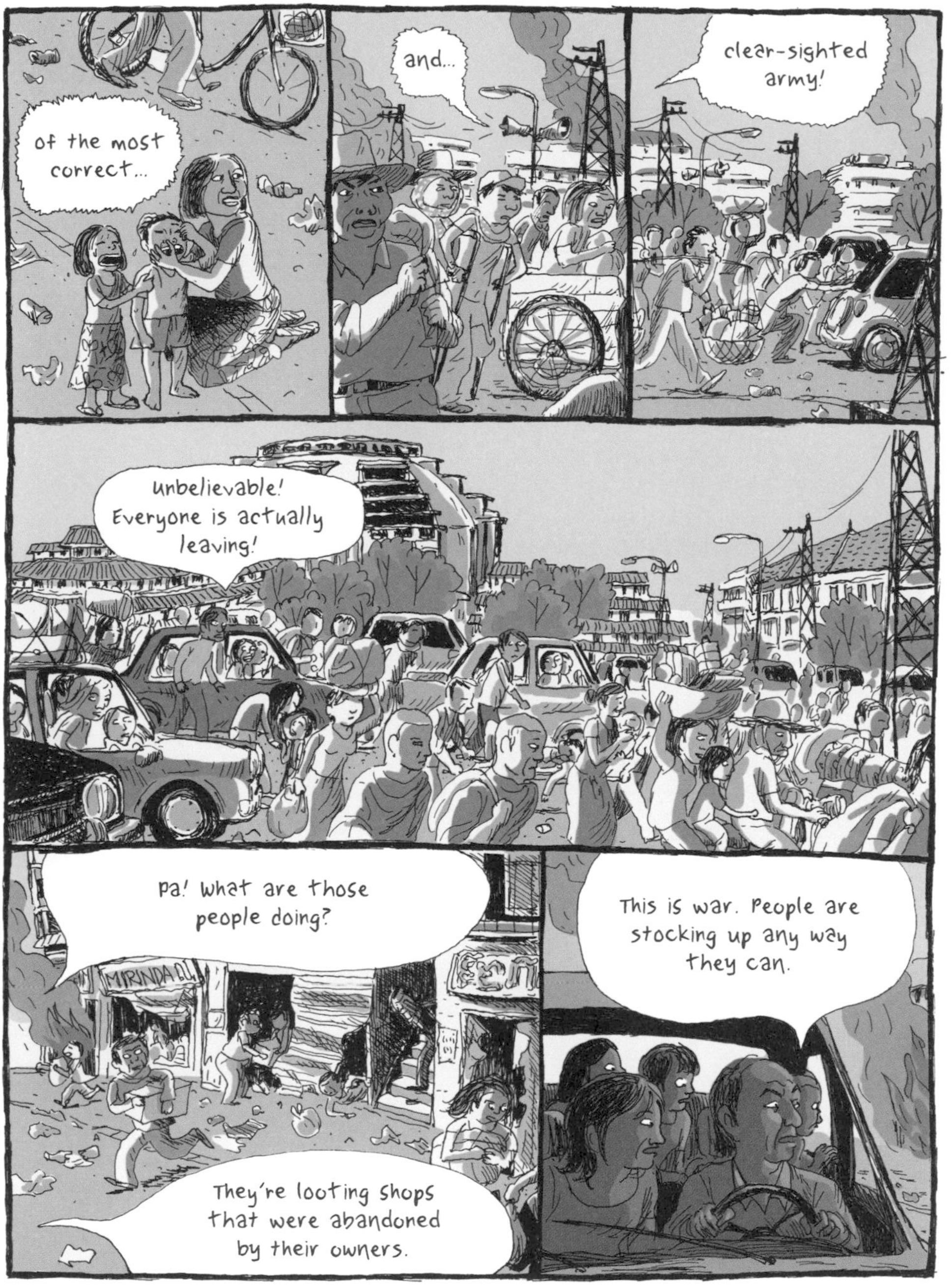
of the most correct...
and...
clear-sighted army!
Unbelievable! Everyone is actually leaving!
Pa! What are those people doing?
They're looting shops that were abandoned by their owners.
This is war. People are stocking up any way they can.

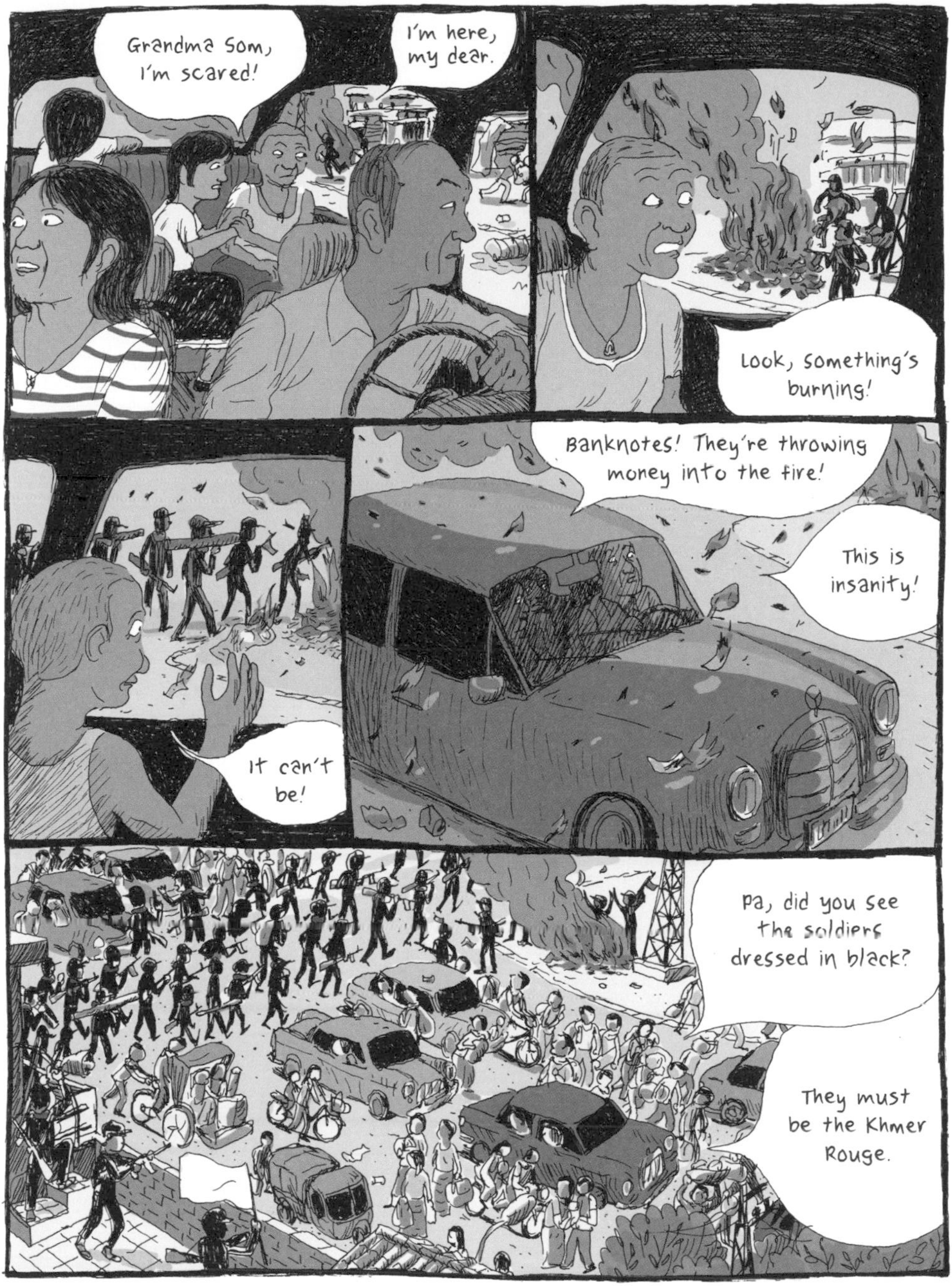
Grandma Som, I'm scared!
I'm here, my dear.
Look, something's burning!
Banknotes! They're throwing money into the fire!
It can't be!
This is insanity!
Pa, did you see the soldiers dressed in black?
They must be the Khmer Rouge.

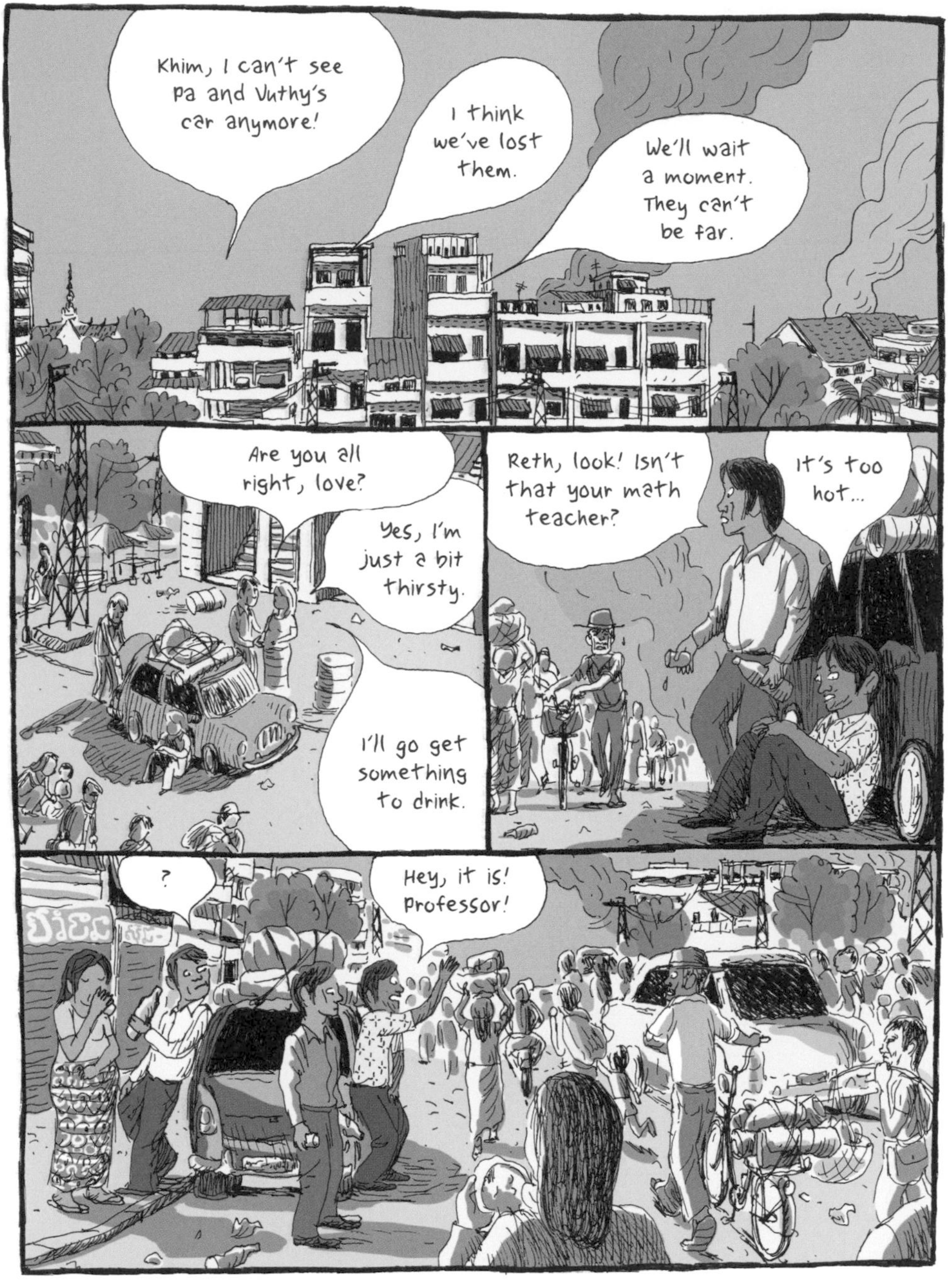

Khim, I can't see pa and Vuthy's car anymore!
I think we've lost them.
We'll wait a moment. They can't be far.
Are you all right, love?
Yes, I'm just a bit thirsty.
I'll go get something to drink.
Reth, look! Isn't that your math teacher?
It's too hot...
?
Hey, it is! Professor!

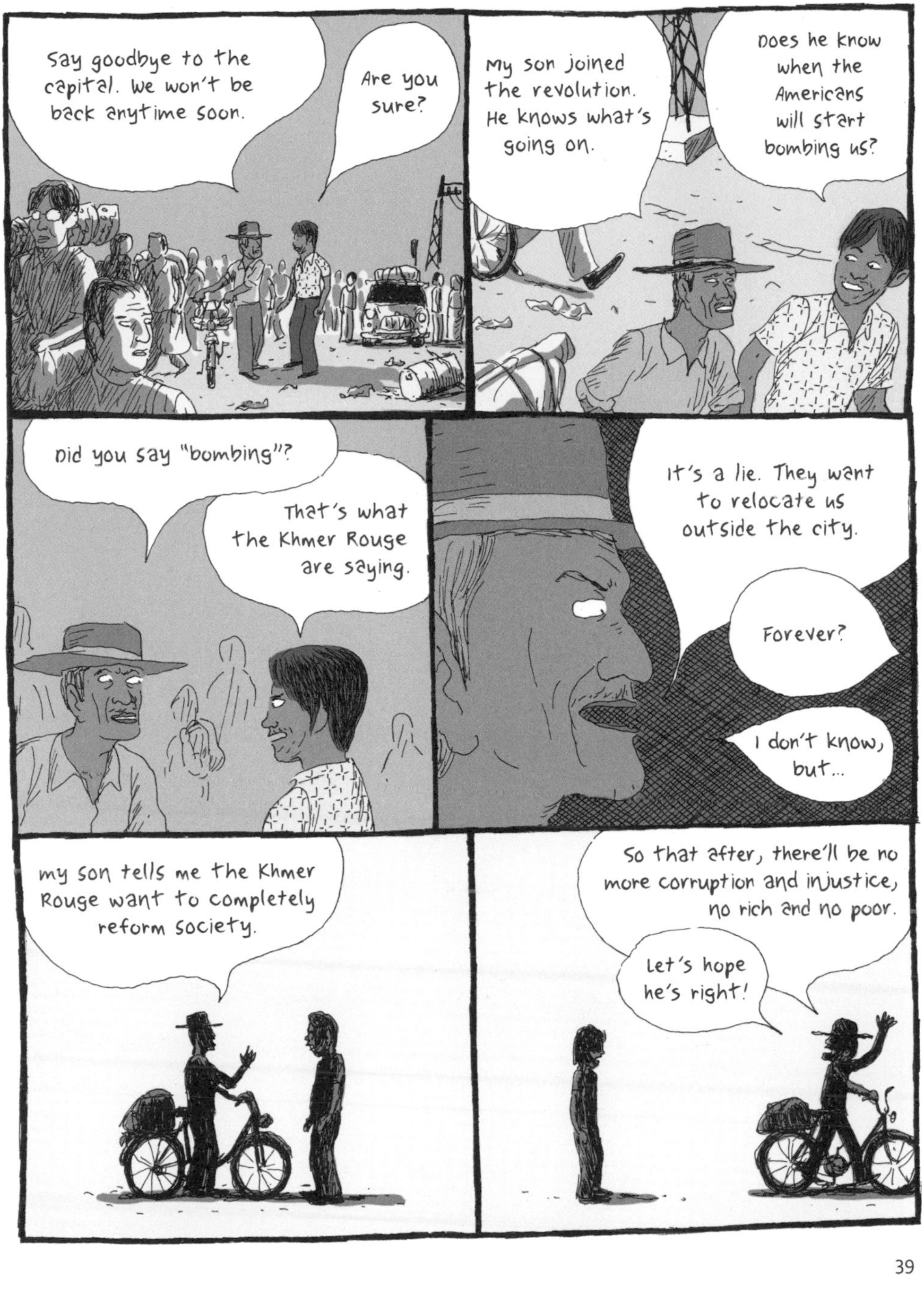
Say goodbye to the capital. We won't be back anytime soon.
Are you sure?
My son joined the revolution. He knows what's going on.
Does he know when the Americans will start bombing us?
Did you say "bombing"?
That's what the Khmer Rouge are saying.
It's a lie. They want to relocate us outside the city.
Forever?
I don't know, but...
My son tells me the Khmer Rouge want to completely reform society.
So that after, there'll be no more corruption and injustice, no rich and no poor.
Let's hope he's right!

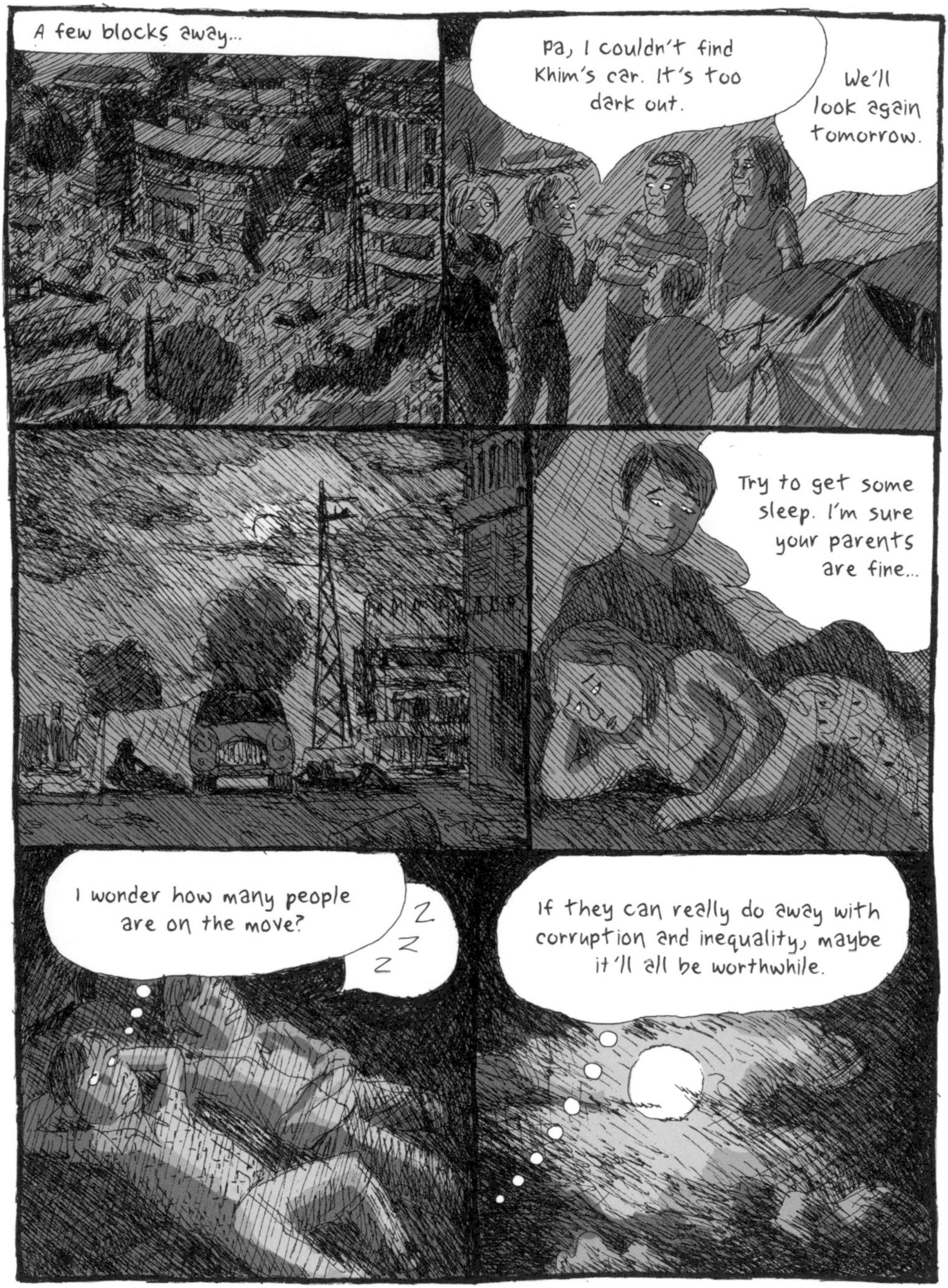
A few blocks away...
Pa, I couldn't find Khim's car. It's too dark out.
We'll look again tomorrow.
Try to get some sleep. I'm sure your parents are fine...
I wonder how many people are on the move?
Z Z Z
If they can really do away with corruption and inequality, maybe it'll all be worthwhile.

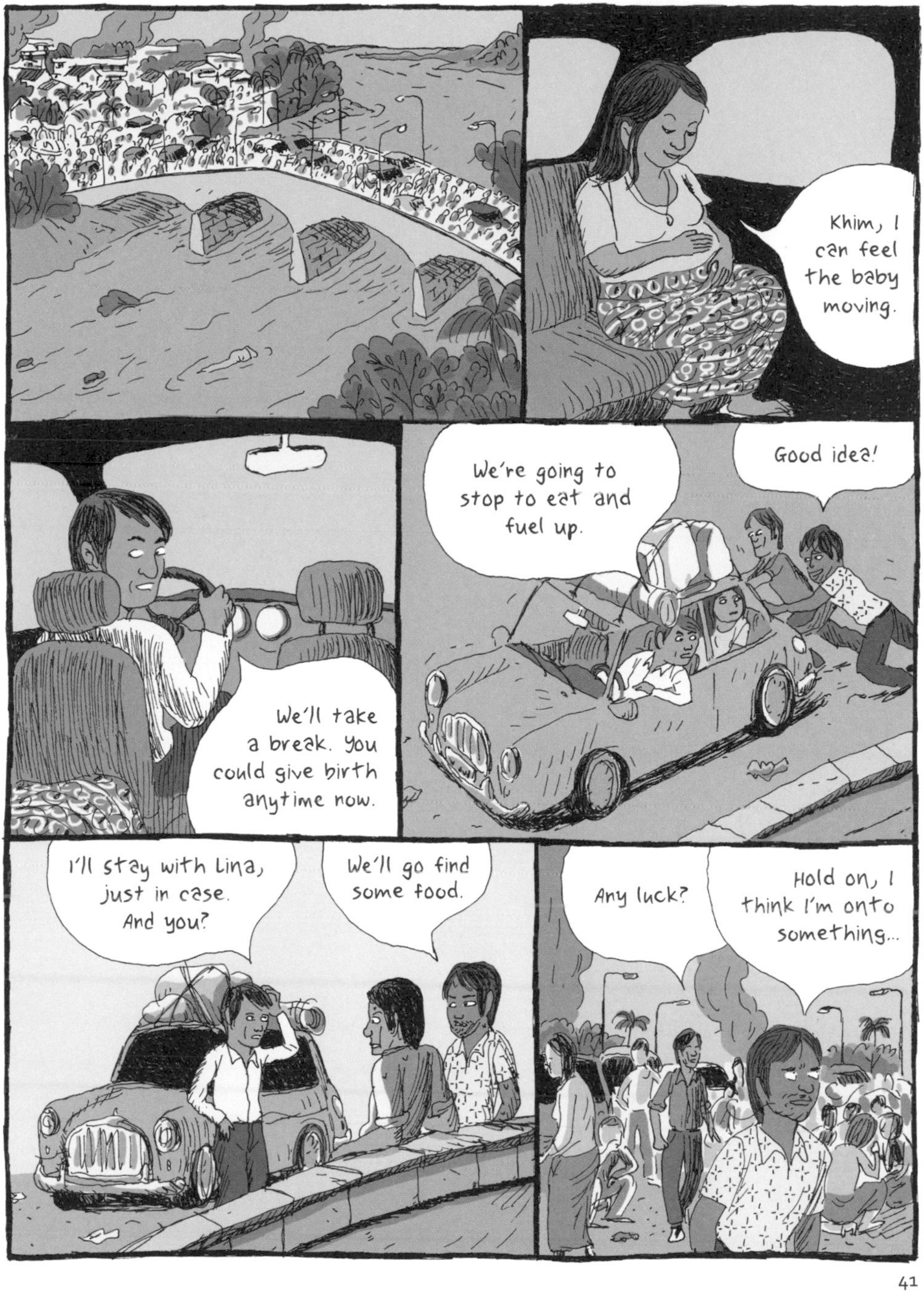
Khim, I can feel the baby moving.
We'll take a break. You could give birth anytime now.
We're going to stop to eat and fuel up.
Good idea!
I'll stay with Lina, just in case. And you?
We'll go find some food.
Any luck?
Hold on, I think I'm onto something...

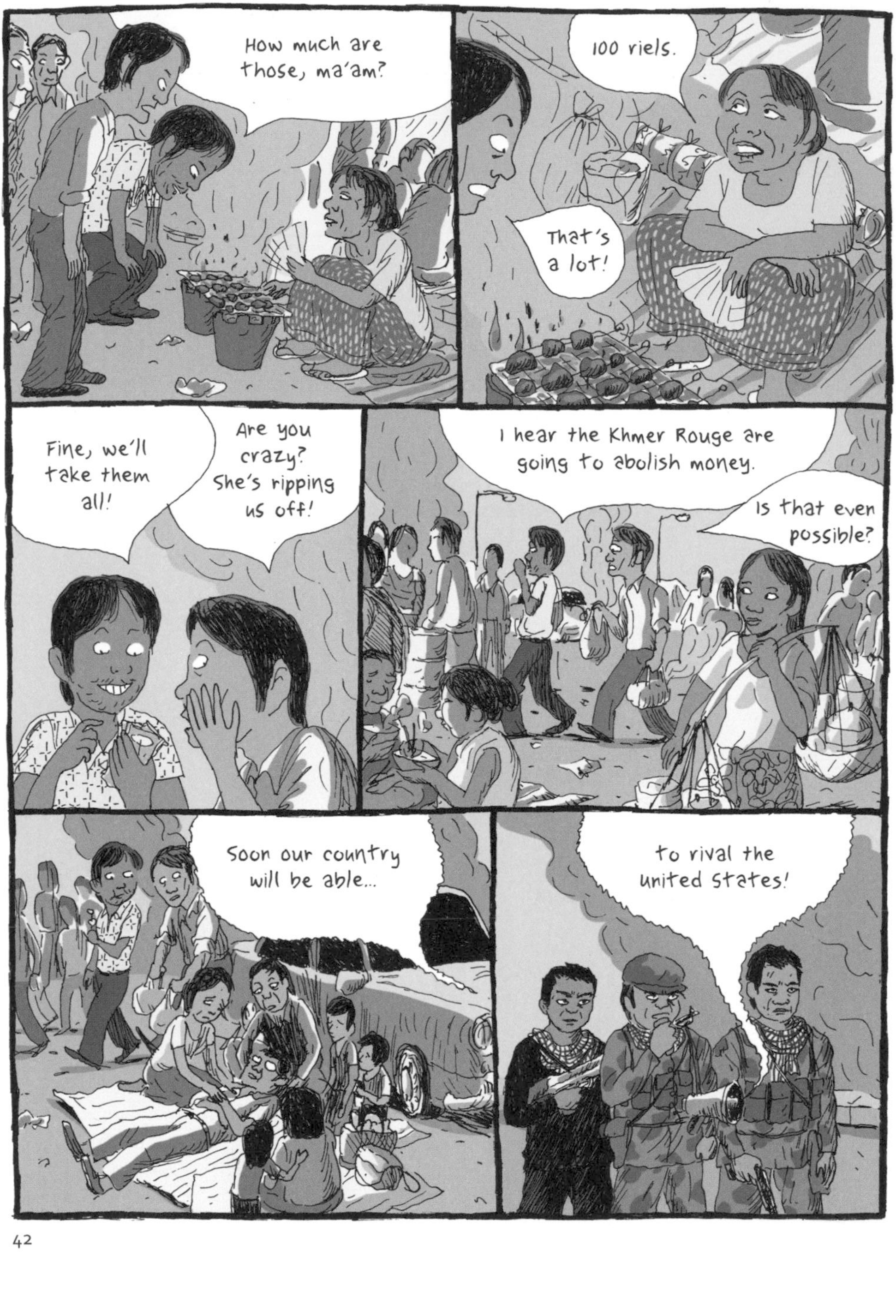
How much are those, ma'am?
100 riels.
That's a lot!
Fine, we'll take them all!
Are you crazy? She's ripping us off!
I hear the Khmer Rouge are going to abolish money.
Is that even possible?
Soon our country will be able...
to rival the United States!

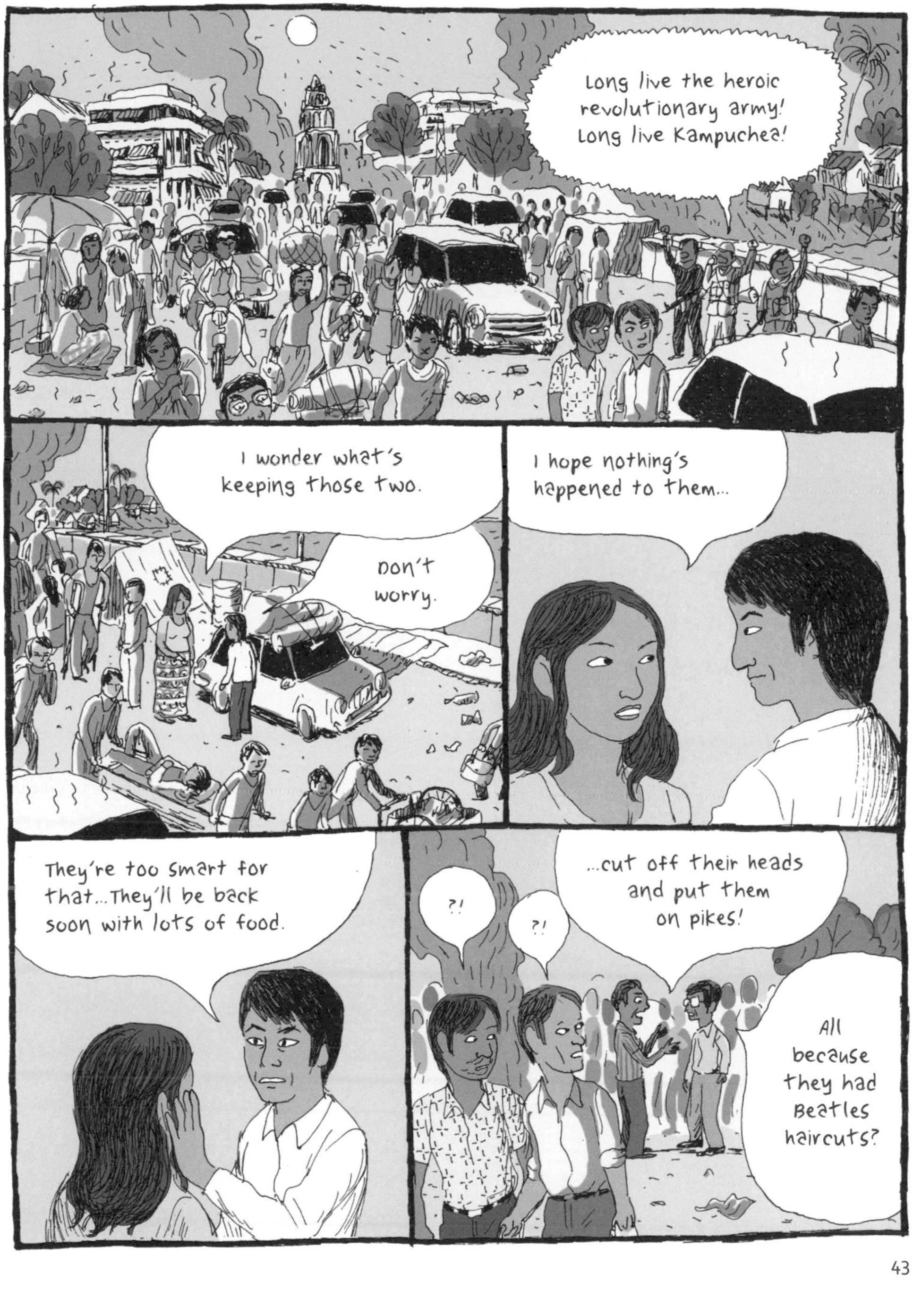

Long live the heroic revolutionary army! Long live Kampuchea!
I wonder what's keeping those two.
Don't worry.
I hope nothing's happened to them...
They're too smart for that... They'll be back soon with lots of food.
?!
?!
...cut off their heads and put them on pikes!
All because they had Beatles haircuts?

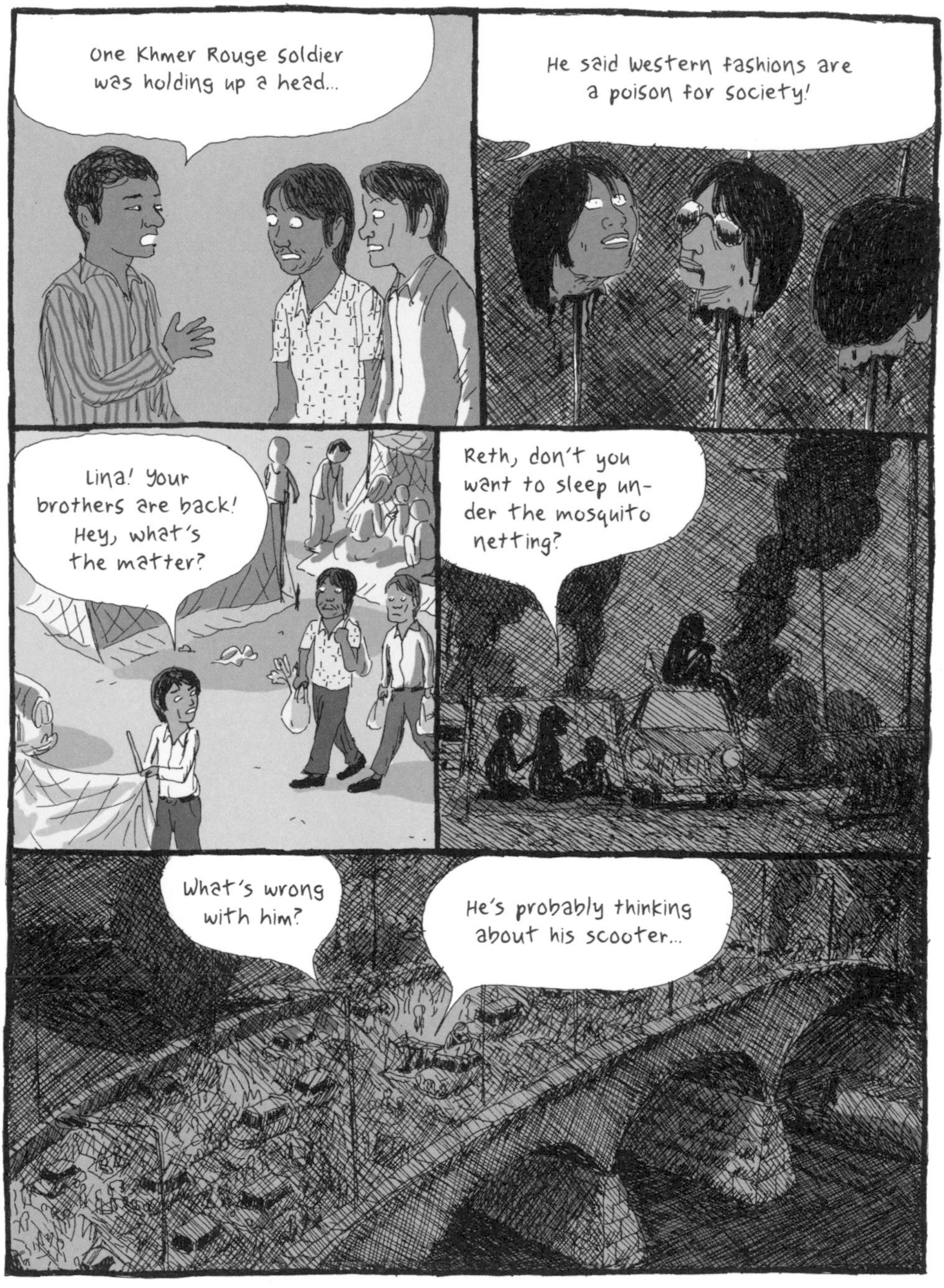
One Khmer Rouge soldier was holding up a head...
He said western fashions are a poison for society!
Lina! Your brothers are back! Hey, what's the matter?
Reth, don't you want to sleep under the mosquito netting?
What's wrong with him?
He's probably thinking about his scooter...

chapter 3

VEASNA

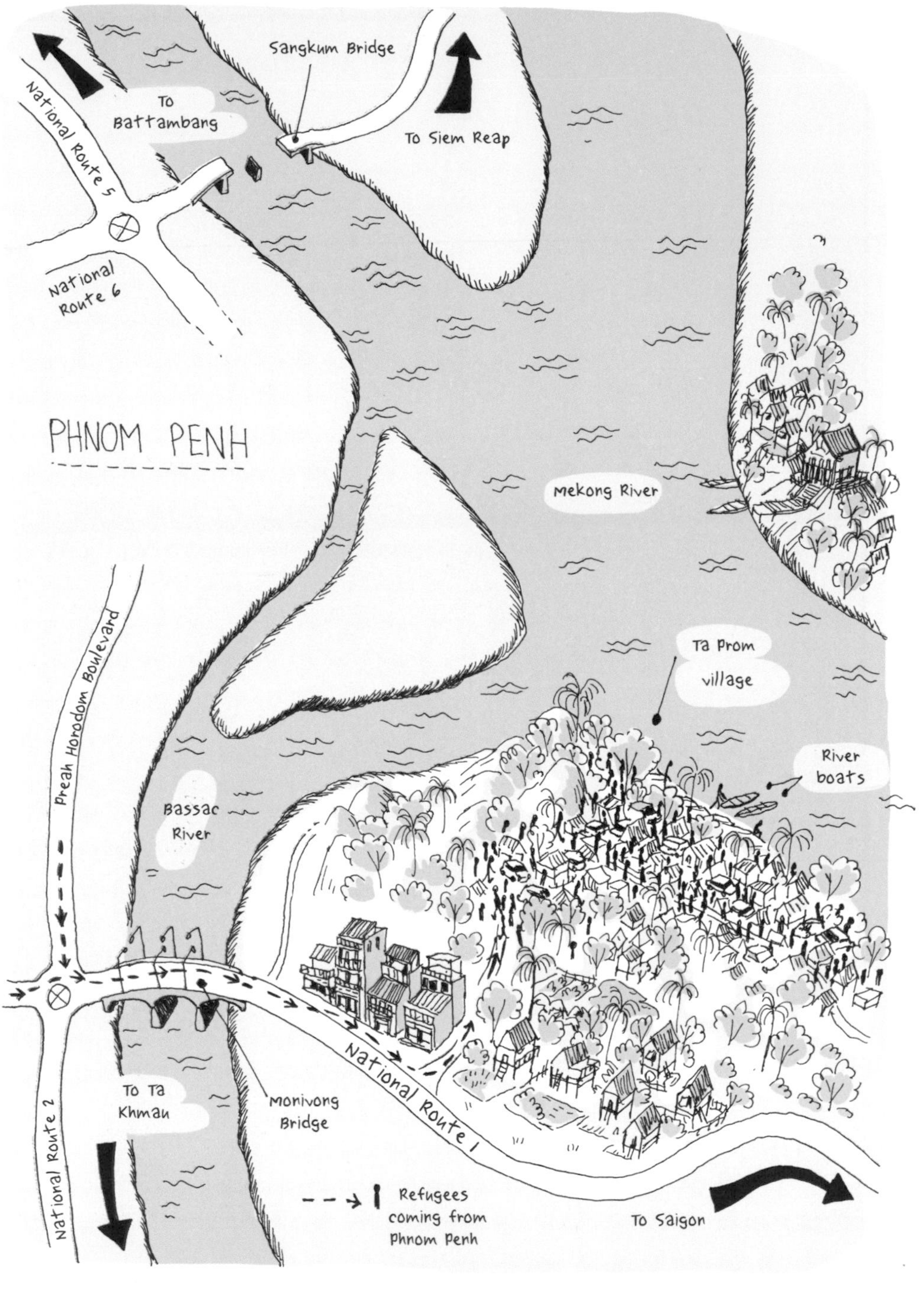
Sangkum Bridge
To Battambang
To Siem Reap
National Route 5
National Route 6
PHNOM PENH
Mekong River
Preah Horodom Boulevard
Ta Prom village
River boats
Bassac River
To Ta Khmau
Monivong Bridge
National Route 1
National Route 2
Refugees coming from Phnom Penh
To Saigon

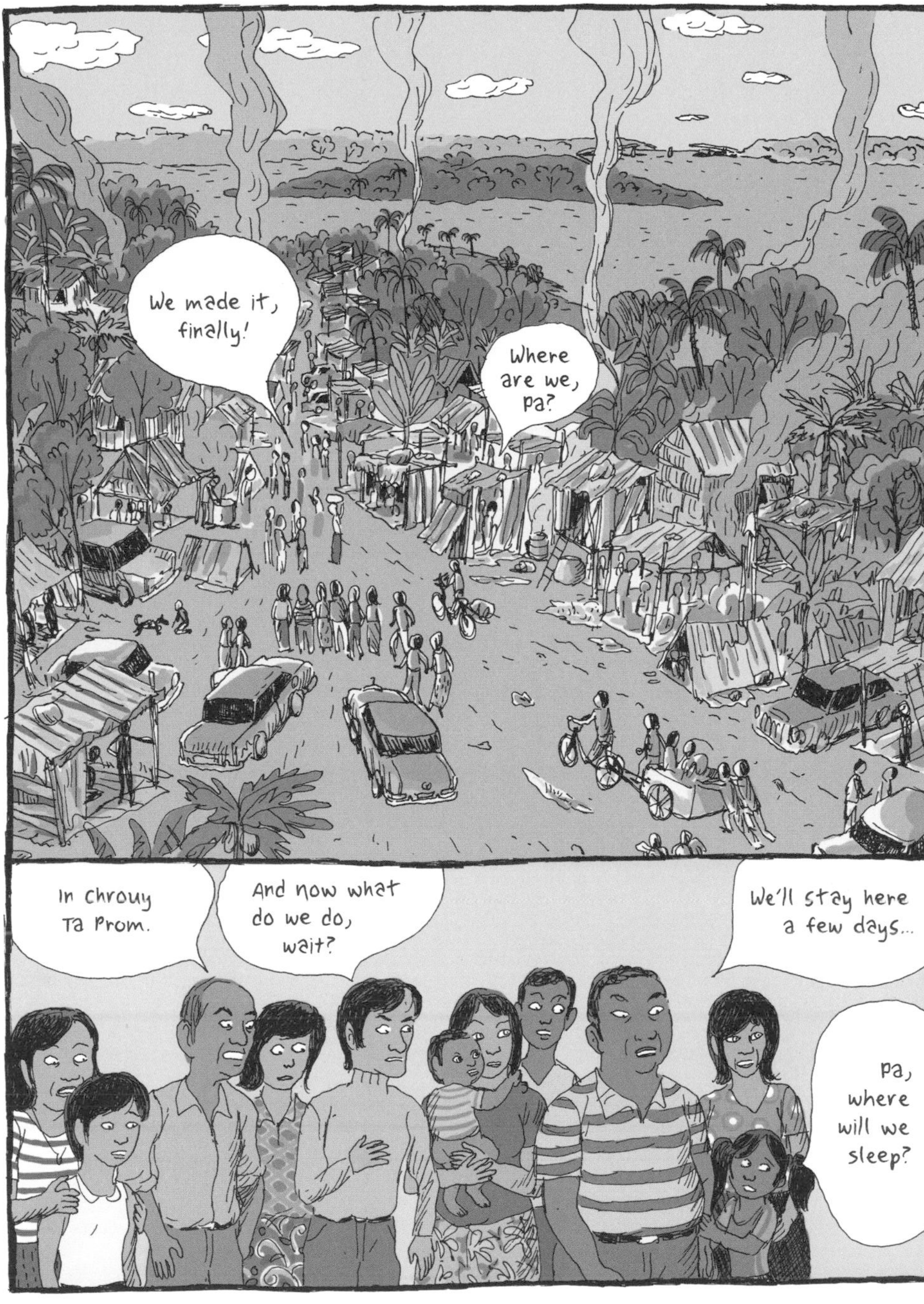
We made it, finally!
Where are we, pa?
In Chrouy Ta Prom.
And now what do we do, wait?
We'll stay here a few days...
Pa, where will we sleep?

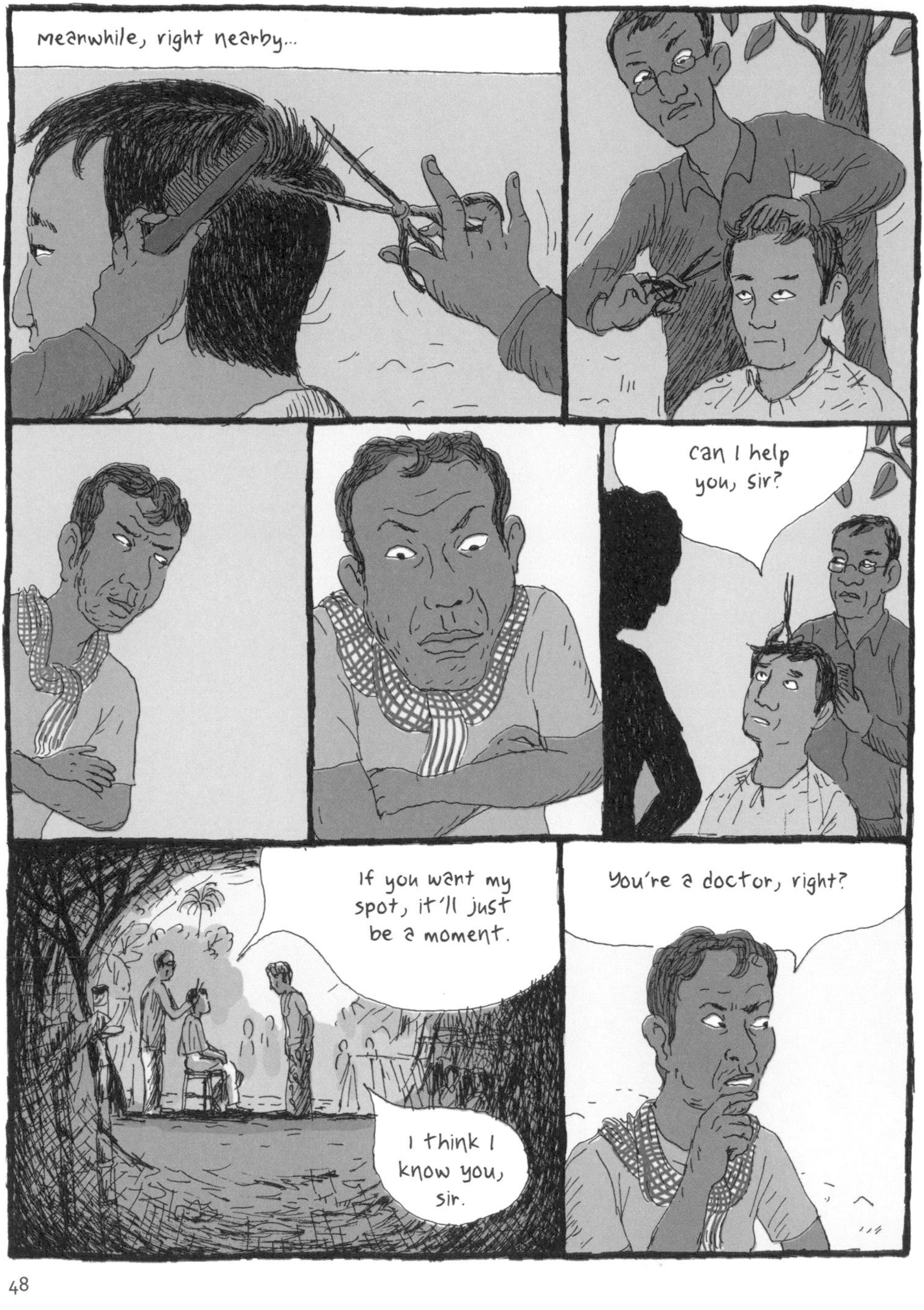
Meanwhile, right nearby...
Can I help you, sir?
If you want my spot, it'll just be a moment.
I think I know you, sir.
You're a doctor, right?

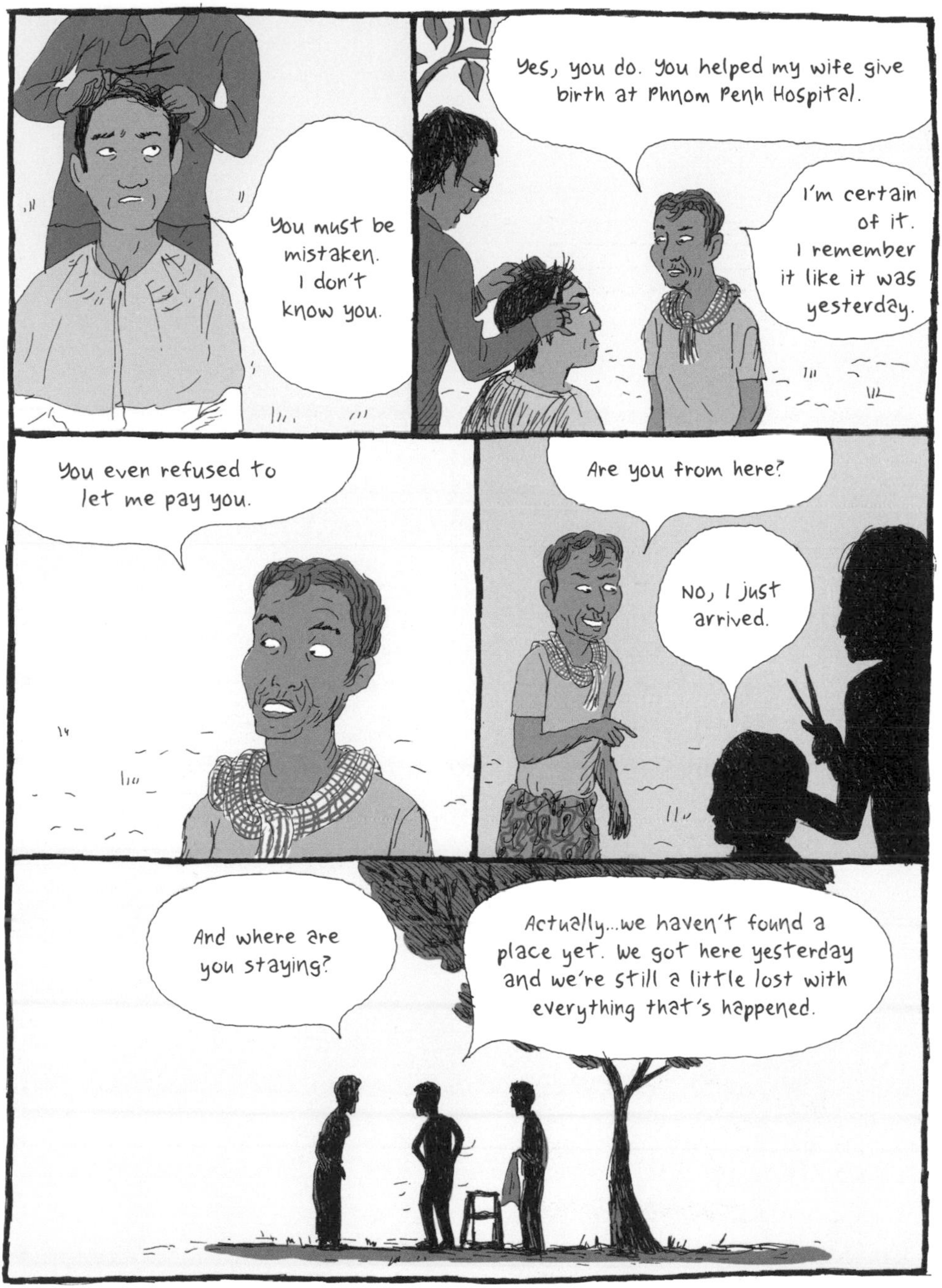
You must be mistaken. I don't know you.
Yes, you do. You helped my wife give birth at Phnom Penh Hospital.
I'm certain of it. I remember it like it was yesterday.
You even refused to let me pay you.
Are you from here?
No, I just arrived.
And where are you staying?
Actually...we haven't found a place yet. We got here yesterday and we're still a little lost with everything that's happened.

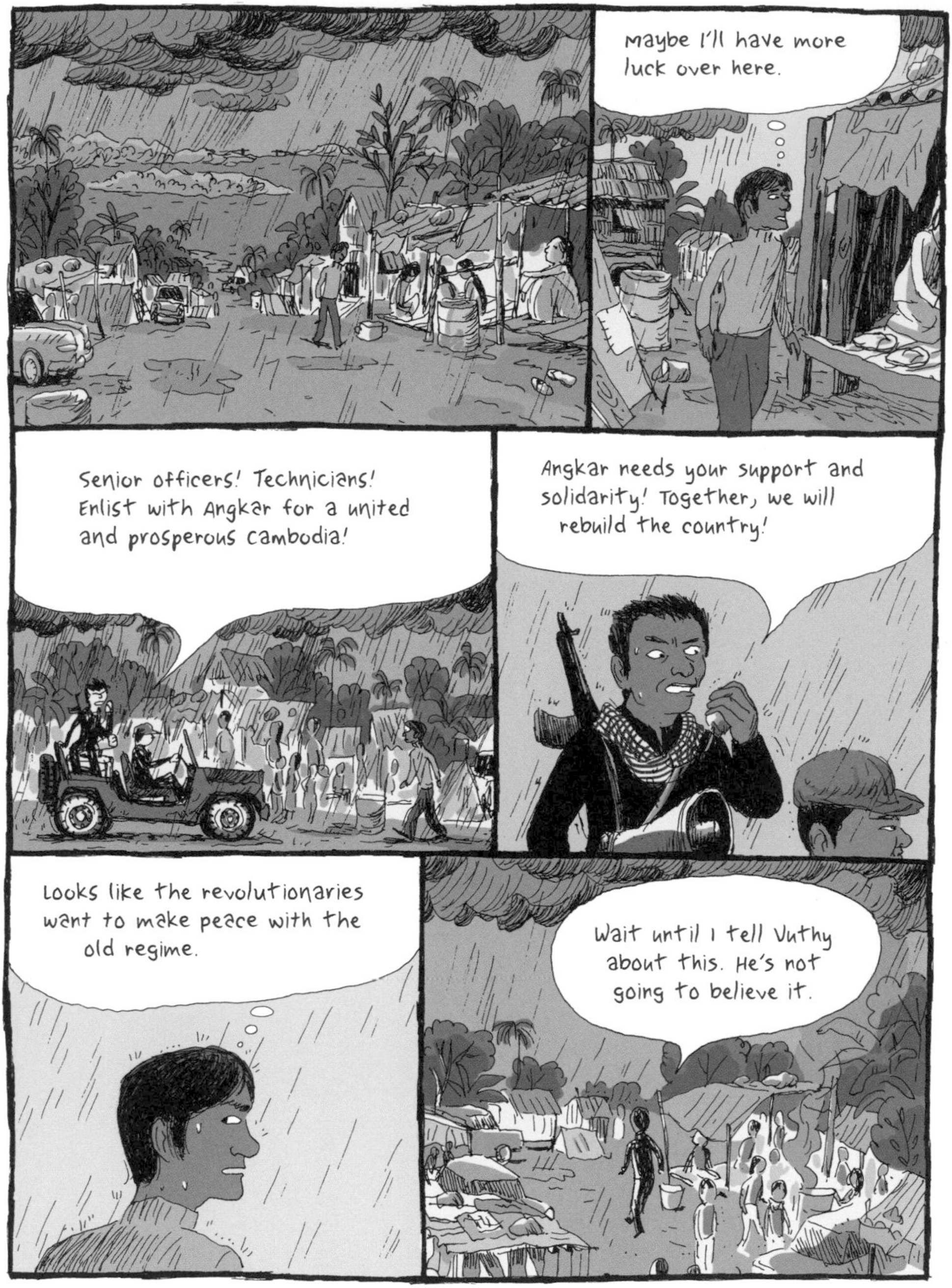

Maybe I'll have more luck over here.
Senior officers! Technicians! Enlist with Angkar for a united and prosperous Cambodia!
Angkar needs your support and solidarity! Together, we will rebuild the country!
Looks like the revolutionaries want to make peace with the old regime.
Wait until I tell Vuthy about this. He's not going to believe it.

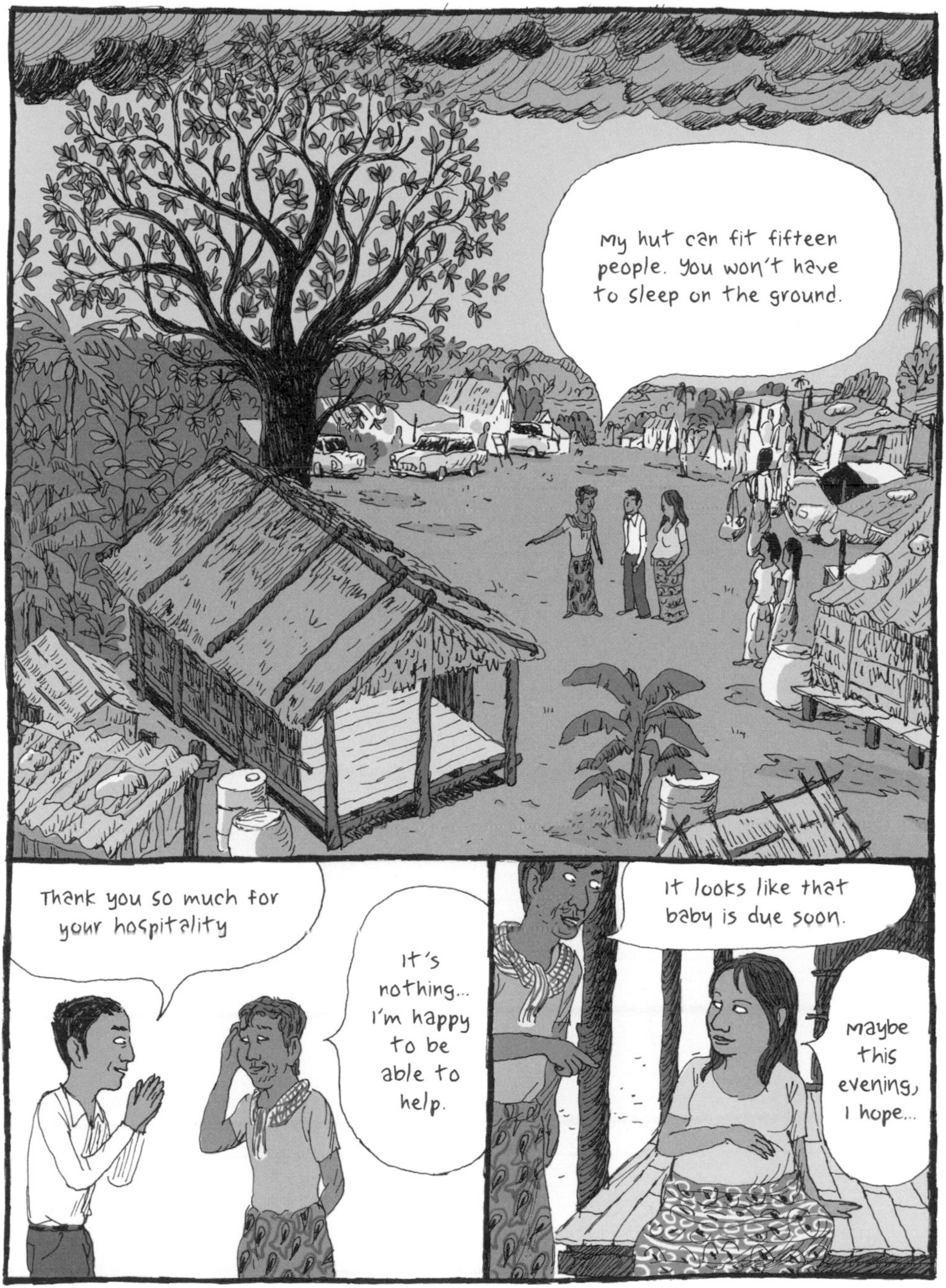
My hut can fit fifteen people. You won't have to sleep on the ground.
Thank you so much for your hospitality
It's nothing... I'm happy to be able to help.
It looks like that baby is due soon.
Maybe this evening, I hope...

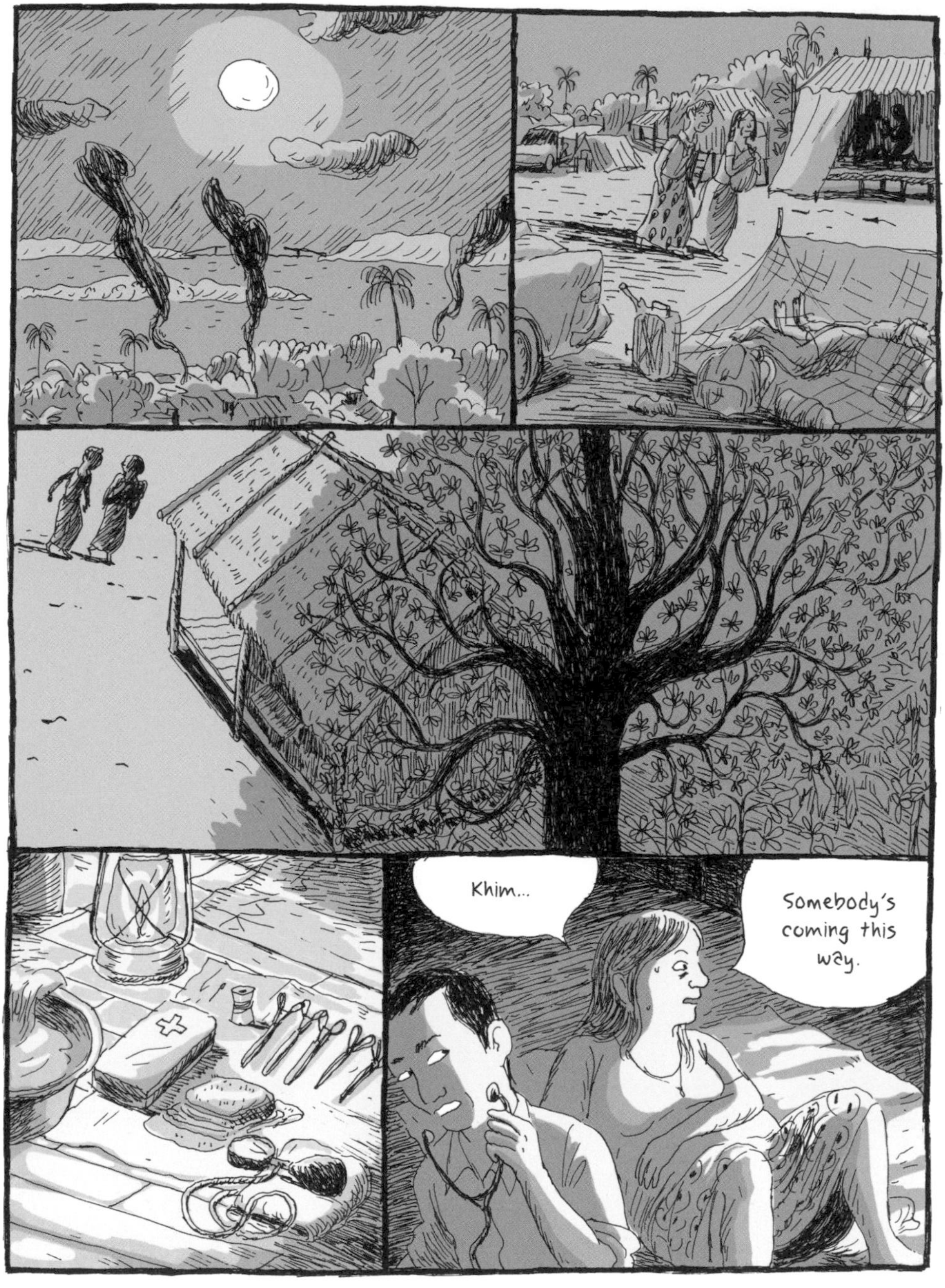
Khim...
Somebody's coming this way.

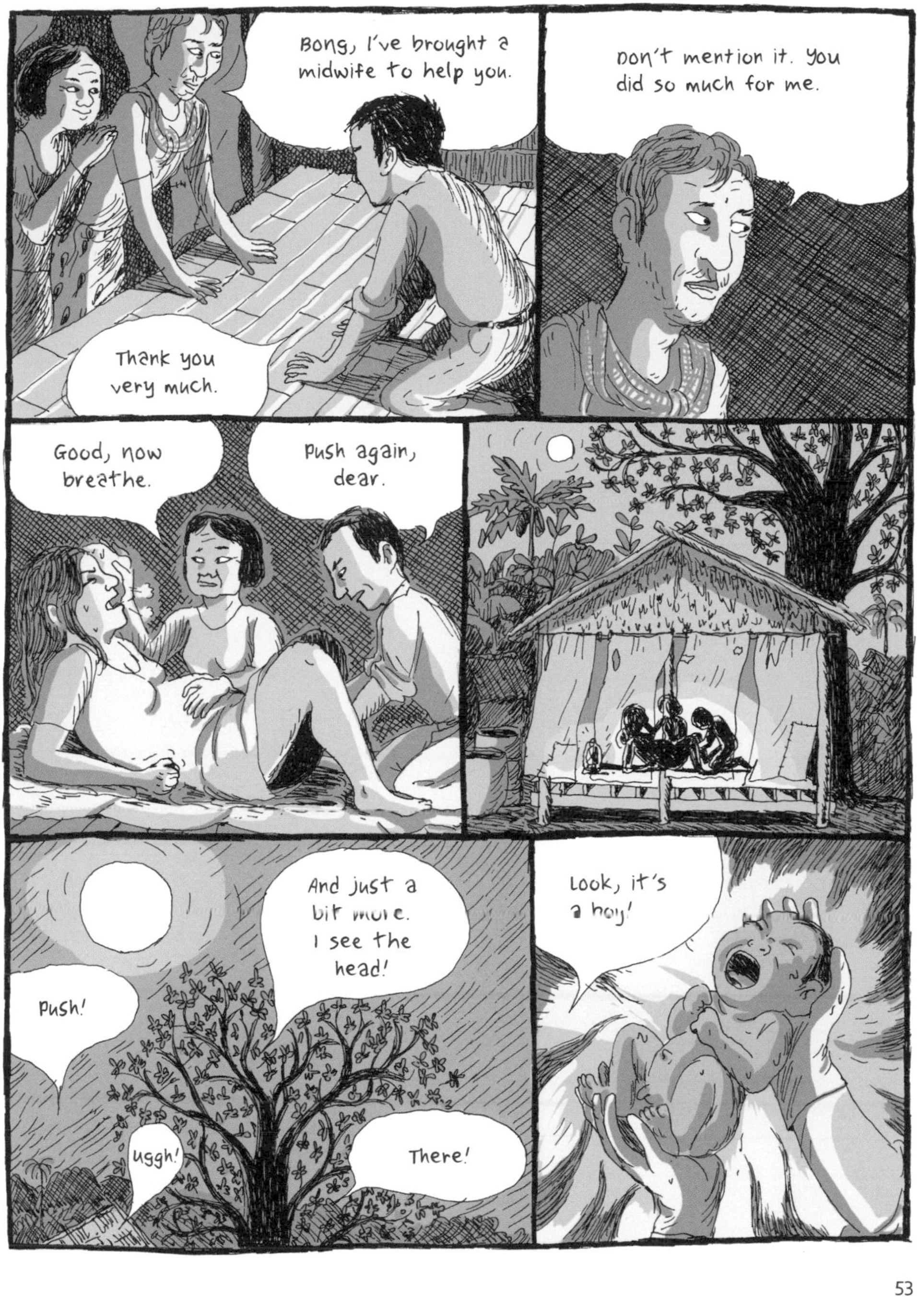

Bong, I've brought a midwife to help you.
Thank you very much.
Don't mention it. You did so much for me.
Good, now breathe.
Push again, dear.
Push!
And just a bit more. I see the head!
Uggh!
There!
Look, it's a boy!

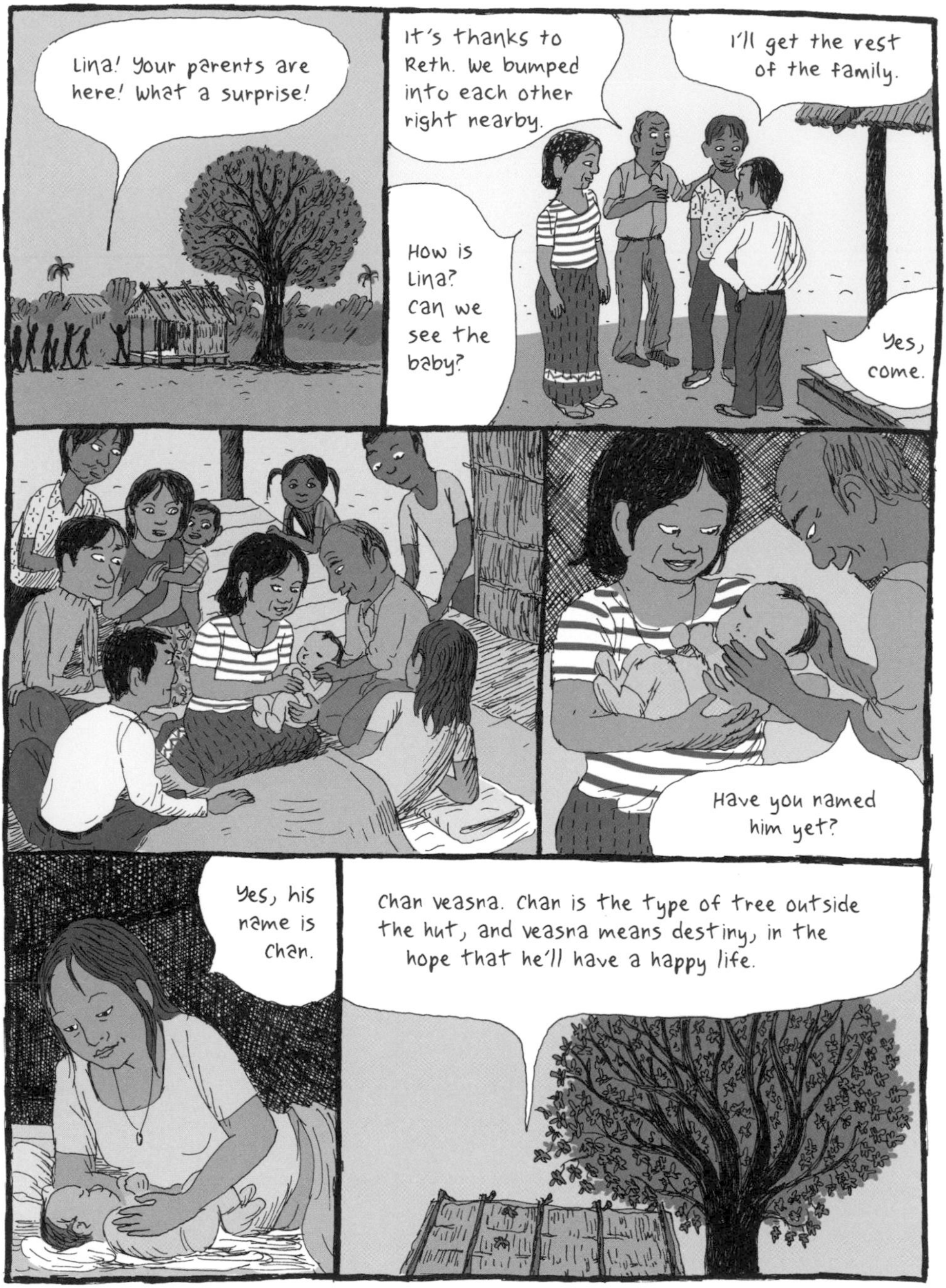
Lina! Your parents are here! What a surprise!
It's thanks to Reth. We bumped into each other right nearby.
I'll get the rest of the family.
How is Lina? Can we see the baby?
Yes, come.
Have you named him yet?
Yes, his name is Chan.
Chan Veasna. Chan is the type of tree outside the hut, and Veasna means destiny, in the hope that he'll have a happy life.

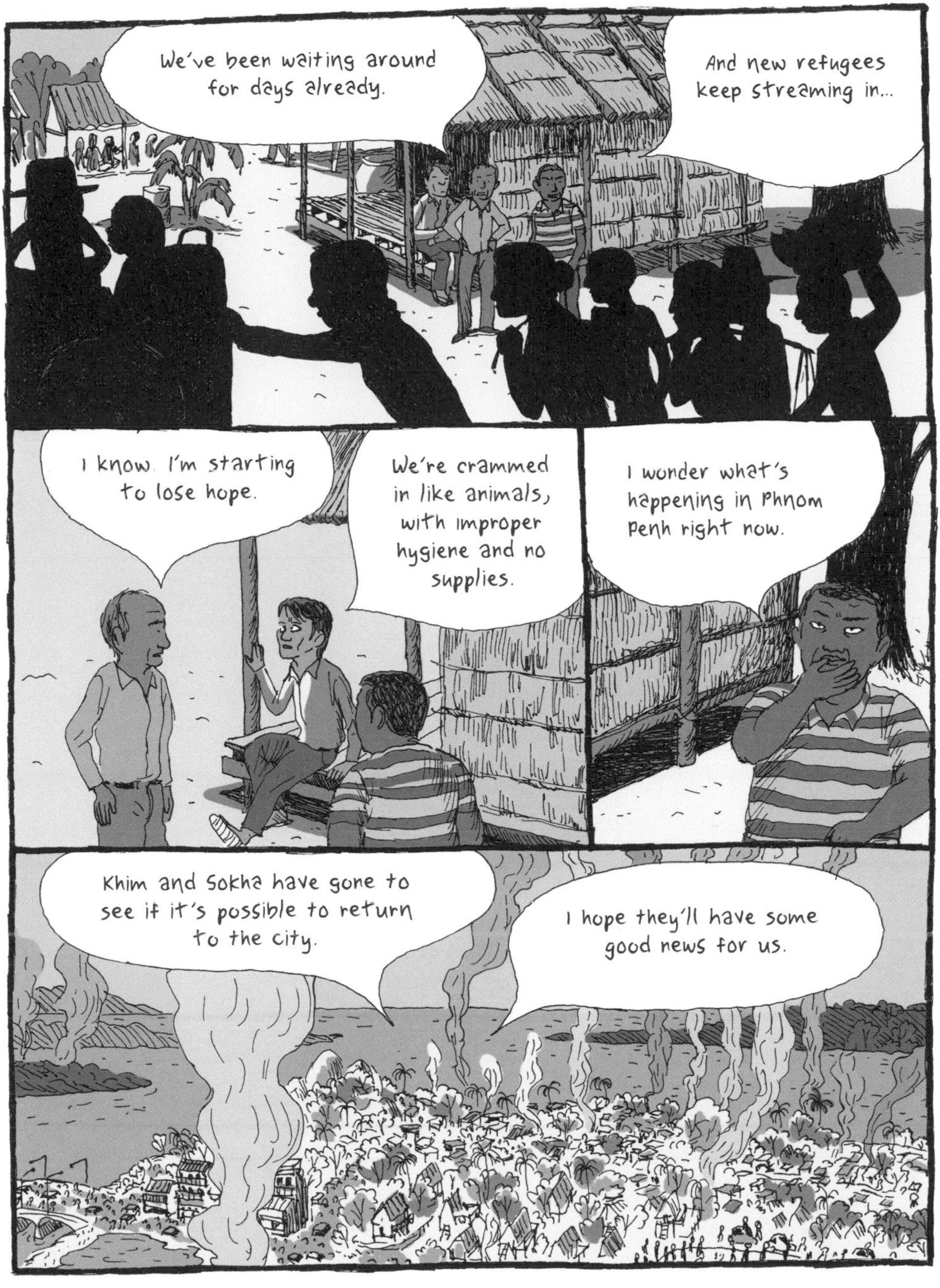
We've been waiting around for days already.
And new refugees keep streaming in...
I know. I'm starting to lose hope.
We're crammed in like animals, with improper hygiene and no supplies.
I wonder what's happening in Phnom Penh right now.
Khim and Sokha have gone to see if it's possible to return to the city.
I hope they'll have some good news for us.

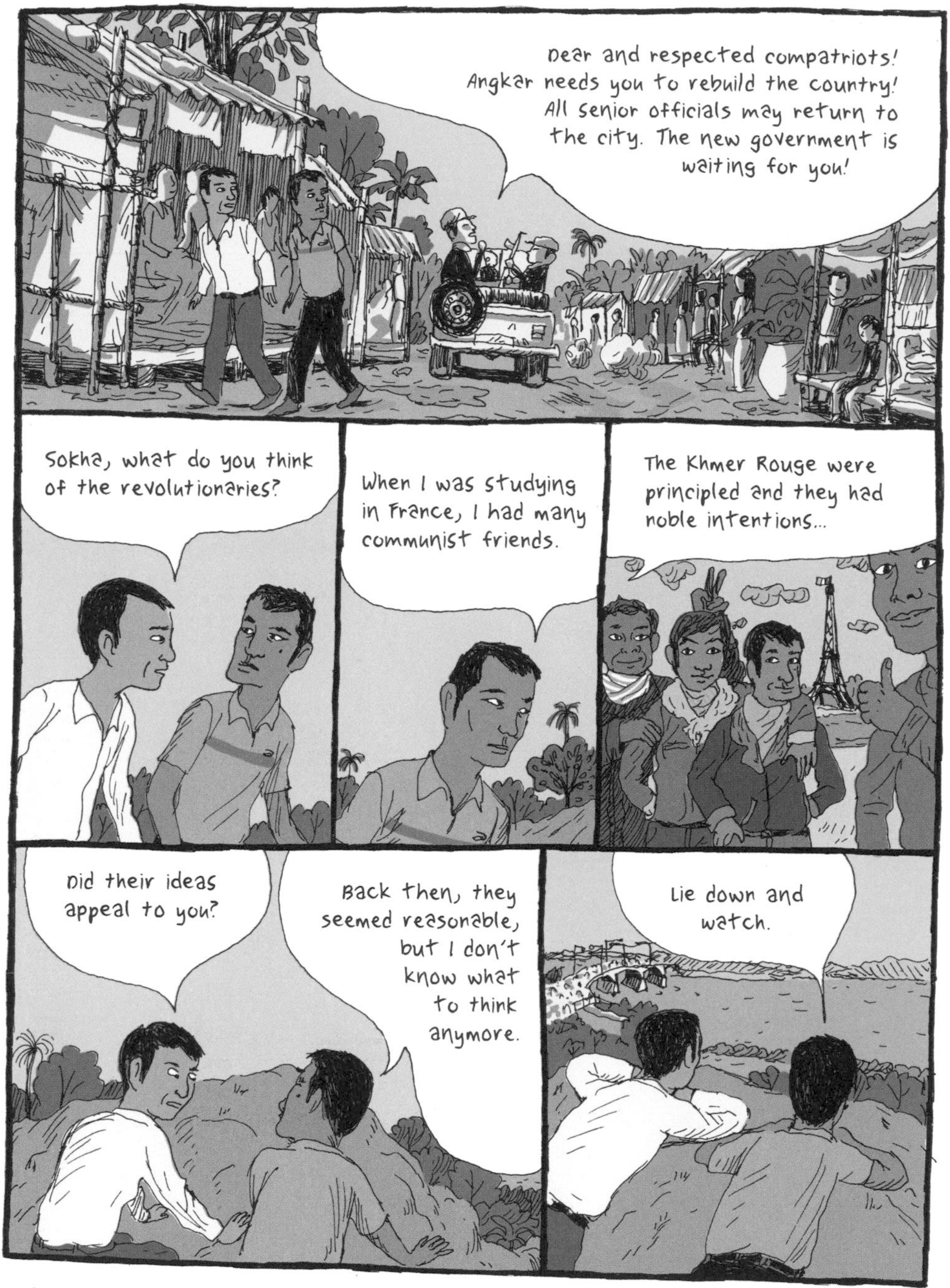

Dear and respected compatriots! Angkar needs you to rebuild the country! All senior officials may return to the city. The new government is waiting for you!
Sokha, what do you think of the revolutionaries?
When I was studying in France, I had many communist friends.
The Khmer Rouge were principled and they had noble intentions...
Did their ideas appeal to you?
Back then, they seemed reasonable, but I don't know what to think anymore.
Lie down and watch.

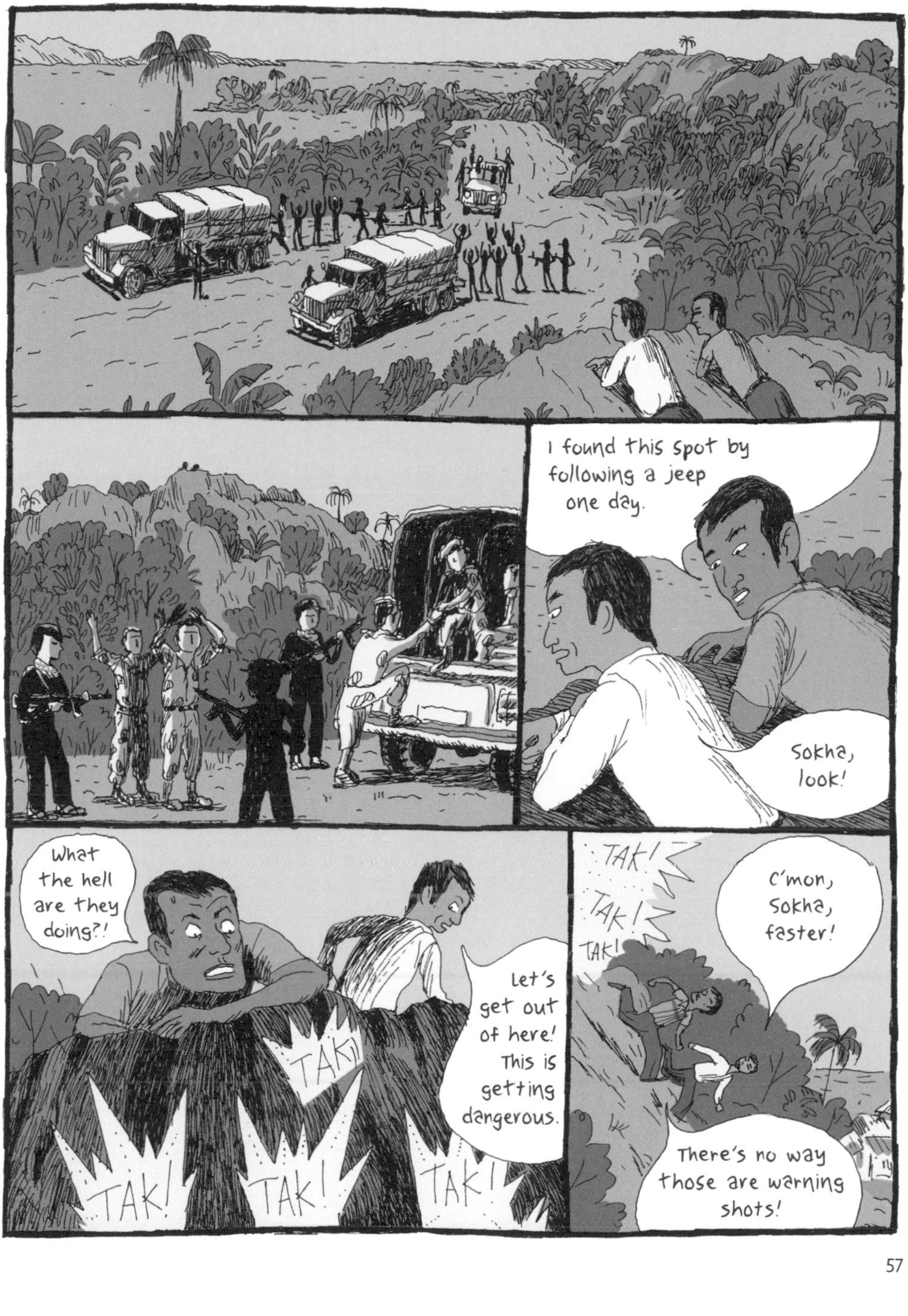
I found this spot by following a jeep one day.
Sokha, look!
What the hell are they doing?!
Let's get out of here! This is getting dangerous.
TAK!
TAK!
TAK!
TAK!
TAK!
TAK!
TAK!
C'mon, Sokha, faster!
There's no way those are warning shots!

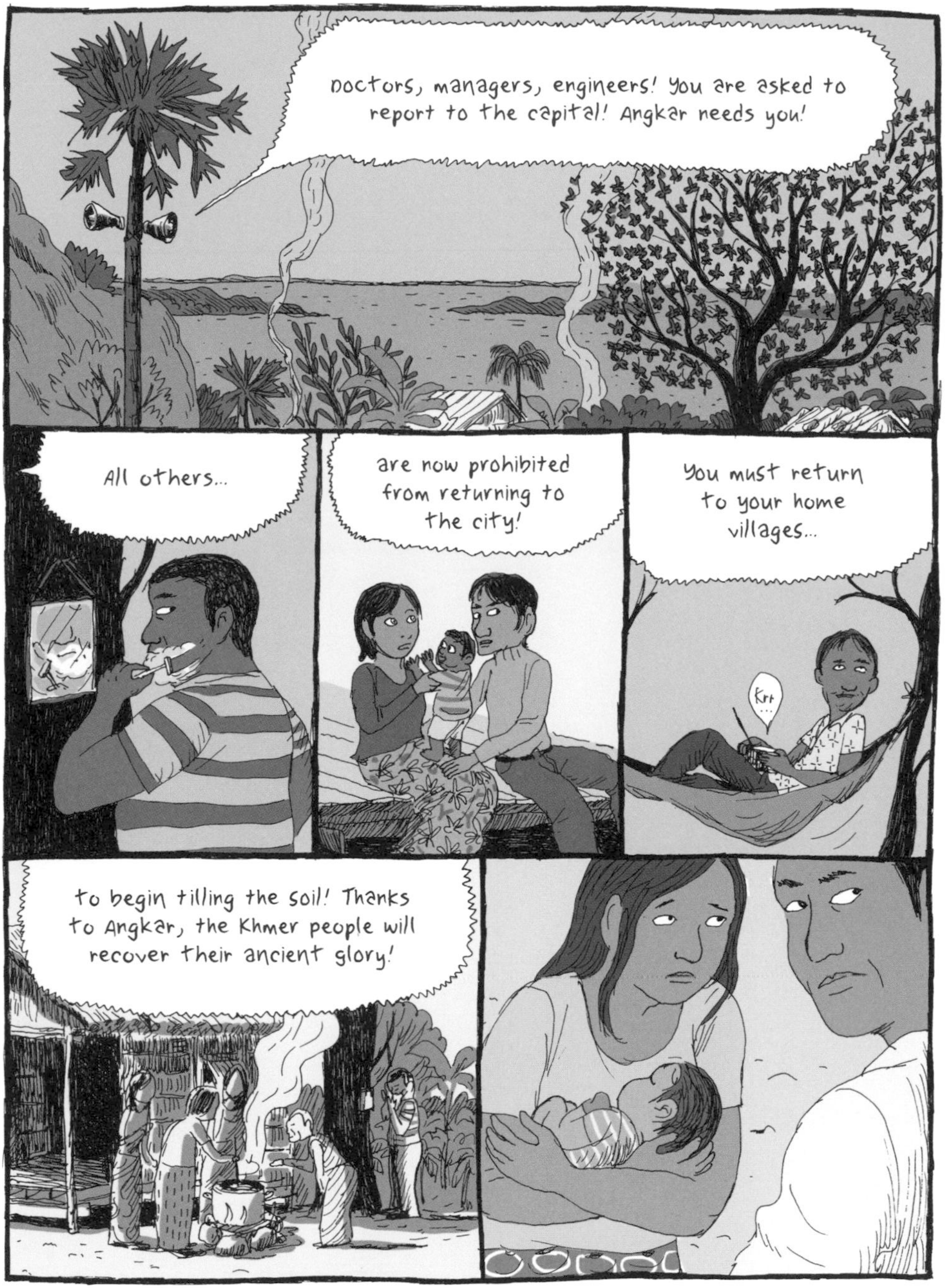

Doctors, managers, engineers! You are asked to report to the capital! Angkar needs you!
All others...
are now prohibited from returning to the city!
You must return to your home villages...
Krr...
to begin tilling the soil! Thanks to Angkar, the Khmer people will recover their ancient glory!

chapter 4

ANGKAR

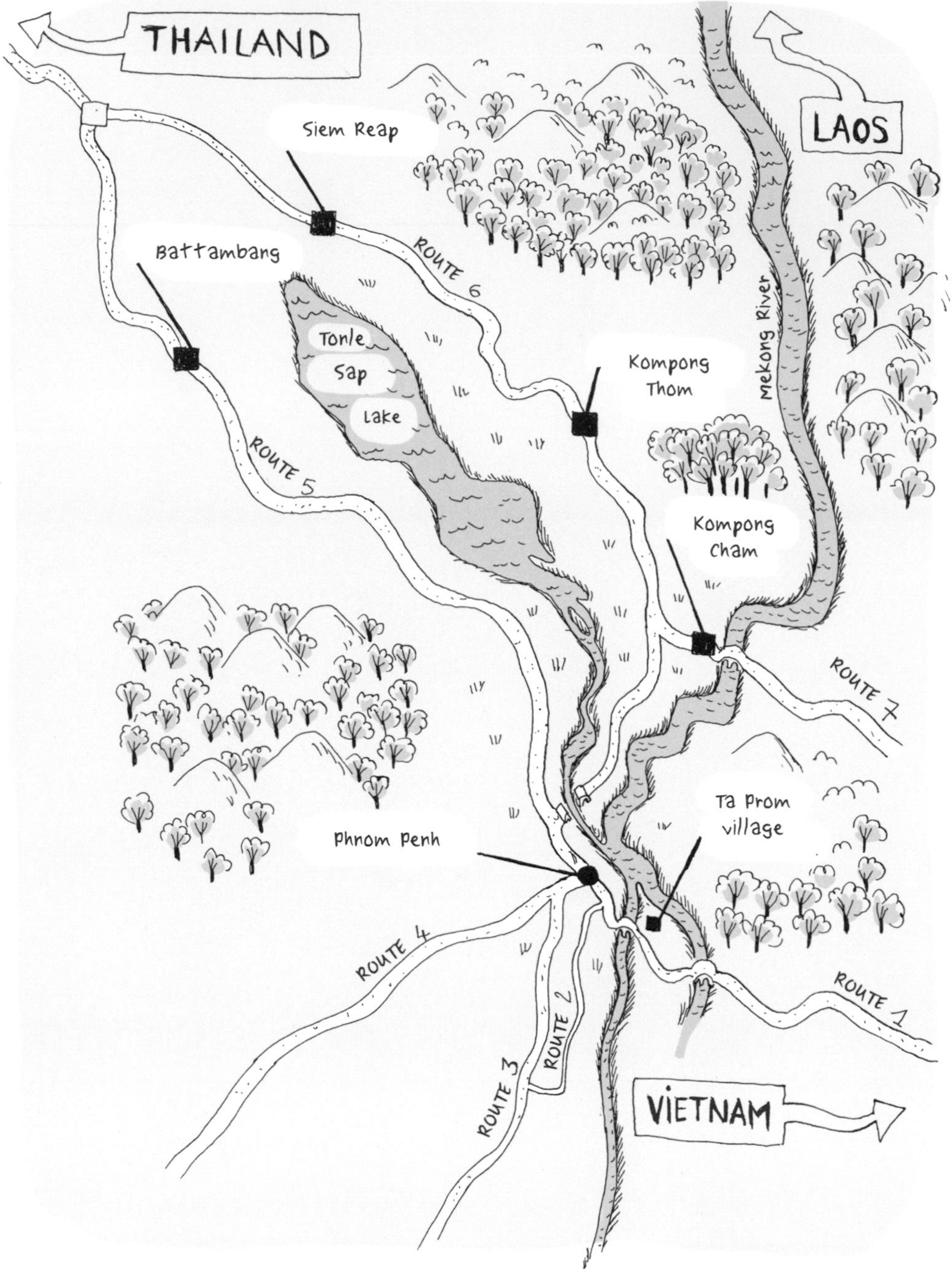
THAILAND
LAOS
Siem Reap
Battambang
ROUTE 6
Tonle
Sap
Lake
Kompong
Thom
Mekong River
ROUTE 5
Kompong
Cham
ROUTE 7
Ta Prom
village
Phnom Penh
ROUTE 4
ROUTE 2
ROUTE 3
ROUTE 1
VIETNAM

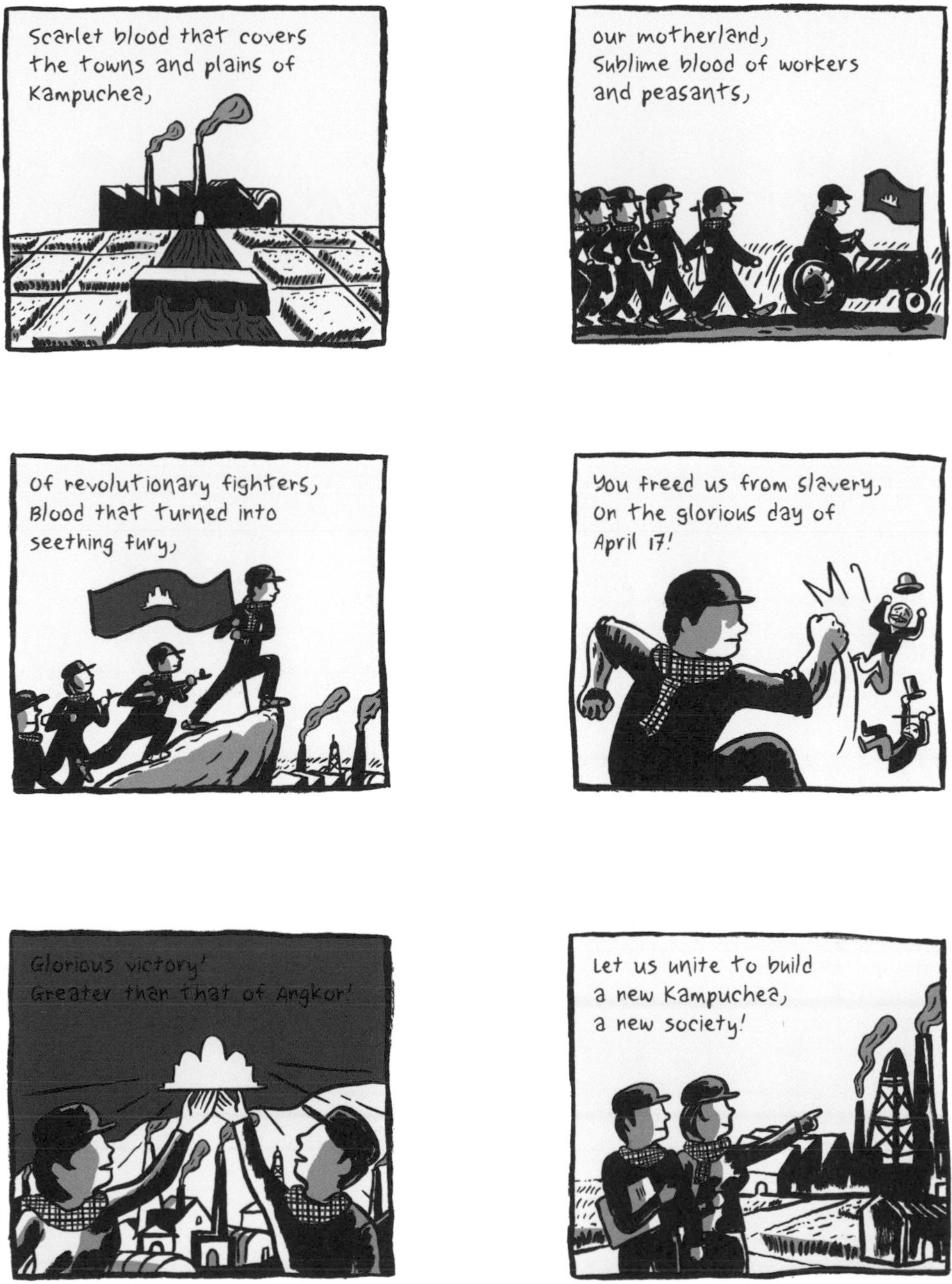
Scarlet blood that covers the towns and plains of Kampuchea,
our motherland, Sublime blood of workers and peasants,
Of revolutionary fighters, Blood that turned into seething fury,
You freed us from slavery, On the glorious day of April 17!
Glorious victory! Greater than that of Angkor!
Let us unite to build a new Kampuchea, a new society!

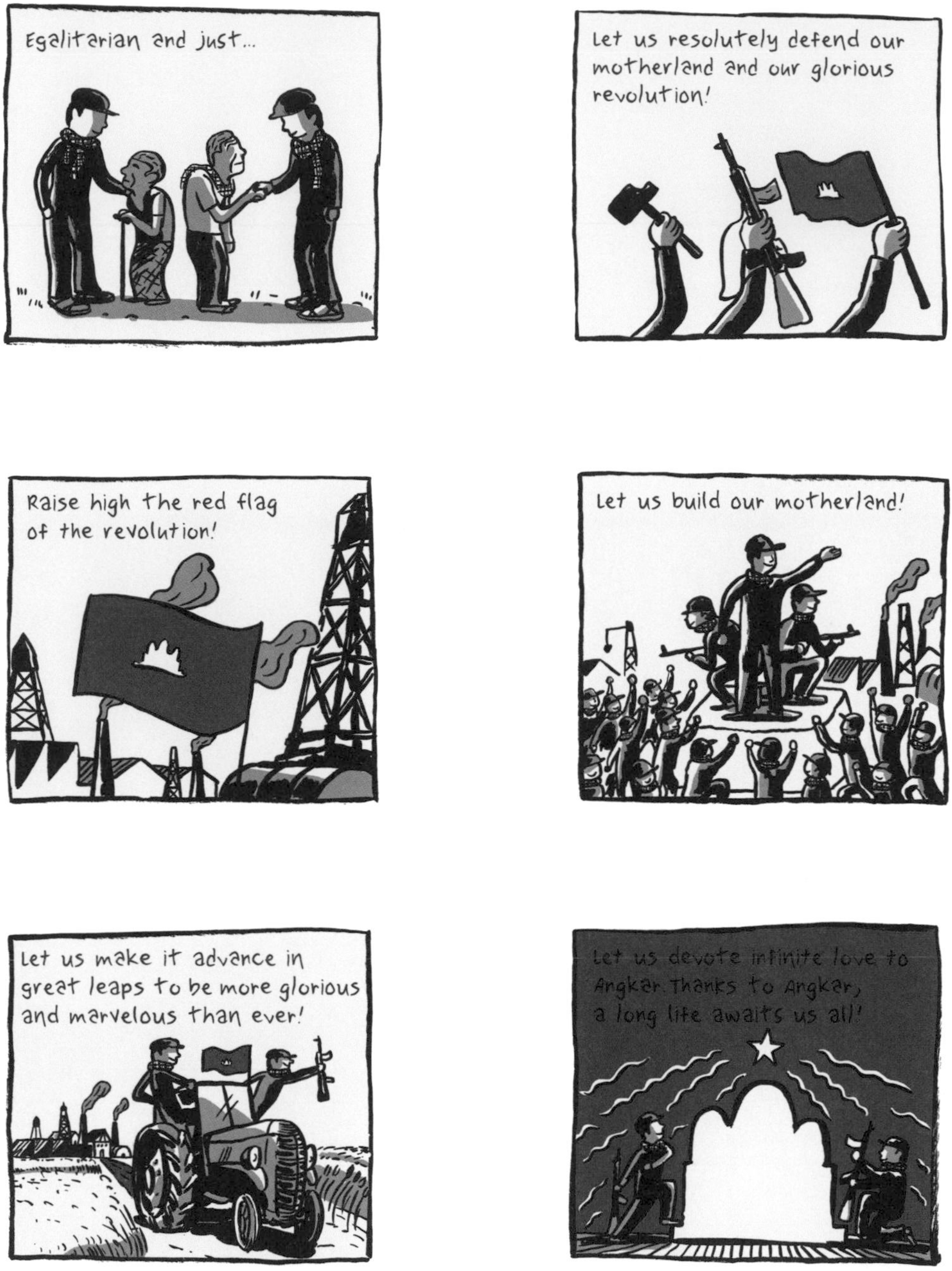
Egalitarian and just...
Let us resolutely defend our motherland and our glorious revolution!
Raise high the red flag of the revolution!
Let us build our motherland!
Let us make it advance in great leaps to be more glorious and marvelous than ever!
Let us devote infinite love to Angkar. Thanks to Angkar, a long life awaits us all!

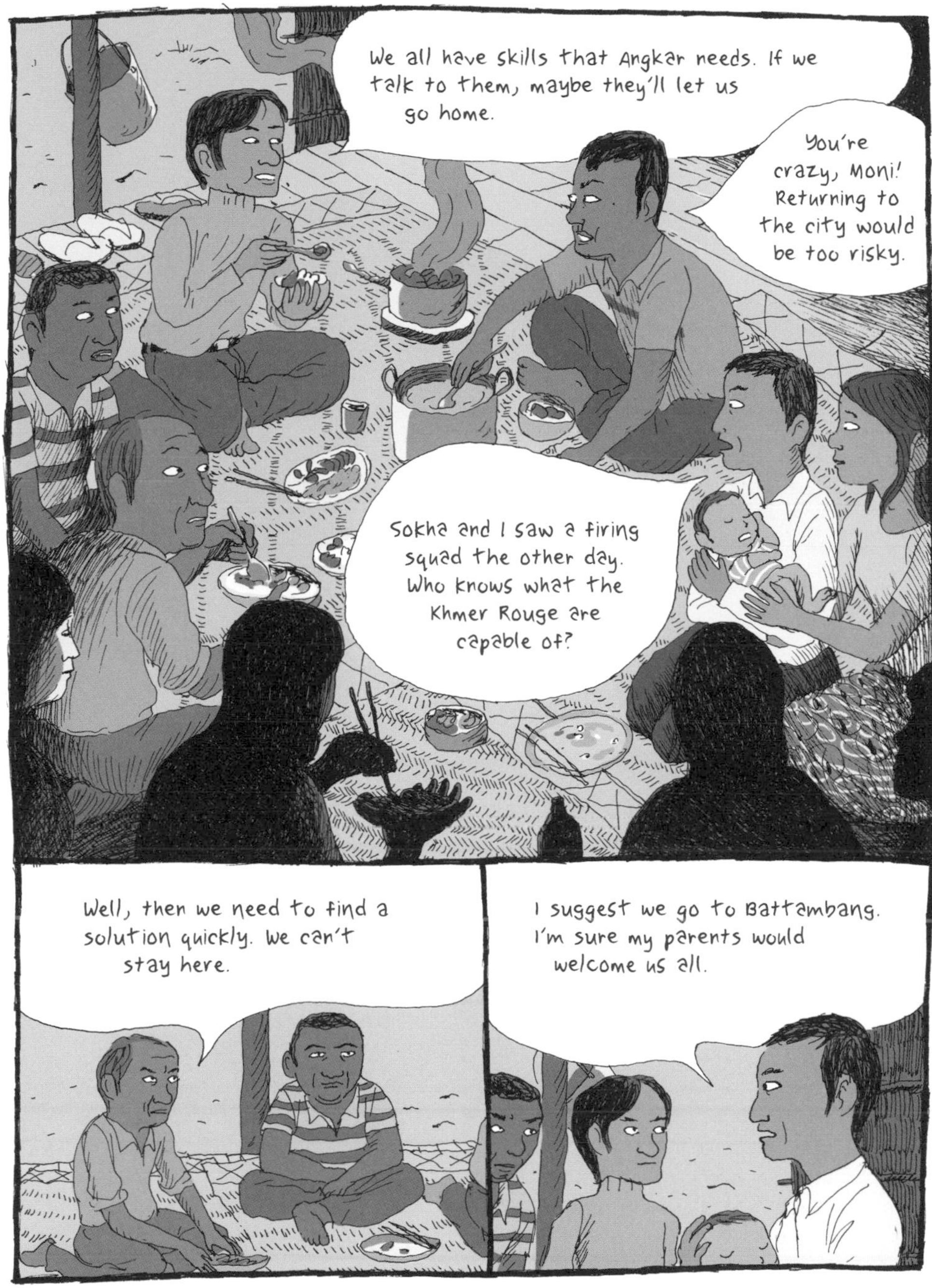
We all have skills that Angkar needs. If we talk to them, maybe they'll let us go home.
You're crazy, Moni! Returning to the city would be too risky.
Sokha and I saw a firing squad the other day. Who knows what the Khmer Rouge are capable of?
Well, then we need to find a solution quickly. We can't stay here.
I suggest we go to Battambang. I'm sure my parents would welcome us all.

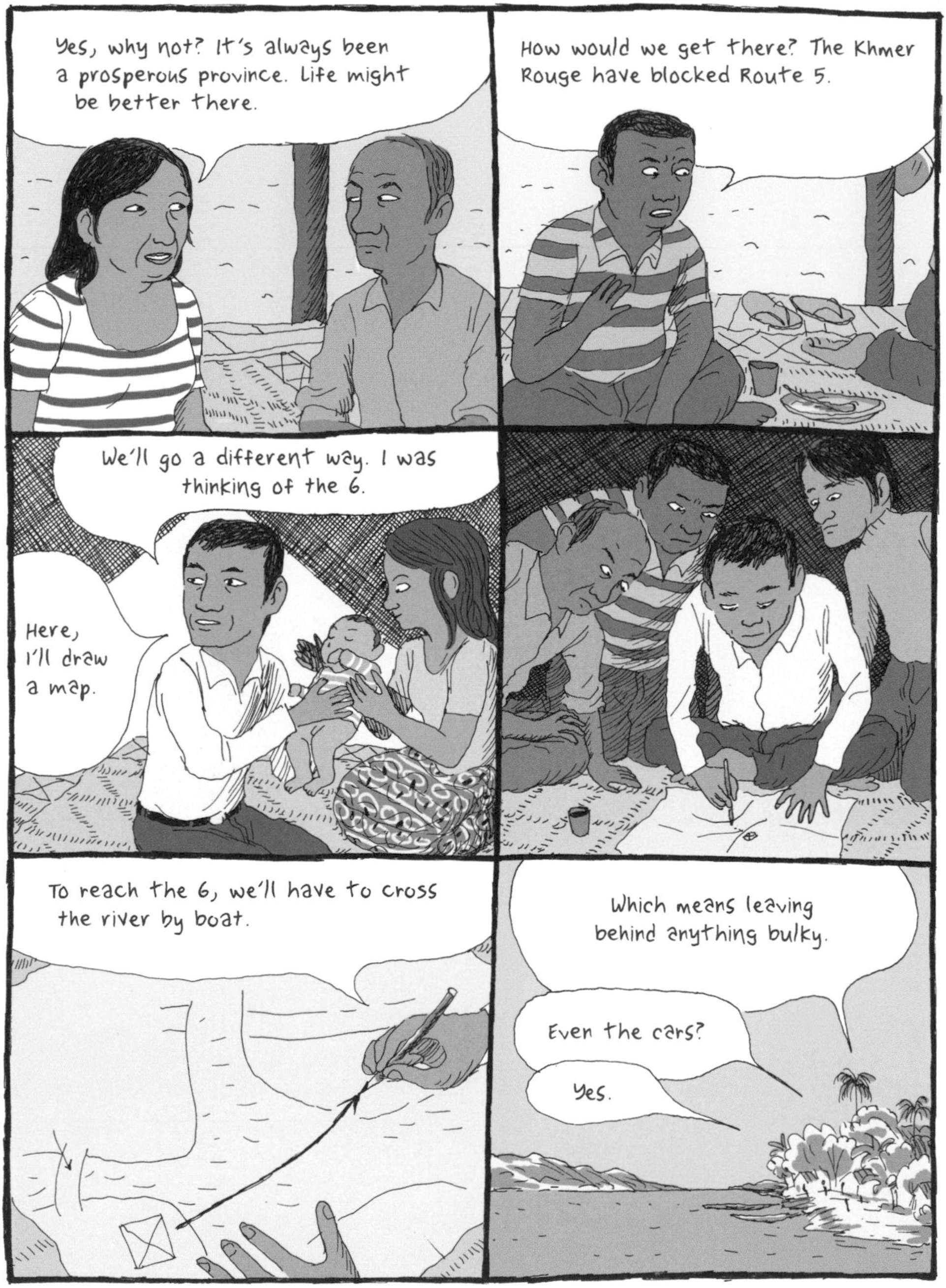
Yes, why not? It's always been a prosperous province. Life might be better there.
How would we get there? The Khmer Rouge have blocked Route 5.
We'll go a different way. I was thinking of the 6.
Here, I'll draw a map.
To reach the 6, we'll have to cross the river by boat.
Which means leaving behind anything bulky.
Even the cars?
Yes.

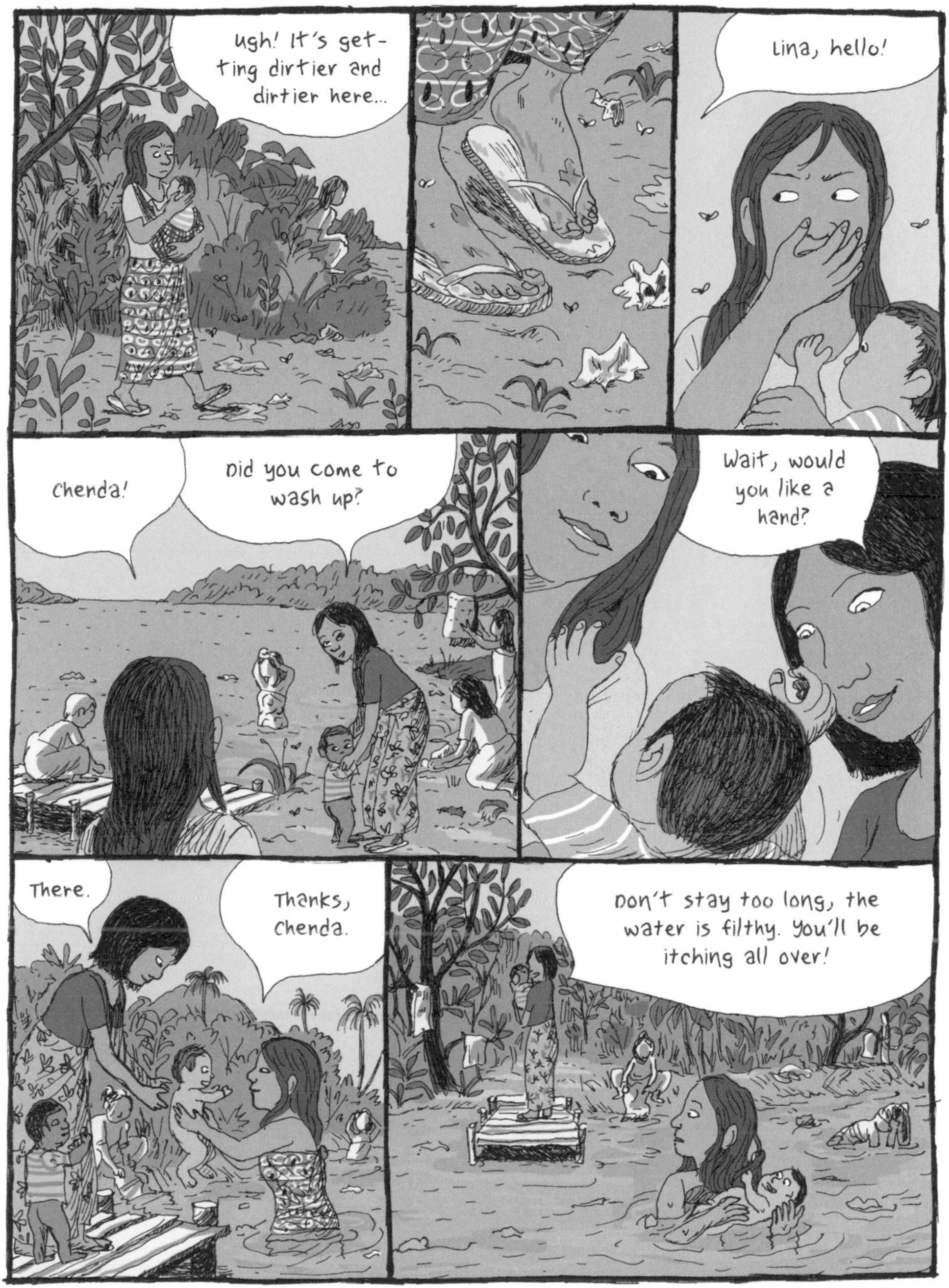
Ugh! It's getting dirtier and dirtier here...
Lina, hello!
Chenda!
Did you come to wash up?
Wait, would you like a hand?
There.
Thanks, Chenda.
Don't stay too long, the water is filthy. You'll be itching all over!

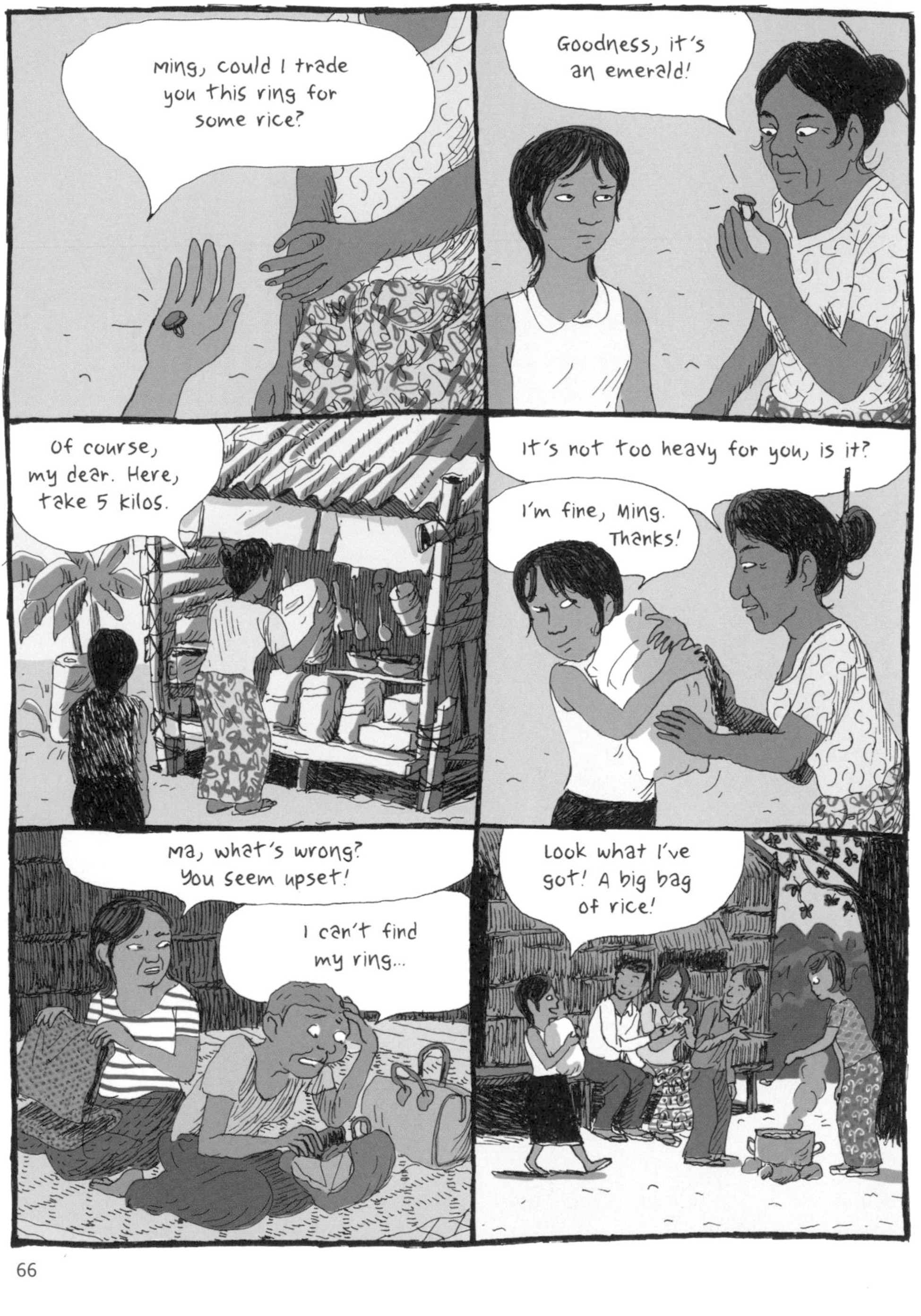
Ming, could I trade you this ring for some rice?
Goodness, it's an emerald!
Of course, my dear. Here, take 5 kilos.
It's not too heavy for you, is it?
I'm fine, Ming. Thanks!
Ma, what's wrong? You seem upset!
I can't find my ring...
Look what I've got! A big bag of rice!

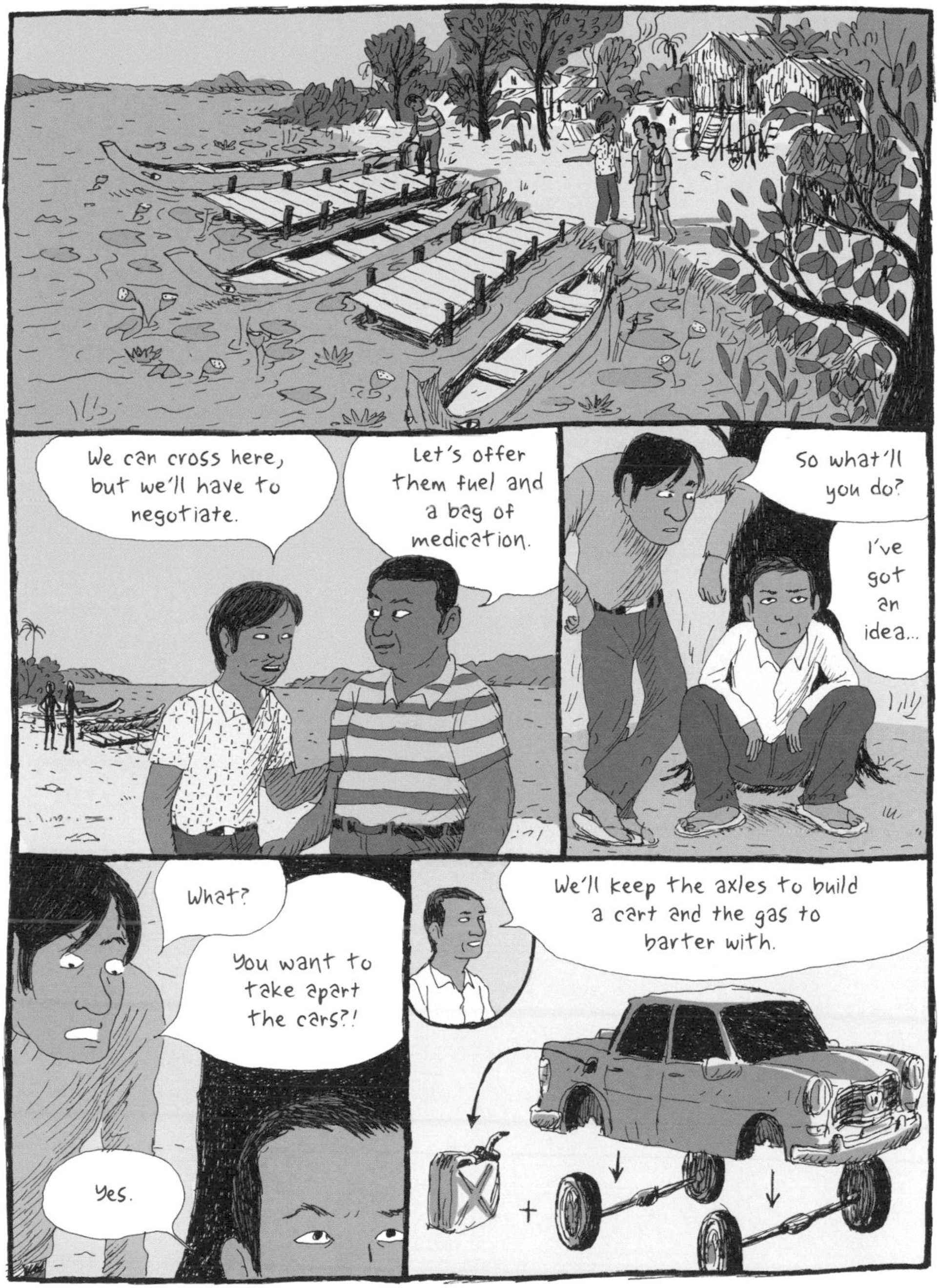
We can cross here, but we'll have to negotiate.
Let's offer them fuel and a bag of medication.
So what'll you do?
I've got an idea...
What?
You want to take apart the cars?!
Yes.
We'll keep the axles to build a cart and the gas to barter with.
+

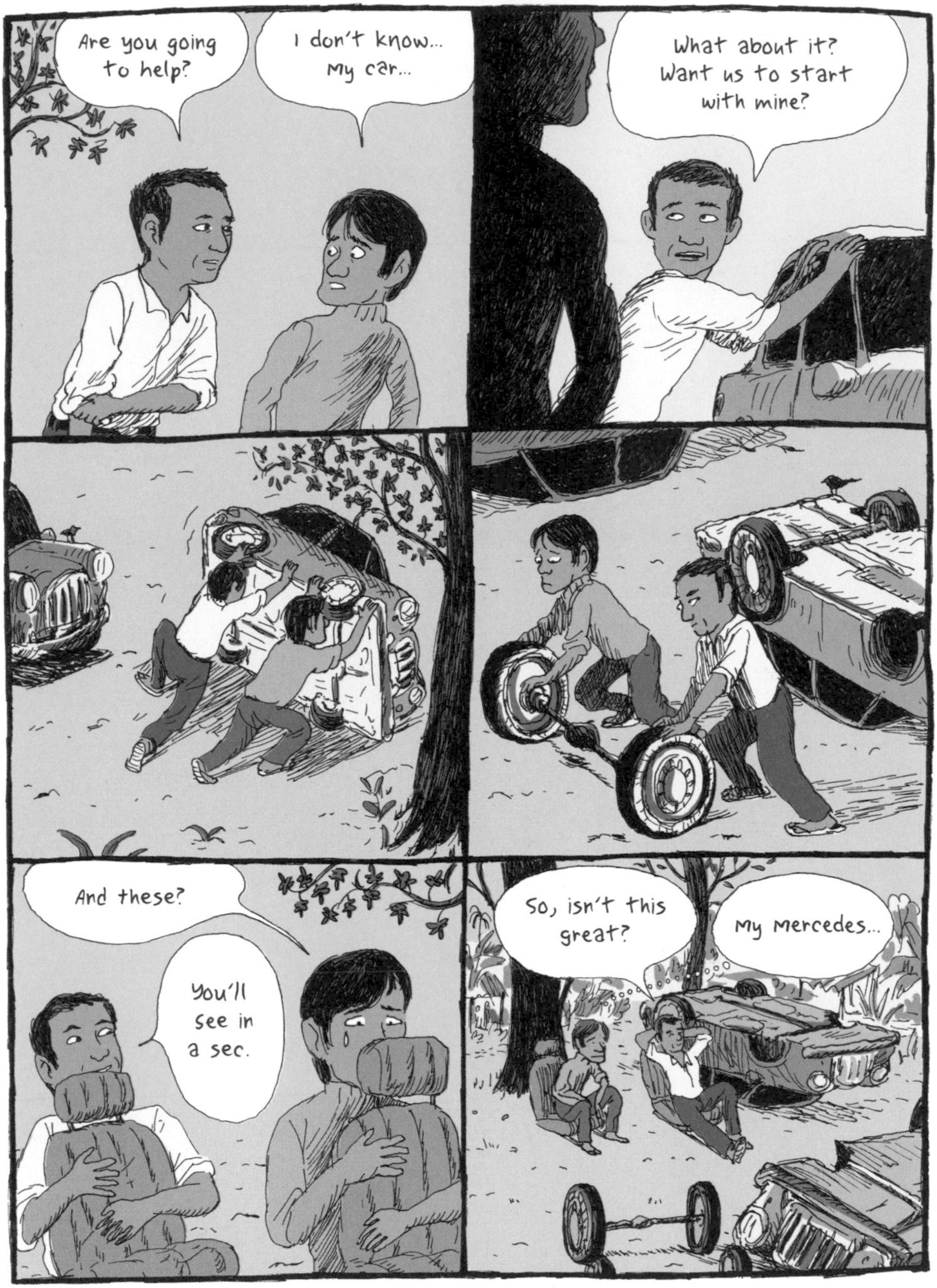

Are you going to help?
I don't know... My car...
What about it? Want us to start with mine?
And these?
You'll see in a sec.
So, isn't this great?
My Mercedes...

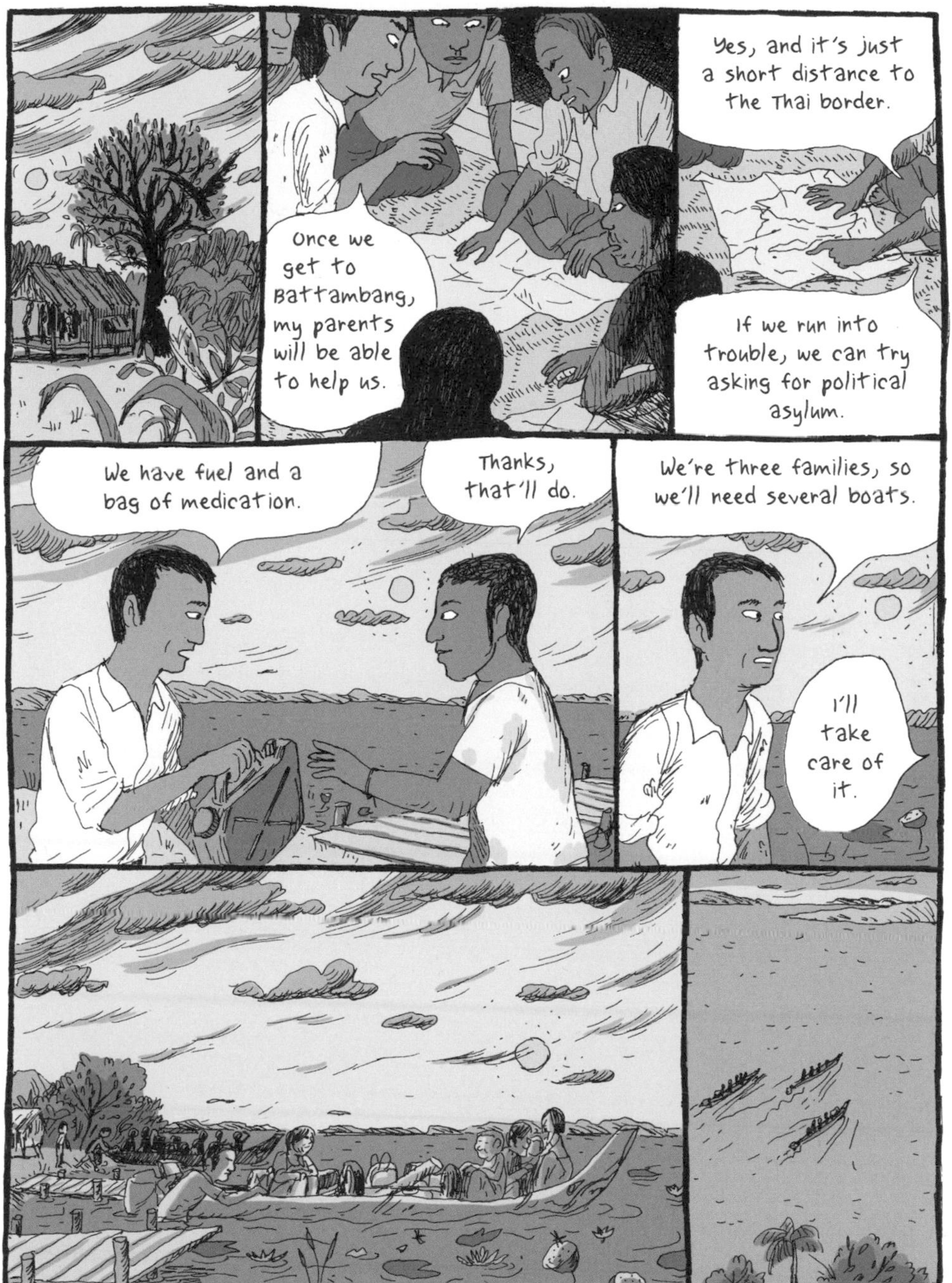
Once we get to Battambang, my parents will be able to help us.
Yes, and it's just a short distance to the Thai border.
If we run into trouble, we can try asking for political asylum.
We have fuel and a bag of medication.
Thanks, that'll do.
We're three families, so we'll need several boats.
I'll take care of it.

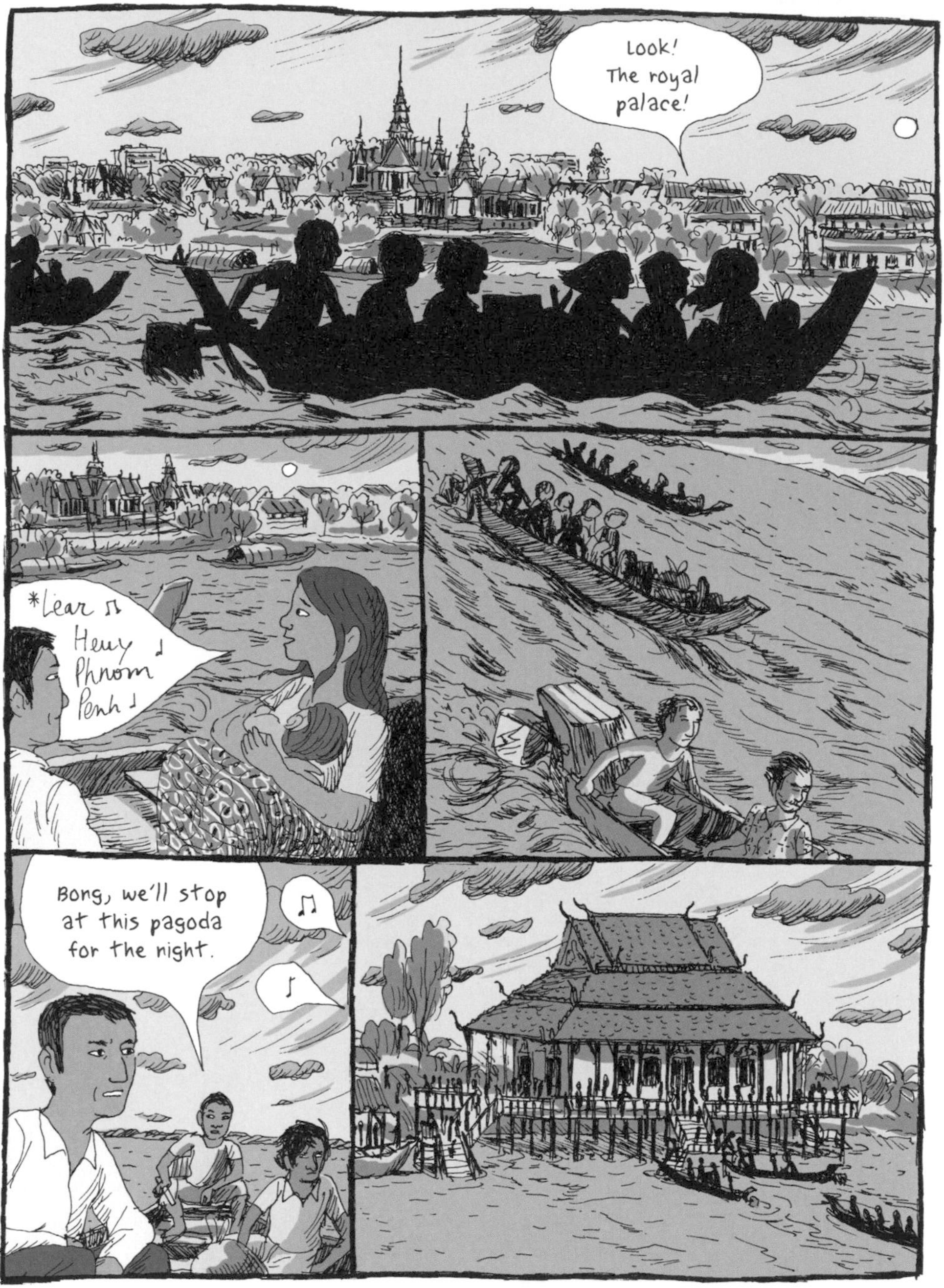
Look! The royal palace!
*Lear ♫ Heuy ♩ Phnom Penh ♩
Bong, we'll stop at this pagoda for the night.
♫
♪

*Lear Heuy Phnom Penh: Goodbye, Phnom Penh

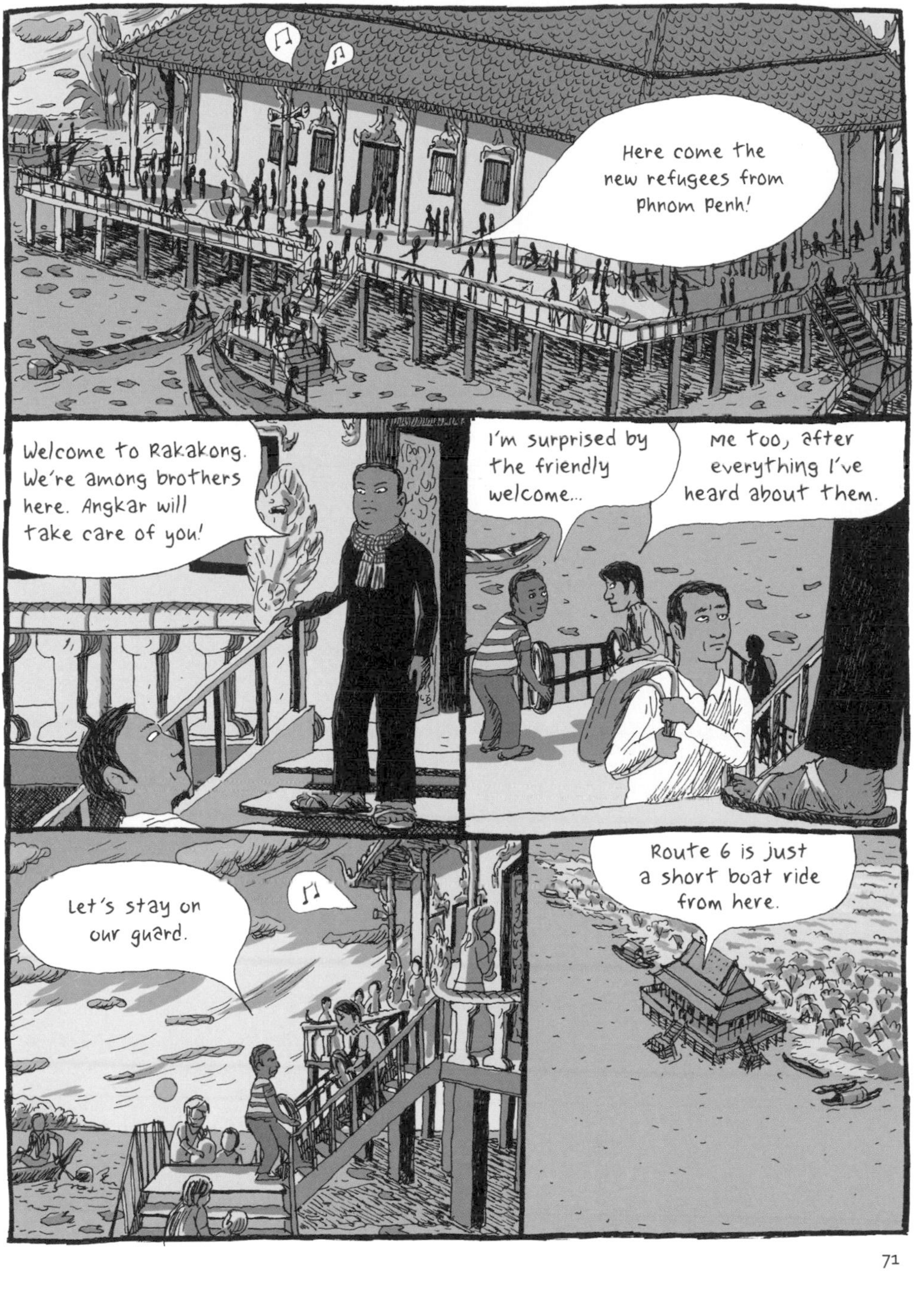
Here come the new refugees from Phnom Penh!
Welcome to Rakakong. We're among brothers here. Angkar will take care of you!
I'm surprised by the friendly welcome...
Me too, after everything I've heard about them.
Let's stay on our guard.
Route 6 is just a short boat ride from here.

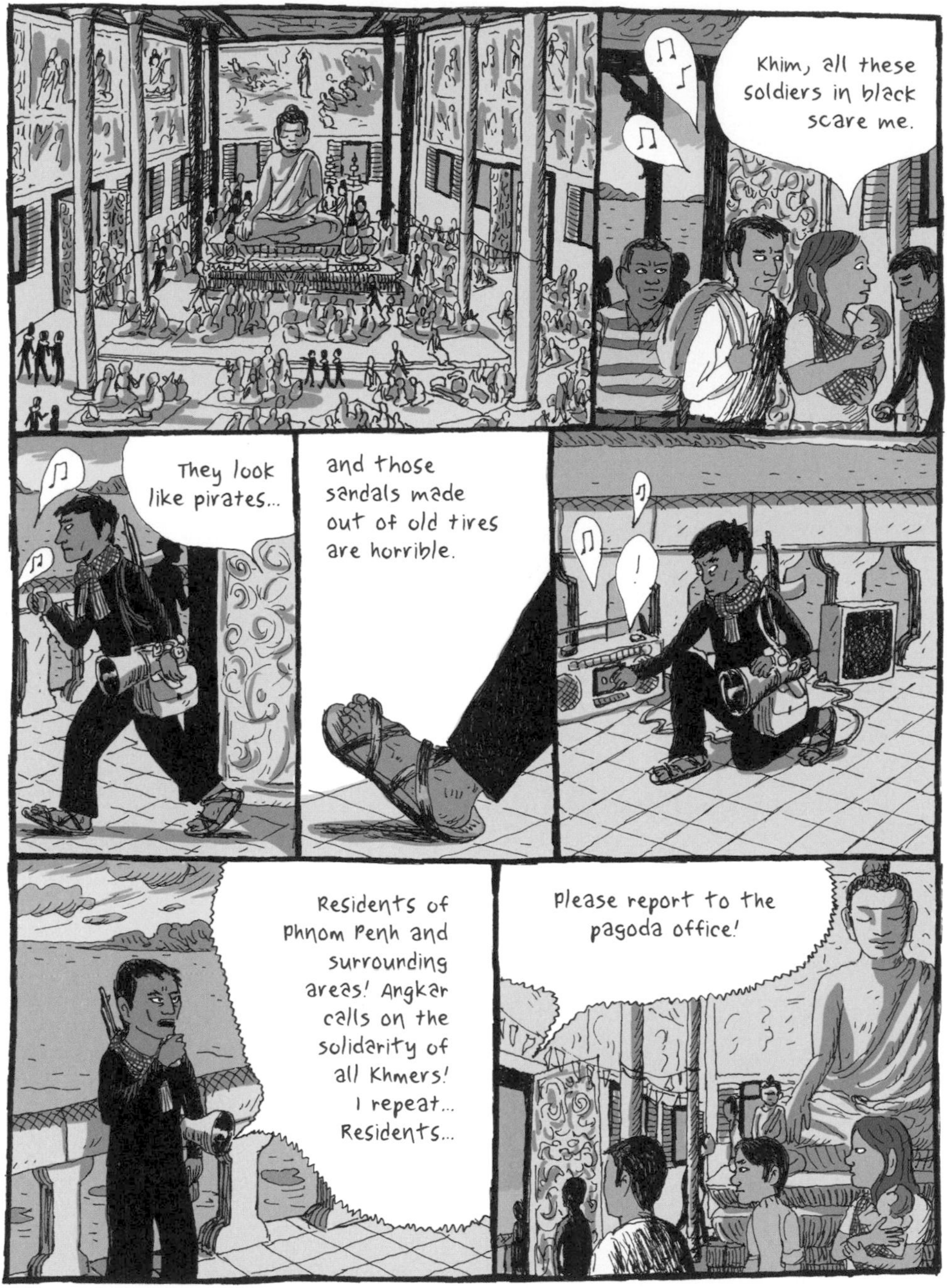
Khim, all these soldiers in black scare me.
They look like pirates...
and those sandals made out of old tires are horrible.
!
Residents of Phnom Penh and surrounding areas! Angkar calls on the solidarity of all Khmers! I repeat... Residents...
Please report to the pagoda office!

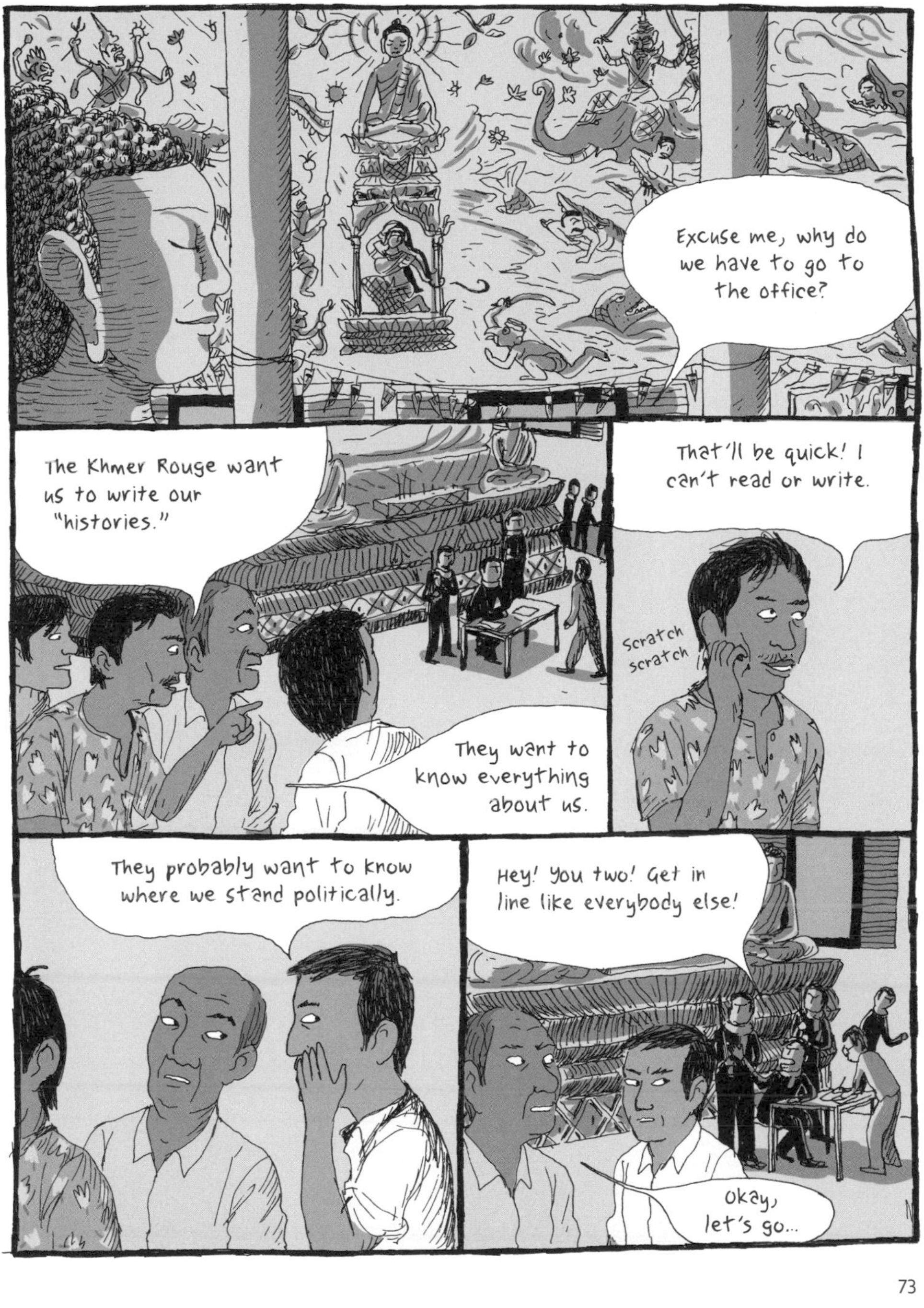
Excuse me, why do we have to go to the office?
The Khmer Rouge want us to write our "histories."
They want to know everything about us.
That'll be quick! I can't read or write.
Scratch scratch
They probably want to know where we stand politically.
Hey! You two! Get in line like everybody else!
Okay, let's go...

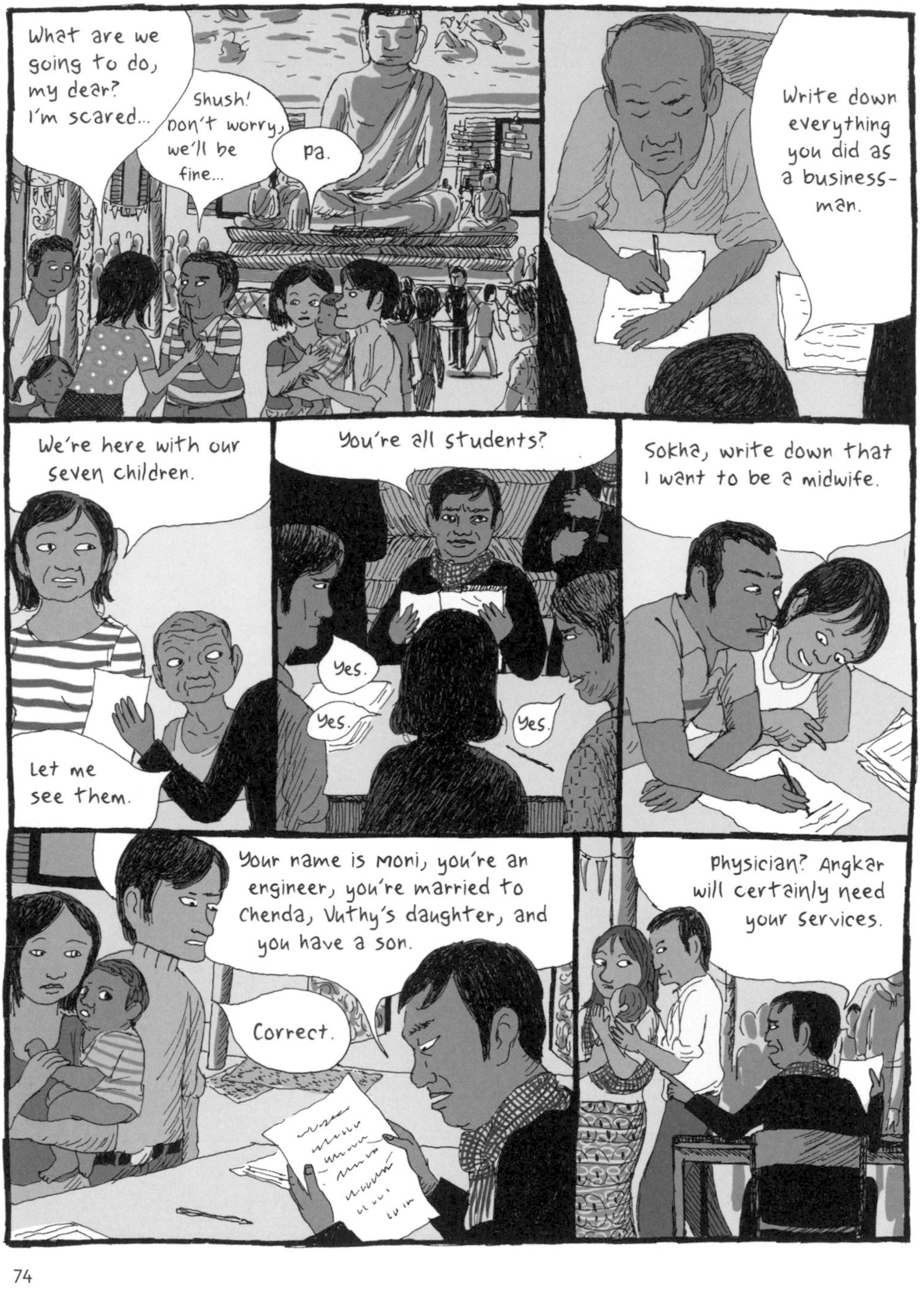
What are we going to do, my dear? I'm scared...
Shush! Don't worry, we'll be fine...
Pa.
Write down everything you did as a business-man.
We're here with our seven children.
Let me see them.
You're all students?
Yes.
Yes.
Yes.
Sokha, write down that I want to be a midwife.
Your name is Moni, you're an engineer, you're married to Chenda, Vuthy's daughter, and you have a son.
Correct.
Physician? Angkar will certainly need your services.

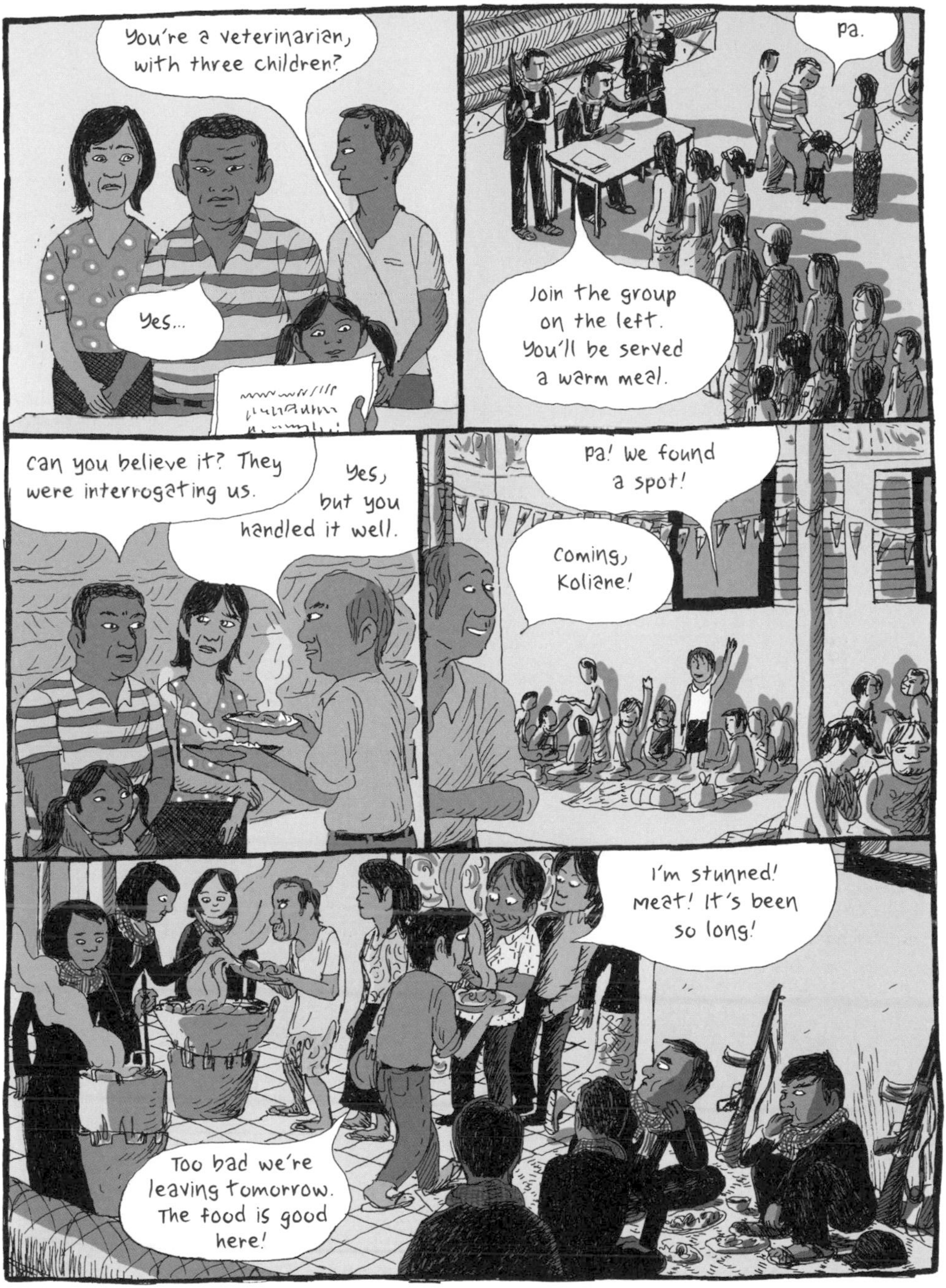

You're a veterinarian, with three children?
Yes...
Pa.
Join the group on the left. You'll be served a warm meal.
Can you believe it? They were interrogating us.
Yes, but you handled it well.
Pa! We found a spot!
Coming, Koliane!
I'm stunned! Meat! It's been so long!
Too bad we're leaving tomorrow. The food is good here!

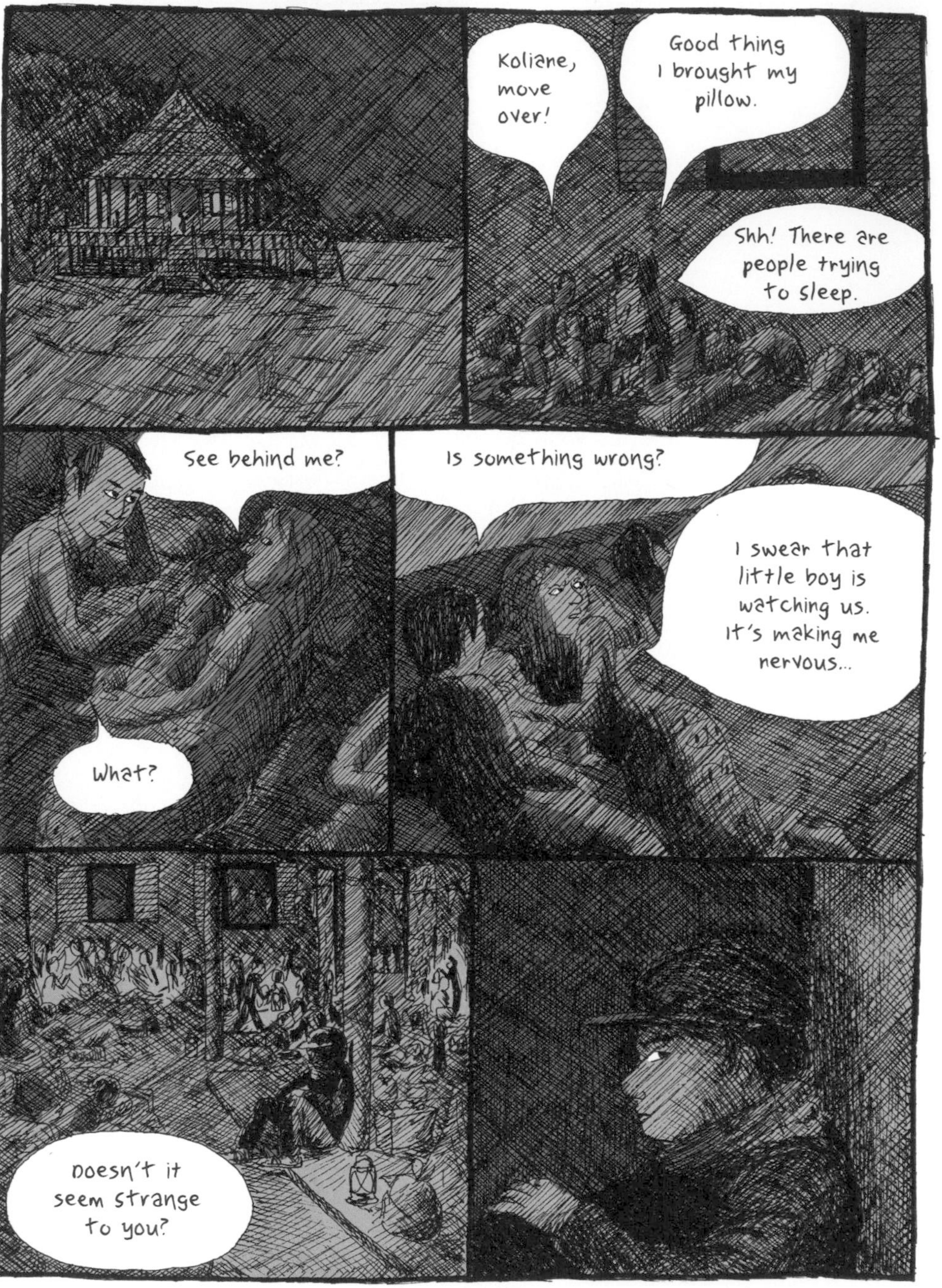
Koliane, move over!
Good thing I brought my pillow.
Shh! There are people trying to sleep.
See behind me?
What?
Is something wrong?
I swear that little boy is watching us. It's making me nervous...
Doesn't it seem strange to you?

chapter 5

PLANT A KAPOK AND A PALM TREE

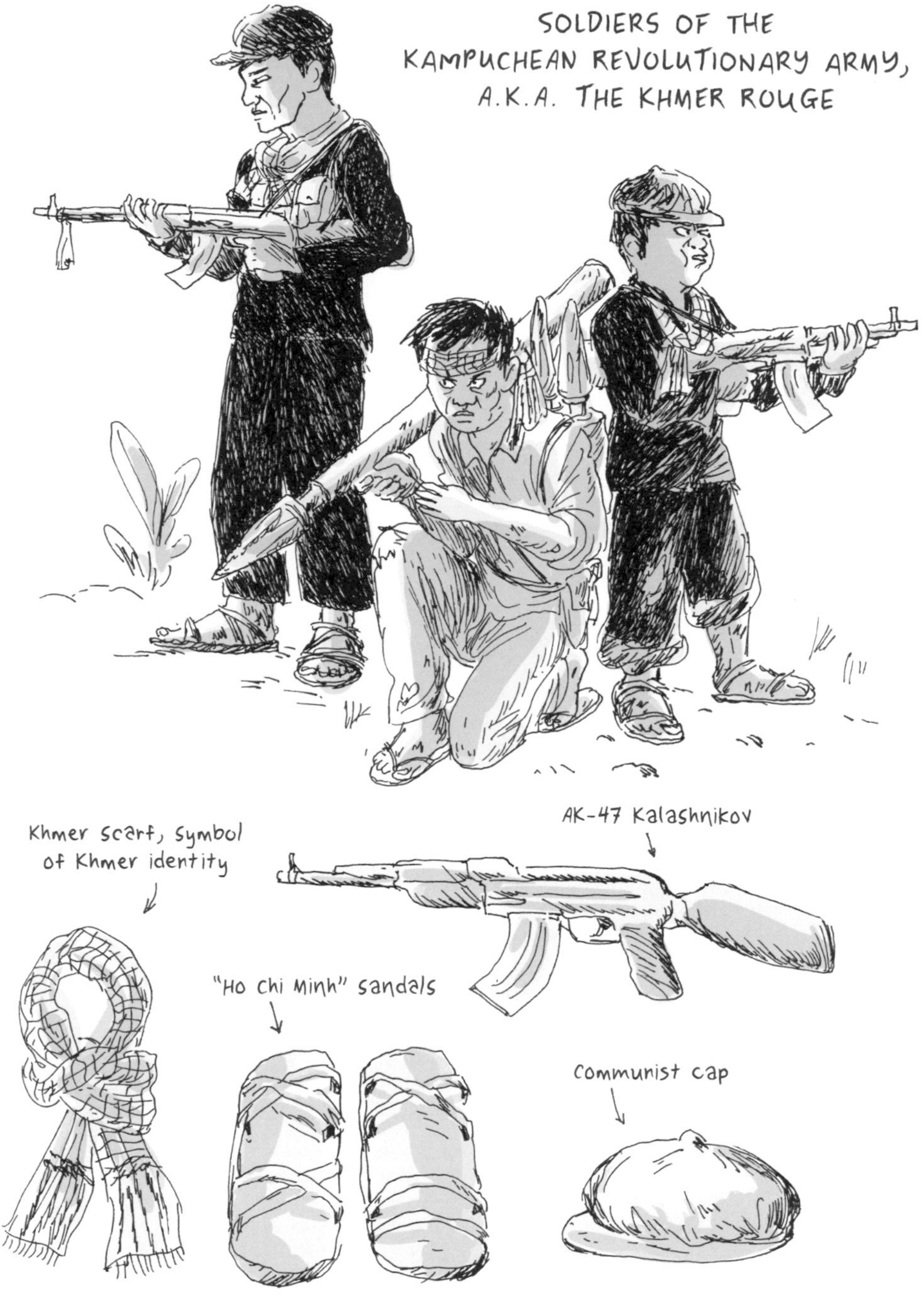
SOLDIERS OF THE KAMPUCHEAN REVOLUTIONARY ARMY, A.K.A. THE KHMER ROUGE
Khmer scarf, symbol of Khmer identity
AK-47 Kalashnikov
"Ho Chi Minh" sandals
Communist cap

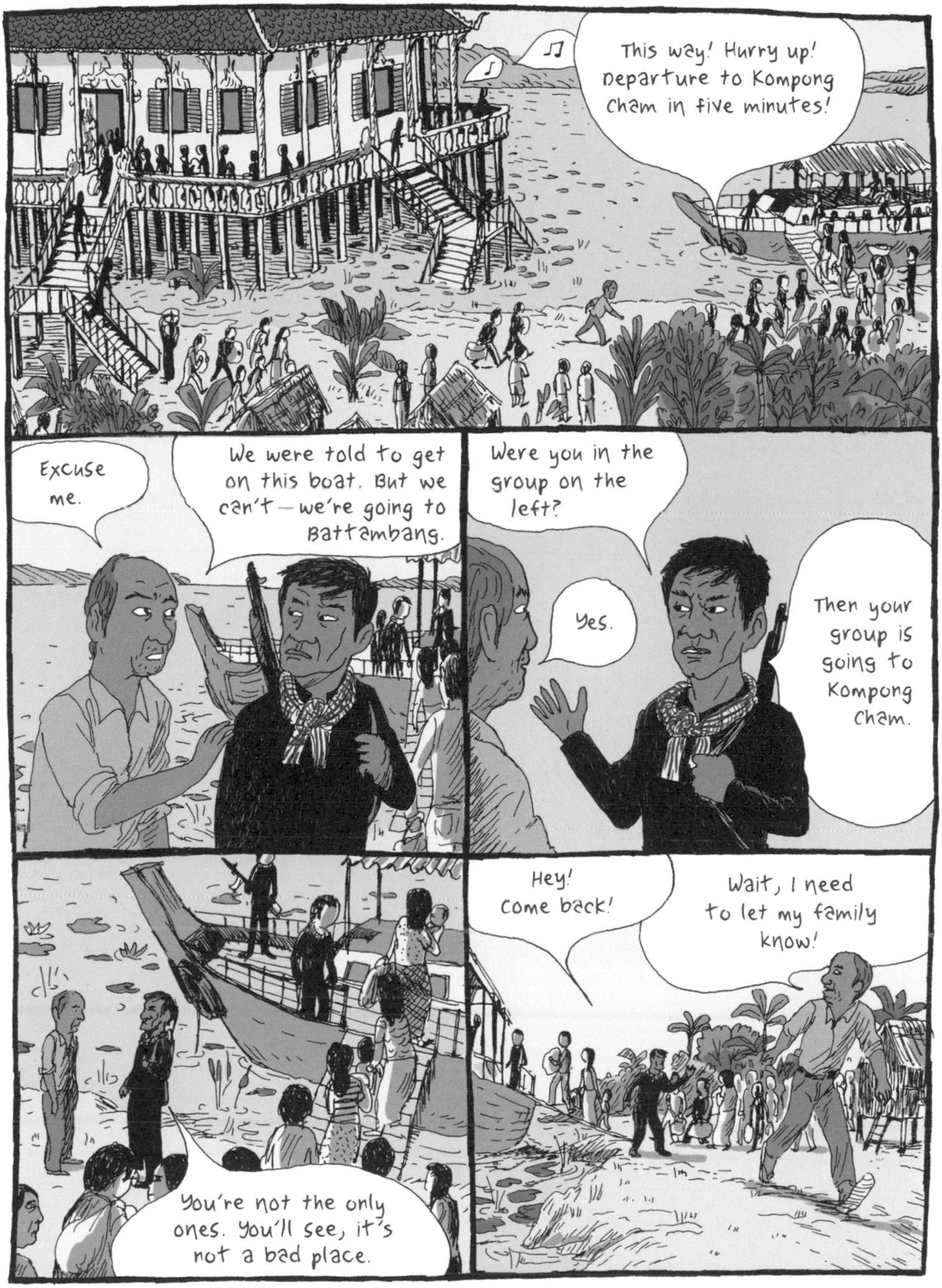
This way! Hurry up! Departure to Kompong Cham in five minutes!
Excuse me.
We were told to get on this boat. But we can't—we're going to Battambang.
Were you in the group on the left?
Yes.
Then your group is going to Kompong Cham.
You're not the only ones. You'll see, it's not a bad place.
Hey! Come back!
Wait, I need to let my family know!

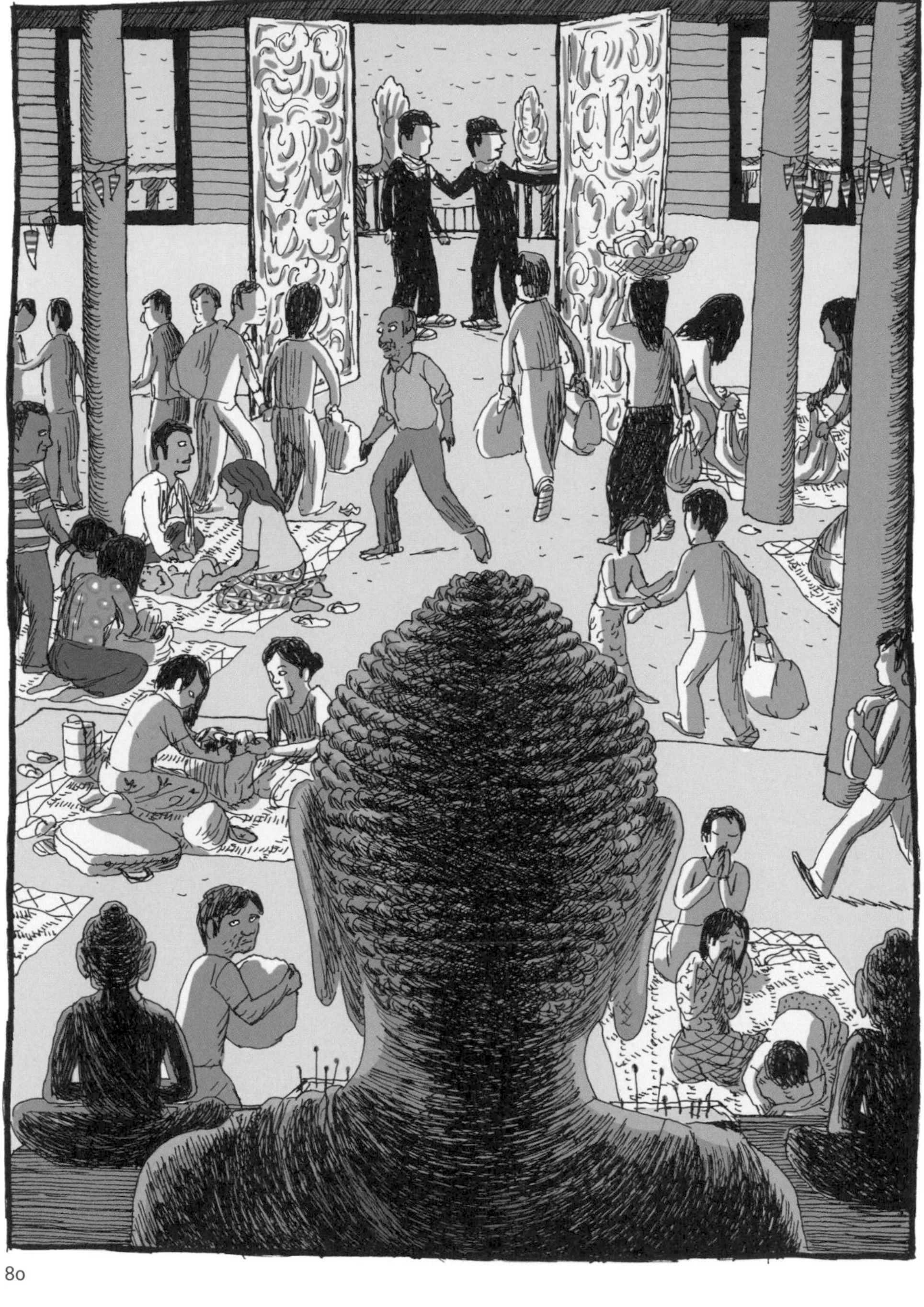

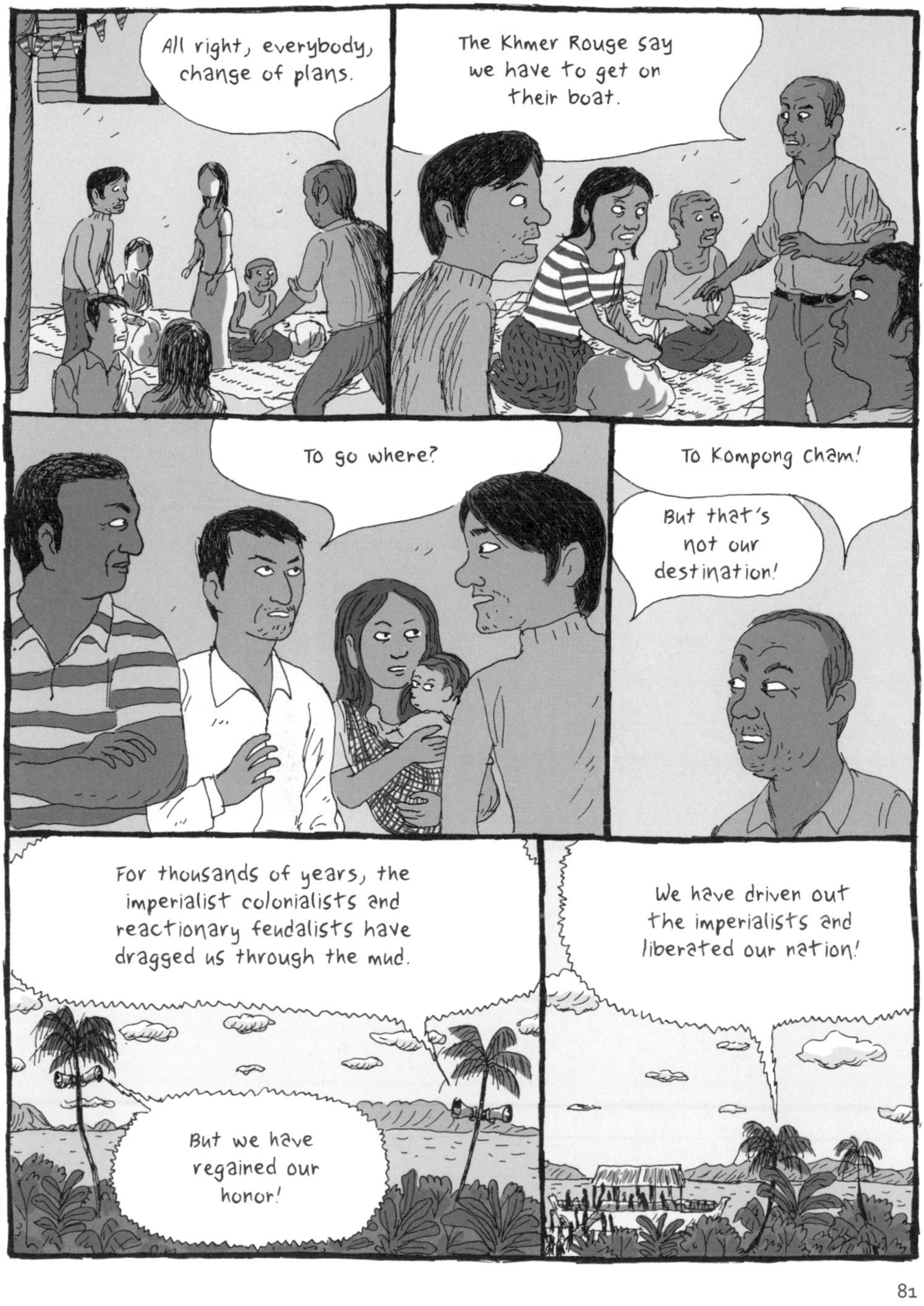
All right, everybody, change of plans.
The Khmer Rouge say we have to get on their boat.
To go where?
To Kompong Cham!
But that's not our destination!
For thousands of years, the imperialist colonialists and reactionary feudalists have dragged us through the mud.
But we have regained our honor!
We have driven out the imperialists and liberated our nation!

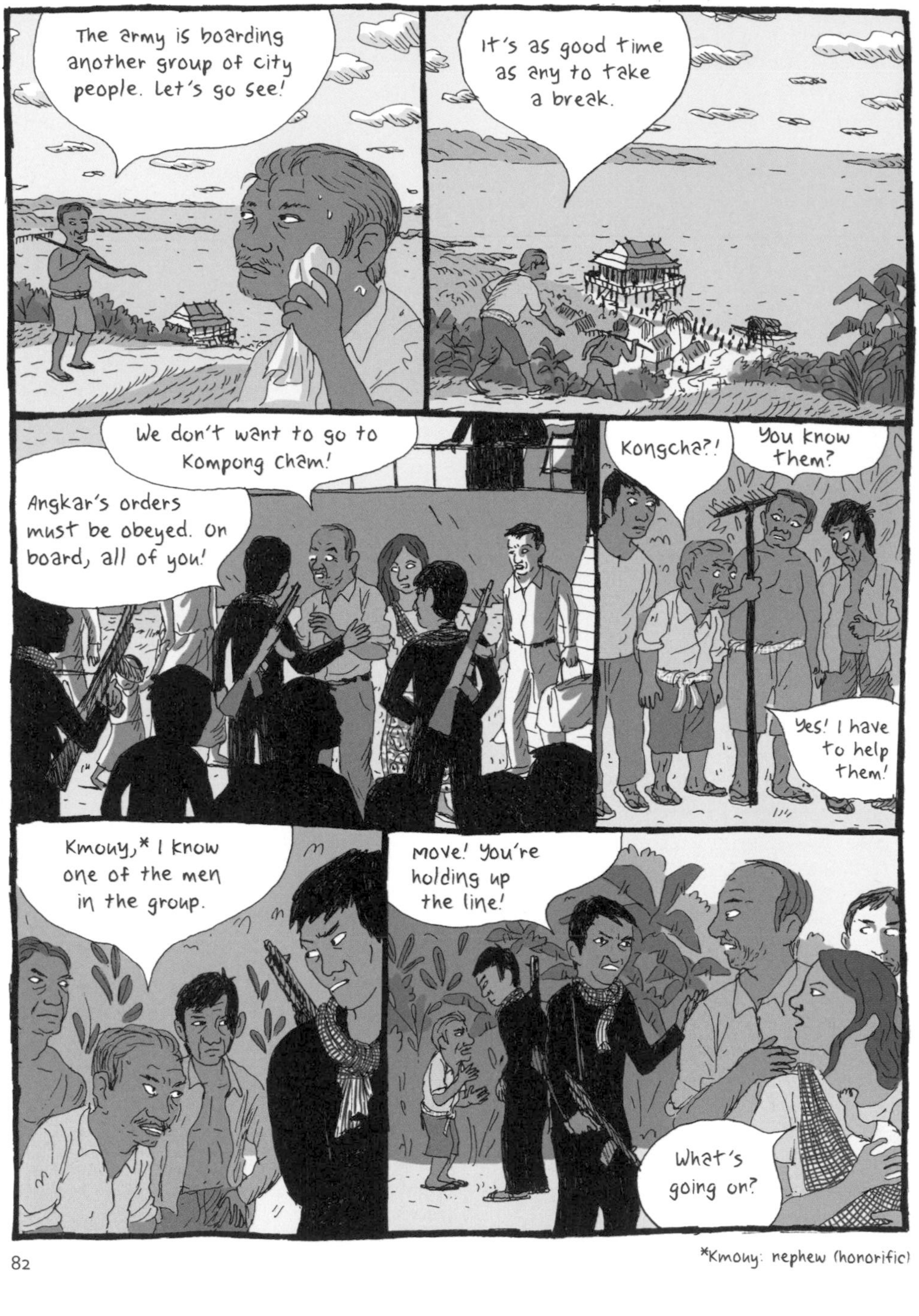
The army is boarding another group of city people. Let's go see!
It's as good time as any to take a break.
We don't want to go to Kompong Cham!
Angkar's orders must be obeyed. On board, all of you!
Kongcha?!
You know them?
Yes! I have to help them!
Kmouy,* I know one of the men in the group.
Move! You're holding up the line!
What's going on?

*Kmouy: nephew (honorific)

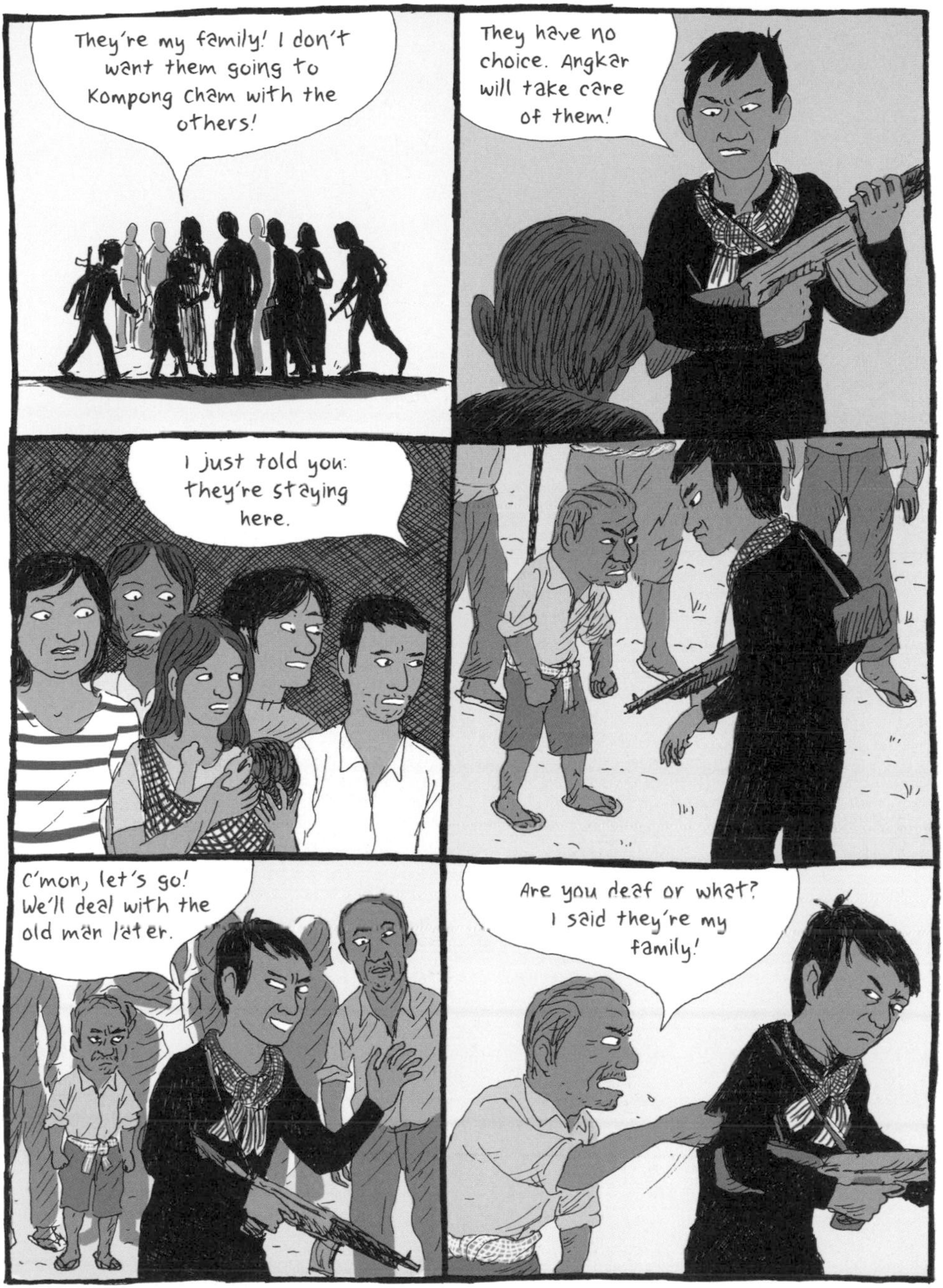
They're my family! I don't want them going to Kompong Cham with the others!
They have no choice. Angkar will take care of them!
I just told you: they're staying here.
C'mon, let's go! We'll deal with the old man later.
Are you deaf or what? I said they're my family!

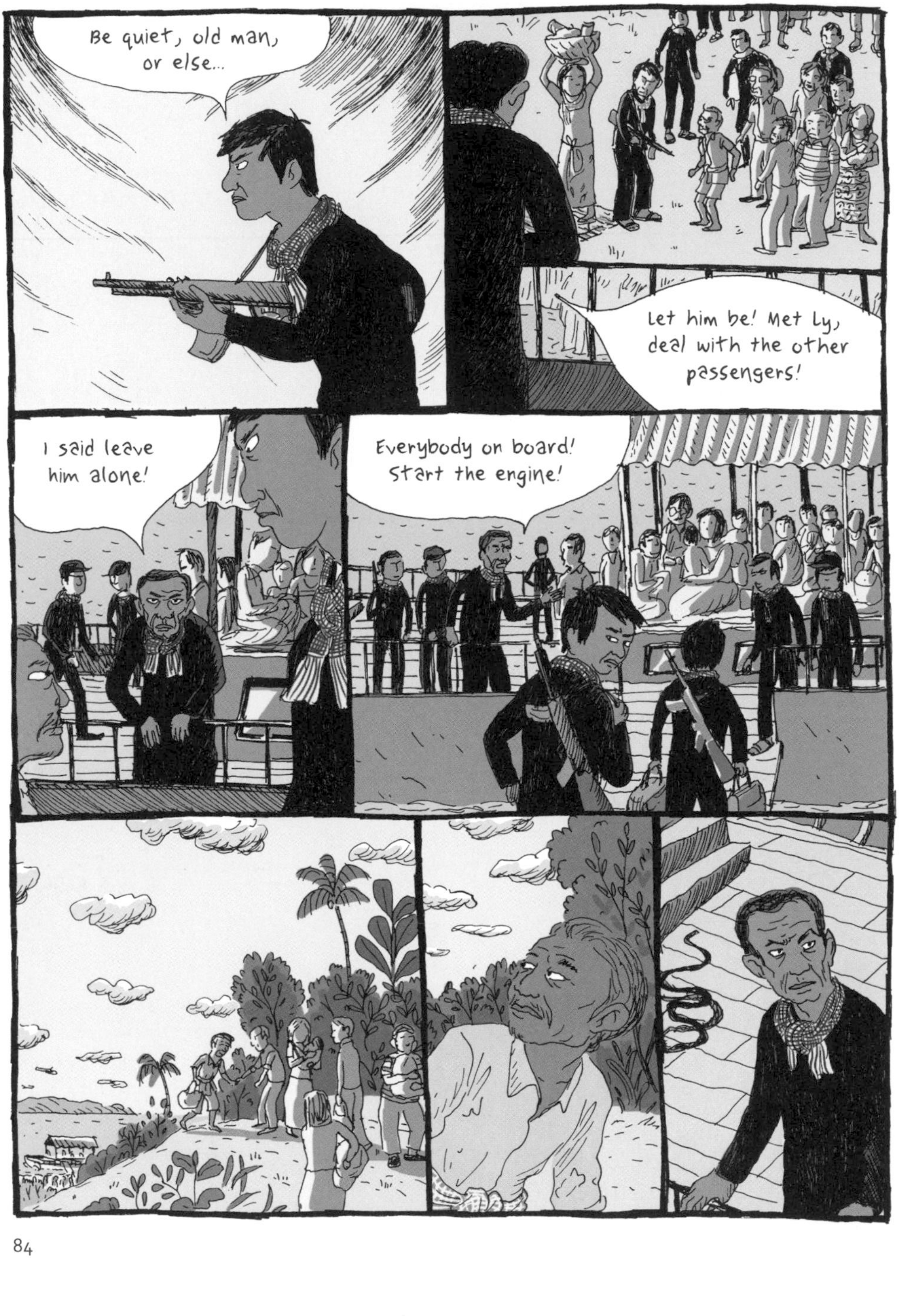
Be quiet, old man, or else...
Let him be! Met Ly, deal with the other passengers!
I said leave him alone!
Everybody on board! Start the engine!

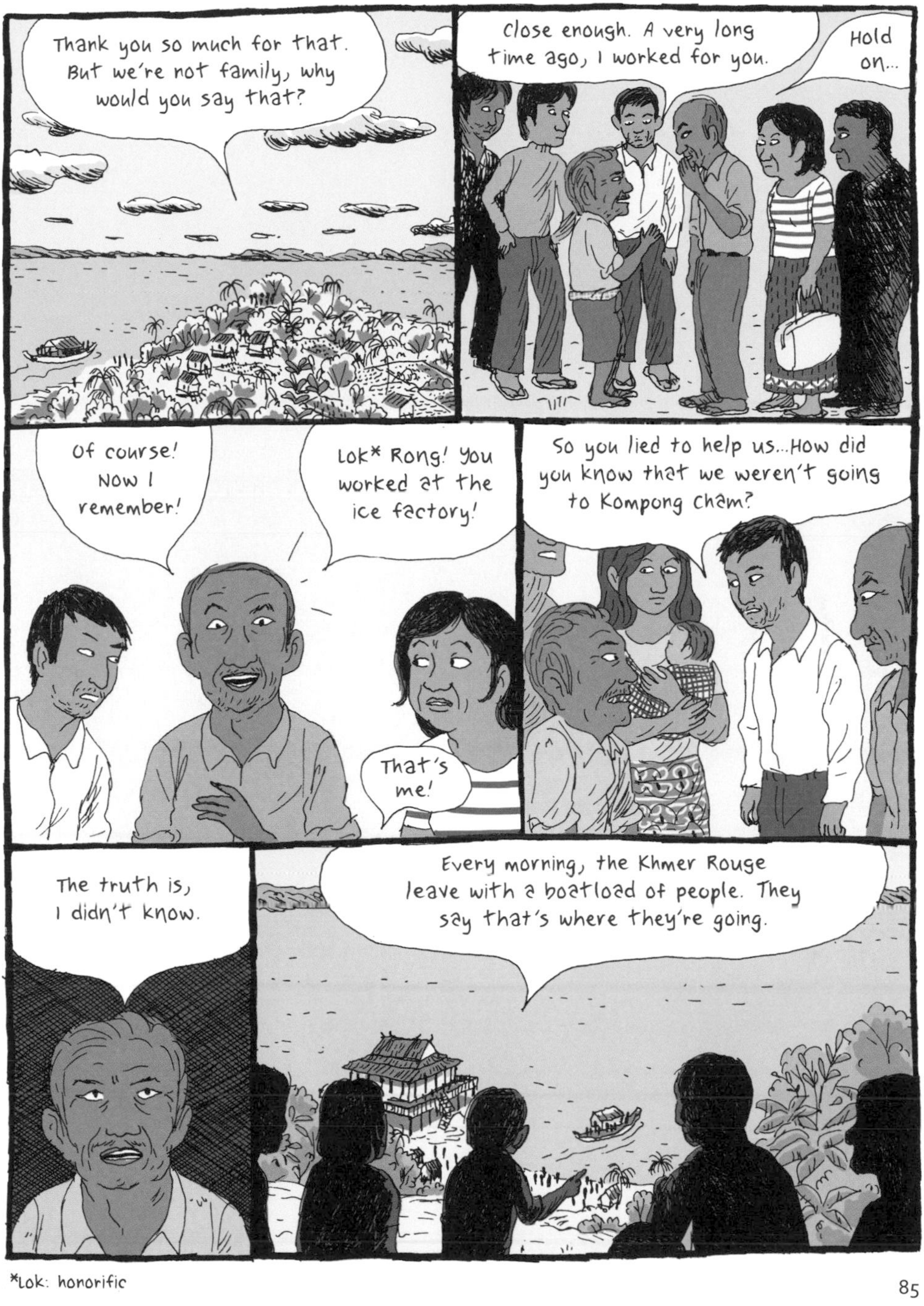
Thank you so much for that. But we're not family, why would you say that?
Close enough. A very long time ago, I worked for you.
Hold on...
Of course! Now I remember!
Lok* Rong! You worked at the ice factory!
That's me!
So you lied to help us...How did you know that we weren't going to Kompong Cham?
The truth is, I didn't know.
Every morning, the Khmer Rouge leave with a boatload of people. They say that's where they're going.

*Lok: honorific

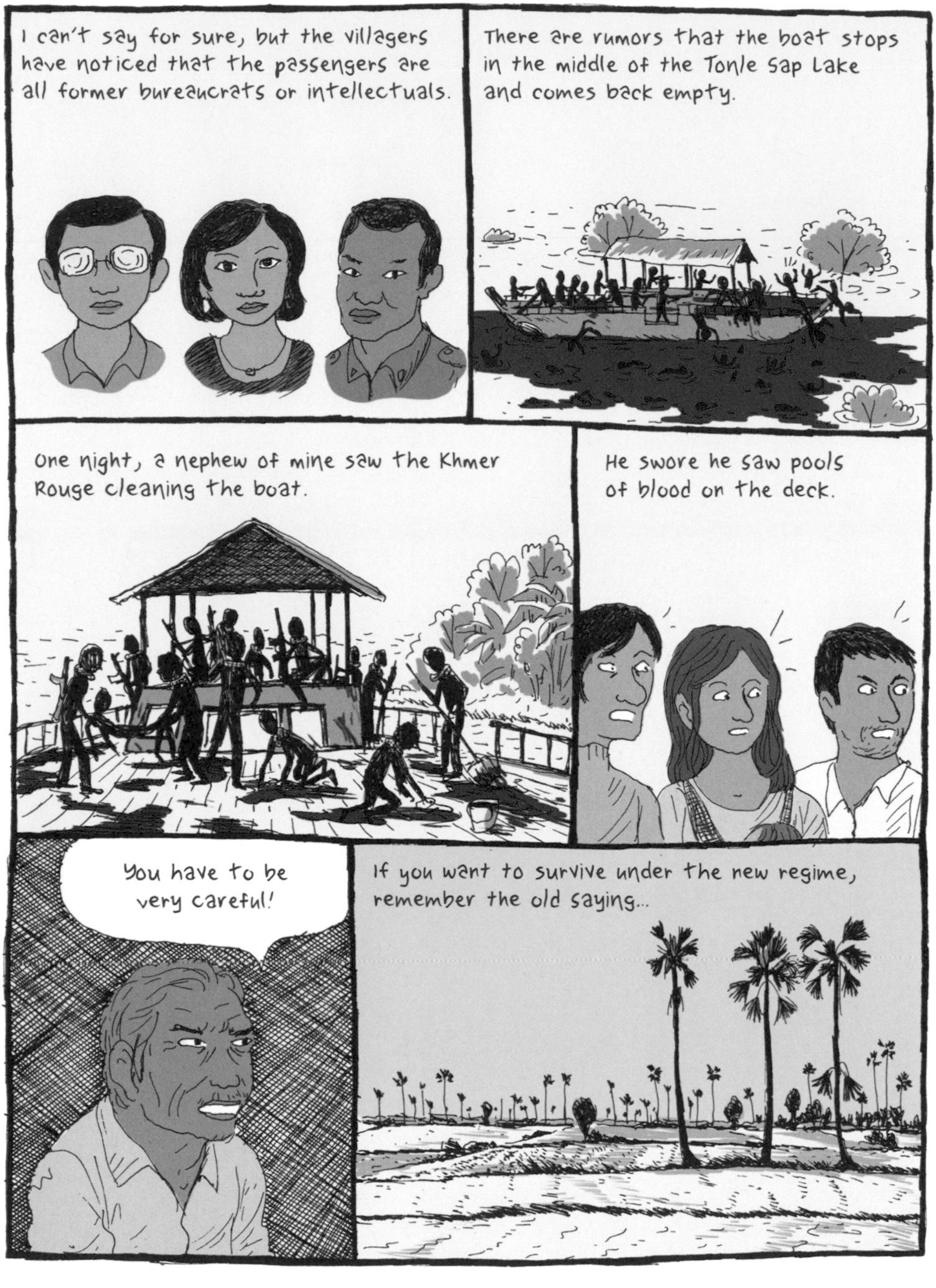
I can't say for sure, but the villagers have noticed that the passengers are all former bureaucrats or intellectuals.
There are rumors that the boat stops in the middle of the Tonle Sap Lake and comes back empty.
One night, a nephew of mine saw the Khmer Rouge cleaning the boat.
He swore he saw pools of blood on the deck.
You have to be very careful!
If you want to survive under the new regime, remember the old saying...

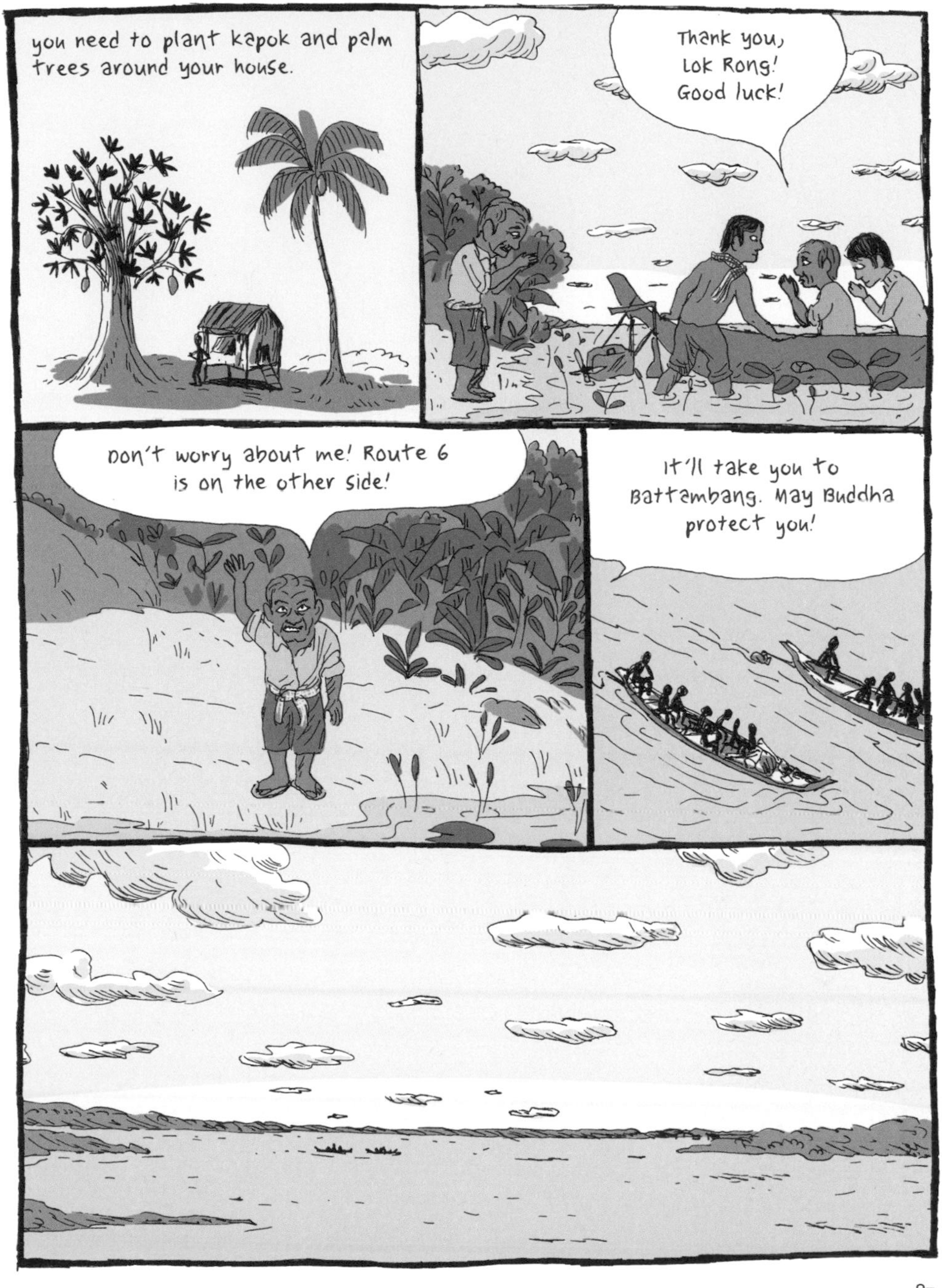
you need to plant kapok and palm trees around your house.
Thank you, Lok Rong! Good luck!
Don't worry about me! Route 6 is on the other side!
It'll take you to Battambang. May Buddha protect you!

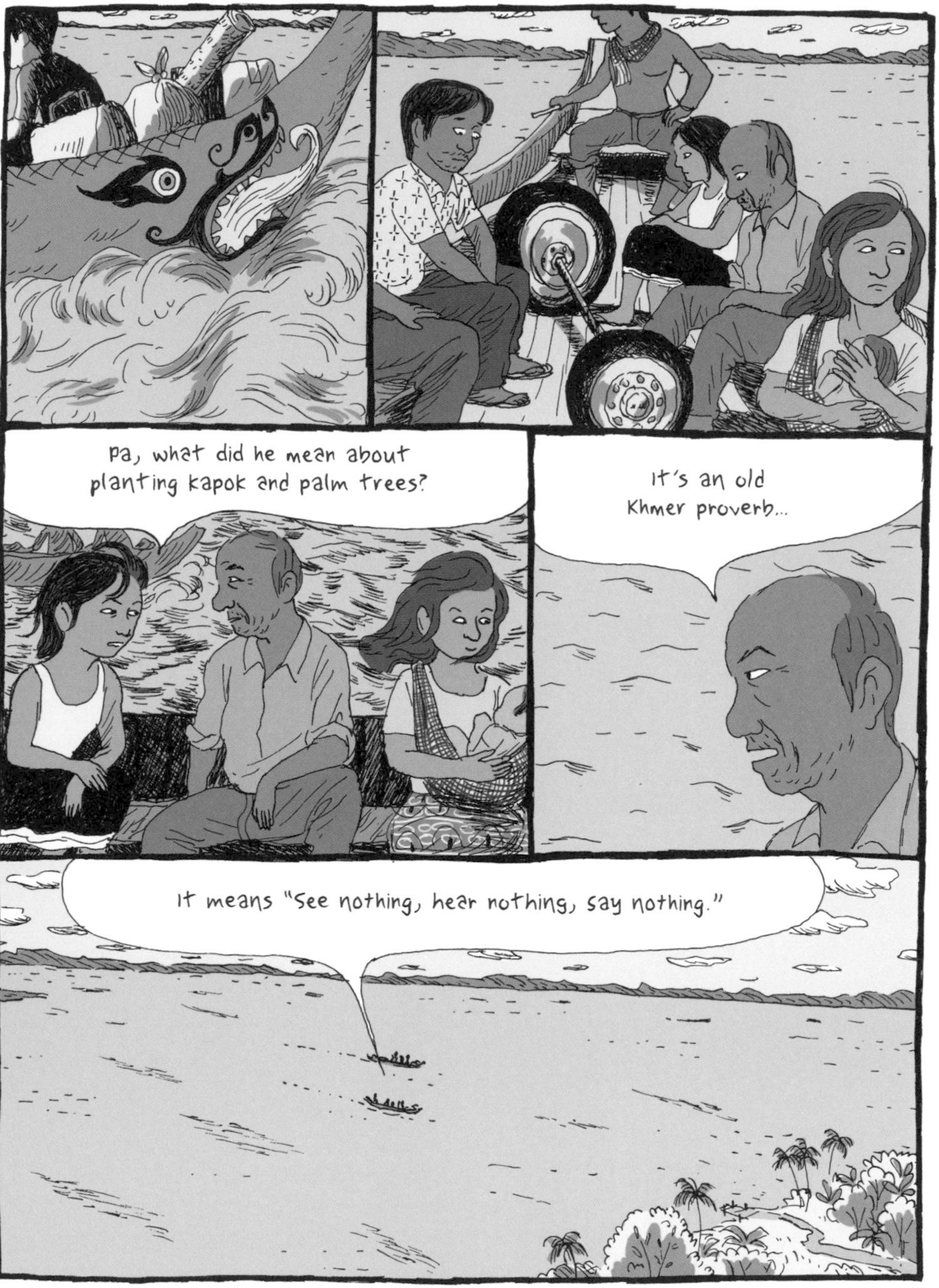
Pa, what did he mean about planting kapok and palm trees?
It's an old Khmer proverb...
It means "See nothing, hear nothing, say nothing."

chapter 6

NATIONAL ROUTE 6

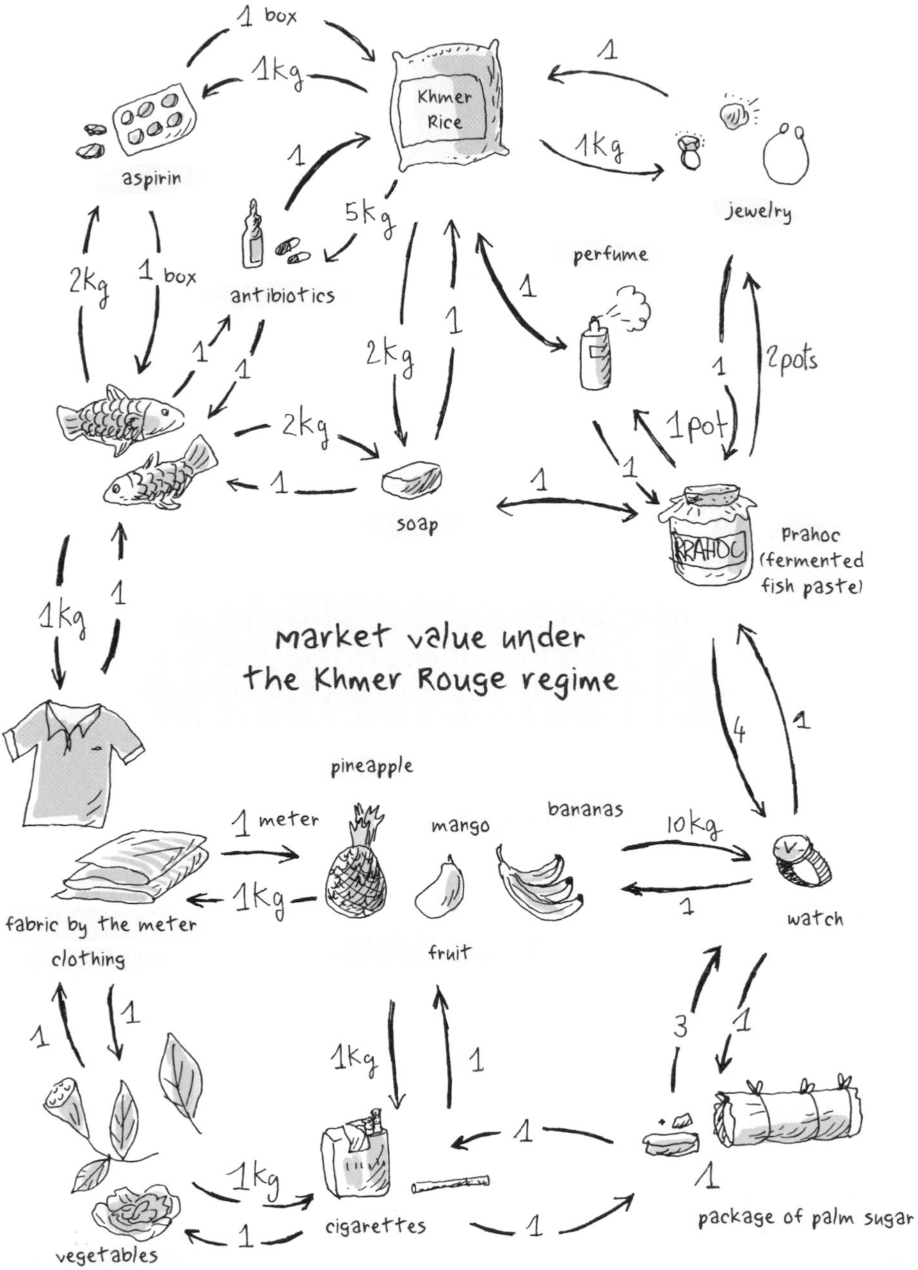
market value under
the Khmer Rouge regime
Khmer Rice
1 box
1kg
1
1kg
aspirin
antibiotics
5kg
2kg
1 box
1
1
2kg
1
1
perfume
jewelry
1
2pots
1pot
1
2kg
1
soap
1
Prahoc (fermented fish paste)
PRAHOC
1kg
1
4
1
pineapple
mango
bananas
1 meter
1kg
10kg
1
watch
fabric by the meter
clothing
fruit
1
1
1kg
1
3
1
1
1
1kg
1
1
vegetables
cigarettes
package of palm sugar

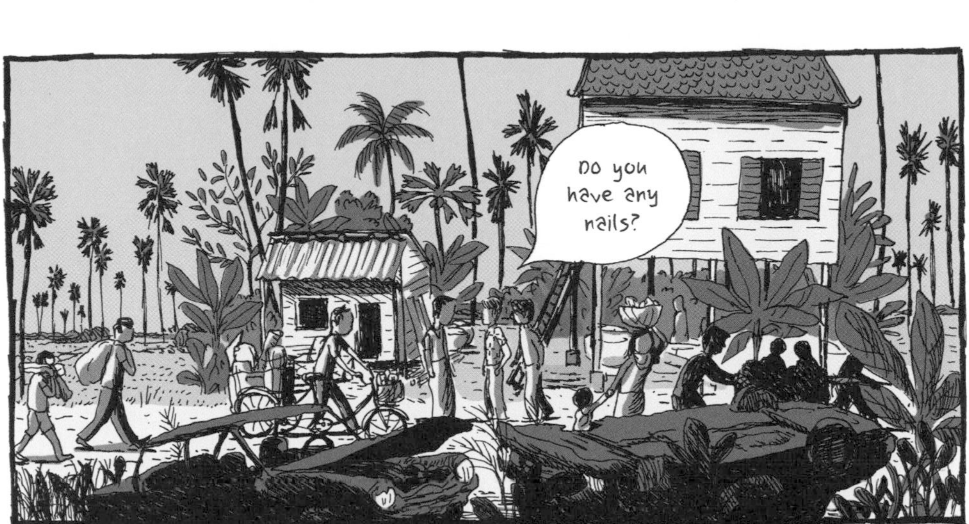
Do you have any nails?

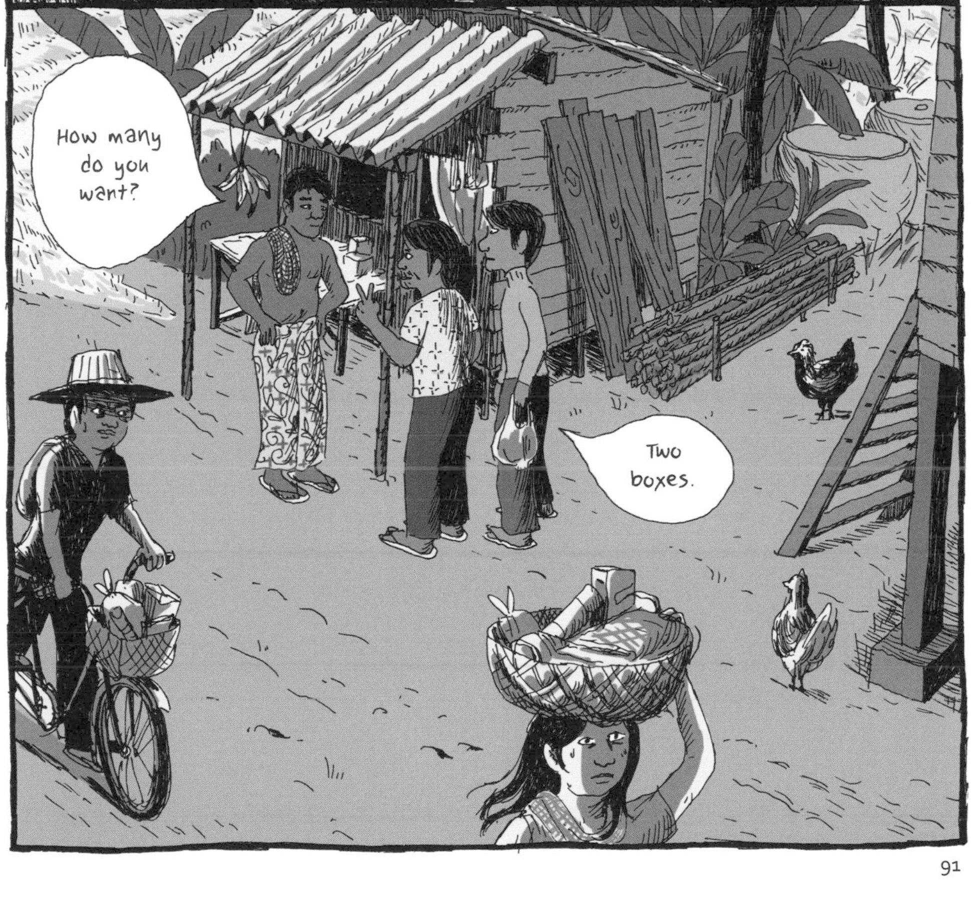
How many do you want?
Two boxes.

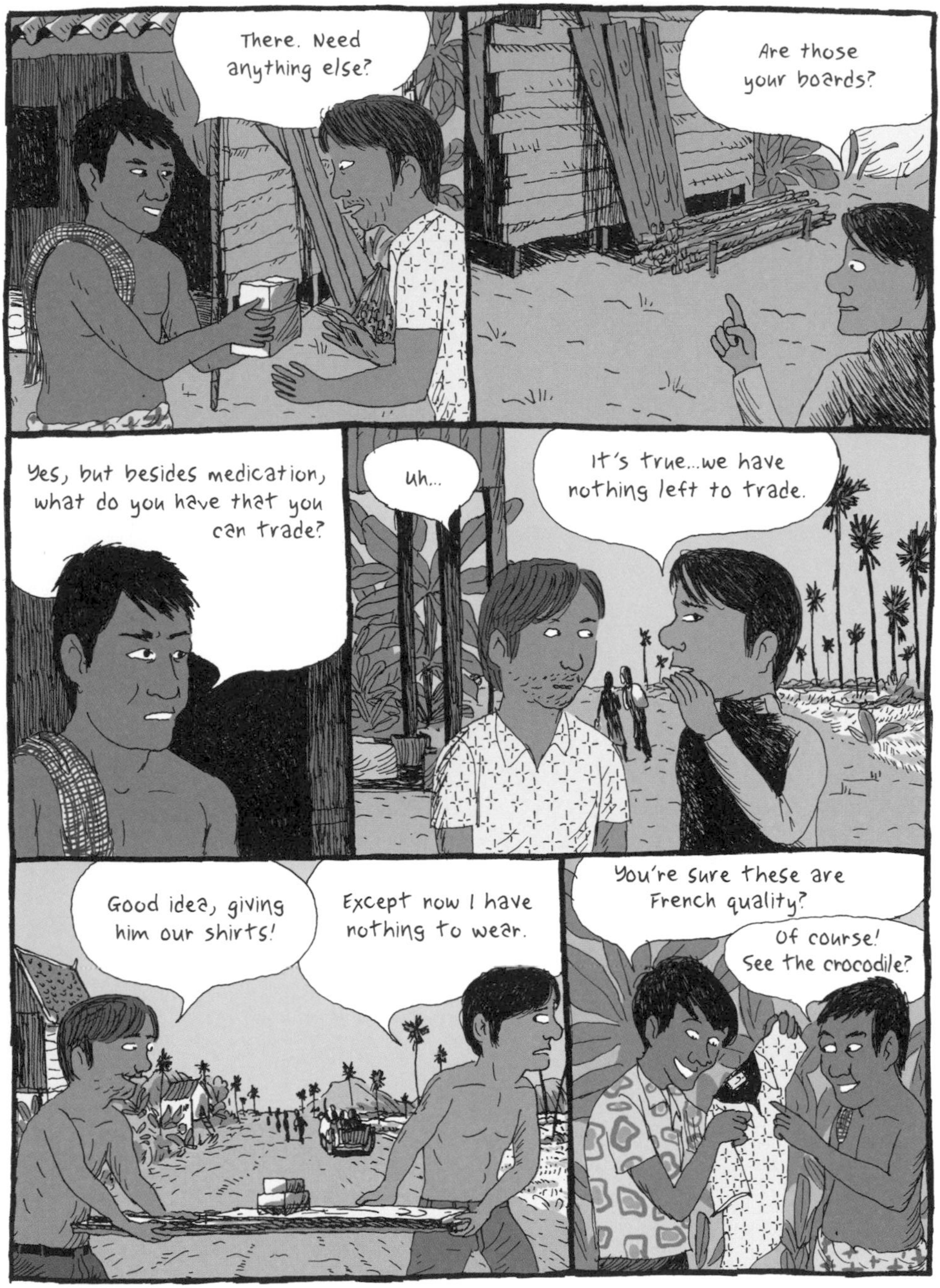
There. Need anything else?
Are those your boards?
Yes, but besides medication, what do you have that you can trade?
Uh...
It's true...we have nothing left to trade.
Good idea, giving him our shirts!
Except now I have nothing to wear.
You're sure these are French quality?
Of course! See the crocodile?

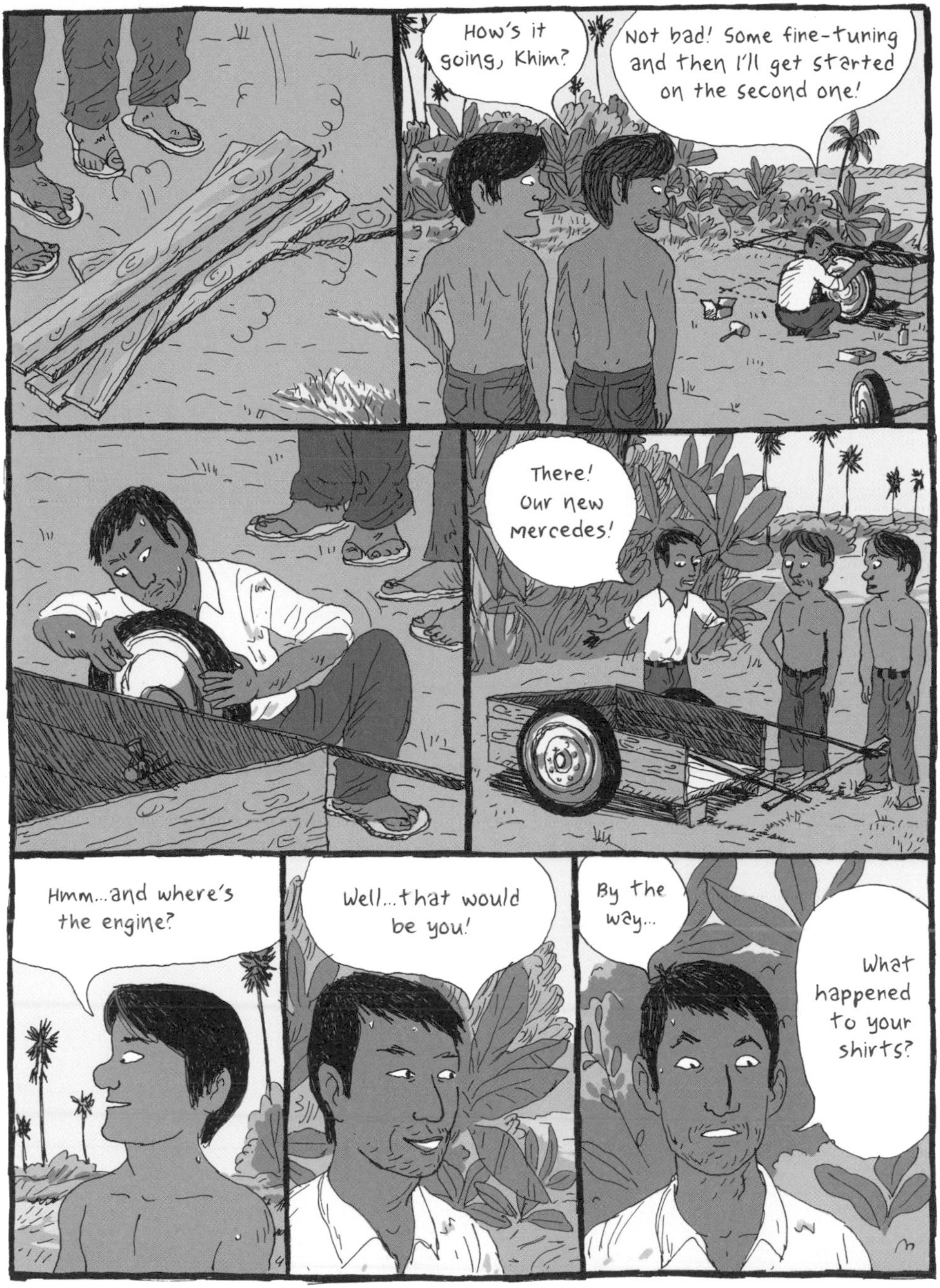
How's it going, Khim?
Not bad! Some fine-tuning and then I'll get started on the second one!
There! Our new Mercedes!
Hmm...and where's the engine?
Well...that would be you!
By the way...
What happened to your shirts?

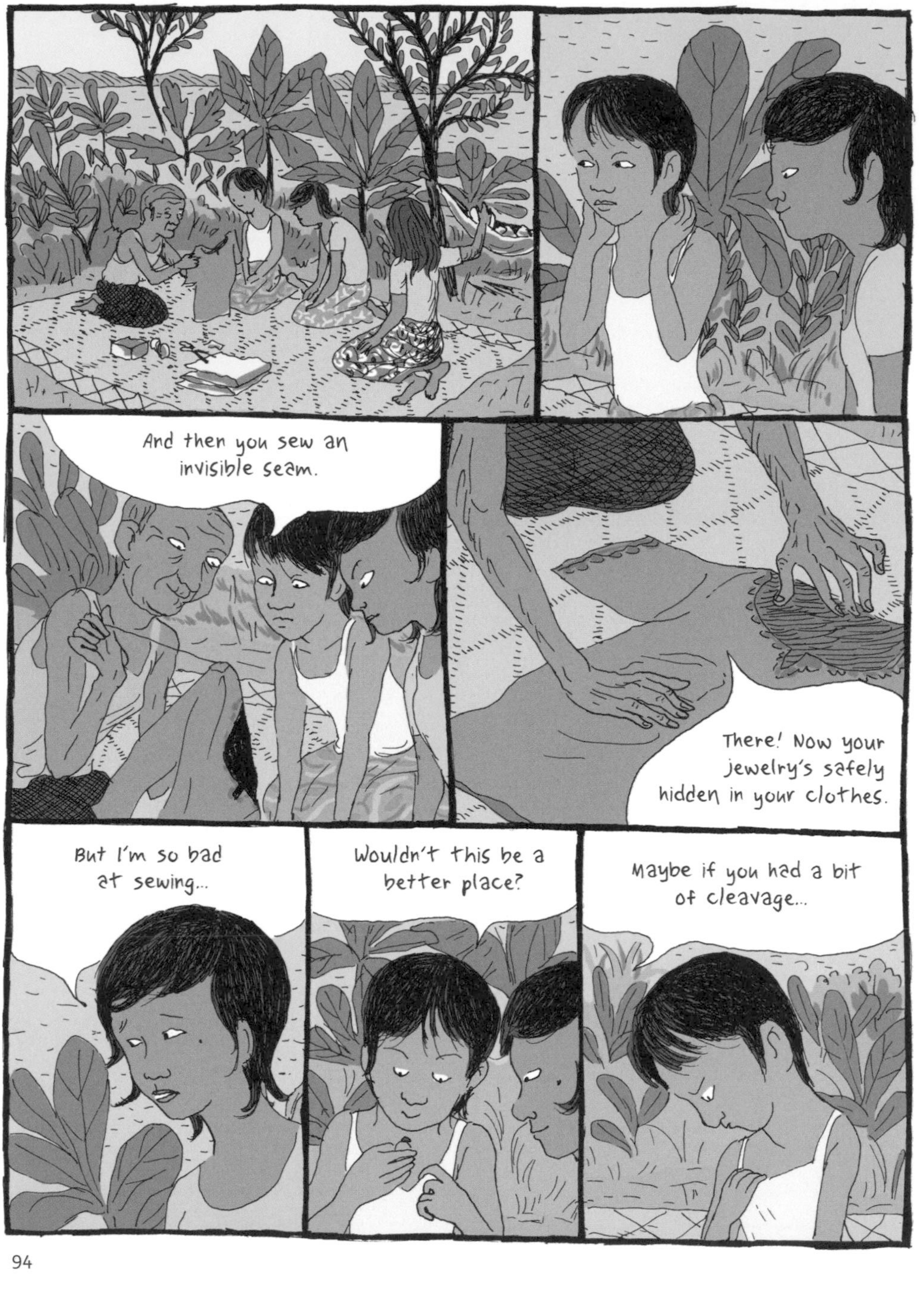
And then you sew an invisible seam.
There! Now your jewelry's safely hidden in your clothes.
But I'm so bad at sewing...
Wouldn't this be a better place?
Maybe if you had a bit of cleavage...

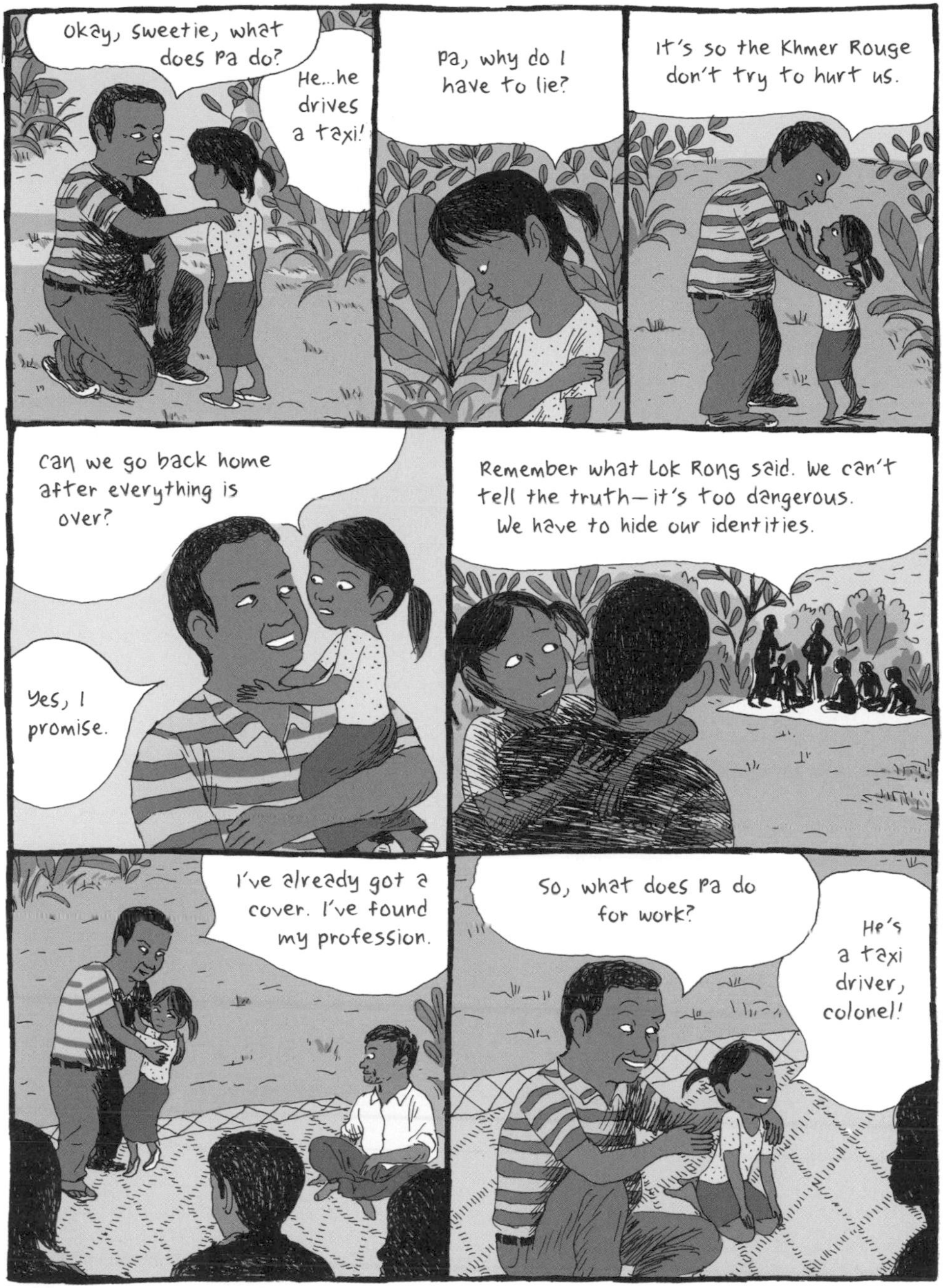
Okay, sweetie, what does Pa do?
He...he drives a taxi!
Pa, why do I have to lie?
It's so the Khmer Rouge don't try to hurt us.
Can we go back home after everything is over?
Yes, I promise.
Remember what Lok Rong said. We can't tell the truth—it's too dangerous. We have to hide our identities.
I've already got a cover. I've found my profession.
So, what does Pa do for work?
He's a taxi driver, colonel!

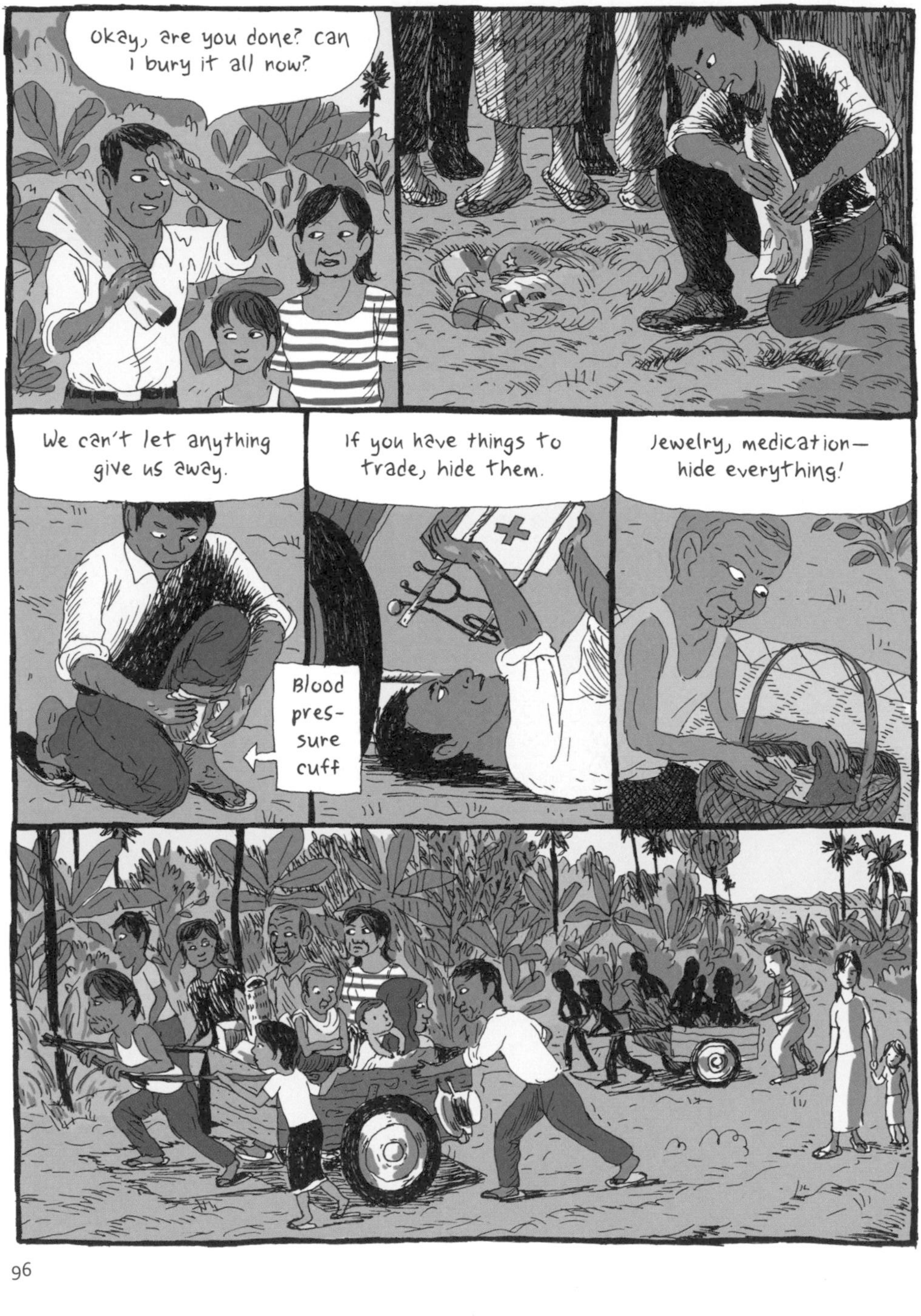
Okay, are you done? Can I bury it all now?
We can't let anything give us away.
If you have things to trade, hide them.
Blood pres-sure cuff
Jewelry, medication—hide everything!

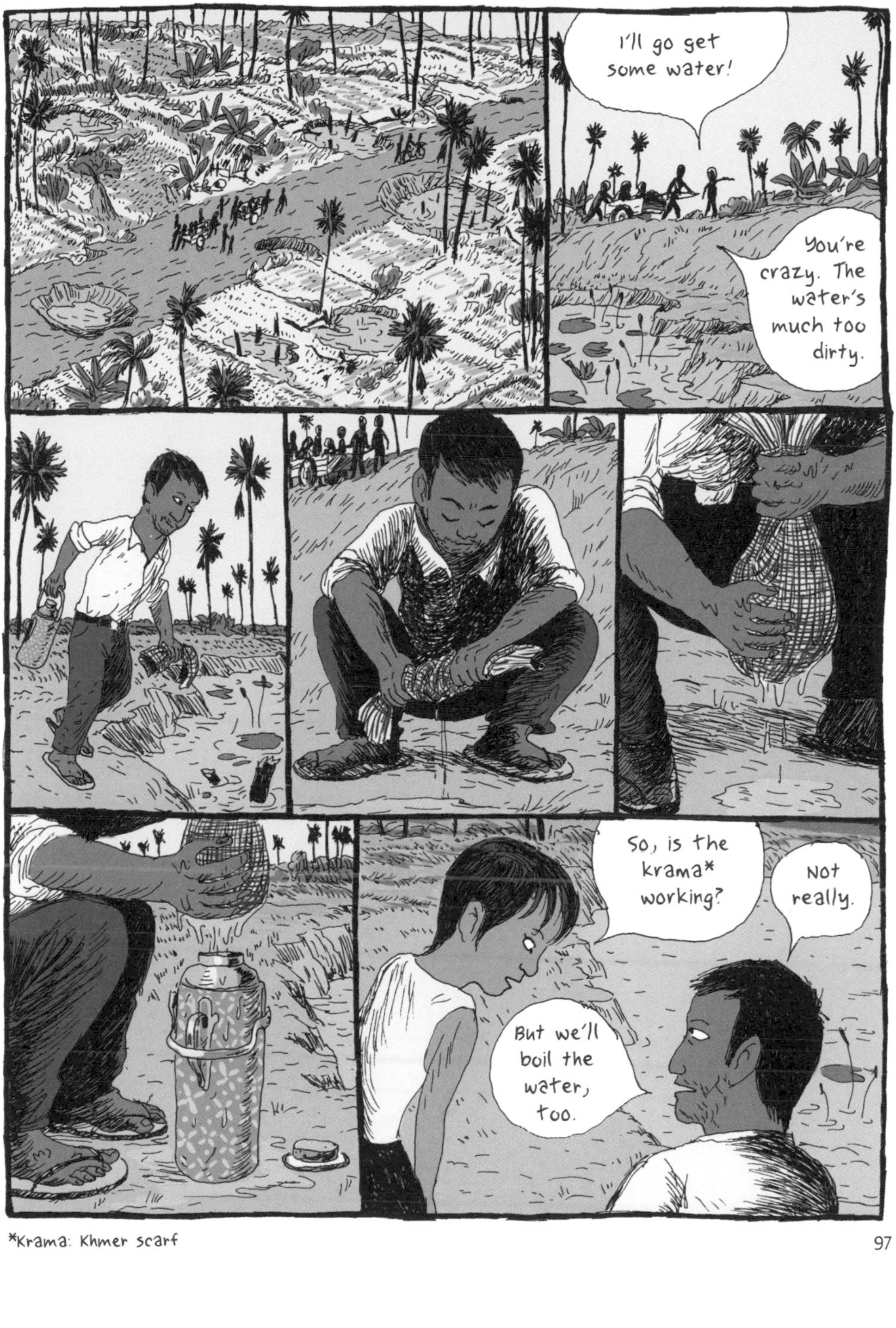
I'll go get some water!
You're crazy. The water's much too dirty.
So, is the krama* working?
Not really.
But we'll boil the water, too.

*Krama: Khmer scarf

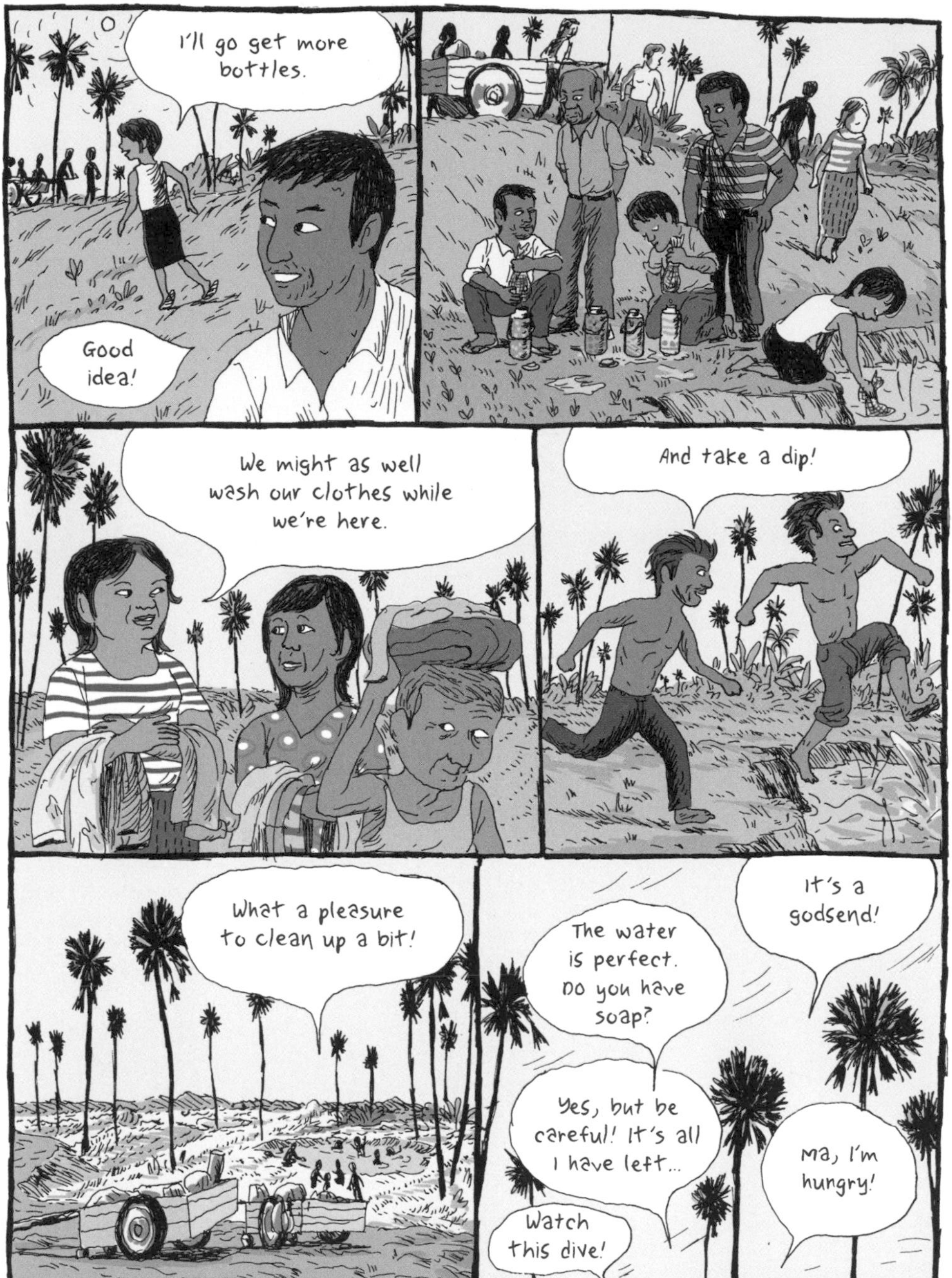
I'll go get more bottles.
Good idea!
We might as well wash our clothes while we're here.
And take a dip!
What a pleasure to clean up a bit!
It's a godsend!
The water is perfect. Do you have soap?
Yes, but be careful! It's all I have left...
Ma, I'm hungry!
Watch this dive!

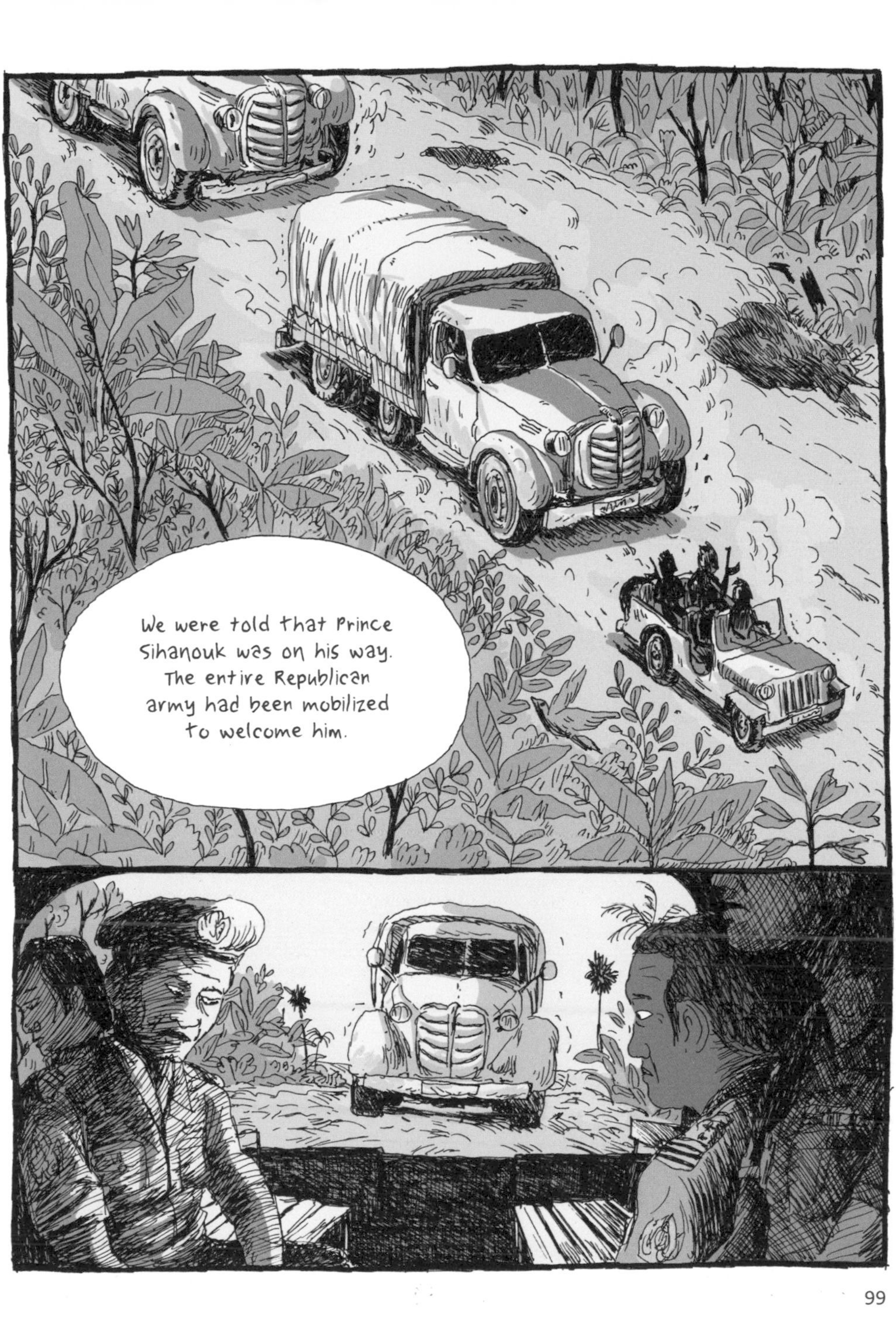
We were told that Prince Sihanouk was on his way. The entire Republican army had been mobilized to welcome him.

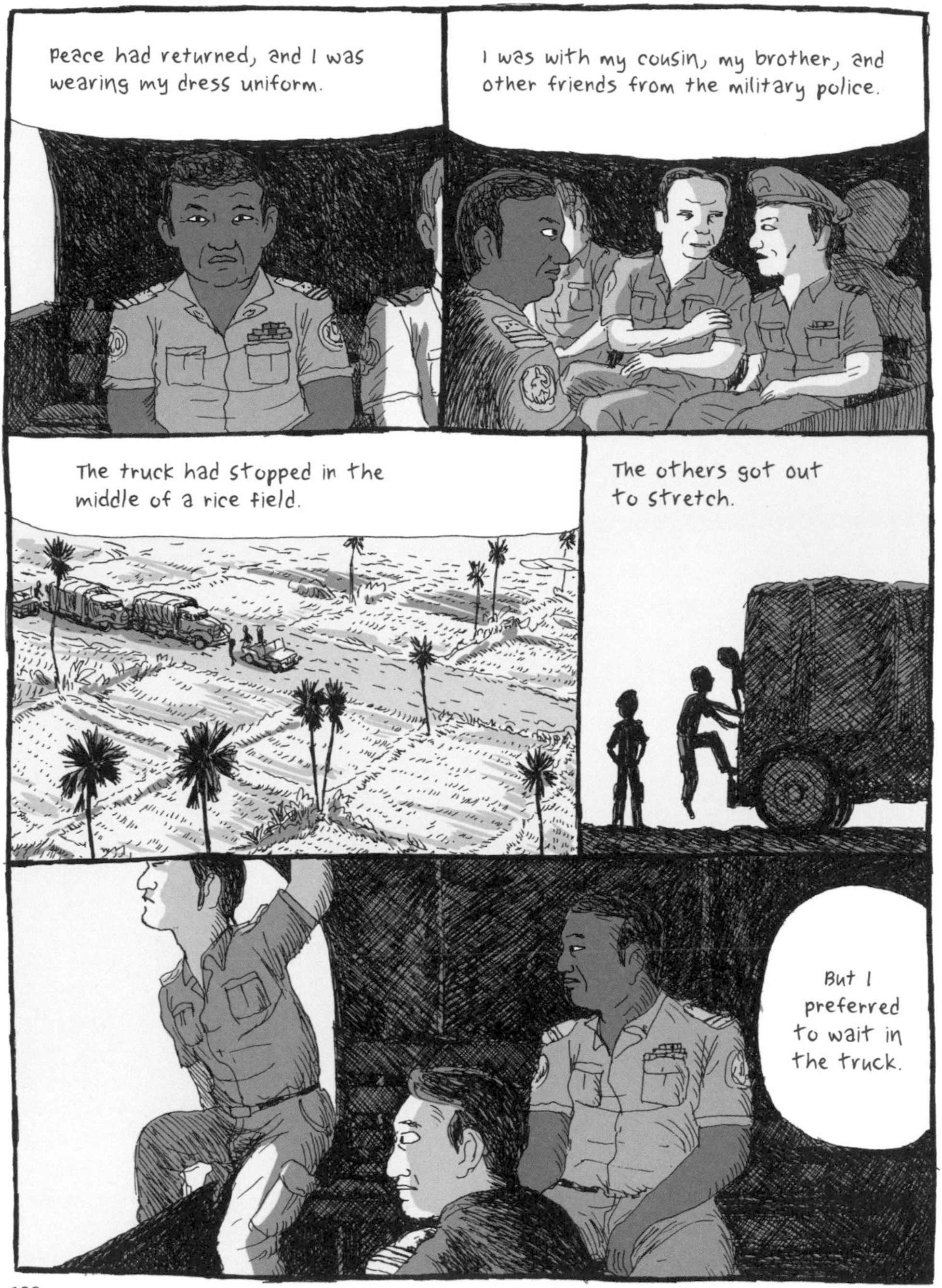
Peace had returned, and I was wearing my dress uniform.
I was with my cousin, my brother, and other friends from the military police.
The truck had stopped in the middle of a rice field.
The others got out to stretch.
But I preferred to wait in the truck.

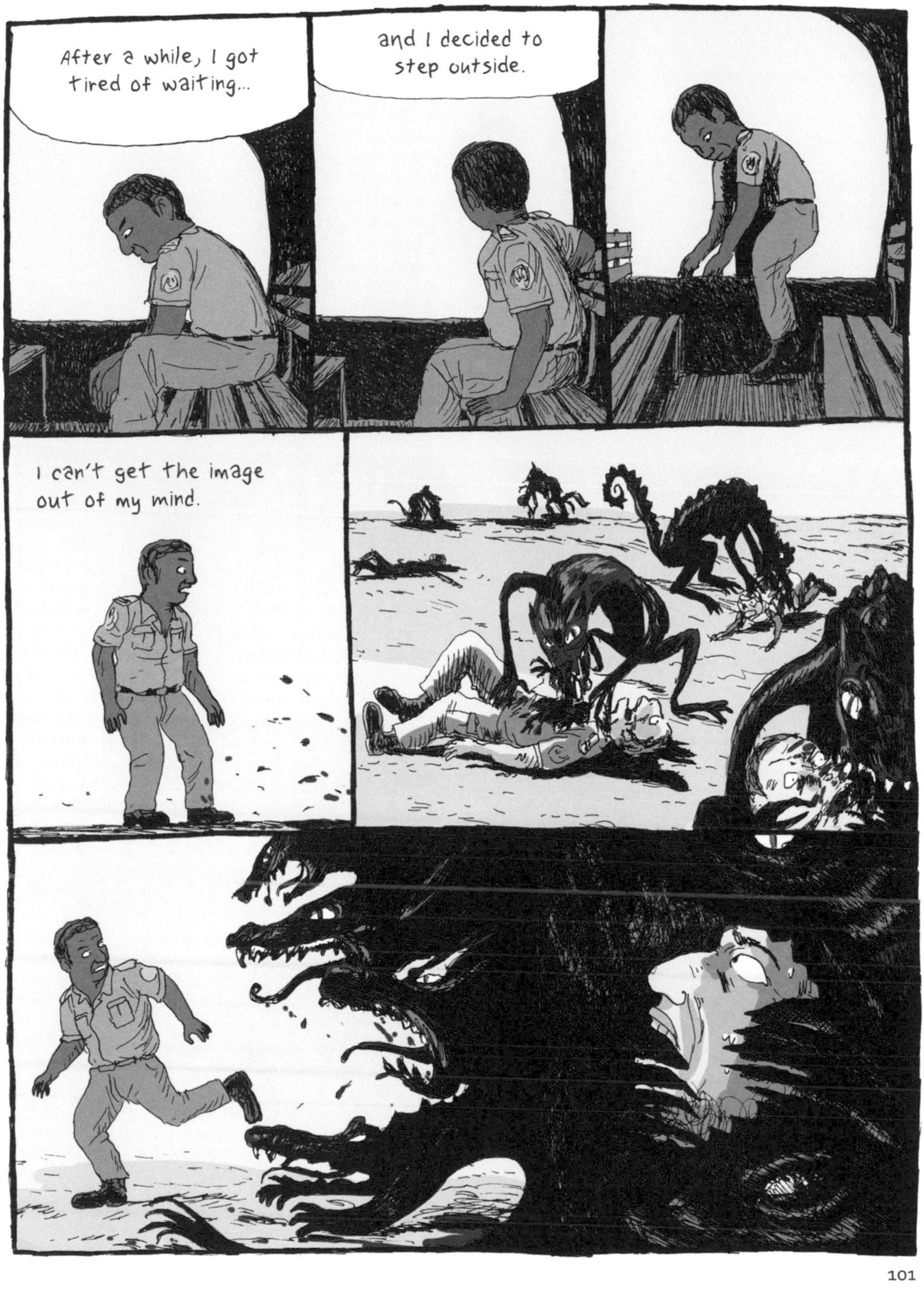
After a while, I got tired of waiting...
and I decided to step outside.
I can't get the image out of my mind.

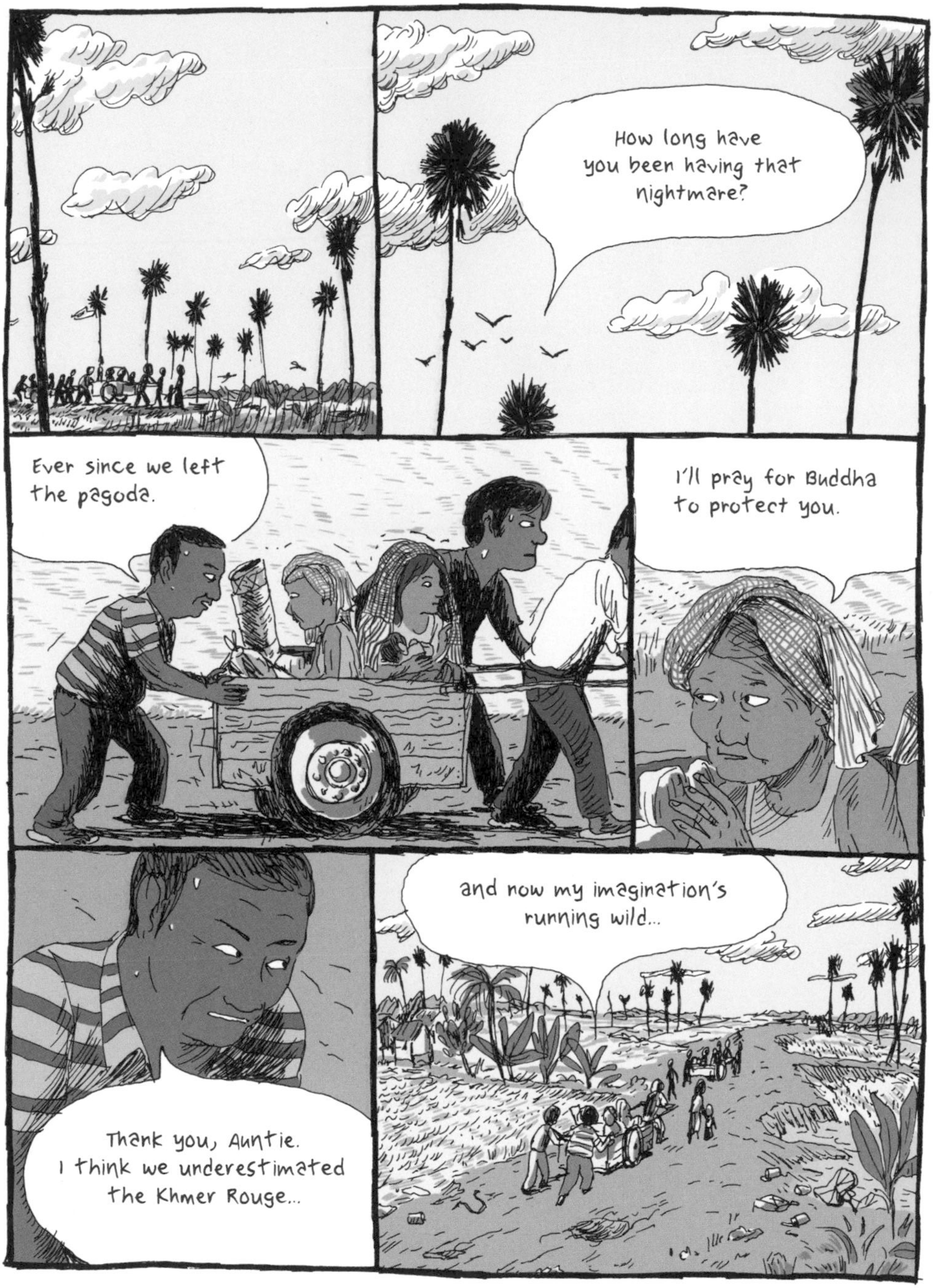
How long have you been having that nightmare?
Ever since we left the pagoda.
I'll pray for Buddha to protect you.
Thank you, Auntie. I think we underestimated the Khmer Rouge...
and now my imagination's running wild...

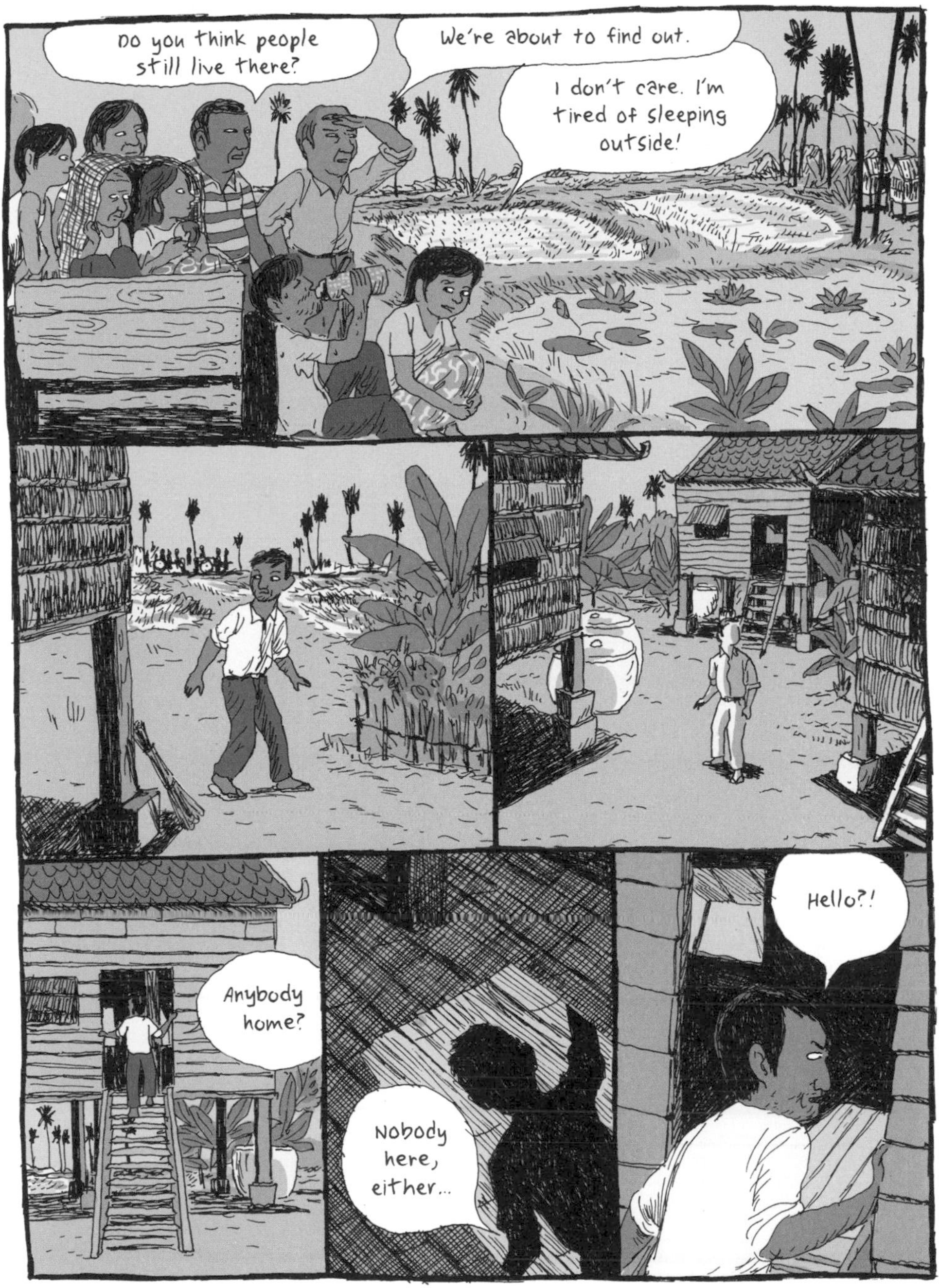
Do you think people still live there?
We're about to find out.
I don't care. I'm tired of sleeping outside!
Anybody home?
Nobody here, either...
Hello?!

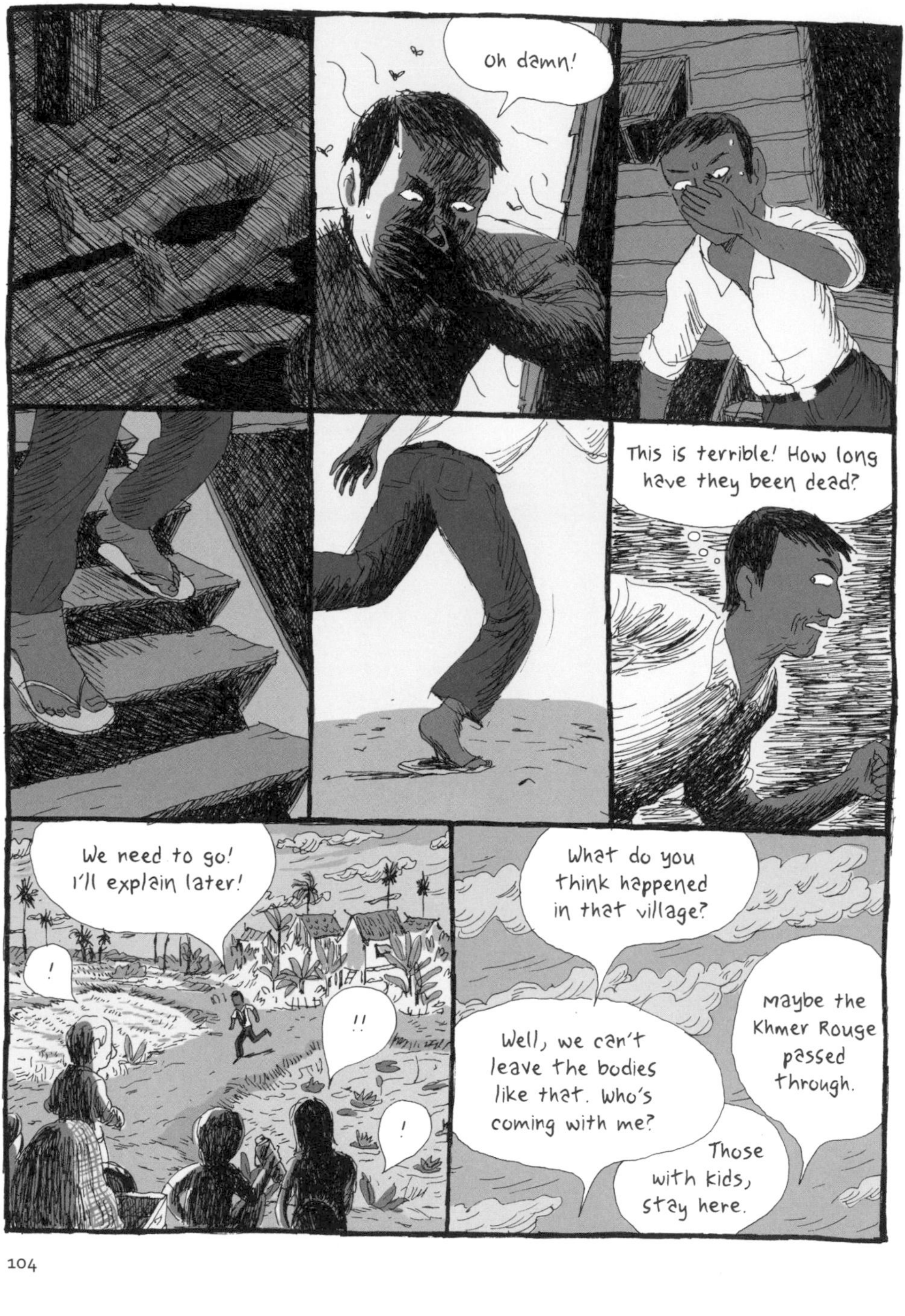

Oh damn!
This is terrible! How long have they been dead?
We need to go! I'll explain later!
!
!!
!
What do you think happened in that village?
Maybe the Khmer Rouge passed through.
Well, we can't leave the bodies like that. Who's coming with me?
Those with kids, stay here.

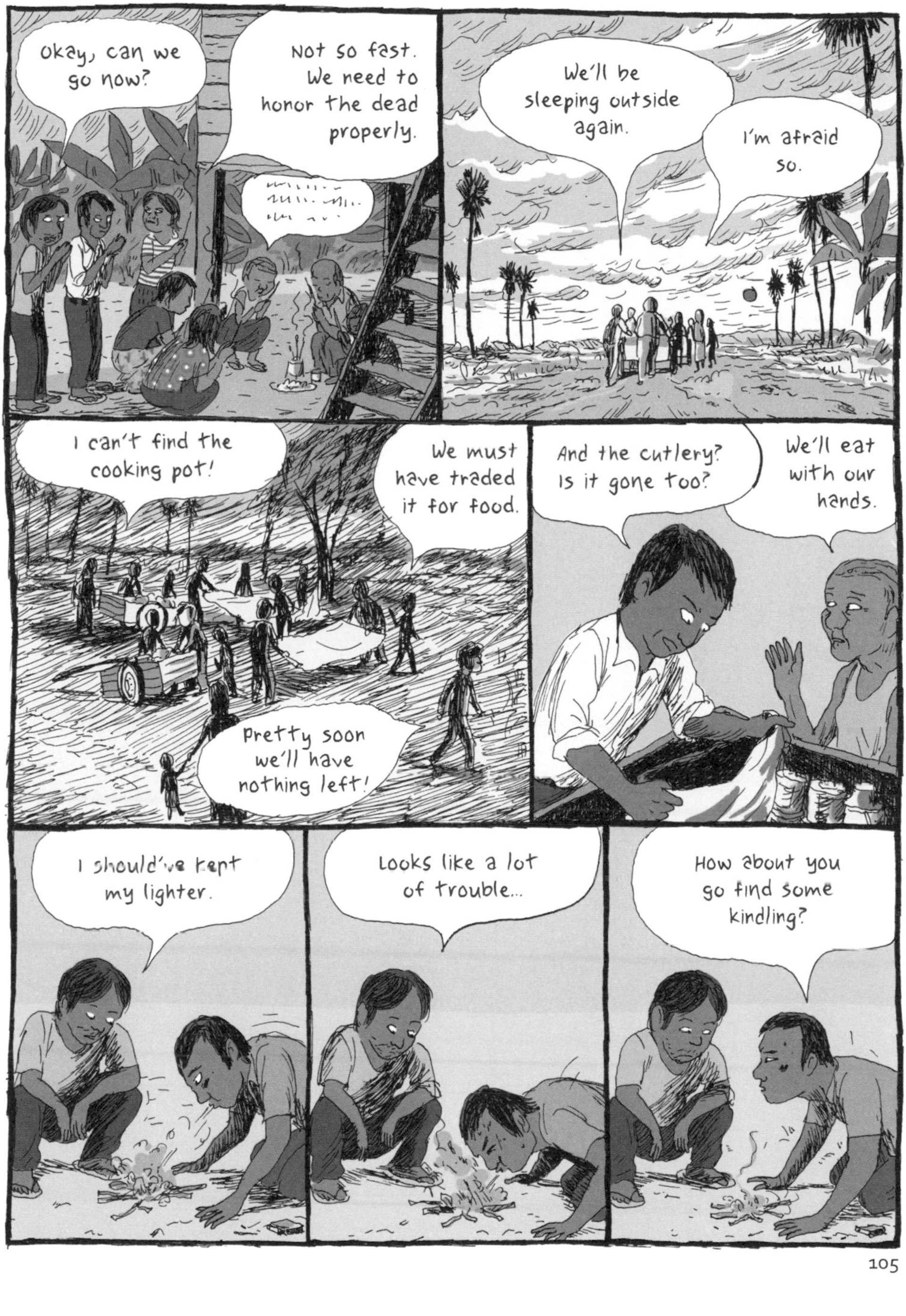

Okay, can we go now?
Not so fast. We need to honor the dead properly.
We'll be sleeping outside again.
I'm afraid so.
I can't find the cooking pot!
We must have traded it for food.
Pretty soon we'll have nothing left!
And the cutlery? Is it gone too?
We'll eat with our hands.
I should've kept my lighter.
Looks like a lot of trouble...
How about you go find some kindling?

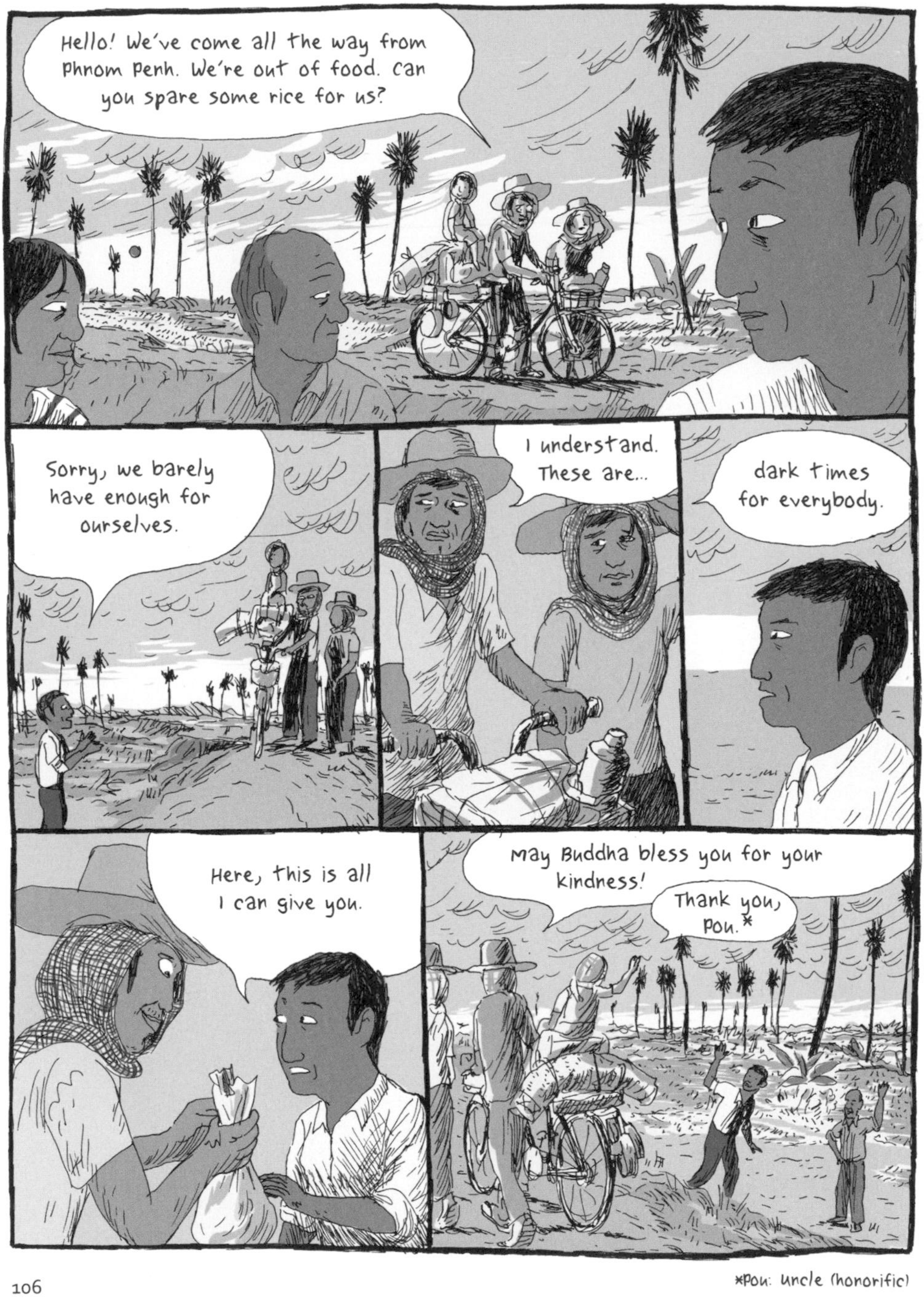
Hello! We've come all the way from Phnom Penh. We're out of food. Can you spare some rice for us?
Sorry, we barely have enough for ourselves.
I understand. These are...
dark times for everybody.
Here, this is all I can give you.
May Buddha bless you for your kindness!
Thank you, Pou.*

*Pou: Uncle (honorific)

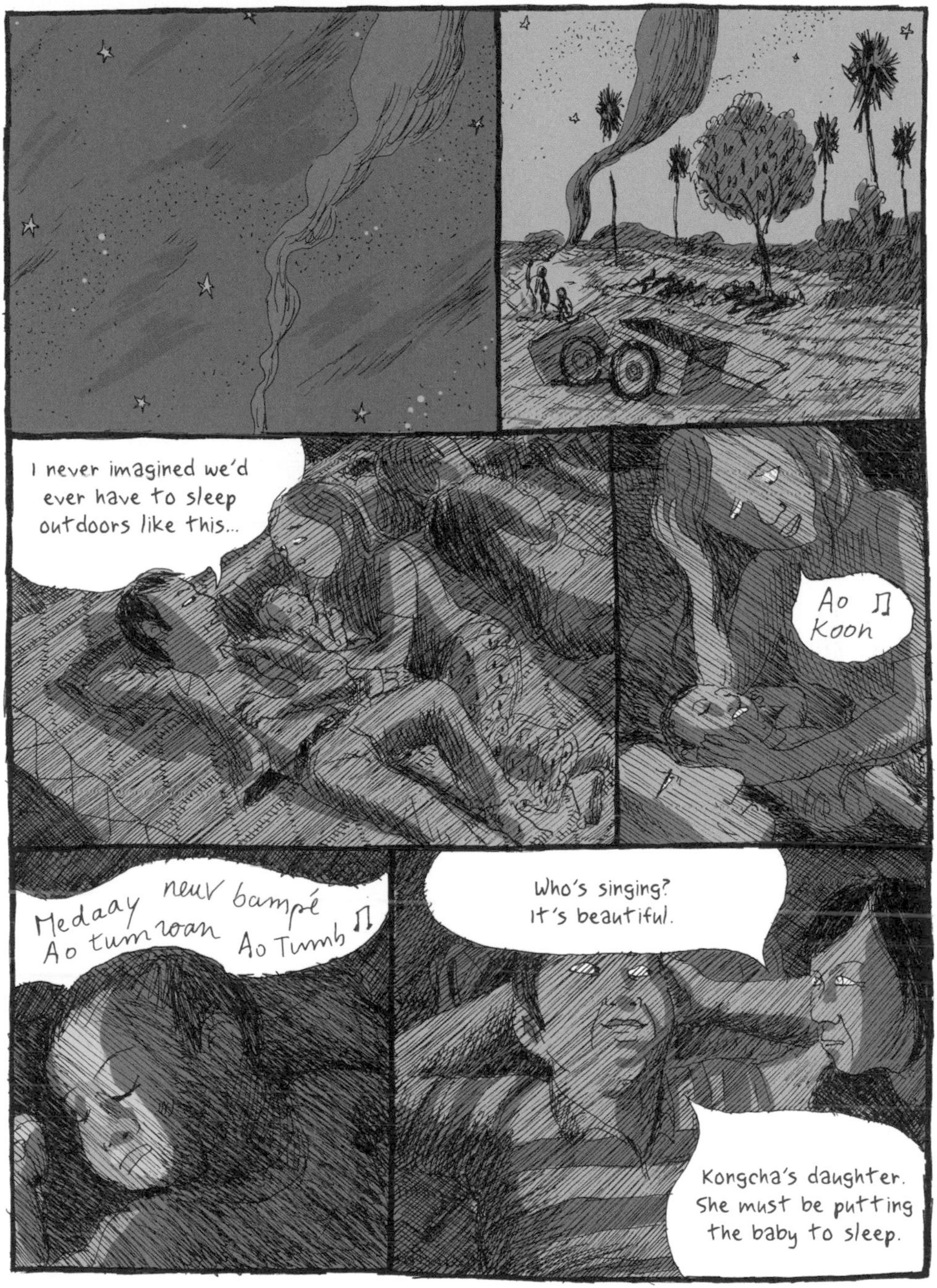
I never imagined we'd ever have to sleep outdoors like this...
Ao ♫ Koon
Medaay neuv bampé Ao tumroan Ao Tumb ♫
Who's singing? It's beautiful.
Kongcha's daughter. She must be putting the baby to sleep.

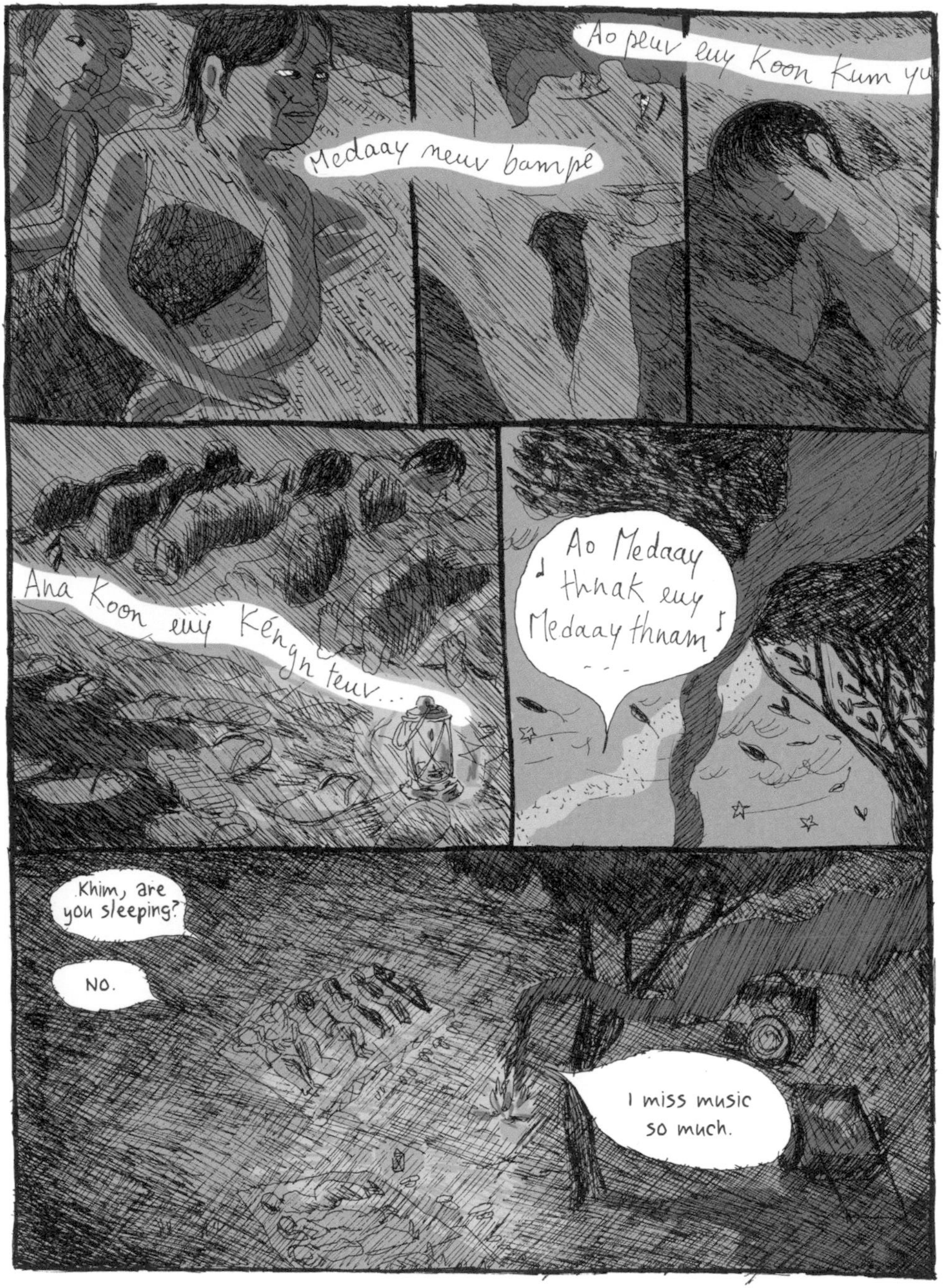
Medaay neuv bampé
Ao peuv euy Koon Kum yu
Ana Koon euy Kéngn teuv...
Ao Medaay thnak euy Medaay thnam ...
Khim, are you sleeping?
No.
I miss music so much.

chapter 7

DESCENT INTO HELL

TO AVOID TROUBLE WITH THE KHMER ROUGE, AVOID CARRYING THE FOLLOWING...

Firearms

military canteen

Photos

Watch

ID

Diploma

Eyeglasses

Radio

military uniform
from the former
regime

Passport

Lighter

Books

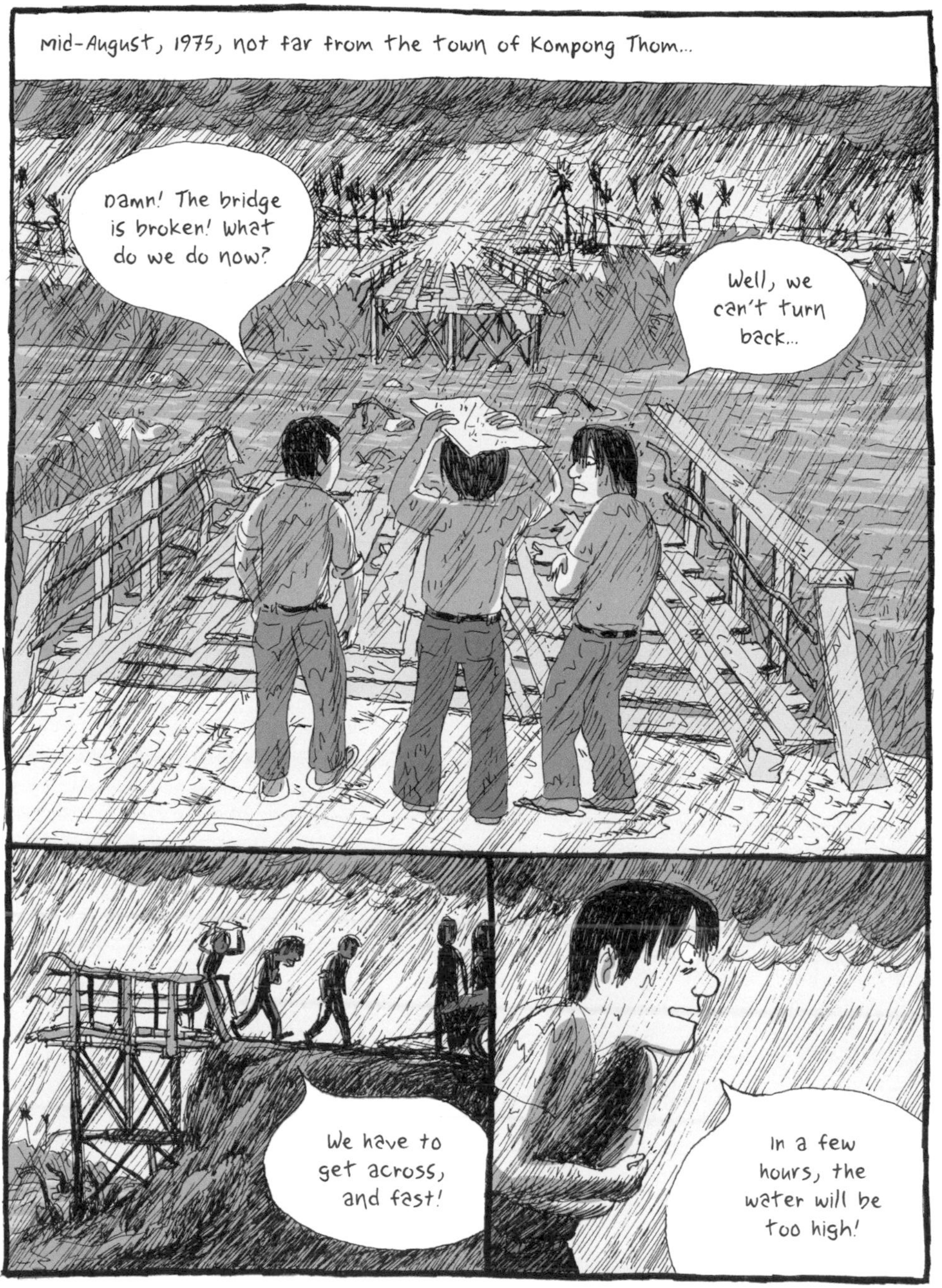

Mid-August, 1975, not far from the town of Kompong Thom...
Damn! The bridge is broken! What do we do now?
Well, we can't turn back...
We have to get across, and fast!
In a few hours, the water will be too high!

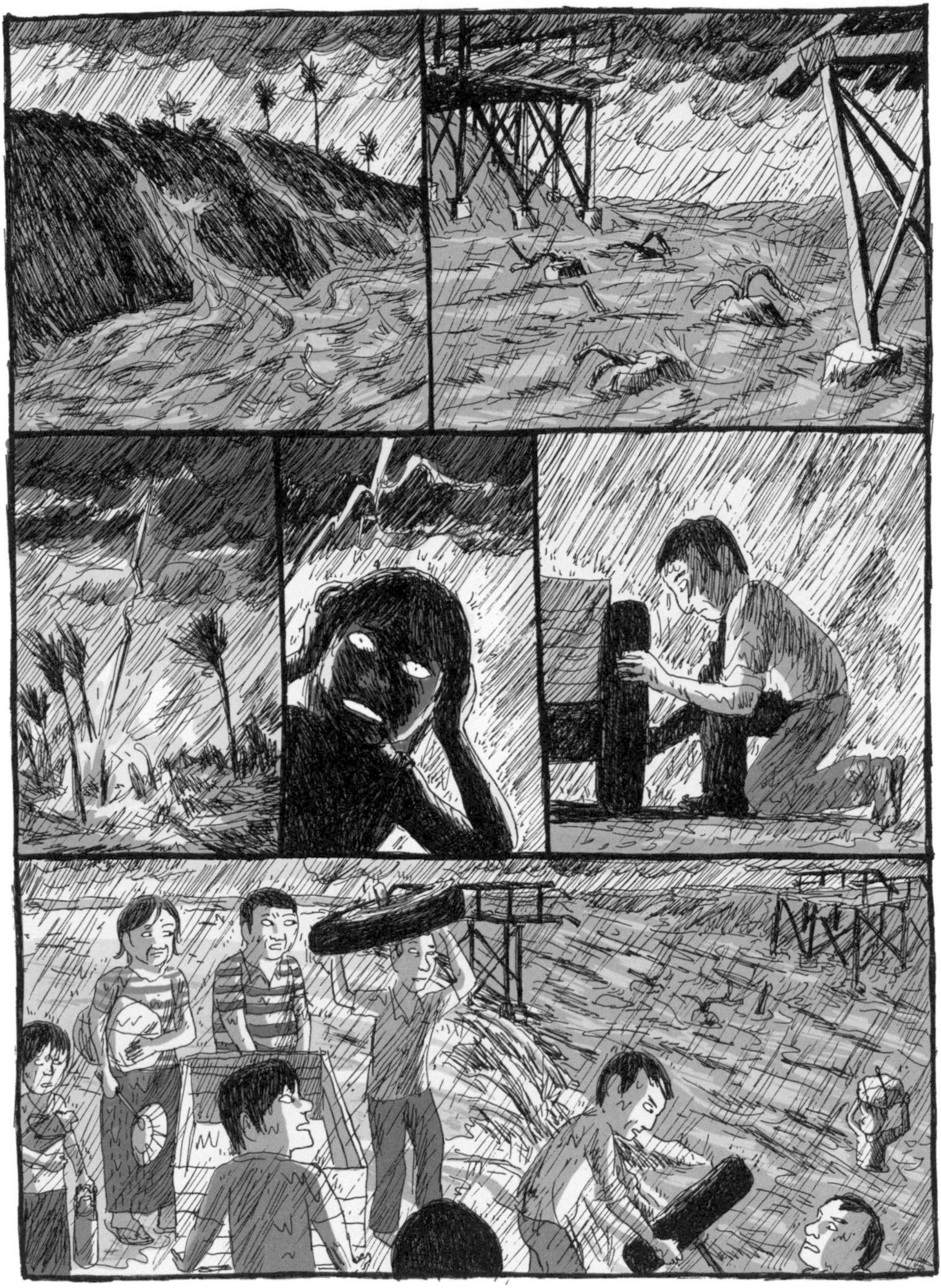

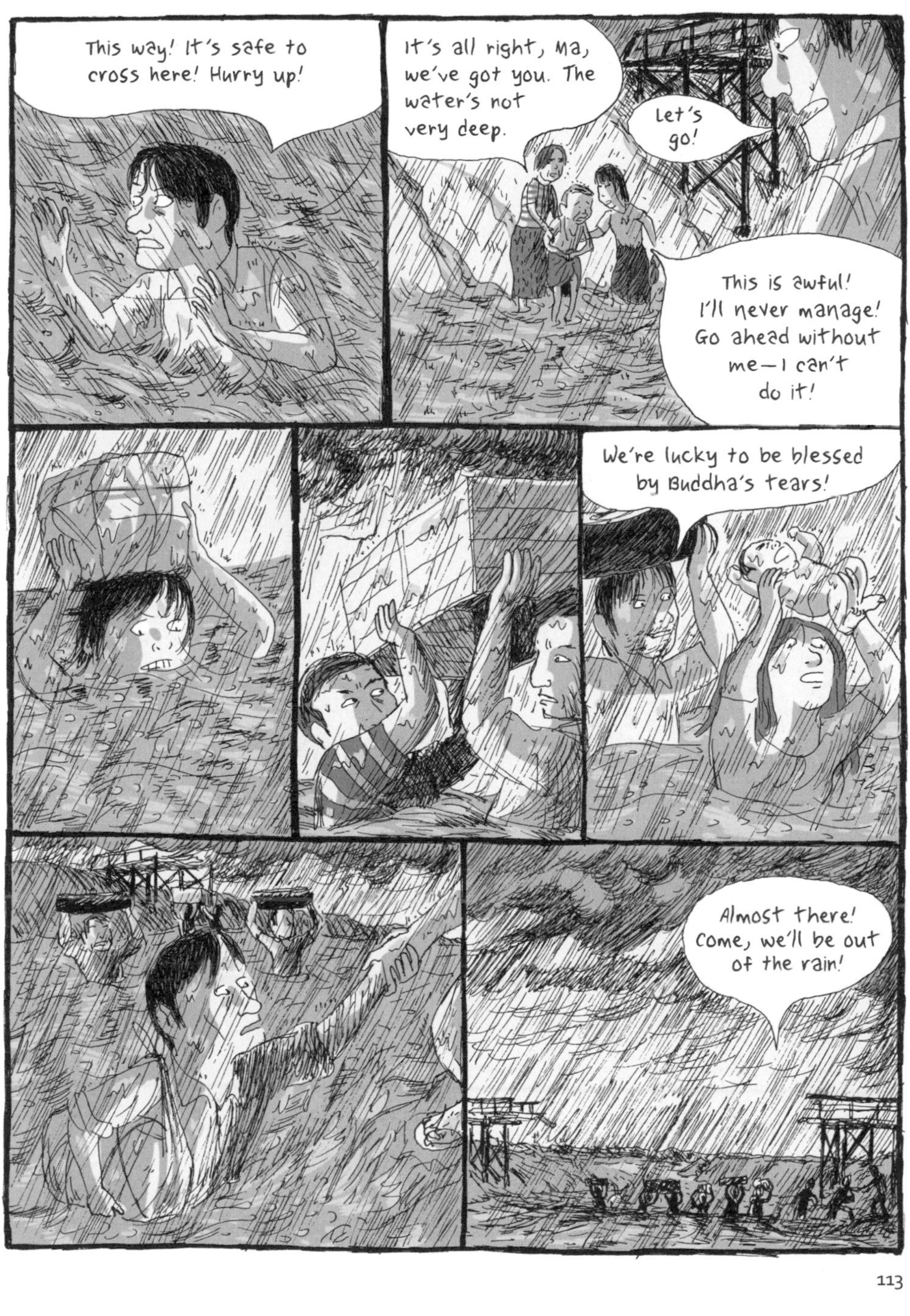

This way! It's safe to cross here! Hurry up!
It's all right, Ma, we've got you. The water's not very deep.
Let's go!
This is awful! I'll never manage! Go ahead without me—I can't do it!
We're lucky to be blessed by Buddha's tears!
Almost there! Come, we'll be out of the rain!

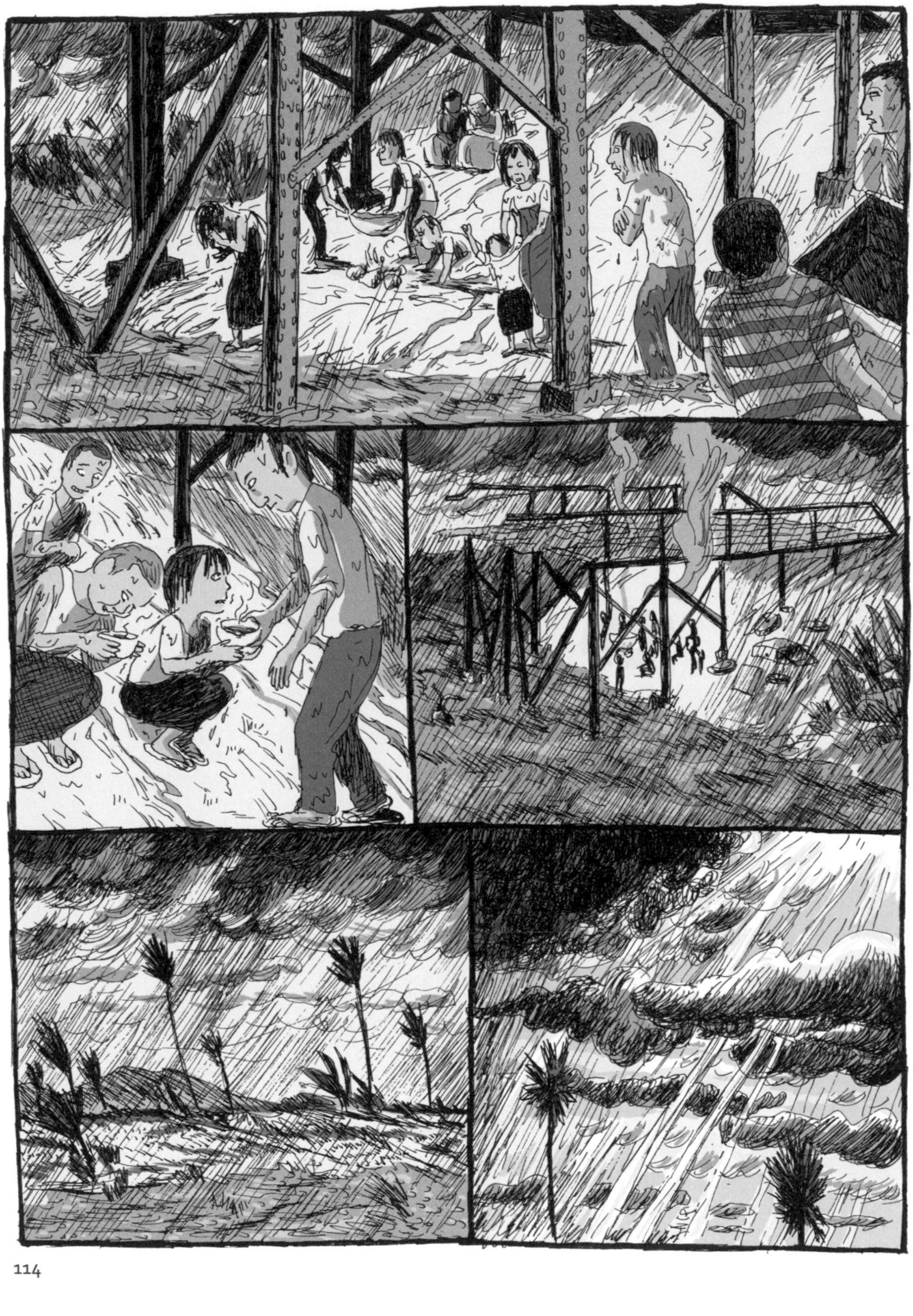

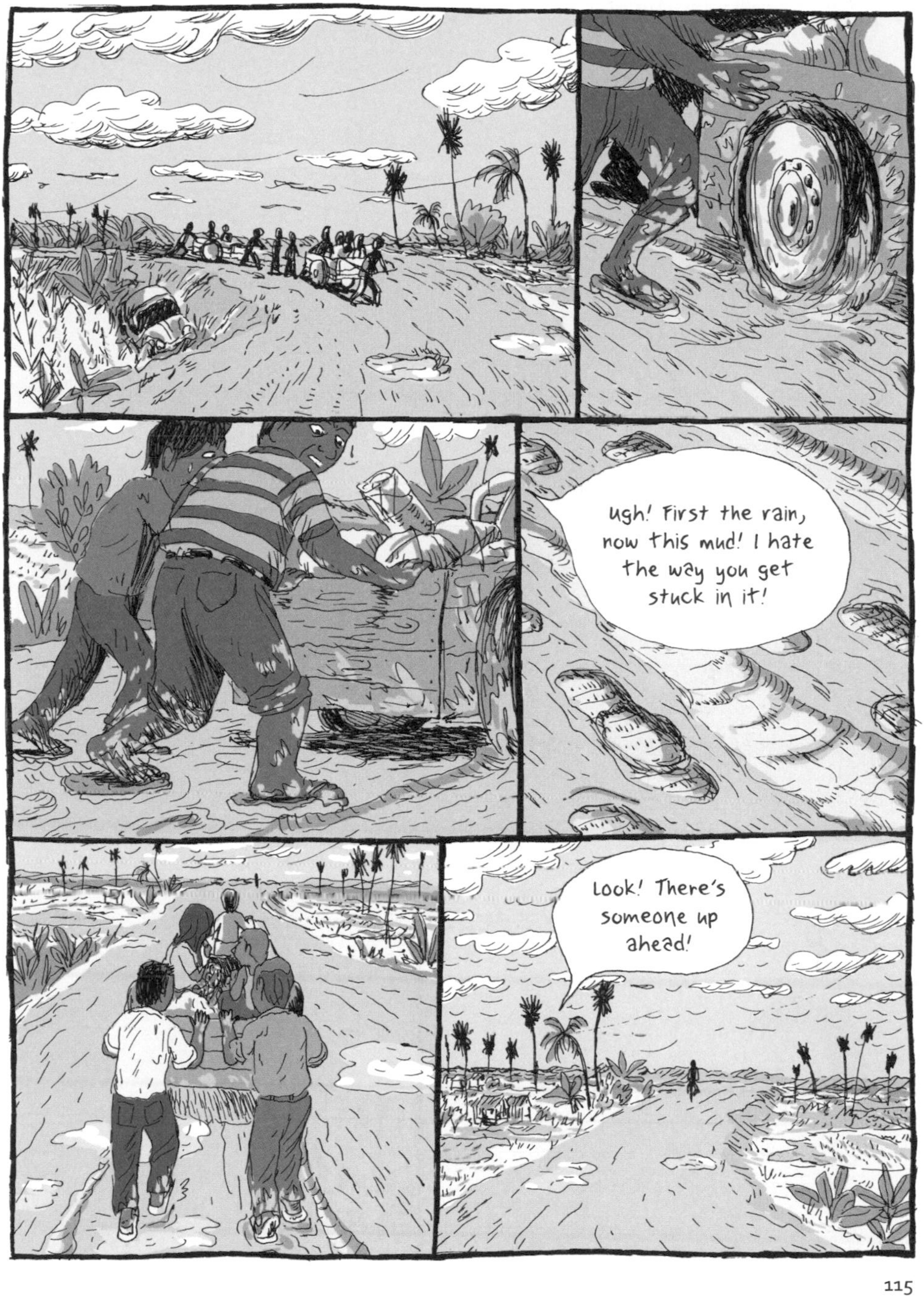
Ugh! First the rain, now this mud! I hate the way you get stuck in it!
Look! There's someone up ahead!

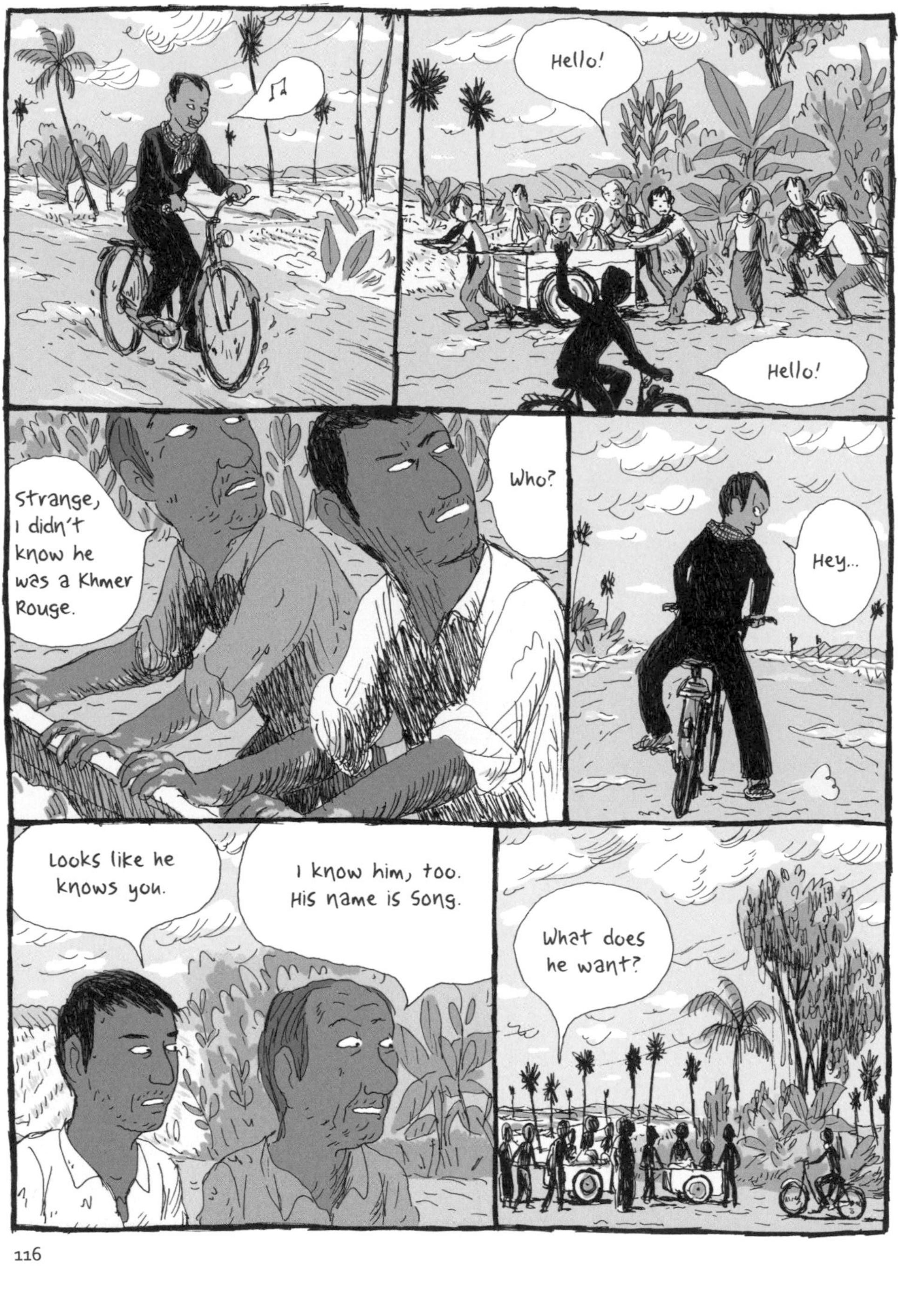
♫
Hello!
Hello!
Strange, I didn't know he was a Khmer Rouge.
Who?
Hey...
Looks like he knows you.
I know him, too. His name is Song.
What does he want?

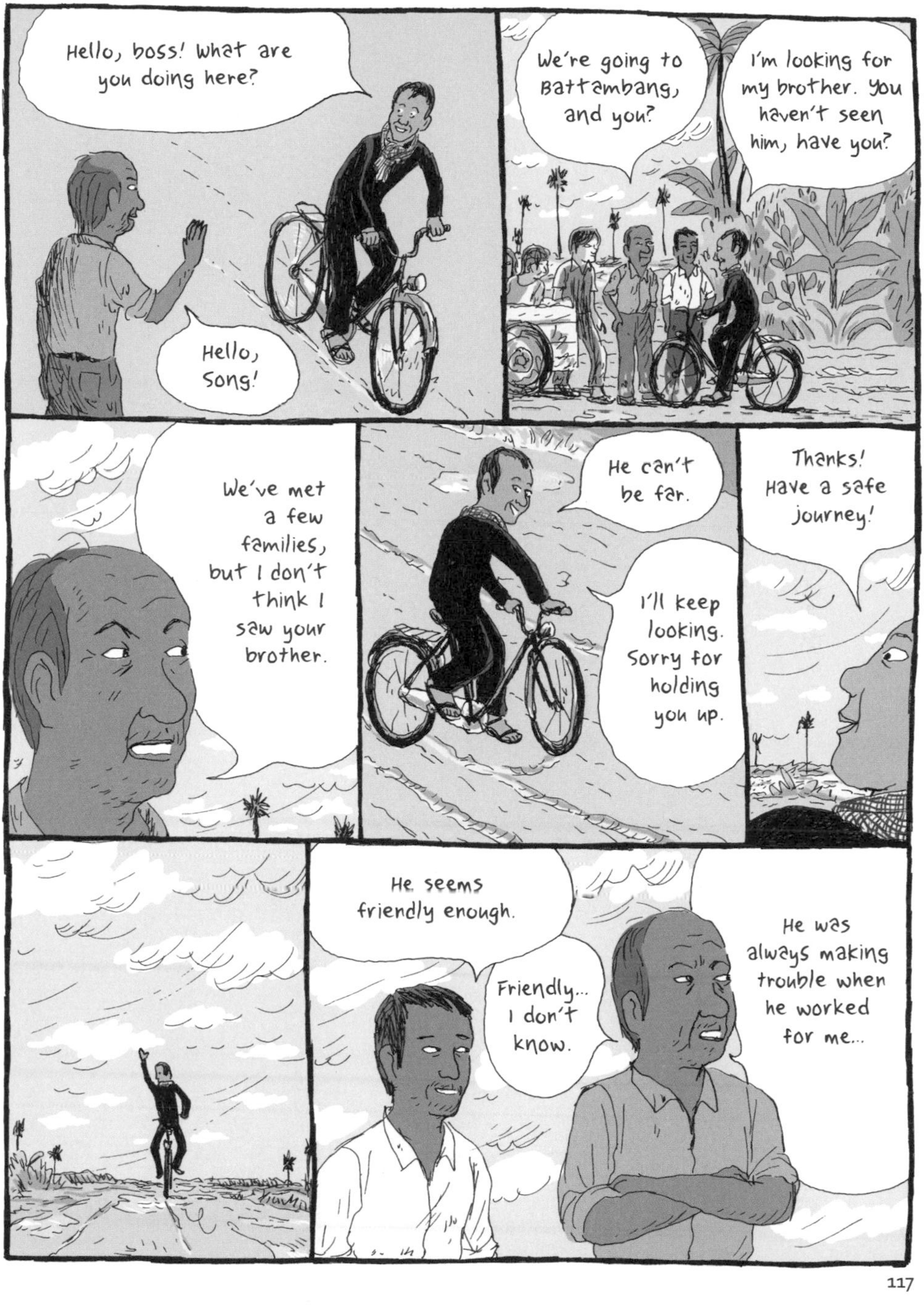

Hello, boss! What are you doing here?
Hello, Song!
We're going to Battambang, and you?
I'm looking for my brother. You haven't seen him, have you?
We've met a few families, but I don't think I saw your brother.
He can't be far.
I'll keep looking. Sorry for holding you up.
Thanks! Have a safe journey!
He seems friendly enough.
Friendly... I don't know.
He was always making trouble when he worked for me...

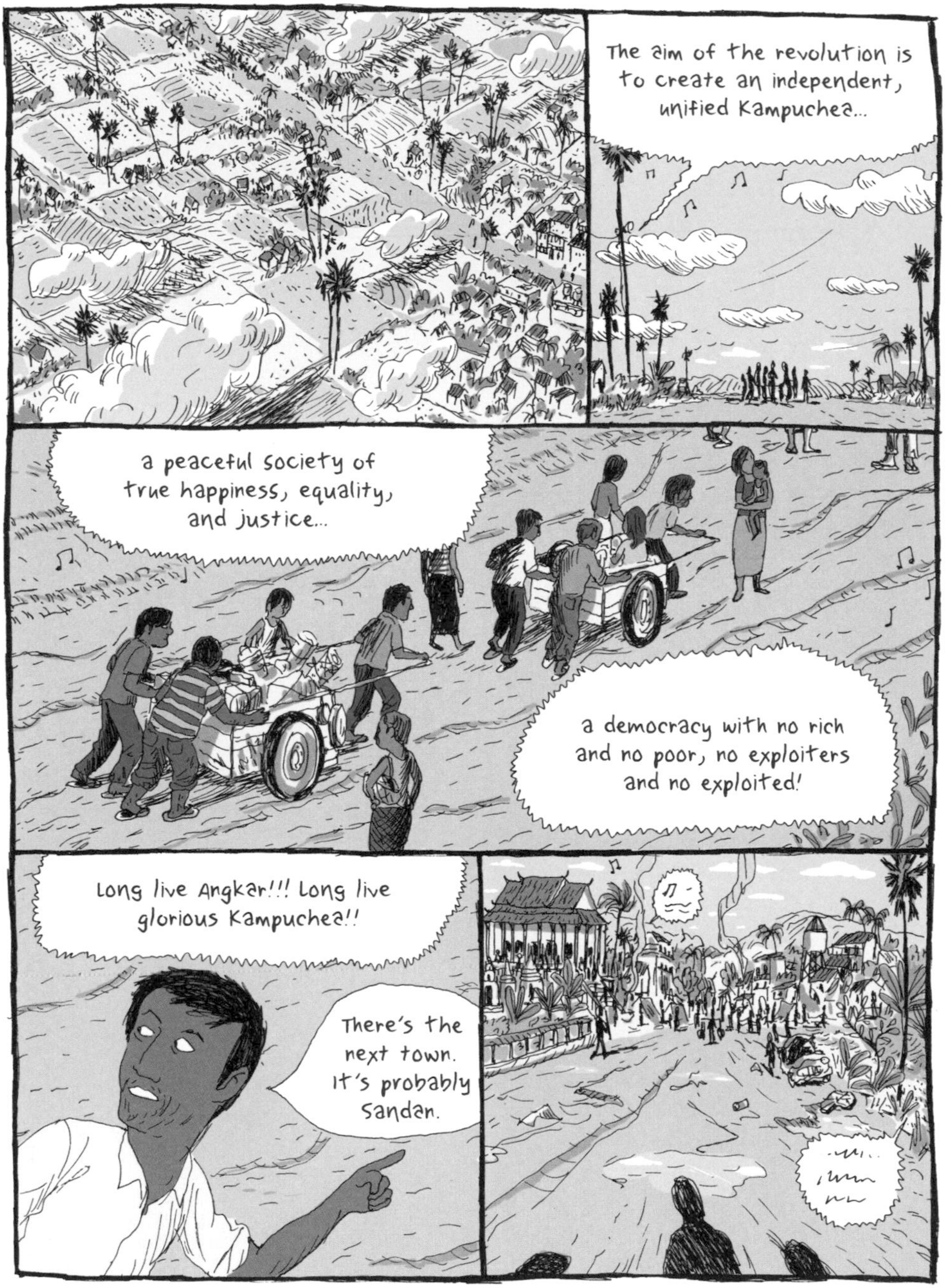
The aim of the revolution is to create an independent, unified Kampuchea...
a peaceful society of true happiness, equality, and justice...
a democracy with no rich and no poor, no exploiters and no exploited!
Long live Angkar!!! Long live glorious Kampuchea!!
There's the next town. It's probably Sandan.

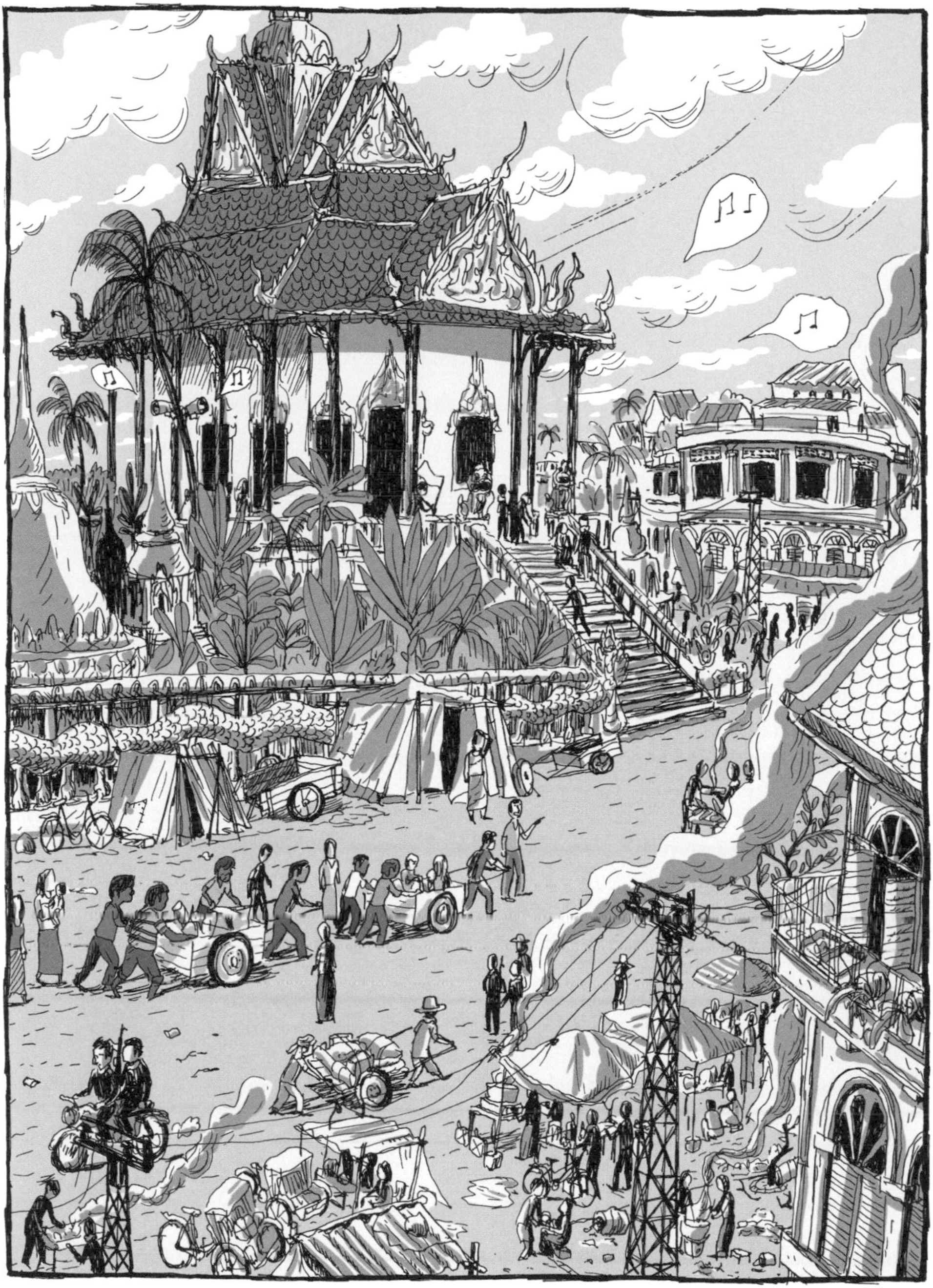

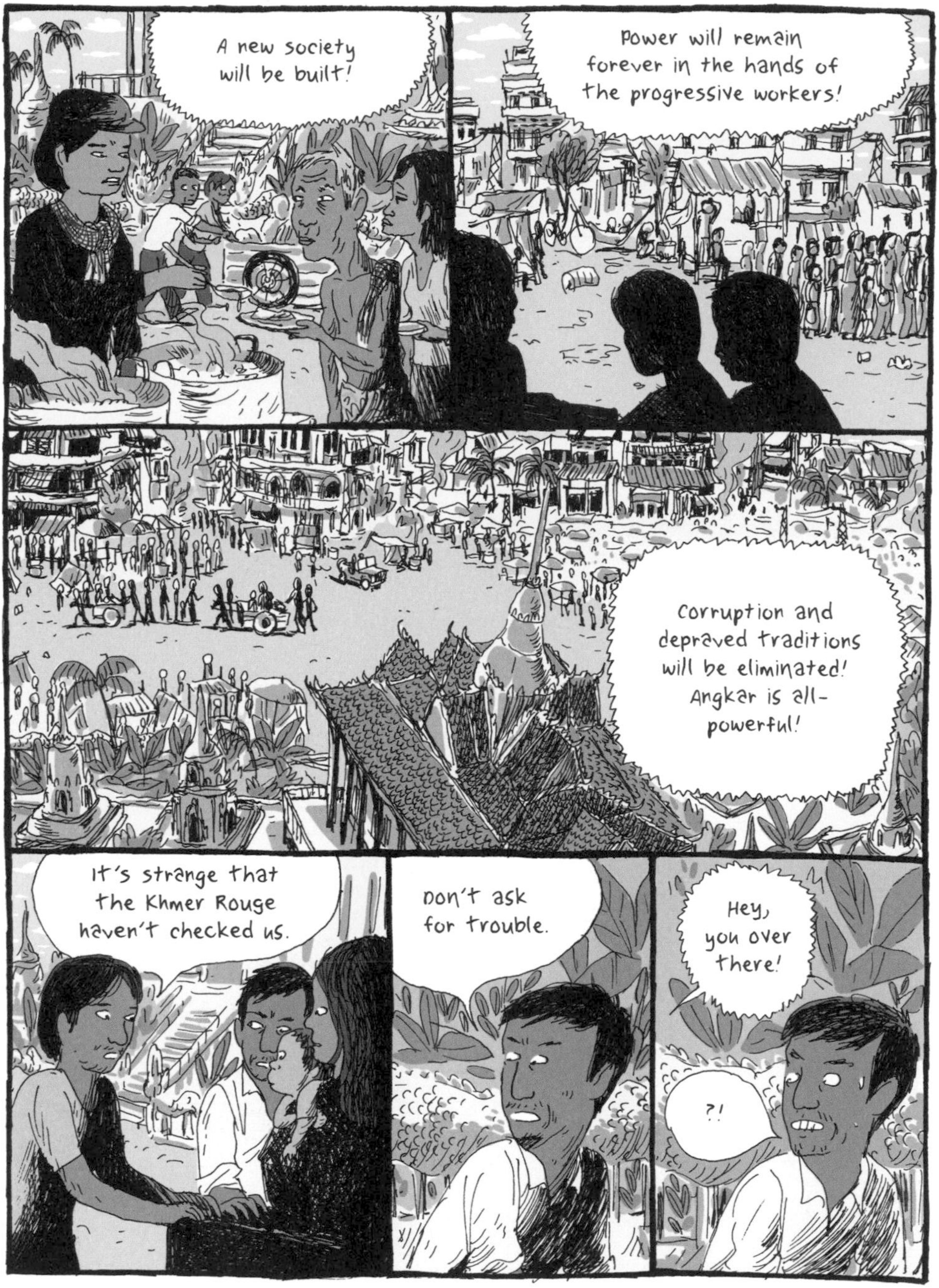
A new society will be built!
Power will remain forever in the hands of the progressive workers!
Corruption and depraved traditions will be eliminated! Angkar is all-powerful!
It's strange that the Khmer Rouge haven't checked us.
Don't ask for trouble.
Hey, you over there!
?!

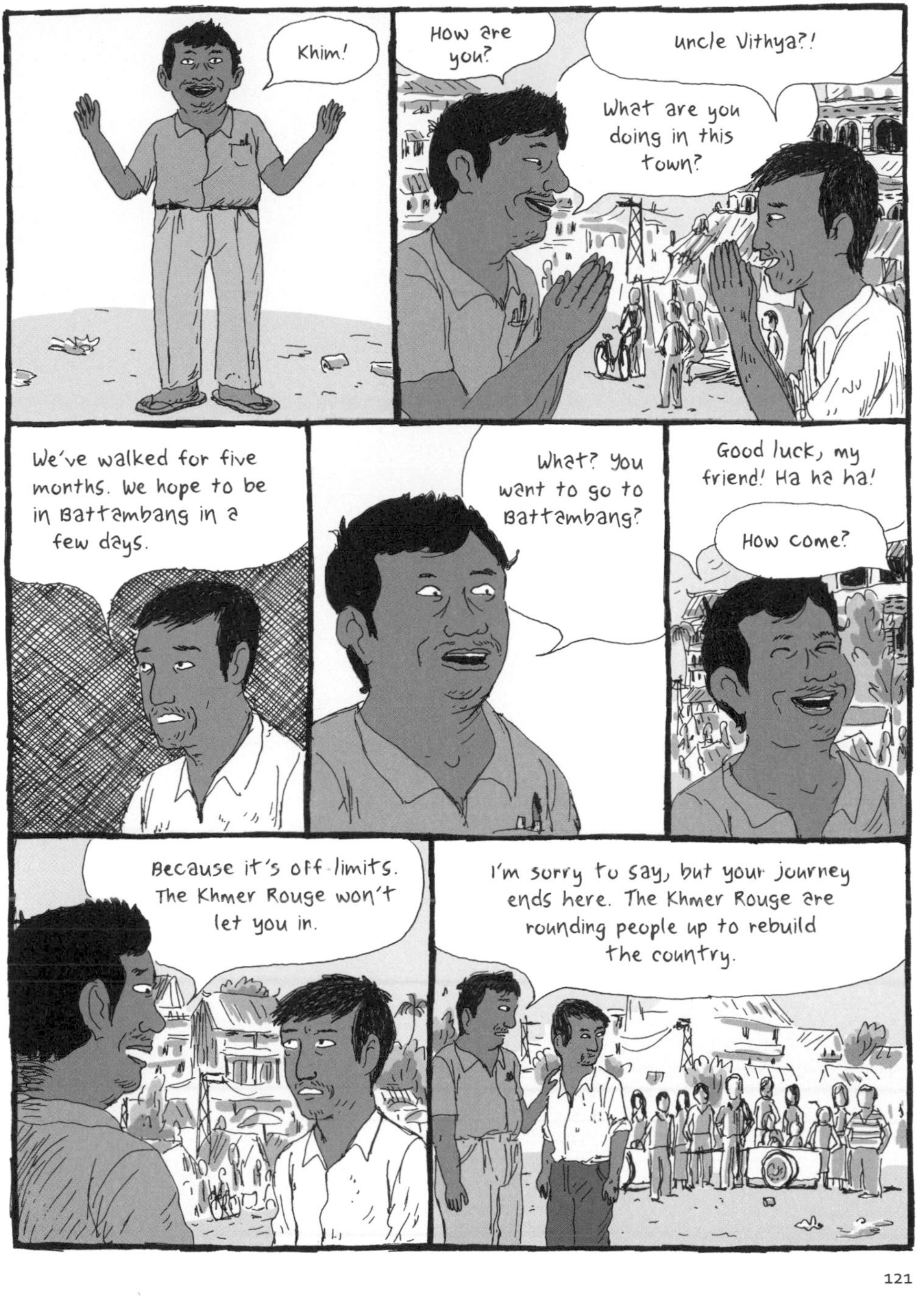

Khim!
How are you?
uncle Vithya?!
What are you doing in this town?
We've walked for five months. We hope to be in Battambang in a few days.
What? You want to go to Battambang?
Good luck, my friend! Ha ha ha!
How come?
Because it's off-limits. The Khmer Rouge won't let you in.
I'm sorry to say, but your journey ends here. The Khmer Rouge are rounding people up to rebuild the country.

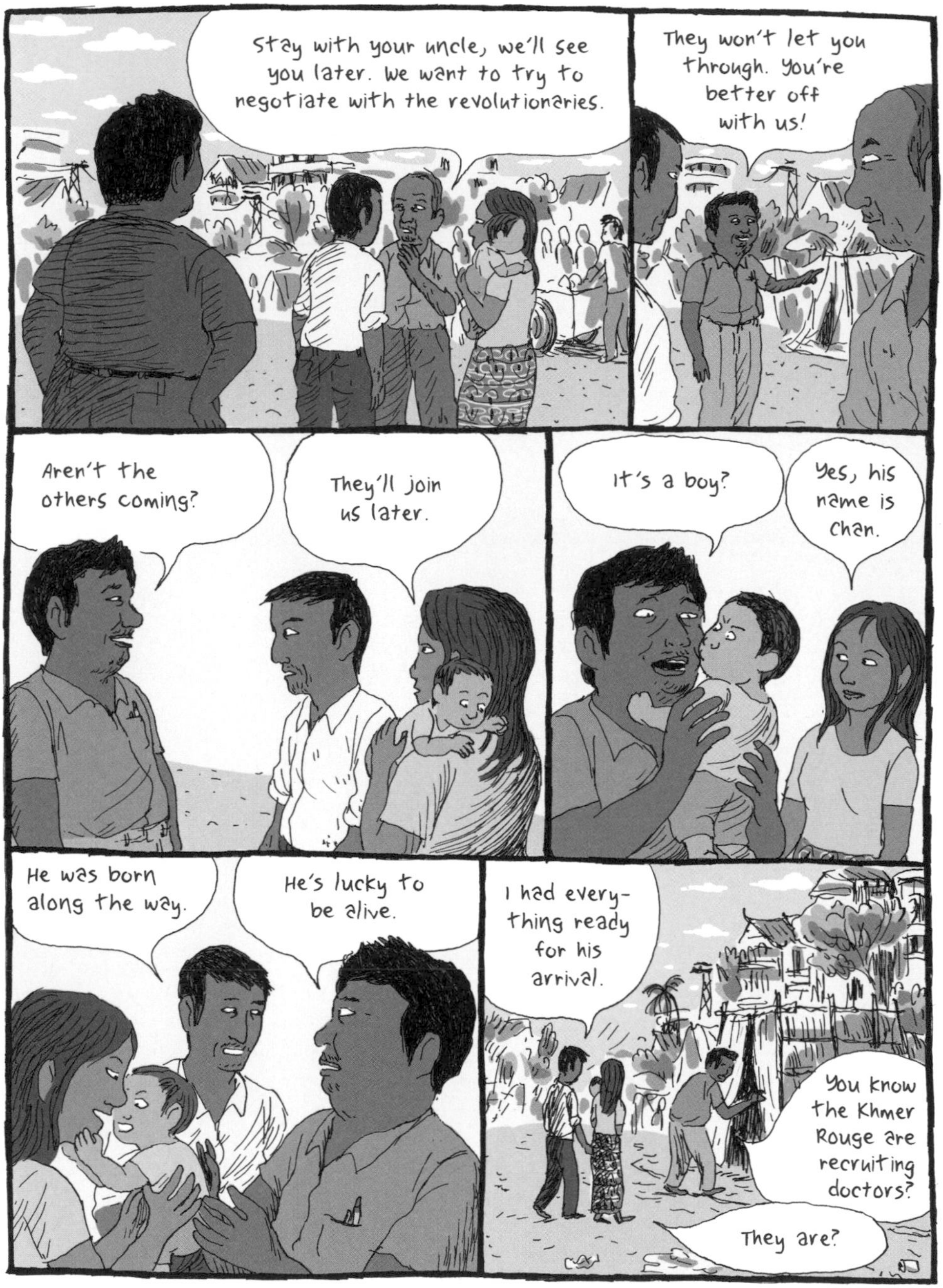
Stay with your uncle, we'll see you later. We want to try to negotiate with the revolutionaries.
They won't let you through. You're better off with us!
Aren't the others coming?
They'll join us later.
It's a boy?
Yes, his name is Chan.
He was born along the way.
He's lucky to be alive.
I had everything ready for his arrival.
You know the Khmer Rouge are recruiting doctors?
They are?

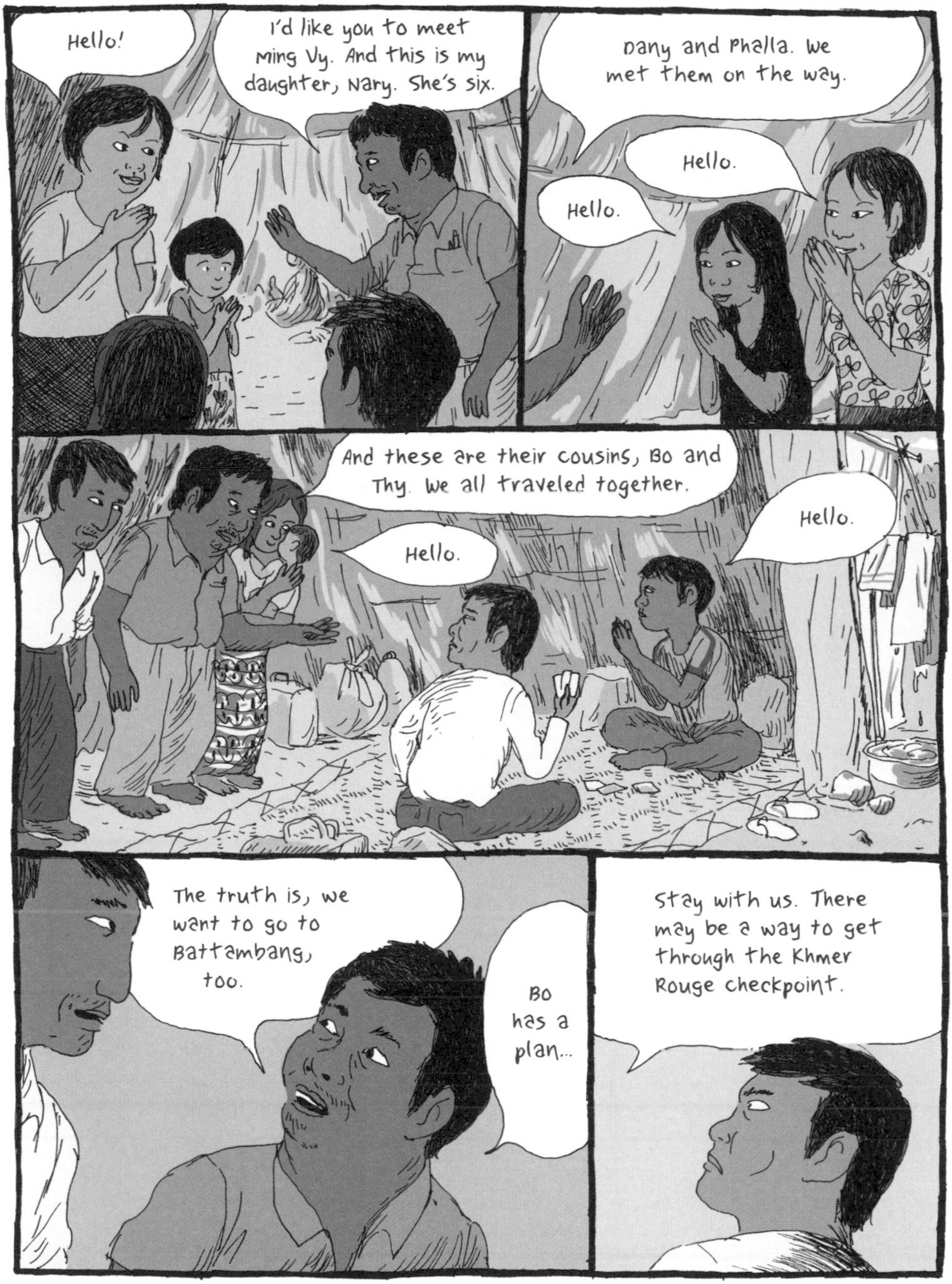
Hello!
I'd like you to meet Ming Vy. And this is my daughter, Nary. She's six.
Dany and Phalla. We met them on the way.
Hello.
Hello.
And these are their cousins, Bo and Thy. We all traveled together.
Hello.
Hello.
The truth is, we want to go to Battambang, too.
Bo has a plan...
Stay with us. There may be a way to get through the Khmer Rouge checkpoint.

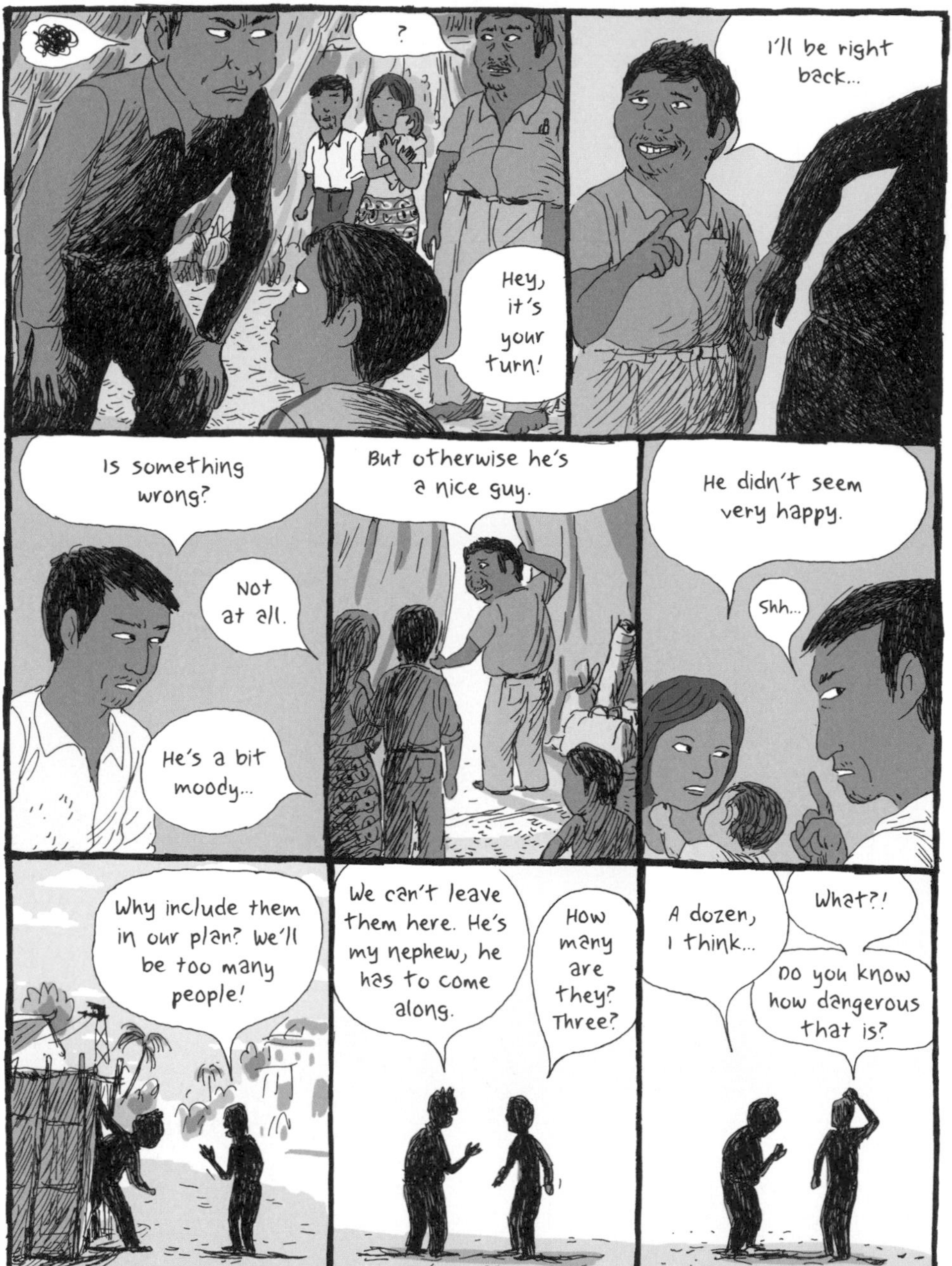
?
Hey, it's your turn!
I'll be right back...
Is something wrong?
Not at all.
He's a bit moody...
But otherwise he's a nice guy.
He didn't seem very happy.
Shh...
Why include them in our plan? We'll be too many people!
We can't leave them here. He's my nephew, he has to come along.
How many are they? Three?
A dozen, I think...
What?!
Do you know how dangerous that is?

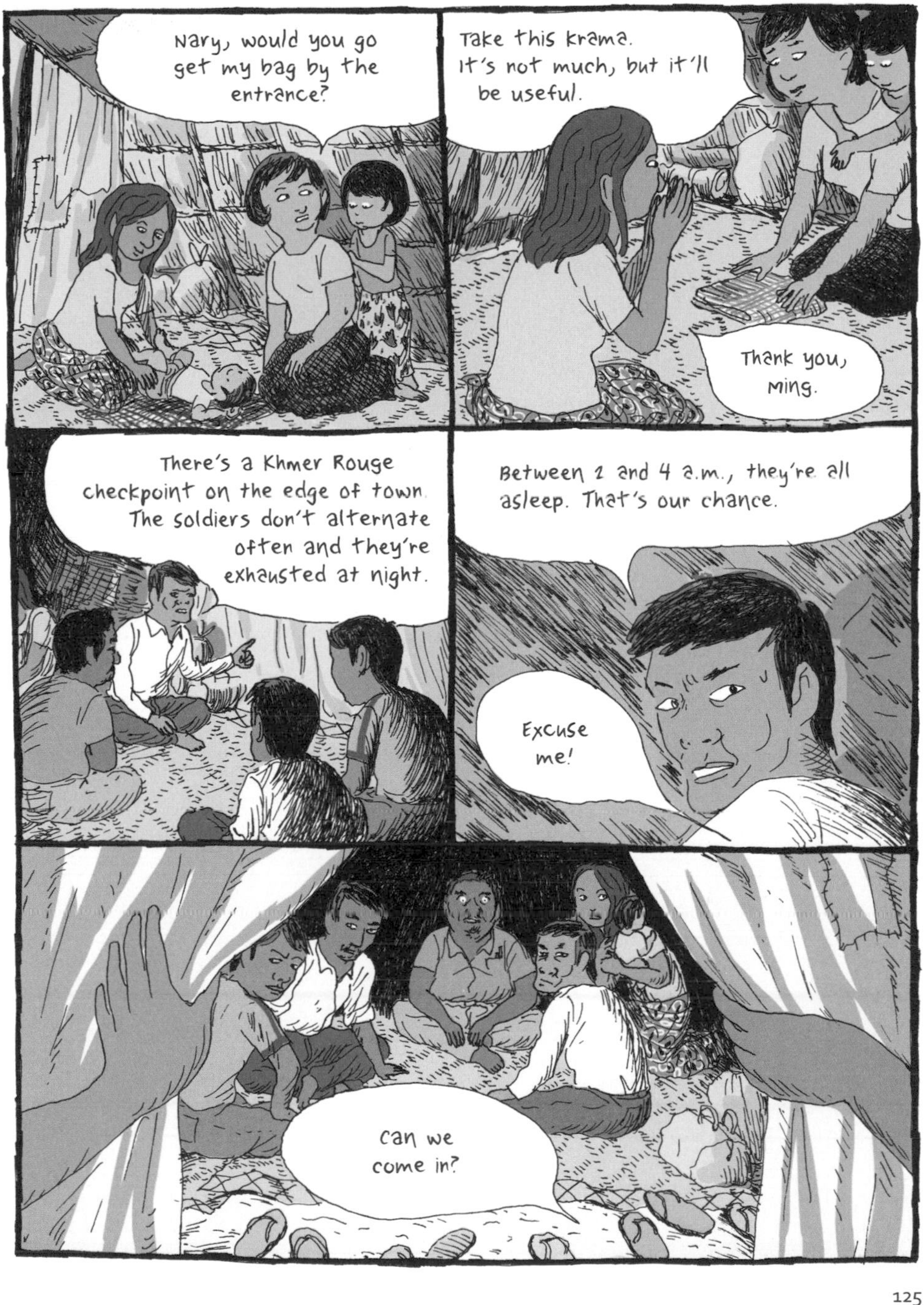
Nary, would you go get my bag by the entrance?
Take this krama. It's not much, but it'll be useful.
Thank you, Ming.
There's a Khmer Rouge checkpoint on the edge of town. The soldiers don't alternate often and they're exhausted at night.
Between 2 and 4 a.m., they're all asleep. That's our chance.
Excuse me!
Can we come in?

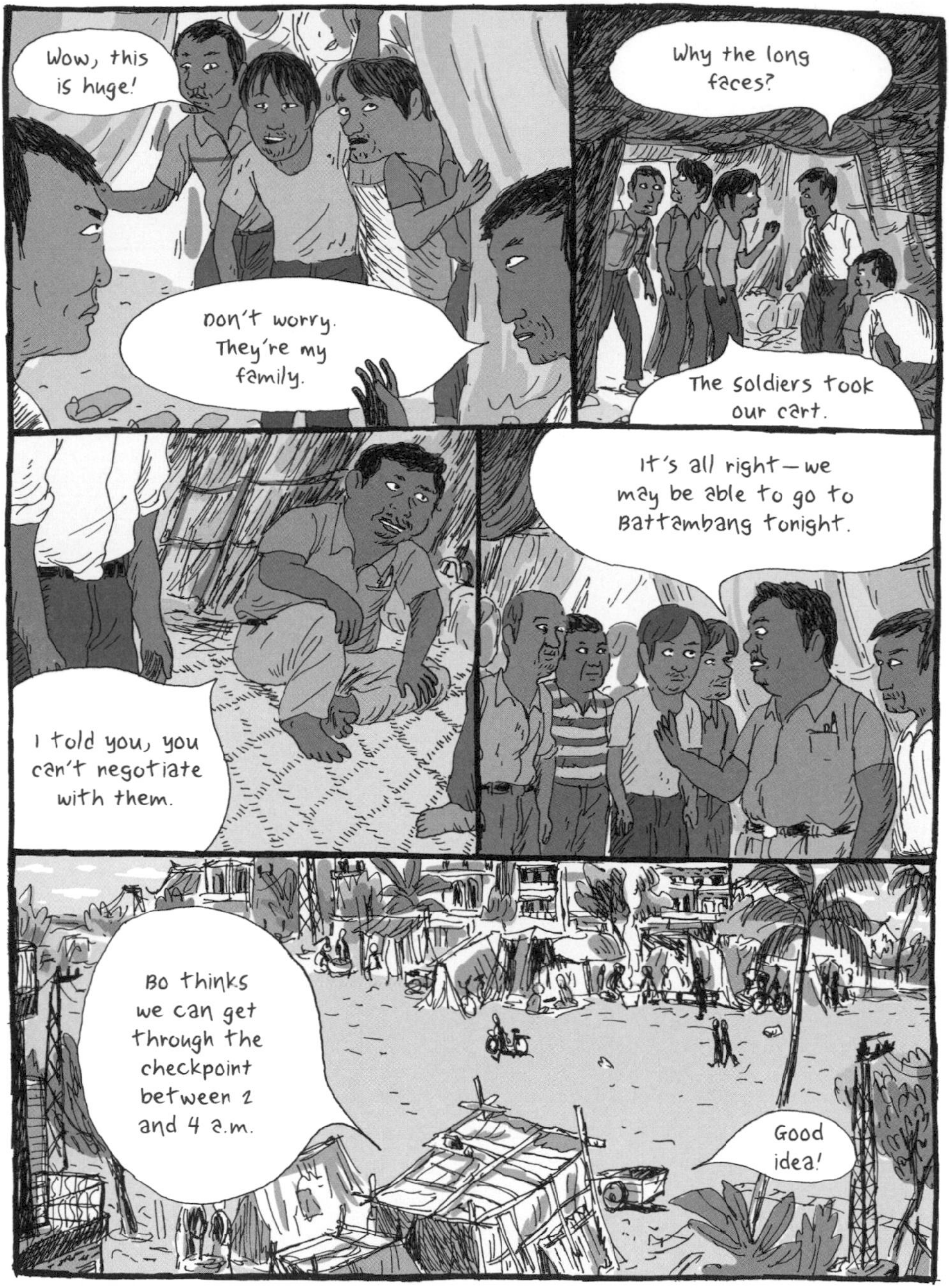
Wow, this is huge!
Don't worry. They're my family.
Why the long faces?
The soldiers took our cart.
I told you, you can't negotiate with them.
It's all right—we may be able to go to Battambang tonight.
Bo thinks we can get through the checkpoint between 2 and 4 a.m.
Good idea!

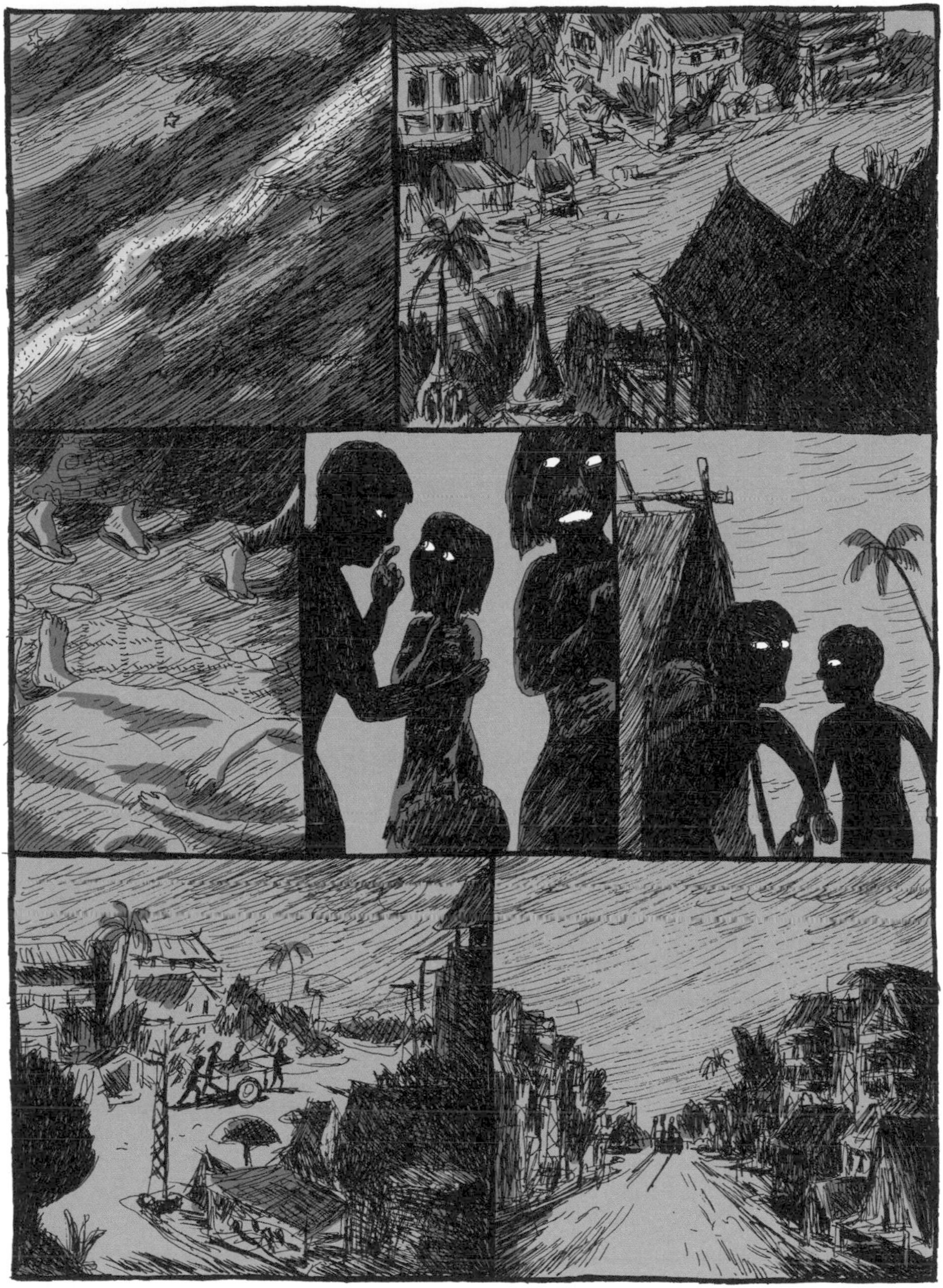

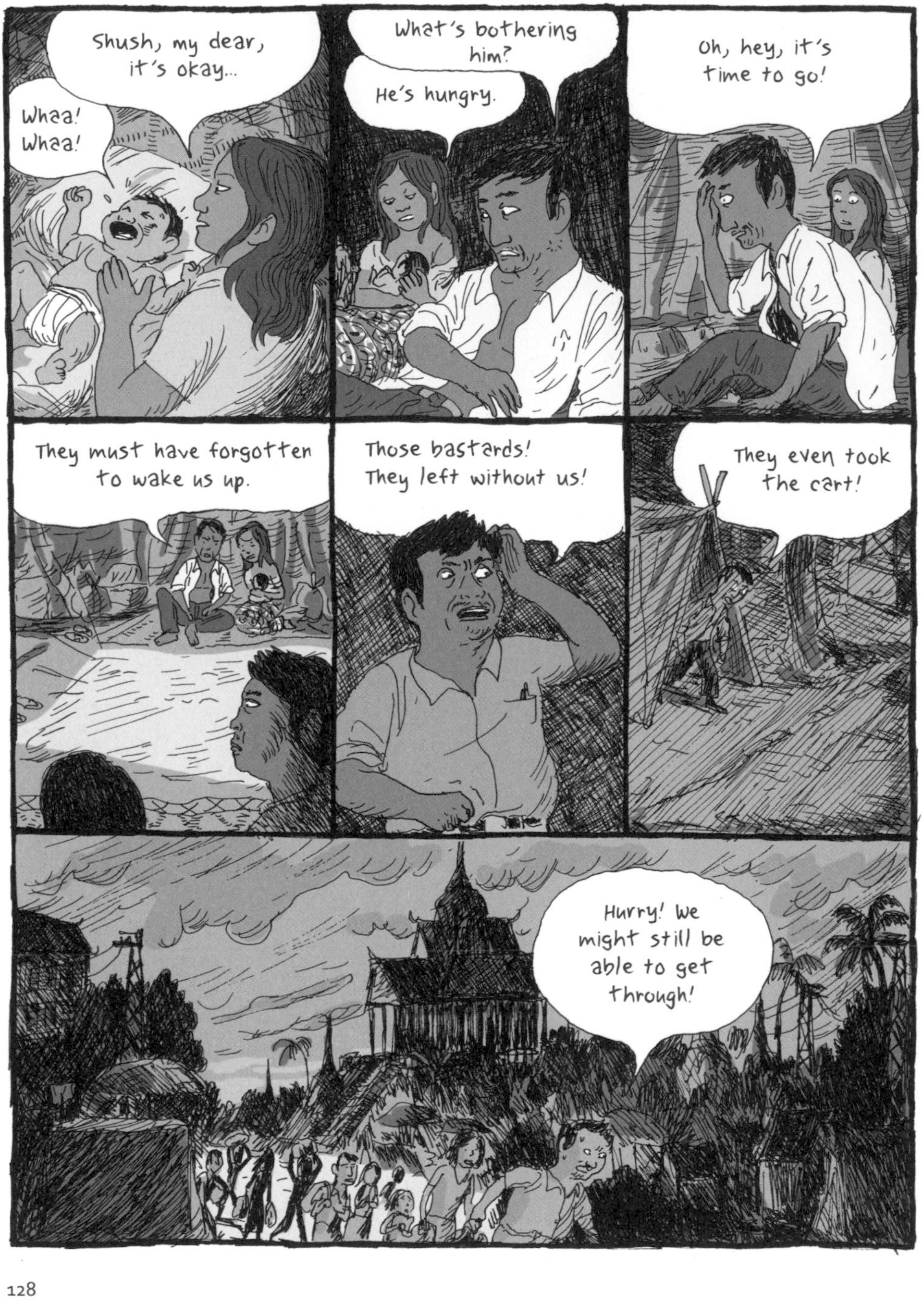
Shush, my dear, it's okay...
Whaa! Whaa!
What's bothering him?
He's hungry.
Oh, hey, it's time to go!
They must have forgotten to wake us up.
Those bastards! They left without us!
They even took the cart!
Hurry! We might still be able to get through!

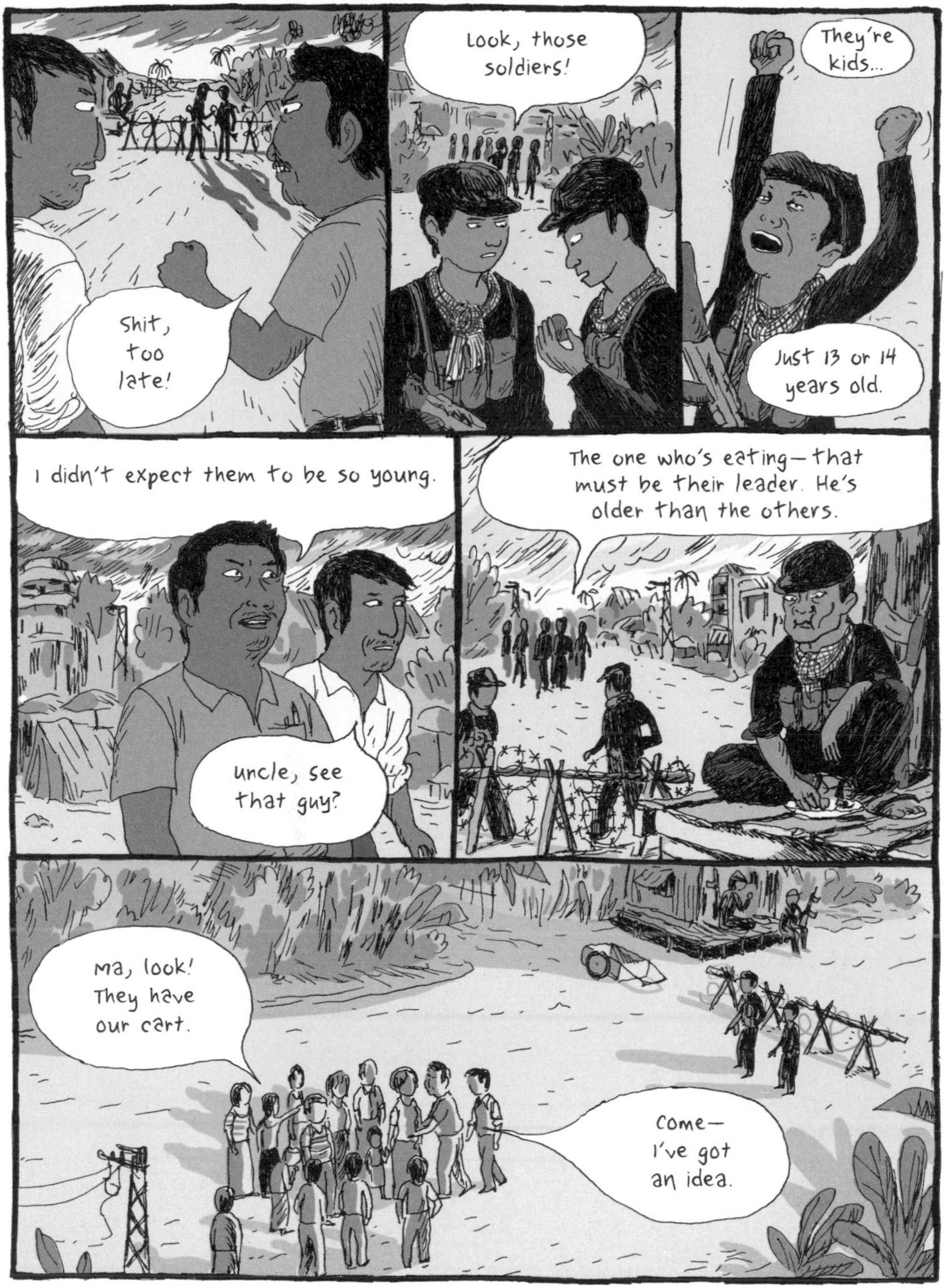
Shit, too late!
Look, those soldiers!
They're kids...
Just 13 or 14 years old.
I didn't expect them to be so young.
Uncle, see that guy?
The one who's eating—that must be their leader. He's older than the others.
Ma, look! They have our cart.
Come— I've got an idea.

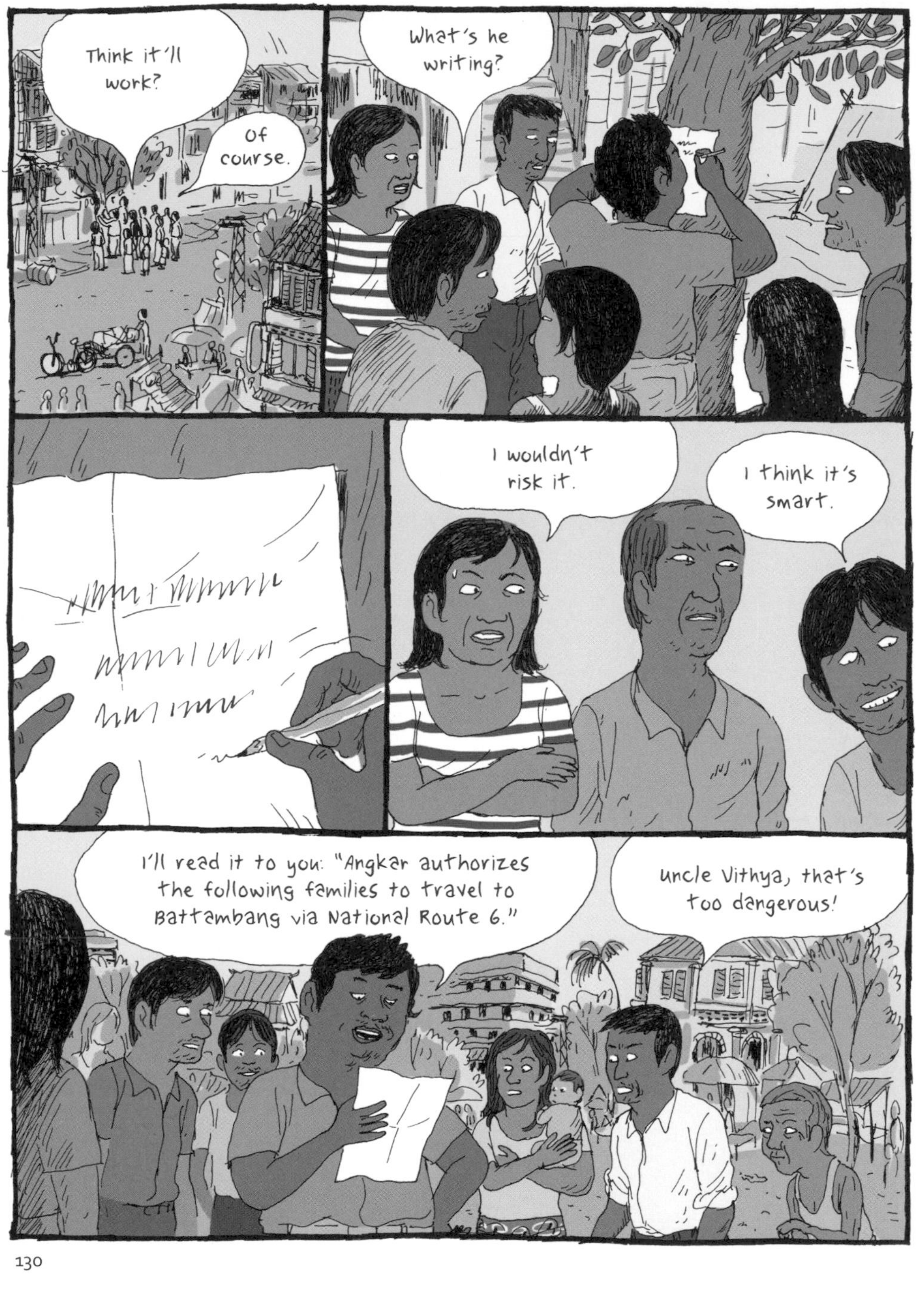
Think it'll work?
Of course.
What's he writing?
I wouldn't risk it.
I think it's smart.
I'll read it to you: "Angkar authorizes the following families to travel to Battambang via National Route 6."
Uncle Vithya, that's too dangerous!

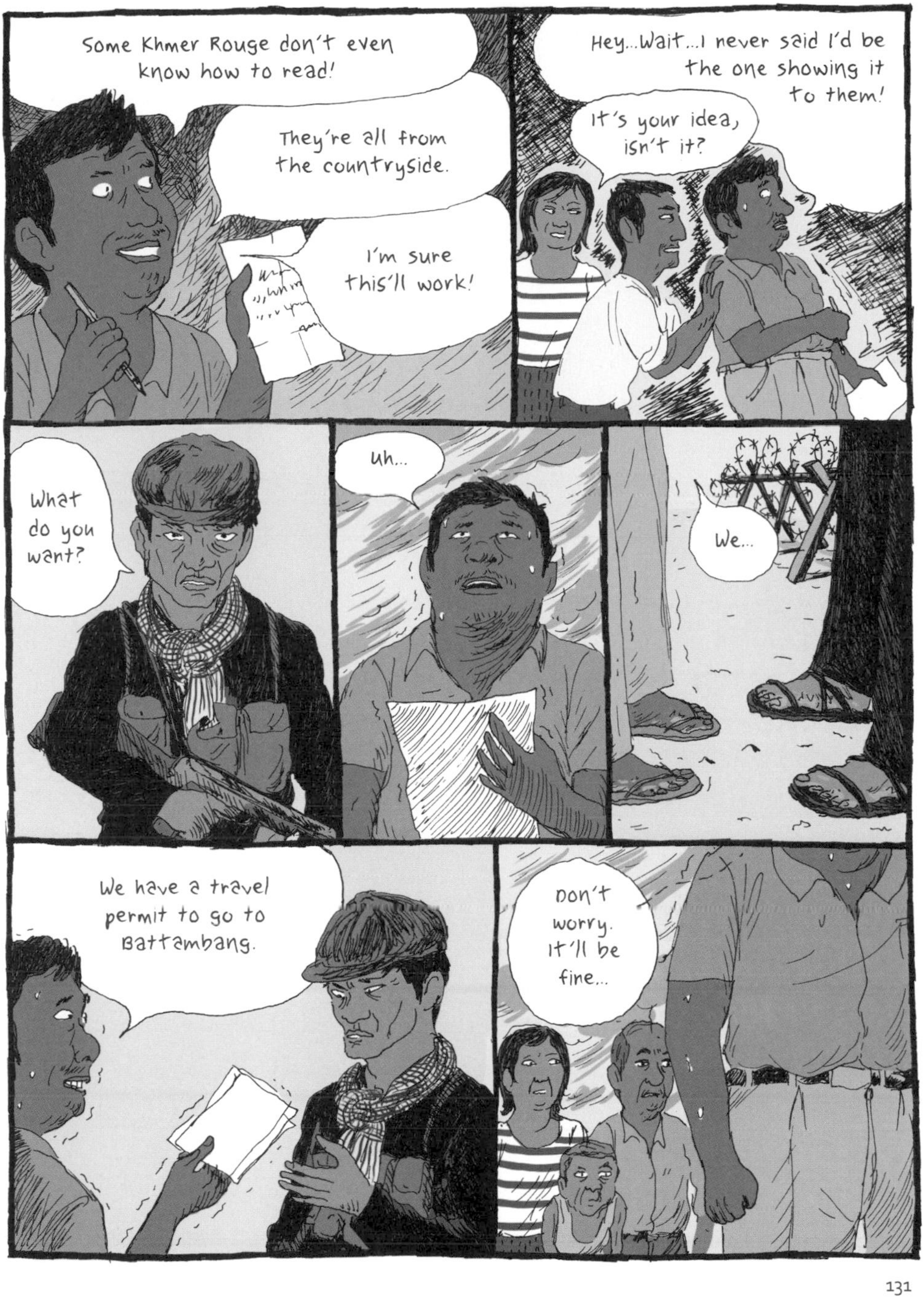
Some Khmer Rouge don't even know how to read!
They're all from the countryside.
I'm sure this'll work!
Hey...Wait...I never said I'd be the one showing it to them!
It's your idea, isn't it?
What do you want?
Uh...
We...
We have a travel permit to go to Battambang.
Don't worry. It'll be fine...

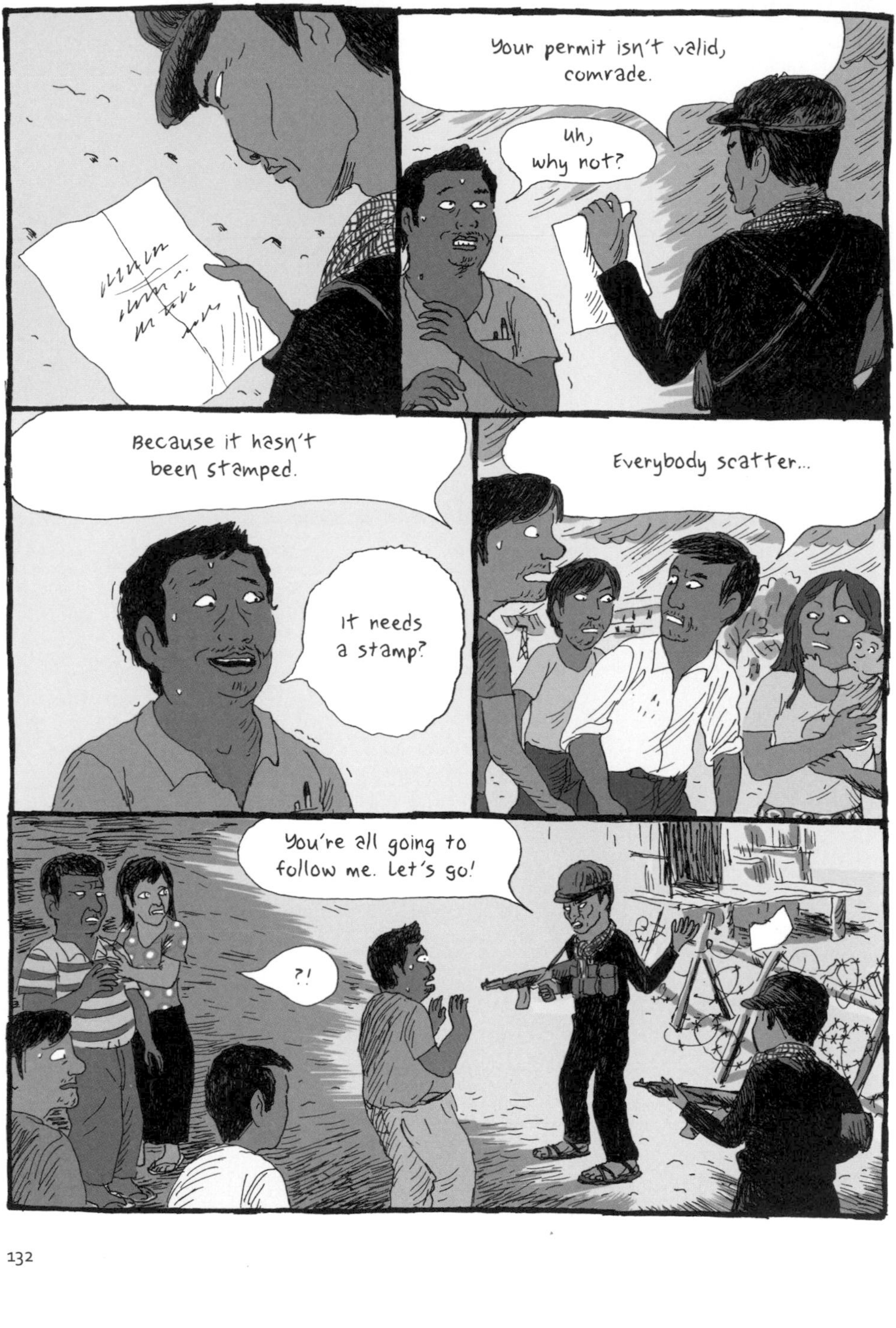

Your permit isn't valid, comrade.
Uh, why not?
Because it hasn't been stamped.
It needs a stamp?
Everybody scatter...
You're all going to follow me. Let's go!
?!

part two

DO NOT WORRY

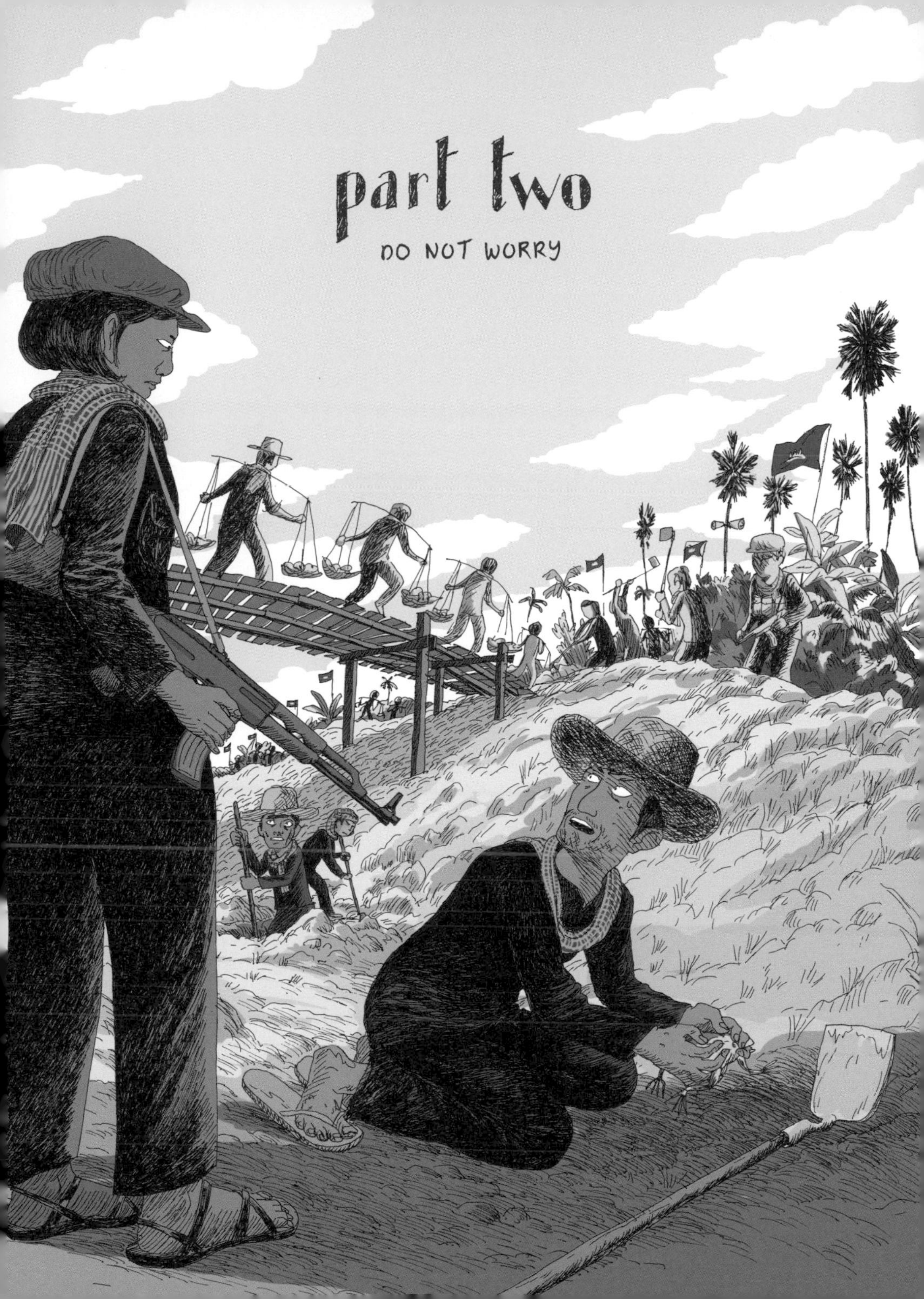

chapter 8

Let us abolish the monarchy and establish Angkar*!
Let us abolish taxes and establish voluntary contributions!
Let us abolish the white and glorify the black!
Let us dignify the ignorant and eradicate the learned!

*Angkar: organization

After their arrest by Khmer Rouge militia, Khim and Vithya's families were sent to a village to be reeducated according to the principles of Angkar. There they again met Song, the young man on the bicycle. As one of the "old people" from the countryside, Song was assigned to help relocate the "new people" from the cities. He suggested that the two families come to his village of Roneam.

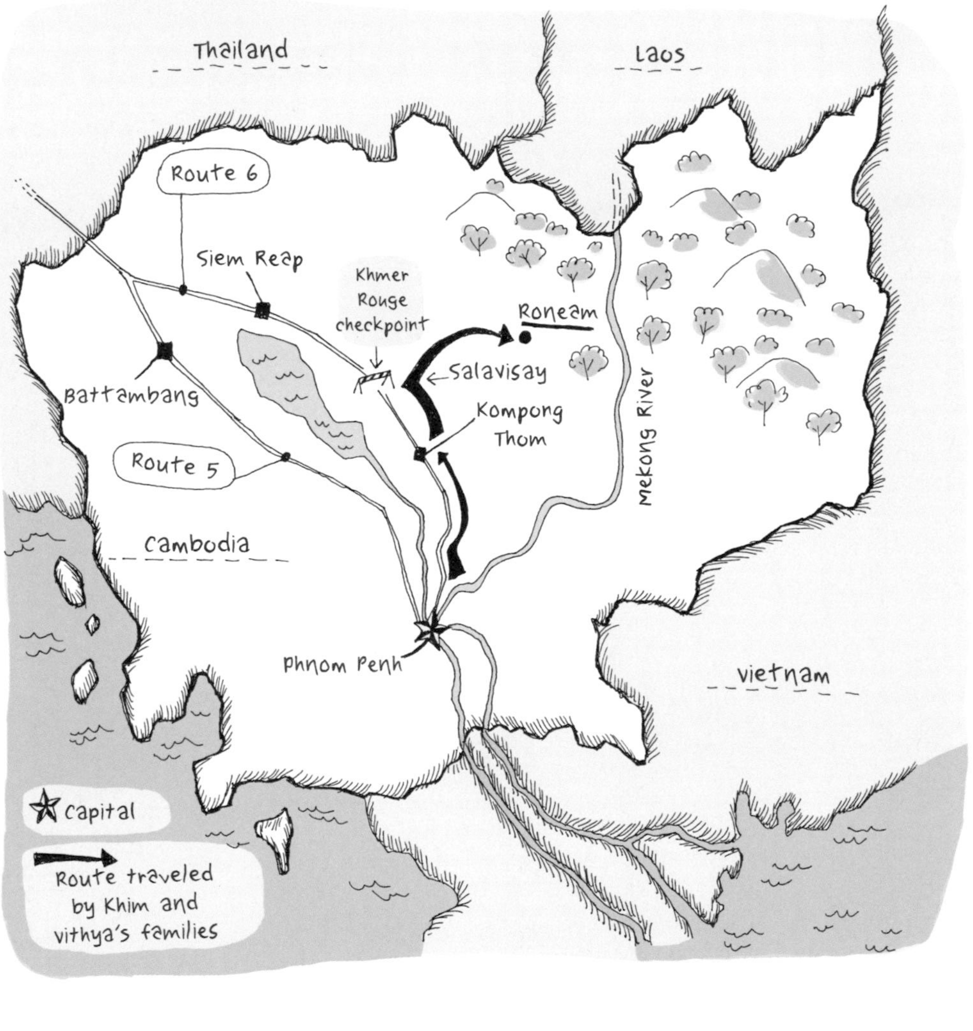

Thailand
Laos
Route 6
Siem Reap
Khmer Rouge checkpoint
Roneam
Battambang
Salavisay
Kompong Thom
Route 5
Mekong River
Cambodia
Phnom Penh
Vietnam
capital
Route traveled by Khim and Vithya's families

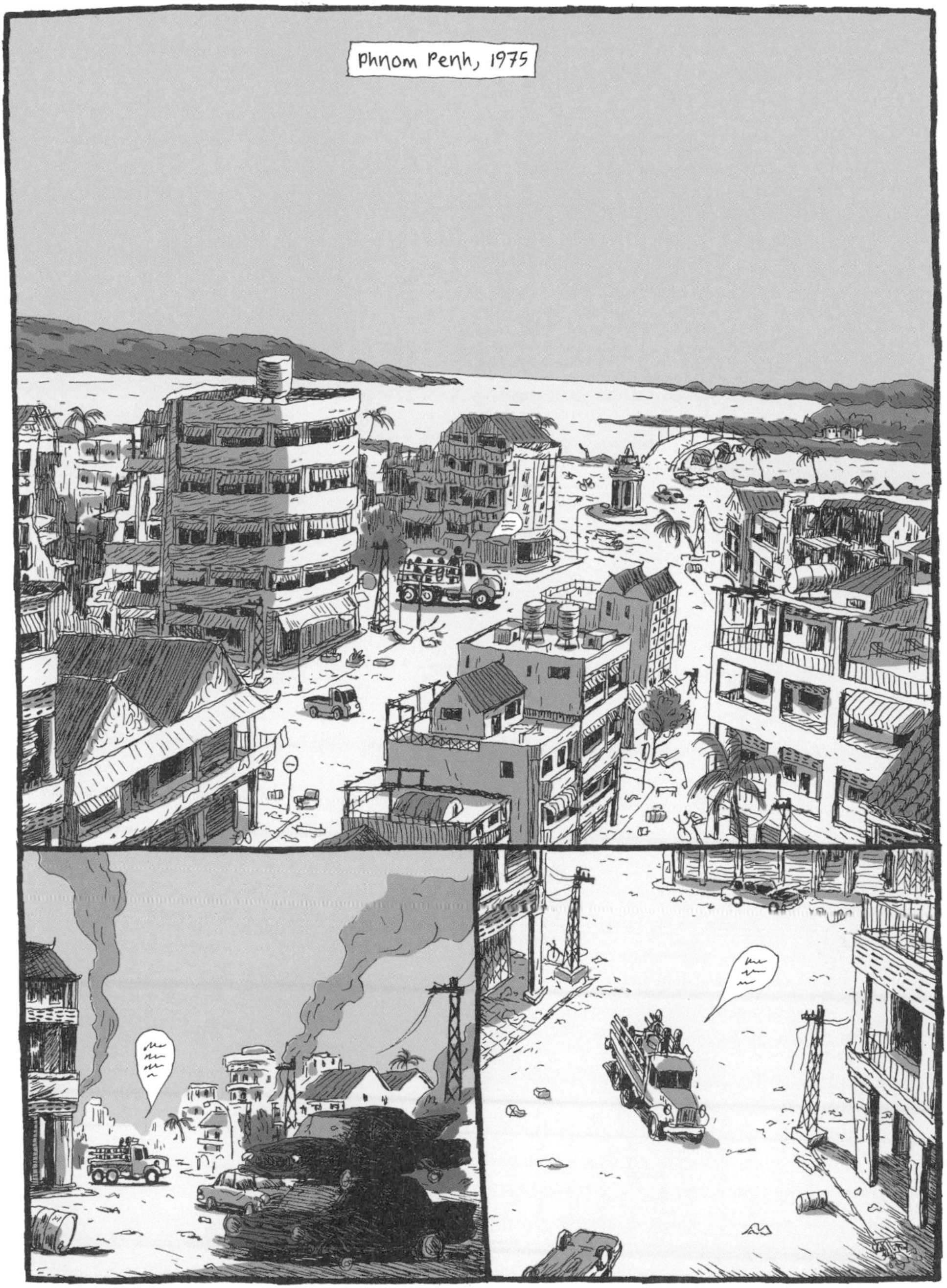
Phnom Penh, 1975

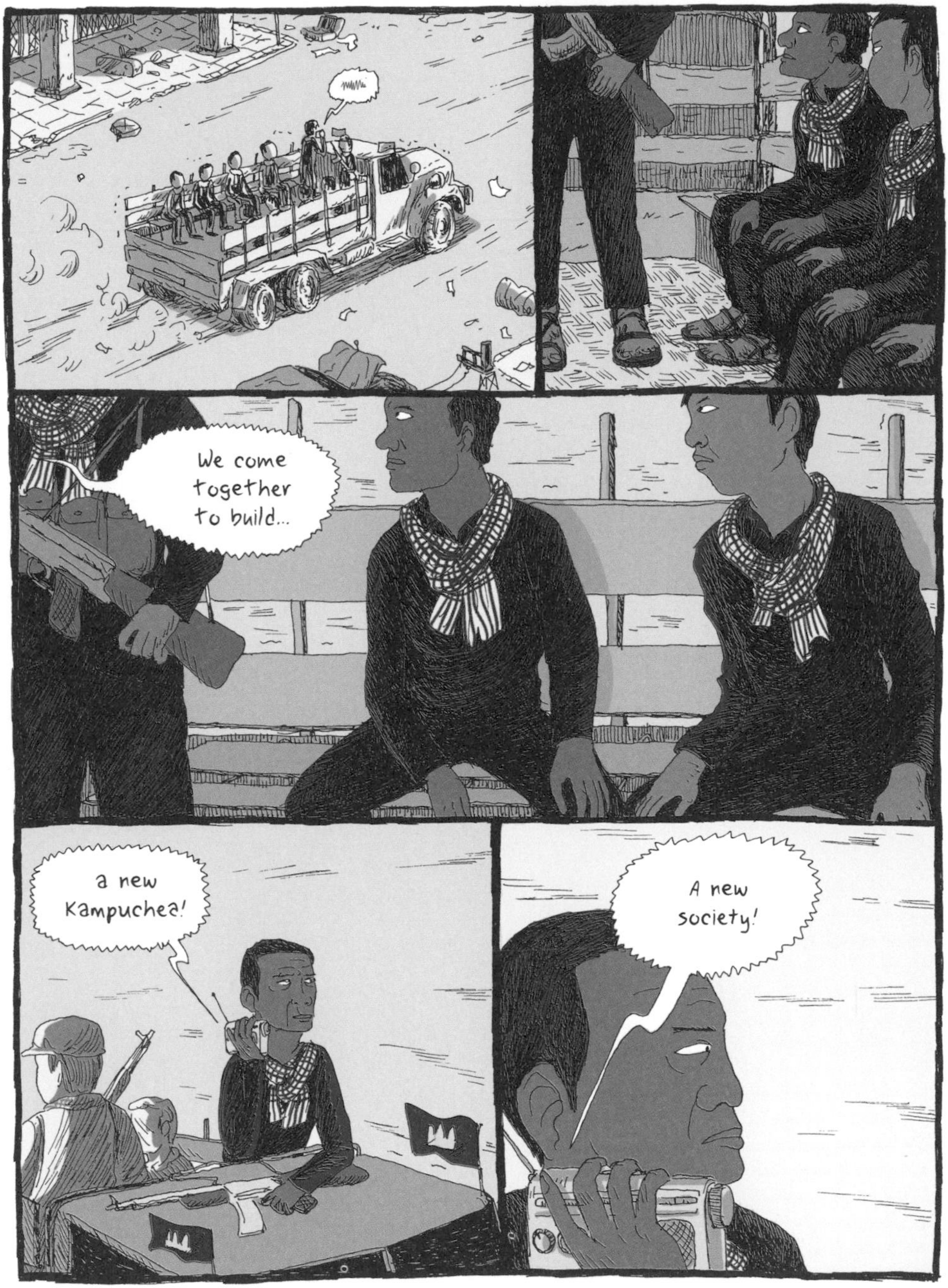
We come together to build...
a new Kampuchea!
A new society!

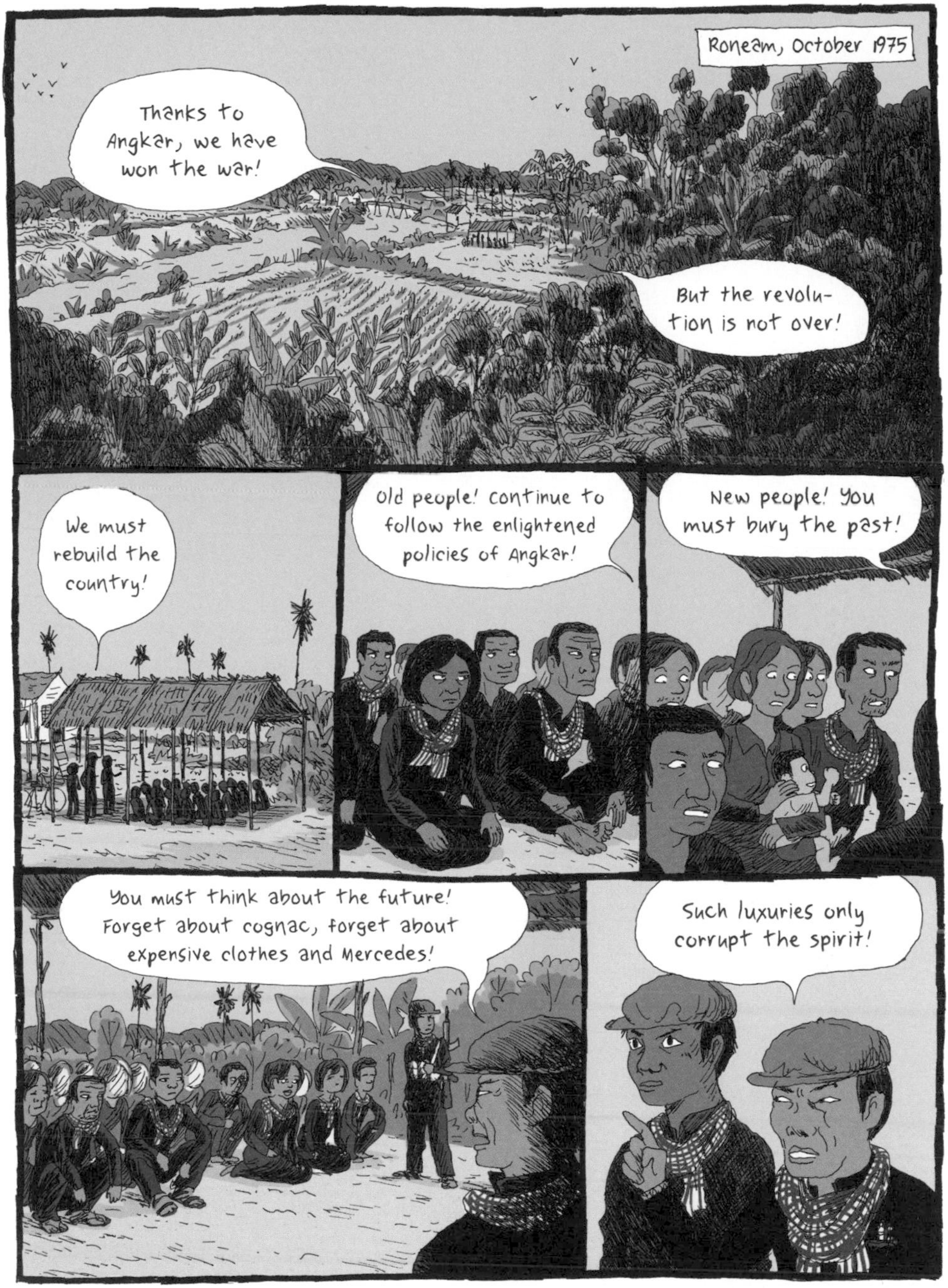

Roneam, October 1975
Thanks to Angkar, we have won the war!
But the revolution is not over!
We must rebuild the country!
Old people! Continue to follow the enlightened policies of Angkar!
New people! You must bury the past!
You must think about the future! Forget about cognac, forget about expensive clothes and Mercedes!
Such luxuries only corrupt the spirit!

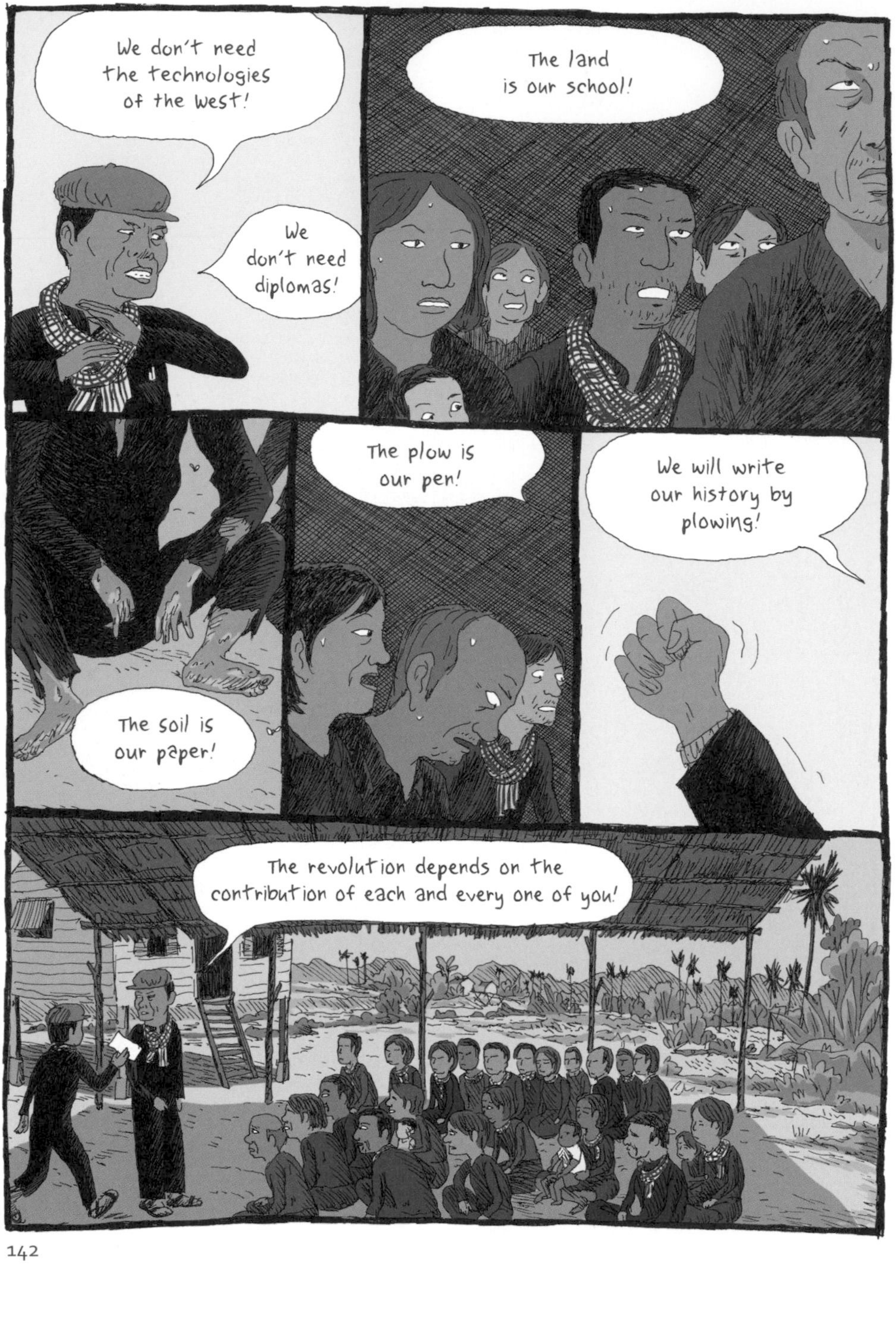
We don't need the technologies of the west!
We don't need diplomas!
The land is our school!
The soil is our paper!
The plow is our pen!
We will write our history by plowing!
The revolution depends on the contribution of each and every one of you!

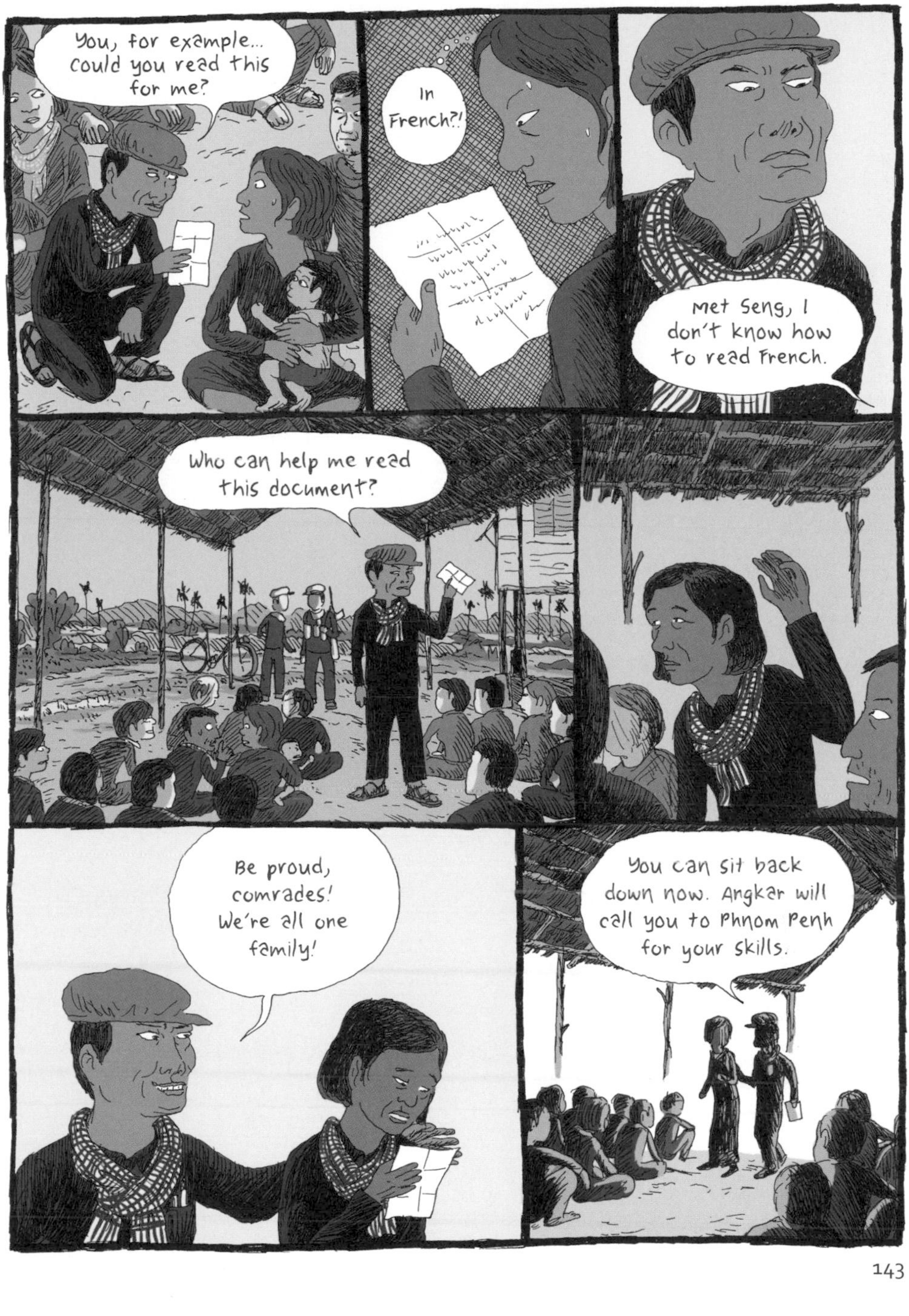
You, for example... could you read this for me?
In French?!
Met Seng, I don't know how to read French.
Who can help me read this document?
Be proud, comrades! We're all one family!
You can sit back down now. Angkar will call you to Phnom Penh for your skills.

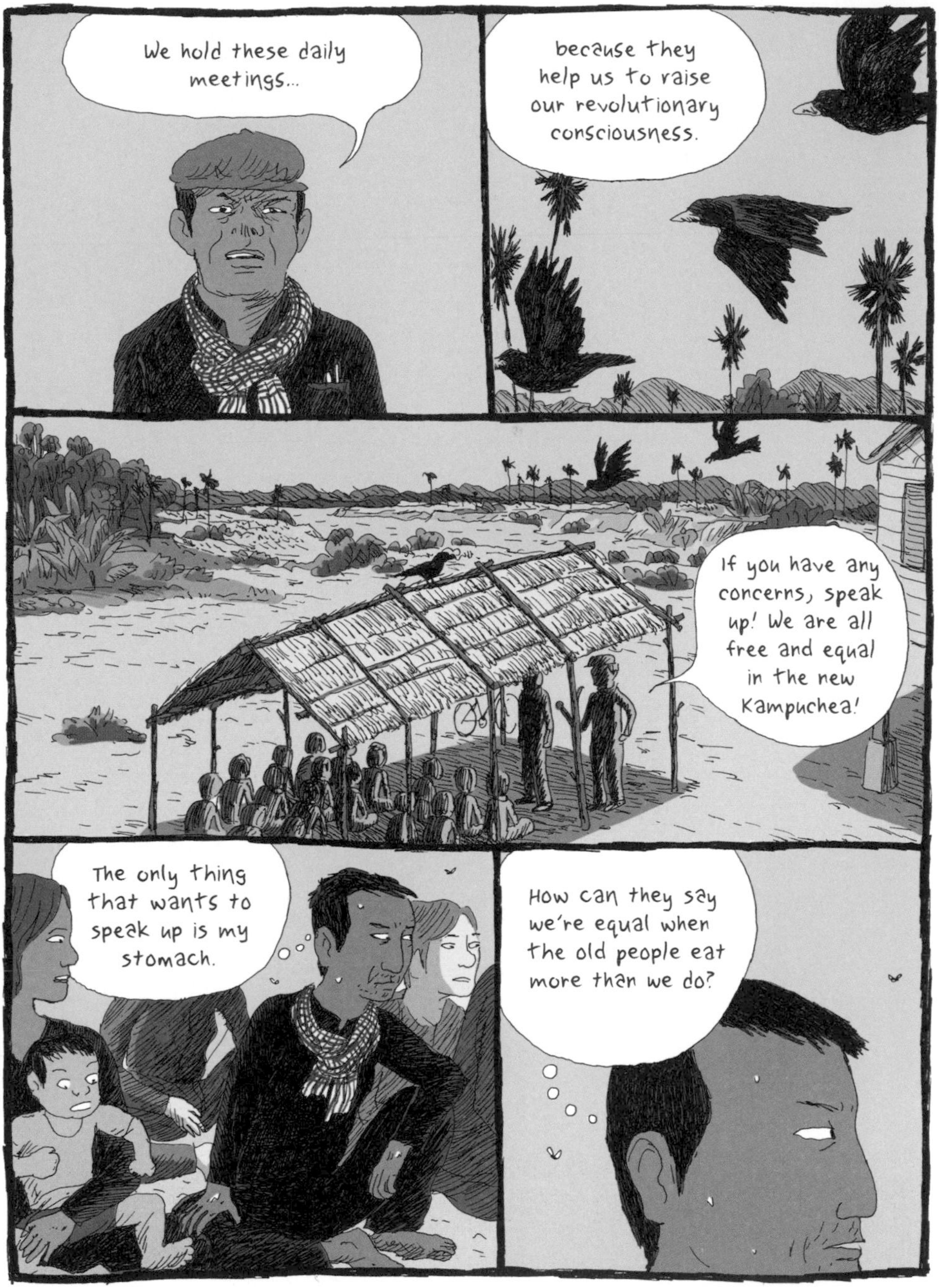
We hold these daily meetings...
because they help us to raise our revolutionary consciousness.
If you have any concerns, speak up! We are all free and equal in the new Kampuchea!
The only thing that wants to speak up is my stomach.
How can they say we're equal when the old people eat more than we do?

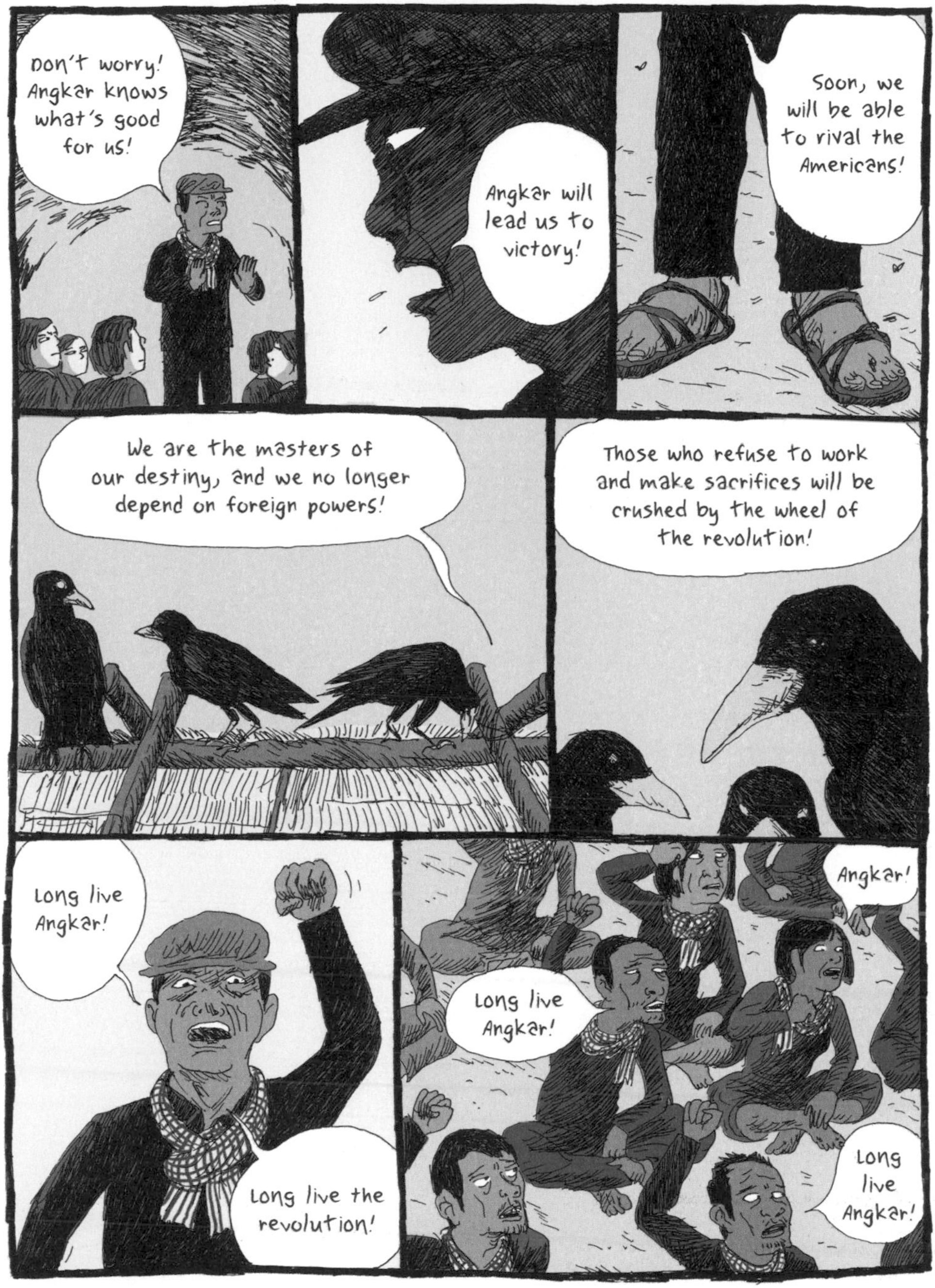
Don't worry! Angkar knows what's good for us!
Angkar will lead us to victory!
Soon, we will be able to rival the Americans!
We are the masters of our destiny, and we no longer depend on foreign powers!
Those who refuse to work and make sacrifices will be crushed by the wheel of the revolution!
Long live Angkar!
Long live the revolution!
Angkar!
Long live Angkar!
Long live Angkar!

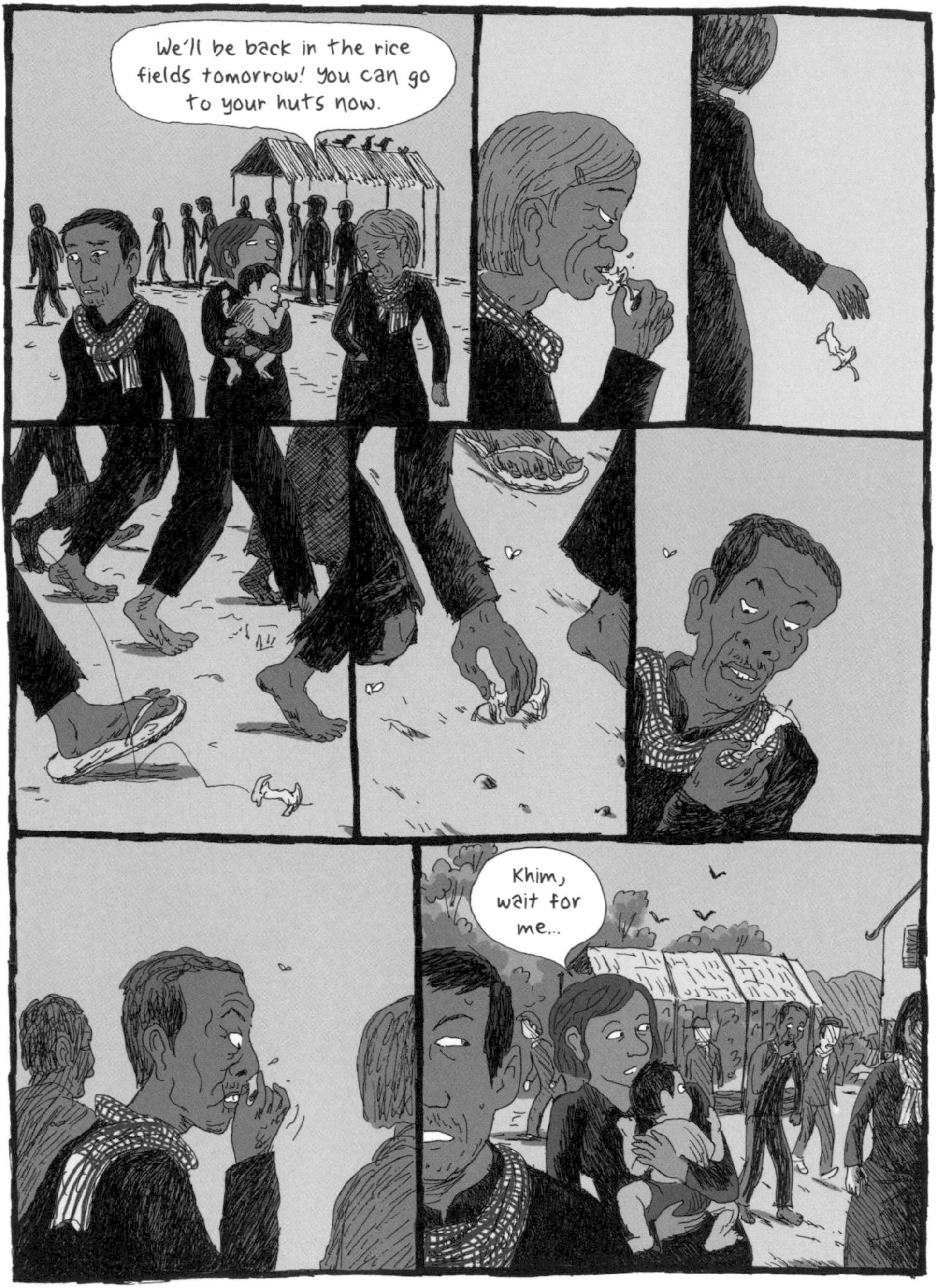
We'll be back in the rice fields tomorrow! You can go to your huts now.
Khim, wait for me...

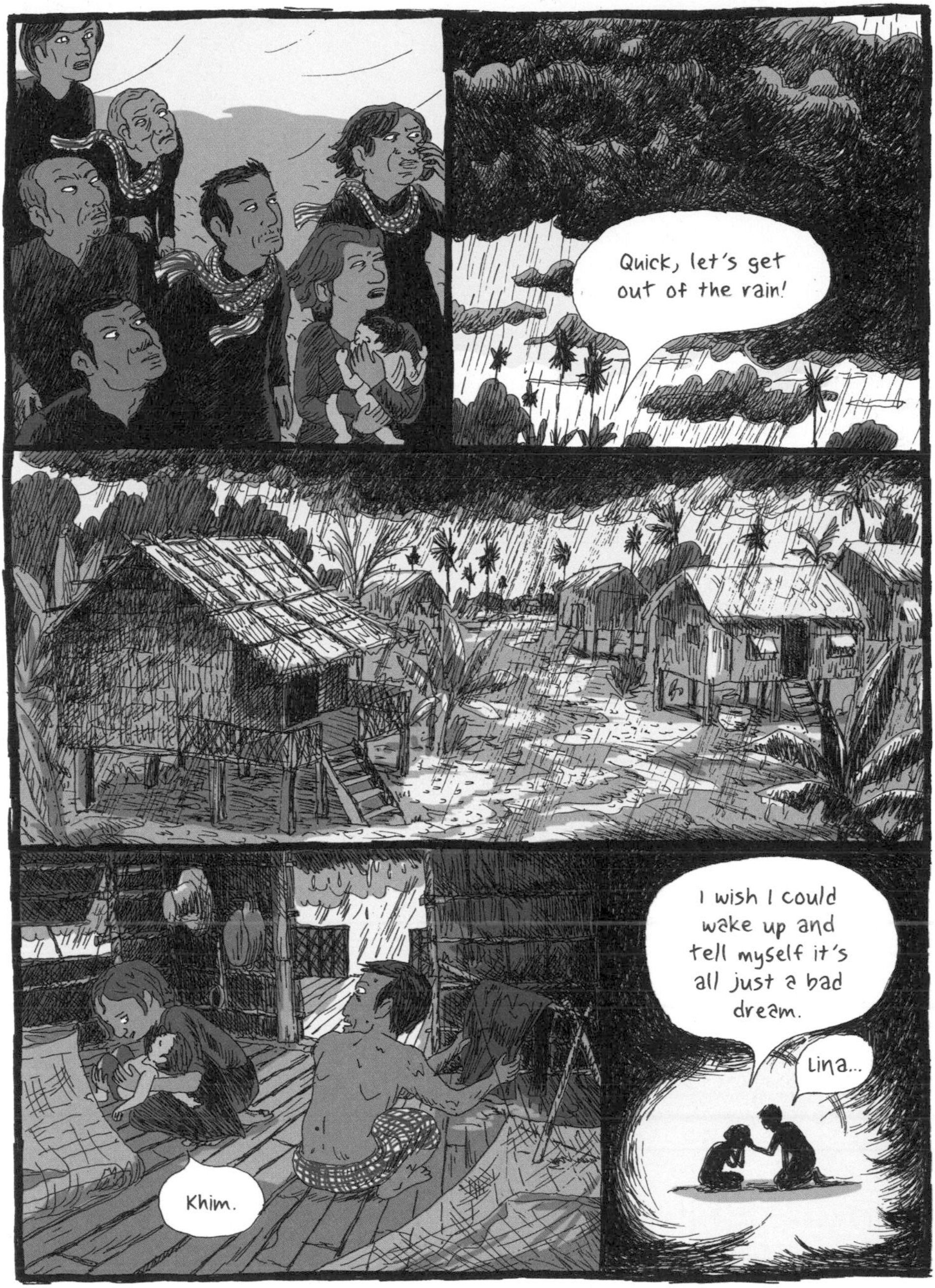
Quick, let's get out of the rain!
Khim.
I wish I could wake up and tell myself it's all just a bad dream.
Lina...

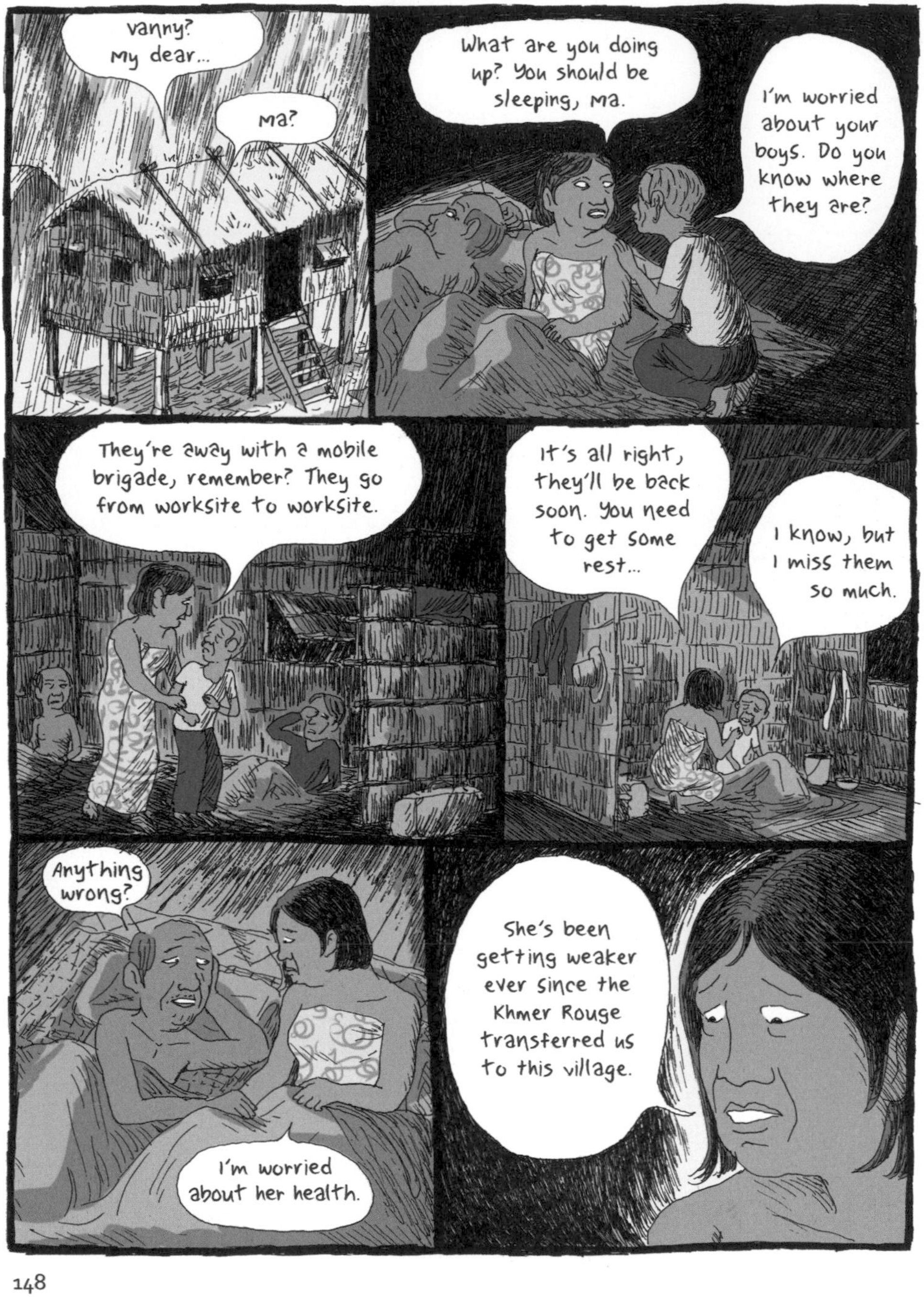
Vanny? My dear...
Ma?
What are you doing up? You should be sleeping, Ma.
I'm worried about your boys. Do you know where they are?
They're away with a mobile brigade, remember? They go from worksite to worksite.
It's all right, they'll be back soon. You need to get some rest...
I know, but I miss them so much.
Anything wrong?
I'm worried about her health.
She's been getting weaker ever since the Khmer Rouge transferred us to this village.

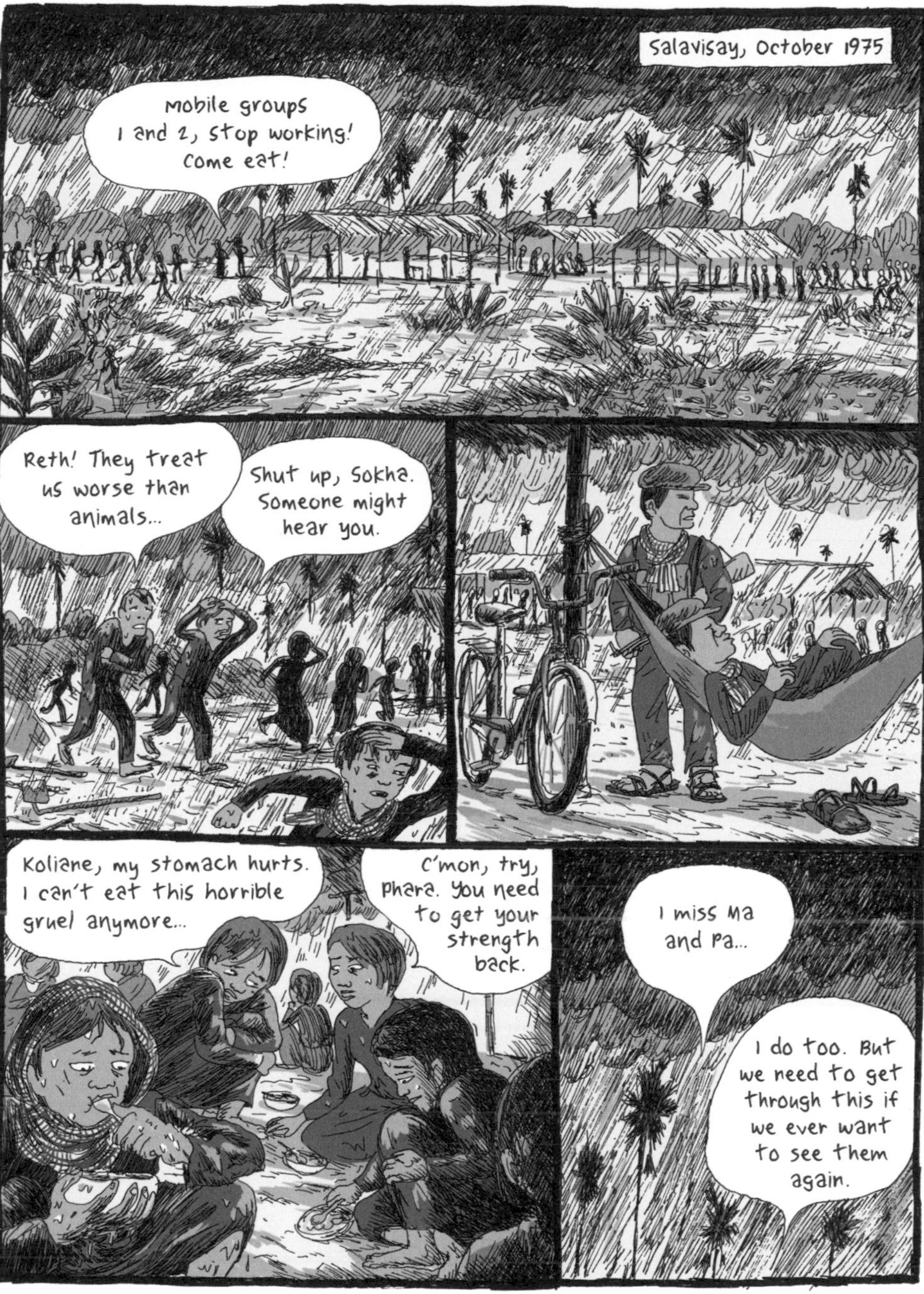

Salavisay, October 1975
Mobile groups 1 and 2, stop working! Come eat!
Reth! They treat us worse than animals...
Shut up, Sokha. Someone might hear you.
Koliane, my stomach hurts. I can't eat this horrible gruel anymore...
C'mon, try, Phara. You need to get your strength back.
I miss Ma and Pa...
I do too. But we need to get through this if we ever want to see them again.

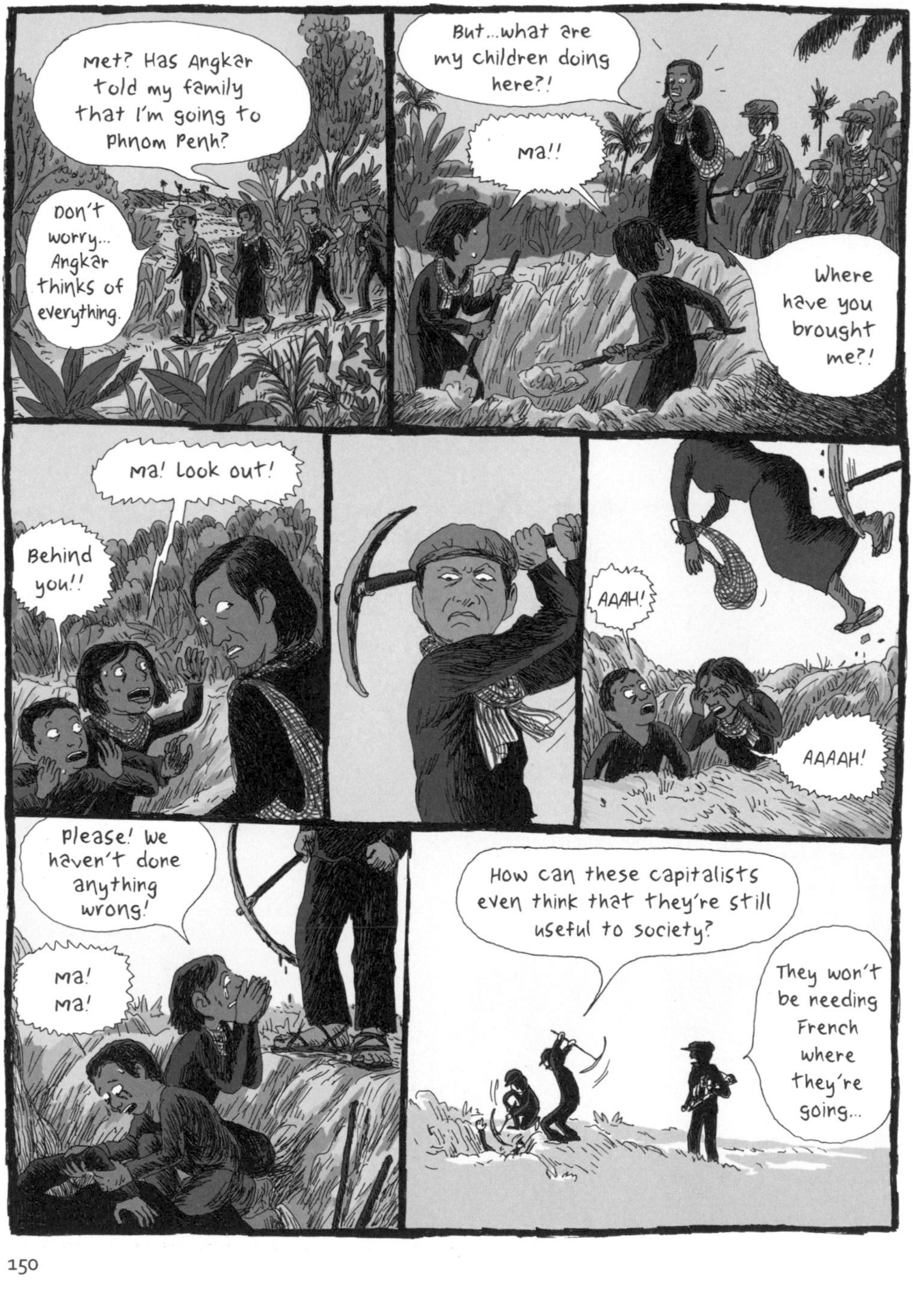
Met? Has Angkar told my family that I'm going to Phnom Penh?
Don't worry... Angkar thinks of everything.
But...what are my children doing here?!
Ma!!
Where have you brought me?!
Ma! Look out!
Behind you!!
AAAH!
AAAAH!
Please! We haven't done anything wrong!
Ma! Ma!
How can these capitalists even think that they're still useful to society?
They won't be needing French where they're going...

chapter 9

CHILDREN ARE LIKE BLANK SHEETS OF PAPER
ON WHICH ANGKAR CAN PRINT WHATEVER IT WANTS.

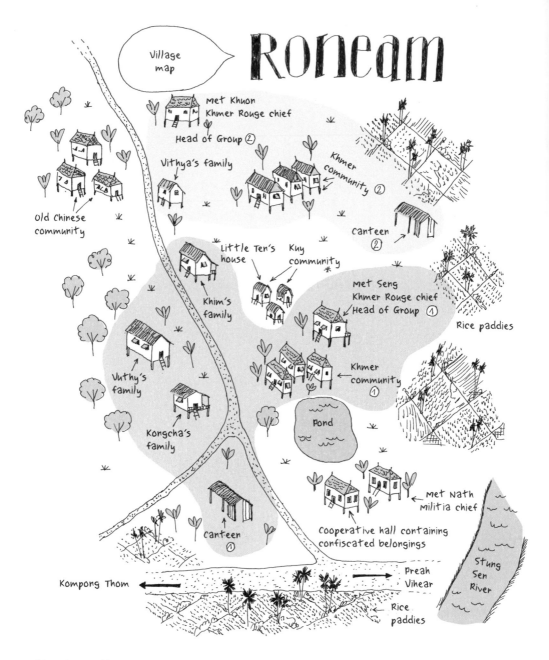

Village map

Roneam

Met Khuon
Khmer Rouge chief
Head of Group ②

Vithya's family

Khmer community ②

canteen ②

Old Chinese community

Little Ten's house

Kuy community *

Khim's family

Met Seng
Khmer Rouge chief
Head of Group ①

Rice paddies

Vuthy's family

Khmer community ①

Kongcha's family

Pond

canteen ①

Met Nath
militia chief

Cooperative hall containing confiscated belongings

Stung Sen River

Kompong Thom ←

Preah Vihear

Rice paddies

*Kuy: Khmer ethnic group

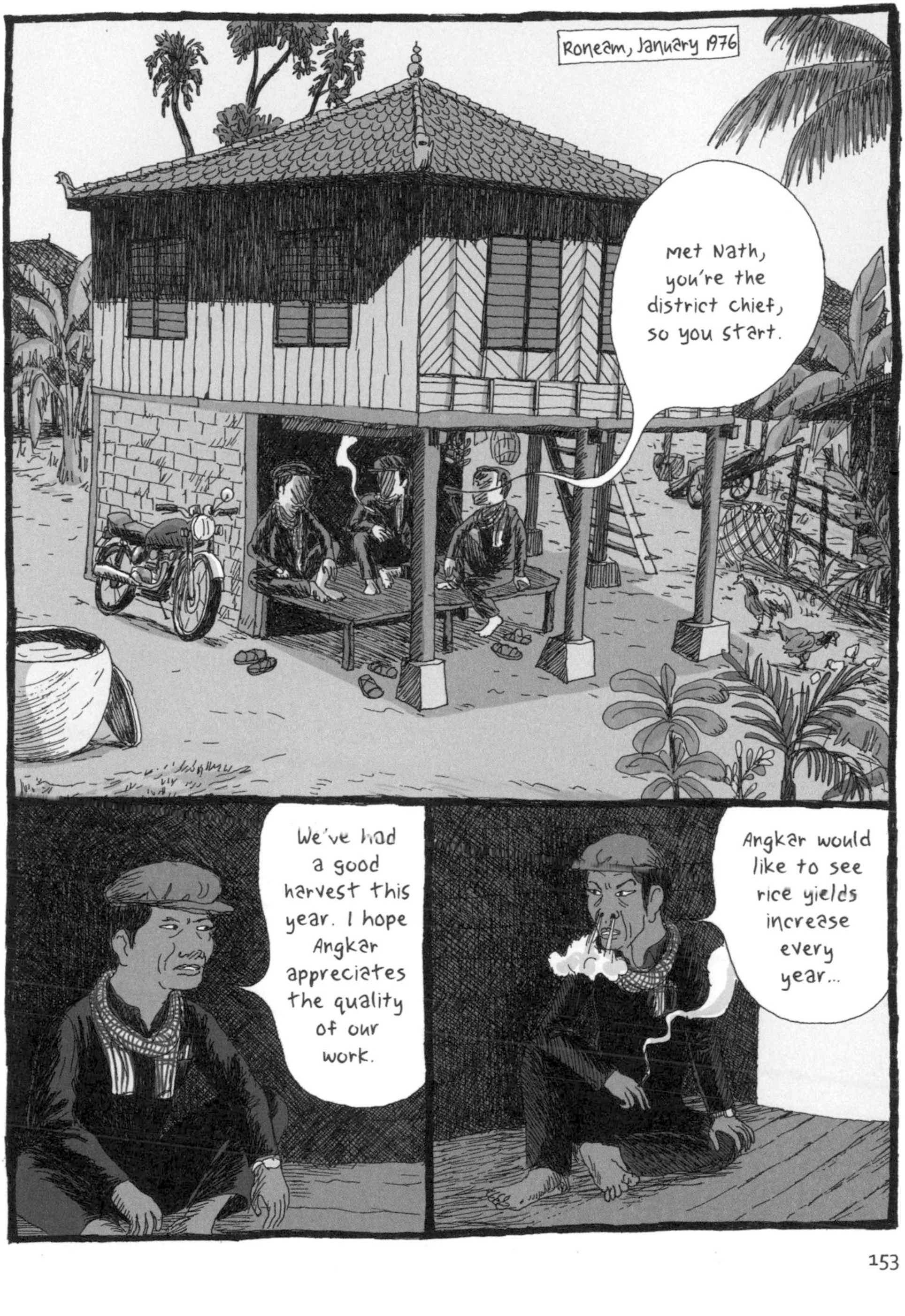
Roneam, January 1976
Met Nath, you're the district chief, so you start.
We've had a good harvest this year. I hope Angkar appreciates the quality of our work.
Angkar would like to see rice yields increase every year...

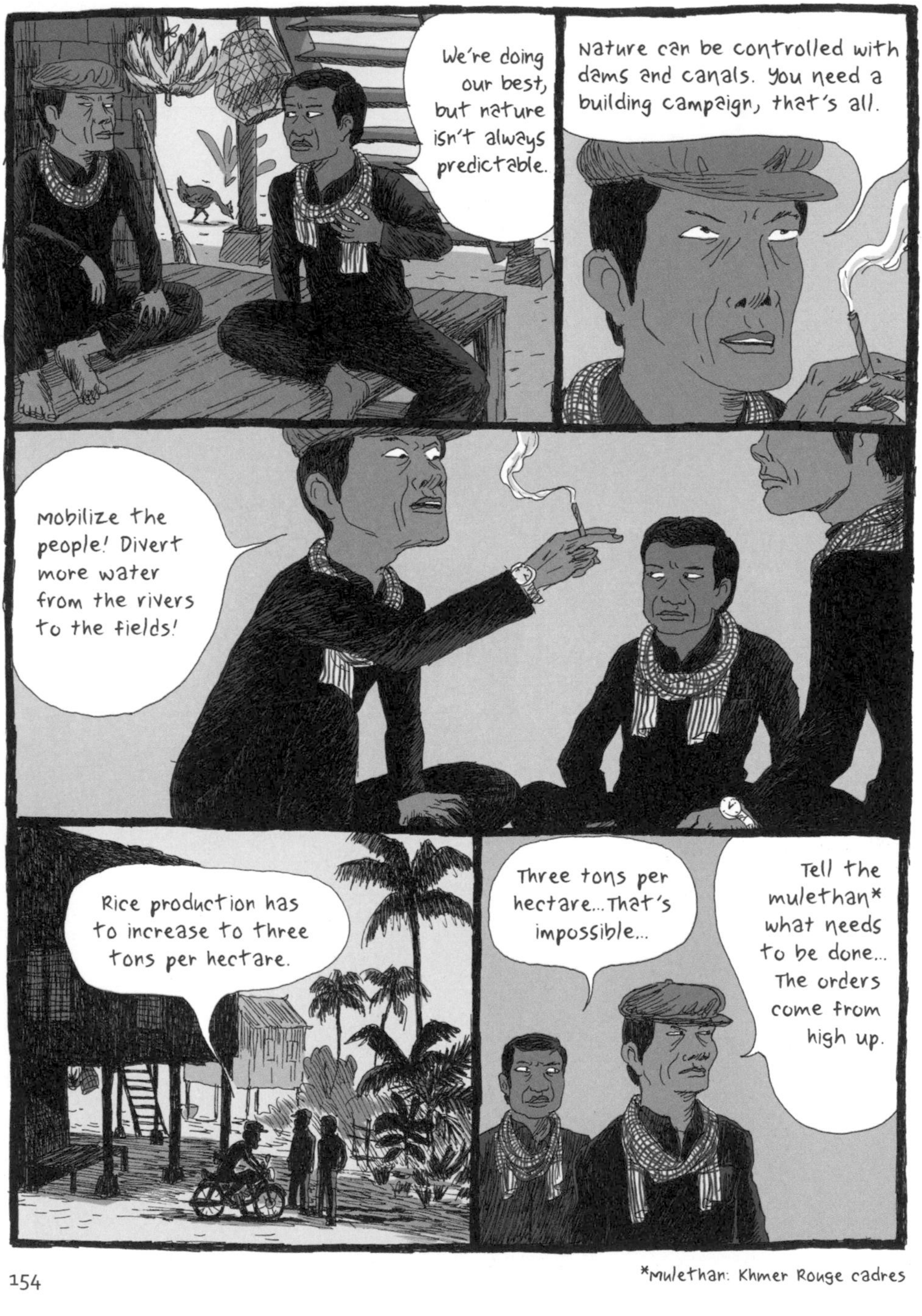
We're doing our best, but nature isn't always predictable.
Nature can be controlled with dams and canals. You need a building campaign, that's all.
Mobilize the people! Divert more water from the rivers to the fields!
Rice production has to increase to three tons per hectare.
Three tons per hectare... That's impossible...
Tell the mulethan* what needs to be done... The orders come from high up.

*Mulethan: Khmer Rouge cadres

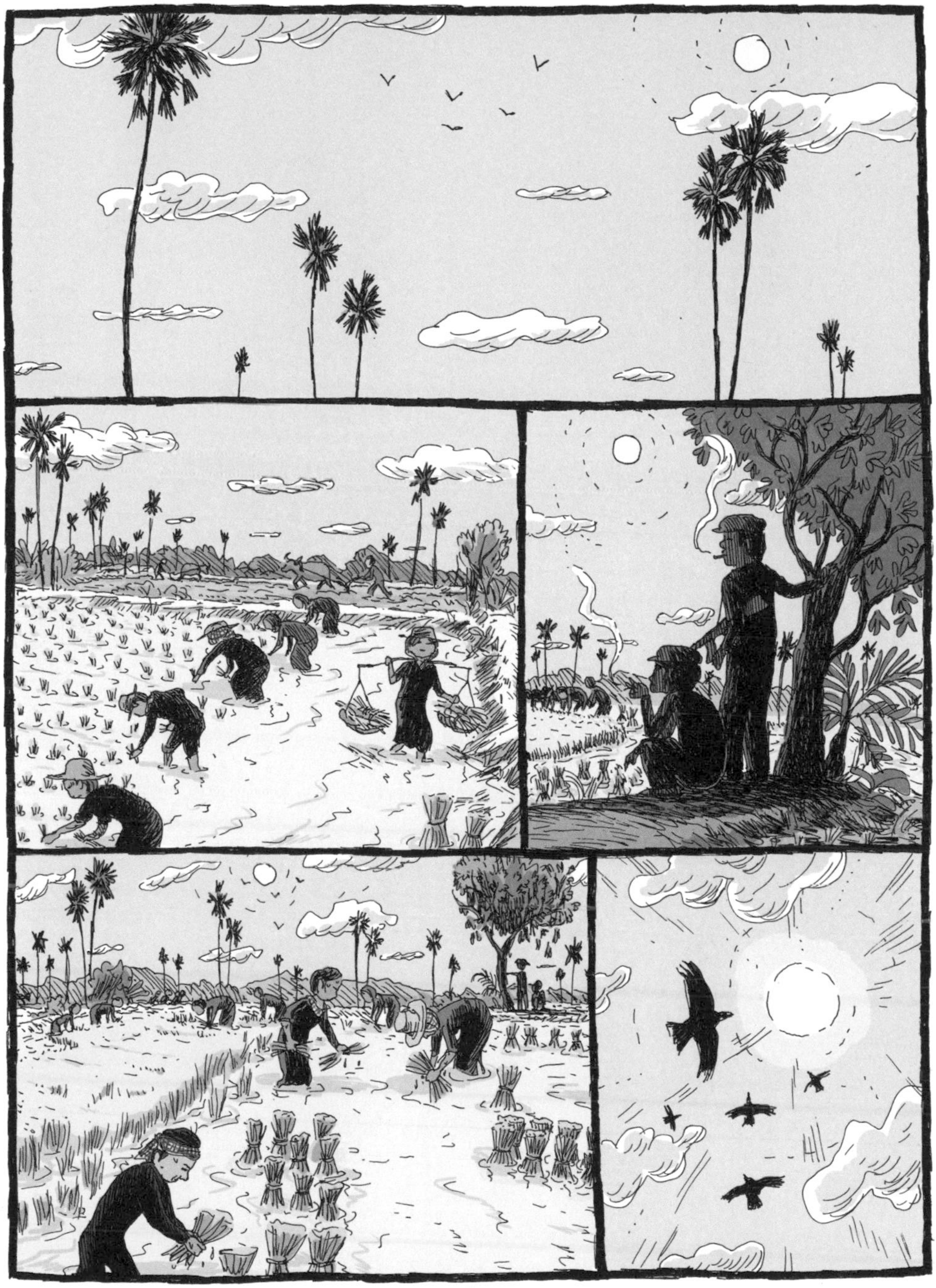

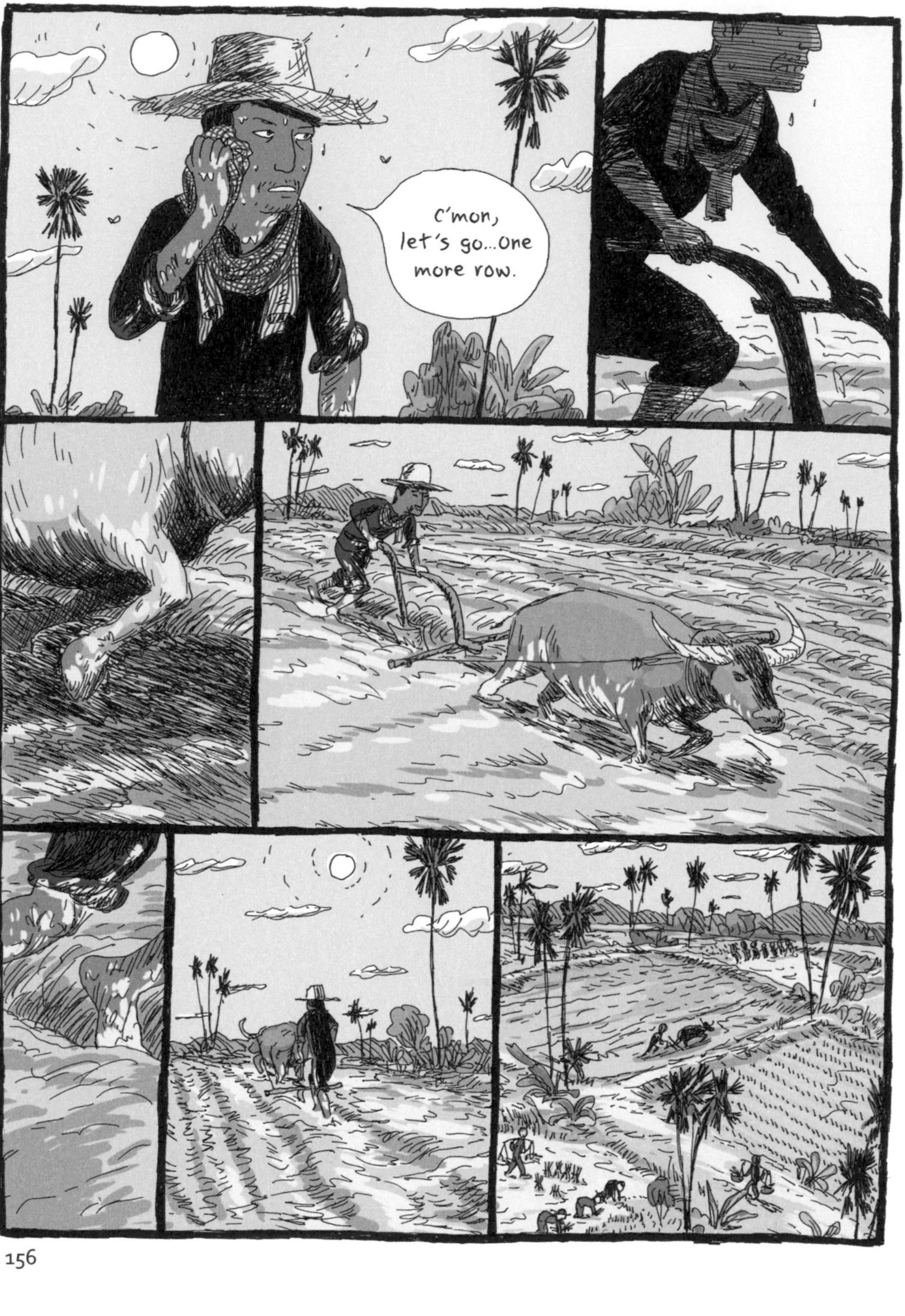
C'mon, let's go...One more row.

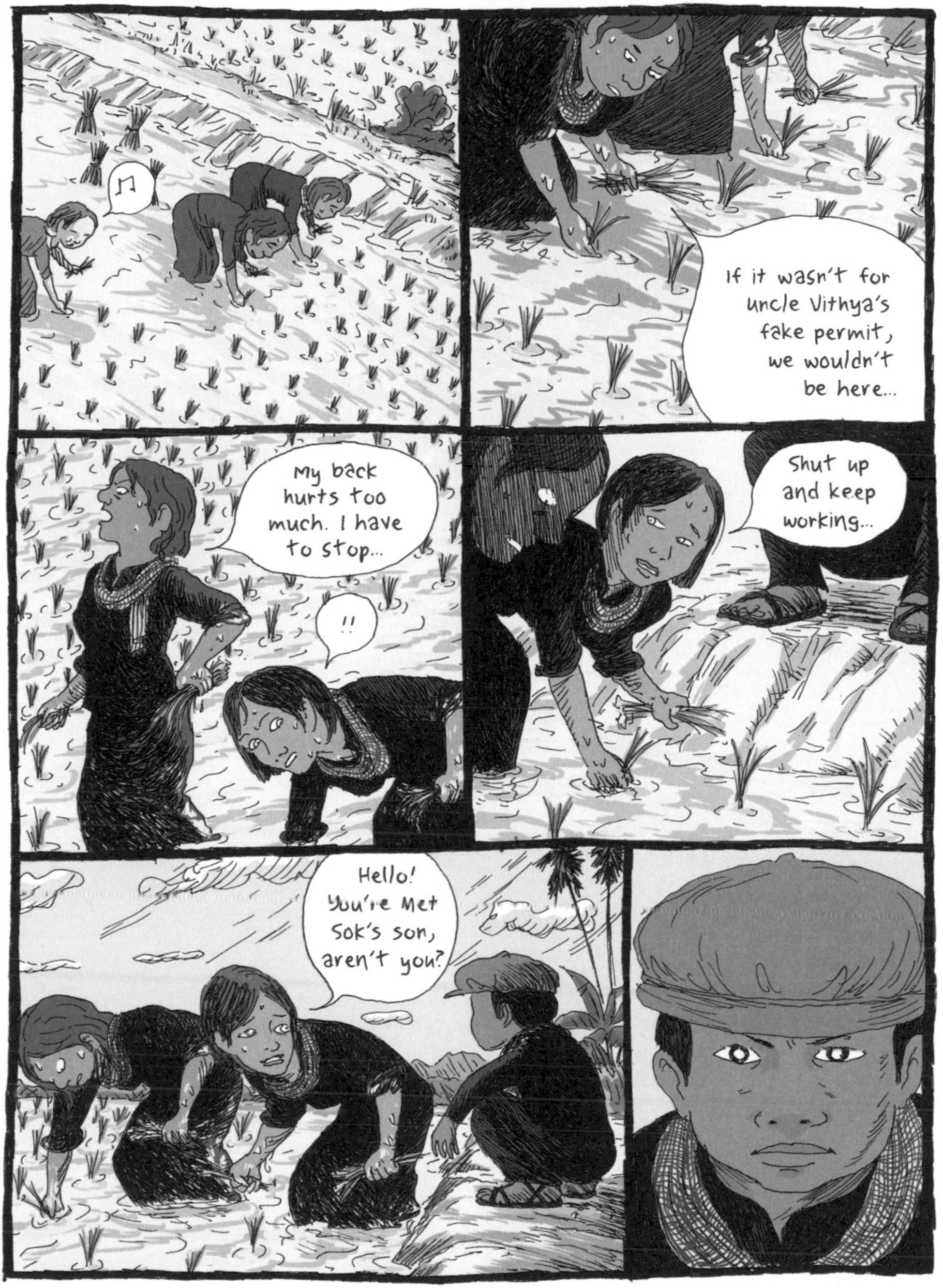
♫
If it wasn't for uncle Vithya's fake permit, we wouldn't be here...
My back hurts too much. I have to stop...
!!
Shut up and keep working...
Hello! You're Met Sok's son, aren't you?

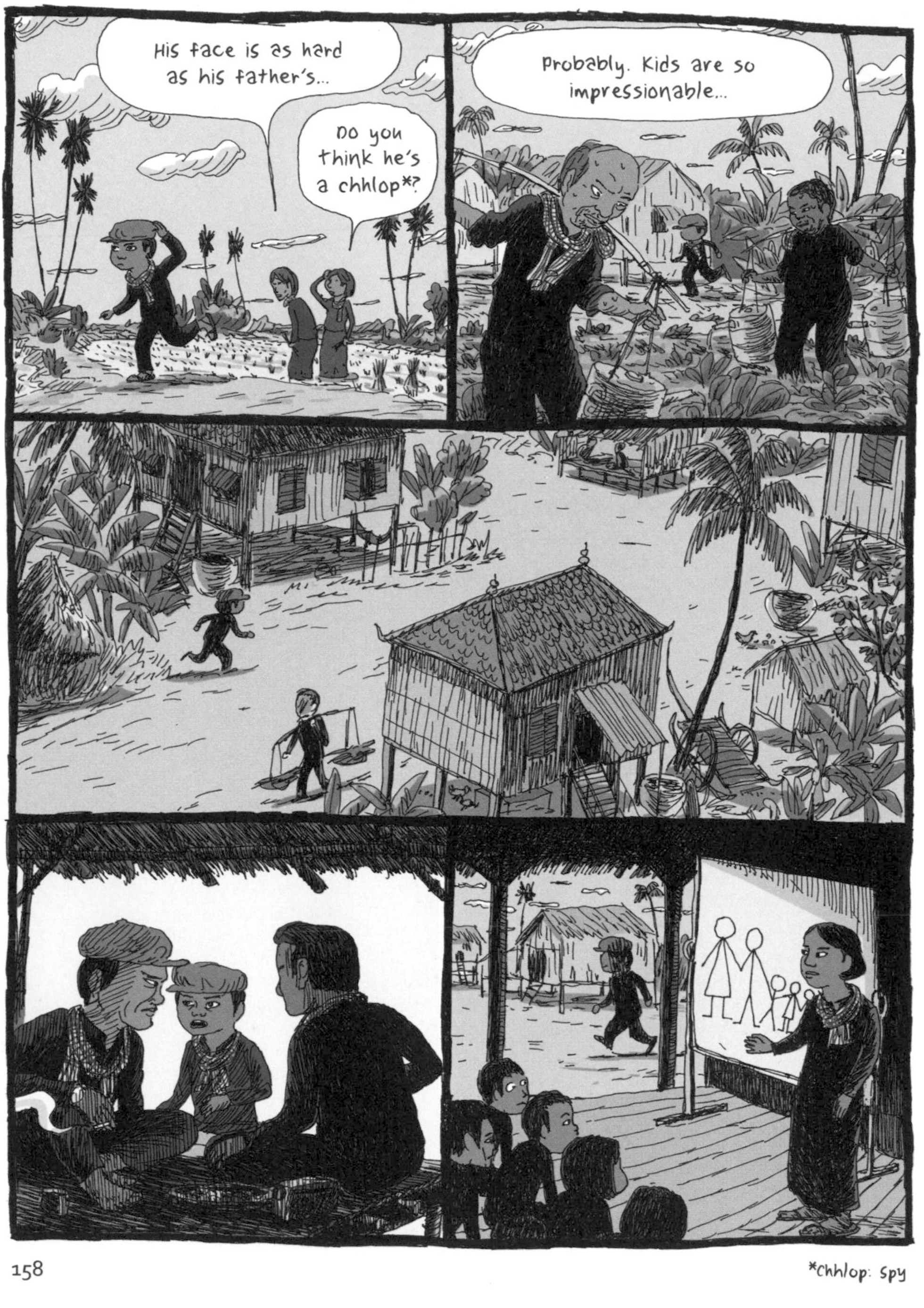
His face is as hard as his father's...
Do you think he's a chhlop*?
Probably. Kids are so impressionable...

*Chhlop: Spy

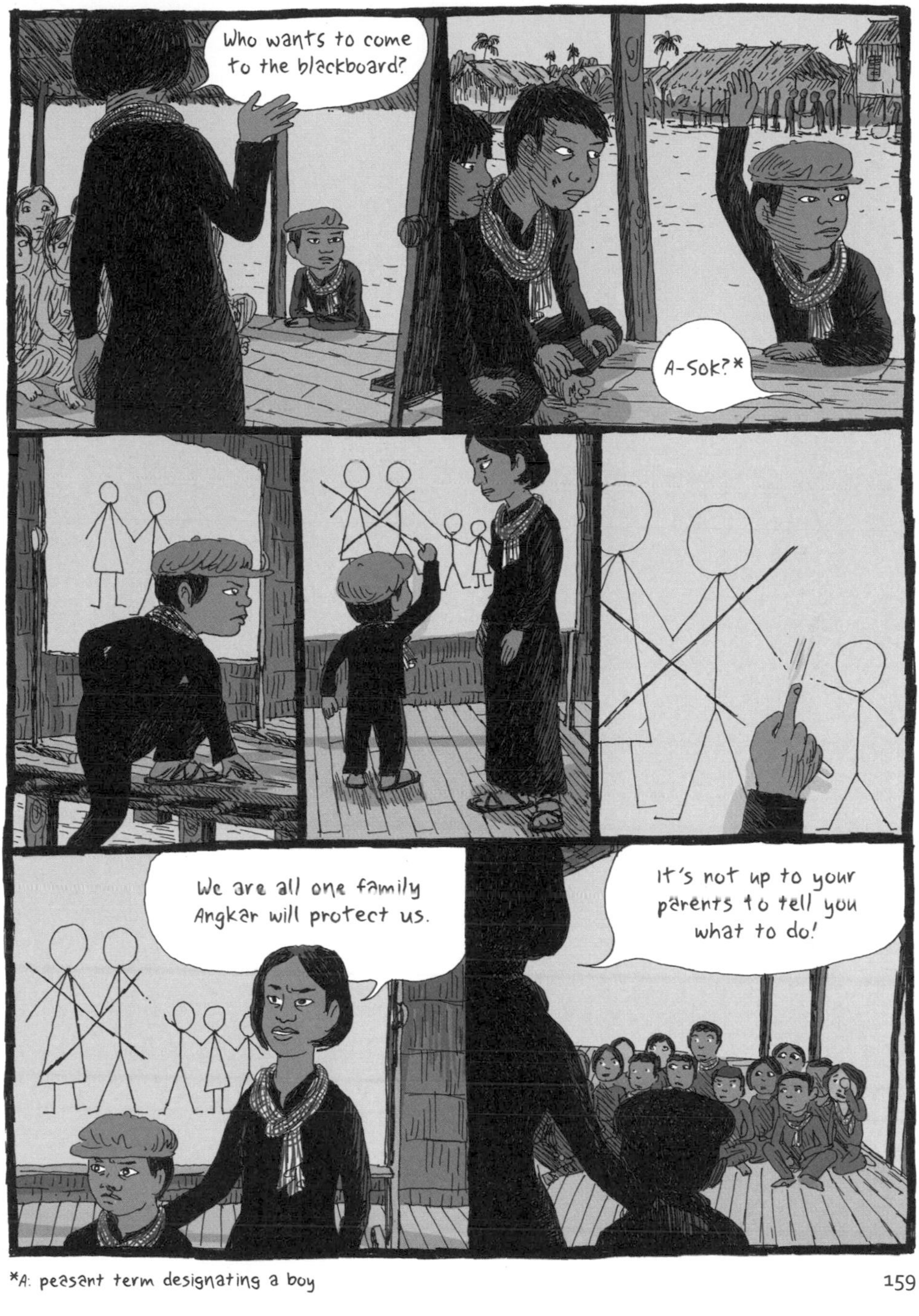
Who wants to come to the blackboard?
A-SOK?*
We are all one family Angkar will protect us.
It's not up to your parents to tell you what to do!

*A: peasant term designating a boy

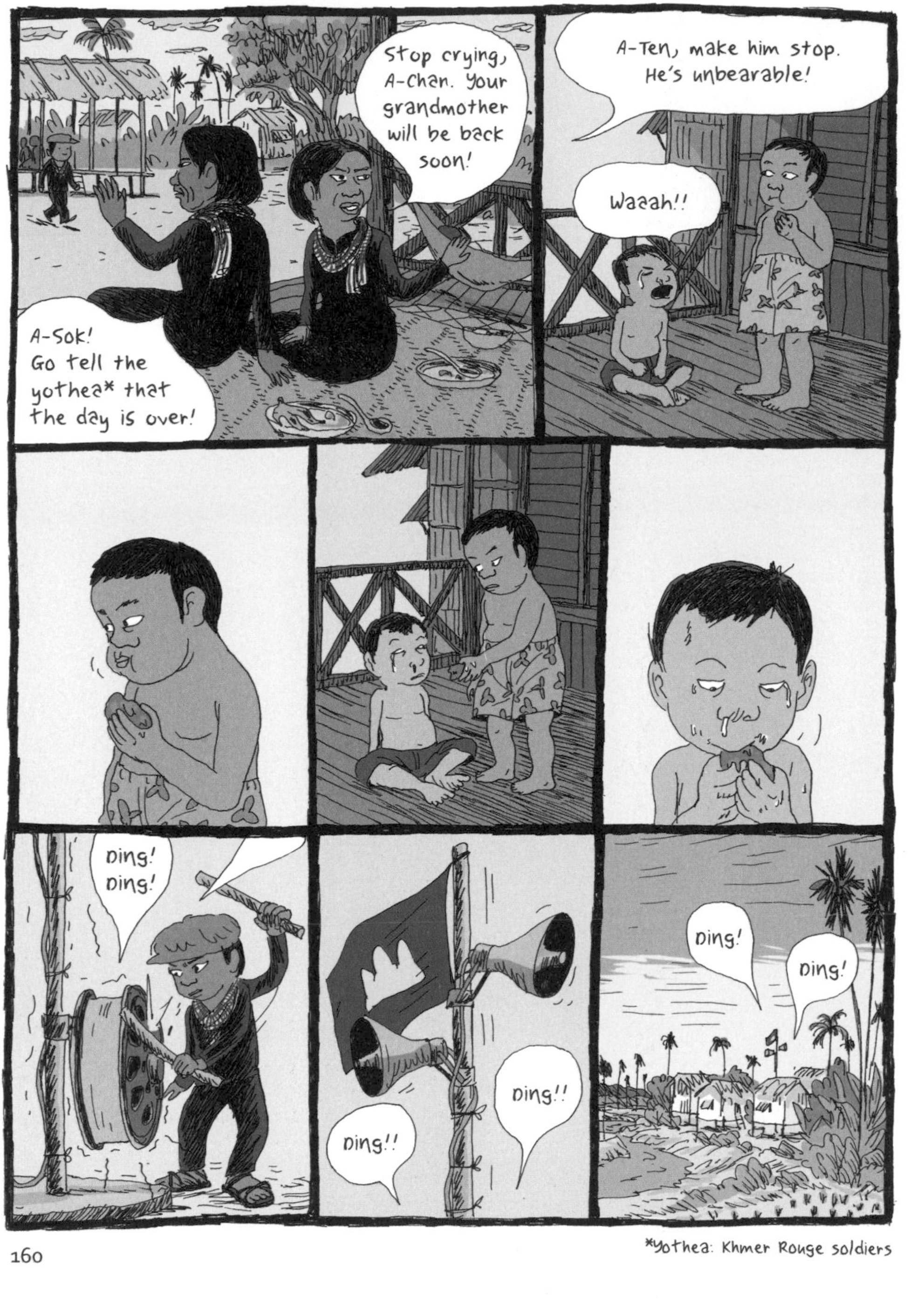
Stop crying, A-Chan. Your grandmother will be back soon!
A-Sok! Go tell the yothea* that the day is over!
A-Ten, make him stop. He's unbearable!
Waaah!!
Ding! Ding!
Ding!!
Ding!!
Ding!
Ding!

*Yothea: Khmer Rouge soldiers

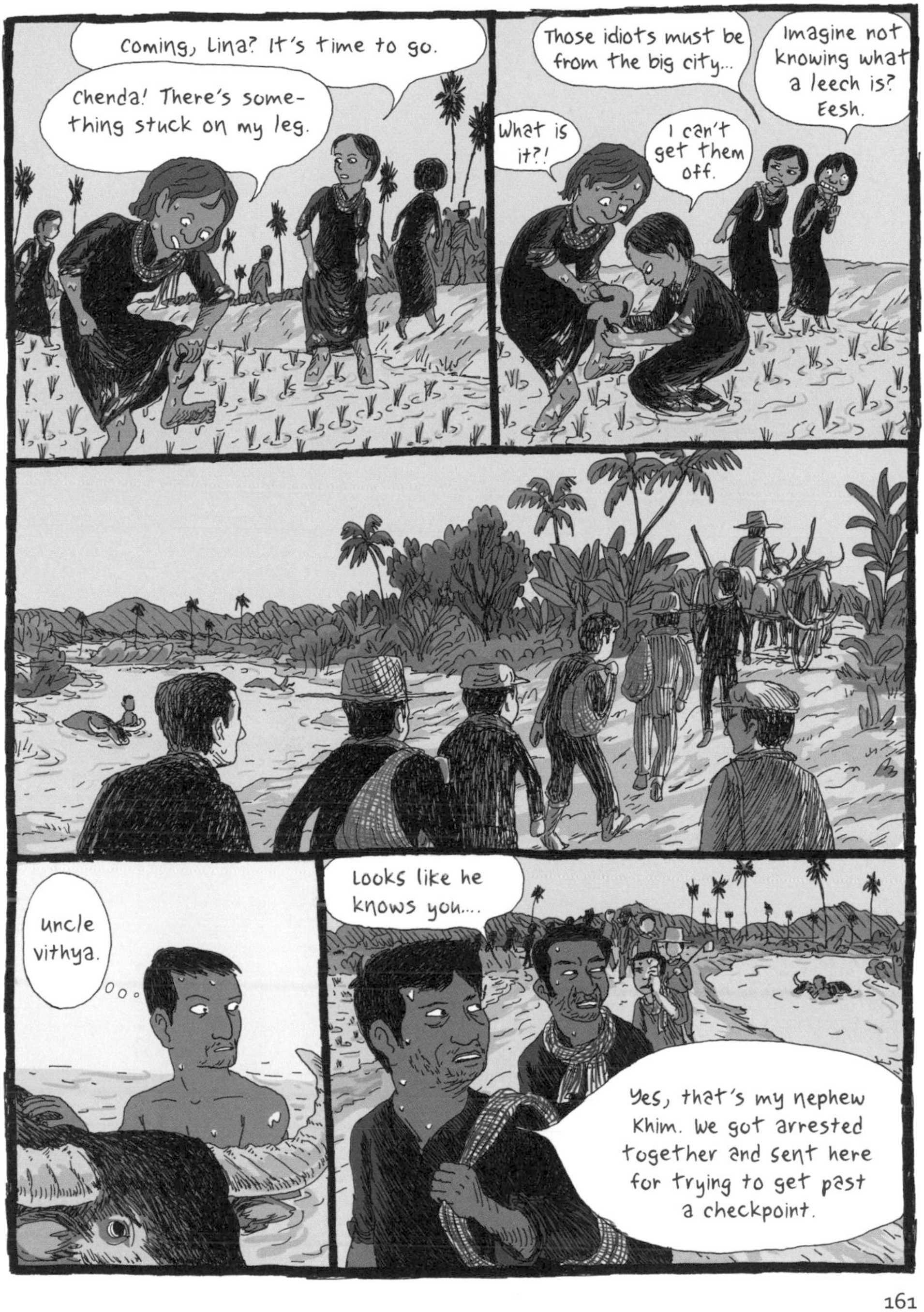
Coming, Lina? It's time to go.
Chenda! There's something stuck on my leg.
Those idiots must be from the big city...
Imagine not knowing what a leech is? Eesh.
What is it?!
I can't get them off.
Uncle Vithya.
Looks like he knows you....
Yes, that's my nephew Khim. We got arrested together and sent here for trying to get past a checkpoint.

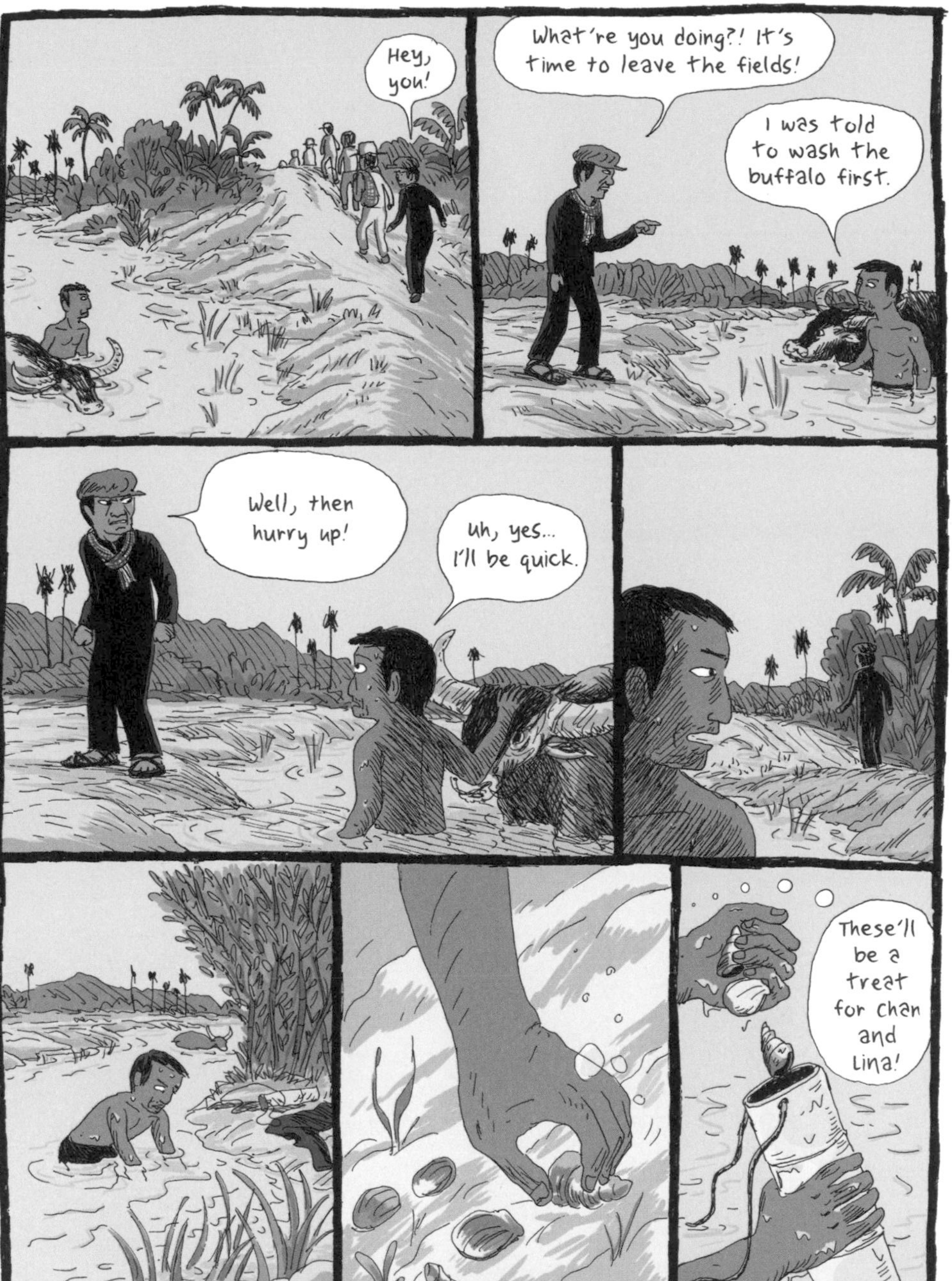
Hey, you!
What're you doing?! It's time to leave the fields!
I was told to wash the buffalo first.
Well, then hurry up!
Uh, yes... I'll be quick.
These'll be a treat for Chan and Lina!

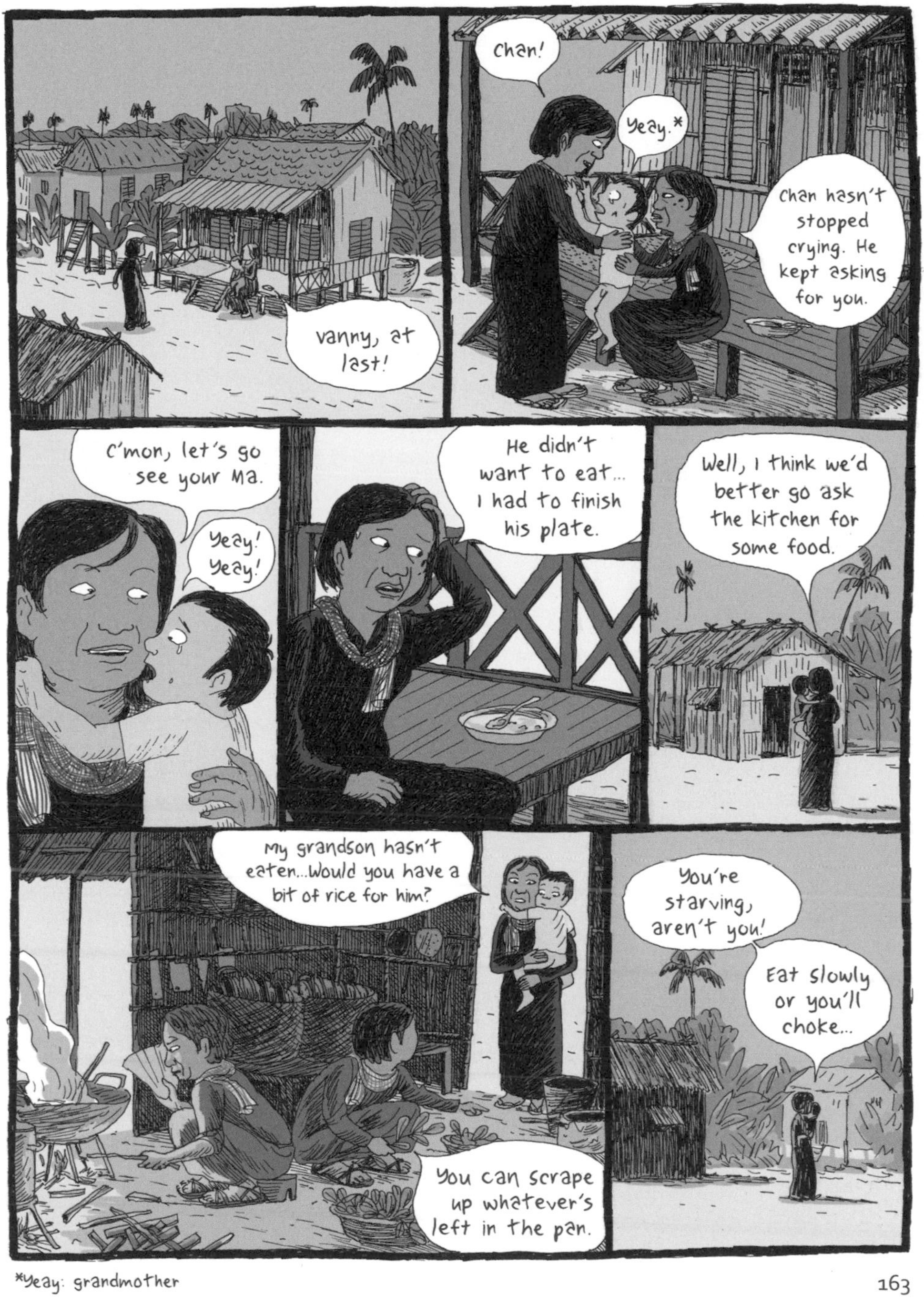
Vanny, at last!
Chan!
Yeay.*
Chan hasn't stopped crying. He kept asking for you.
C'mon, let's go see your Ma.
Yeay! Yeay!
He didn't want to eat... I had to finish his plate.
Well, I think we'd better go ask the kitchen for some food.
My grandson hasn't eaten...Would you have a bit of rice for him?
You can scrape up whatever's left in the pan.
You're starving, aren't you!
Eat slowly or you'll choke...

*Yeay: grandmother

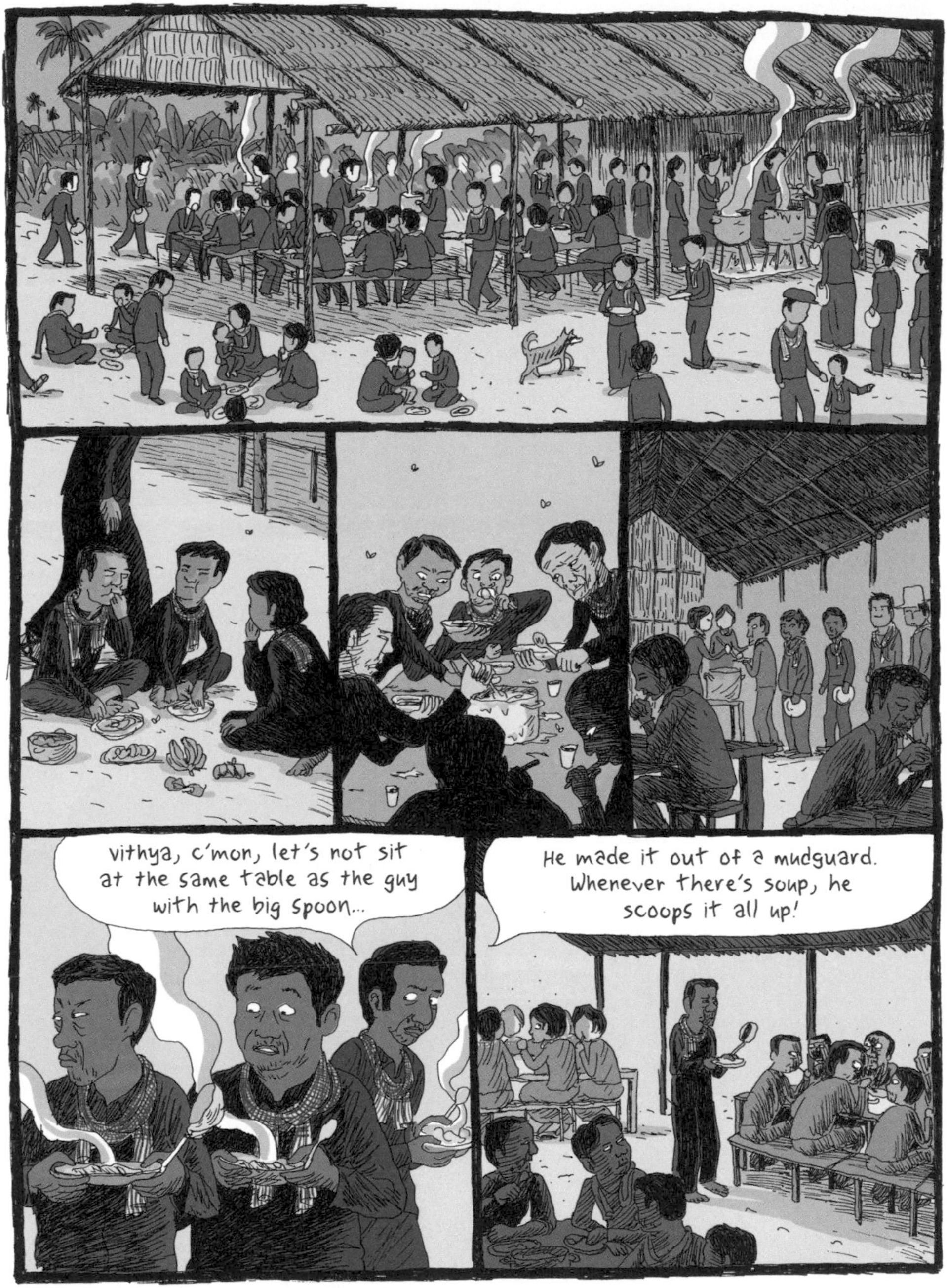
Vithya, c'mon, let's not sit at the same table as the guy with the big spoon...
He made it out of a mudguard. Whenever there's soup, he scoops it all up!

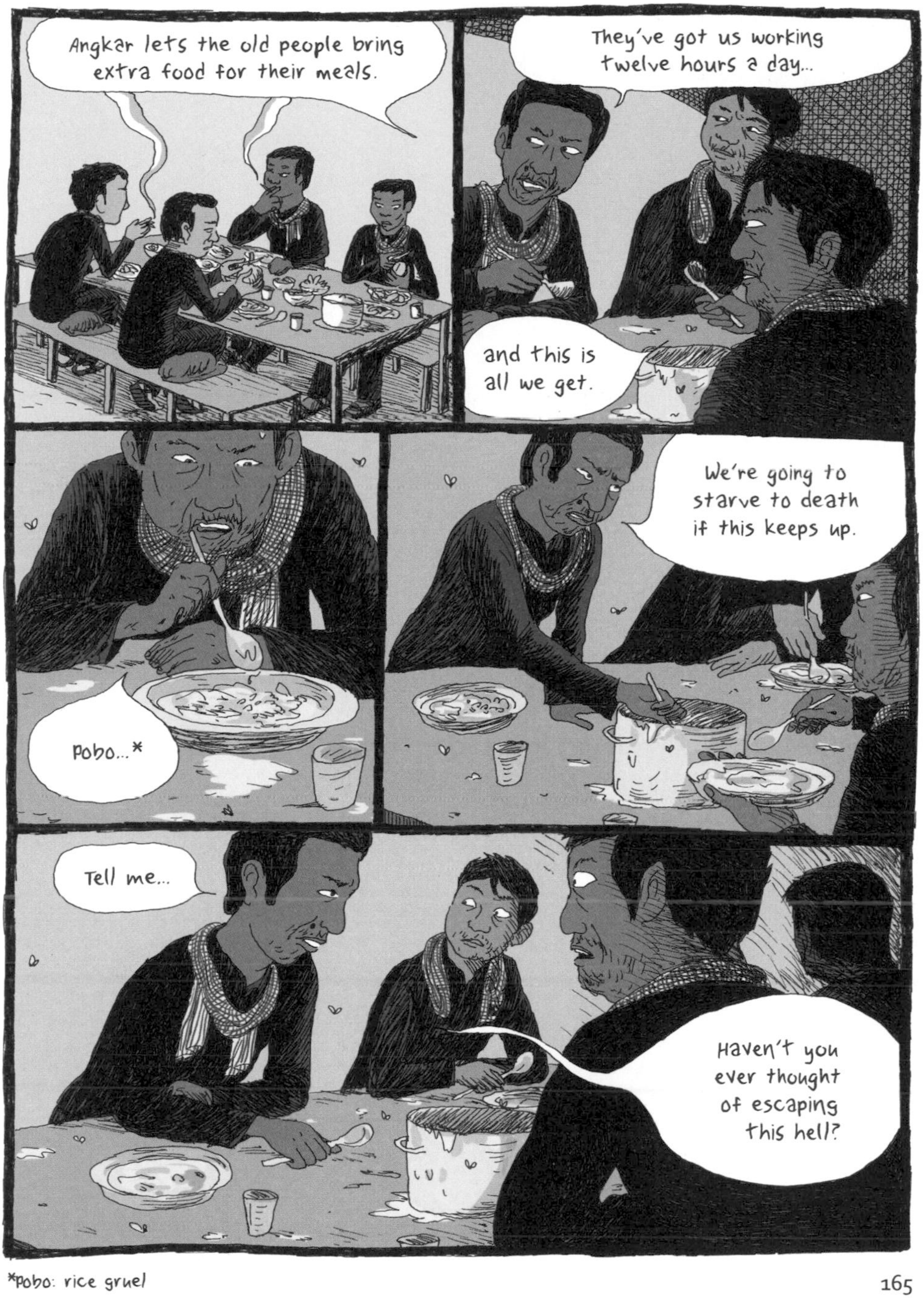
Angkar lets the old people bring extra food for their meals.
They've got us working twelve hours a day...
and this is all we get.
Pobo...*
We're going to starve to death if this keeps up.
Tell me...
Haven't you ever thought of escaping this hell?

*Pobo: rice gruel

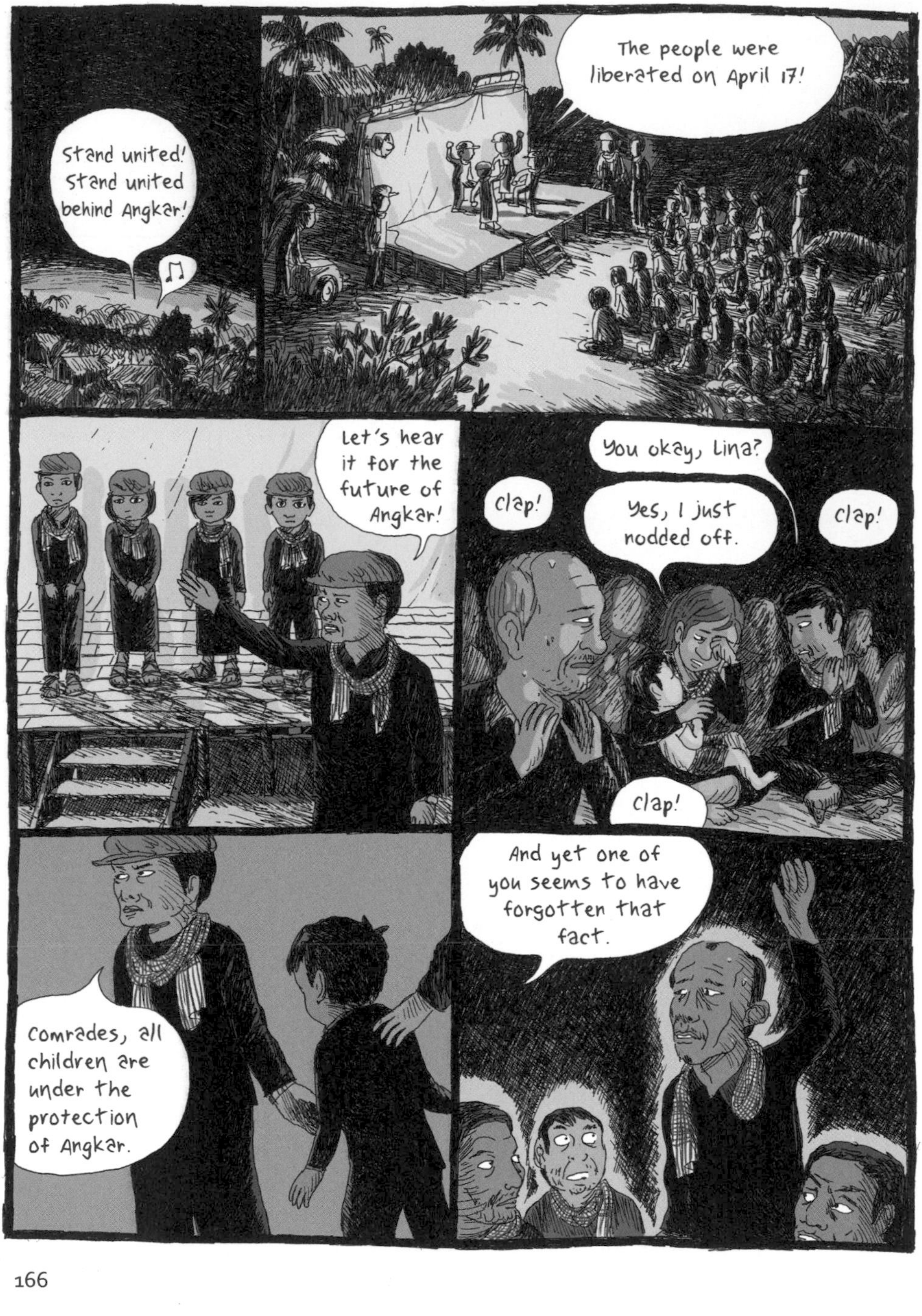
Stand united! Stand united behind Angkar!
The people were liberated on April 17!
Let's hear it for the future of Angkar!
You okay, Lina?
Clap!
Yes, I just nodded off.
Clap!
Clap!
Comrades, all children are under the protection of Angkar.
And yet one of you seems to have forgotten that fact.

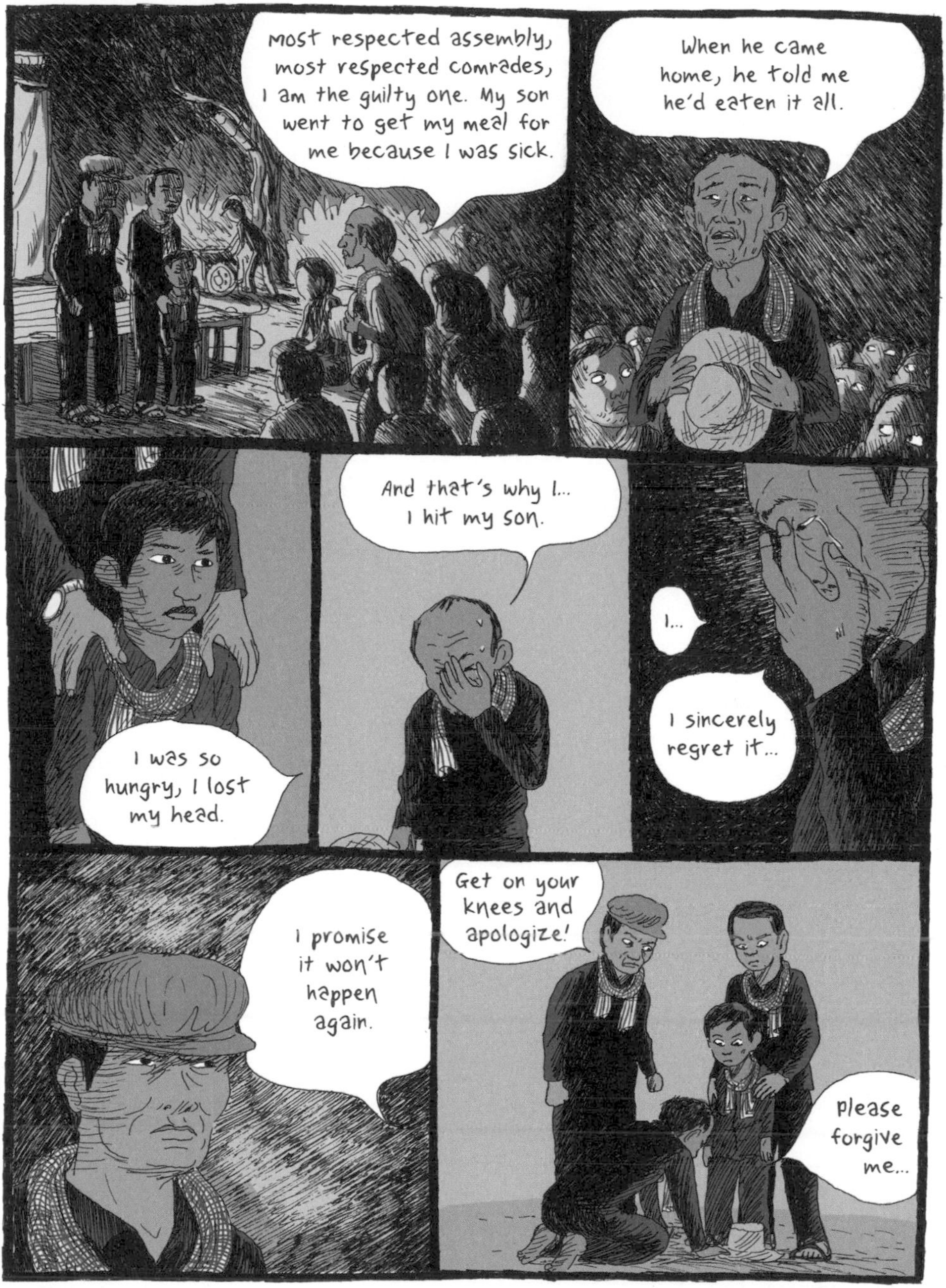
Most respected assembly, most respected comrades, I am the guilty one. My son went to get my meal for me because I was sick.
When he came home, he told me he'd eaten it all.
I was so hungry, I lost my head.
And that's why I... I hit my son.
I...
I sincerely regret it...
I promise it won't happen again.
Get on your knees and apologize!
Please forgive me...

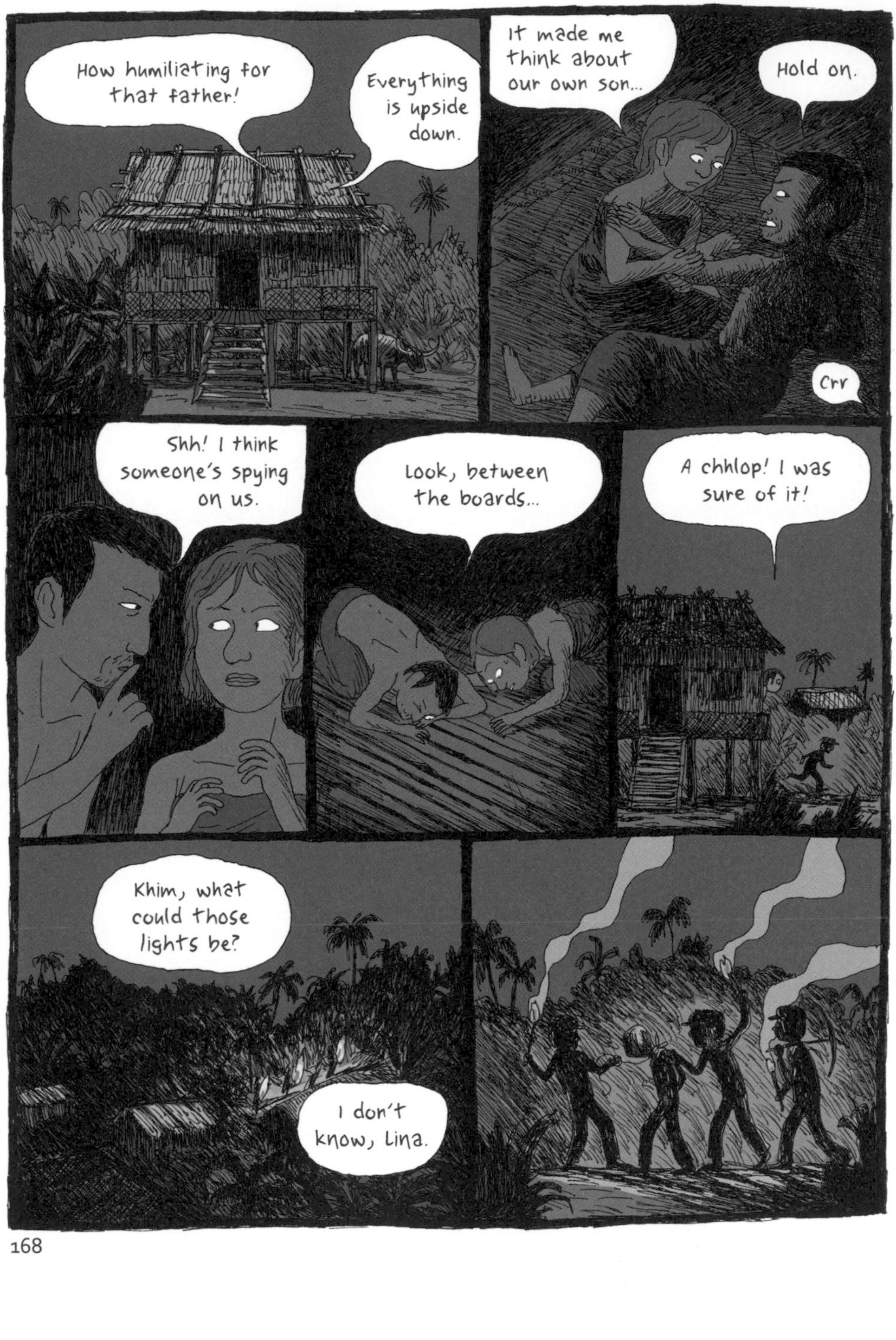
How humiliating for that father!
Everything is upside down.
It made me think about our own son...
Hold on.
Crr
Shh! I think someone's spying on us.
Look, between the boards...
A chhlop! I was sure of it!
Khim, what could those lights be?
I don't know, Lina.

chapter 10

ANGKAR CARES FOR ALL!
BROTHERS AND SISTERS, FATHERS AND MOTHERS!
THE PEOPLE ARE ANGKAR'S BRAIN!

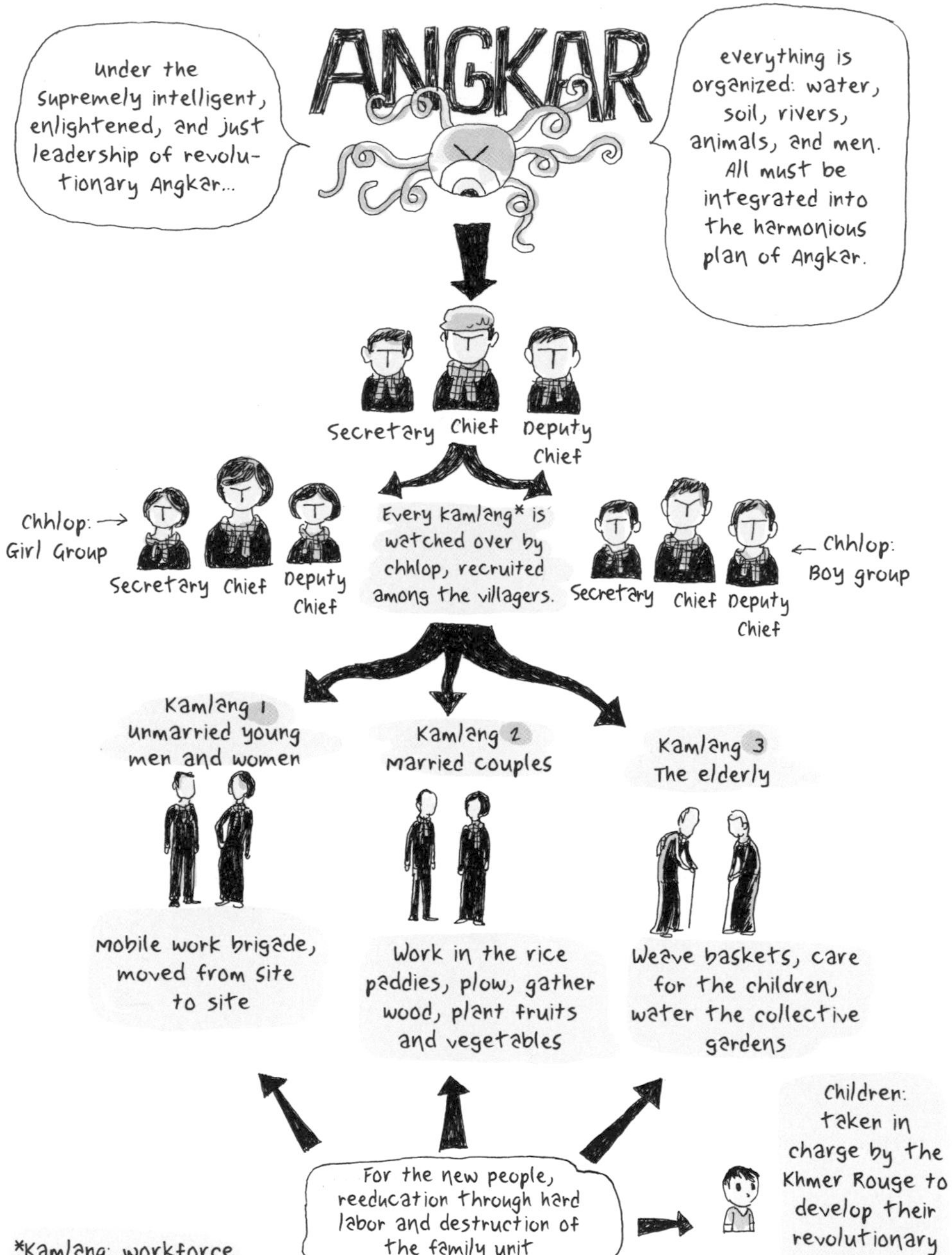
ANGKAR
Under the supremely intelligent, enlightened, and just leadership of revolutionary Angkar...
everything is organized: water, soil, rivers, animals, and men. All must be integrated into the harmonious plan of Angkar.
Secretary
Chief
Deputy Chief
Chhlop: Girl Group
Secretary
Chief
Deputy Chief
Every kamlang* is watched over by chhlop, recruited among the villagers.
Secretary
Chief
Deputy Chief
Chhlop: Boy group
Kamlang 1 Unmarried young men and women
Kamlang 2 Married couples
Kamlang 3 The elderly
Mobile work brigade, moved from site to site
Work in the rice paddies, plow, gather wood, plant fruits and vegetables
Weave baskets, care for the children, water the collective gardens
For the new people, reeducation through hard labor and destruction of the family unit
Children: taken in charge by the Khmer Rouge to develop their revolutionary spirit
*Kamlang: workforce

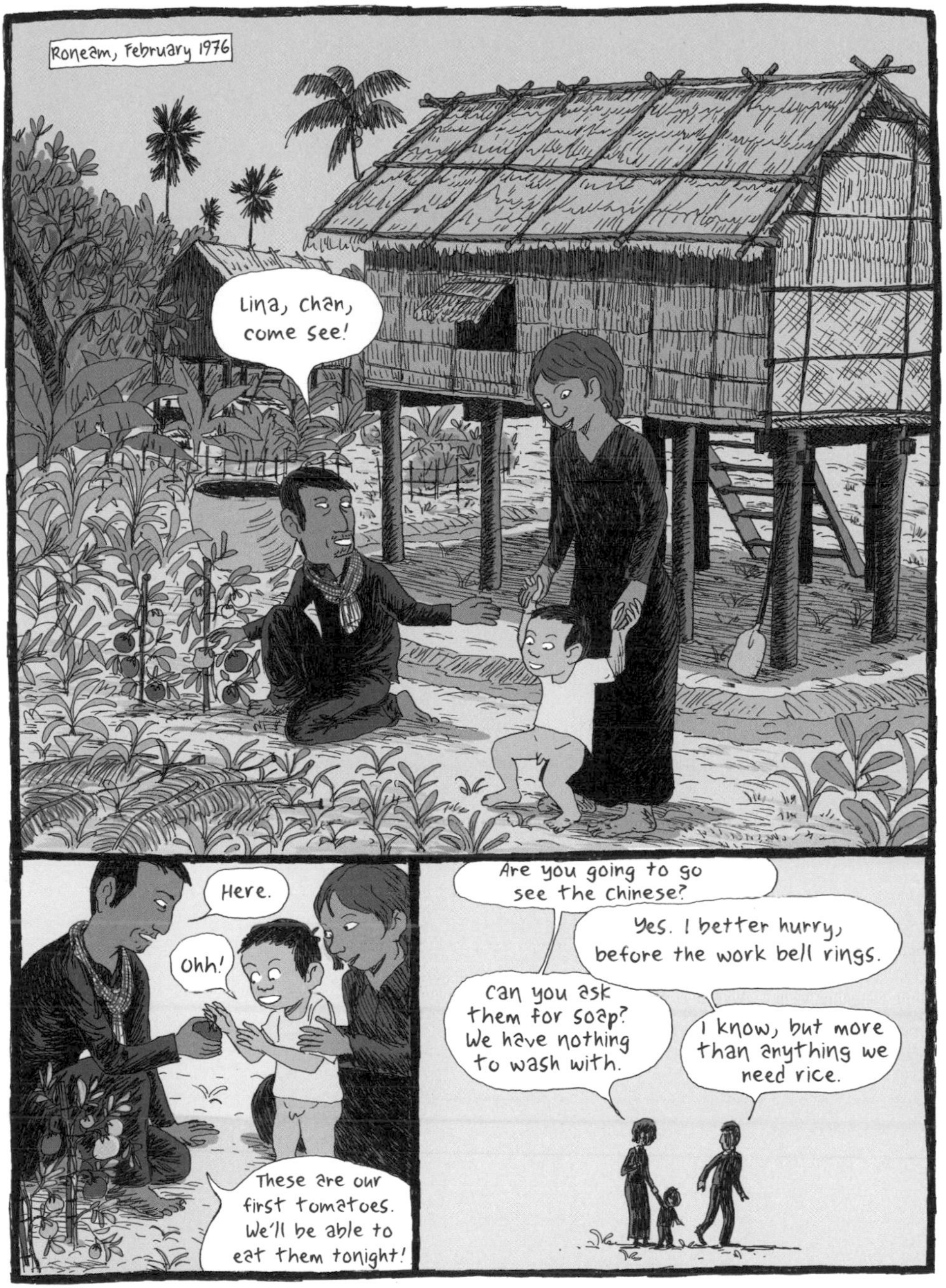
Roneam, February 1976
Lina, Chan, come see!
Here.
Ohh!
These are our first tomatoes. We'll be able to eat them tonight!
Are you going to go see the Chinese?
Yes. I better hurry, before the work bell rings.
Can you ask them for soap? We have nothing to wash with.
I know, but more than anything we need rice.

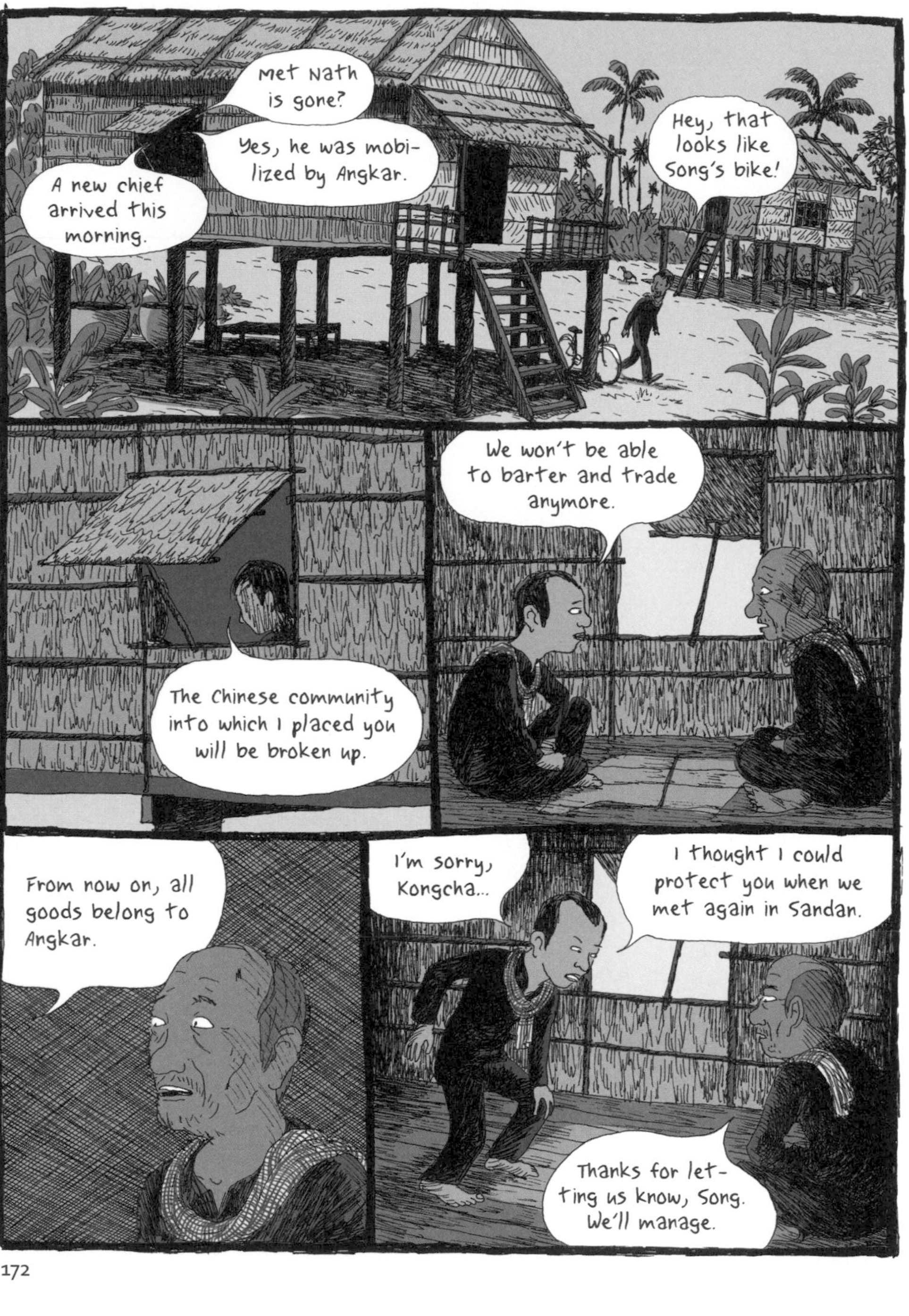
Met Nath is gone?
Yes, he was mobilized by Angkar.
A new chief arrived this morning.
Hey, that looks like Song's bike!
We won't be able to barter and trade anymore.
The Chinese community into which I placed you will be broken up.
From now on, all goods belong to Angkar.
I'm sorry, Kongcha...
I thought I could protect you when we met again in Sandan.
Thanks for letting us know, Song. We'll manage.

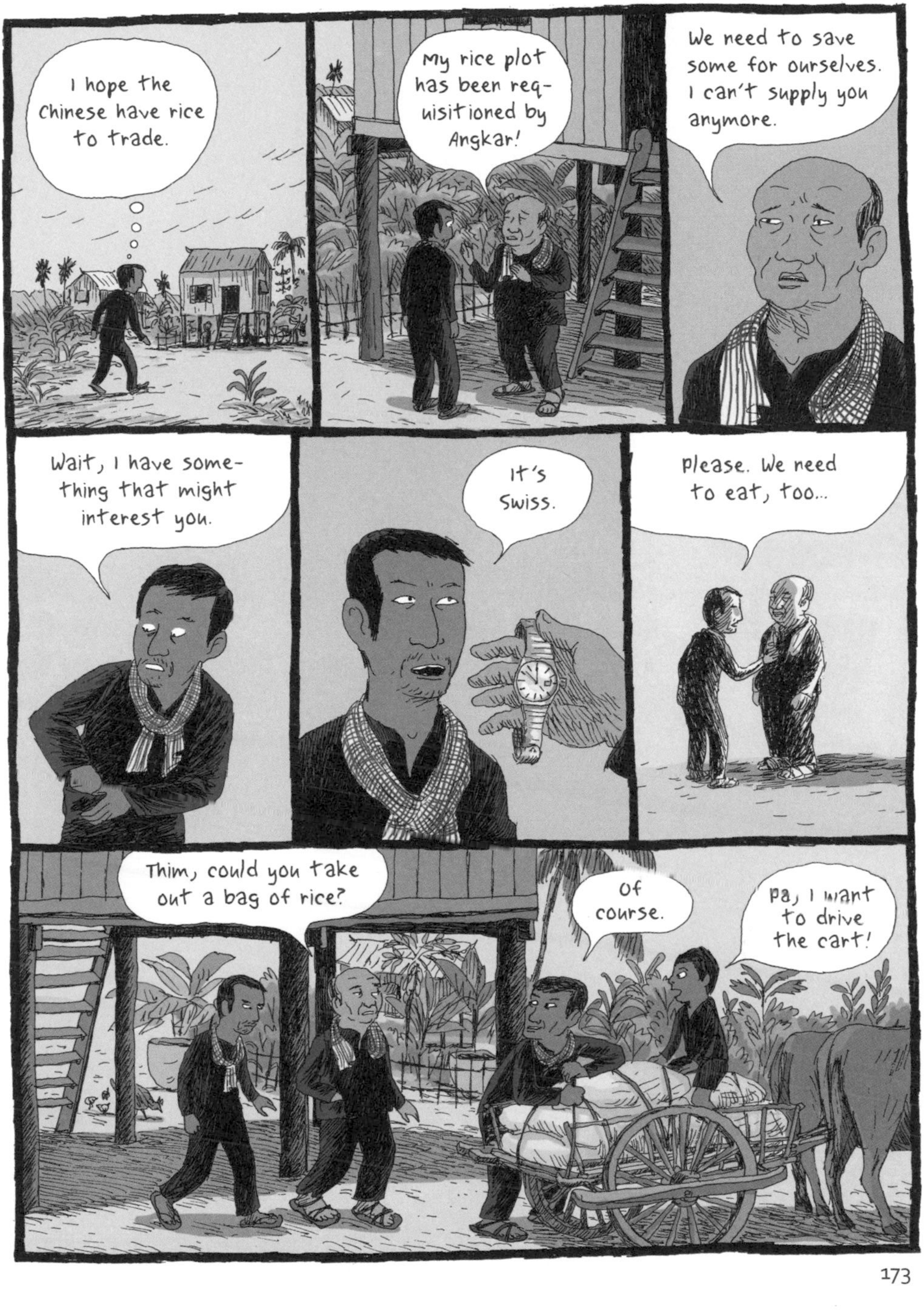
I hope the Chinese have rice to trade.
My rice plot has been requisitioned by Angkar!
We need to save some for ourselves. I can't supply you anymore.
Wait, I have something that might interest you.
It's Swiss.
Please. We need to eat, too...
Thim, could you take out a bag of rice?
Of course.
Pa, I want to drive the cart!

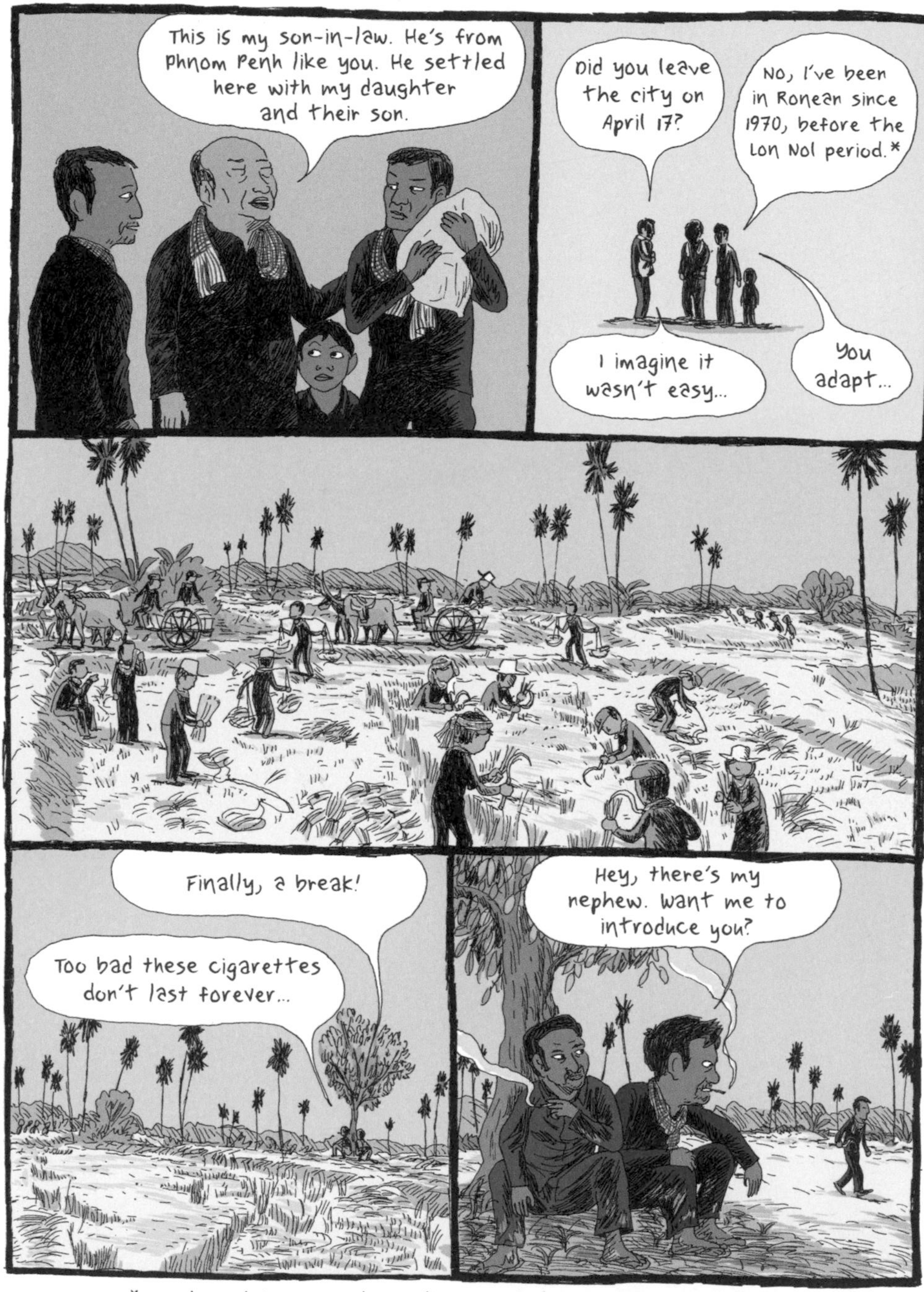
This is my son-in-law. He's from Phnom Penh like you. He settled here with my daughter and their son.
Did you leave the city on April 17?
No, I've been in Ronean since 1970, before the Lon Nol period.*
I imagine it wasn't easy...
You adapt...
Finally, a break!
Too bad these cigarettes don't last forever...
Hey, there's my nephew. Want me to introduce you?

*Lon Nol period: from General Lon Nol's U.S.-backed coup in 1970 to the fall of Phnom Penh in 1975

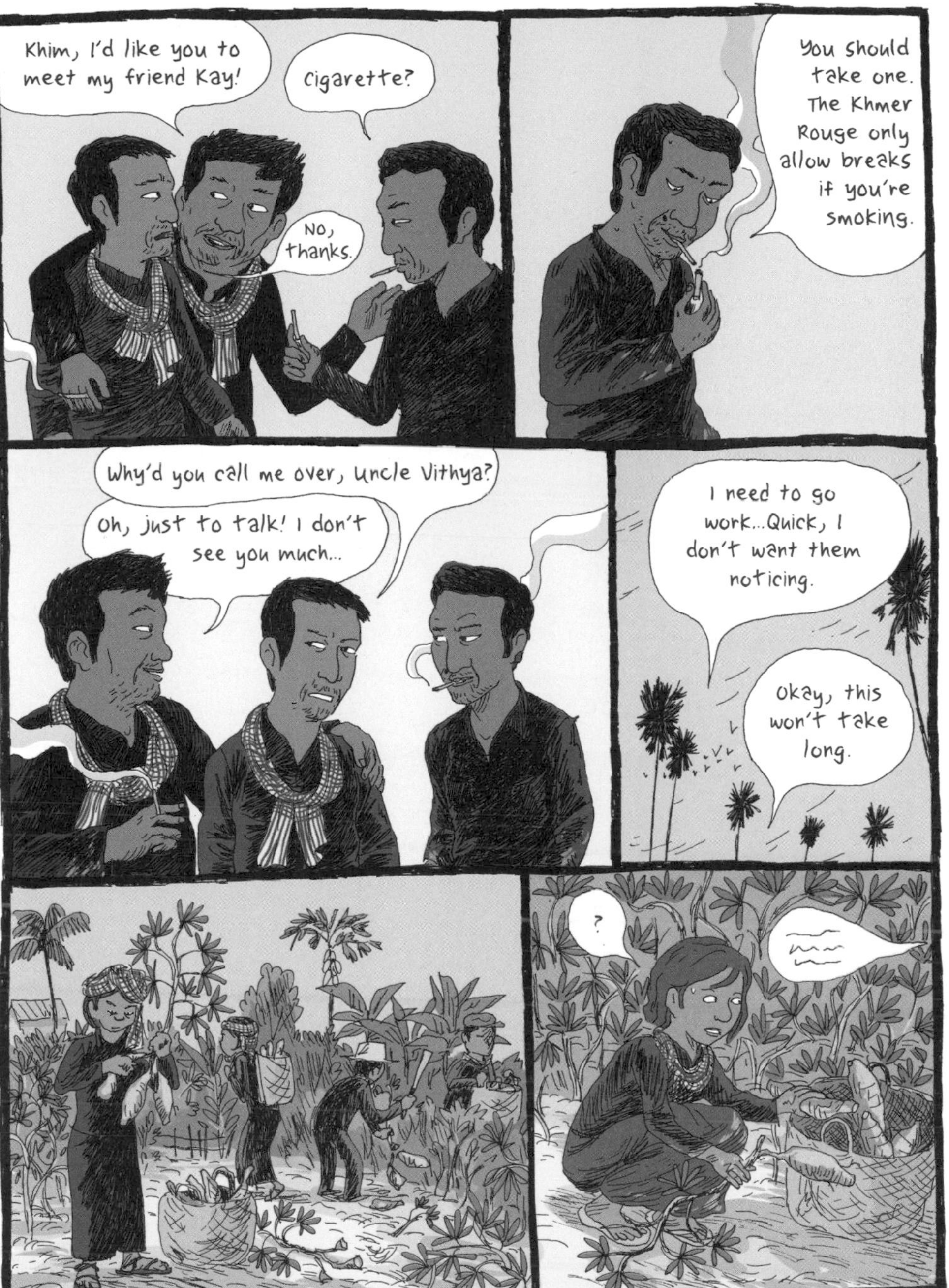
Khim, I'd like you to meet my friend Kay!
Cigarette?
No, thanks.
You should take one. The Khmer Rouge only allow breaks if you're smoking.
Why'd you call me over, Uncle Vithya?
Oh, just to talk! I don't see you much...
I need to go work... Quick, I don't want them noticing.
Okay, this won't take long.
?

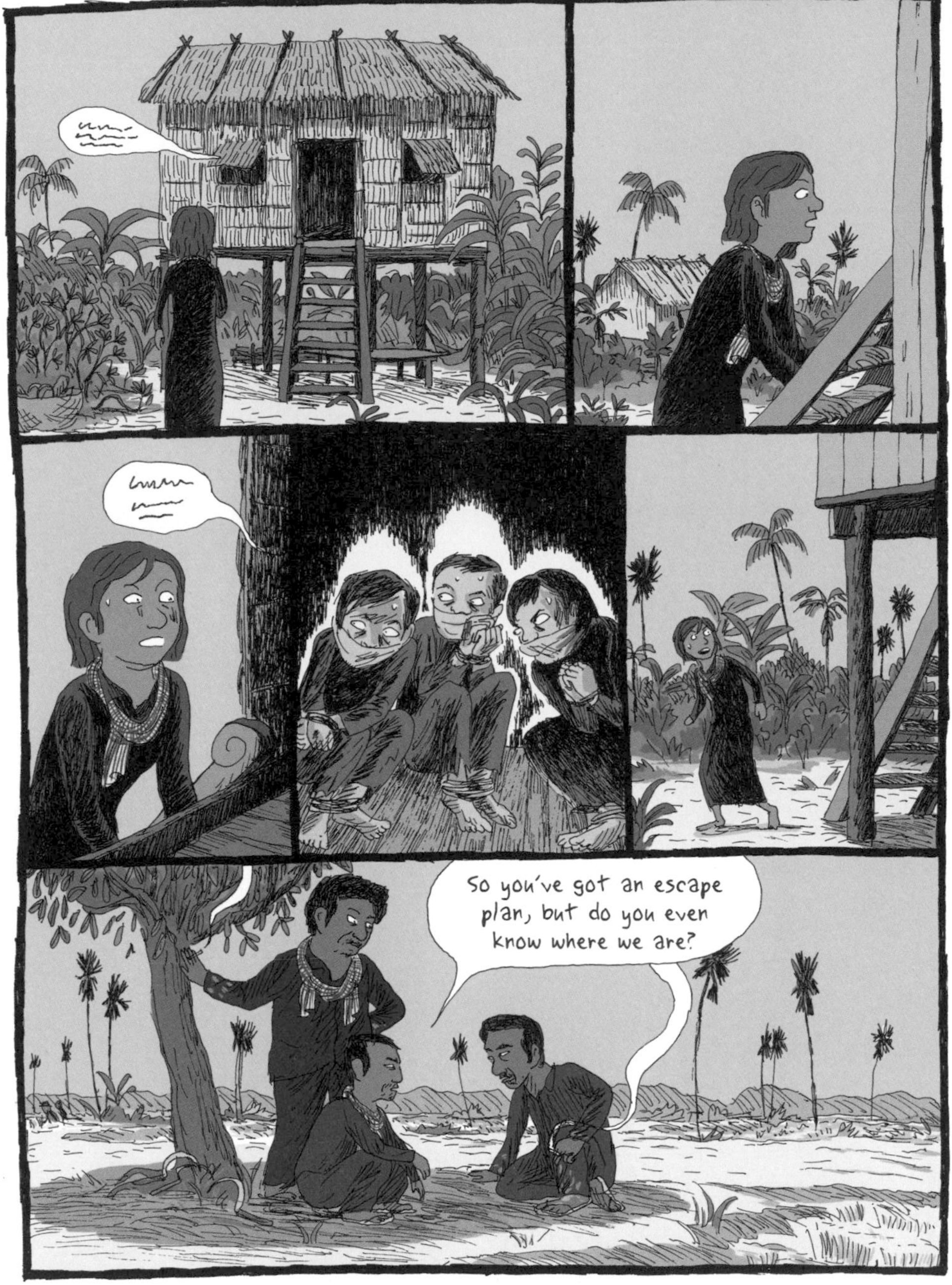
So you've got an escape plan, but do you even know where we are?

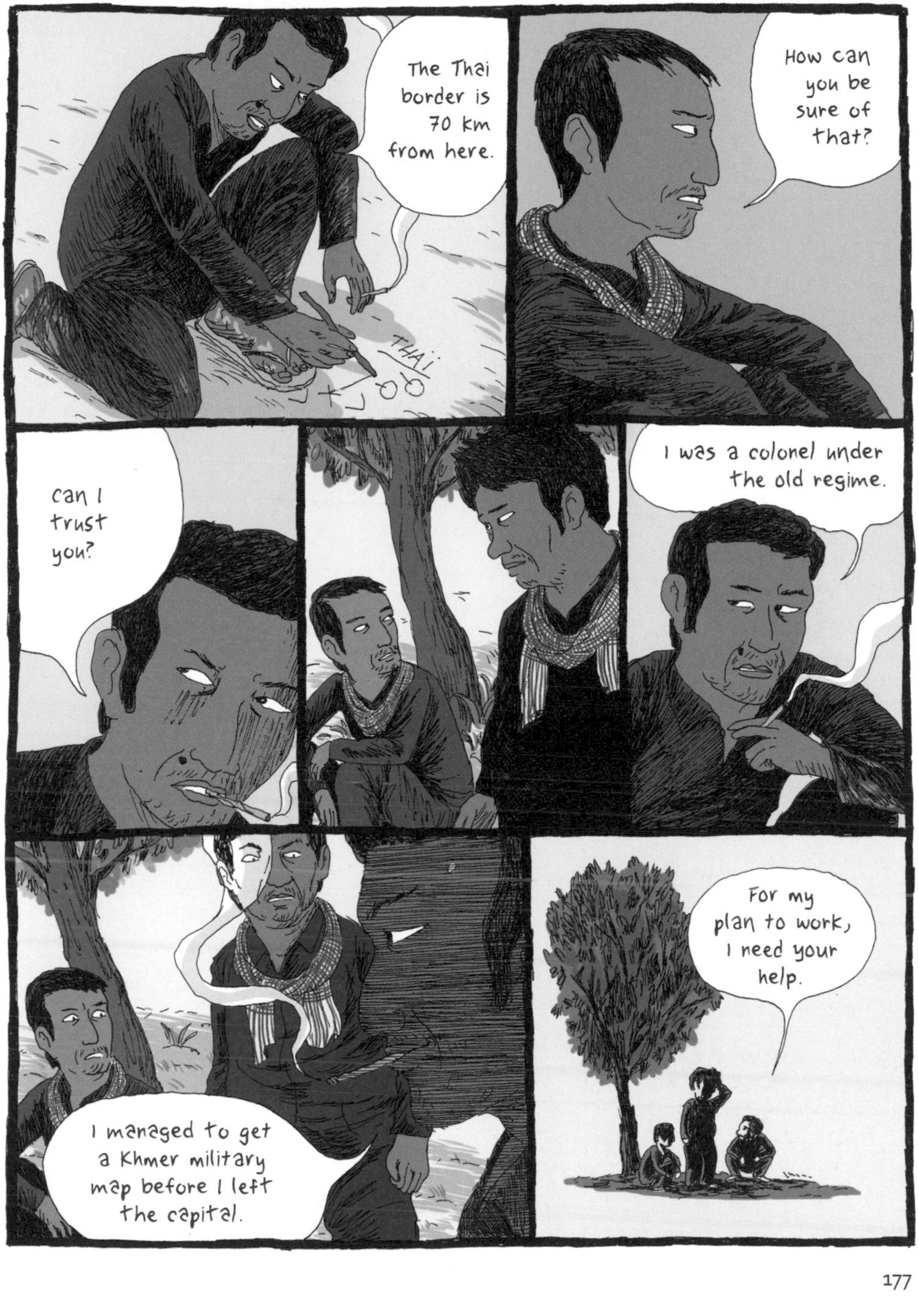
The Thai border is 70 km from here.
THAI
How can you be sure of that?
Can I trust you?
I was a colonel under the old regime.
I managed to get a Khmer military map before I left the capital.
For my plan to work, I need your help.

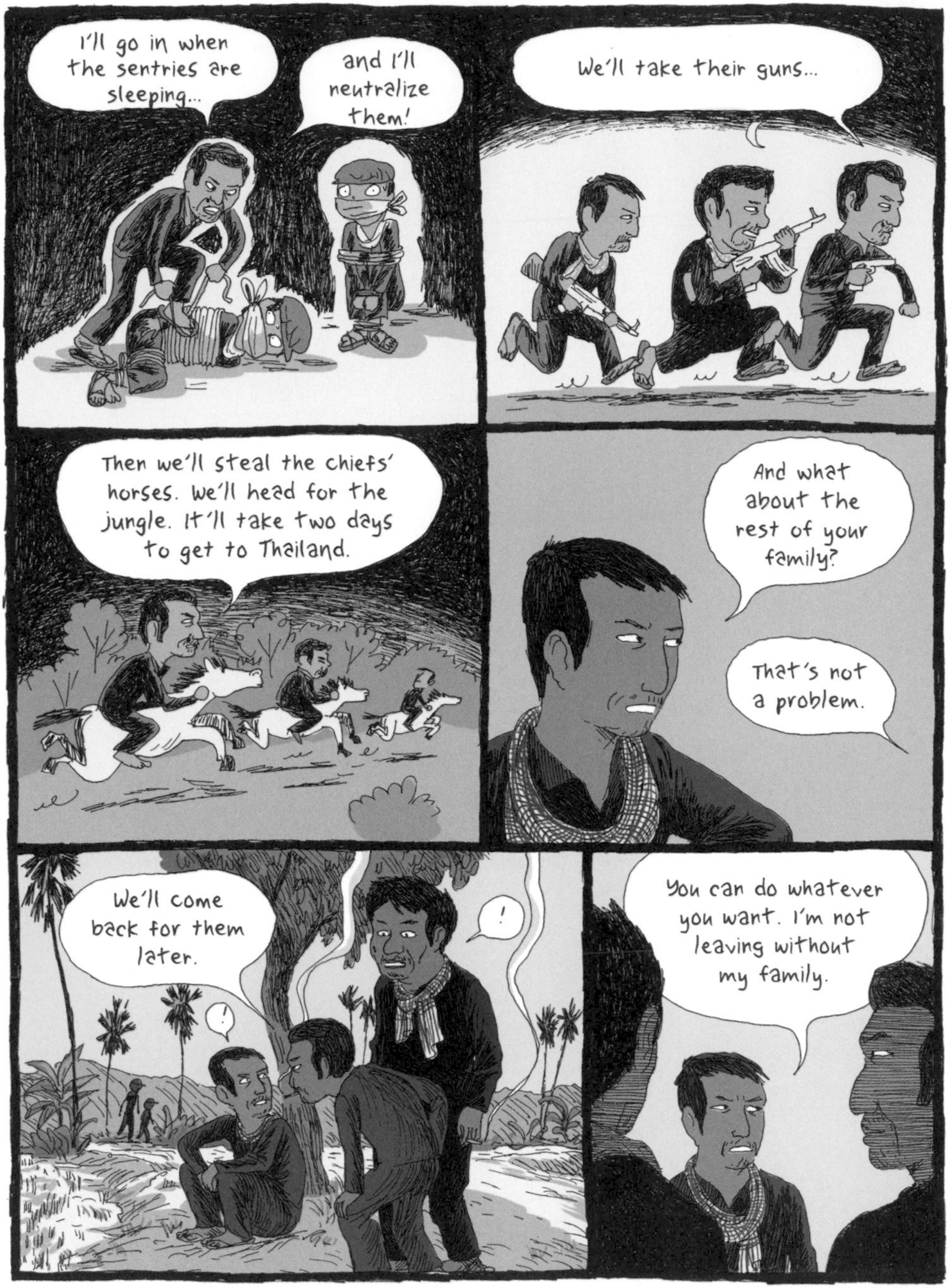
I'll go in when the sentries are sleeping...
and I'll neutralize them!
We'll take their guns...
Then we'll steal the chiefs' horses. We'll head for the jungle. It'll take two days to get to Thailand.
And what about the rest of your family?
That's not a problem.
We'll come back for them later.
!
!
You can do whatever you want. I'm not leaving without my family.

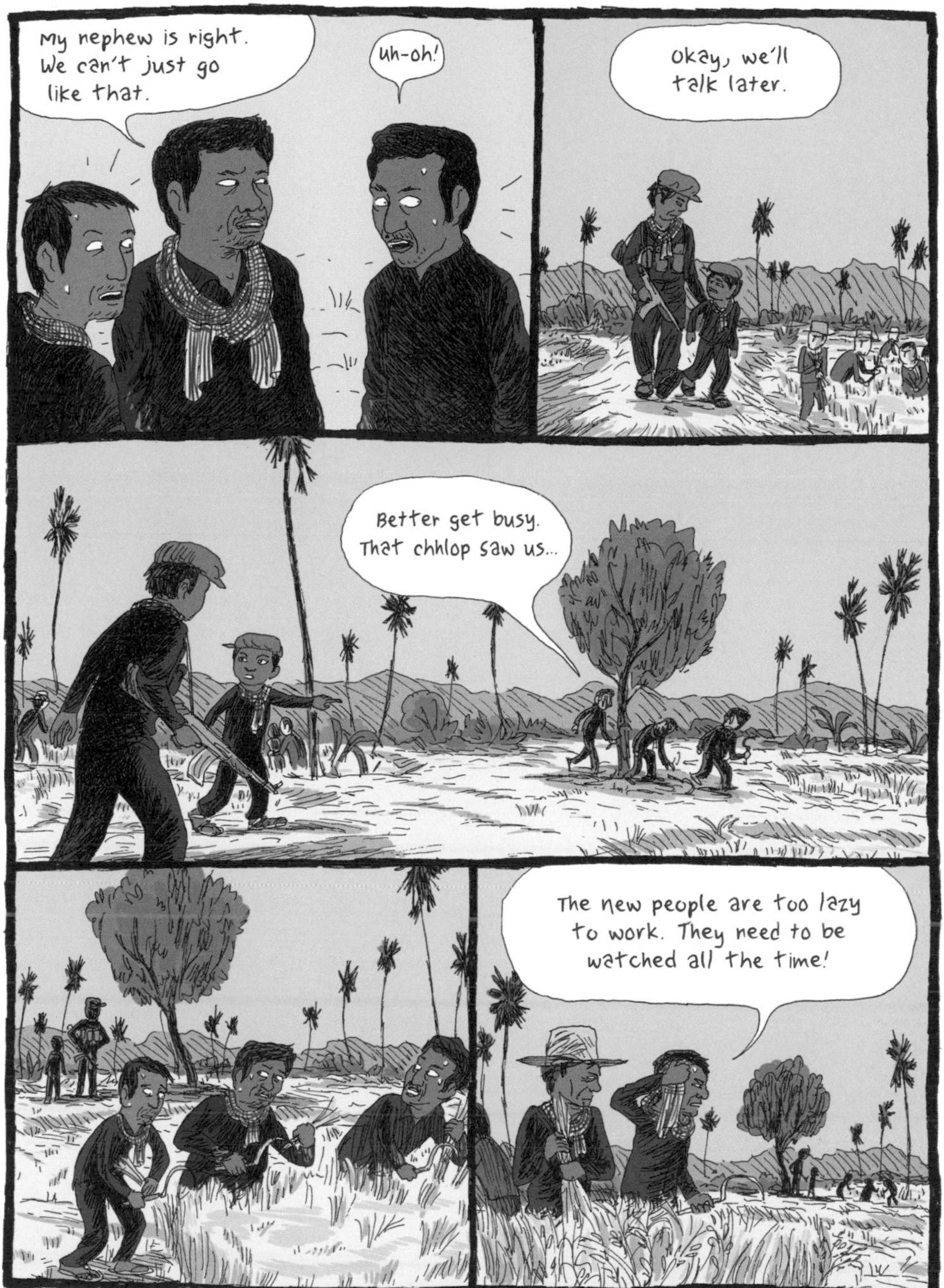
My nephew is right. We can't just go like that.
Uh-oh!
Okay, we'll talk later.
Better get busy. That chhlop saw us...
The new people are too lazy to work. They need to be watched all the time!

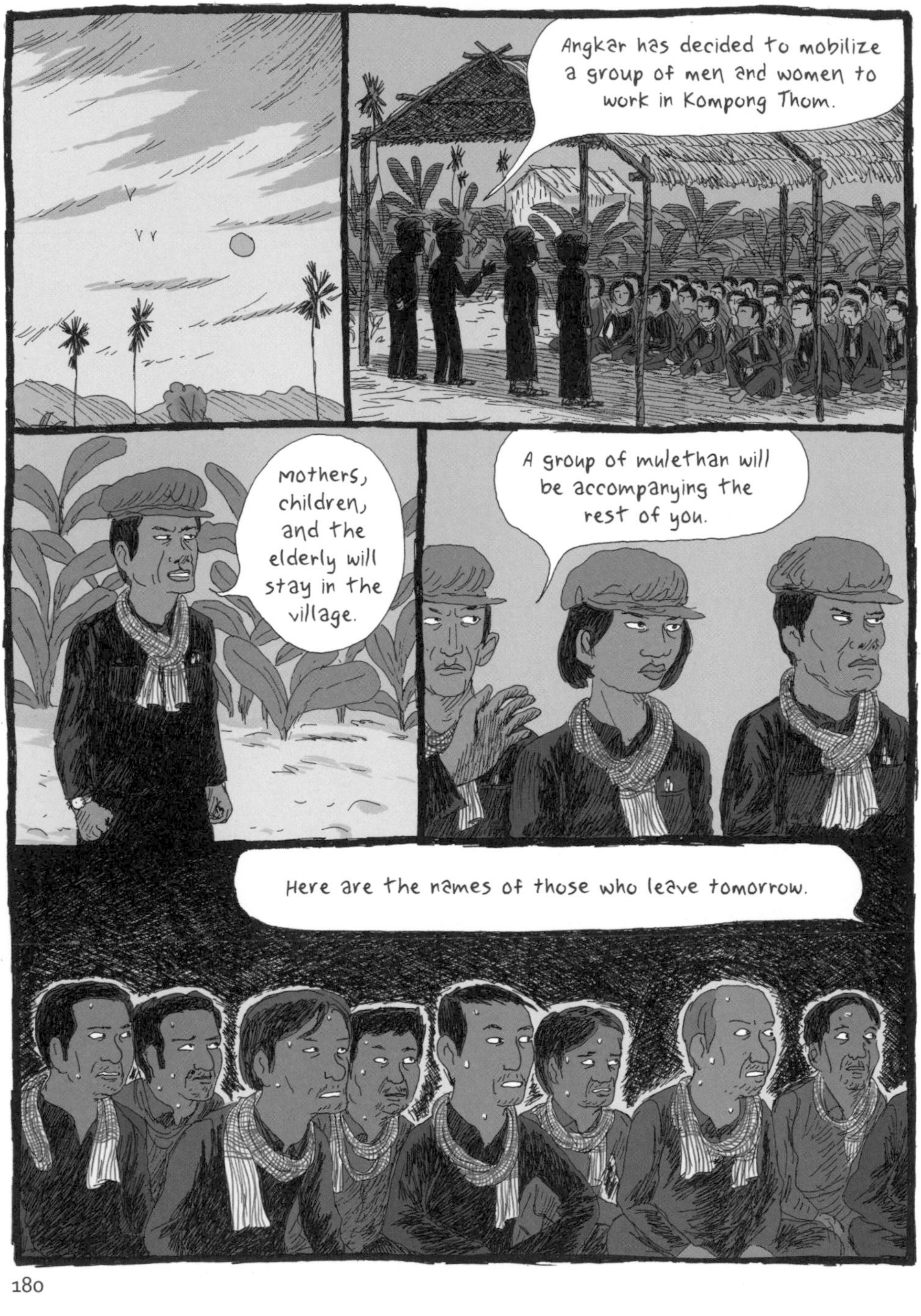
Angkar has decided to mobilize a group of men and women to work in Kompong Thom.
Mothers, children, and the elderly will stay in the village.
A group of mulethan will be accompanying the rest of you.
Here are the names of those who leave tomorrow.

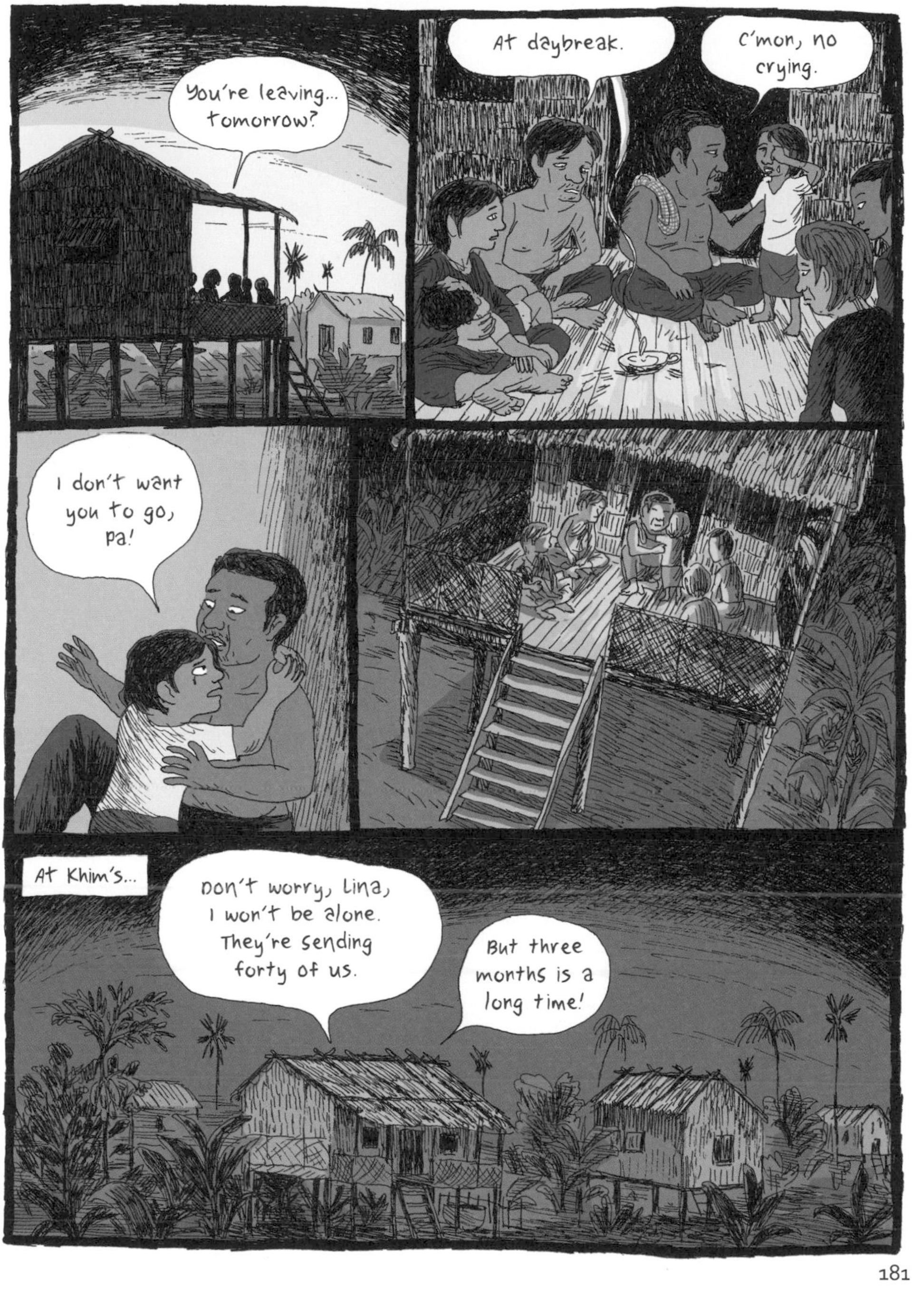
You're leaving... tomorrow?
At daybreak.
C'mon, no crying.
I don't want you to go, pa!
At Khim's...
Don't worry, Lina, I won't be alone. They're sending forty of us.
But three months is a long time!

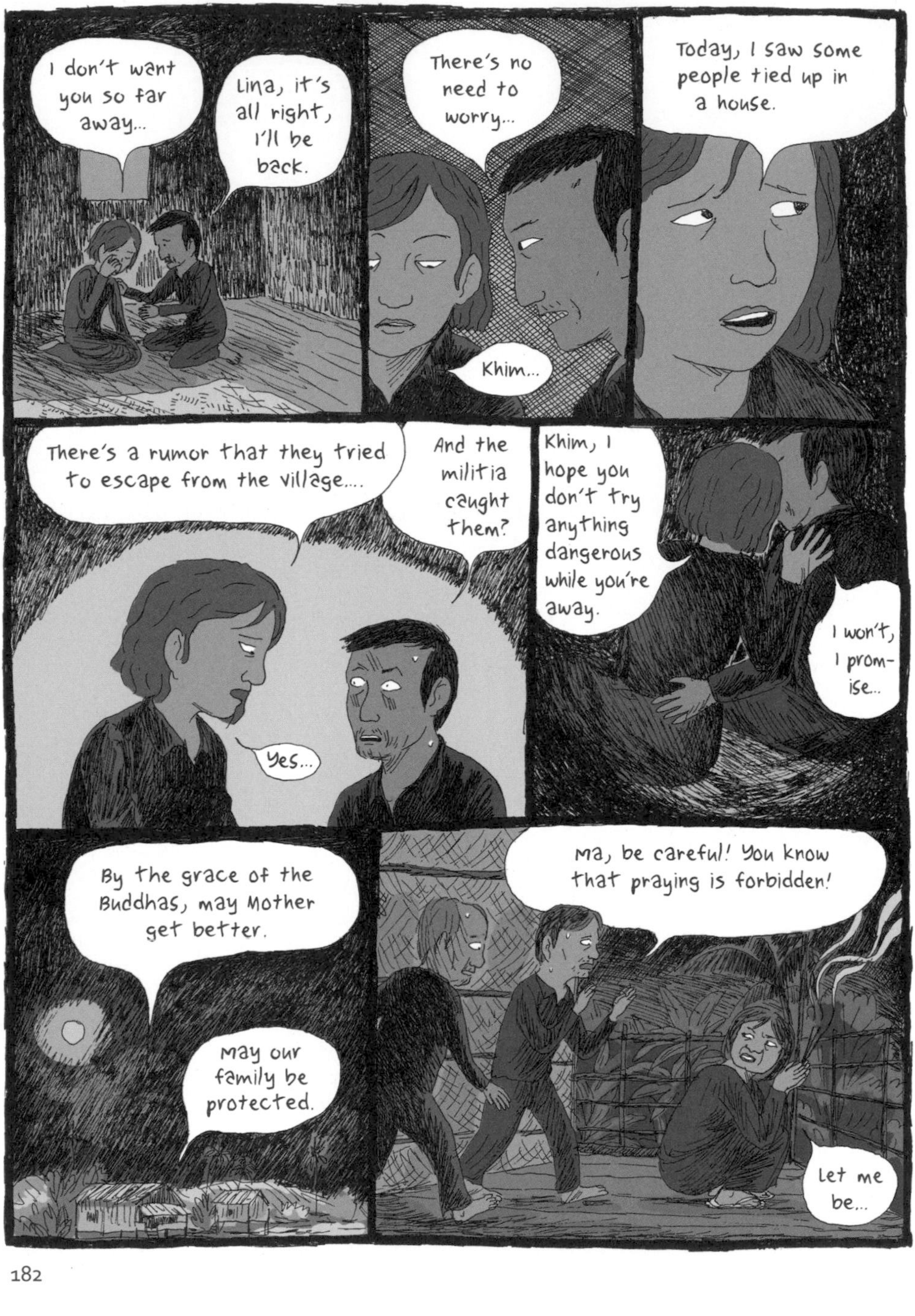
I don't want you so far away...
Lina, it's all right, I'll be back.
There's no need to worry...
Khim...
Today, I saw some people tied up in a house.
There's a rumor that they tried to escape from the village....
And the militia caught them?
Yes...
Khim, I hope you don't try anything dangerous while you're away.
I won't, I promise...
By the grace of the Buddhas, may Mother get better.
May our family be protected.
Ma, be careful! You know that praying is forbidden!
Let me be...

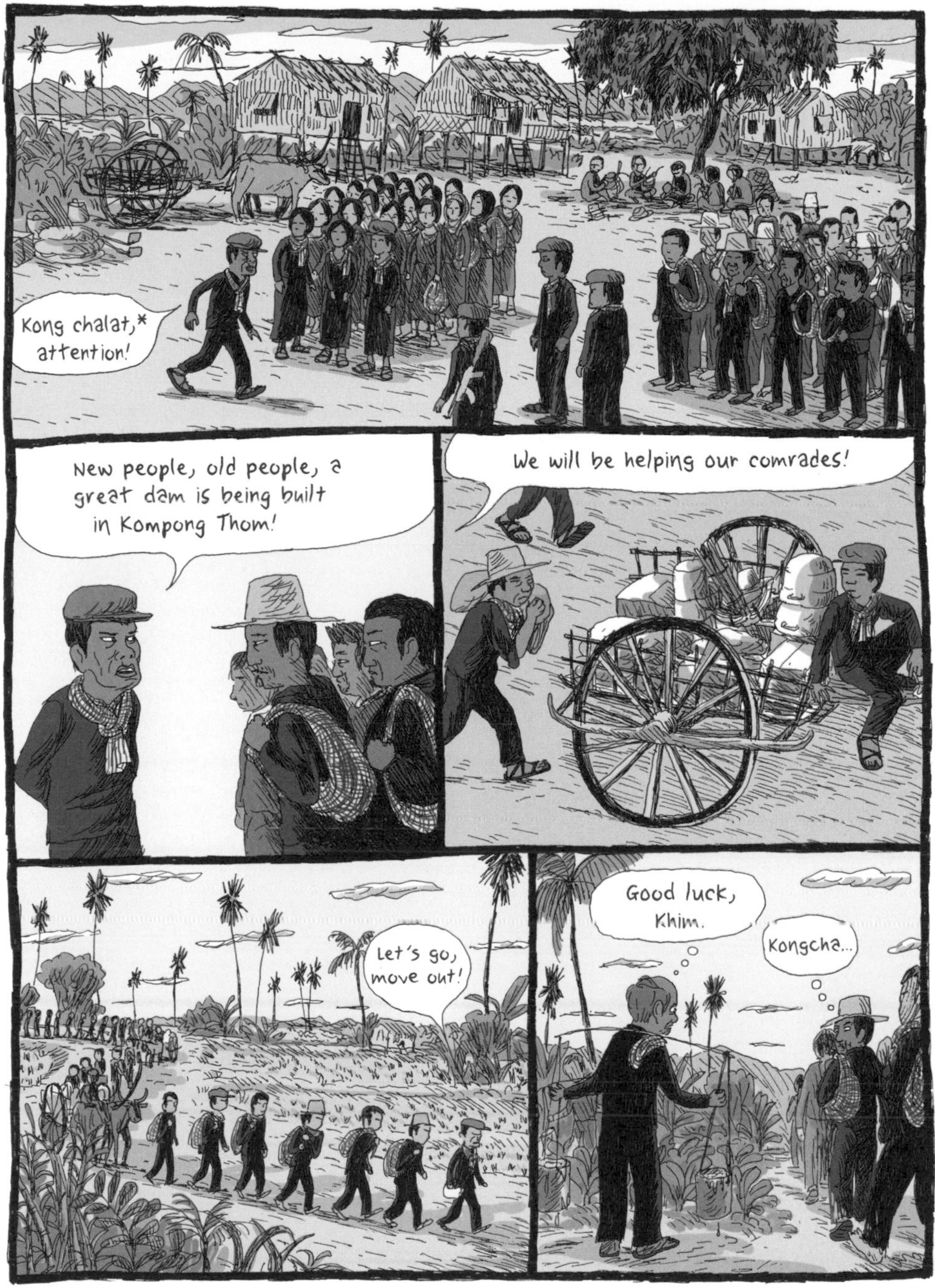
Kong chalat,* attention!
New people, old people, a great dam is being built in Kompong Thom!
We will be helping our comrades!
Let's go, move out!
Good luck, Khim.
Kongcha...

*Kong chalat: mobile brigade

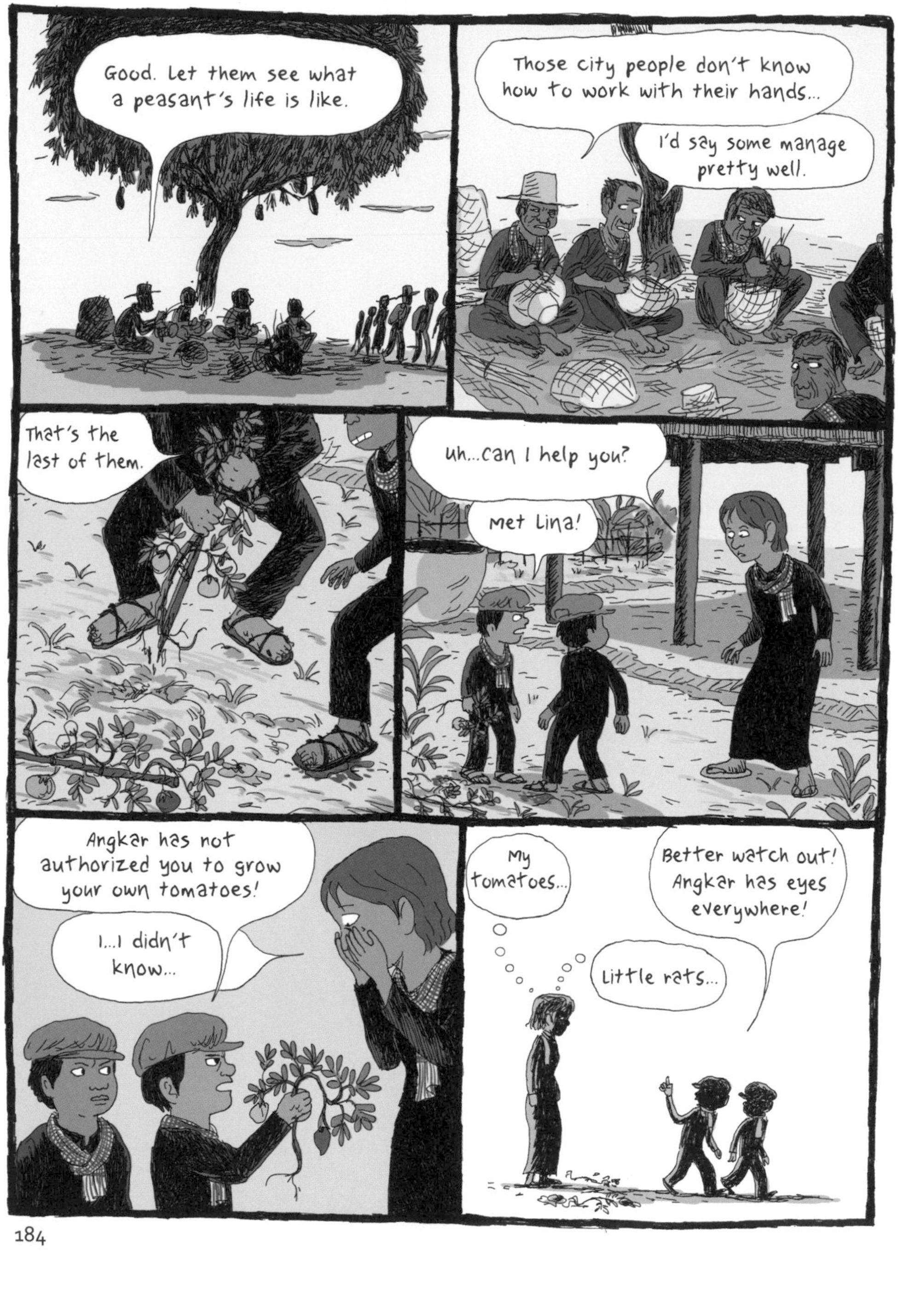
Good. Let them see what a peasant's life is like.
Those city people don't know how to work with their hands...
I'd say some manage pretty well.
That's the last of them.
Uh...can I help you?
Met Lina!
Angkar has not authorized you to grow your own tomatoes!
I...I didn't know...
My tomatoes...
Better watch out! Angkar has eyes everywhere!
Little rats...

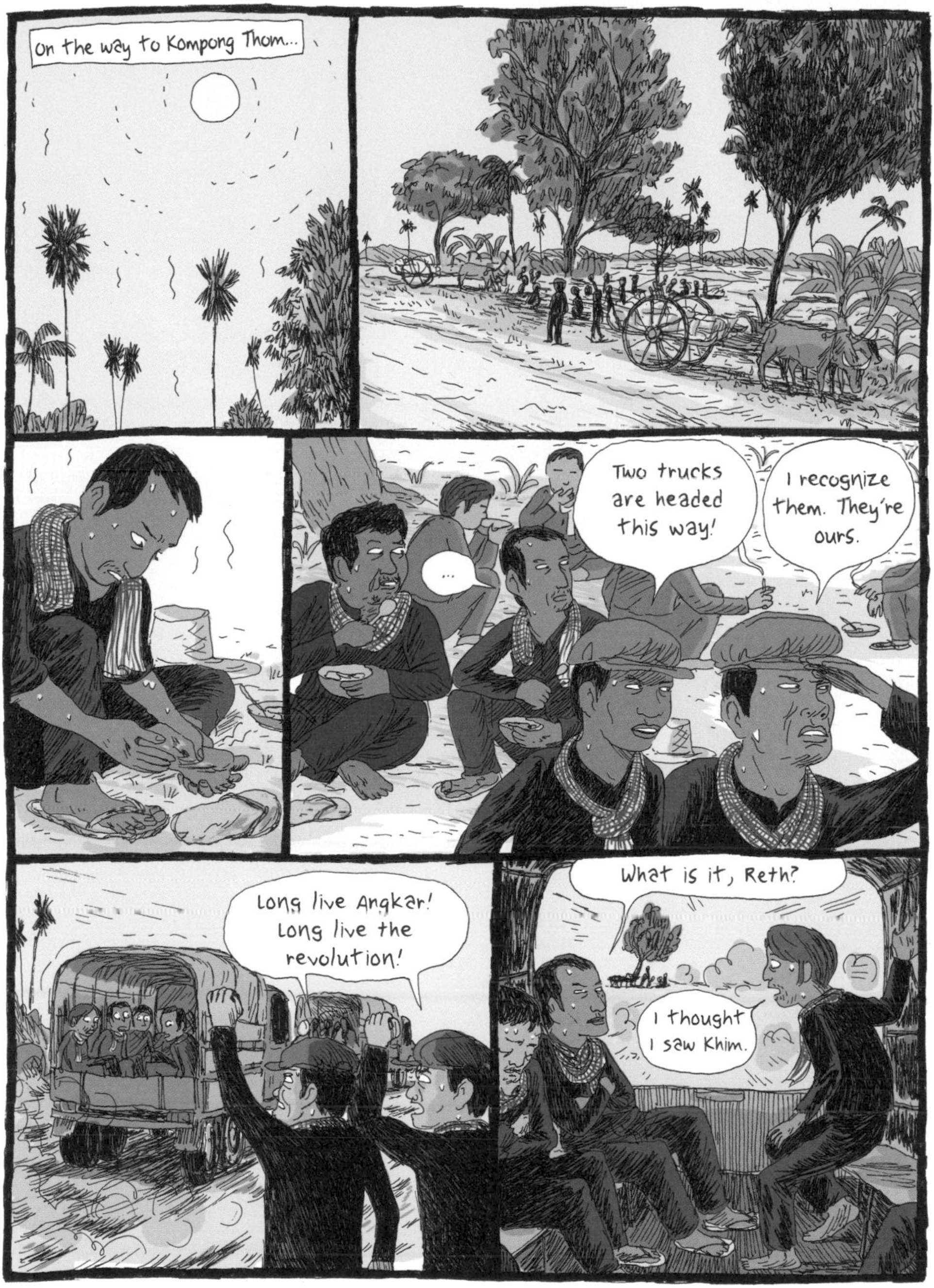
On the way to Kompong Thom...
...
Two trucks are headed this way!
I recognize them. They're ours.
Long live Angkar! Long live the revolution!
What is it, Reth?
I thought I saw Khim.

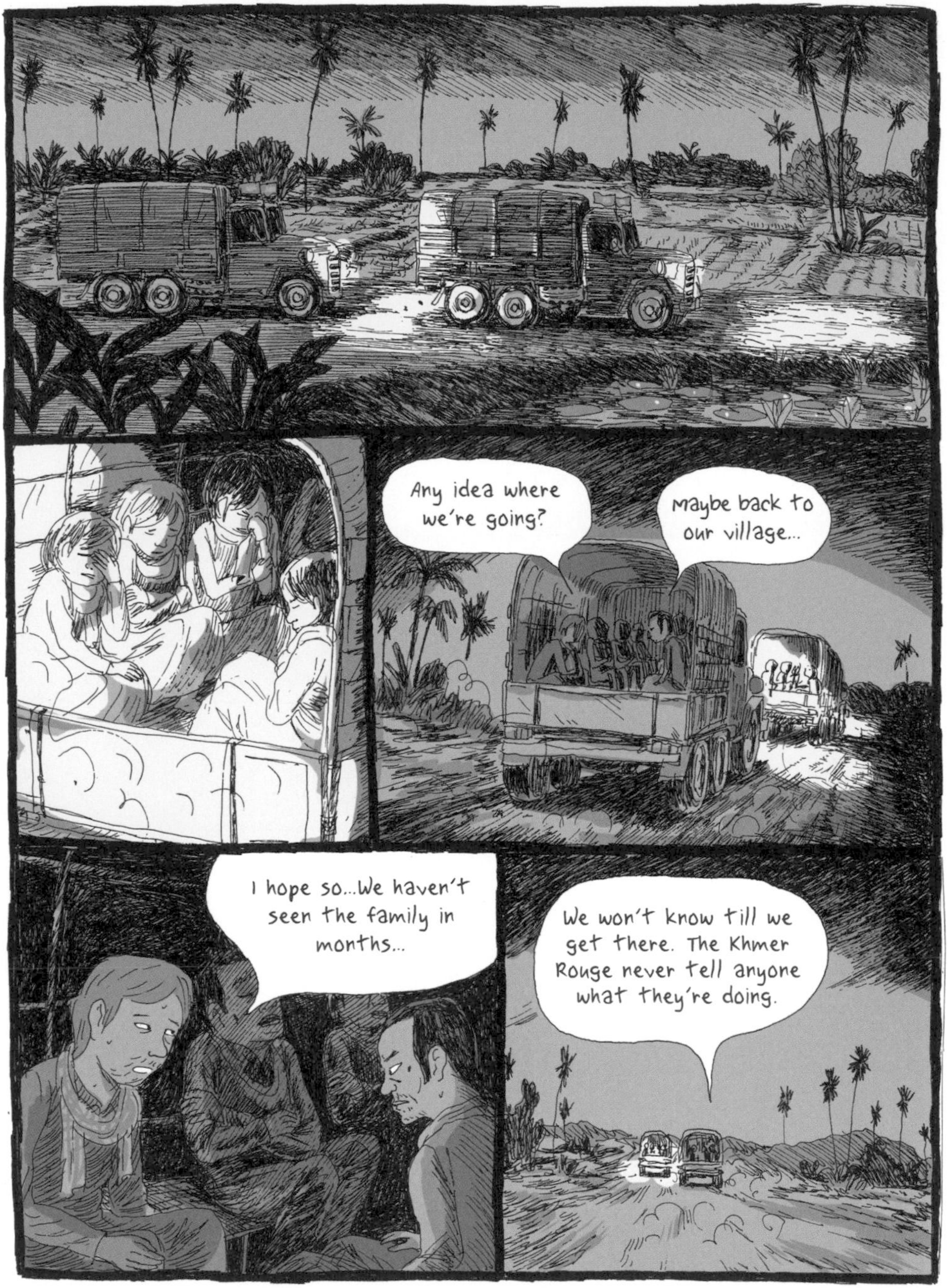
Any idea where we're going?
Maybe back to our village...
I hope so...We haven't seen the family in months...
We won't know till we get there. The Khmer Rouge never tell anyone what they're doing.

chapter 11

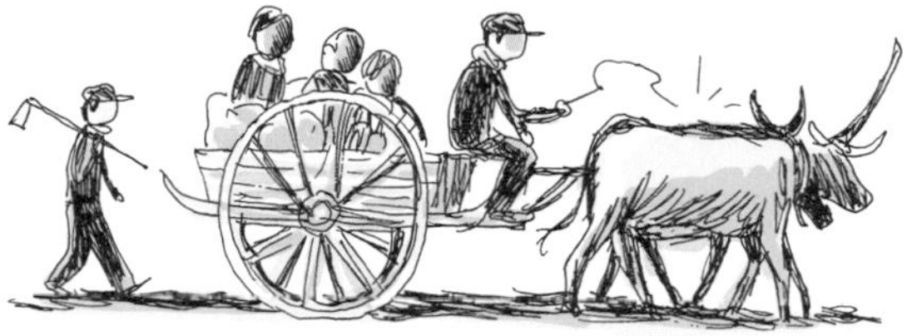

THERE ARE NO CAMPS OR PRISONS
IN DEMOCRATIC KAMPUCHEA.
WHATEVER THE CRIME,
THE ONLY PUNISHMENT IS DEATH.

PERSONAL BELONGINGS OF THE NEW PEOPLE IN DEMOCRATIC KAMPUCHEA

After their relocation to the countryside, the new people have to adapt and improvise to survive the hardships and dictates imposed by Angkar.

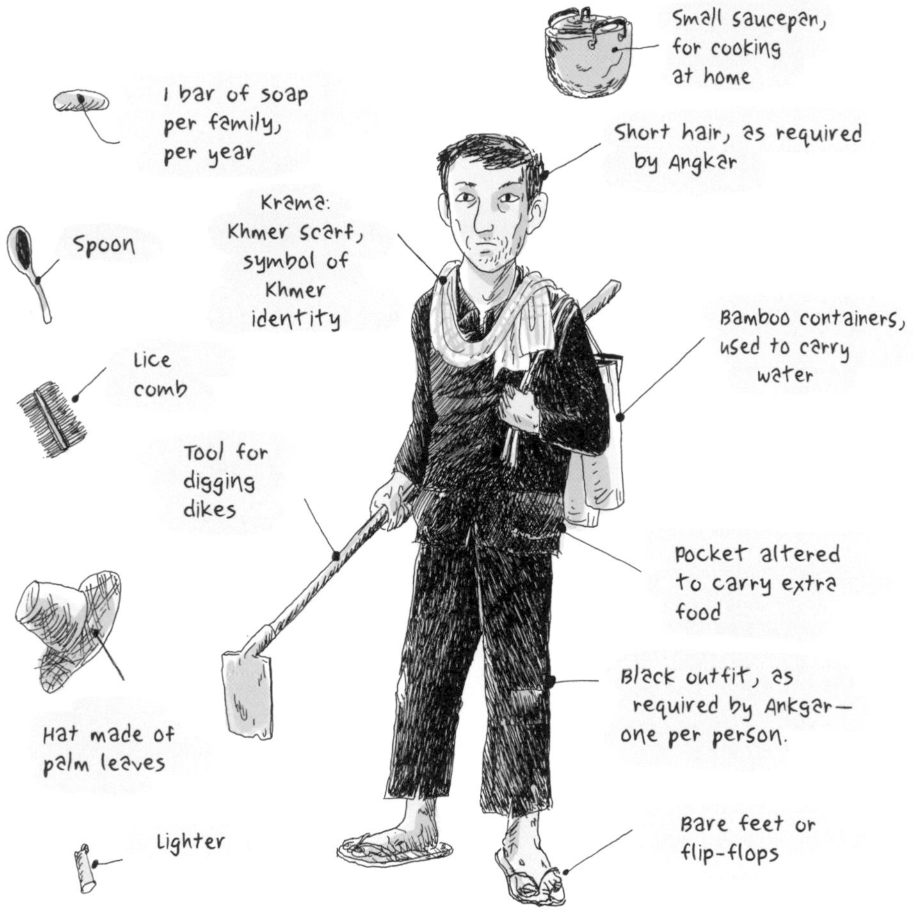
Small saucepan, for cooking at home
1 bar of soap per family, per year
Short hair, as required by Angkar
Krama: Khmer scarf, symbol of Khmer identity
Spoon
Bamboo containers, used to carry water
Lice comb
Tool for digging dikes
Pocket altered to carry extra food
Black outfit, as required by Ankgar— one per person.
Hat made of palm leaves
Lighter
Bare feet or flip-flops

All other belongings are confiscated and stored in cooperative warehouses. Everything belongs to Angkar...

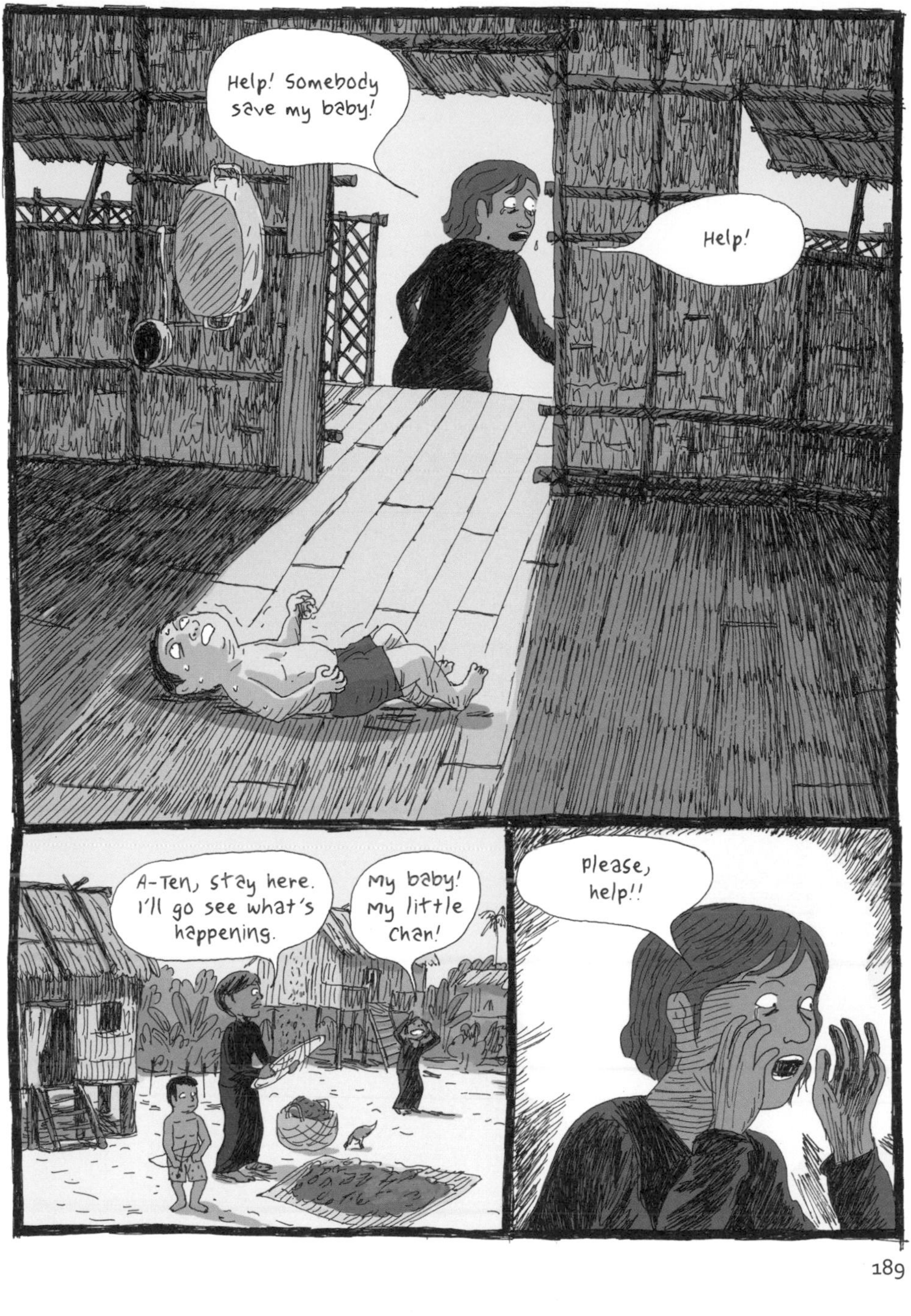
Help! Somebody save my baby!
Help!
A-Ten, stay here. I'll go see what's happening.
My baby! My little Chan!
Please, help!!

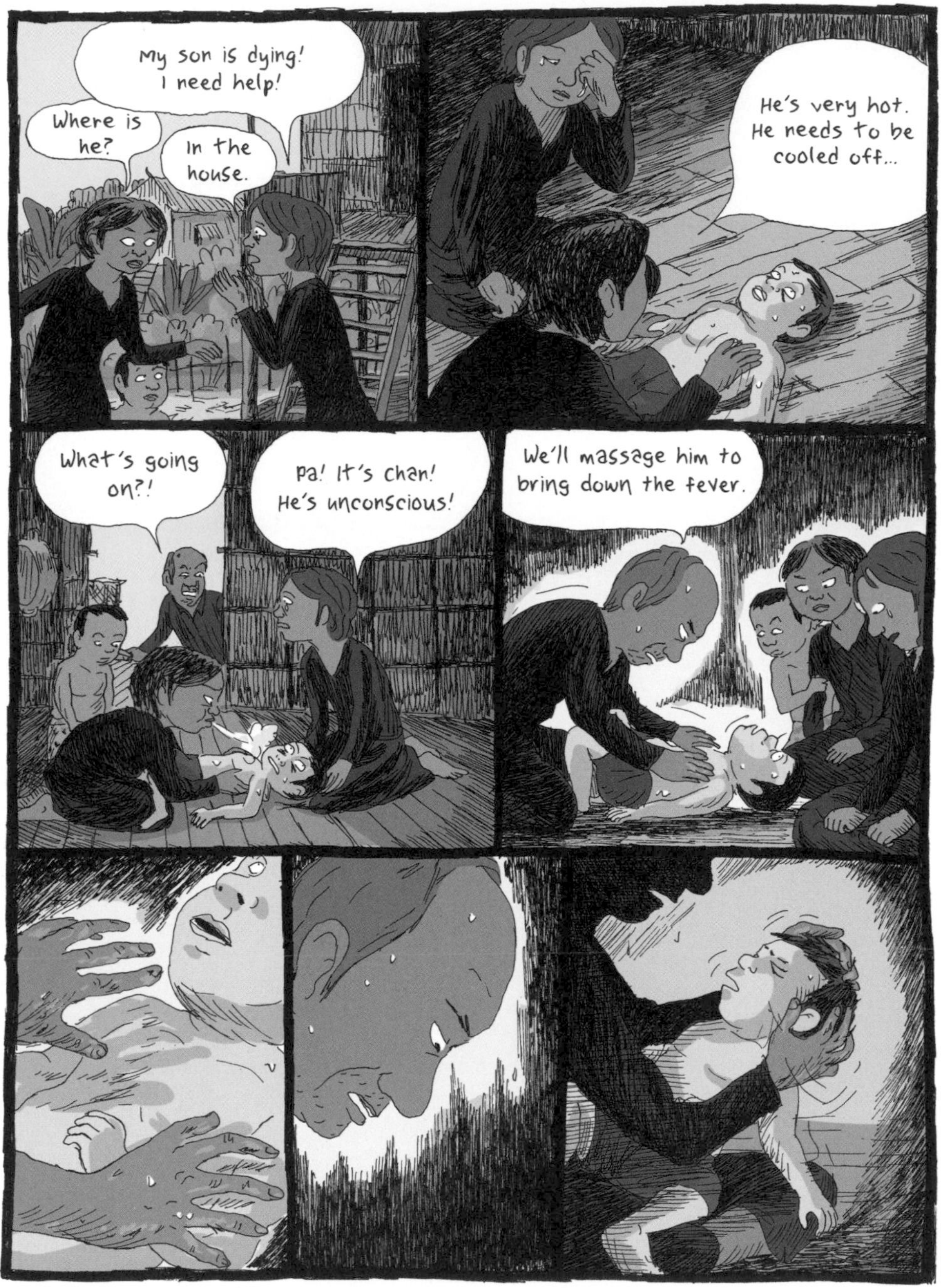
My son is dying! I need help!
Where is he?
In the house.
He's very hot. He needs to be cooled off...
What's going on?!
Pa! It's Chan! He's unconscious!
We'll massage him to bring down the fever.

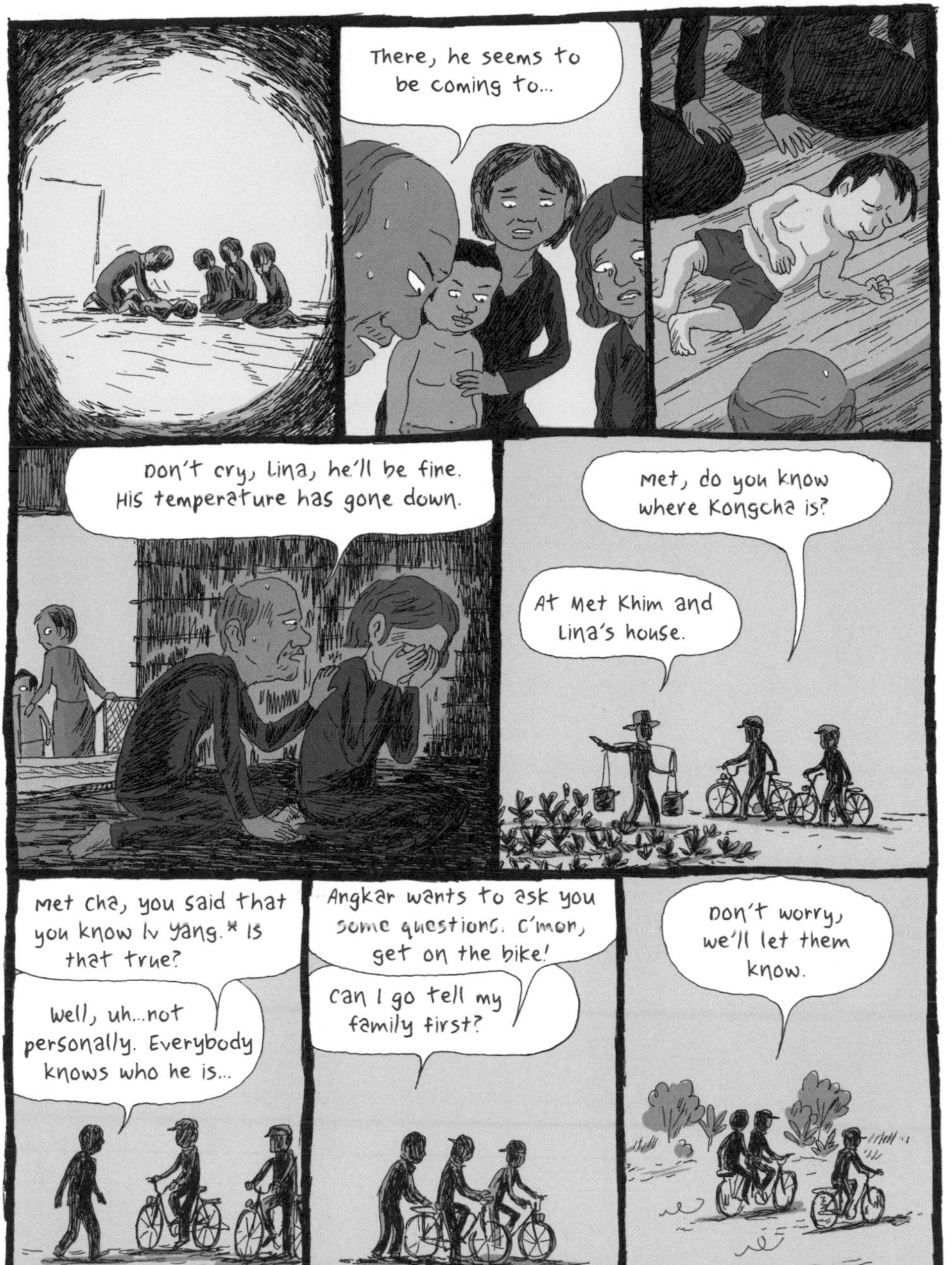
There, he seems to be coming to...
Don't cry, Lina, he'll be fine. His temperature has gone down.
Met, do you know where Kongcha is?
At Met Khim and Lina's house.
Met Cha, you said that you know Iv Yang.* Is that true?
Well, uh...not personally. Everybody knows who he is...
Angkar wants to ask you some questions. C'mon, get on the bike!
Can I go tell my family first?
Don't worry, we'll let them know.

*Iv Yang: minister of Finance under the old regime

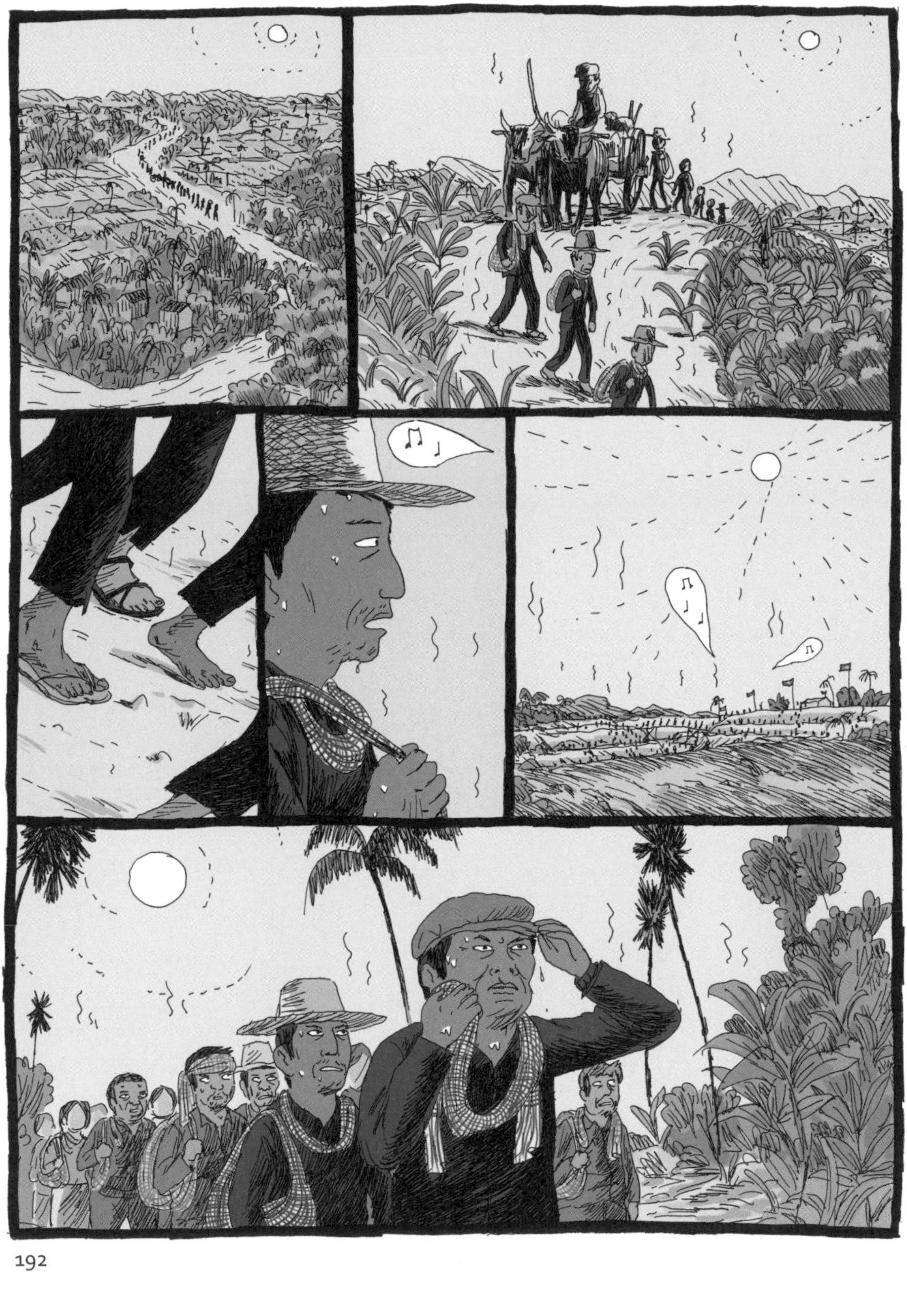

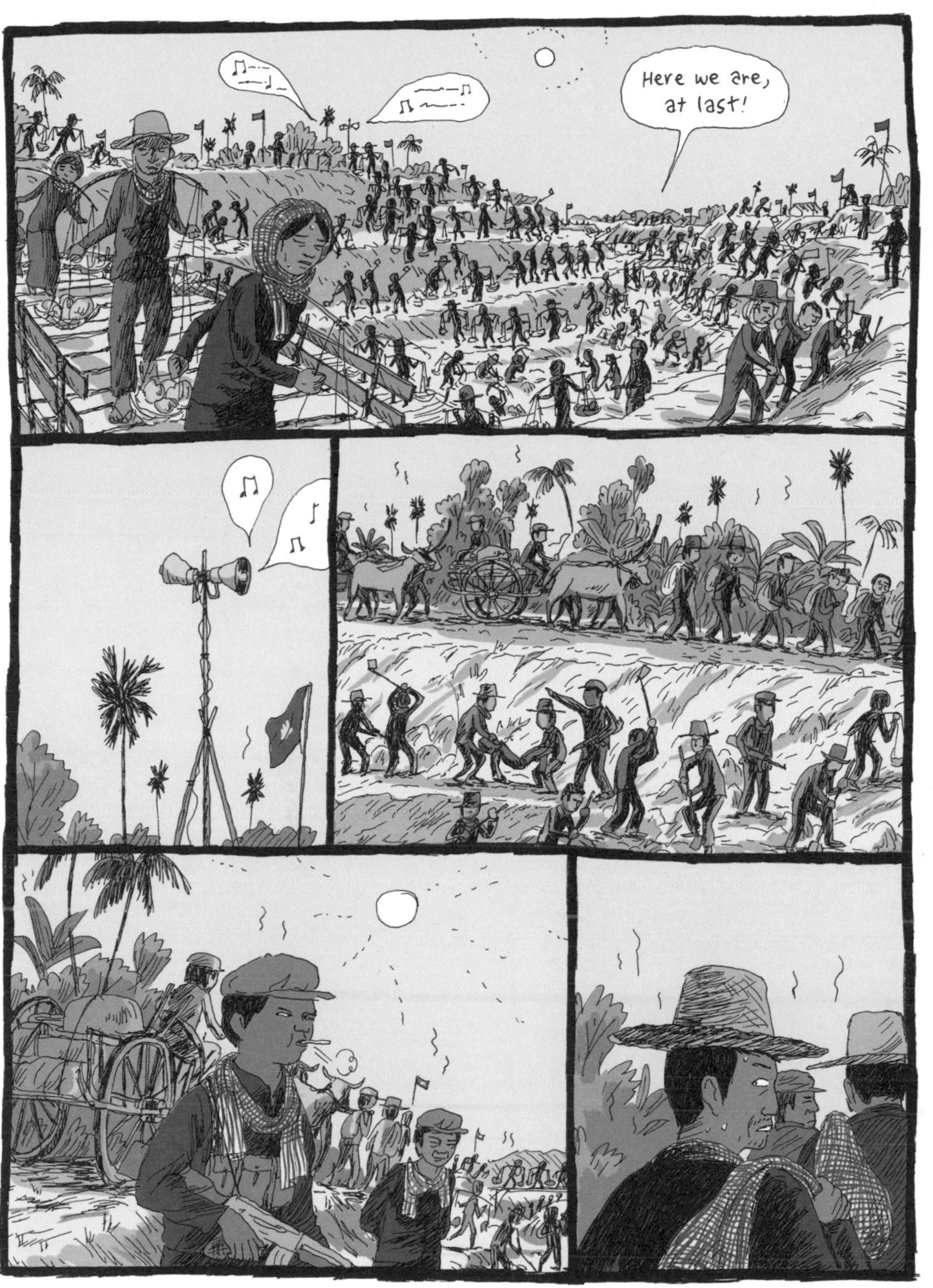
Here we are, at last!

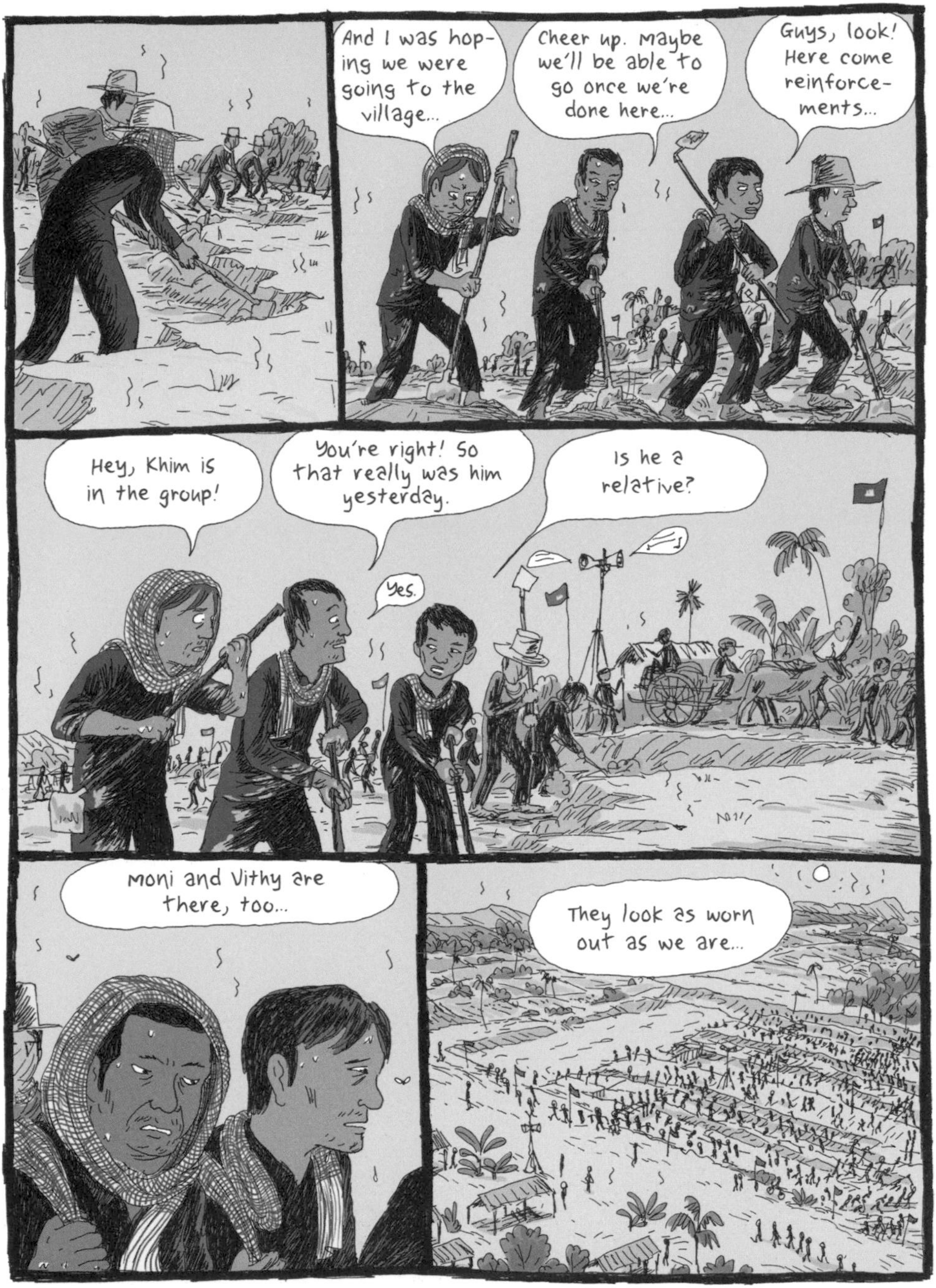
And I was hoping we were going to the village...
Cheer up. Maybe we'll be able to go once we're done here...
Guys, look! Here come reinforcements...
Hey, Khim is in the group!
You're right! So that really was him yesterday.
Yes.
Is he a relative?
Moni and Vithy are there, too...
They look as worn out as we are...

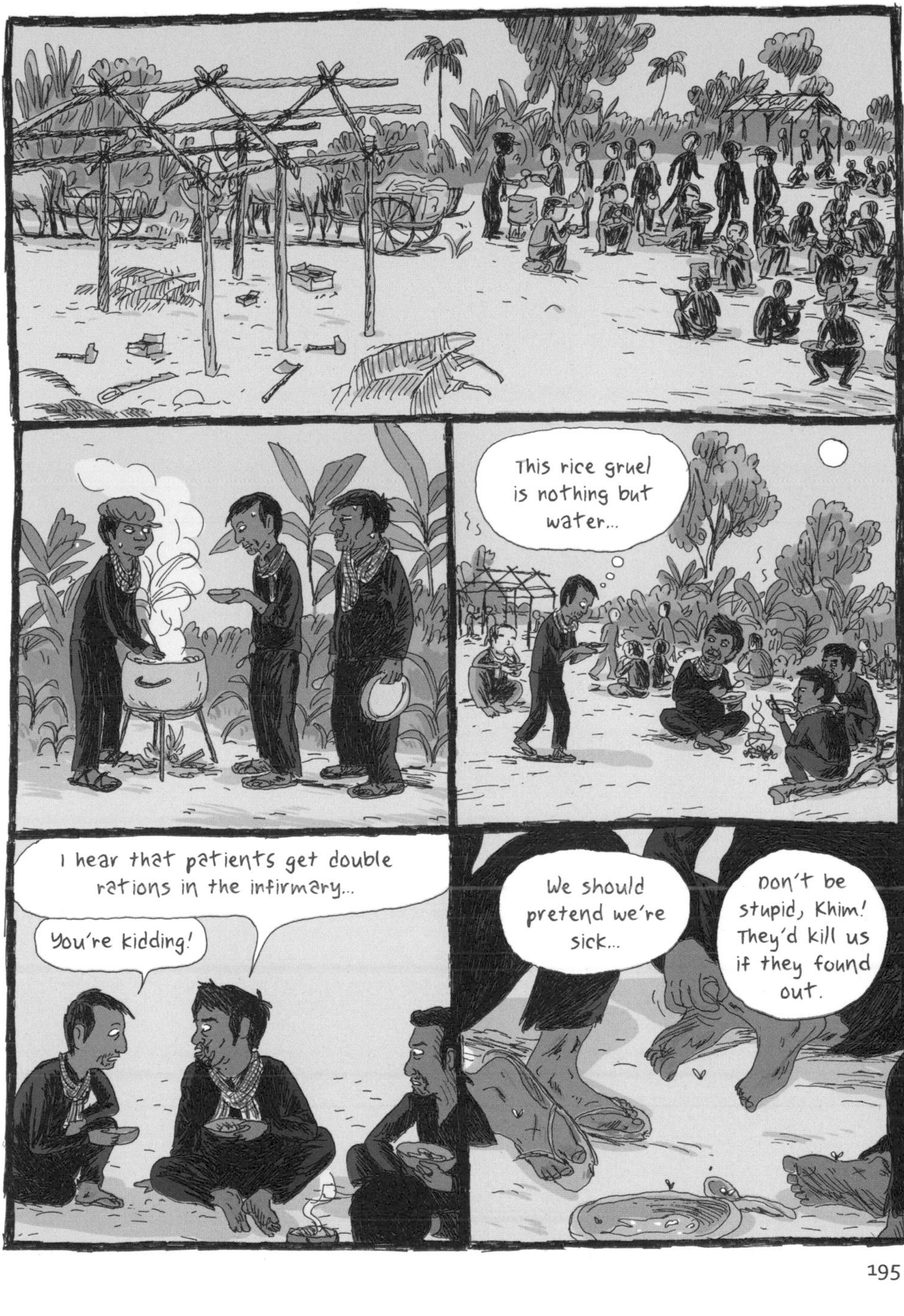
This rice gruel is nothing but water...
I hear that patients get double rations in the infirmary...
You're kidding!
We should pretend we're sick...
Don't be stupid, Khim! They'd kill us if they found out.

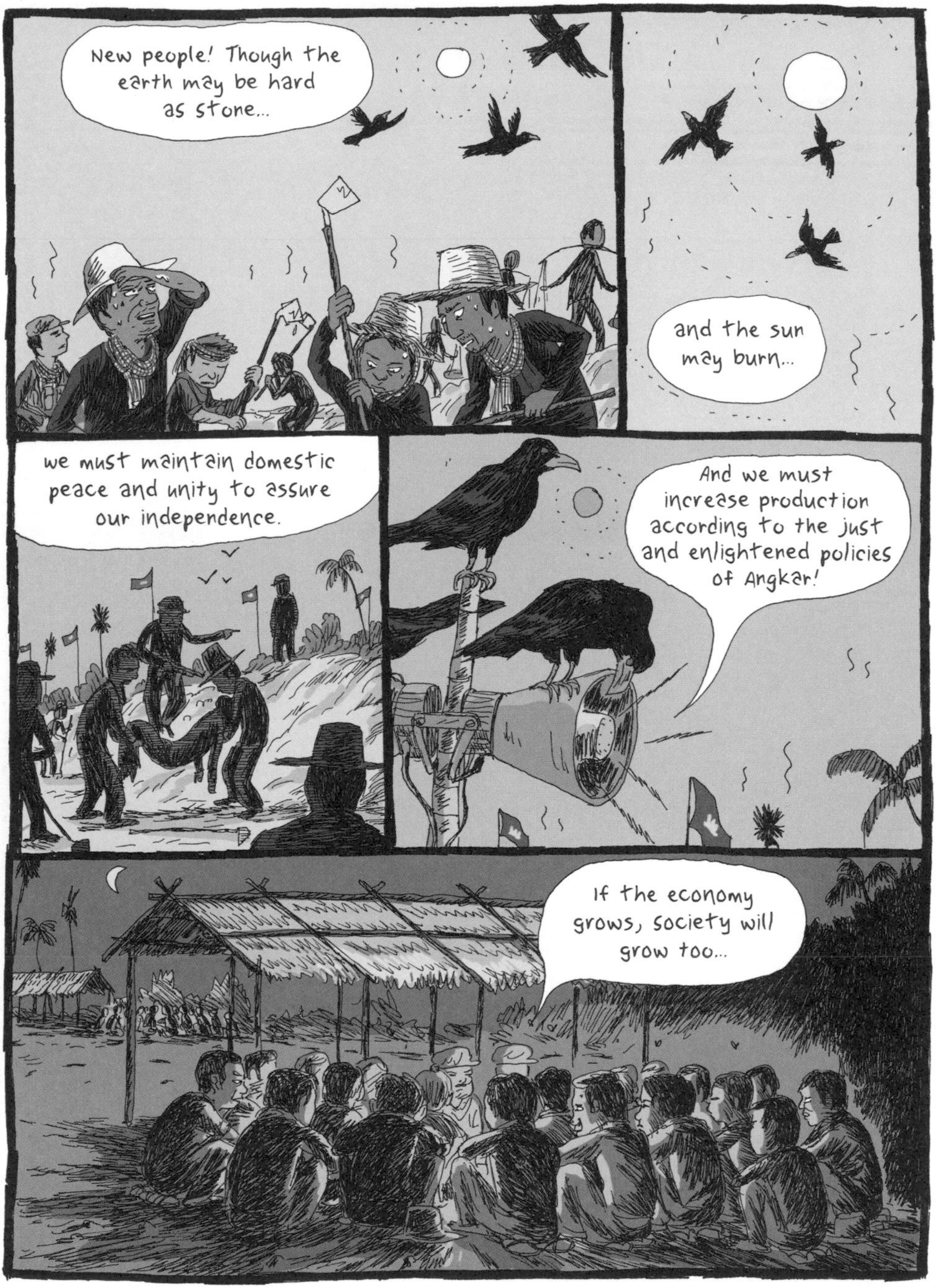
New people! Though the earth may be hard as stone...
and the sun may burn...
we must maintain domestic peace and unity to assure our independence.
And we must increase production according to the just and enlightened policies of Angkar!
If the economy grows, society will grow too...

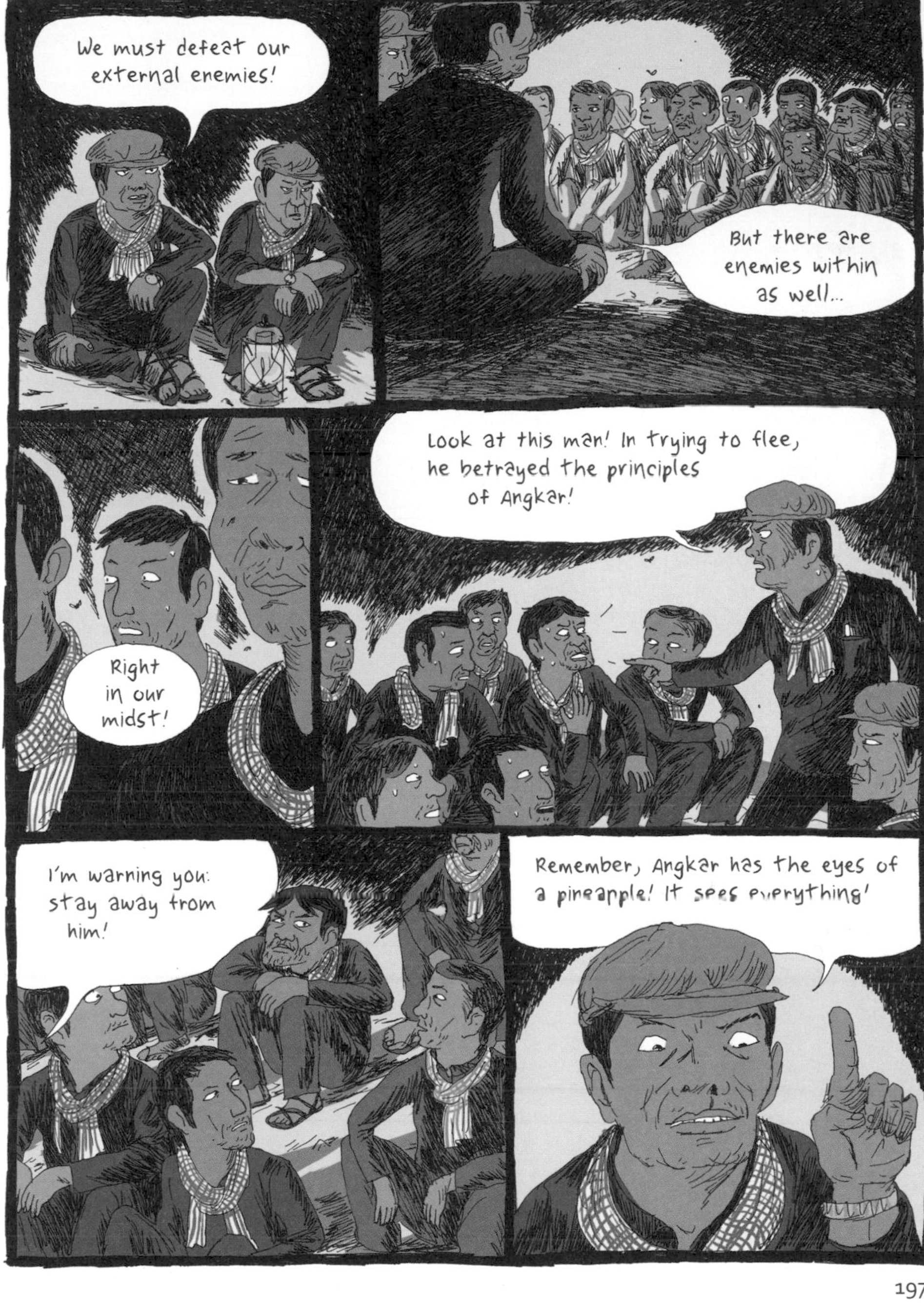
We must defeat our external enemies!
But there are enemies within as well...
Right in our midst!
Look at this man! In trying to flee, he betrayed the principles of Angkar!
I'm warning you: stay away from him!
Remember, Angkar has the eyes of a pineapple! It sees everything!

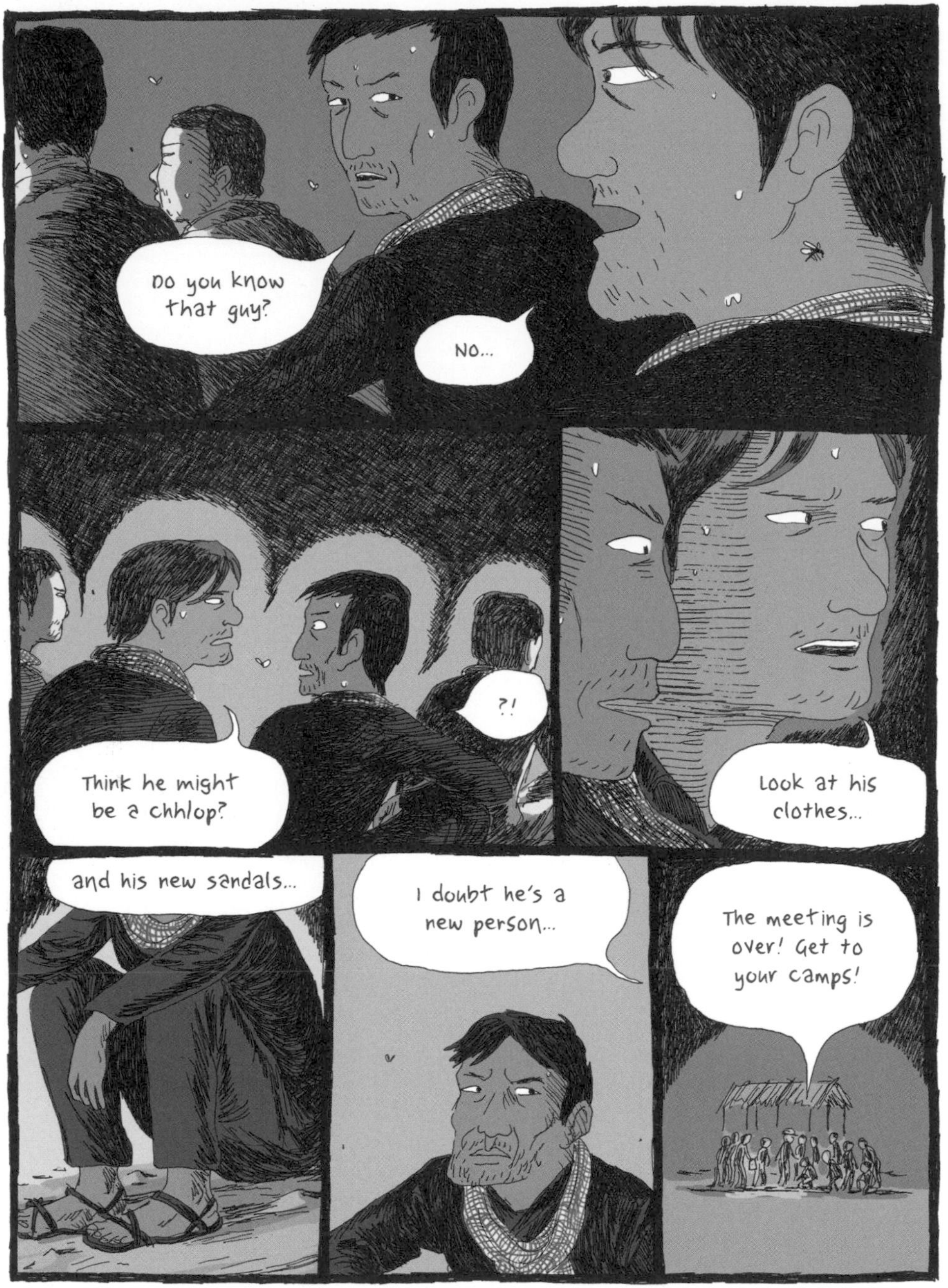
Do you know that guy?
No...
Think he might be a chhlop?
?!
Look at his clothes...
and his new sandals...
I doubt he's a new person...
The meeting is over! Get to your camps!

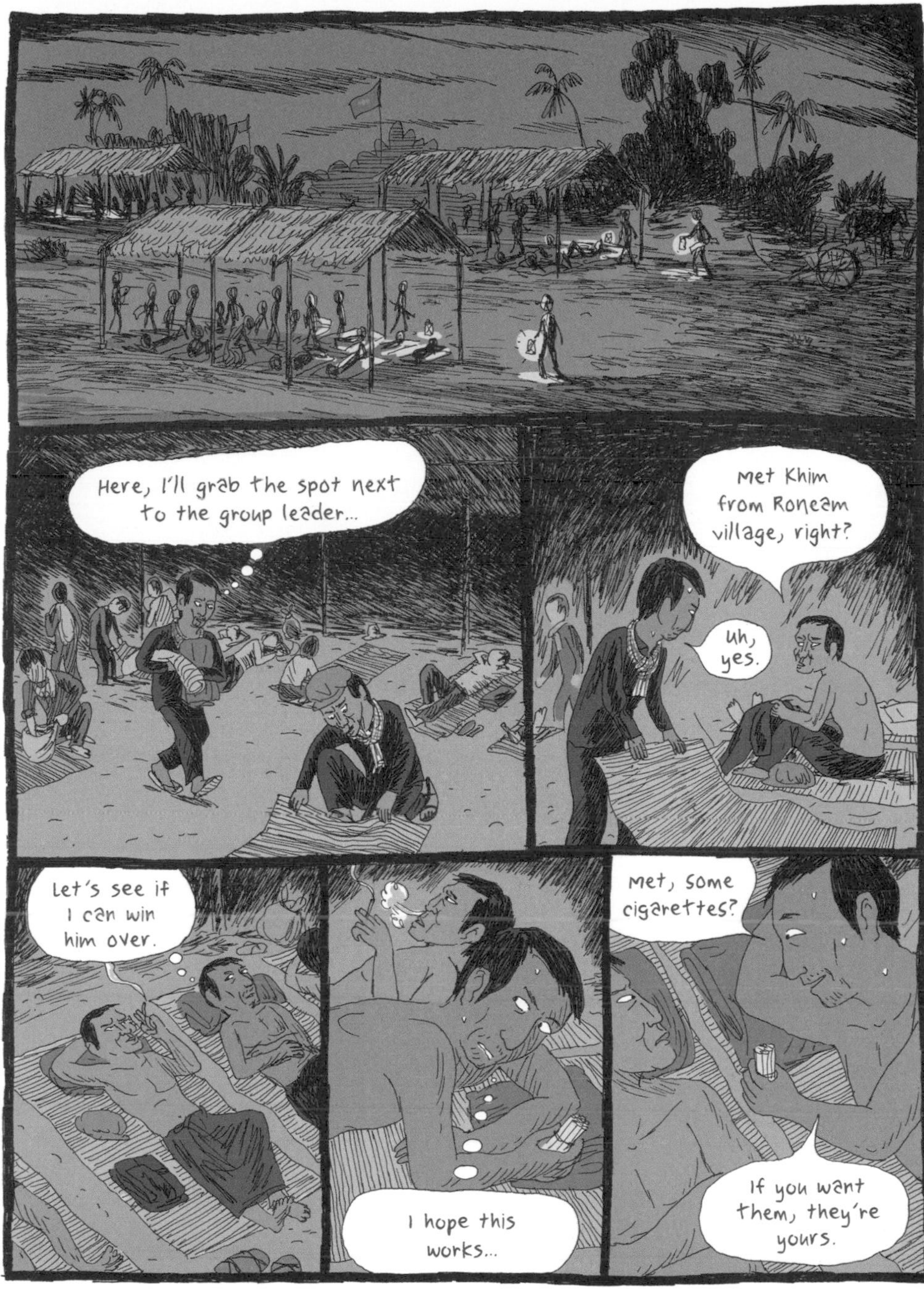
Here, I'll grab the spot next to the group leader...
Met Khim from Roneam village, right?
Uh, yes.
Let's see if I can win him over.
I hope this works...
Met, some cigarettes?
If you want them, they're yours.

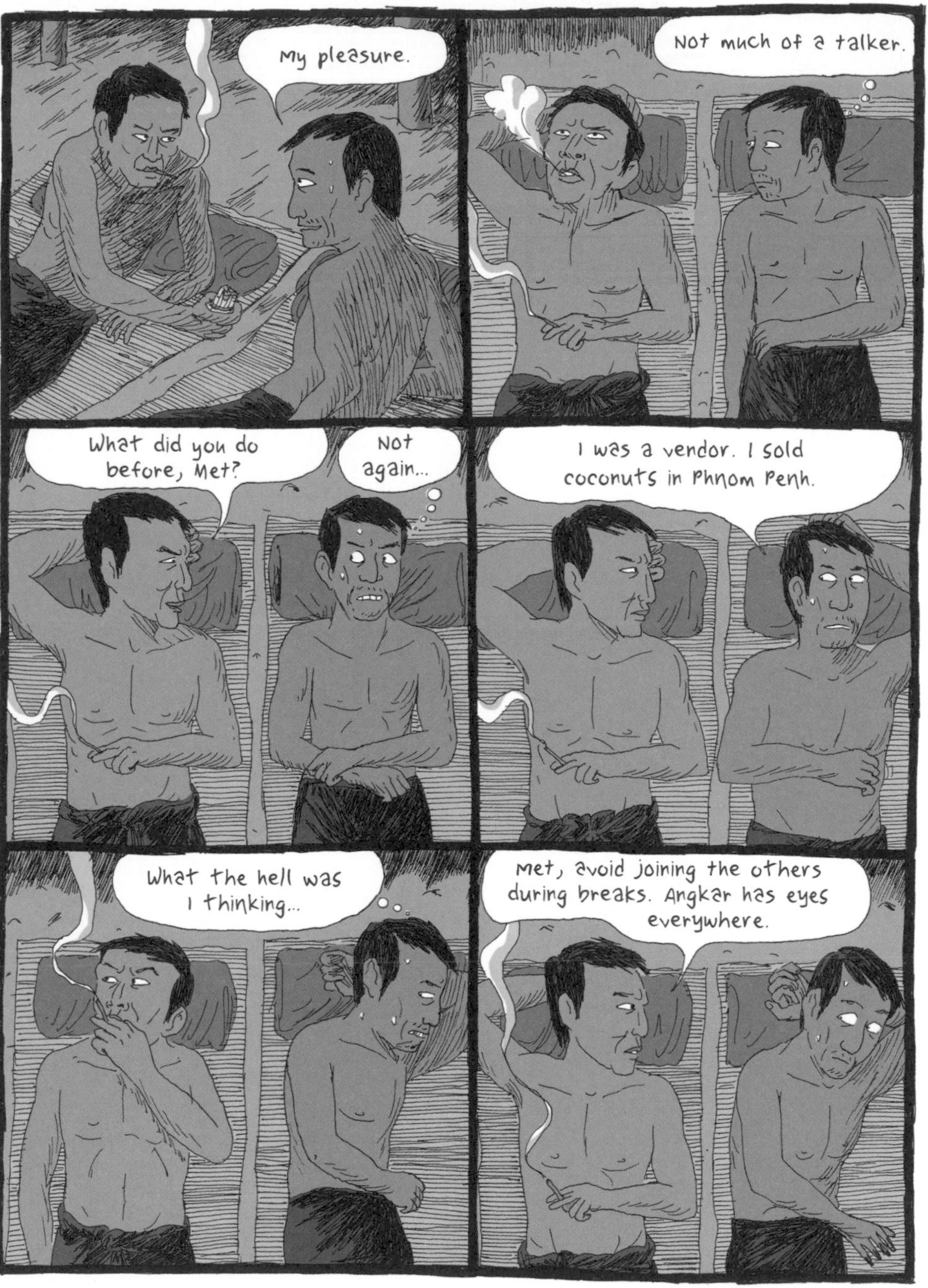
My pleasure.
Not much of a talker.
What did you do before, Met?
Not again...
I was a vendor. I sold coconuts in Phnom Penh.
What the hell was I thinking...
Met, avoid joining the others during breaks. Angkar has eyes everywhere.

chapter 12

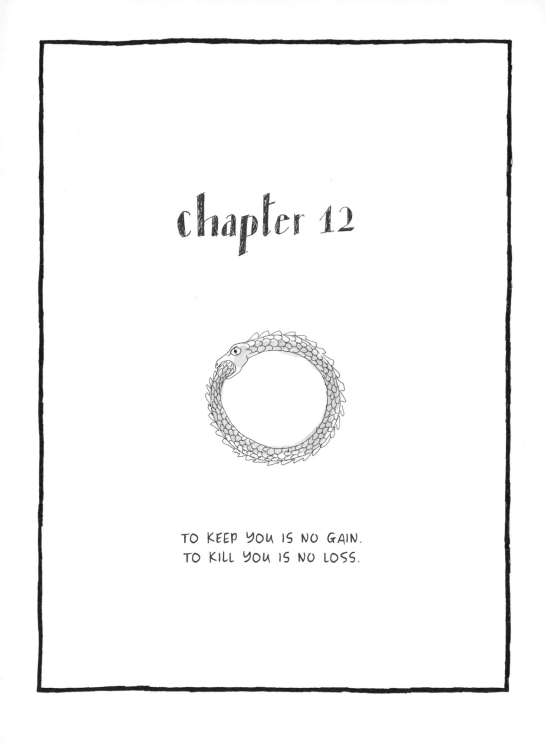

TO KEEP YOU IS NO GAIN.
TO KILL YOU IS NO LOSS.

A DAY IN THE LIFE OF THE NEW PEOPLE...

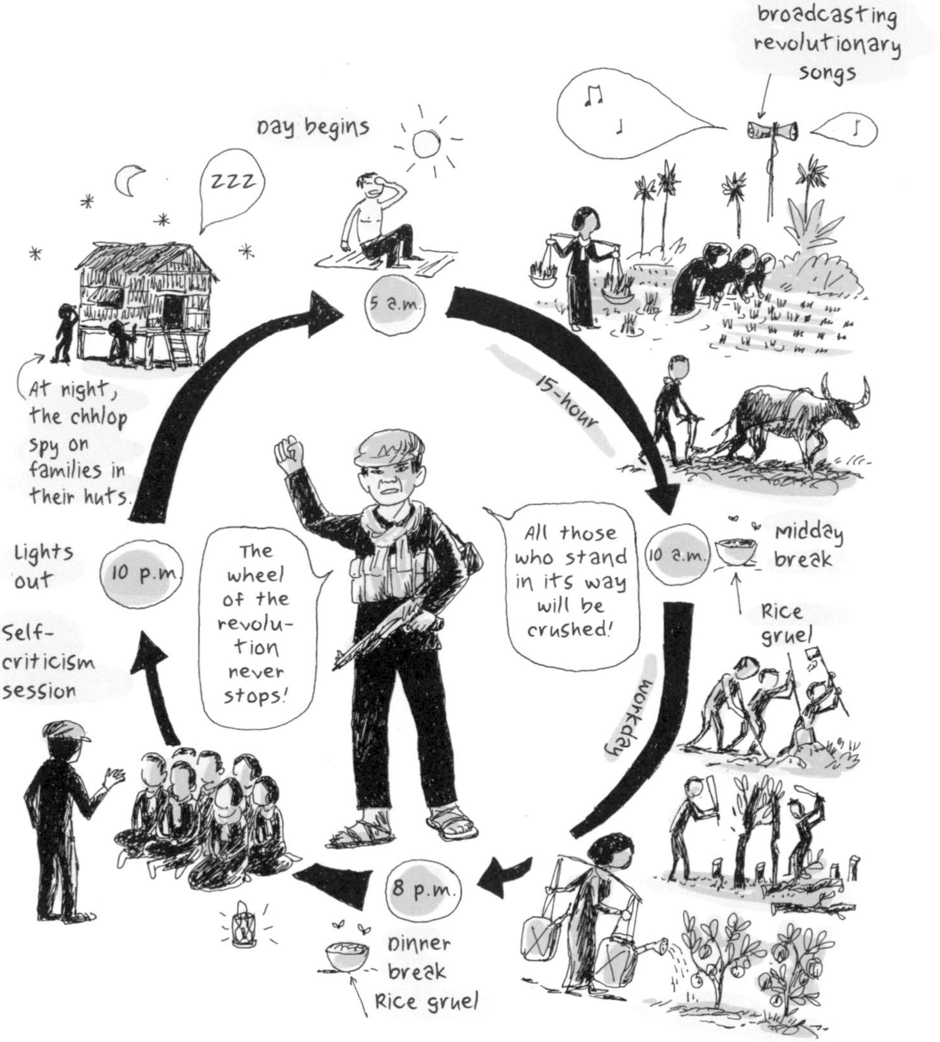
Khmer radio broadcasting revolutionary songs
Day begins
5 a.m.
15-hour
workday
10 a.m.
Midday break
Rice gruel
8 p.m.
Dinner break
Rice gruel
Self-criticism session
10 p.m.
Lights out
At night, the chhlop spy on families in their huts.
zzz
The wheel of the revolution never stops!
All those who stand in its way will be crushed!

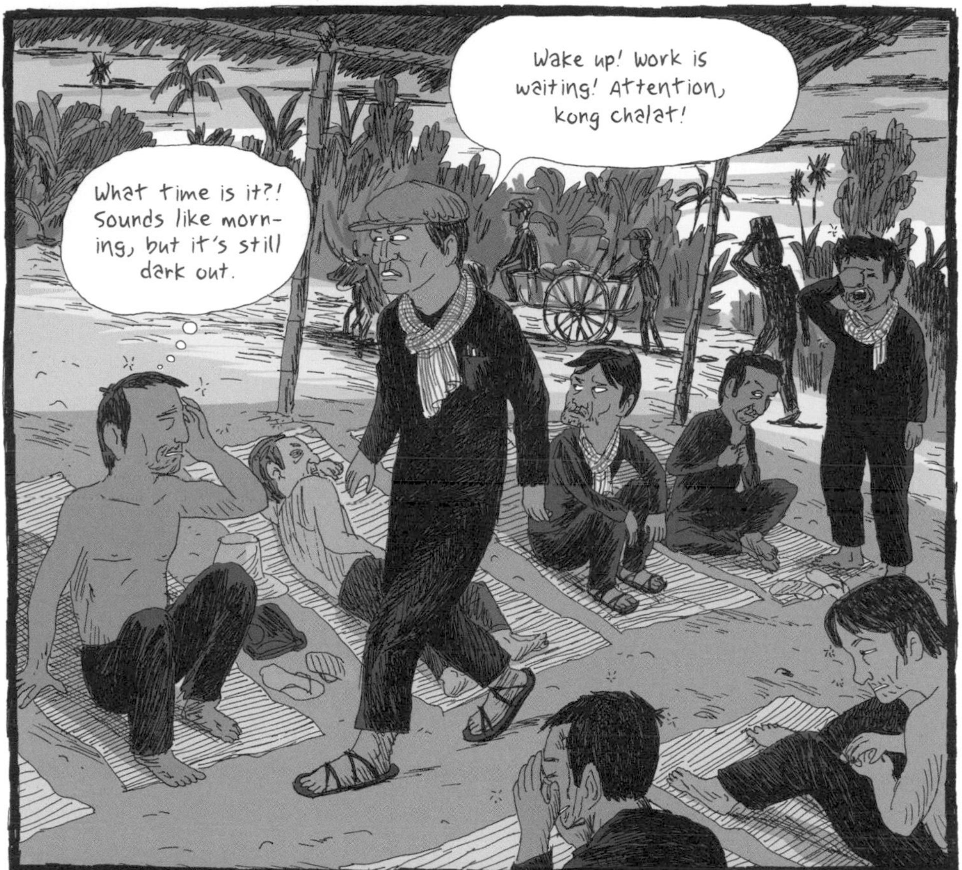
Wake up! Work is waiting! Attention, kong chalat!
What time is it?! Sounds like morning, but it's still dark out.

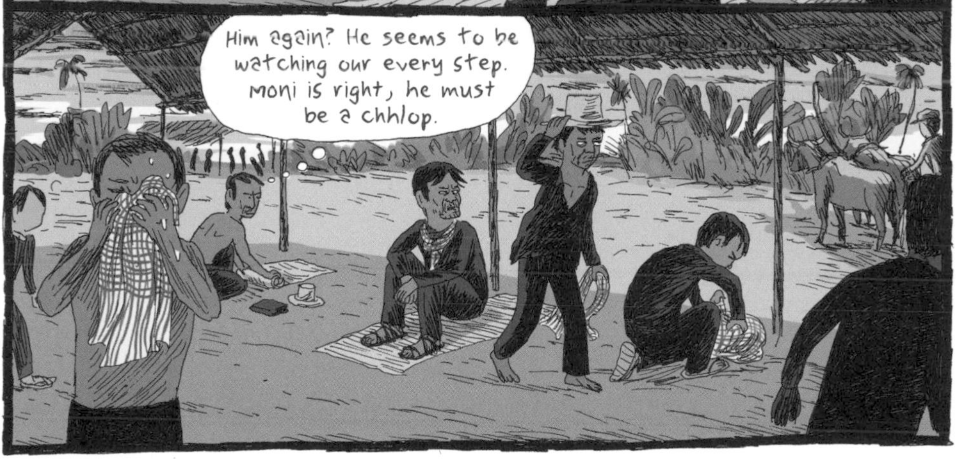
Him again? He seems to be watching our every step. Moni is right, he must be a chhlop.

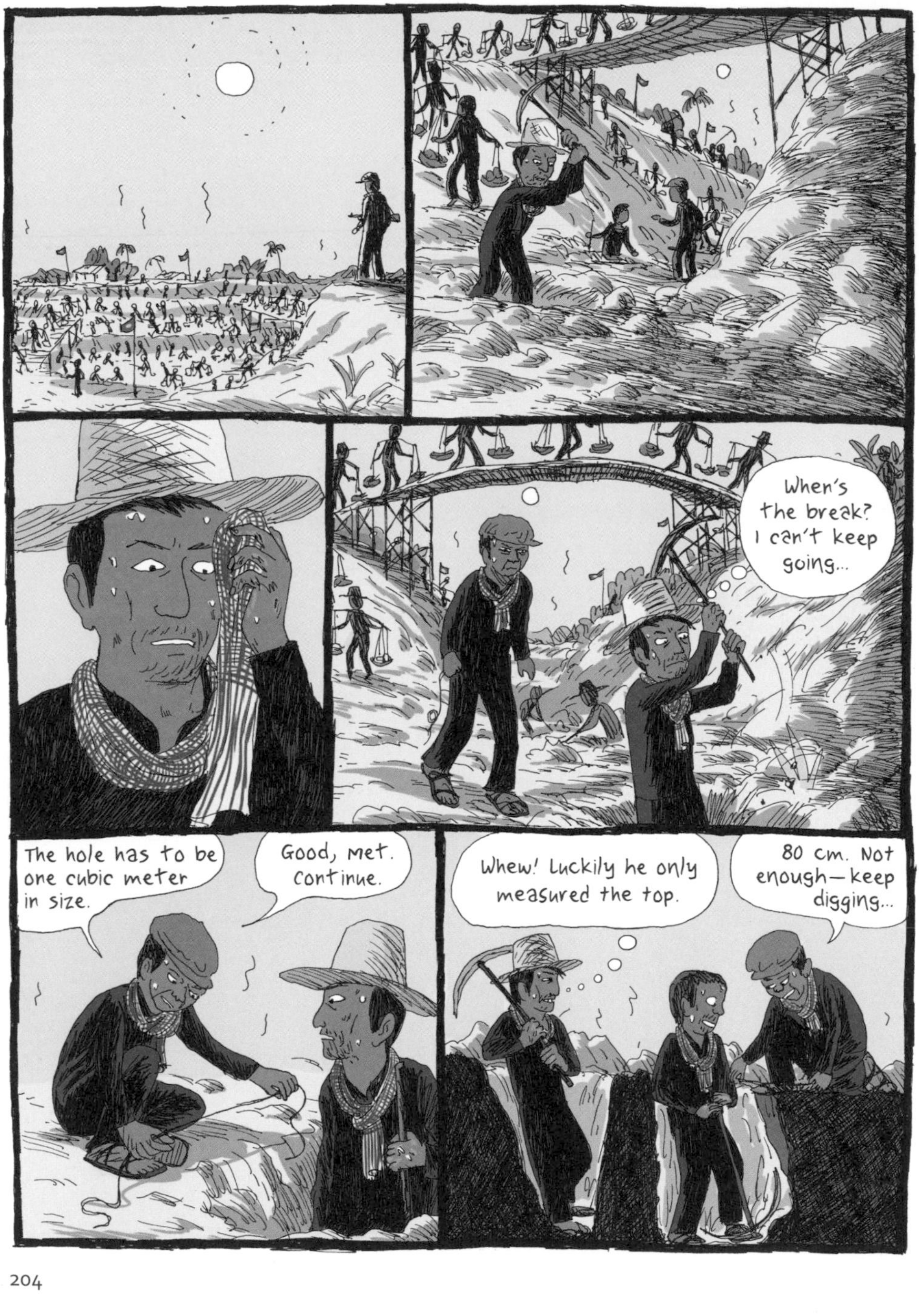
When's the break? I can't keep going...
The hole has to be one cubic meter in size.
Good, met. Continue.
Whew! Luckily he only measured the top.
80 cm. Not enough—keep digging...

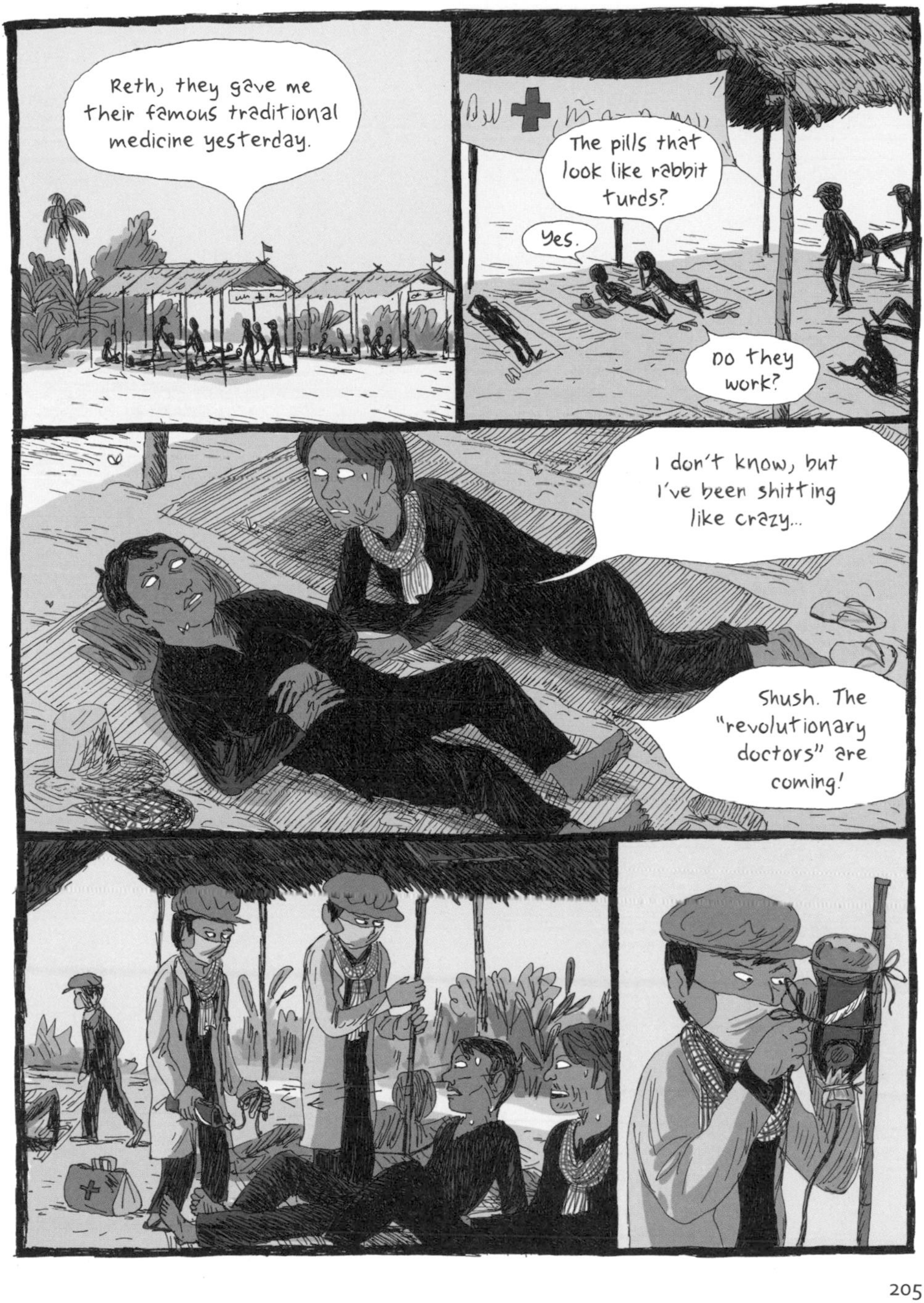
Reth, they gave me their famous traditional medicine yesterday.
The pills that look like rabbit turds?
Yes.
Do they work?
I don't know, but I've been shitting like crazy...
Shush. The "revolutionary doctors" are coming!

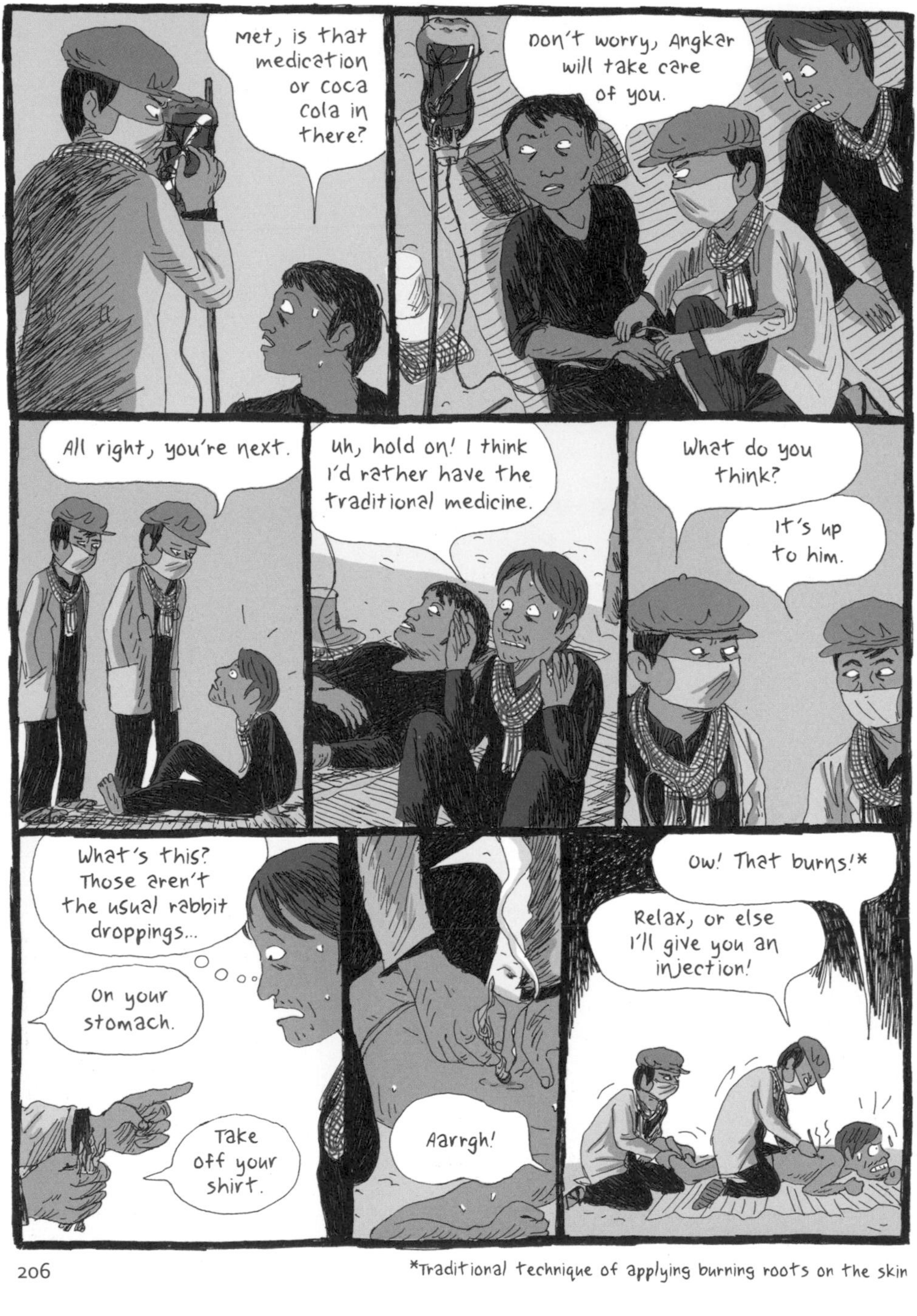
Met, is that medication or coca cola in there?
Don't worry, Angkar will take care of you.
All right, you're next.
Uh, hold on! I think I'd rather have the traditional medicine.
What do you think?
It's up to him.
What's this? Those aren't the usual rabbit droppings...
On your stomach.
Take off your shirt.
Aarrgh!
Ow! That burns!*
Relax, or else I'll give you an injection!

*Traditional technique of applying burning roots on the skin

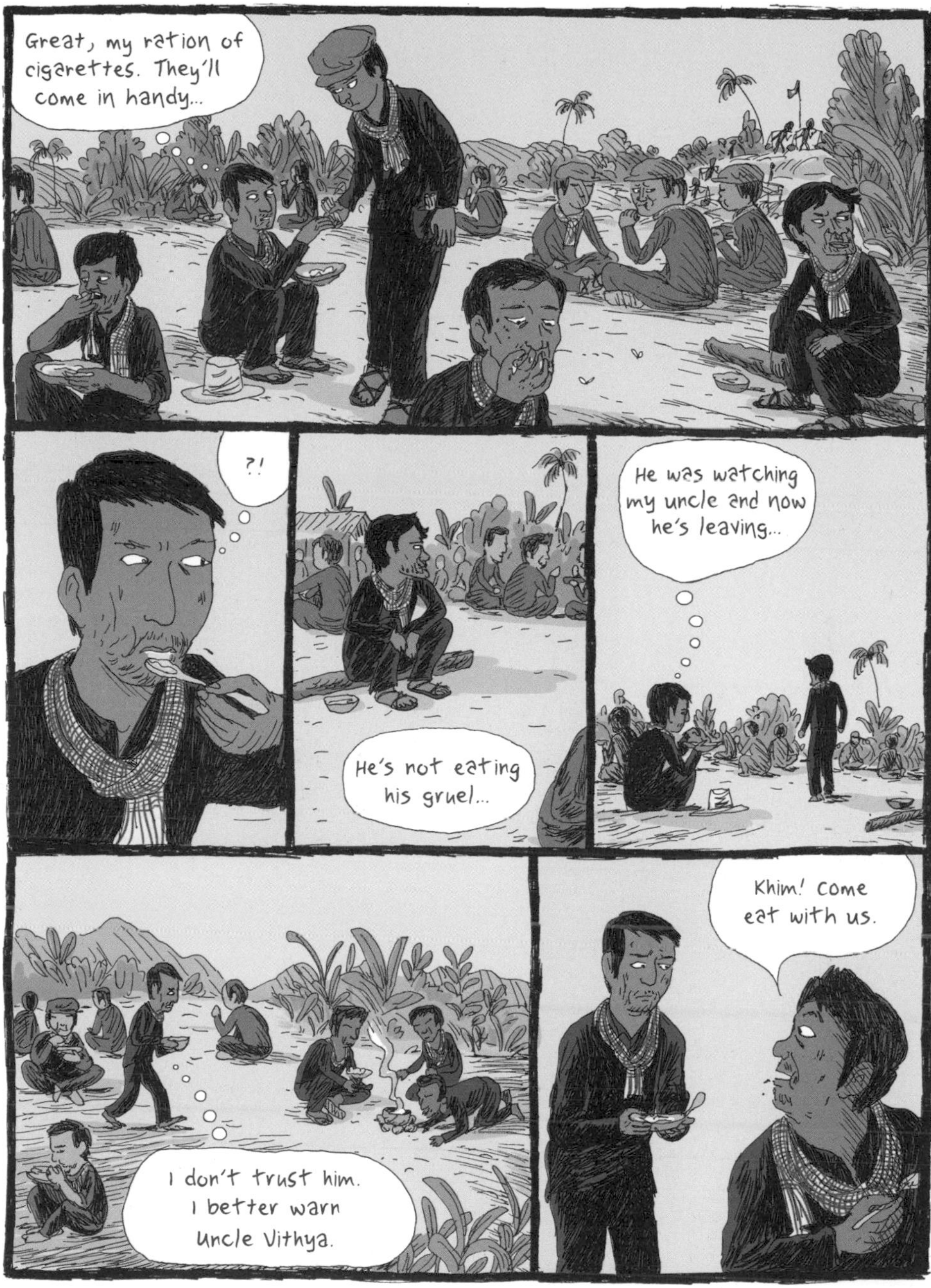
Great, my ration of cigarettes. They'll come in handy...
?!
He's not eating his gruel...
He was watching my uncle and now he's leaving...
I don't trust him. I better warn Uncle Vithya.
Khim! Come eat with us.

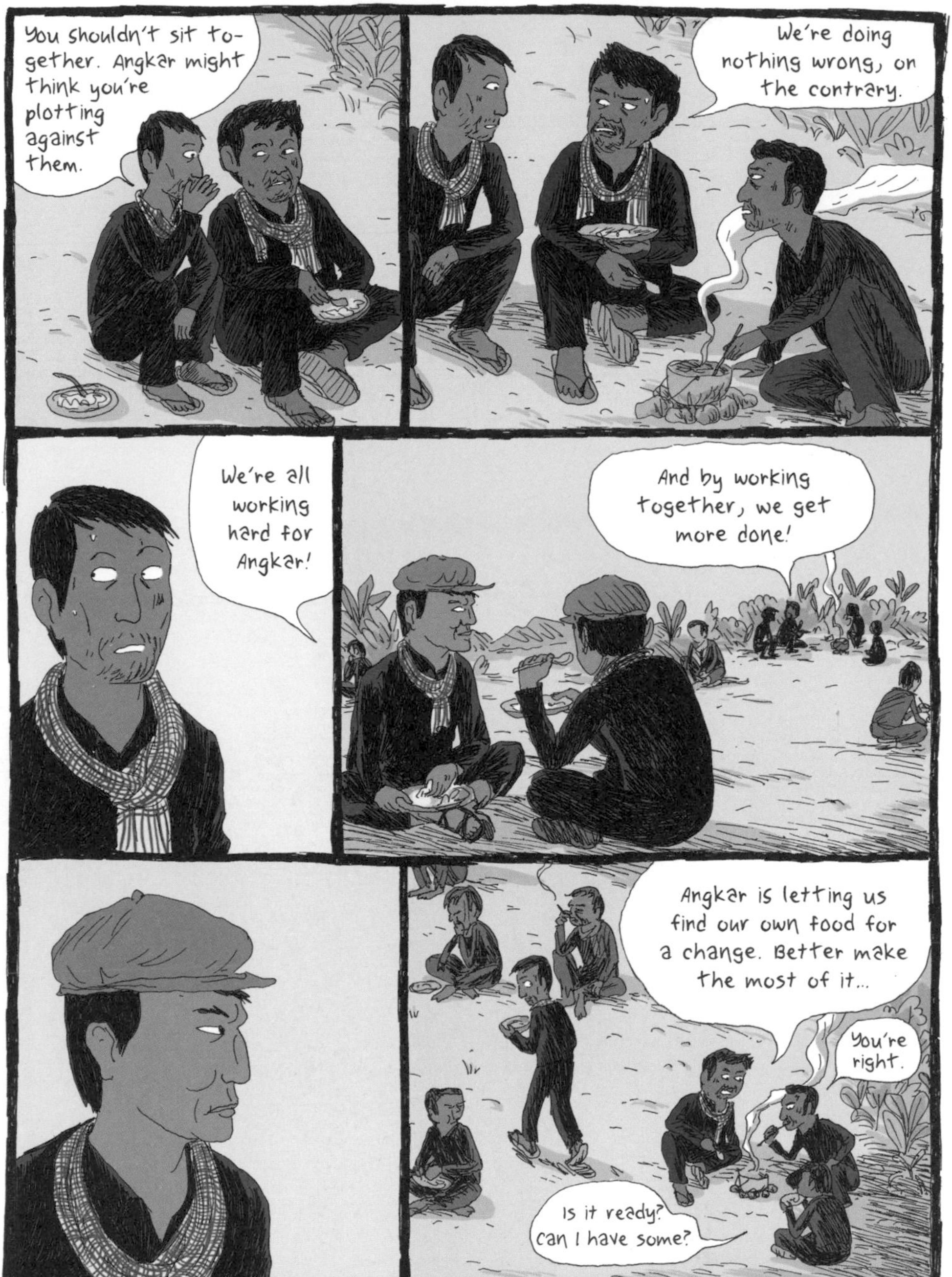

You shouldn't sit together. Angkar might think you're plotting against them.
We're doing nothing wrong, on the contrary.
We're all working hard for Angkar!
And by working together, we get more done!
Angkar is letting us find our own food for a change. Better make the most of it...
You're right.
Is it ready? Can I have some?

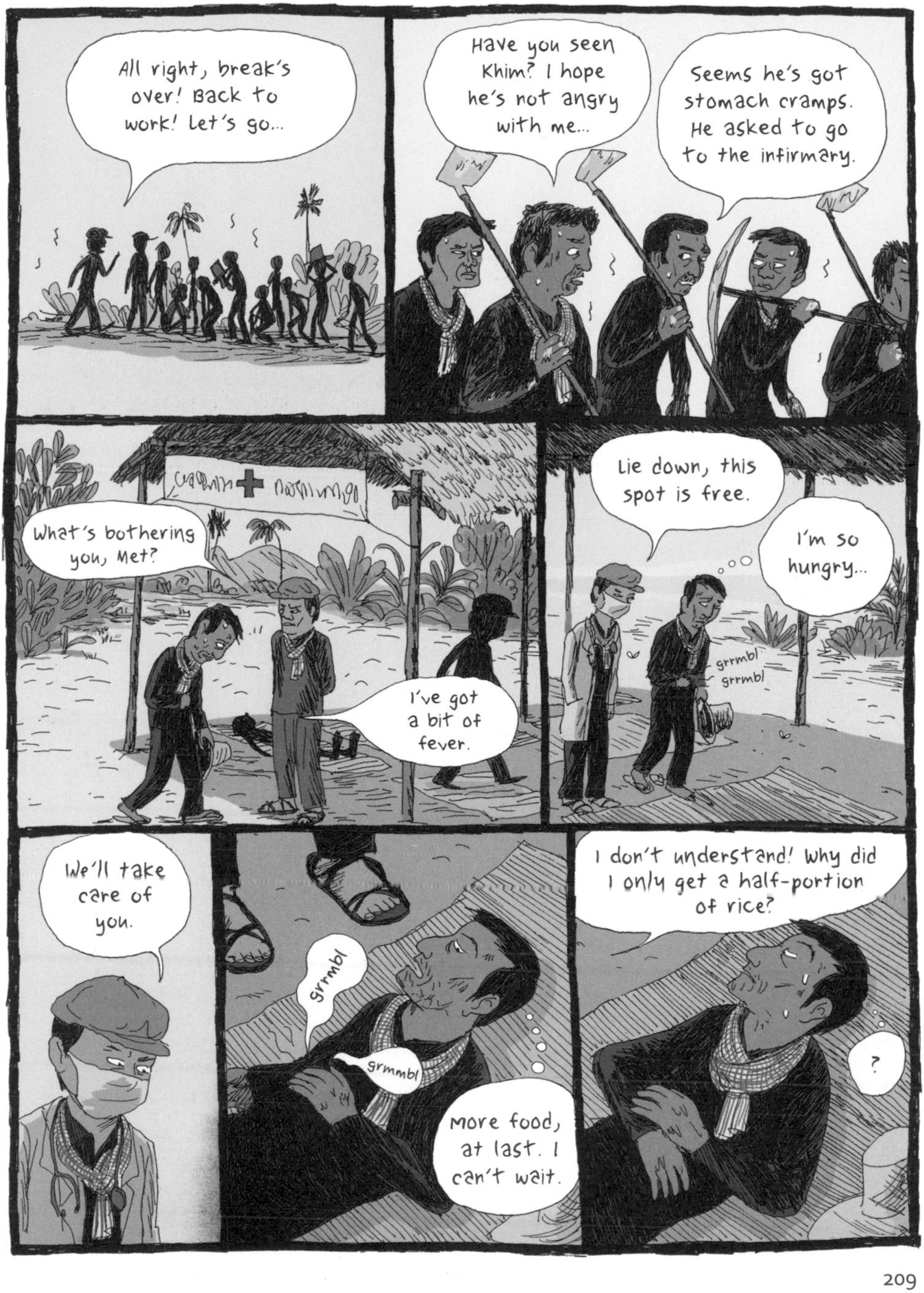

All right, break's over! Back to work! Let's go...
Have you seen Khim? I hope he's not angry with me...
Seems he's got stomach cramps. He asked to go to the infirmary.
What's bothering you, Met?
I've got a bit of fever.
Lie down, this spot is free.
I'm so hungry...
grrmbl grrmbl
We'll take care of you.
grrmbl
grmmbl
More food, at last. I can't wait.
I don't understand! Why did I only get a half-portion of rice?
?

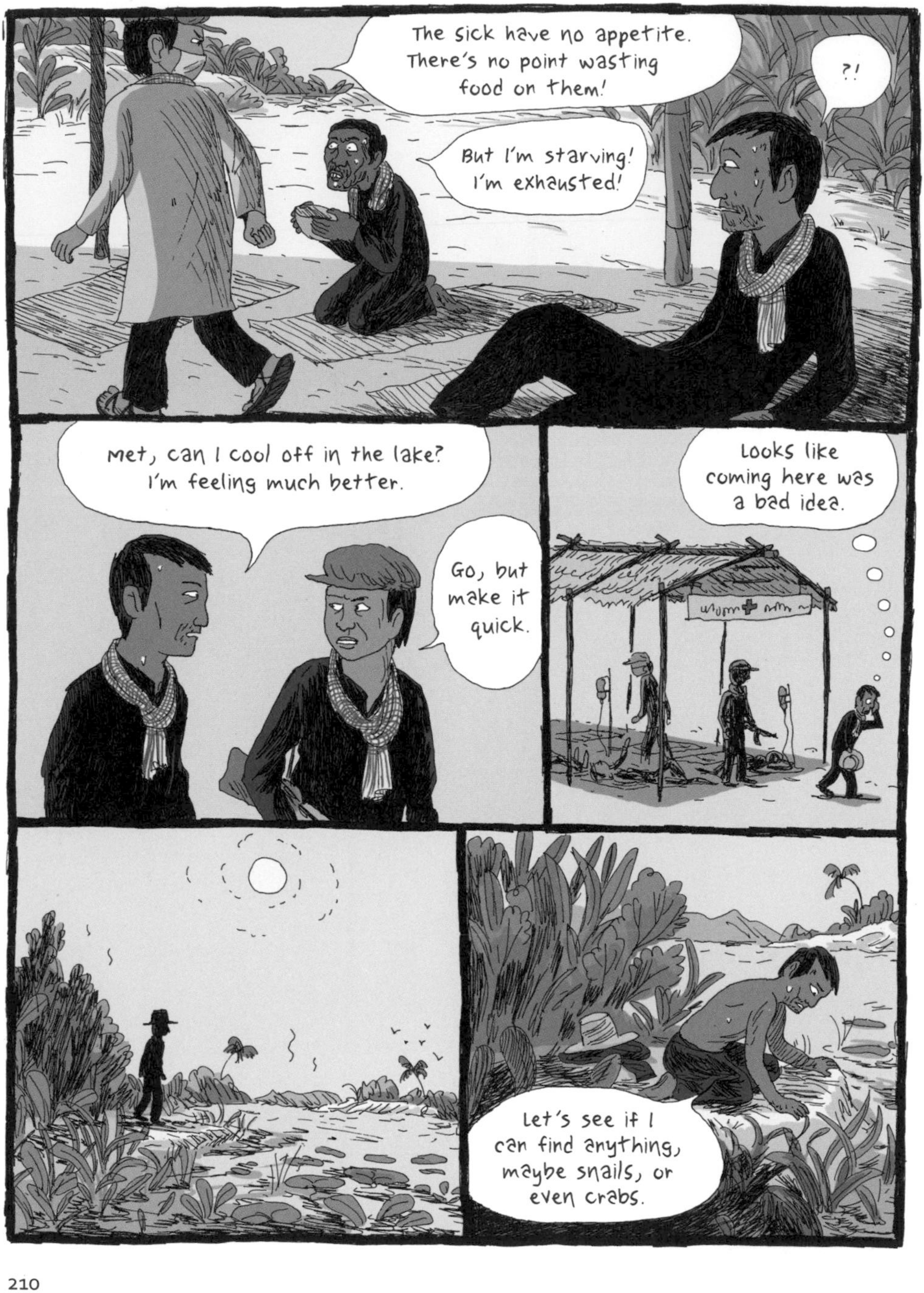
The sick have no appetite. There's no point wasting food on them!
But I'm starving! I'm exhausted!
?!
Met, can I cool off in the lake? I'm feeling much better.
Go, but make it quick.
Looks like coming here was a bad idea.
Let's see if I can find anything, maybe snails, or even crabs.

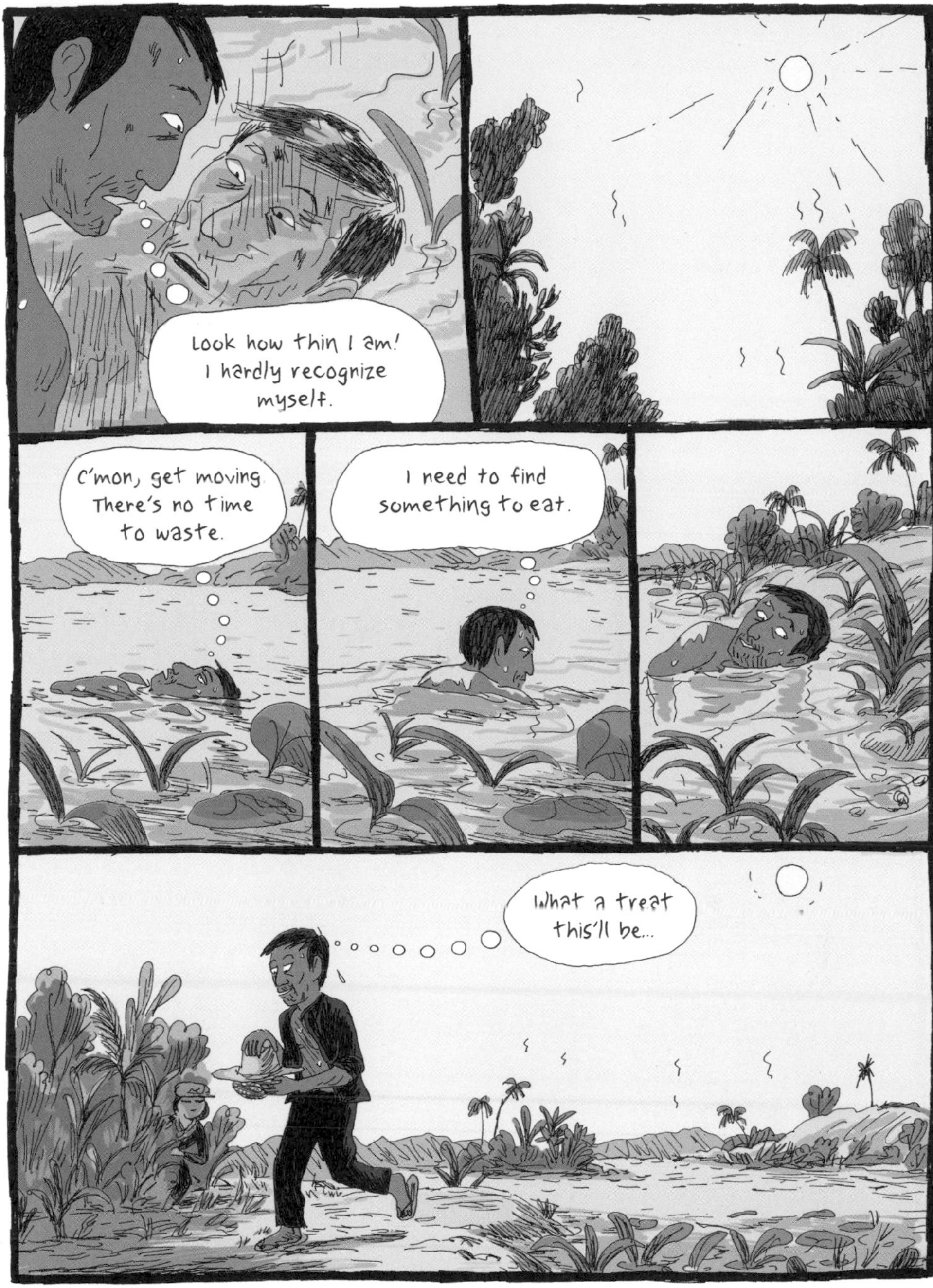

Look how thin I am! I hardly recognize myself.
C'mon, get moving. There's no time to waste.
I need to find something to eat.
What a treat this'll be...

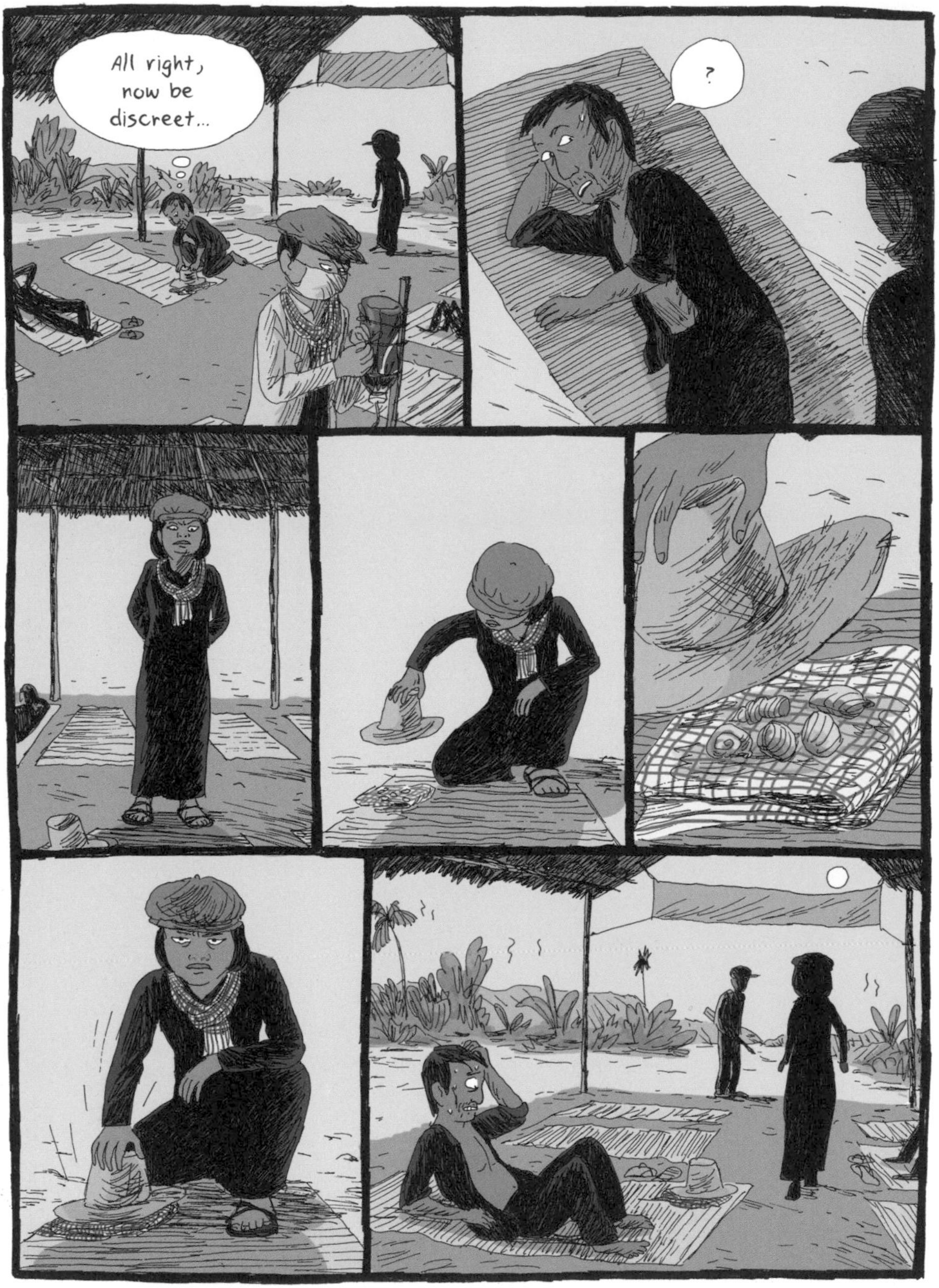
All right, now be discreet...
?

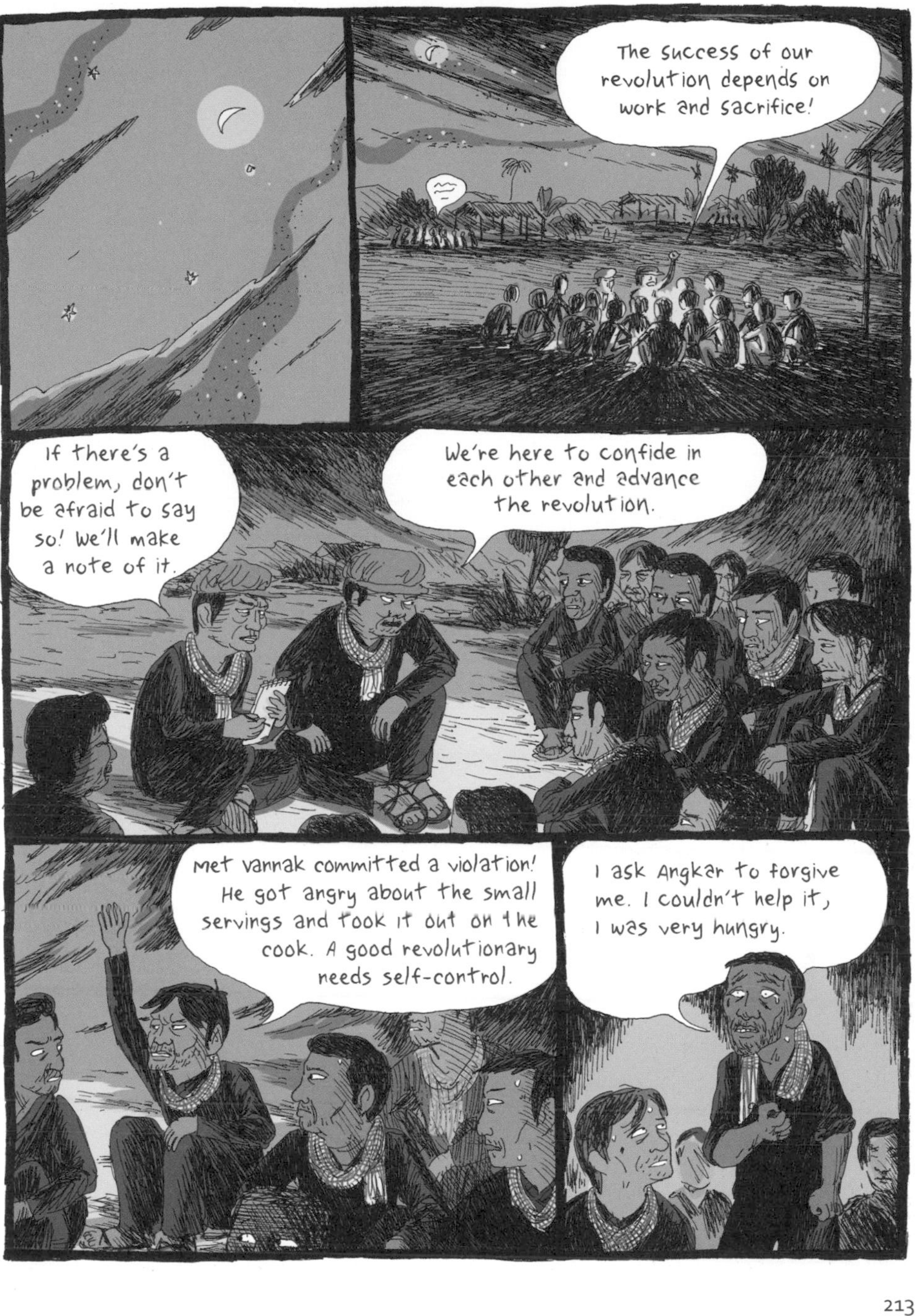
The success of our revolution depends on work and sacrifice!
If there's a problem, don't be afraid to say so! We'll make a note of it.
We're here to confide in each other and advance the revolution.
Met Vannak committed a violation! He got angry about the small servings and took it out on the cook. A good revolutionary needs self-control.
I ask Angkar to forgive me. I couldn't help it, I was very hungry.

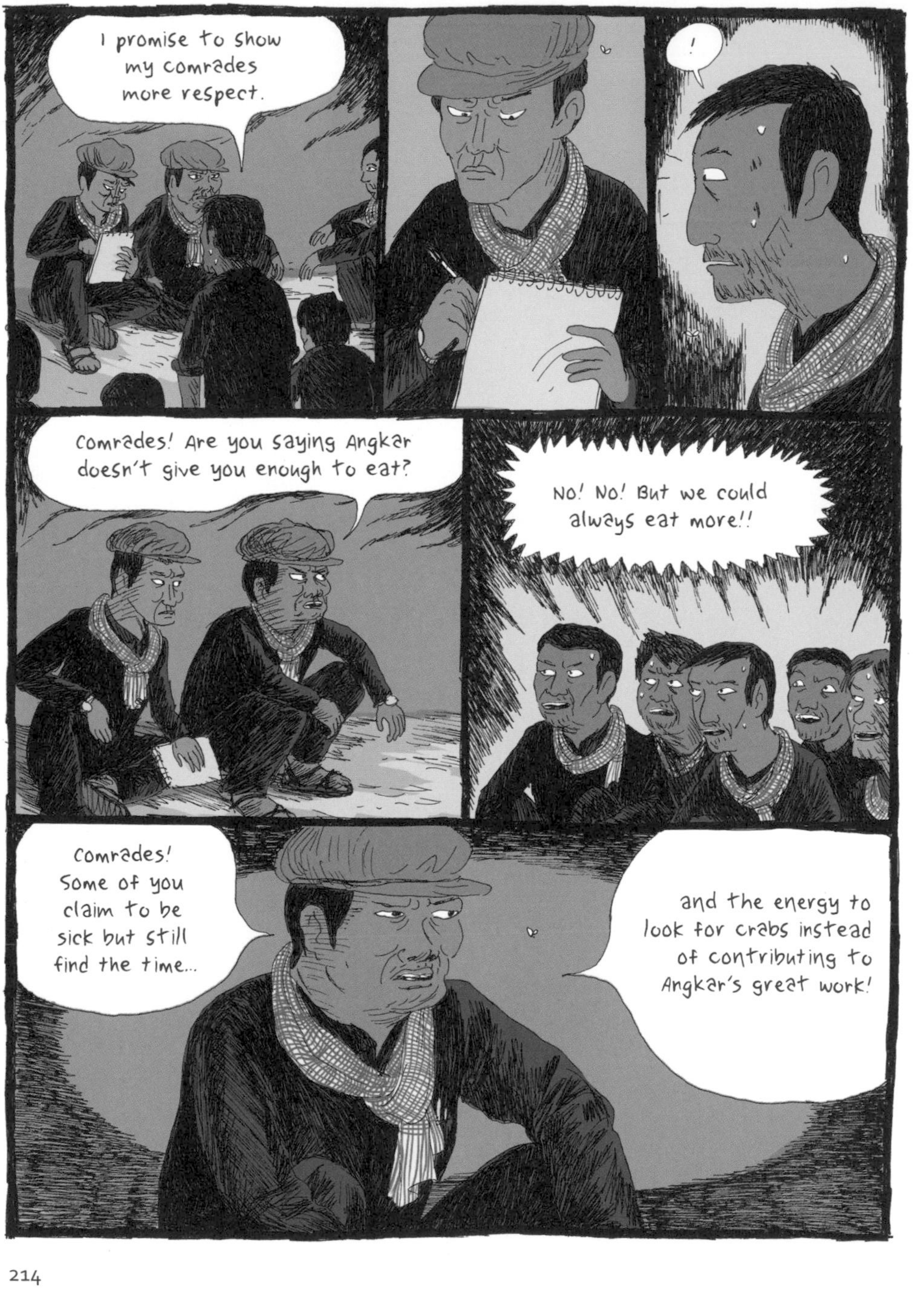
I promise to show my comrades more respect.
!
Comrades! Are you saying Angkar doesn't give you enough to eat?
No! No! But we could always eat more!!
Comrades! Some of you claim to be sick but still find the time...
and the energy to look for crabs instead of contributing to Angkar's great work!

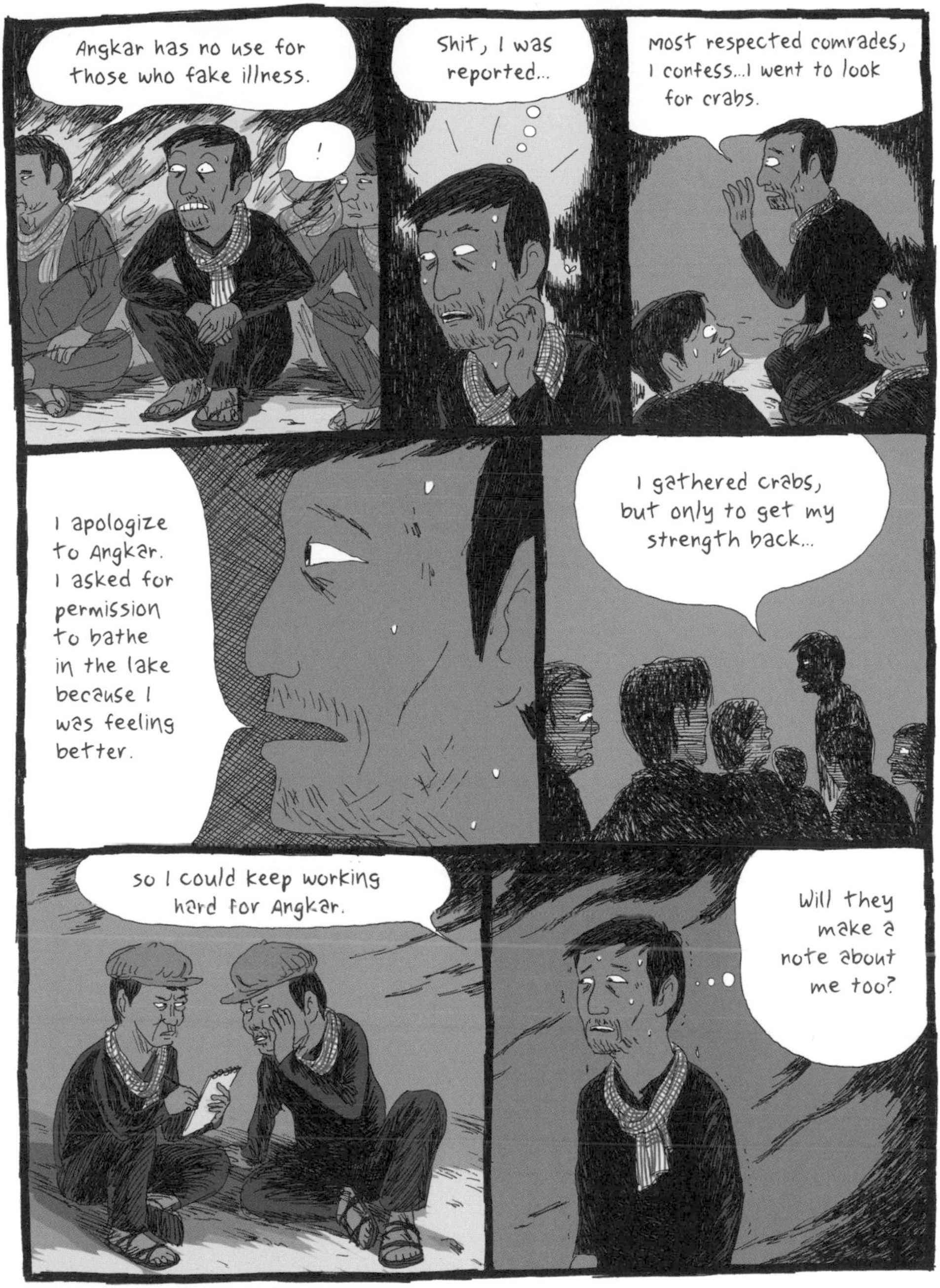
Angkar has no use for those who fake illness.
!
Shit, I was reported...
Most respected comrades, I confess...I went to look for crabs.
I apologize to Angkar. I asked for permission to bathe in the lake because I was feeling better.
I gathered crabs, but only to get my strength back...
so I could keep working hard for Angkar.
Will they make a note about me too?

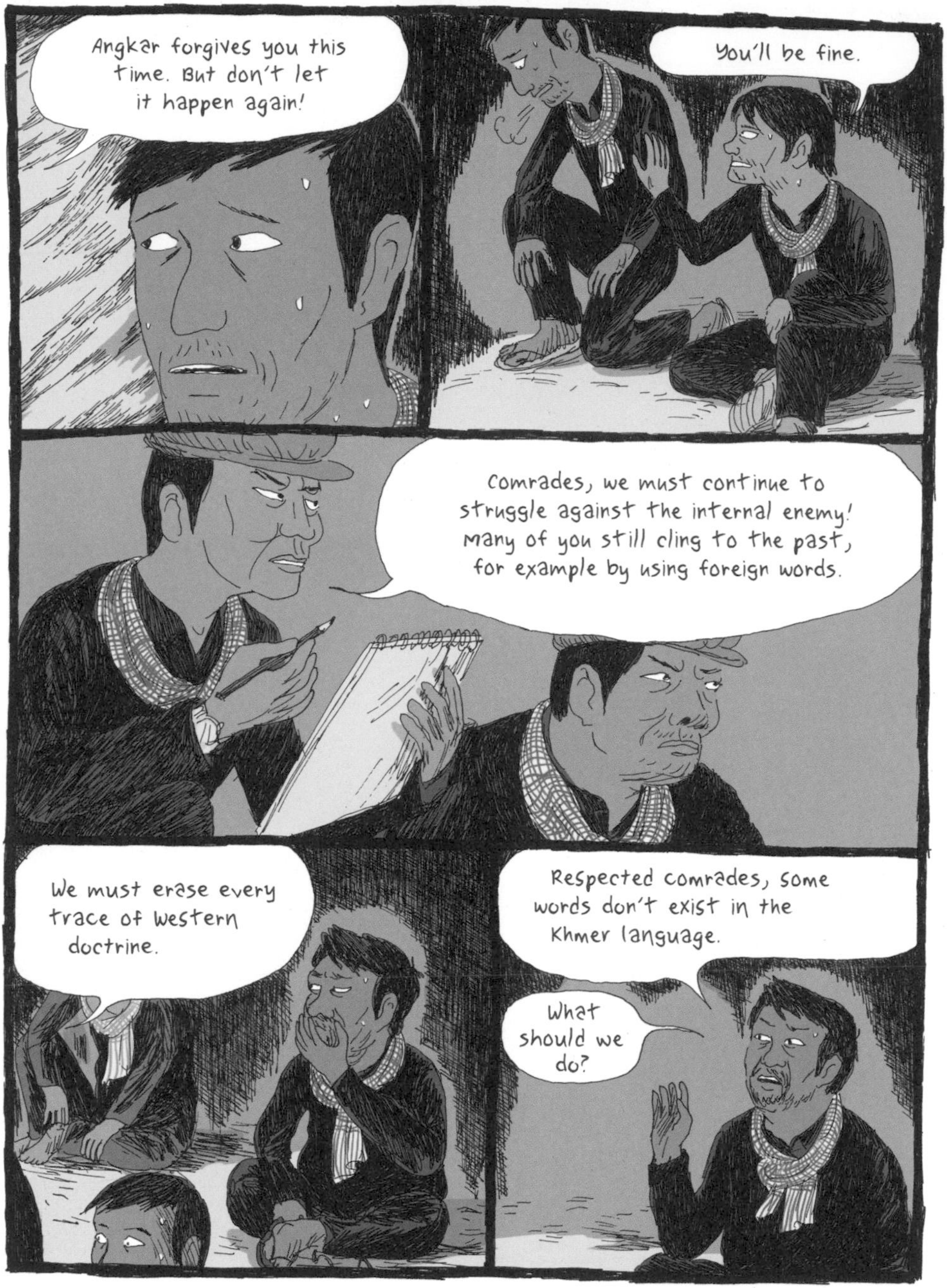
Angkar forgives you this time. But don't let it happen again!
You'll be fine.
Comrades, we must continue to struggle against the internal enemy! Many of you still cling to the past, for example by using foreign words.
We must erase every trace of Western doctrine.
Respected comrades, some words don't exist in the Khmer language.
What should we do?

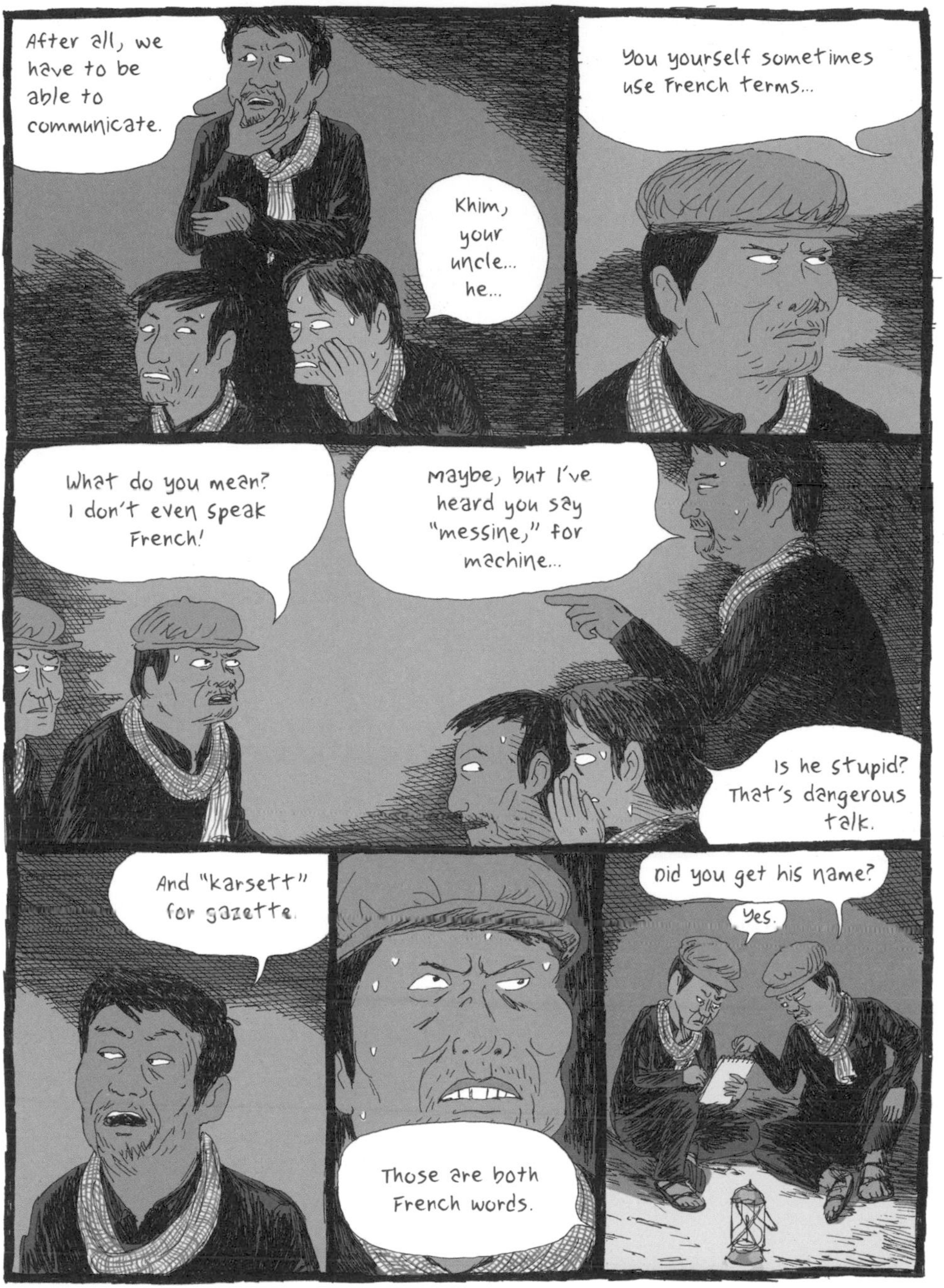

After all, we have to be able to communicate.
Khim, your uncle... he...
You yourself sometimes use French terms...
What do you mean? I don't even speak French!
Maybe, but I've heard you say "messine," for machine...
Is he stupid? That's dangerous talk.
And "karsett" for gazette.
Those are both French words.
Did you get his name?
Yes.

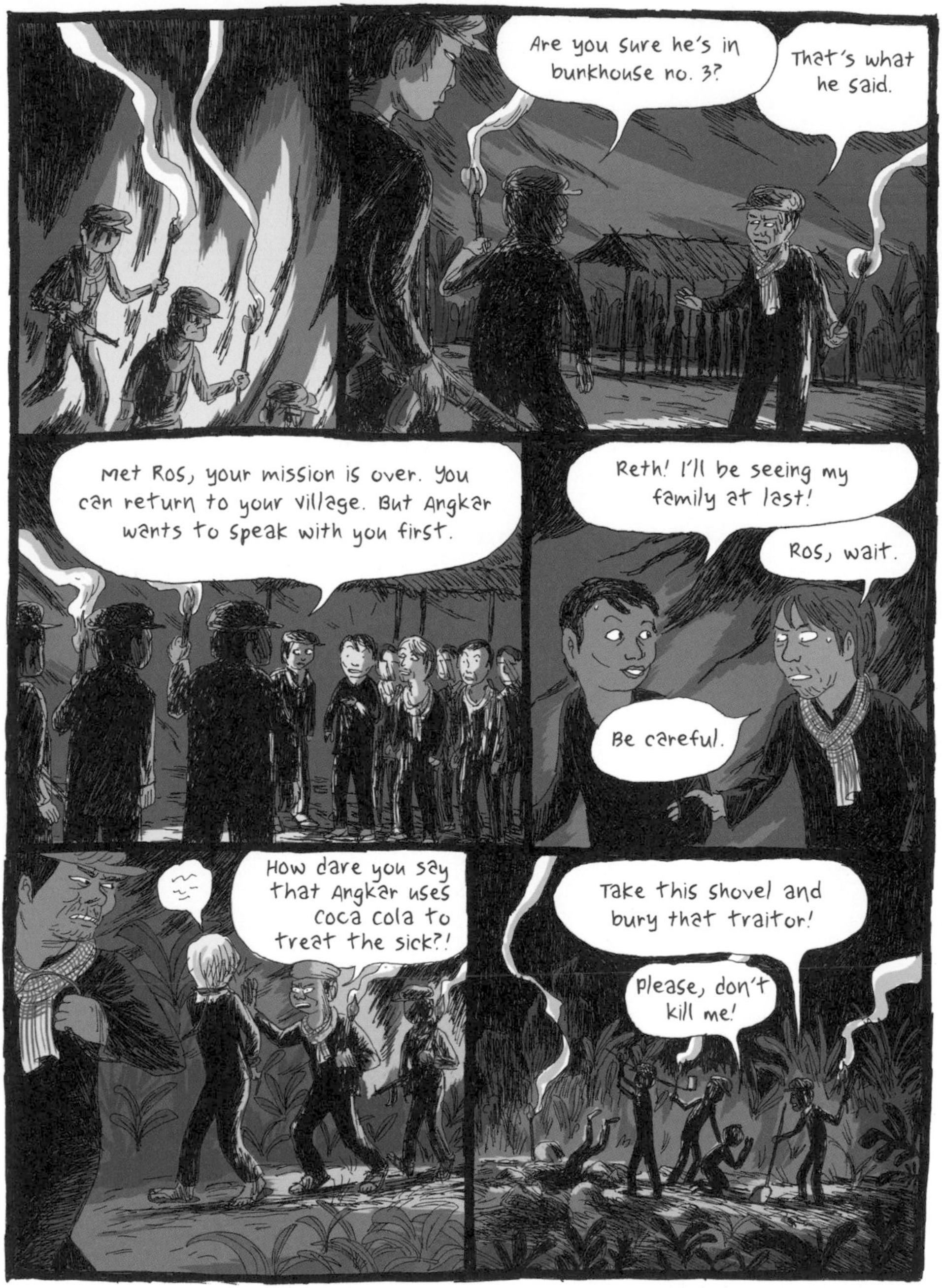
Are you sure he's in bunkhouse no. 3?
That's what he said.
Met Ros, your mission is over. You can return to your village. But Angkar wants to speak with you first.
Reth! I'll be seeing my family at last!
Ros, wait.
Be careful.
How dare you say that Angkar uses Coca Cola to treat the sick?!
Take this shovel and bury that traitor!
Please, don't kill me!

chapter 13

BETTER A LESS POPULATED CAMBODIA
THAN A COUNTRY OF INCOMPETENTS.

HOW TO LOOK LIKE A HIDDEN ENEMY OF ANGKAR

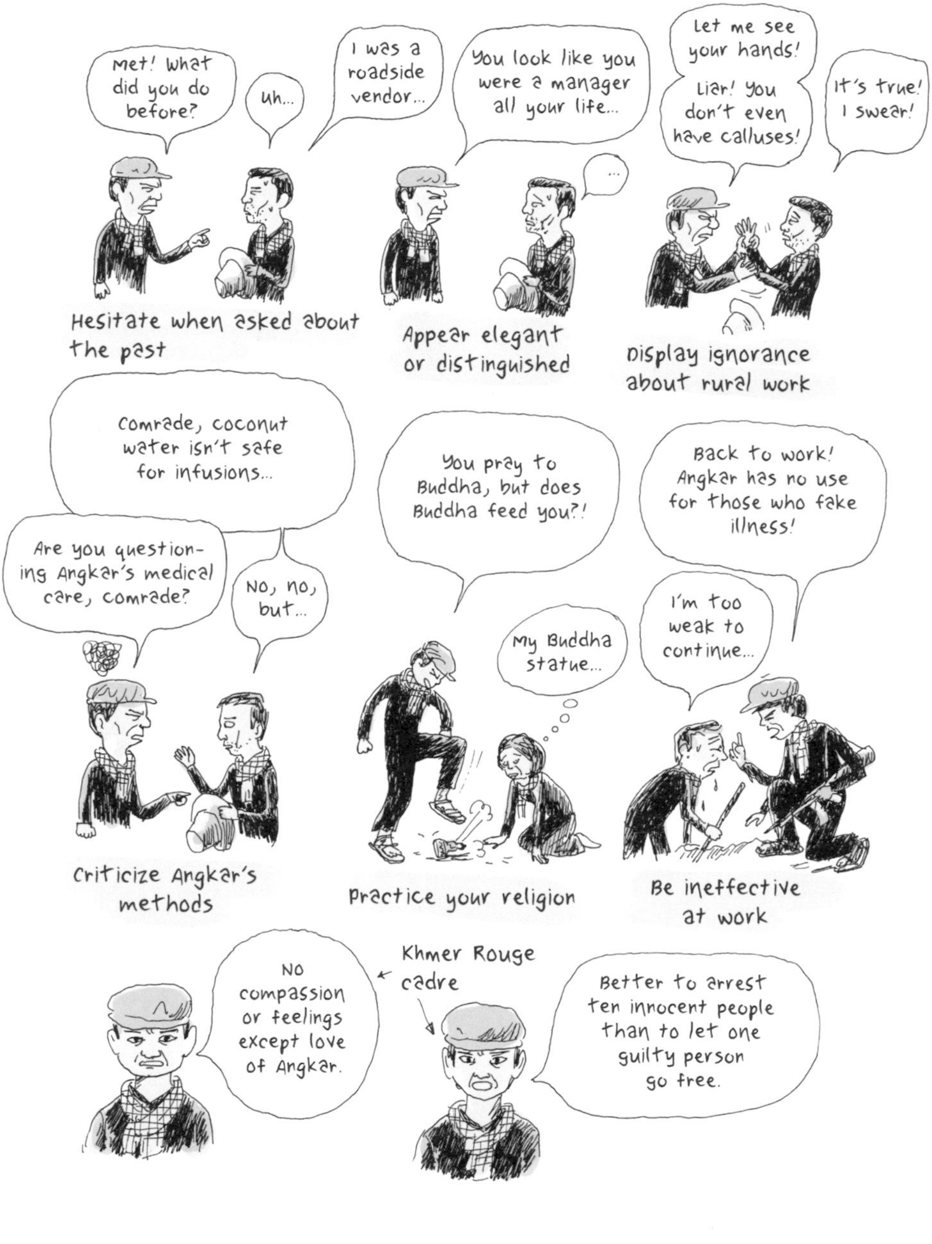

Met! What did you do before?
Uh...
I was a roadside vendor...
Hesitate when asked about the past
You look like you were a manager all your life...
...
Appear elegant or distinguished
Let me see your hands!
Liar! You don't even have calluses!
It's true! I swear!
Display ignorance about rural work
Comrade, coconut water isn't safe for infusions...
Are you questioning Angkar's medical care, comrade?
No, no, but...
Criticize Angkar's methods
You pray to Buddha, but does Buddha feed you?!
My Buddha statue...
Practice your religion
Back to work! Angkar has no use for those who fake illness!
I'm too weak to continue...
Be ineffective at work
No compassion or feelings except love of Angkar.
Khmer Rouge cadre
Better to arrest ten innocent people than to let one guilty person go free.

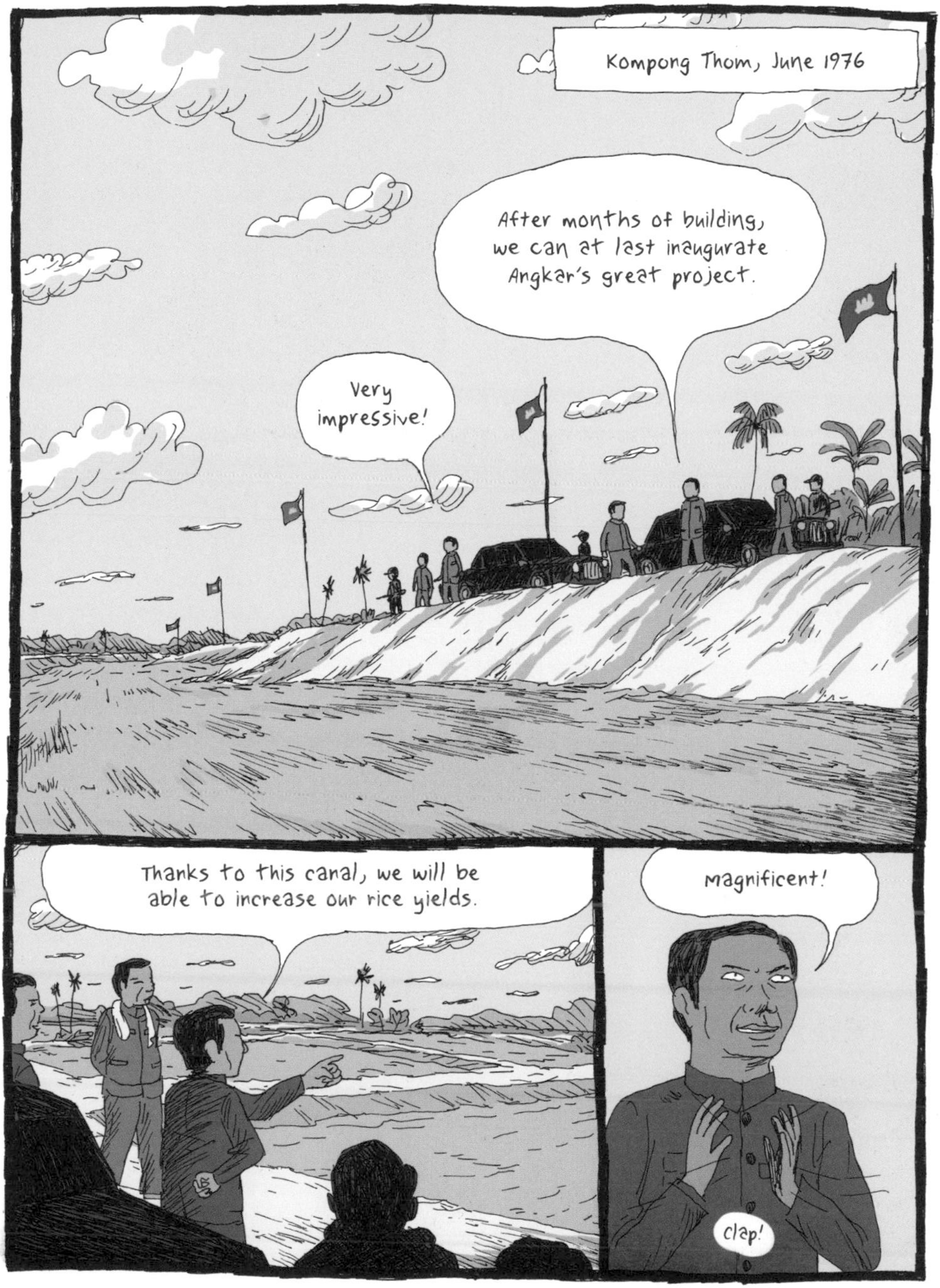
Kompong Thom, June 1976
After months of building, we can at last inaugurate Angkar's great project.
Very impressive!
Thanks to this canal, we will be able to increase our rice yields.
Magnificent!
clap!

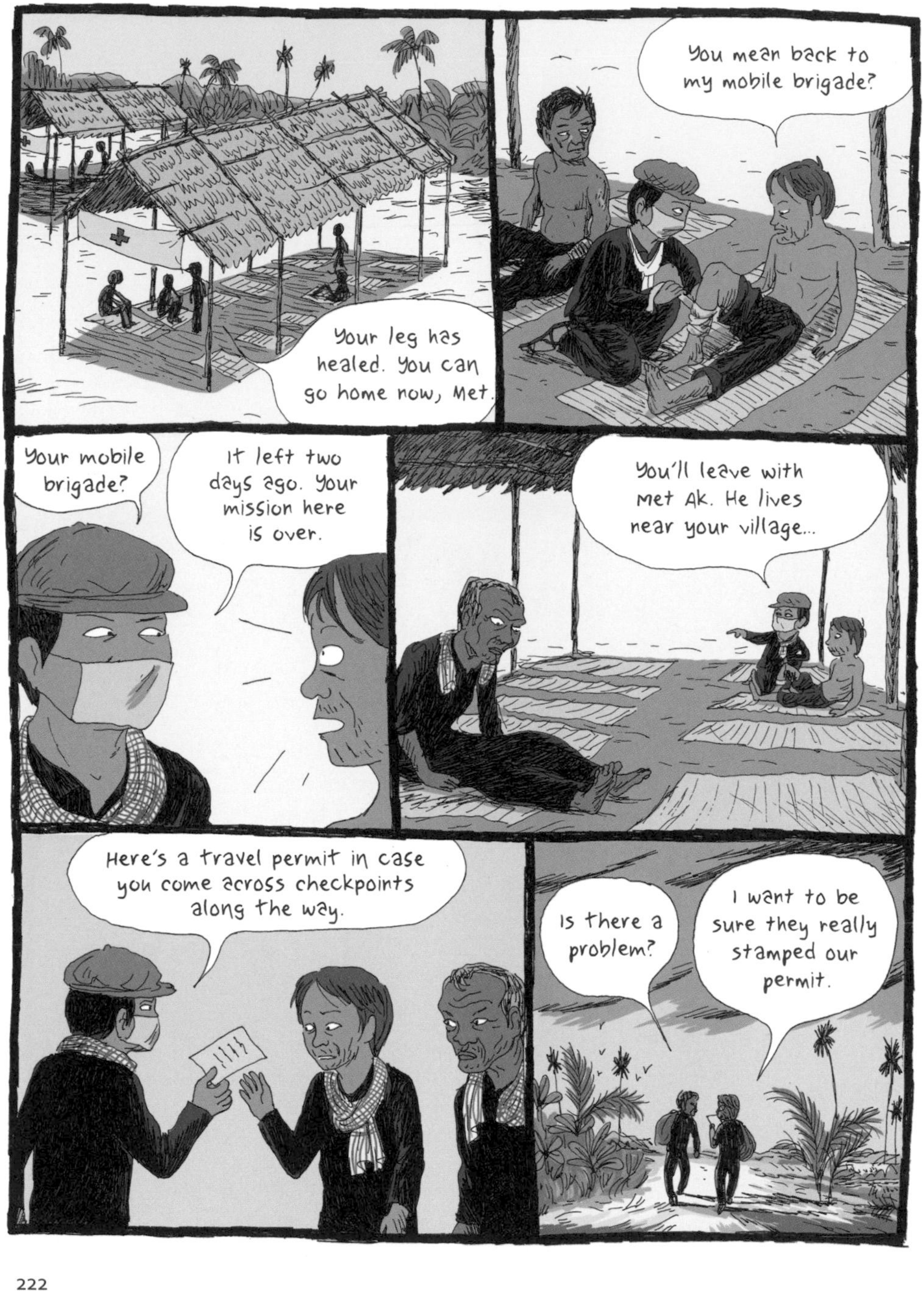
Your leg has healed. You can go home now, Met.
You mean back to my mobile brigade?
Your mobile brigade?
It left two days ago. Your mission here is over.
You'll leave with Met Ak. He lives near your village...
Here's a travel permit in case you come across checkpoints along the way.
Is there a problem?
I want to be sure they really stamped our permit.

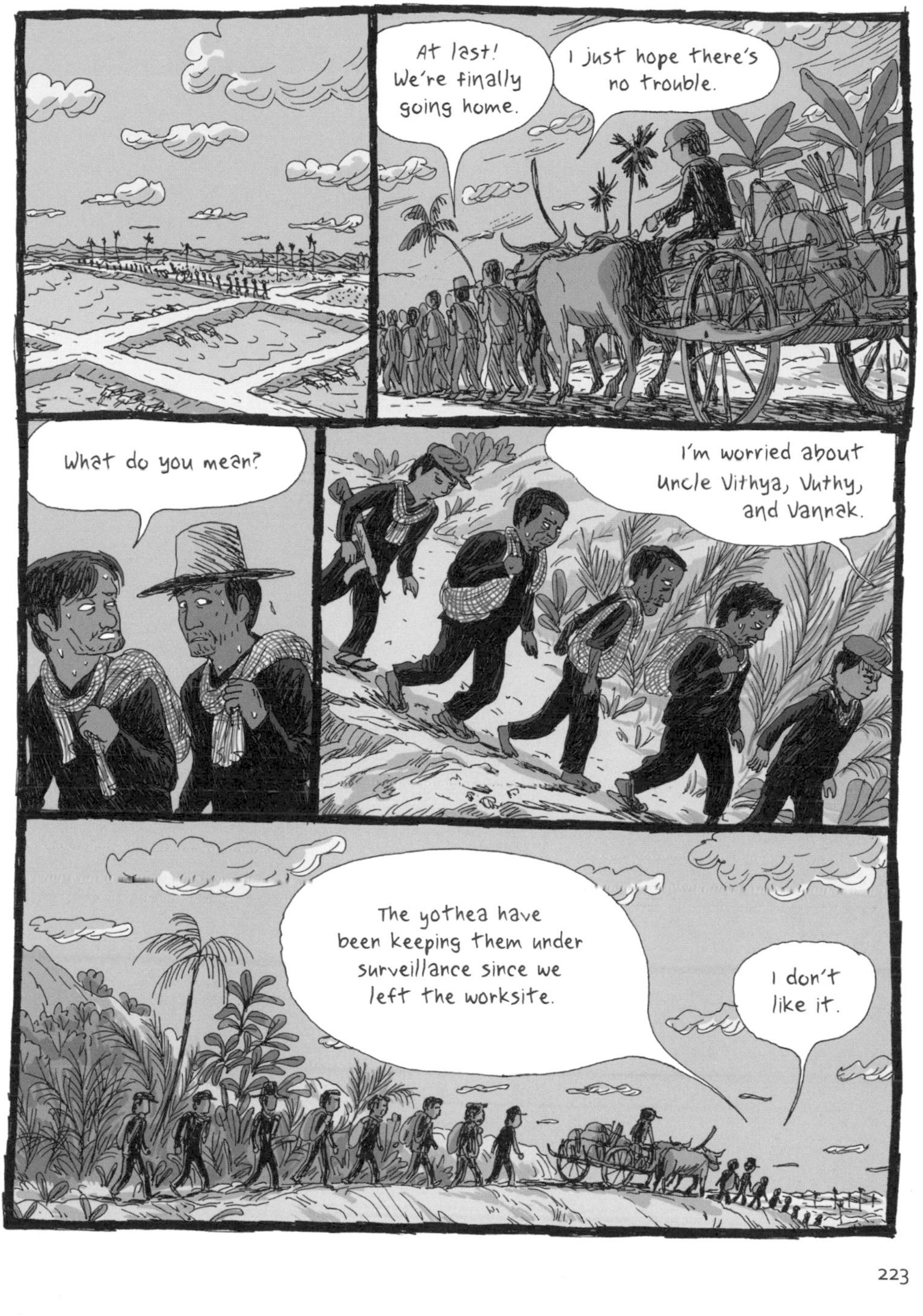
At last! We're finally going home.
I just hope there's no trouble.
What do you mean?
I'm worried about Uncle Vithya, Vuthy, and Vannak.
The yothea have been keeping them under surveillance since we left the worksite.
I don't like it.

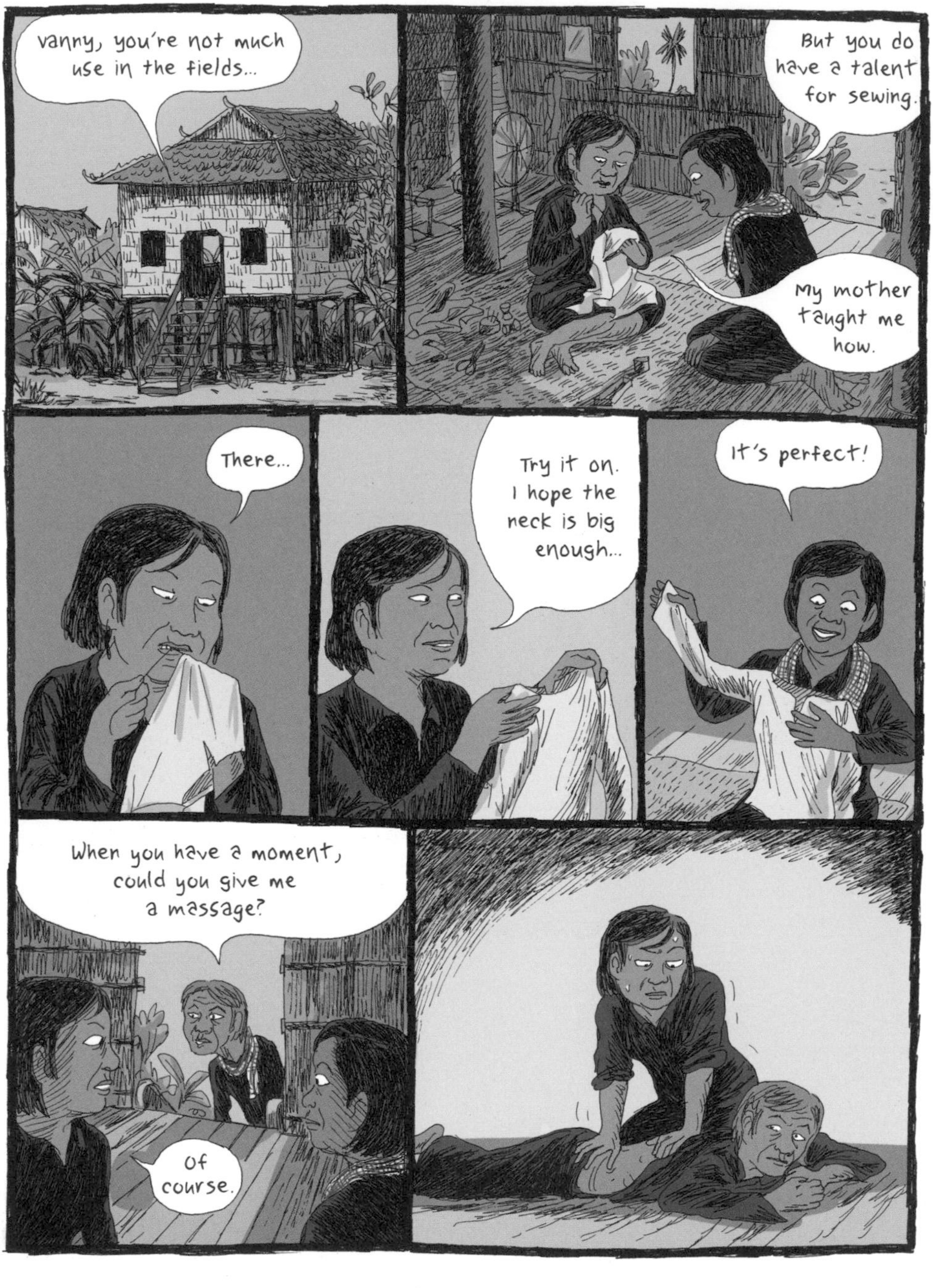
Vanny, you're not much use in the fields...
But you do have a talent for sewing.
My mother taught me how.
There...
Try it on. I hope the neck is big enough...
It's perfect!
When you have a moment, could you give me a massage?
Of course.

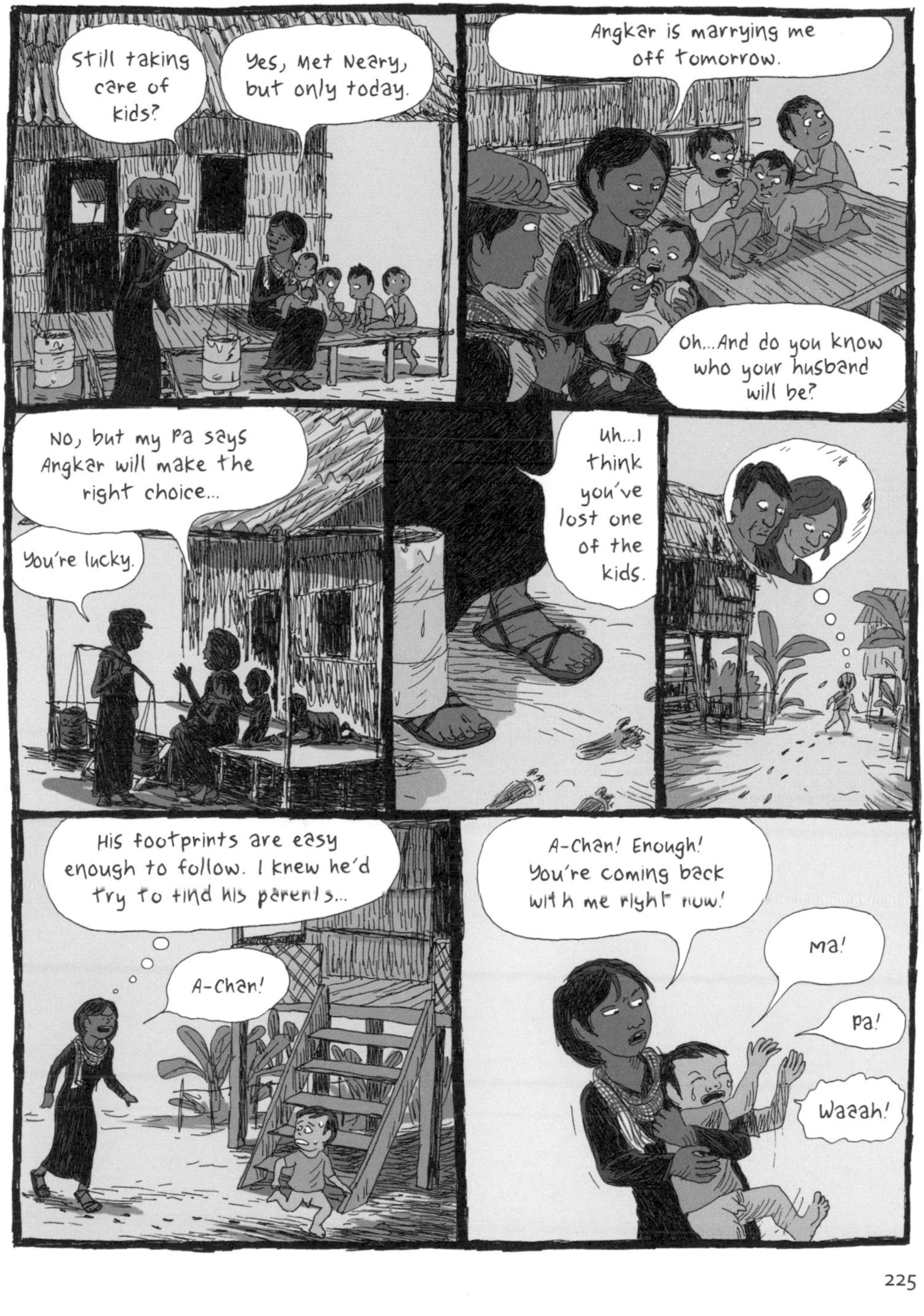
Still taking care of kids?
Yes, Met Neary, but only today.
Angkar is marrying me off tomorrow.
Oh... And do you know who your husband will be?
No, but my Pa says Angkar will make the right choice...
You're lucky.
Uh... I think you've lost one of the kids.
His footprints are easy enough to follow. I knew he'd try to find his parents...
A-Chan!
A-Chan! Enough! You're coming back with me right now!
Ma!
Pa!
Waaah!

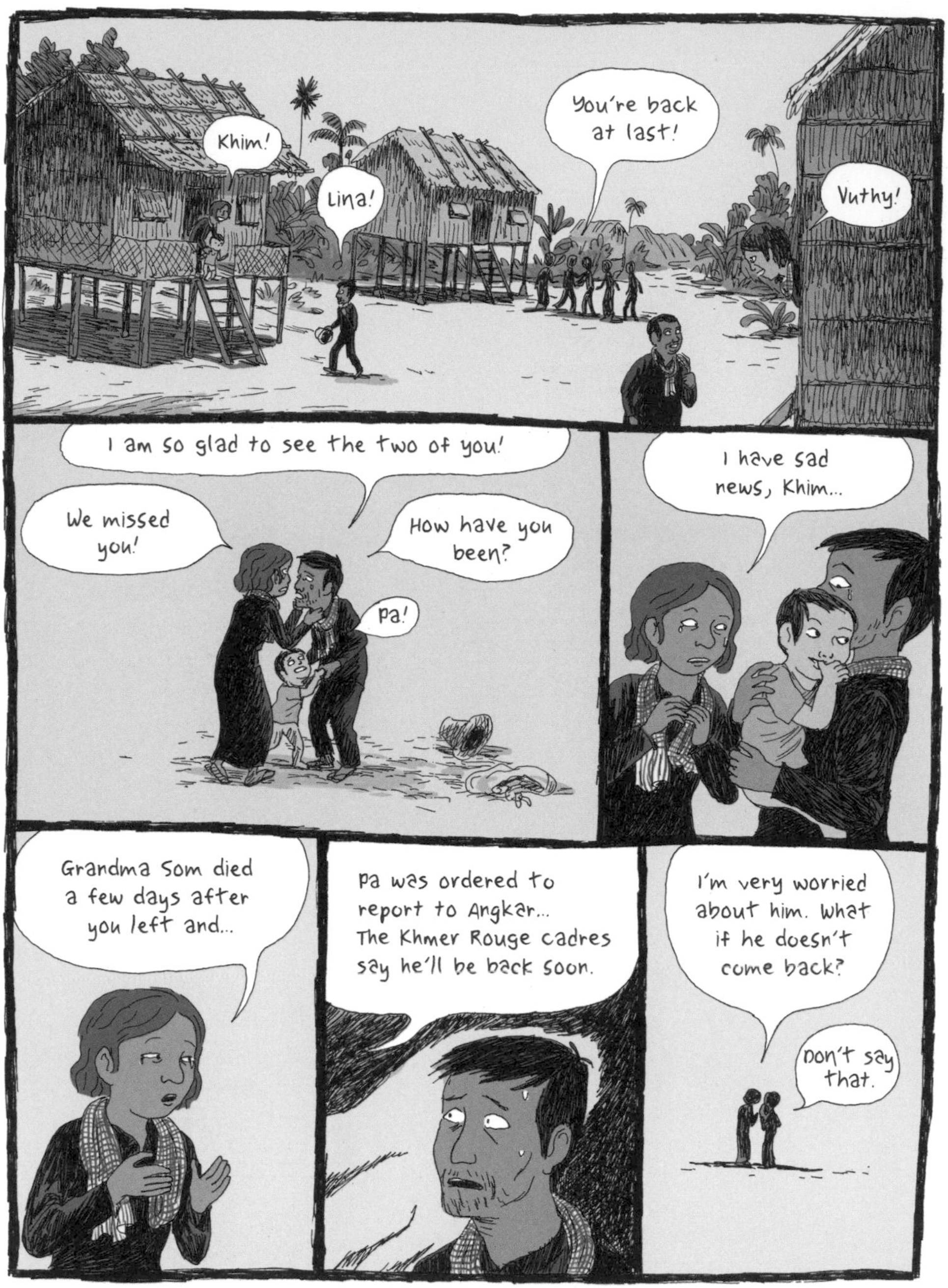
Khim!
Lina!
You're back at last!
Vuthy!
I am so glad to see the two of you!
We missed you!
How have you been?
Pa!
I have sad news, Khim...
Grandma Som died a few days after you left and...
Pa was ordered to report to Angkar... The Khmer Rouge cadres say he'll be back soon.
I'm very worried about him. What if he doesn't come back?
Don't say that.

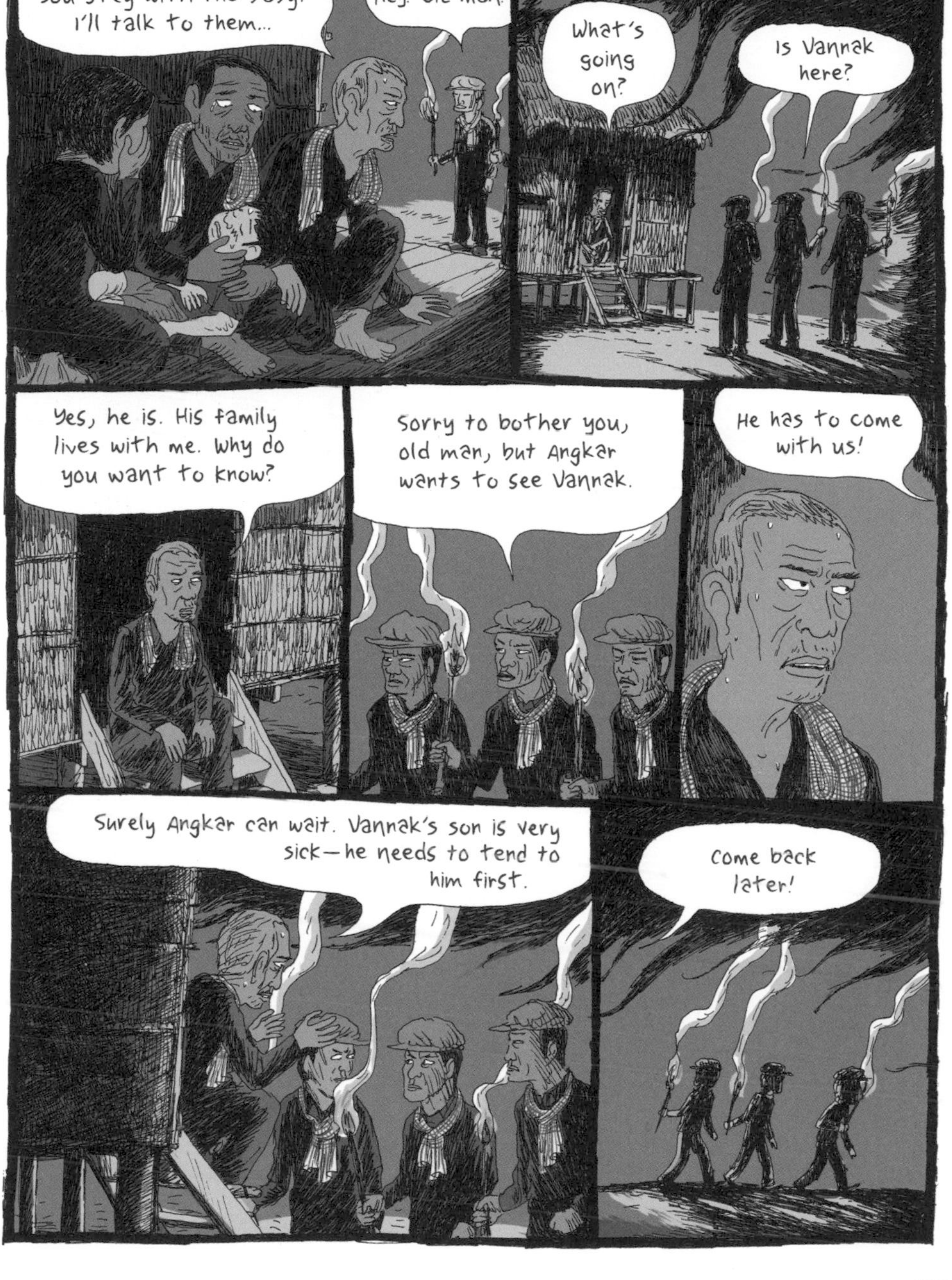
You stay with the baby. I'll talk to them...
Hey! Old man!
What's going on?
Is Vannak here?
Yes, he is. His family lives with me. Why do you want to know?
Sorry to bother you, old man, but Angkar wants to see Vannak.
He has to come with us!
Surely Angkar can wait. Vannak's son is very sick—he needs to tend to him first.
Come back later!

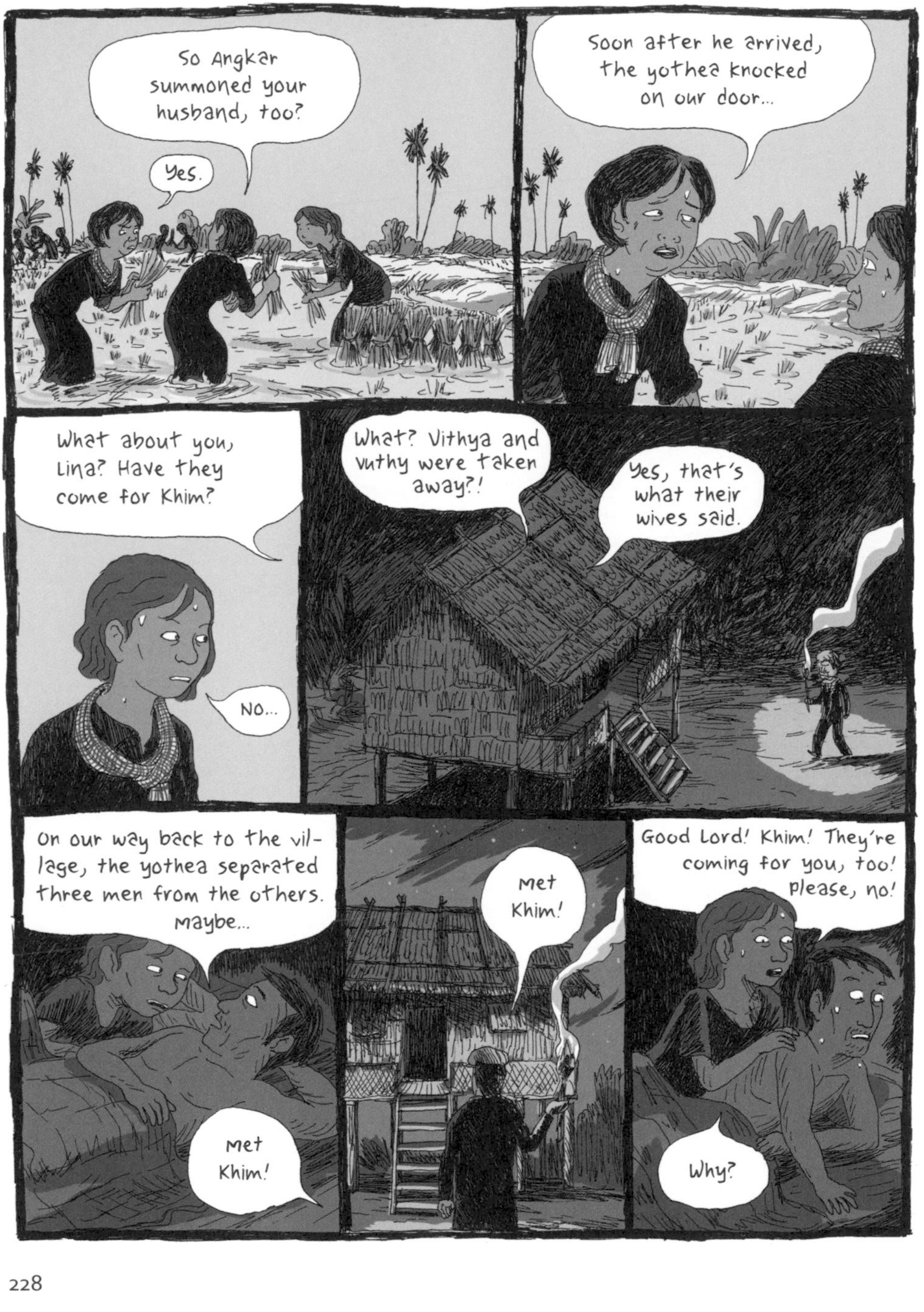
So Angkar summoned your husband, too?
Yes.
Soon after he arrived, the yothea knocked on our door...
What about you, Lina? Have they come for Khim?
No...
What? Vithya and Vuthy were taken away?!
Yes, that's what their wives said.
On our way back to the village, the yothea separated three men from the others. Maybe...
Met Khim!
Met Khim!
Good Lord! Khim! They're coming for you, too! Please, no!
Why?

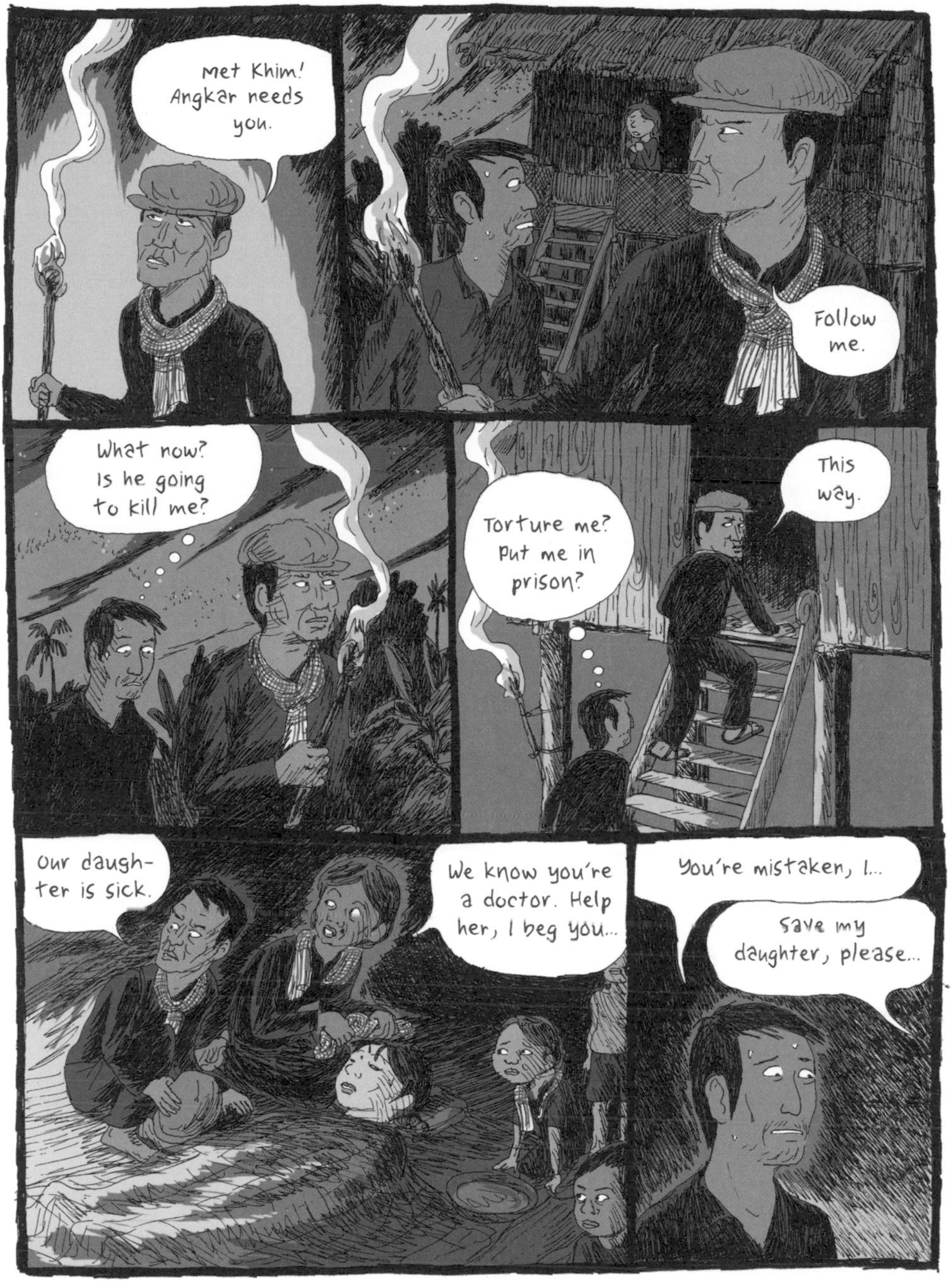
Met Khim! Angkar needs you.
Follow me.
What now? Is he going to kill me?
Torture me? Put me in prison?
This way.
Our daughter is sick.
We know you're a doctor. Help her, I beg you...
You're mistaken, I...
Save my daughter, please...

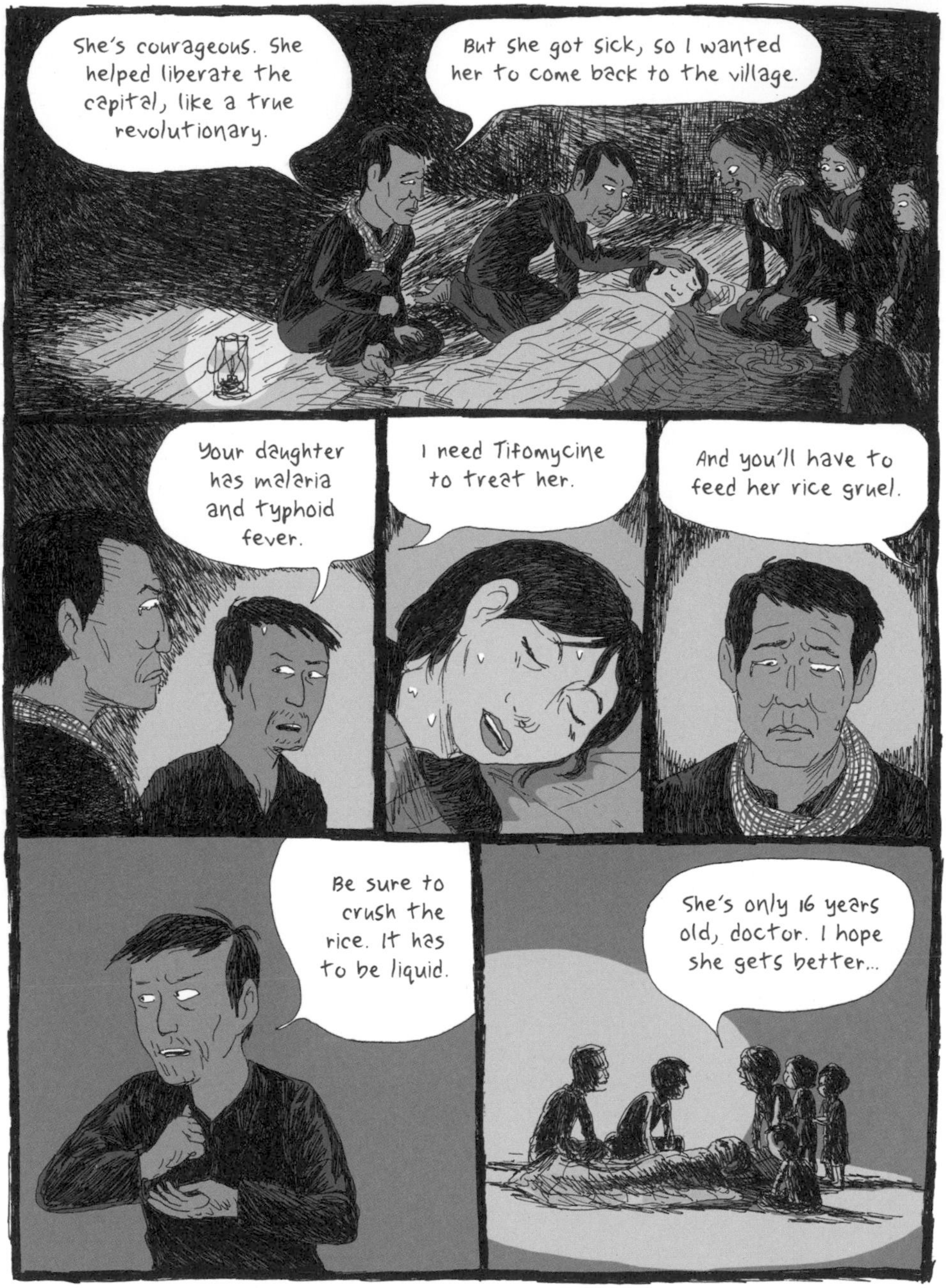
She's courageous. She helped liberate the capital, like a true revolutionary.
But she got sick, so I wanted her to come back to the village.
Your daughter has malaria and typhoid fever.
I need Tifomycine to treat her.
And you'll have to feed her rice gruel.
Be sure to crush the rice. It has to be liquid.
She's only 16 years old, doctor. I hope she gets better...

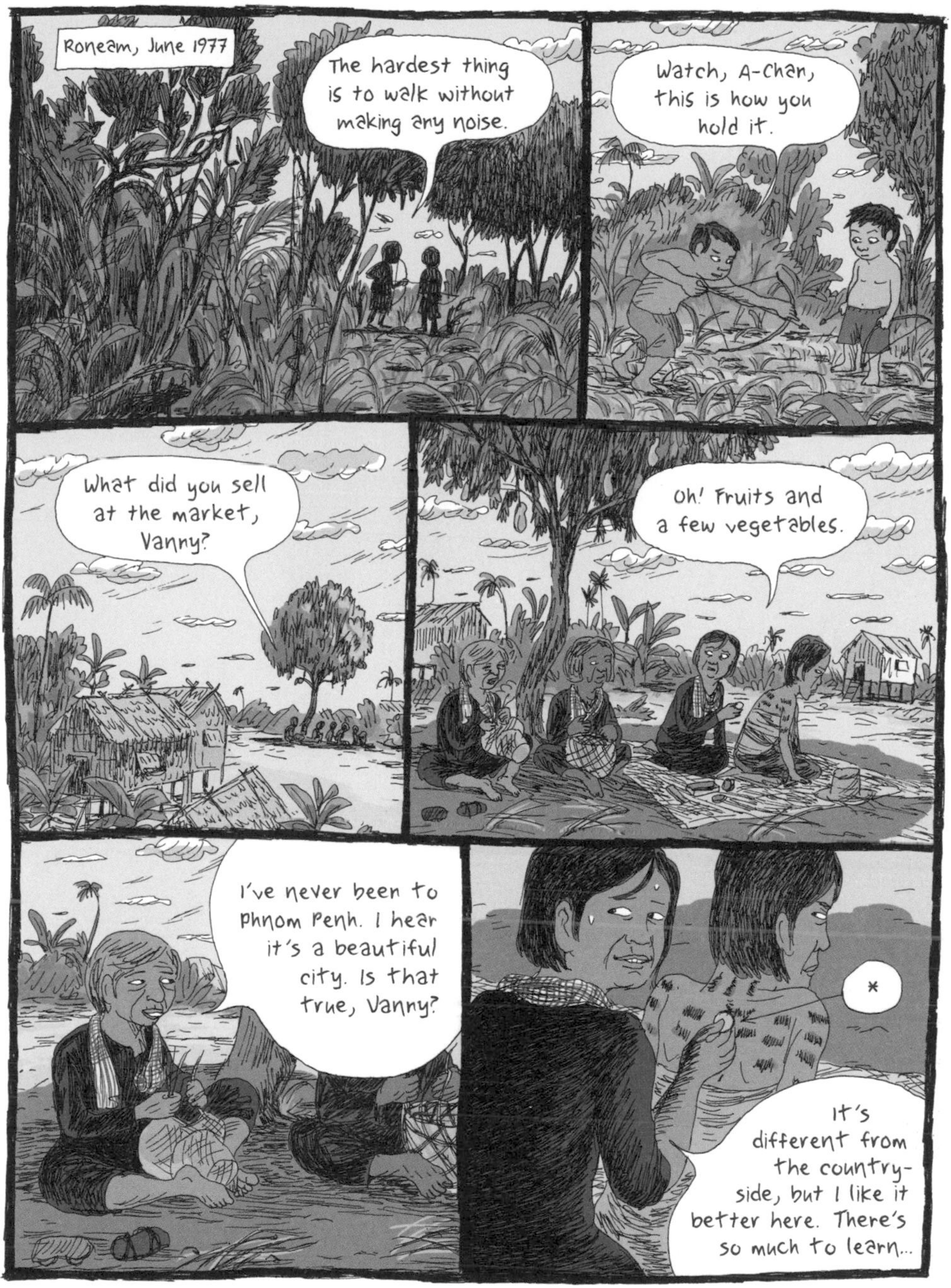
Roneam, June 1977
The hardest thing is to walk without making any noise.
Watch, A-Chan, this is how you hold it.
What did you sell at the market, Vanny?
Oh! Fruits and a few vegetables.
I've never been to Phnom Penh. I hear it's a beautiful city. Is that true, Vanny?
*
It's different from the country-side, but I like it better here. There's so much to learn...

*"Koh khchal" or "rubbing the wind": a traditional healing technique that consists of rubbing the skin with an oiled coin

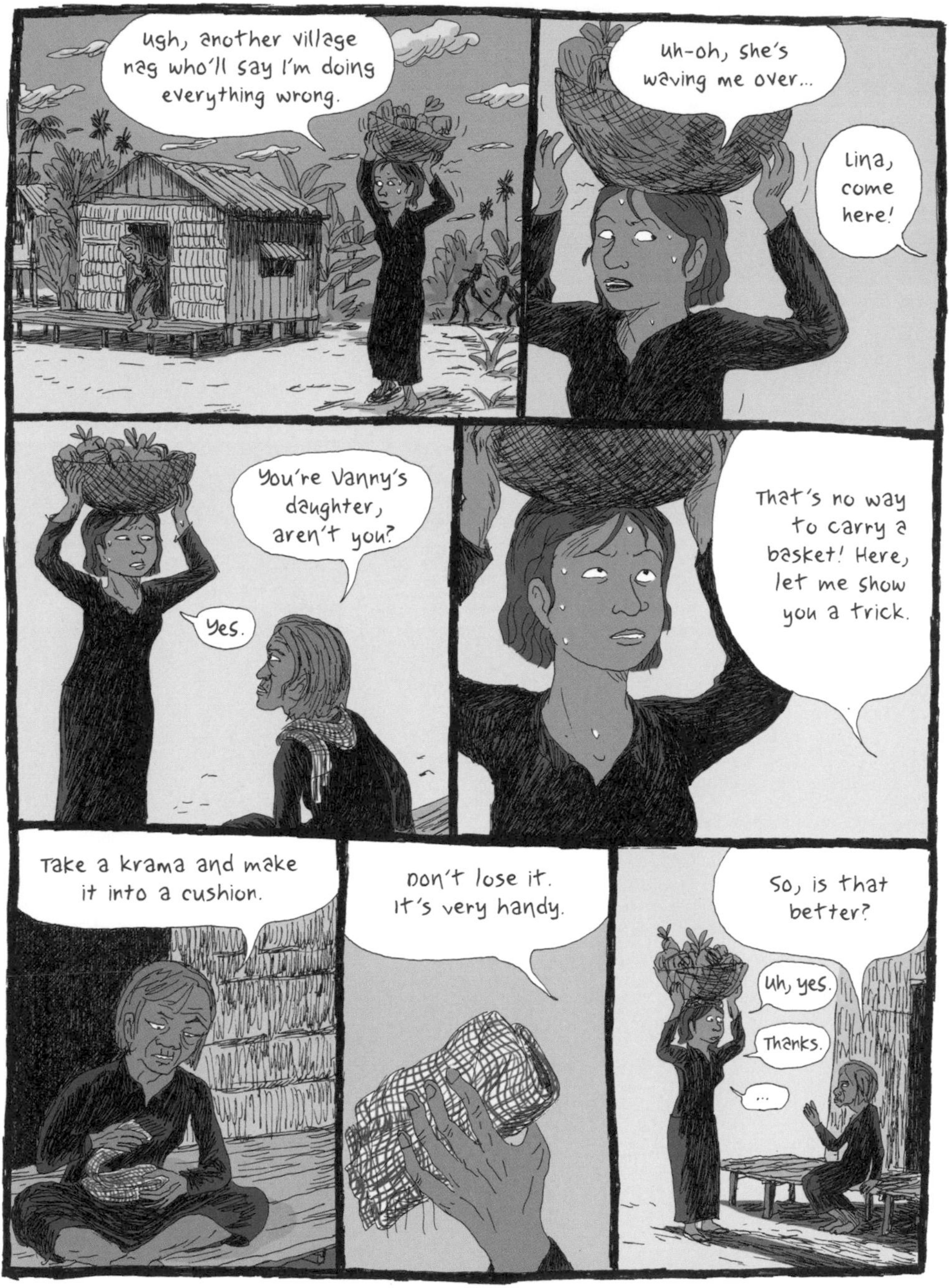
Ugh, another village nag who'll say I'm doing everything wrong.
Uh-oh, she's waving me over...
Lina, come here!
You're Vanny's daughter, aren't you?
Yes.
That's no way to carry a basket! Here, let me show you a trick.
Take a krama and make it into a cushion.
Don't lose it. It's very handy.
So, is that better?
Uh, yes.
Thanks.
...

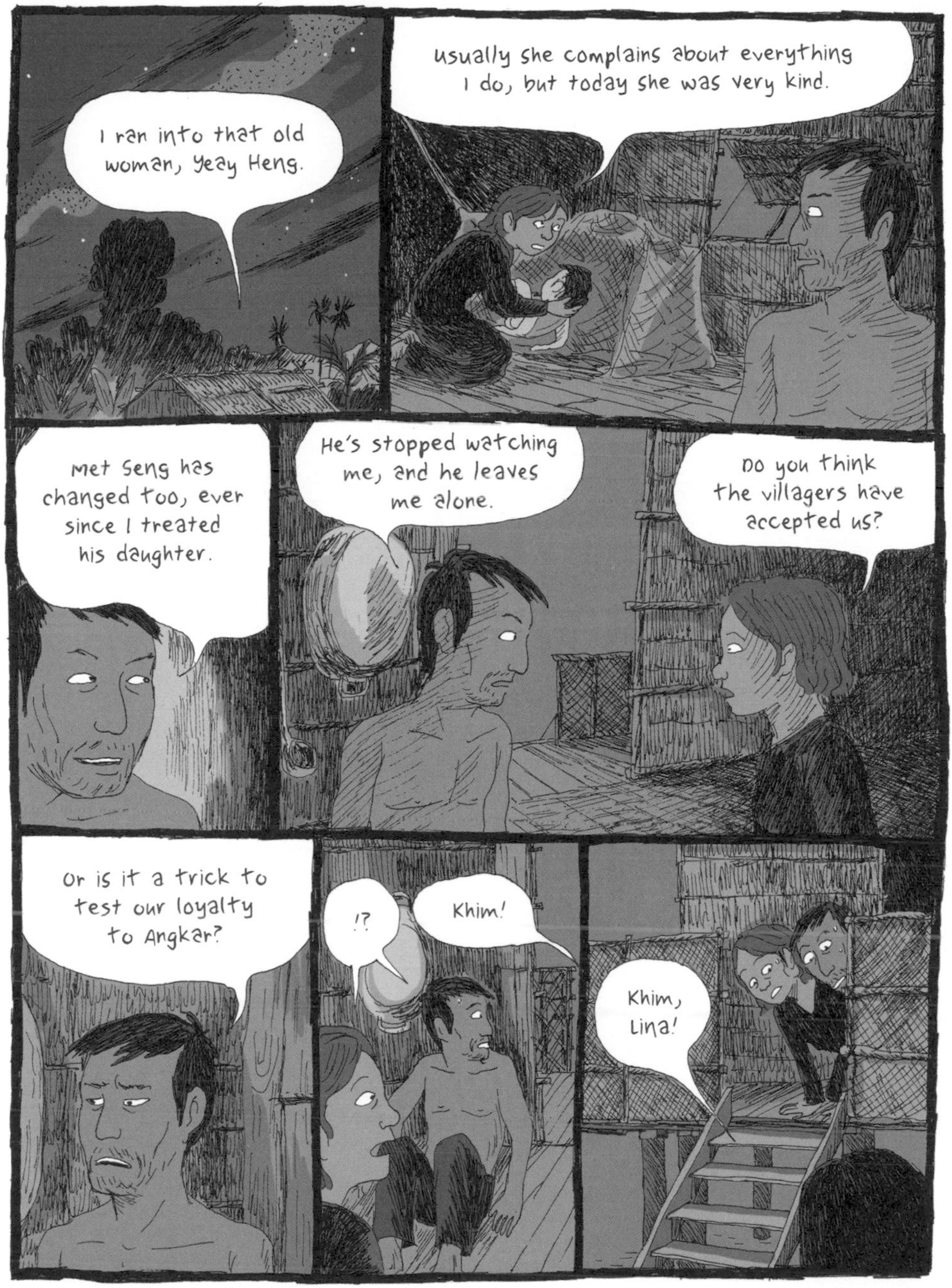
I ran into that old woman, Yeay Heng.
Usually she complains about everything I do, but today she was very kind.
Met Seng has changed too, ever since I treated his daughter.
He's stopped watching me, and he leaves me alone.
Do you think the villagers have accepted us?
Or is it a trick to test our loyalty to Angkar?
!?
Khim!
Khim, Lina!

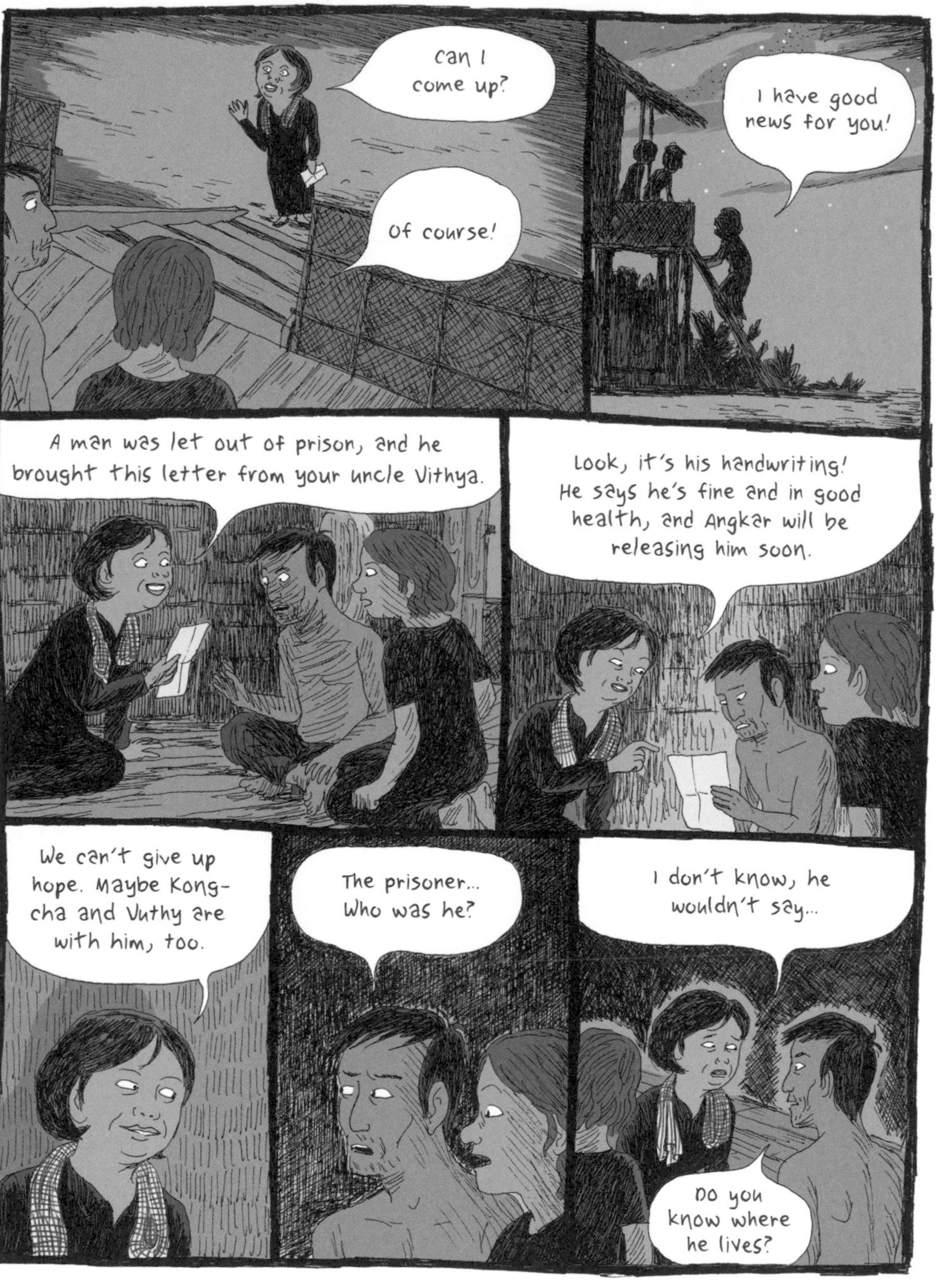
Can I come up?
Of course!
I have good news for you!
A man was let out of prison, and he brought this letter from your uncle Vithya.
Look, it's his handwriting! He says he's fine and in good health, and Angkar will be releasing him soon.
We can't give up hope. Maybe Kong-cha and Vuthy are with him, too.
The prisoner... Who was he?
I don't know, he wouldn't say...
Do you know where he lives?

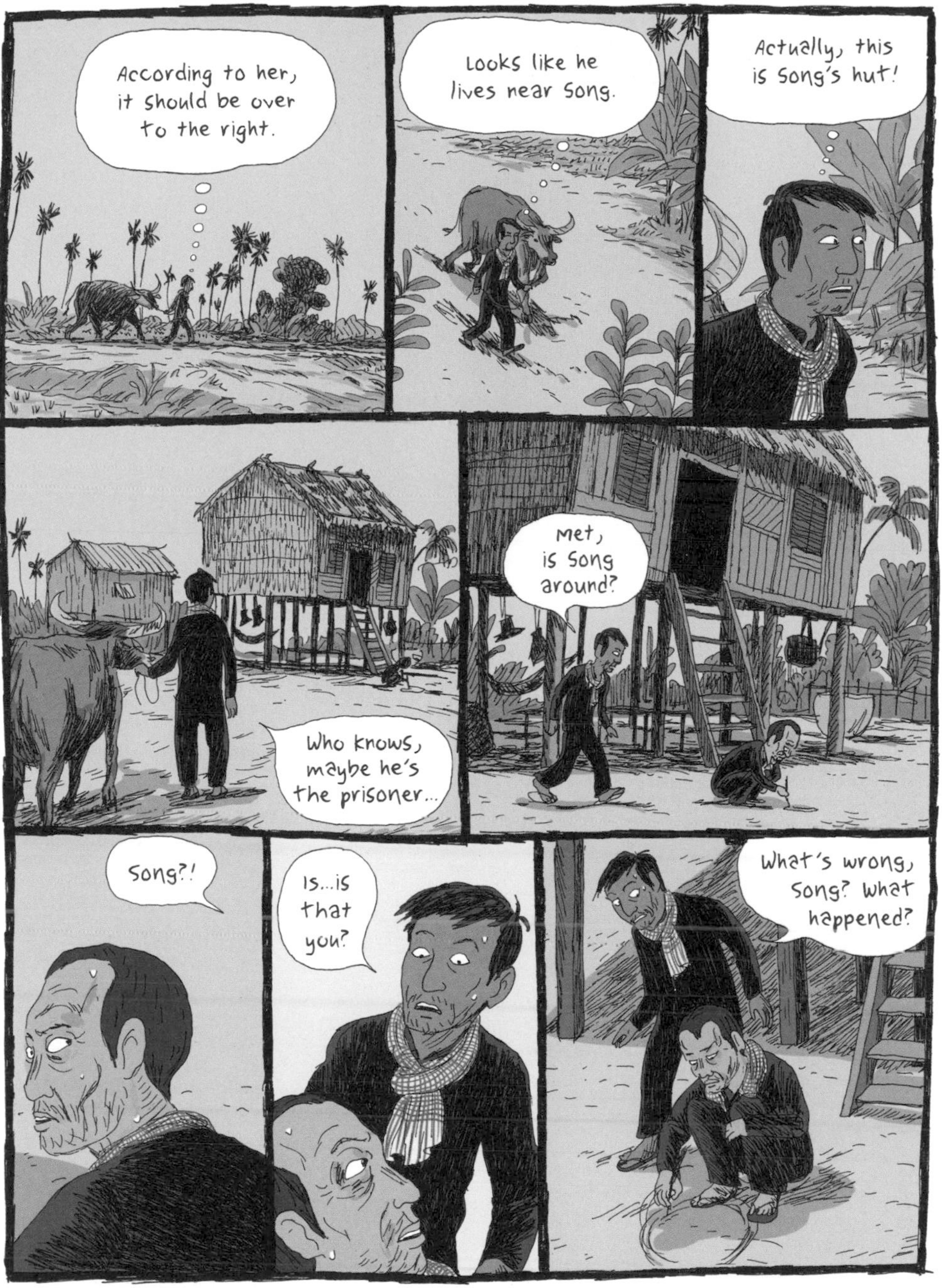
According to her, it should be over to the right.
Looks like he lives near Song.
Actually, this is Song's hut!
Who knows, maybe he's the prisoner...
Met, is Song around?
Song?!
Is...is that you?
What's wrong, Song? What happened?

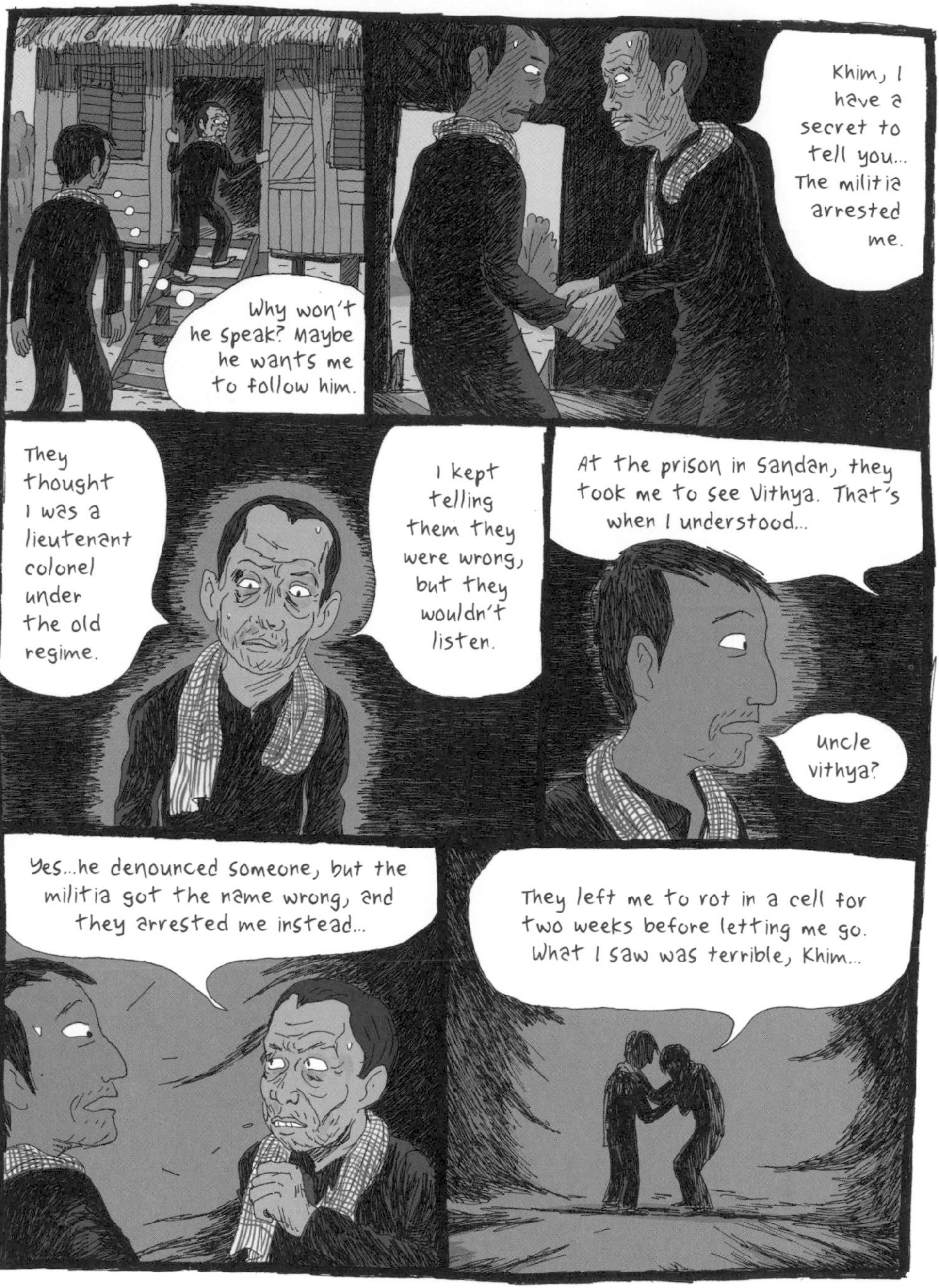
Why won't he speak? Maybe he wants me to follow him.
Khim, I have a secret to tell you... The militia arrested me.
They thought I was a lieutenant colonel under the old regime.
I kept telling them they were wrong, but they wouldn't listen.
At the prison in Sandan, they took me to see Vithya. That's when I understood...
Uncle Vithya?
Yes...he denounced someone, but the militia got the name wrong, and they arrested me instead...
They left me to rot in a cell for two weeks before letting me go. What I saw was terrible, Khim...

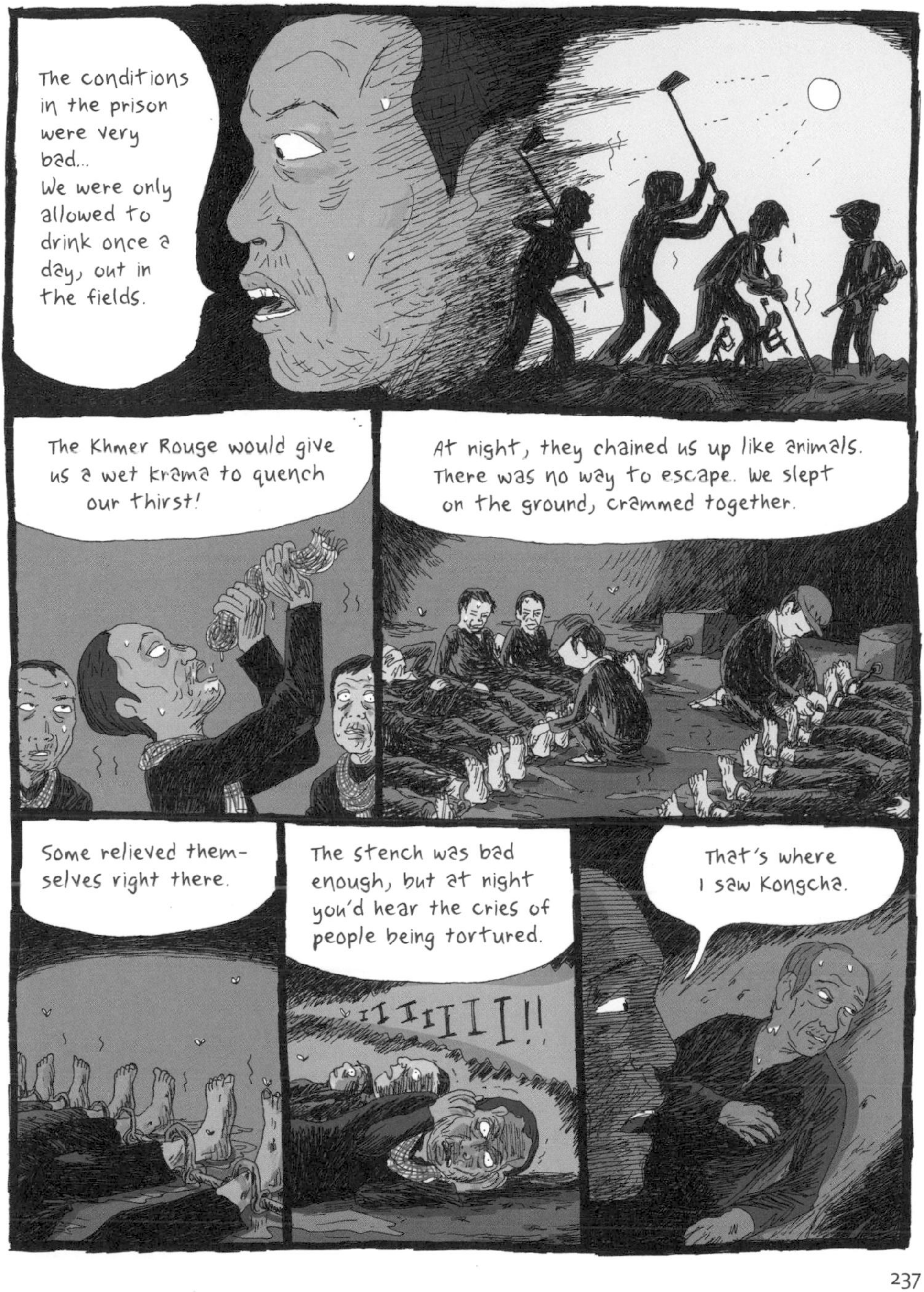
The conditions in the prison were very bad... We were only allowed to drink once a day, out in the fields.
The Khmer Rouge would give us a wet krama to quench our thirst!
At night, they chained us up like animals. There was no way to escape. We slept on the ground, crammed together.
Some relieved themselves right there.
The stench was bad enough, but at night you'd hear the cries of people being tortured.
IIIIIII!!
That's where I saw Kongcha.

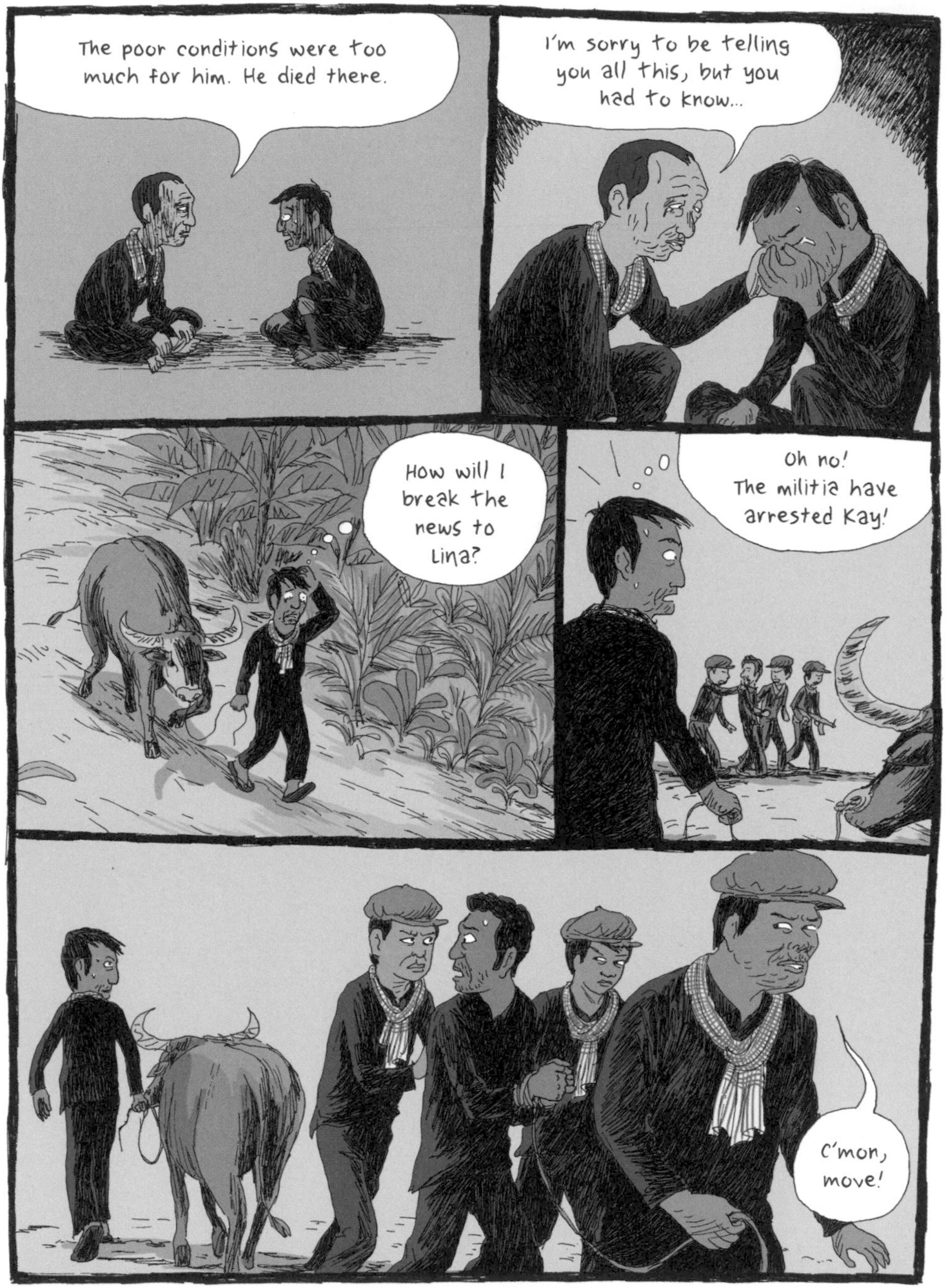
The poor conditions were too much for him. He died there.
I'm sorry to be telling you all this, but you had to know...
How will I break the news to Lina?
Oh no! The militia have arrested Kay!
C'mon, move!

chapter 14

CUTTING A WEED IS NOT ENOUGH—
IT MUST BE PULLED UP BY THE ROOTS.

KHIM'S TIPS AND TRICKS

Starting a fire can be difficult. Usually a lighter will do, but if you don't have one on hand, you can try getting fire from a neighbor...

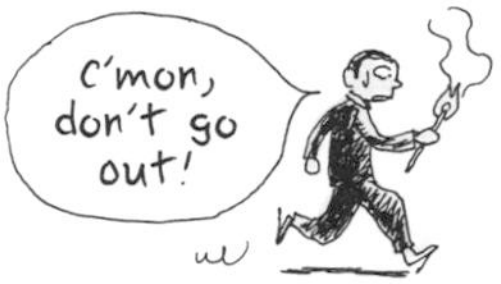
C'mon, don't go out!

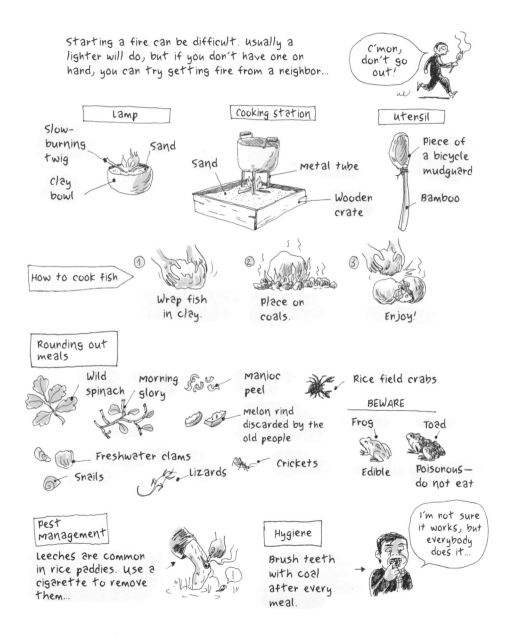

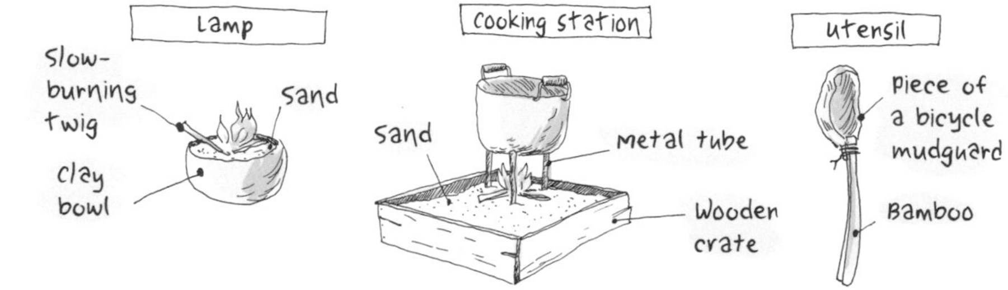
Lamp
Slow-burning twig
Sand
Clay bowl
Cooking station
Sand
Metal tube
Wooden crate
Utensil
Piece of a bicycle mudguard
Bamboo

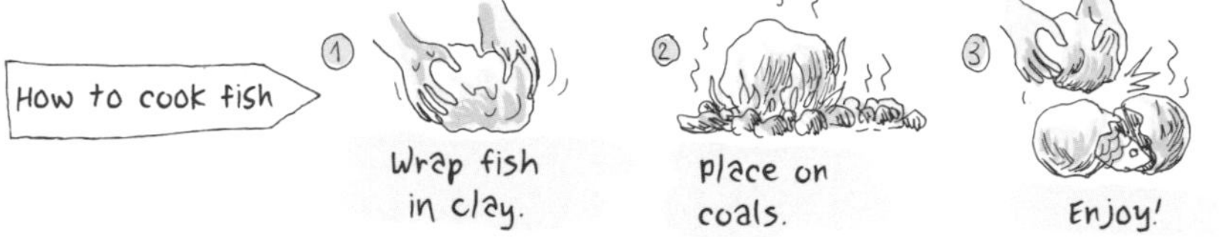
How to cook fish
1
Wrap fish in clay.
2
Place on coals.
3
Enjoy!

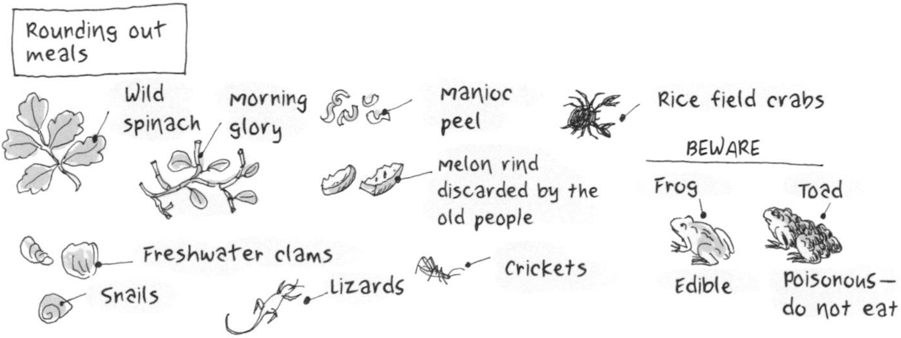
Rounding out meals
Wild spinach
Morning glory
Manioc peel
Rice field crabs
Melon rind discarded by the old people
BEWARE
Frog
Toad
Edible
Poisonous— do not eat
Freshwater clams
Snails
Lizards
Crickets

Pest management

Leeches are common in rice paddies. Use a cigarette to remove them...

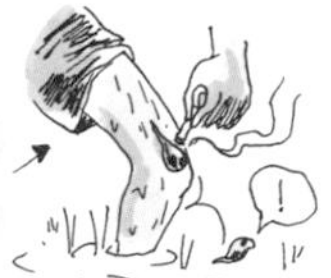
!

Hygiene

Brush teeth with coal after every meal.

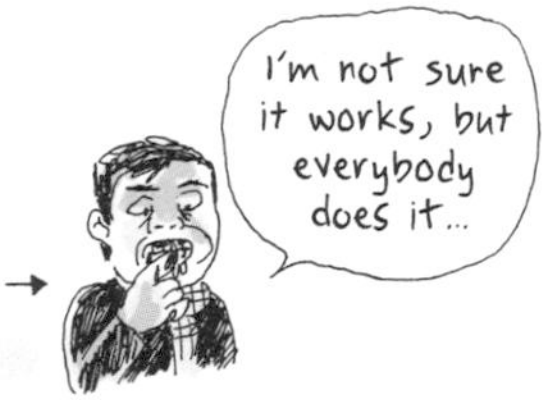
I'm not sure it works, but everybody does it...

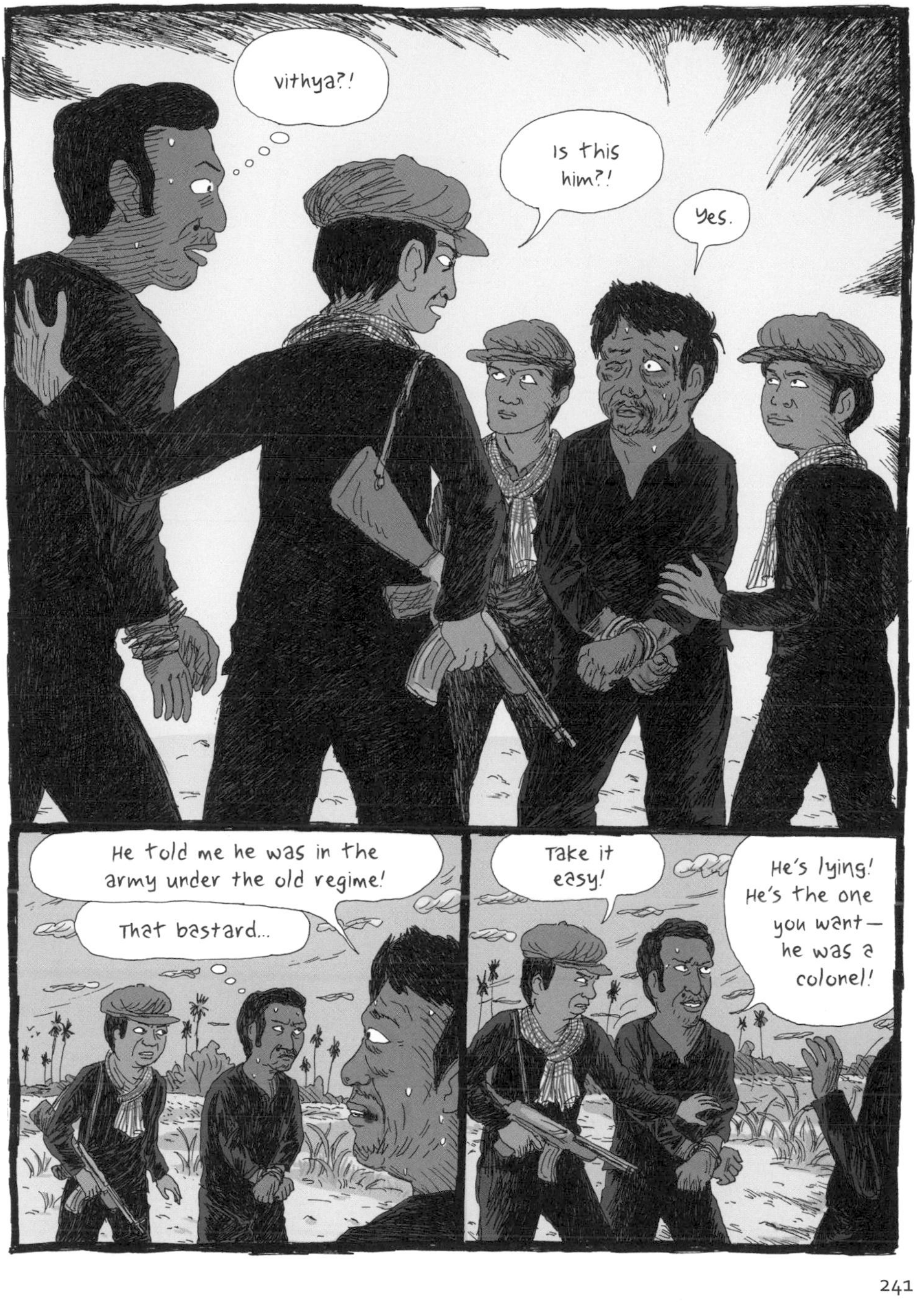
vithya?!
Is this him?!
Yes.
He told me he was in the army under the old regime!
That bastard...
Take it easy!
He's lying! He's the one you want—he was a colonel!

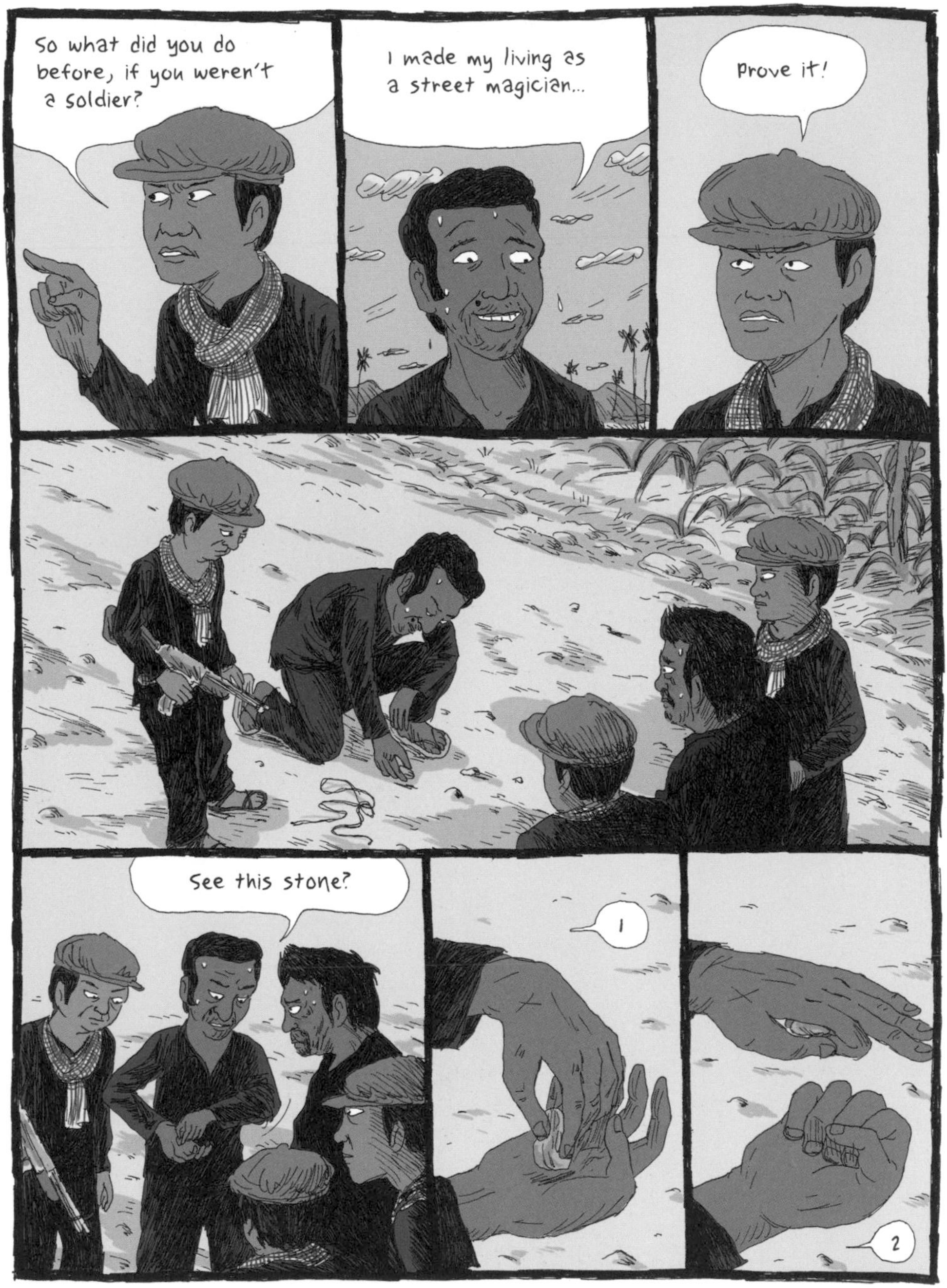
So what did you do before, if you weren't a soldier?
I made my living as a street magician...
Prove it!
See this stone?
1
2

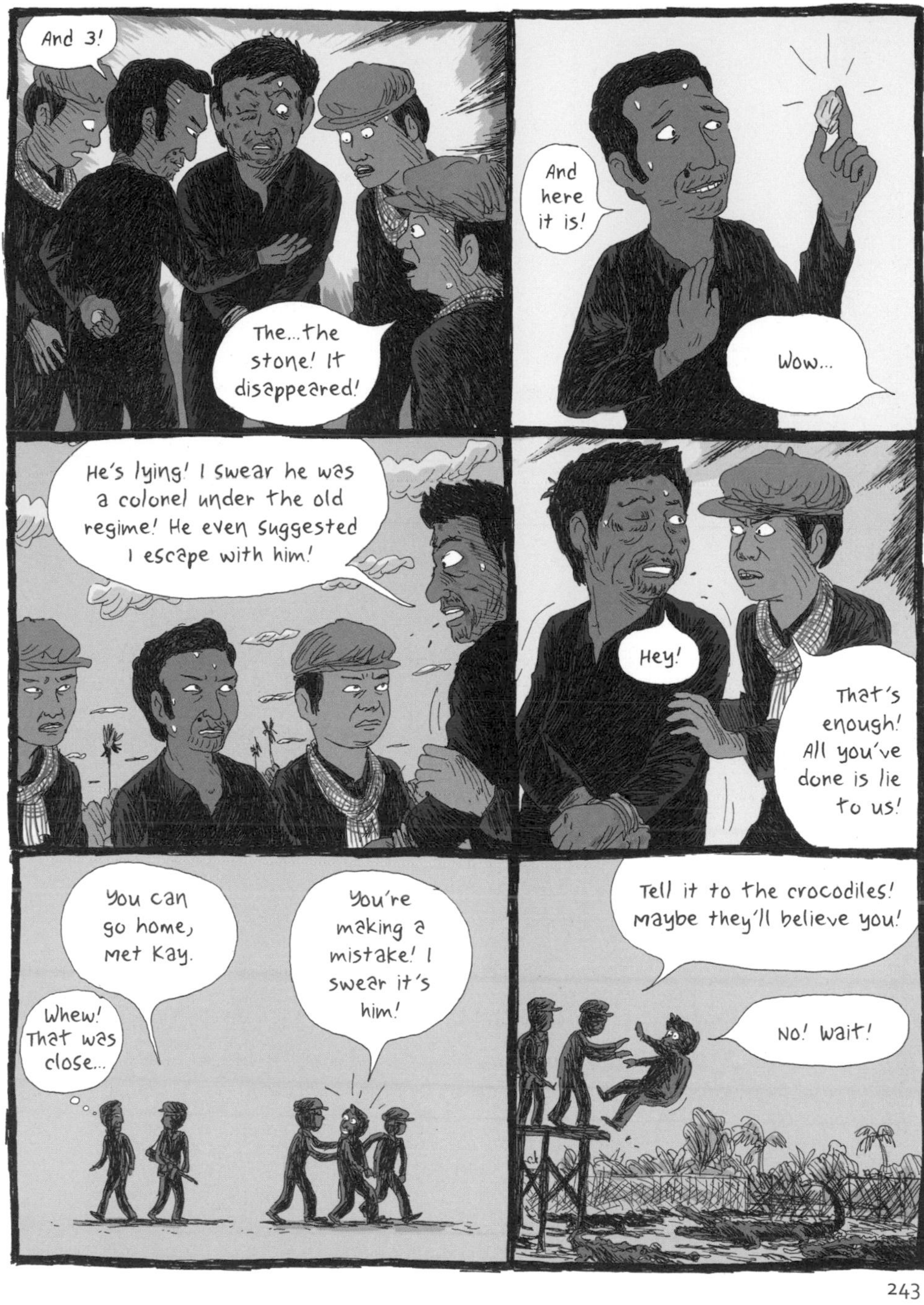
And 3!
The...the stone! It disappeared!
And here it is!
Wow...
He's lying! I swear he was a colonel under the old regime! He even suggested I escape with him!
Hey!
That's enough! All you've done is lie to us!
You can go home, Met Kay.
Whew! That was close...
You're making a mistake! I swear it's him!
Tell it to the crocodiles! Maybe they'll believe you!
No! Wait!

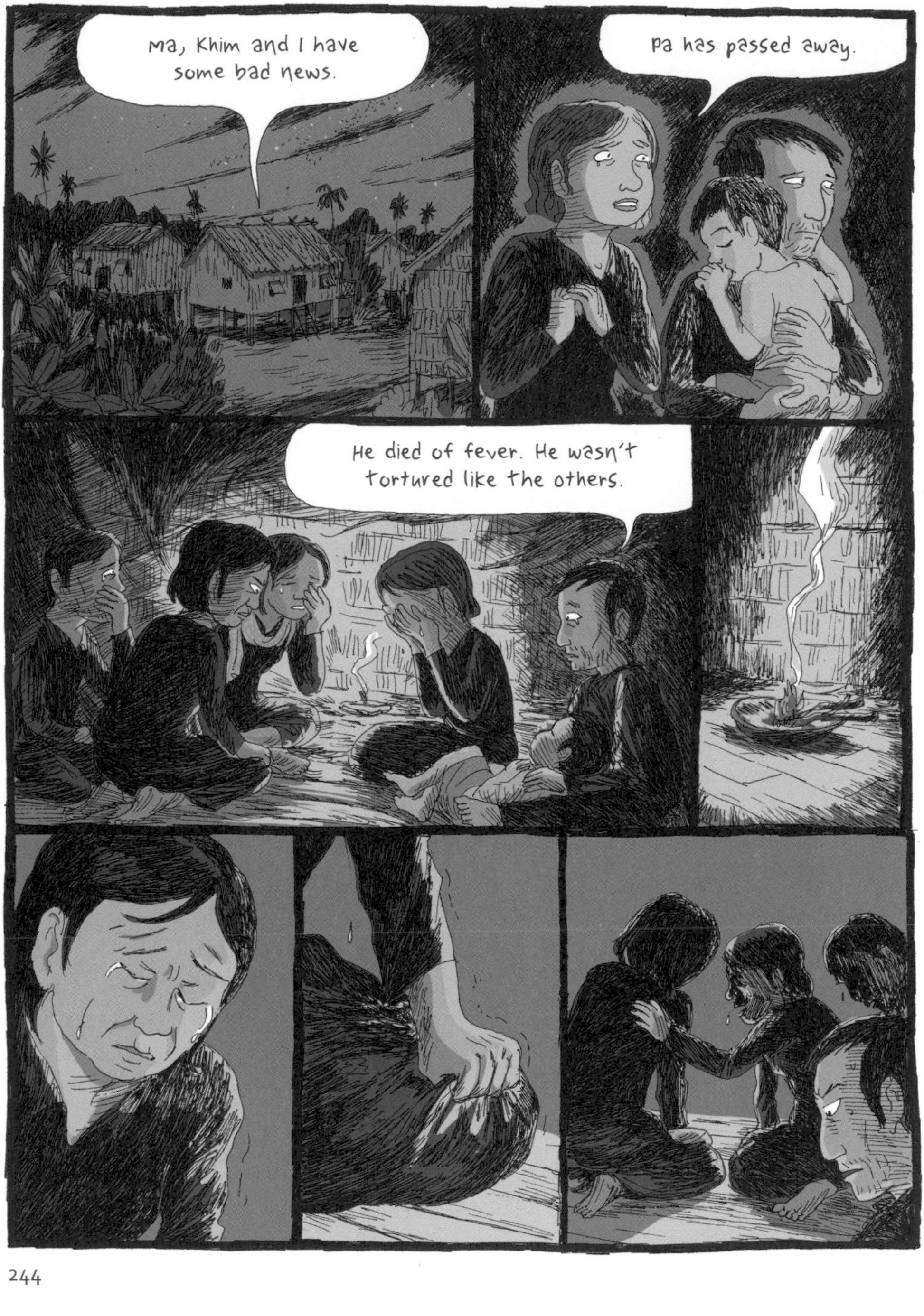
Ma, Khim and I have some bad news.
Pa has passed away.
He died of fever. He wasn't tortured like the others.

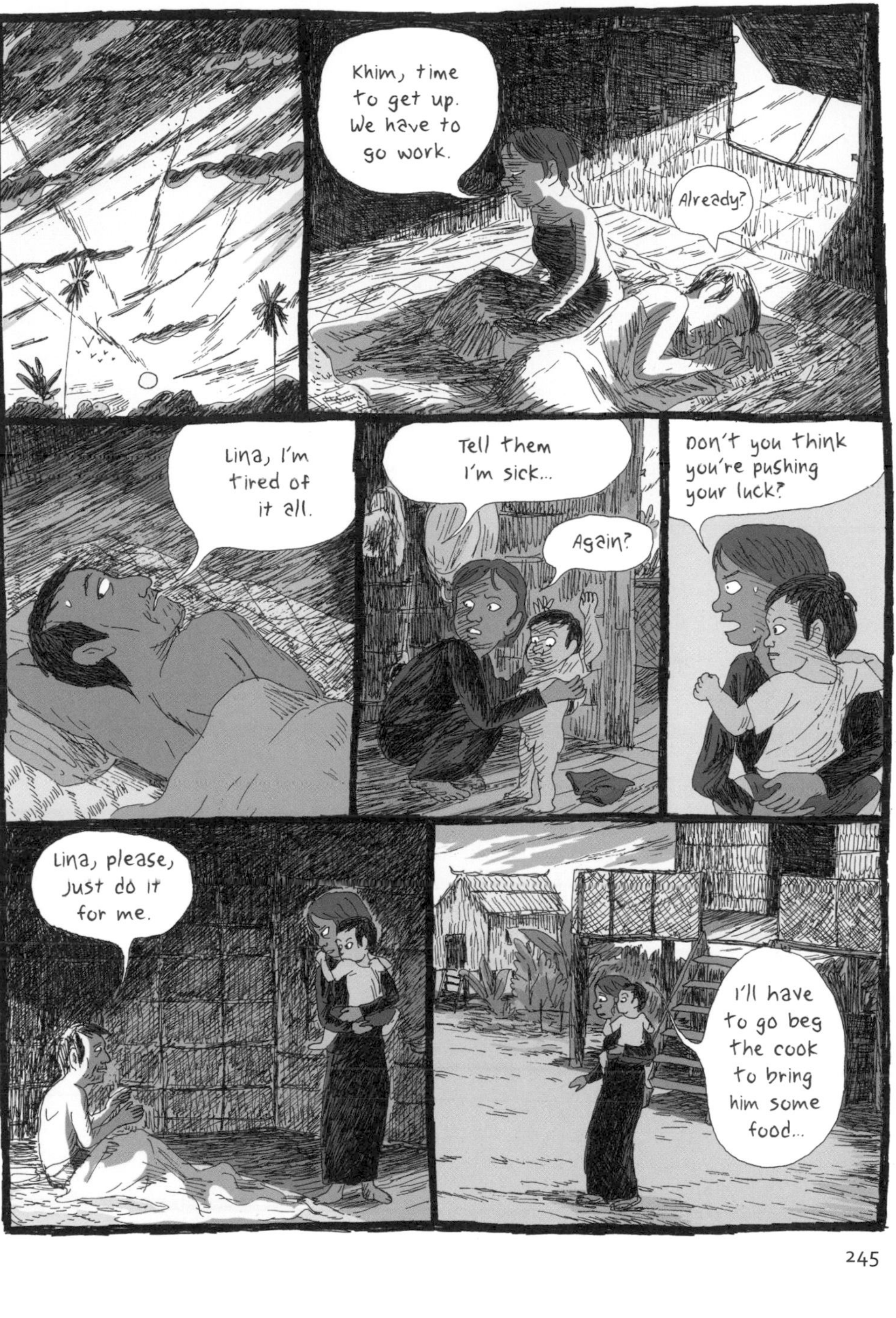
Khim, time to get up. We have to go work.
Already?
Lina, I'm tired of it all.
Tell them I'm sick...
Again?
Don't you think you're pushing your luck?
Lina, please, just do it for me.
I'll have to go beg the cook to bring him some food...

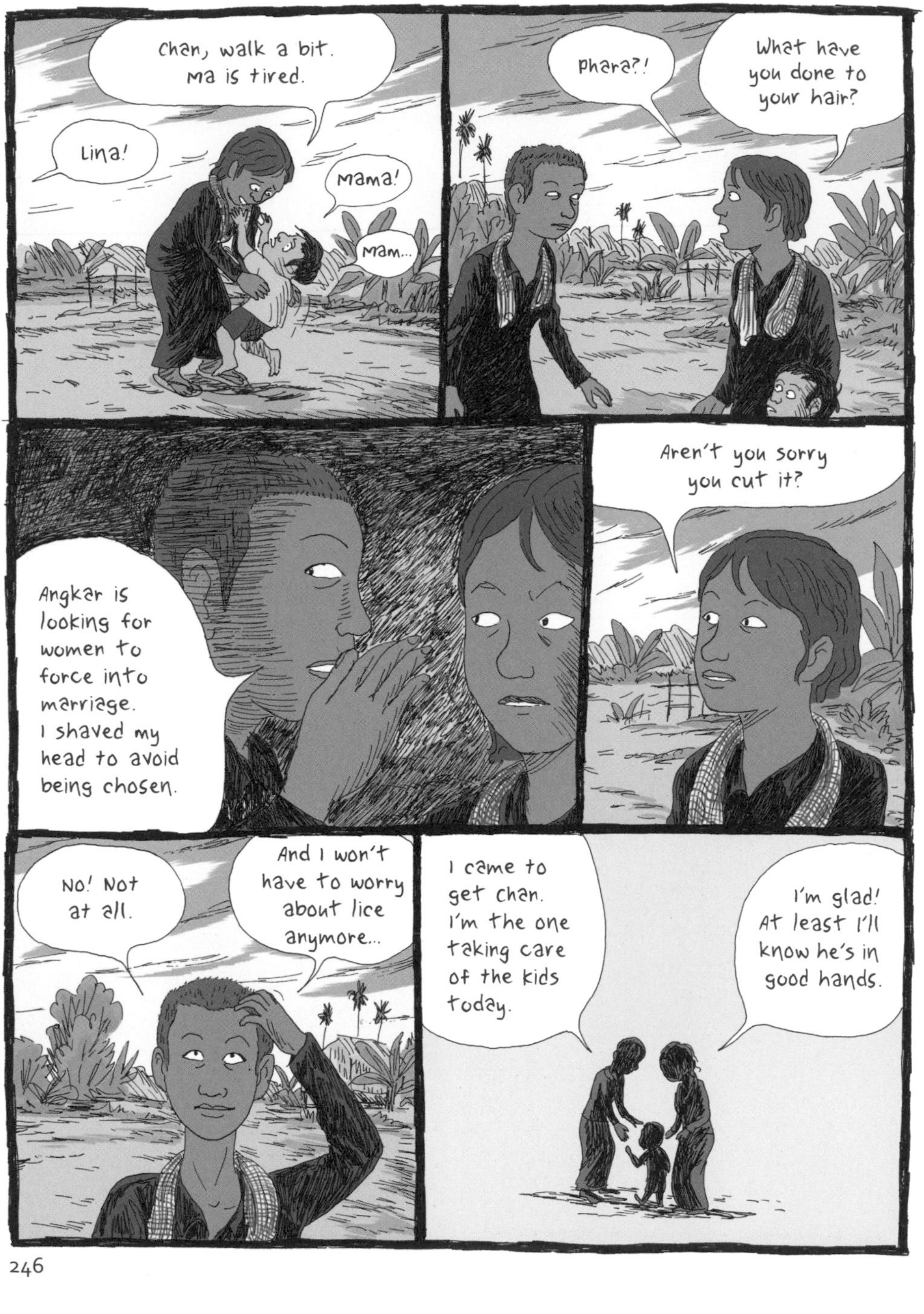
Chan, walk a bit. Ma is tired.
Lina!
Mama!
Mam...
Phara?!
What have you done to your hair?
Angkar is looking for women to force into marriage. I shaved my head to avoid being chosen.
Aren't you sorry you cut it?
No! Not at all.
And I won't have to worry about lice anymore...
I came to get Chan. I'm the one taking care of the kids today.
I'm glad! At least I'll know he's in good hands.

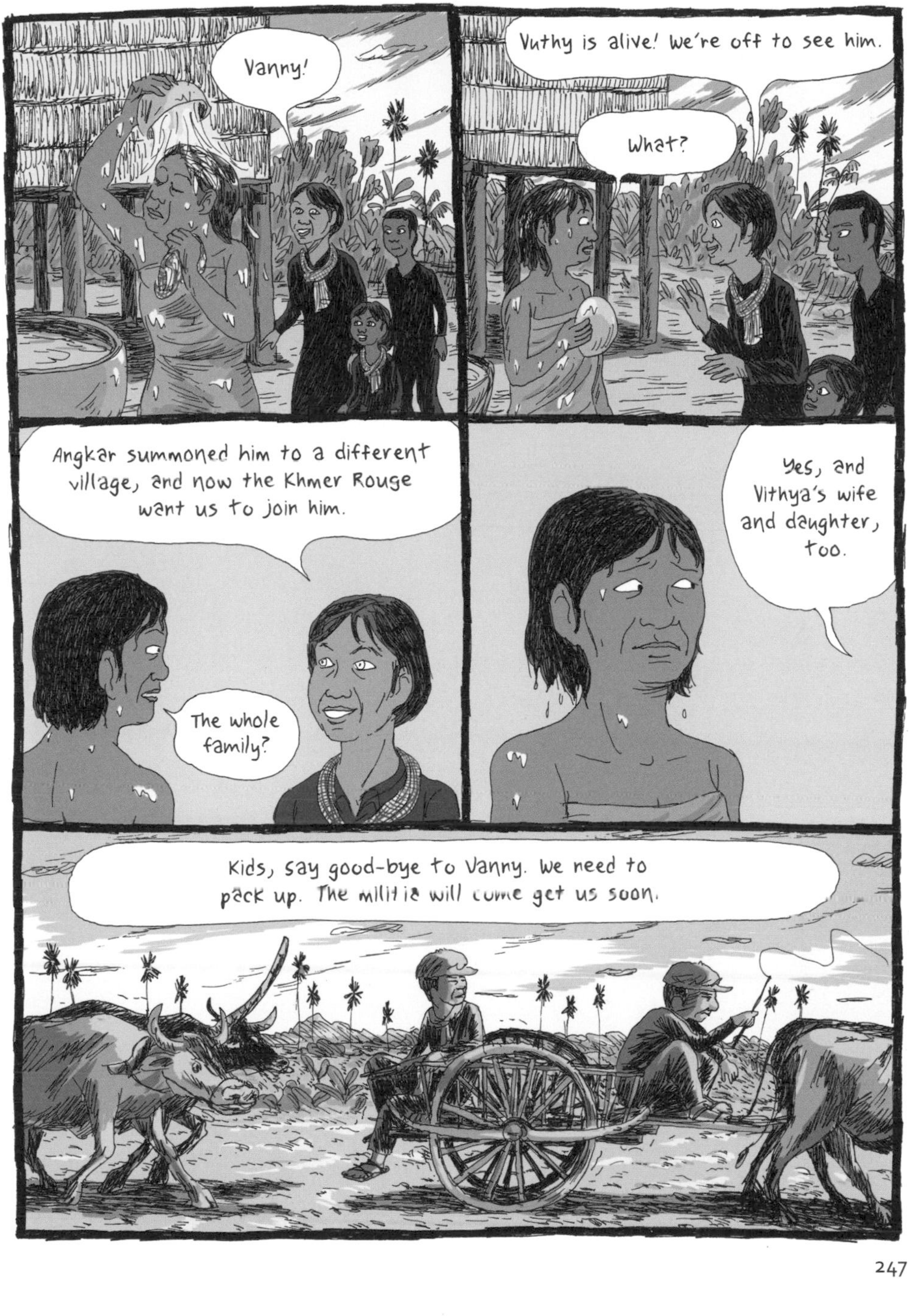
Vanny!
Vuthy is alive! We're off to see him.
What?
Angkar summoned him to a different village, and now the Khmer Rouge want us to join him.
The whole family?
Yes, and Vithya's wife and daughter, too.
Kids, say good-bye to Vanny. We need to pack up. The militia will come get us soon.

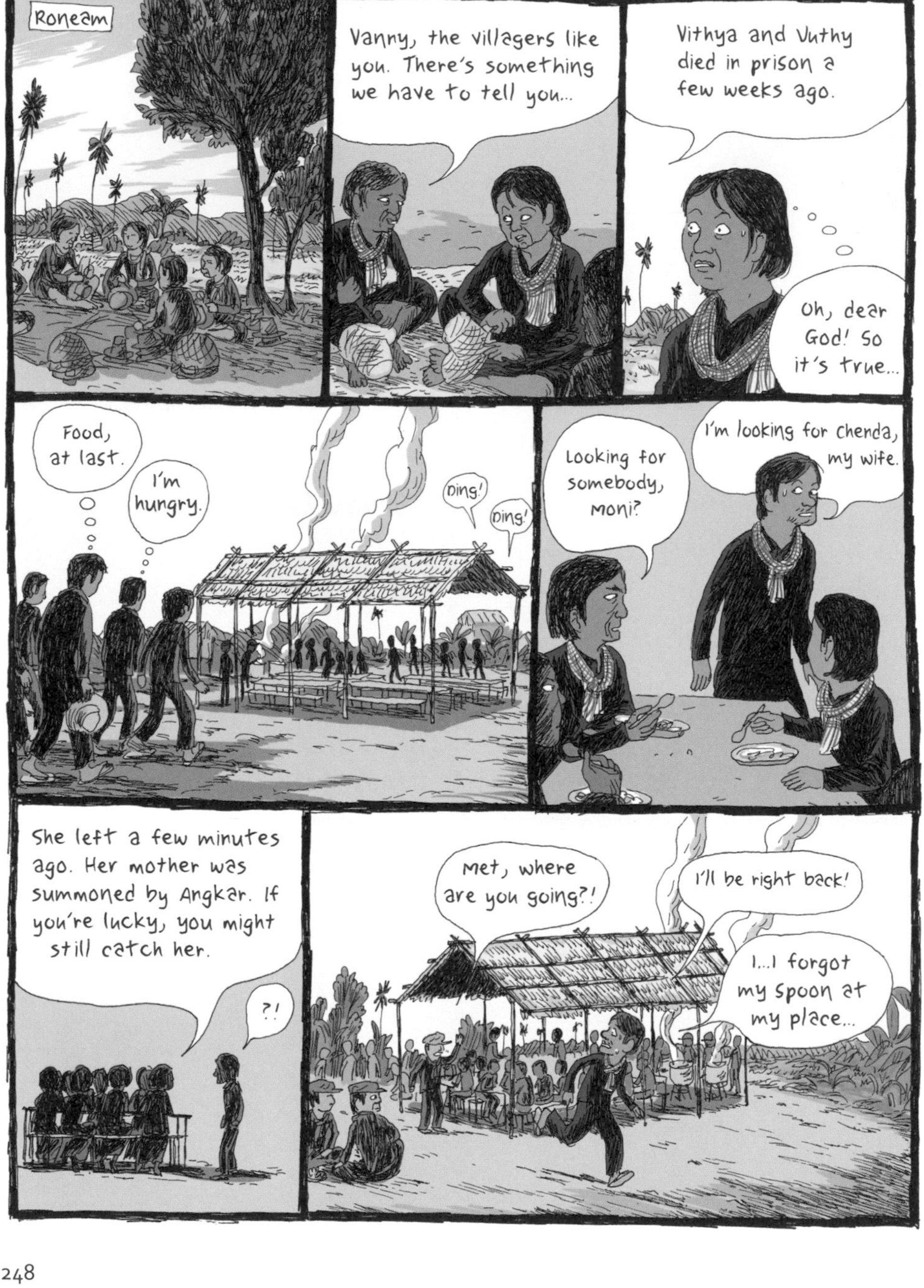
Roneam
Vanny, the villagers like you. There's something we have to tell you...
Vithya and Vuthy died in prison a few weeks ago.
Oh, dear God! So it's true...
Food, at last.
I'm hungry.
Ding!
Ding!
Looking for somebody, Moni?
I'm looking for Chenda, my wife.
She left a few minutes ago. Her mother was summoned by Angkar. If you're lucky, you might still catch her.
?!
Met, where are you going?!
I'll be right back!
I...I forgot my spoon at my place...

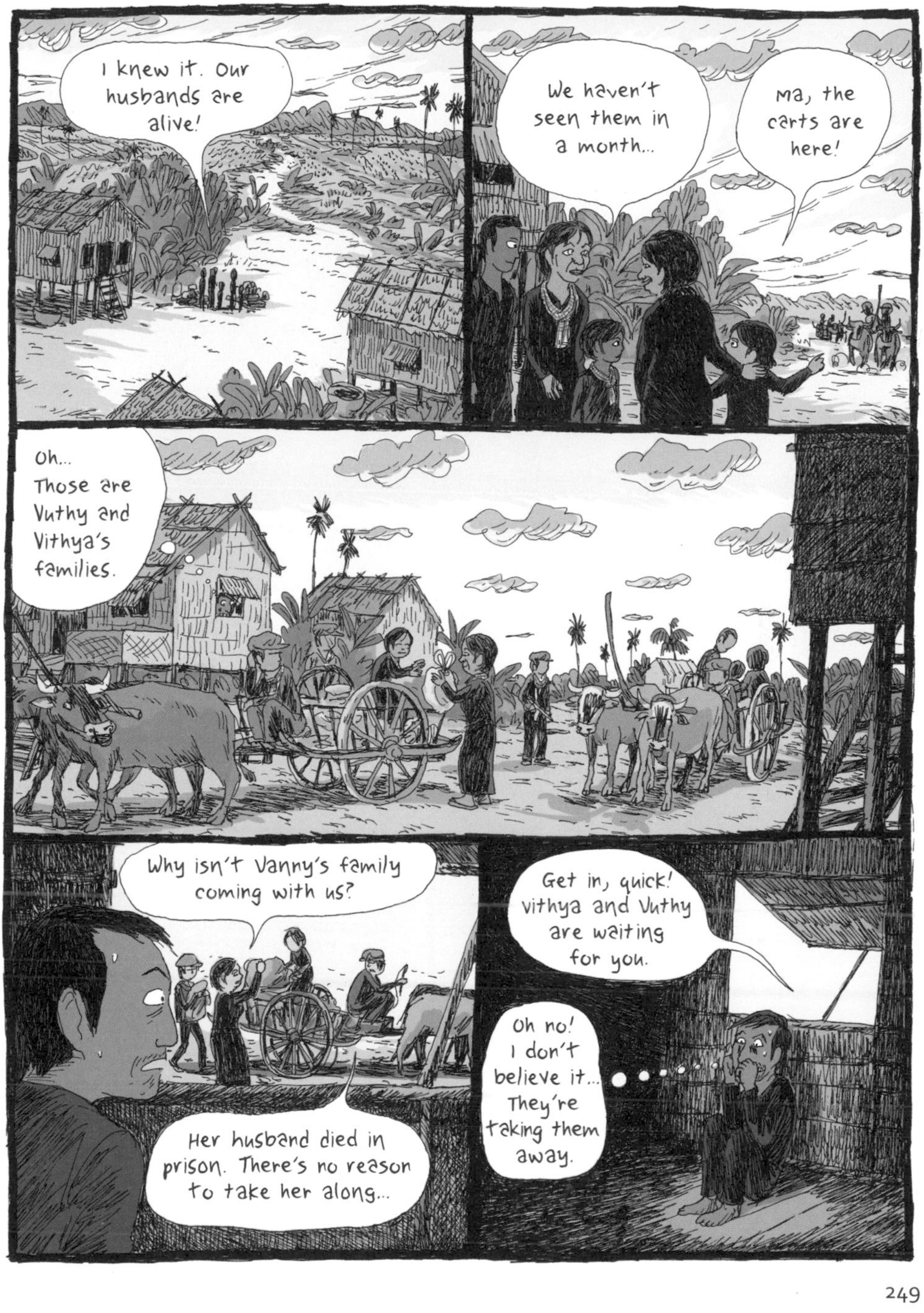
I knew it. Our husbands are alive!
We haven't seen them in a month...
Ma, the carts are here!
Oh... Those are Vuthy and Vithya's families.
Why isn't Vanny's family coming with us?
Her husband died in prison. There's no reason to take her along...
Get in, quick! Vithya and Vuthy are waiting for you.
Oh no! I don't believe it... They're taking them away.

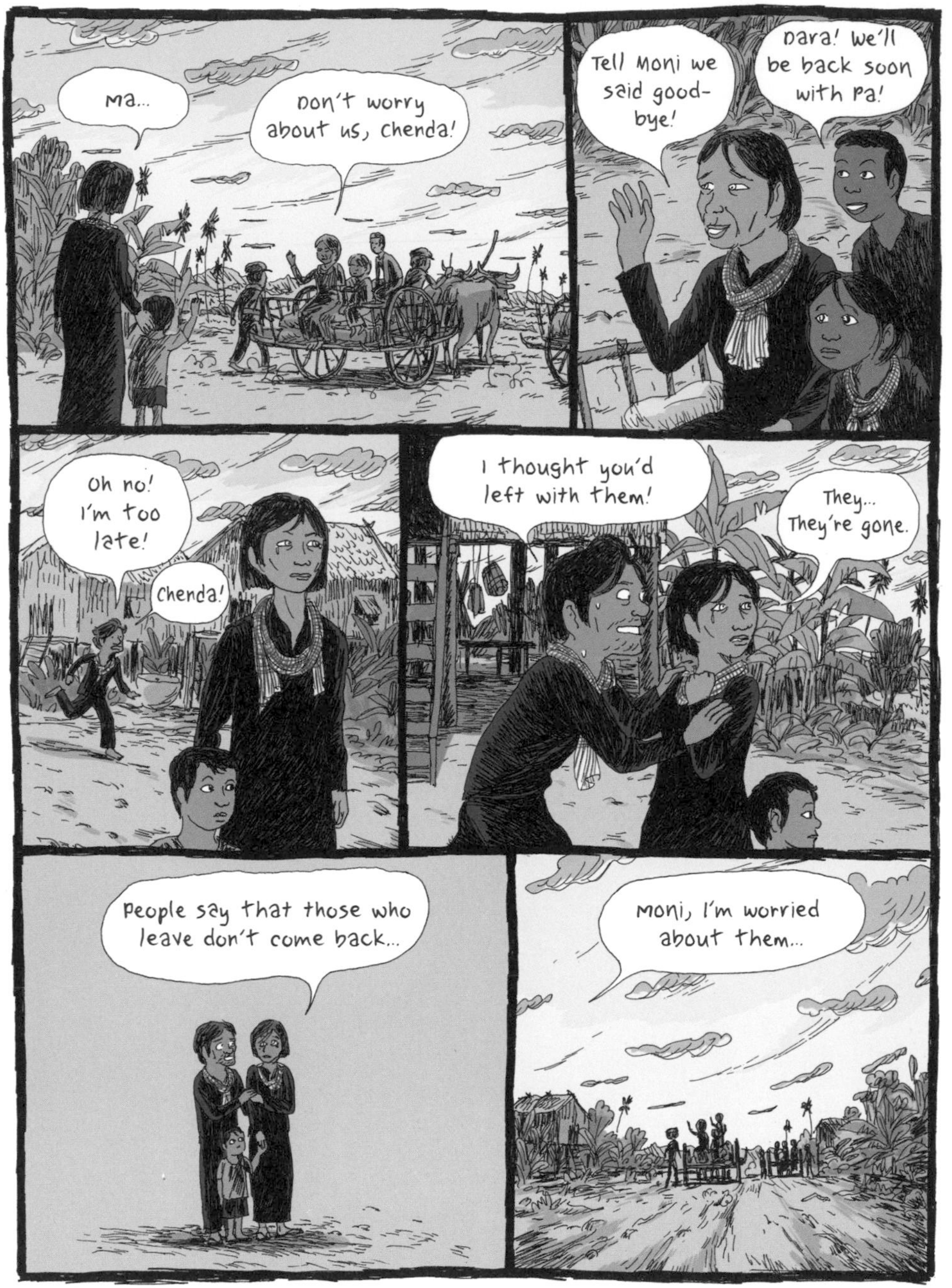
Ma...
Don't worry about us, Chenda!
Tell Moni we said good-bye!
Dara! We'll be back soon with Pa!
Oh no! I'm too late!
Chenda!
I thought you'd left with them!
They... They're gone.
People say that those who leave don't come back...
Moni, I'm worried about them...

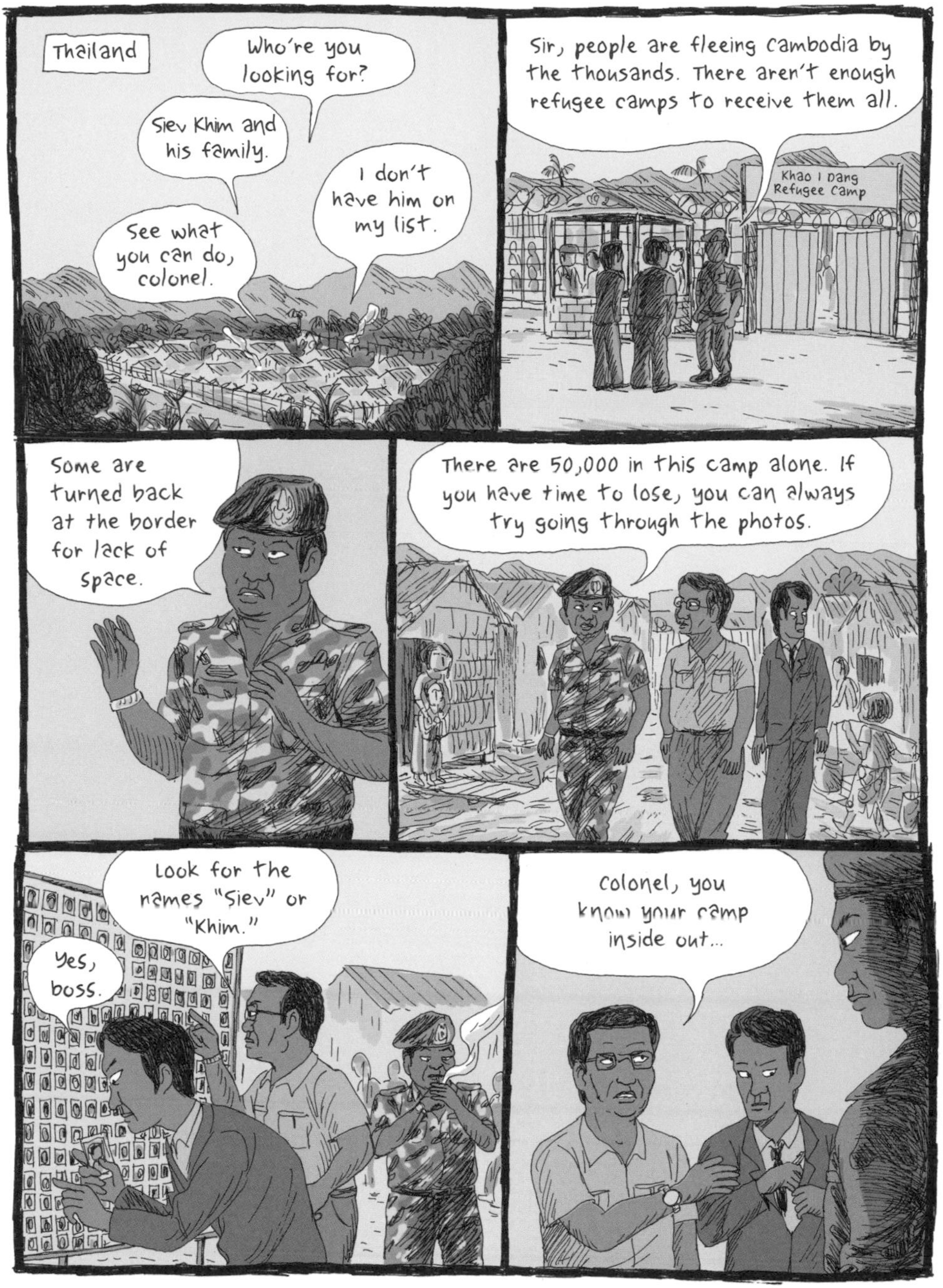
Thailand
Who're you looking for?
Siev Khim and his family.
See what you can do, colonel.
I don't have him on my list.
Khao I Dang Refugee Camp
Sir, people are fleeing Cambodia by the thousands. There aren't enough refugee camps to receive them all.
Some are turned back at the border for lack of space.
There are 50,000 in this camp alone. If you have time to lose, you can always try going through the photos.
Look for the names "Siev" or "Khim."
Yes, boss.
Colonel, you know your camp inside out...

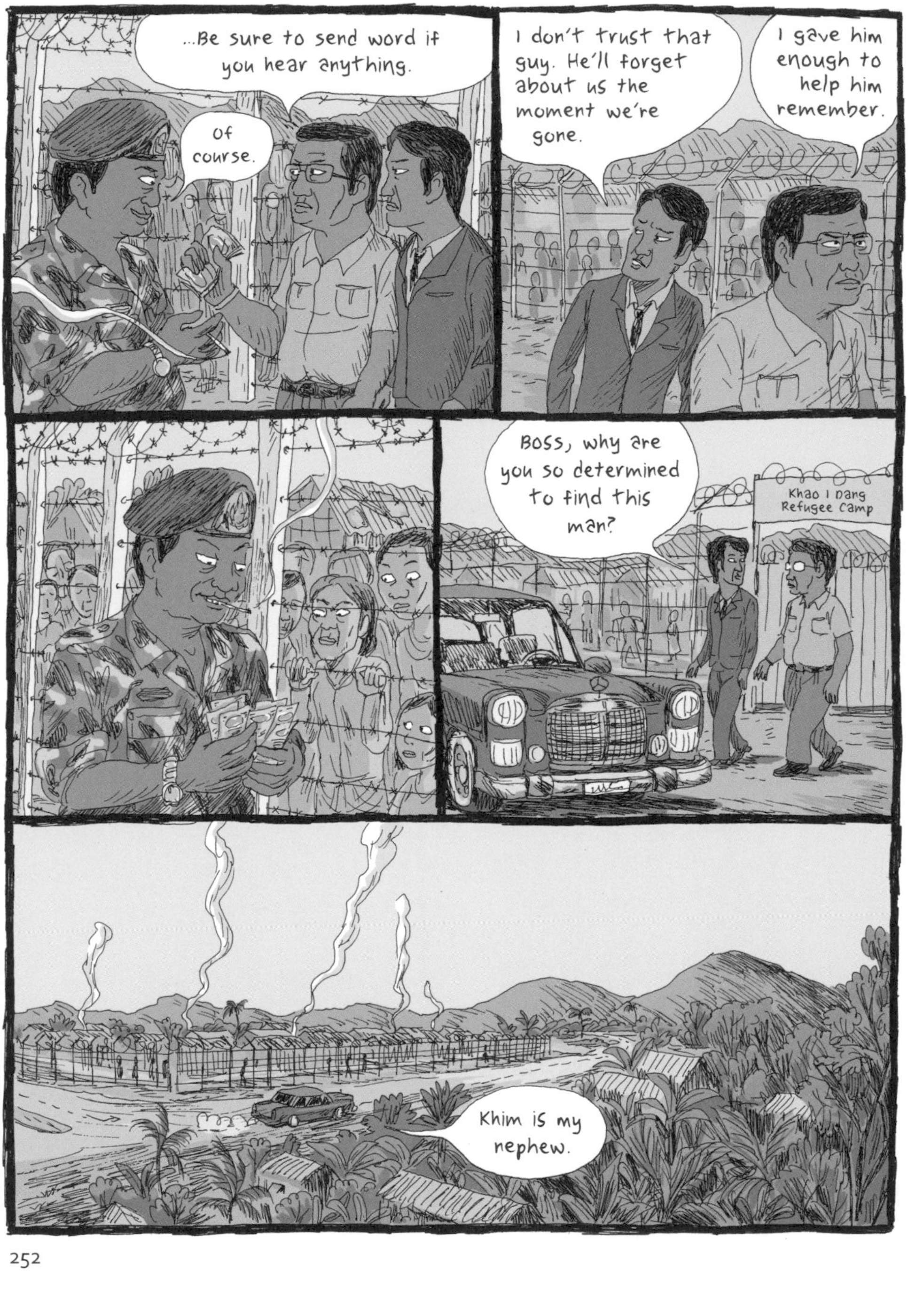
...Be sure to send word if you hear anything.
Of course.
I don't trust that guy. He'll forget about us the moment we're gone.
I gave him enough to help him remember.
Boss, why are you so determined to find this man?
Khao I Dang Refugee Camp
Khim is my nephew.

Souvenir album pre-1975

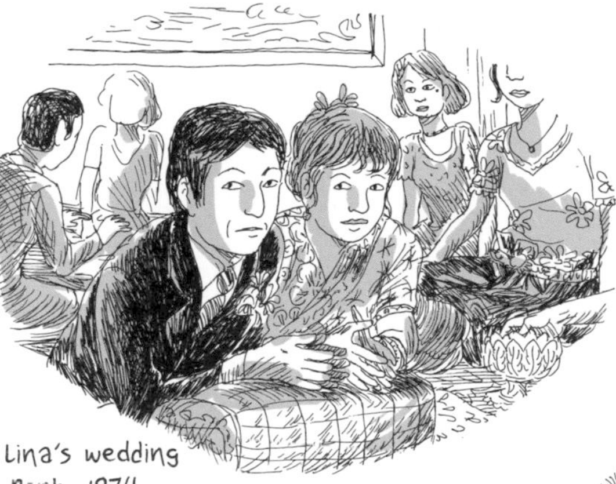

Khim and Lina's wedding
Phnom Penh, 1974

Lina's brothers,
1972

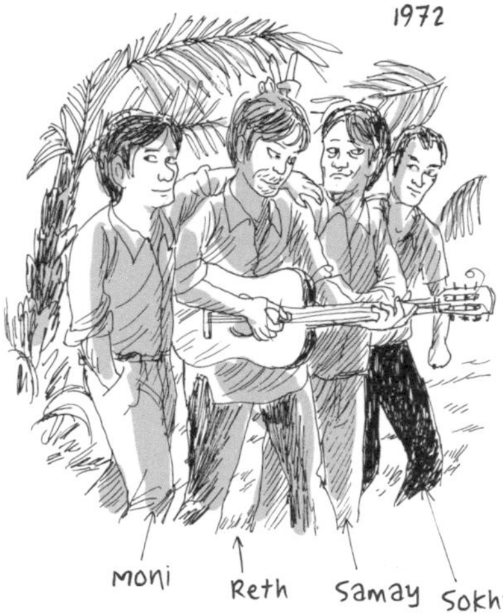
Moni
Reth
Samay
Sokha

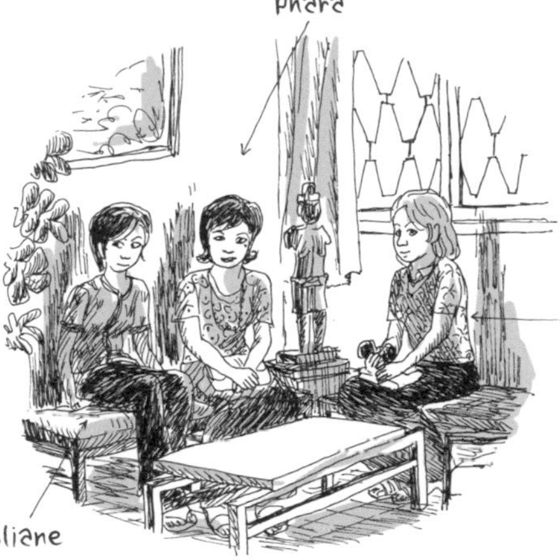
Phara
Lina
Koliane

Lina and her sisters in their
family home—Phnom Penh, 1970

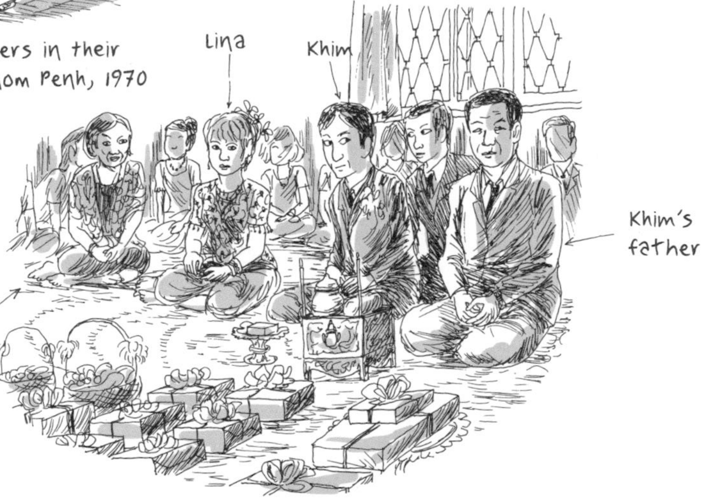
Lina
Khim
Khim's father
Khim's mother

Wedding ceremony
in Lina's family
home, 1974

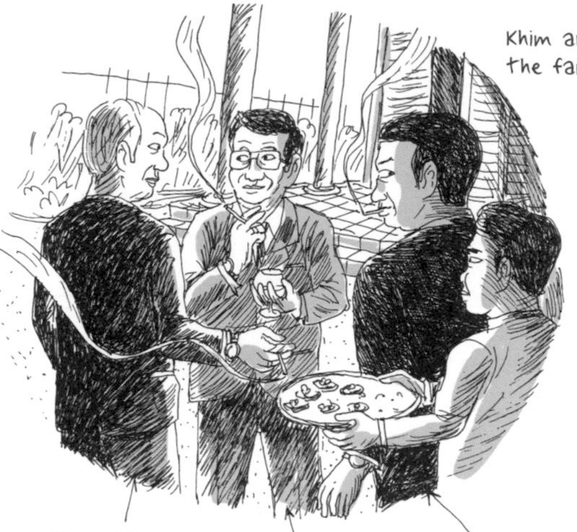
Kongcha
Khim's uncle
Vuthy

Khim and Lina's wedding in the family home, 1974

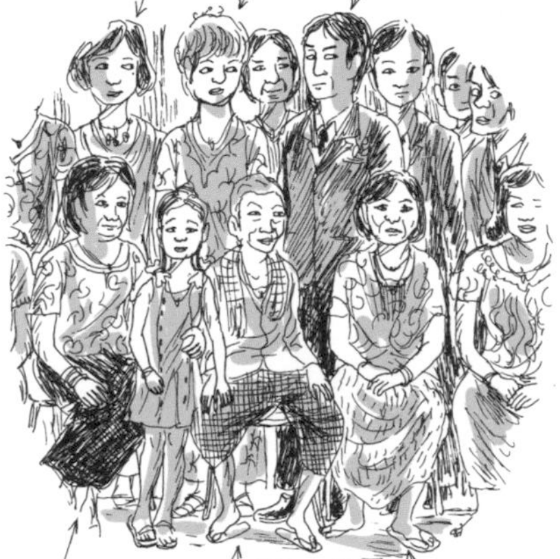
Phara
Lina
Khim
Vanny
Ma Som, in traditional attire
Khim's mother

Group photo Khim's wedding, 1974

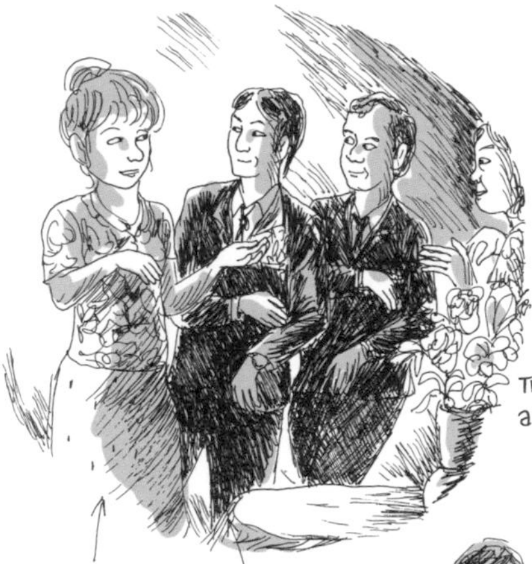
Lina
Khim

Traditional dance at Khim and Lina's wedding, 1974

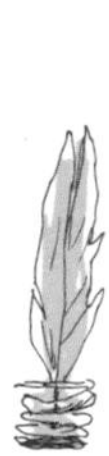

Sei is a popular Cambodian game. Players kick the "sei"—made of feathers attached to disks—to keep it in the air as long as possible.

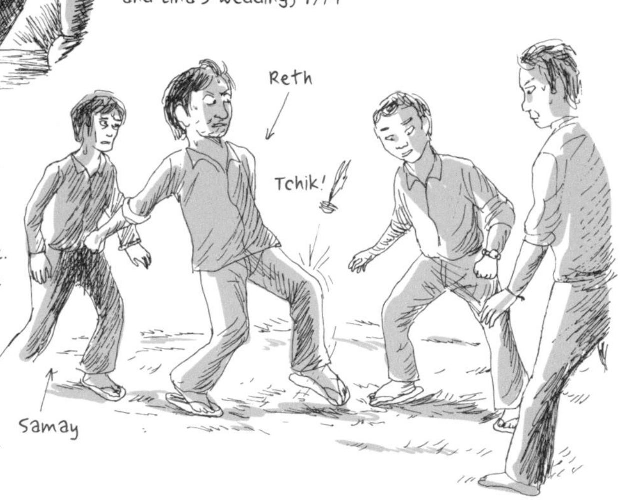
Reth
Tchik!
Samay

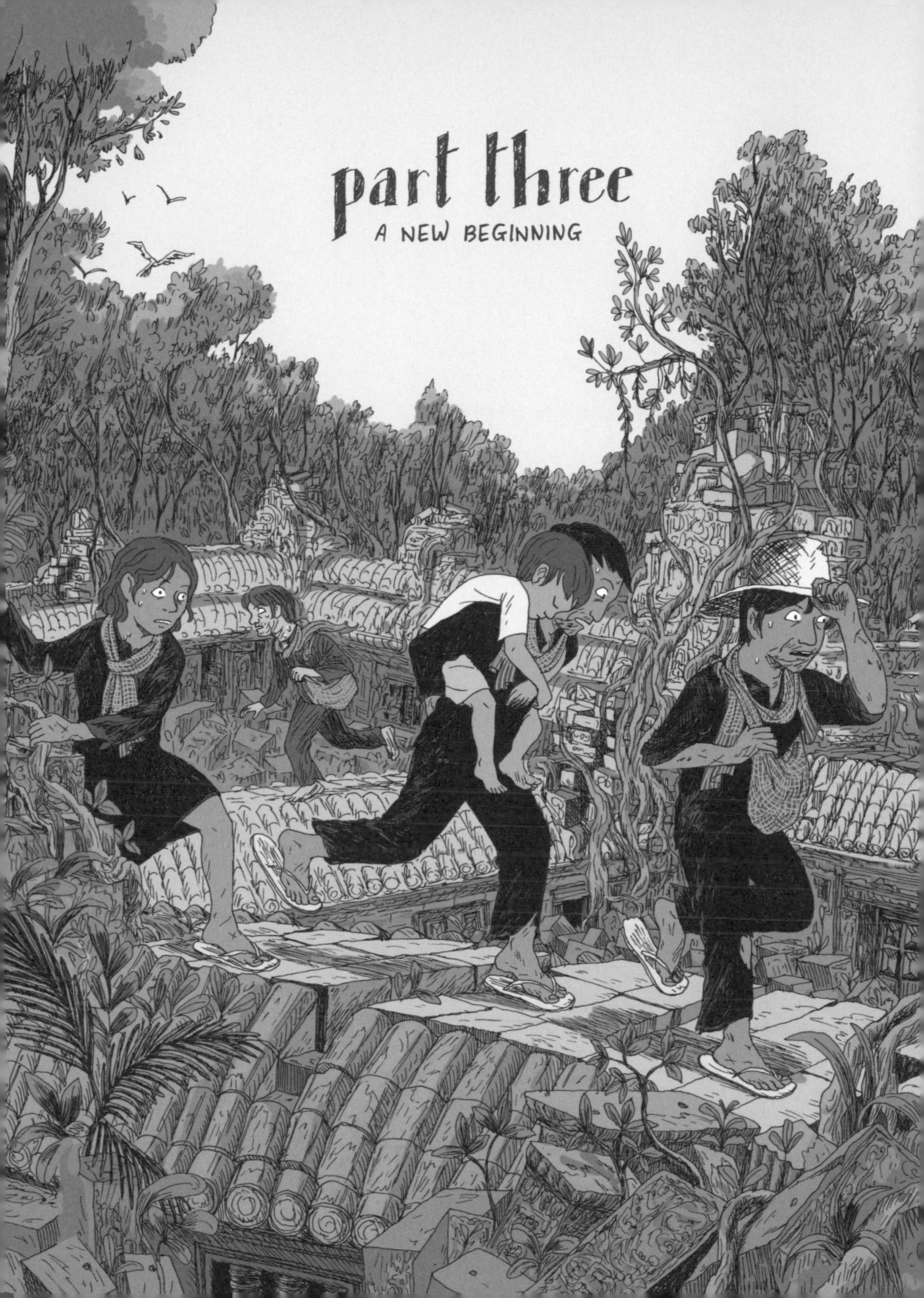
part three
A NEW BEGINNING

chapter 15

THE PURGE

THE KHMER ROUGE MACHINE

The Khmer Rouge machine began to jam. Angkar continued to eliminate the regime's opponents. After the new people, they moved onto those close to power. The purges started. Since the events, 191 political prisons have been identified. The most infamous were Thma Kup (M-13) and Tuol Sleng (S-21).

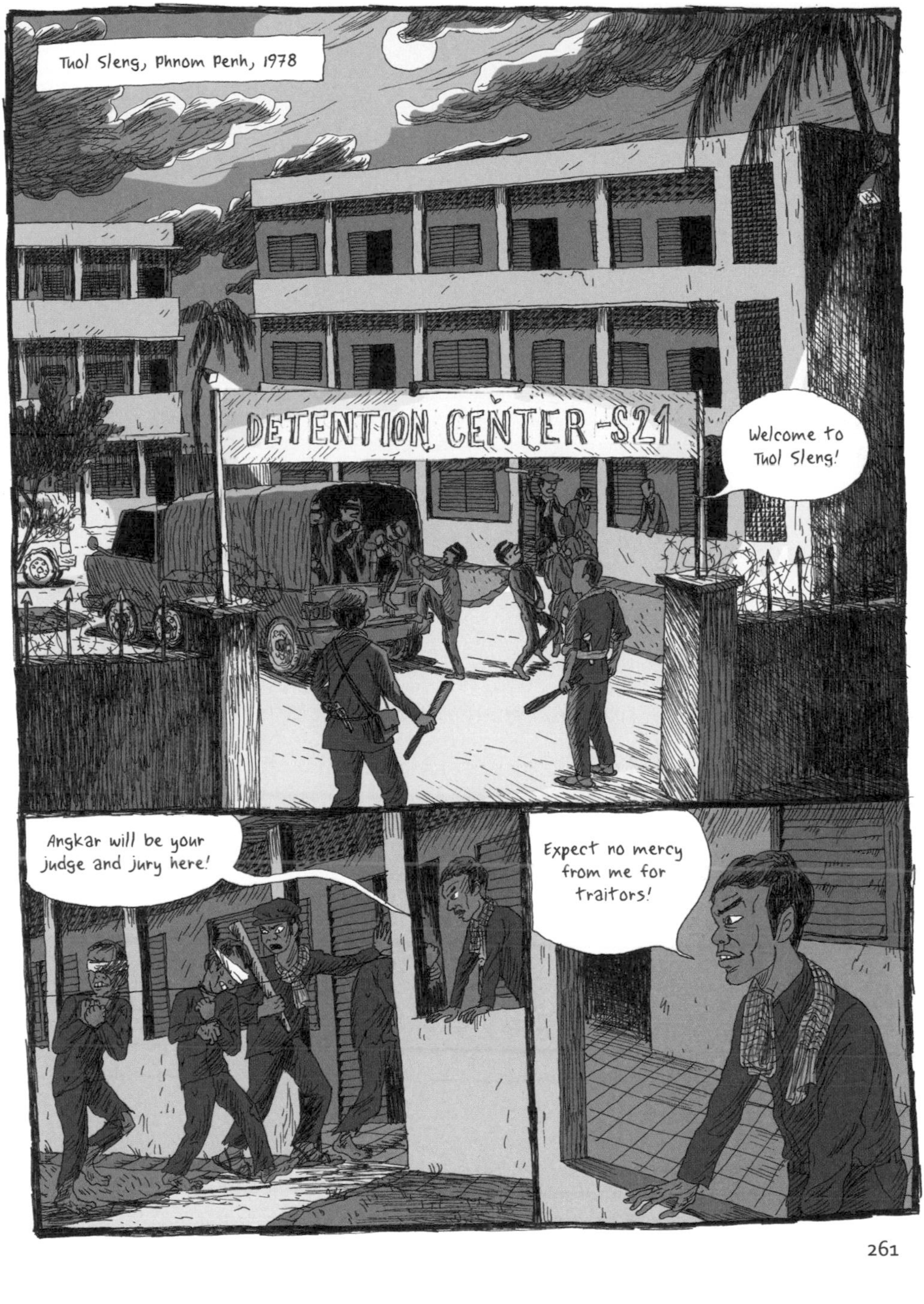
Tuol Sleng, Phnom Penh, 1978
DETENTION CENTER-S21
Welcome to Tuol Sleng!
Angkar will be your judge and jury here!
Expect no mercy from me for traitors!

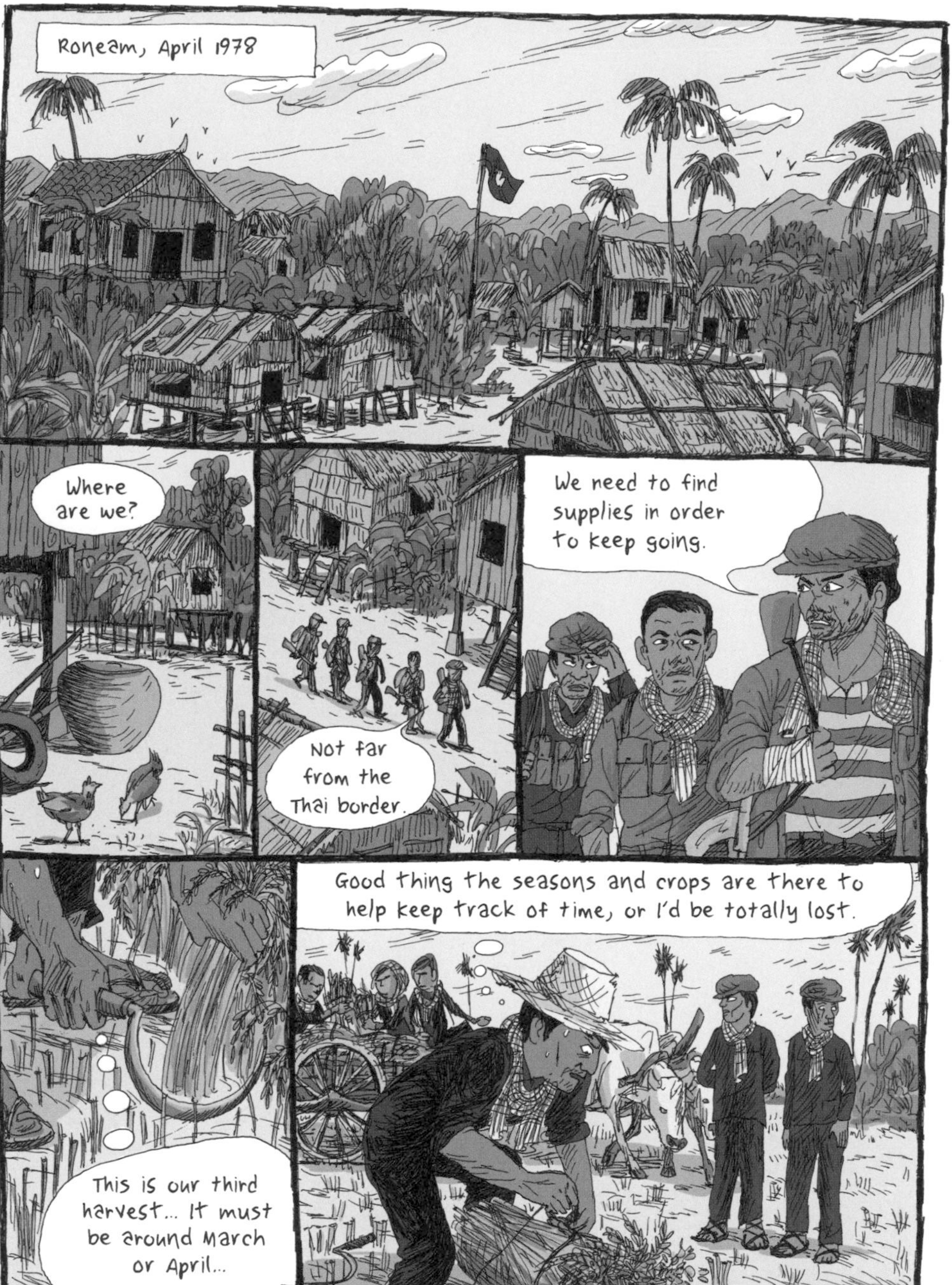

Roneam, April 1978
Where are we?
Not far from the Thai border.
We need to find supplies in order to keep going.
Good thing the seasons and crops are there to help keep track of time, or I'd be totally lost.
This is our third harvest... It must be around March or April...

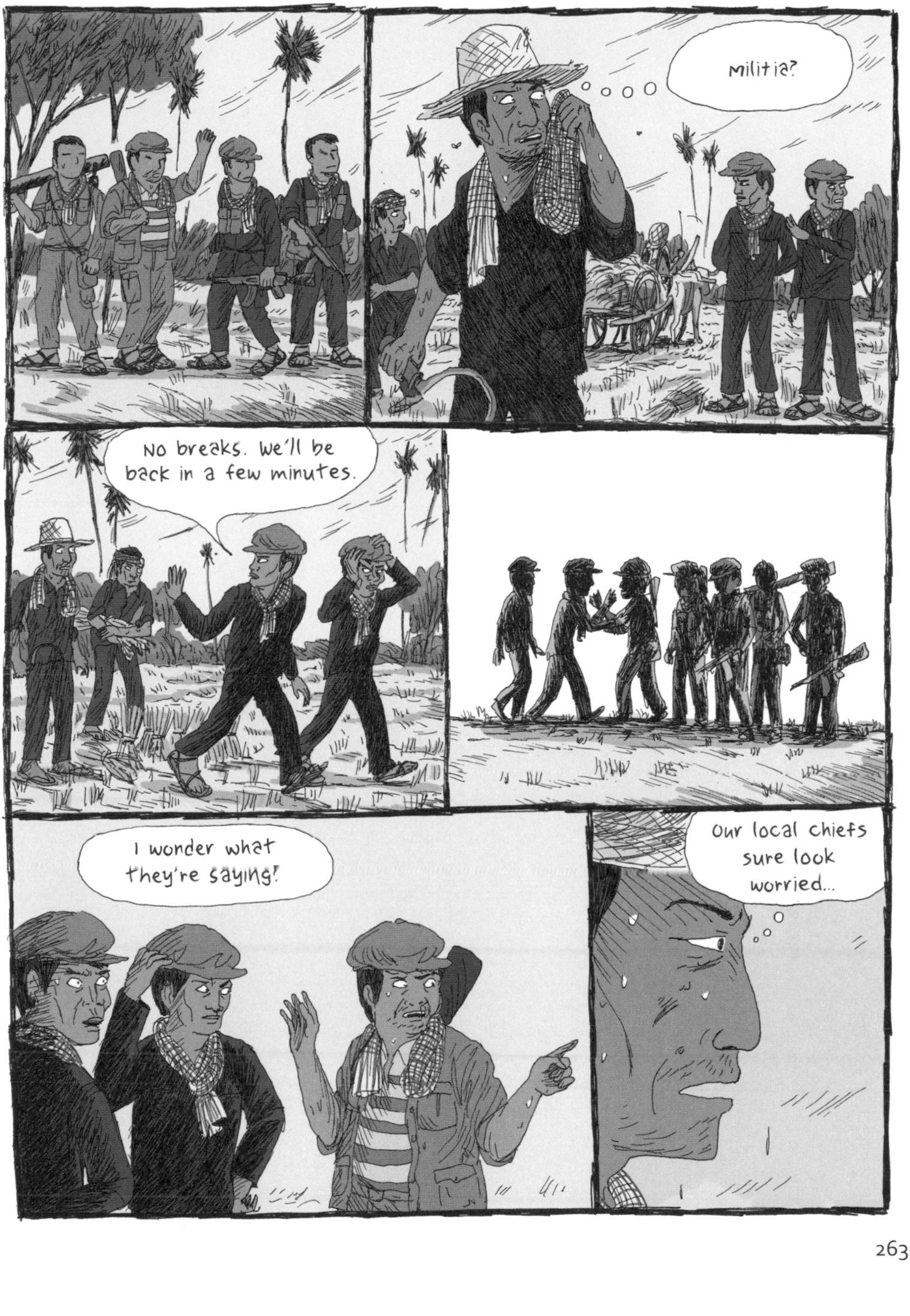
Militia?
No breaks. We'll be back in a few minutes.
I wonder what they're saying!
Our local chiefs sure look worried...

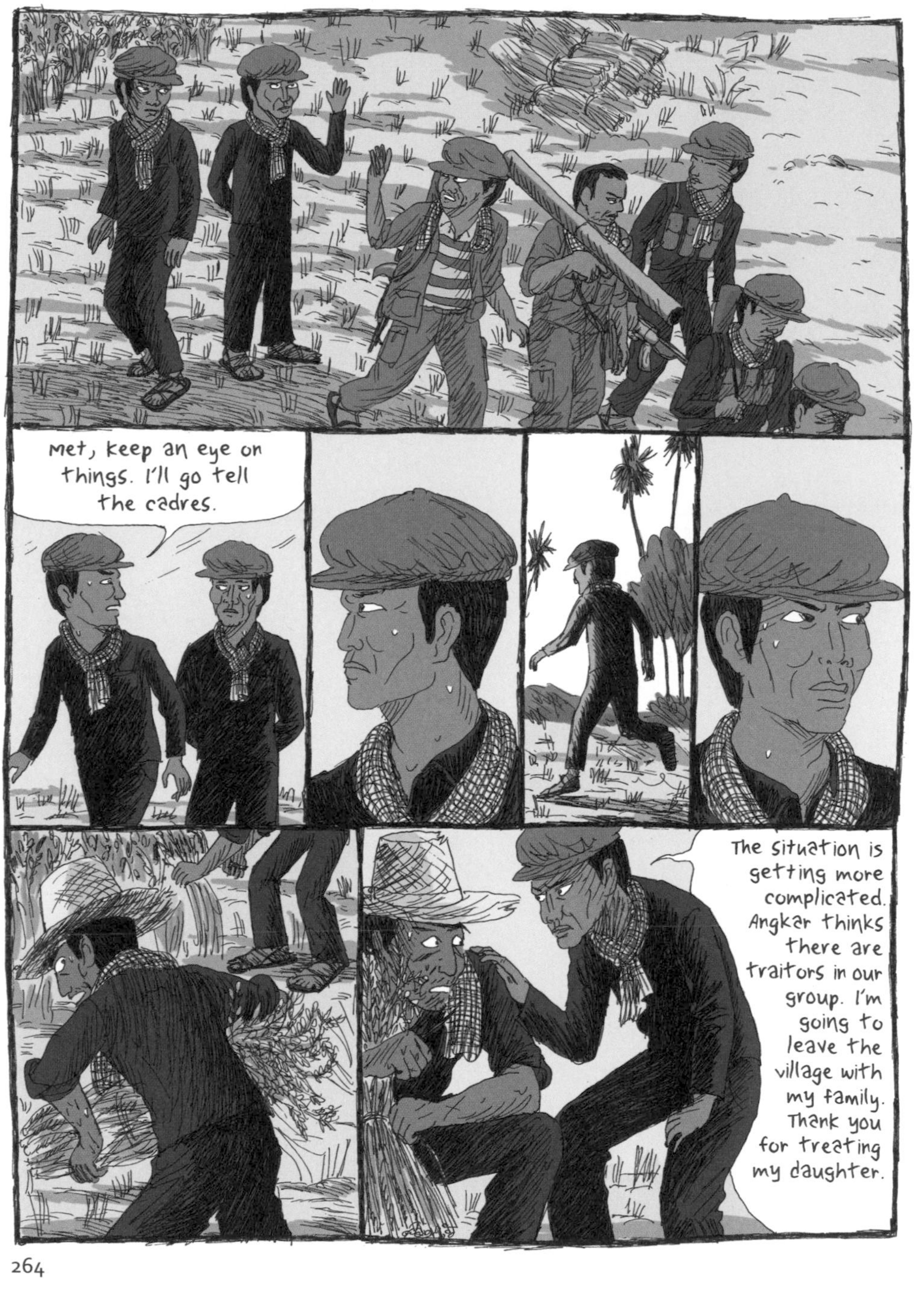

Met, keep an eye on things. I'll go tell the cadres.
The situation is getting more complicated. Angkar thinks there are traitors in our group. I'm going to leave the village with my family. Thank you for treating my daughter.

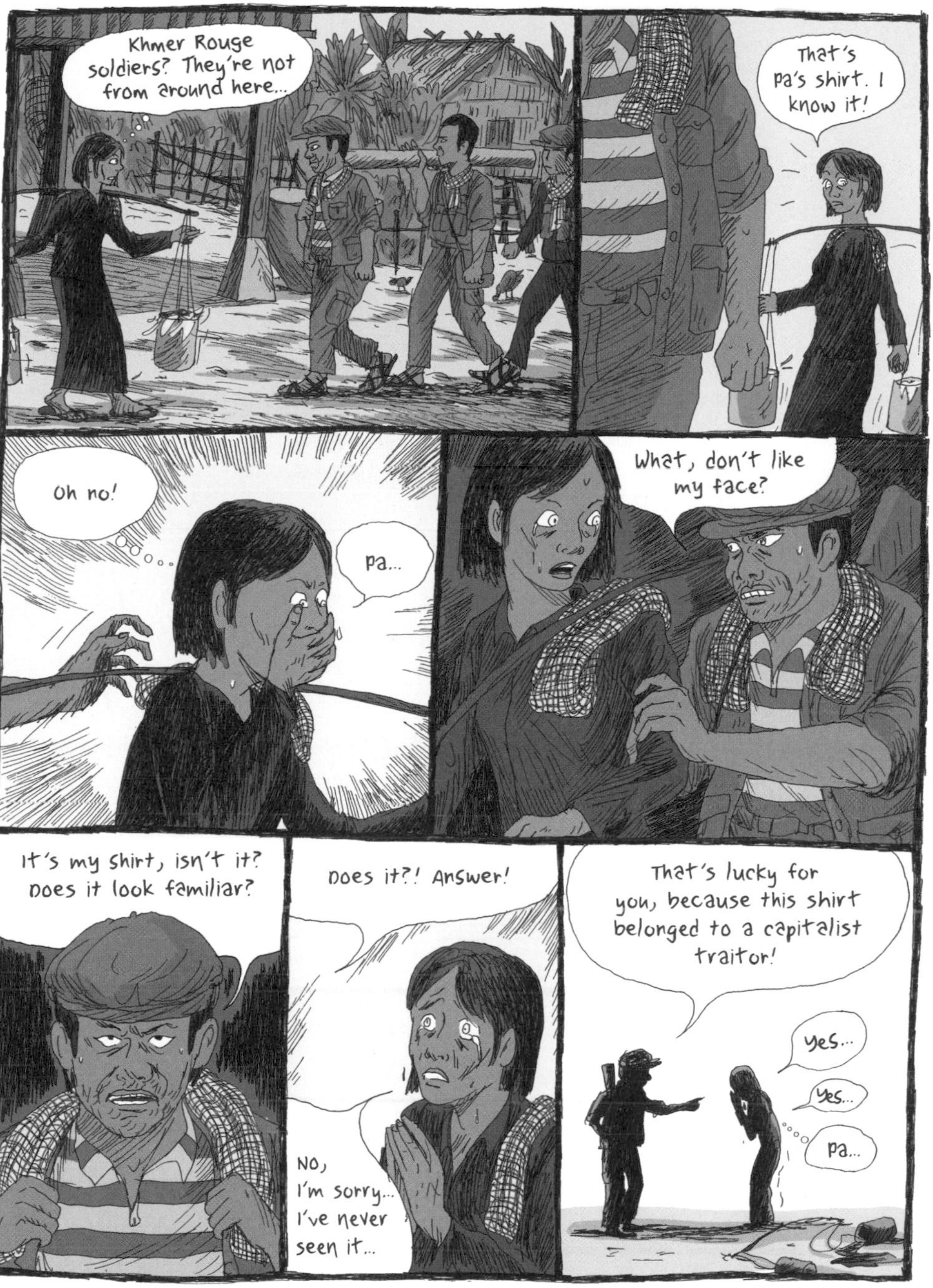
Khmer Rouge soldiers? They're not from around here...
That's pa's shirt. I know it!
Oh no!
pa...
What, don't like my face?
It's my shirt, isn't it? Does it look familiar?
Does it?! Answer!
No, I'm sorry... I've never seen it...
That's lucky for you, because this shirt belonged to a capitalist traitor!
Yes...
Yes...
pa...

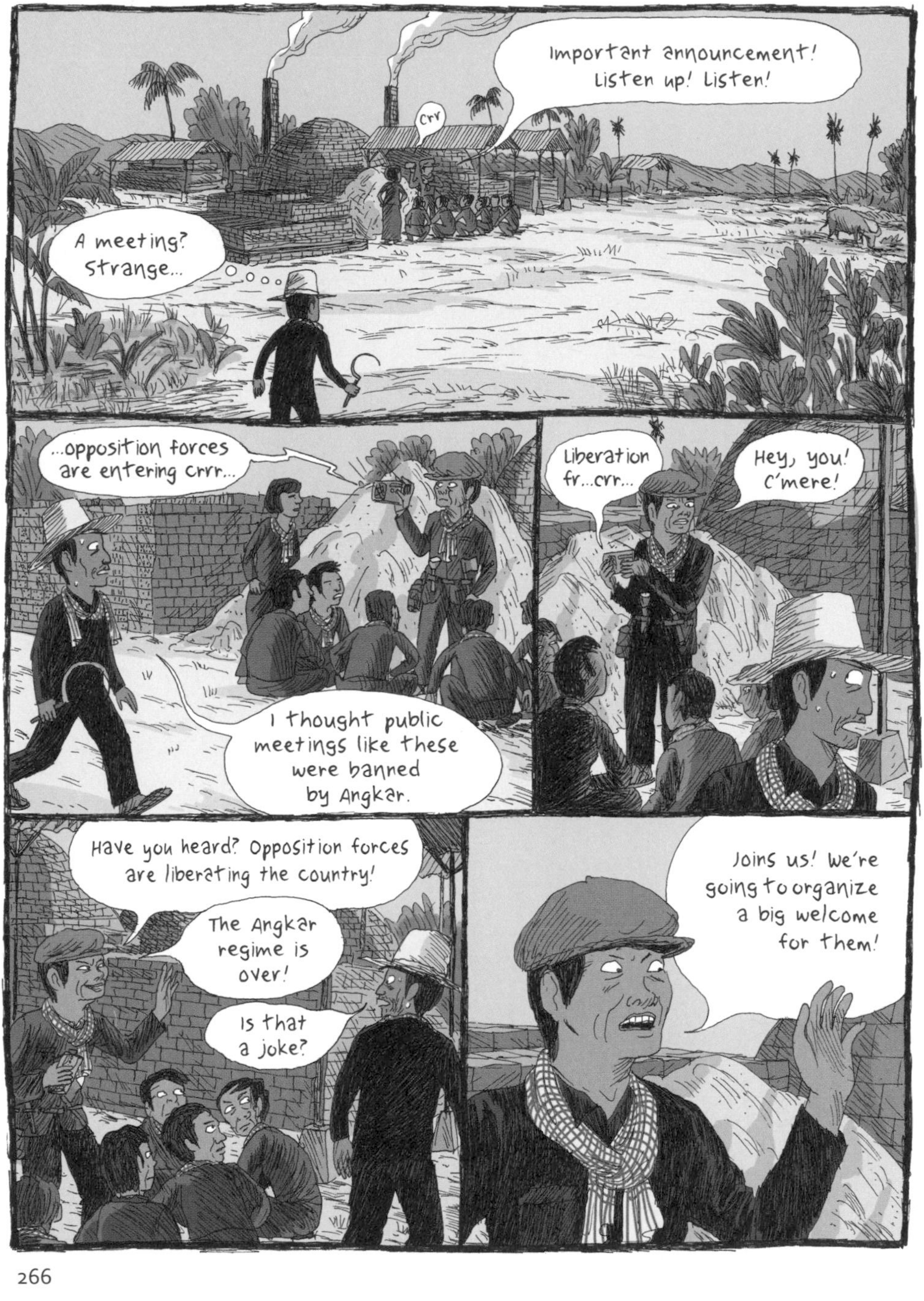

Important announcement! Listen up! Listen!
Crr
A meeting? Strange...
...opposition forces are entering crrr...
I thought public meetings like these were banned by Angkar.
Liberation fr...crr...
Hey, you! C'mere!
Have you heard? Opposition forces are liberating the country!
The Angkar regime is over!
Is that a joke?
Joins us! We're going to organize a big welcome for them!

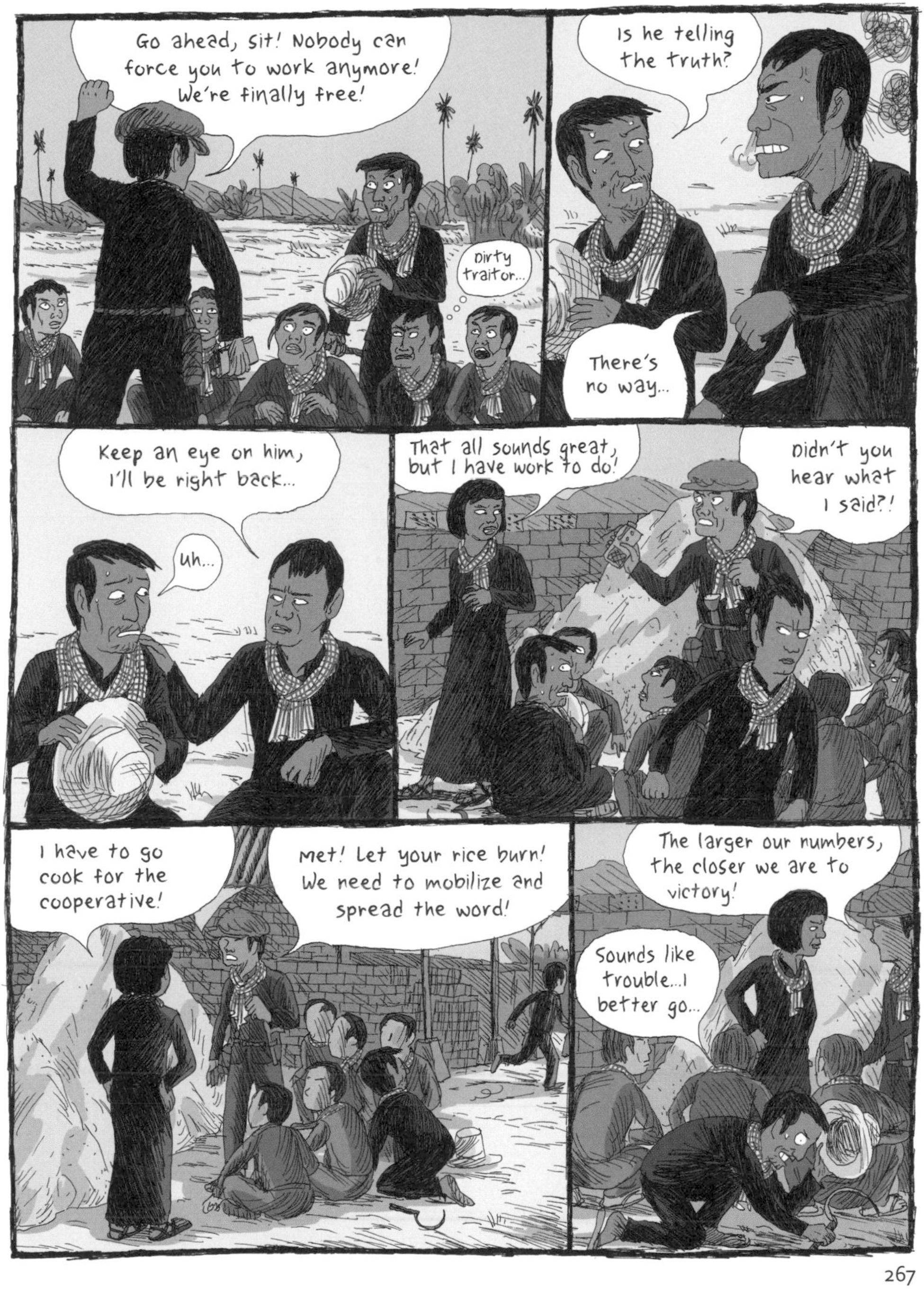
Go ahead, sit! Nobody can force you to work anymore! We're finally free!
Dirty traitor...
Is he telling the truth?
There's no way...
Keep an eye on him, I'll be right back...
Uh...
That all sounds great, but I have work to do!
Didn't you hear what I said?!
I have to go cook for the cooperative!
Met! Let your rice burn! We need to mobilize and spread the word!
The larger our numbers, the closer we are to victory!
Sounds like trouble...I better go...

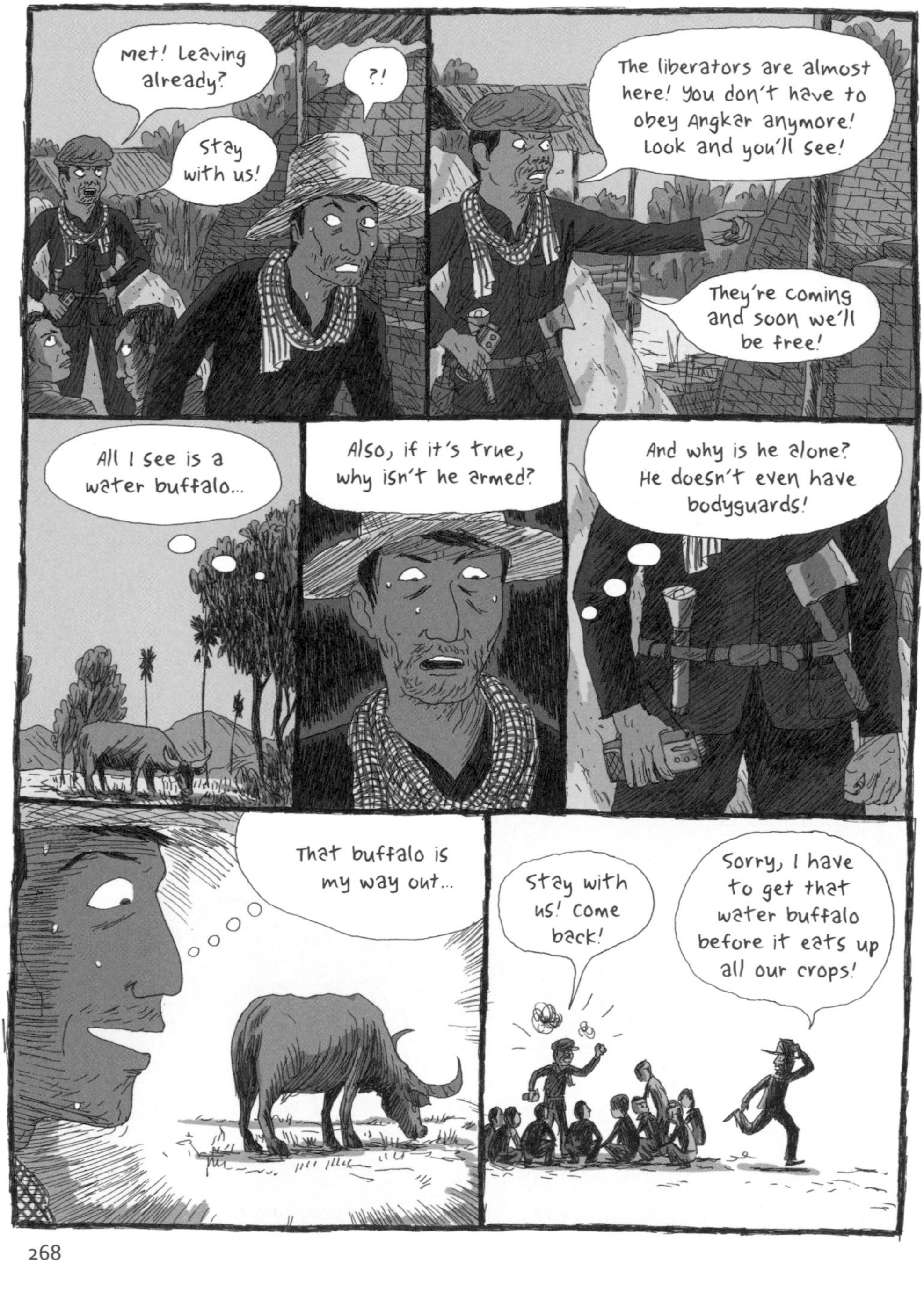
Met! Leaving already?
Stay with us!
?!
The liberators are almost here! You don't have to obey Angkar anymore! Look and you'll see!
They're coming and soon we'll be free!
All I see is a water buffalo...
Also, if it's true, why isn't he armed?
And why is he alone? He doesn't even have bodyguards!
That buffalo is my way out...
Stay with us! Come back!
Sorry, I have to get that water buffalo before it eats up all our crops!

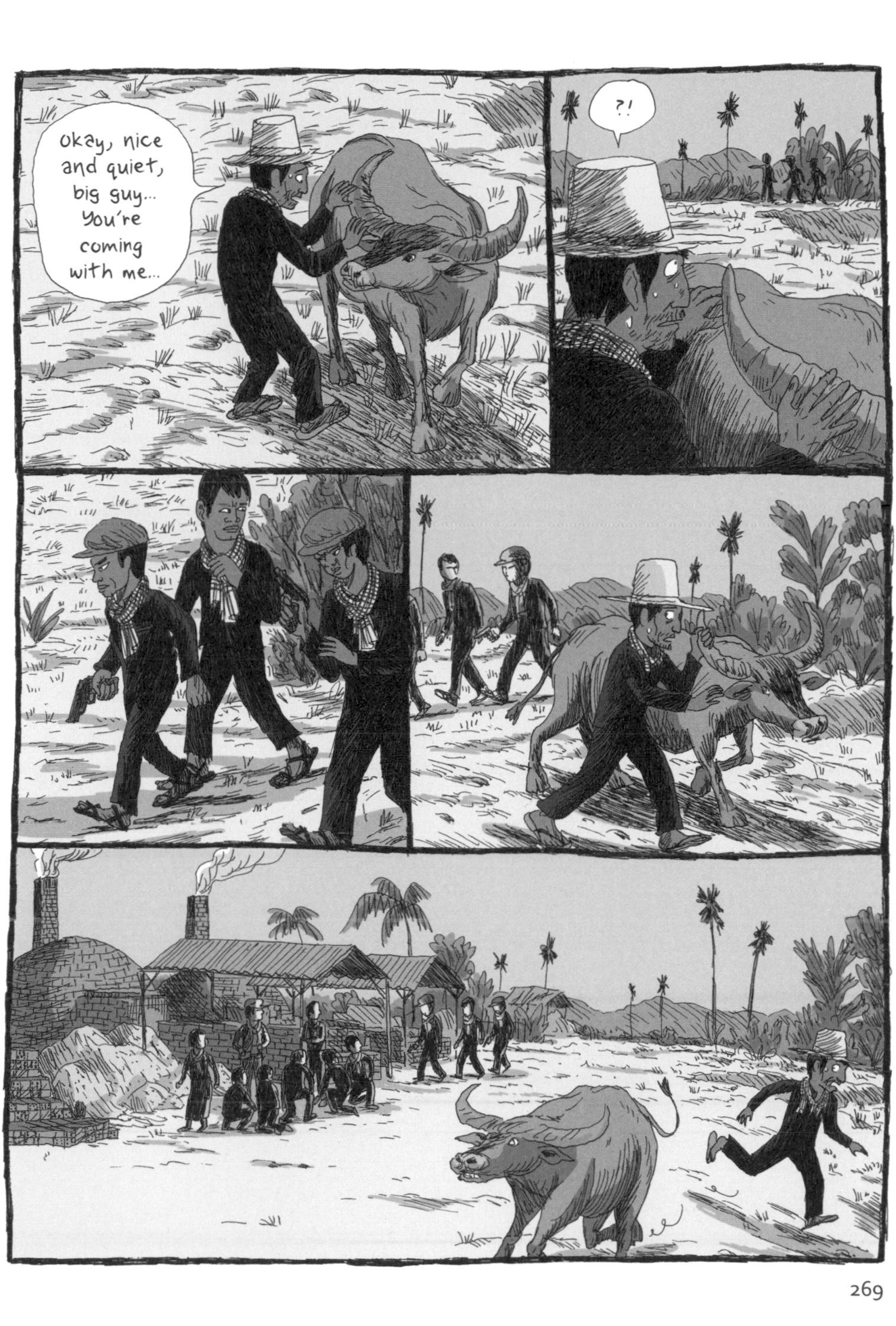
Okay, nice and quiet, big guy... You're coming with me...
?!

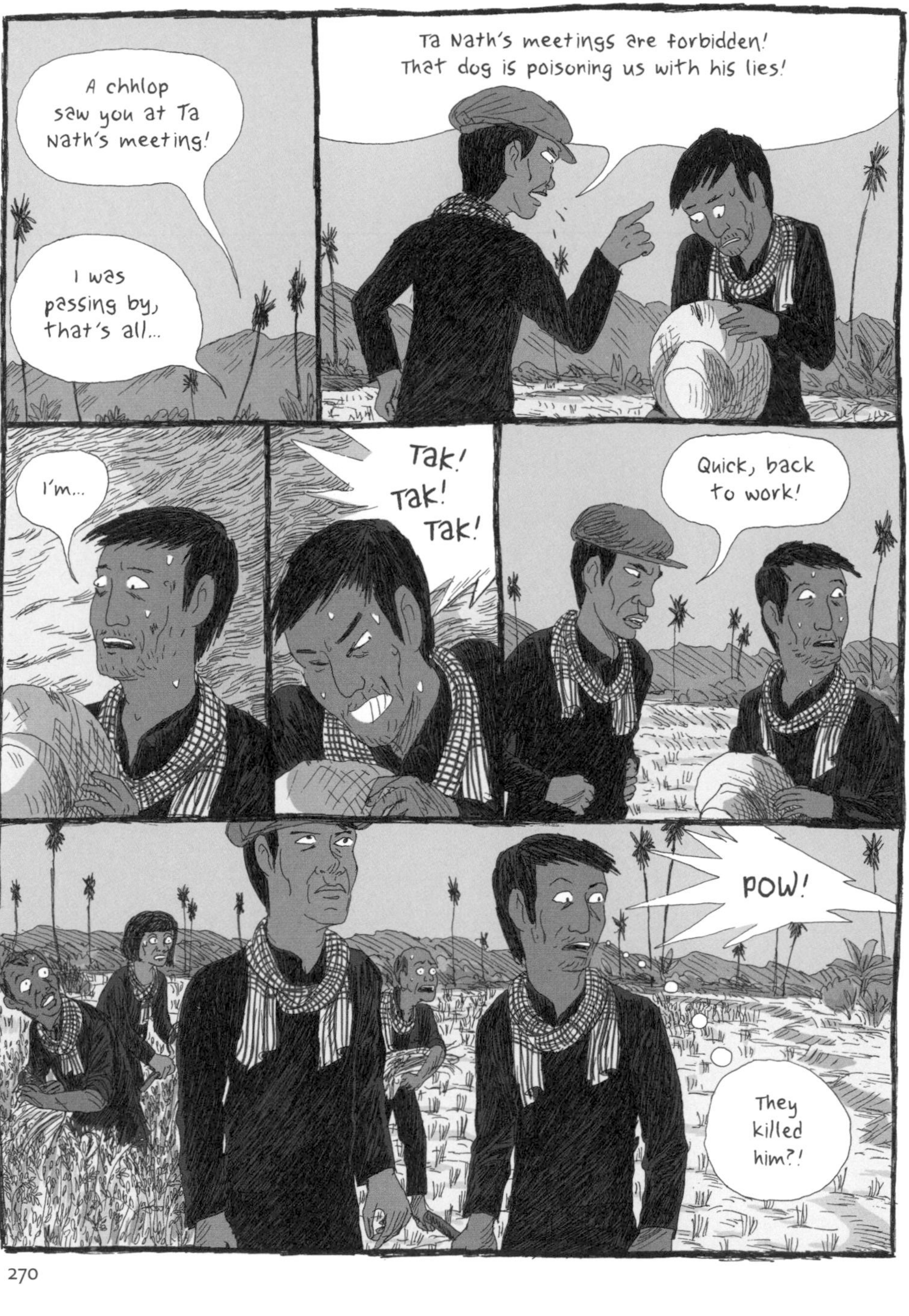
A chhlop saw you at Ta Nath's meeting!
I was passing by, that's all...
Ta Nath's meetings are forbidden! That dog is poisoning us with his lies!
I'm...
Tak! Tak! Tak!
Quick, back to work!
POW!
They killed him?!

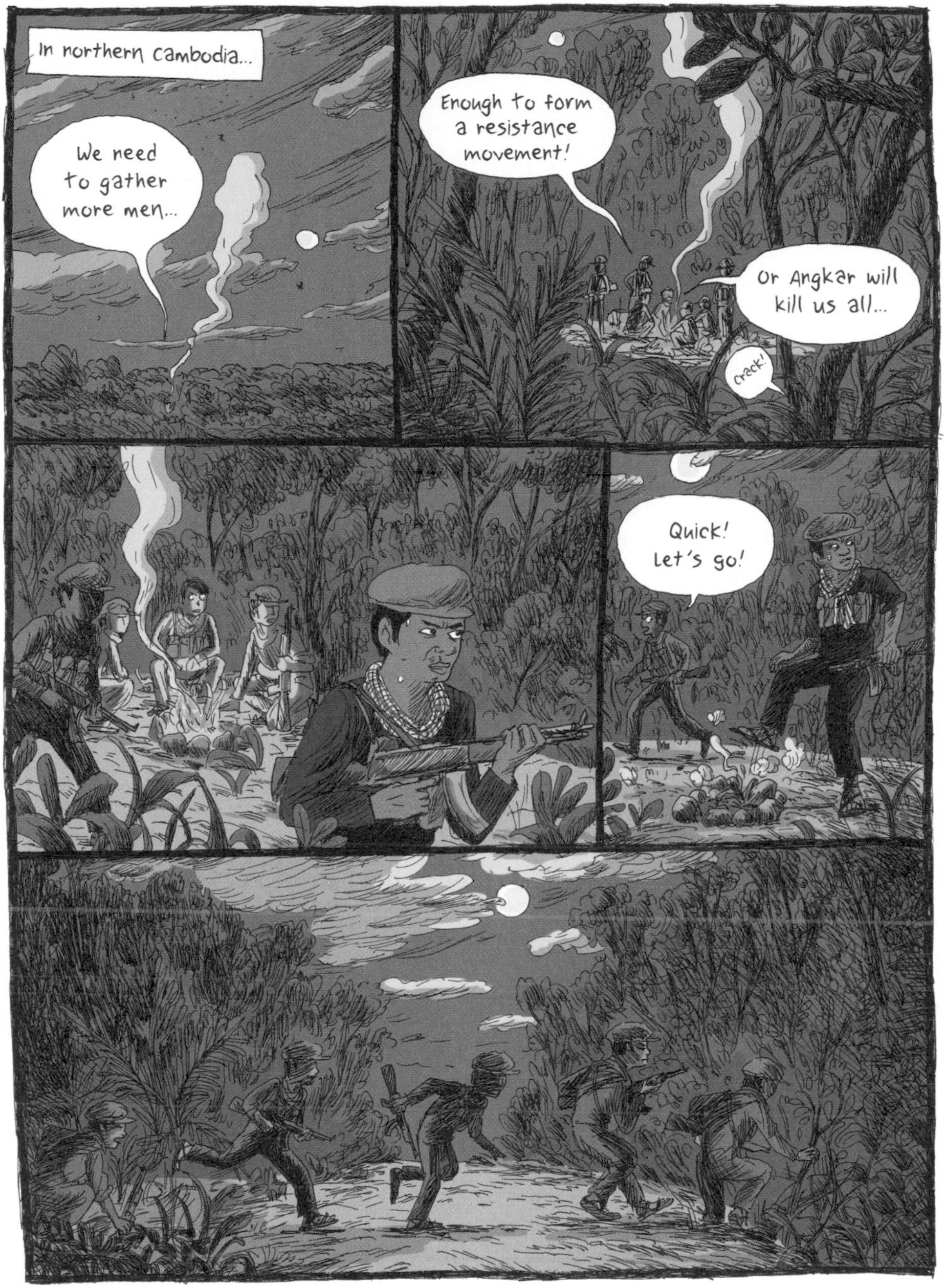
In northern cambodia...
We need to gather more men...
Enough to form a resistance movement!
Or Angkar will kill us all...
Crack!
Quick! Let's go!

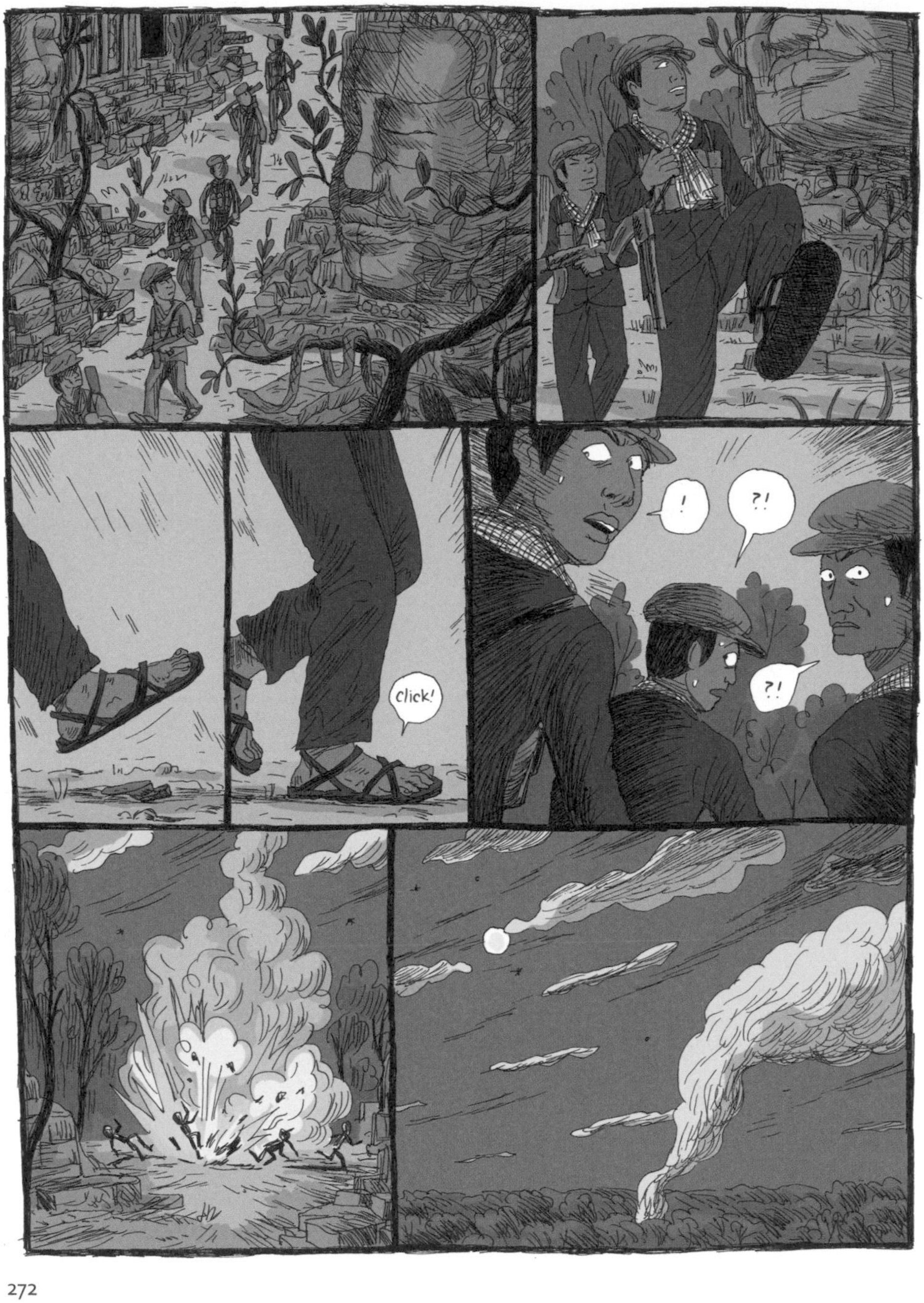
Click!
!
?!
?!

chapter 16

LIBERATION

BEHIND THE BANNER OF ANGKAR: THE CENTRAL COMMITTEE OF THE COMMUNIST PARTY OF KAMPUCHEA

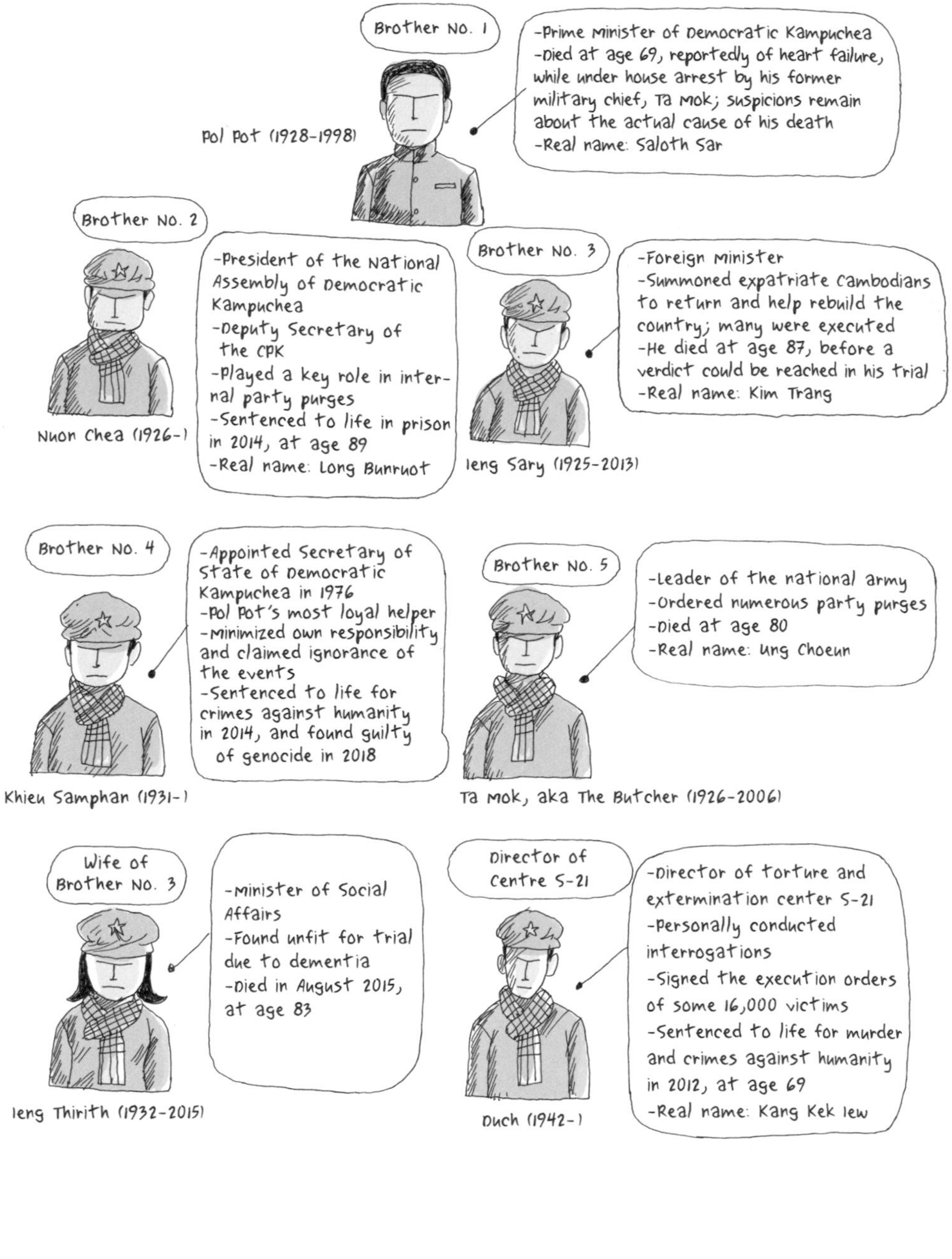

Brother No. 1
Pol Pot (1928-1998)
-Prime Minister of Democratic Kampuchea
-Died at age 69, reportedly of heart failure, while under house arrest by his former military chief, Ta Mok; suspicions remain about the actual cause of his death
-Real name: Saloth Sar
Brother No. 2
Nuon Chea (1926-)
-President of the National Assembly of Democratic Kampuchea
-Deputy Secretary of the CPK
-Played a key role in internal party purges
-Sentenced to life in prison in 2014, at age 89
-Real name: Long Bunruot
Brother No. 3
Ieng Sary (1925-2013)
-Foreign Minister
-Summoned expatriate Cambodians to return and help rebuild the country; many were executed
-He died at age 87, before a verdict could be reached in his trial
-Real name: Kim Trang
Brother No. 4
Khieu Samphan (1931-)
-Appointed Secretary of State of Democratic Kampuchea in 1976
-Pol Pot's most loyal helper
-Minimized own responsibility and claimed ignorance of the events
-Sentenced to life for crimes against humanity in 2014, and found guilty of genocide in 2018
Brother No. 5
Ta Mok, aka The Butcher (1926-2006)
-Leader of the national army
-Ordered numerous party purges
-Died at age 80
-Real name: Ung Choeun
Wife of Brother No. 3
Ieng Thirith (1932-2015)
-Minister of Social Affairs
-Found unfit for trial due to dementia
-Died in August 2015, at age 83
Director of Centre S-21
Duch (1942-)
-Director of torture and extermination center S-21
-Personally conducted interrogations
-Signed the execution orders of some 16,000 victims
-Sentenced to life for murder and crimes against humanity in 2012, at age 69
-Real name: Kang Kek Iew

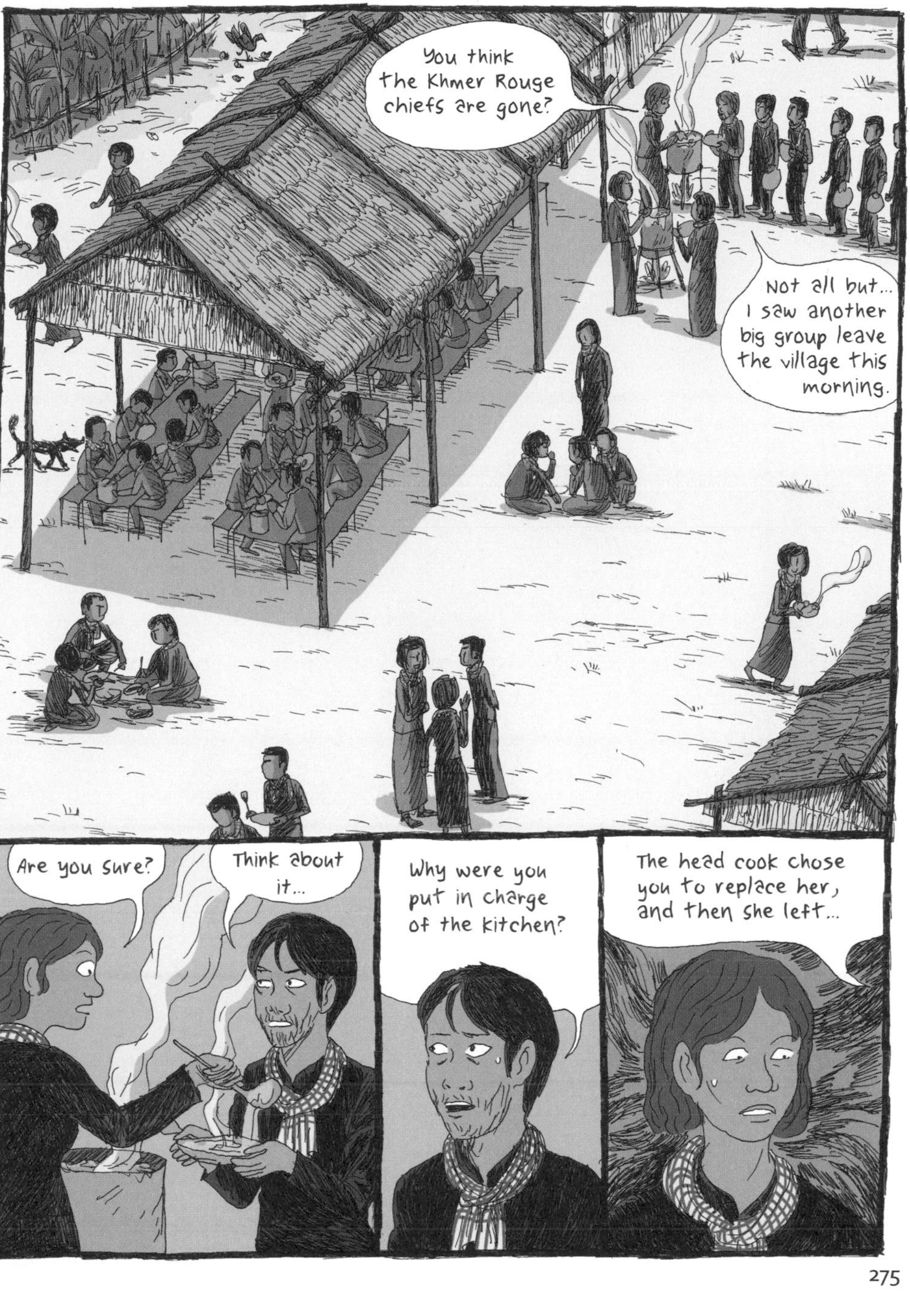
You think the Khmer Rouge chiefs are gone?
Not all but... I saw another big group leave the village this morning.
Are you sure?
Think about it...
Why were you put in charge of the kitchen?
The head cook chose you to replace her, and then she left...

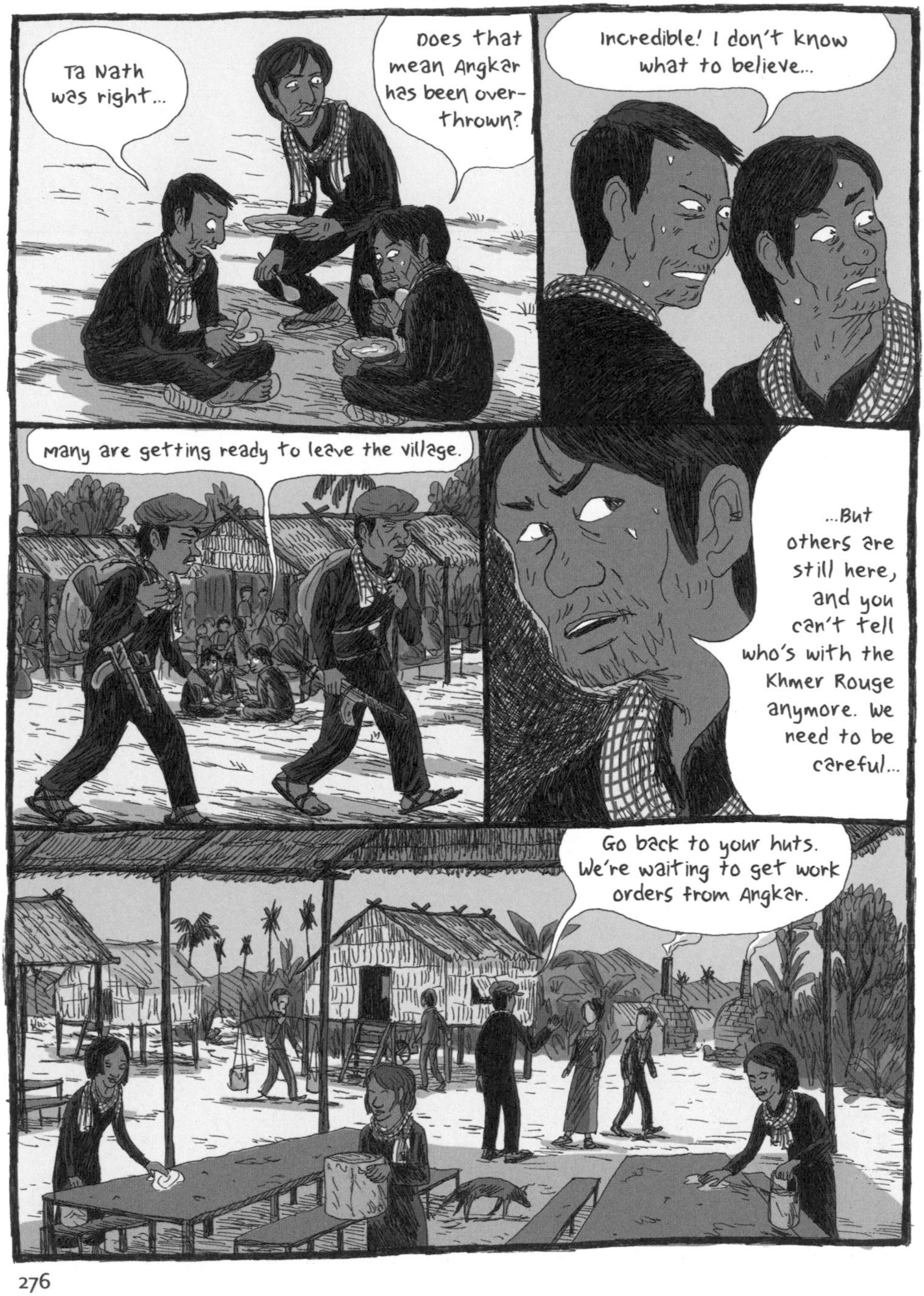
Ta Nath was right...
Does that mean Angkar has been overthrown?
Incredible! I don't know what to believe...
Many are getting ready to leave the village.
...But others are still here, and you can't tell who's with the Khmer Rouge anymore. We need to be careful...
Go back to your huts. We're waiting to get work orders from Angkar.

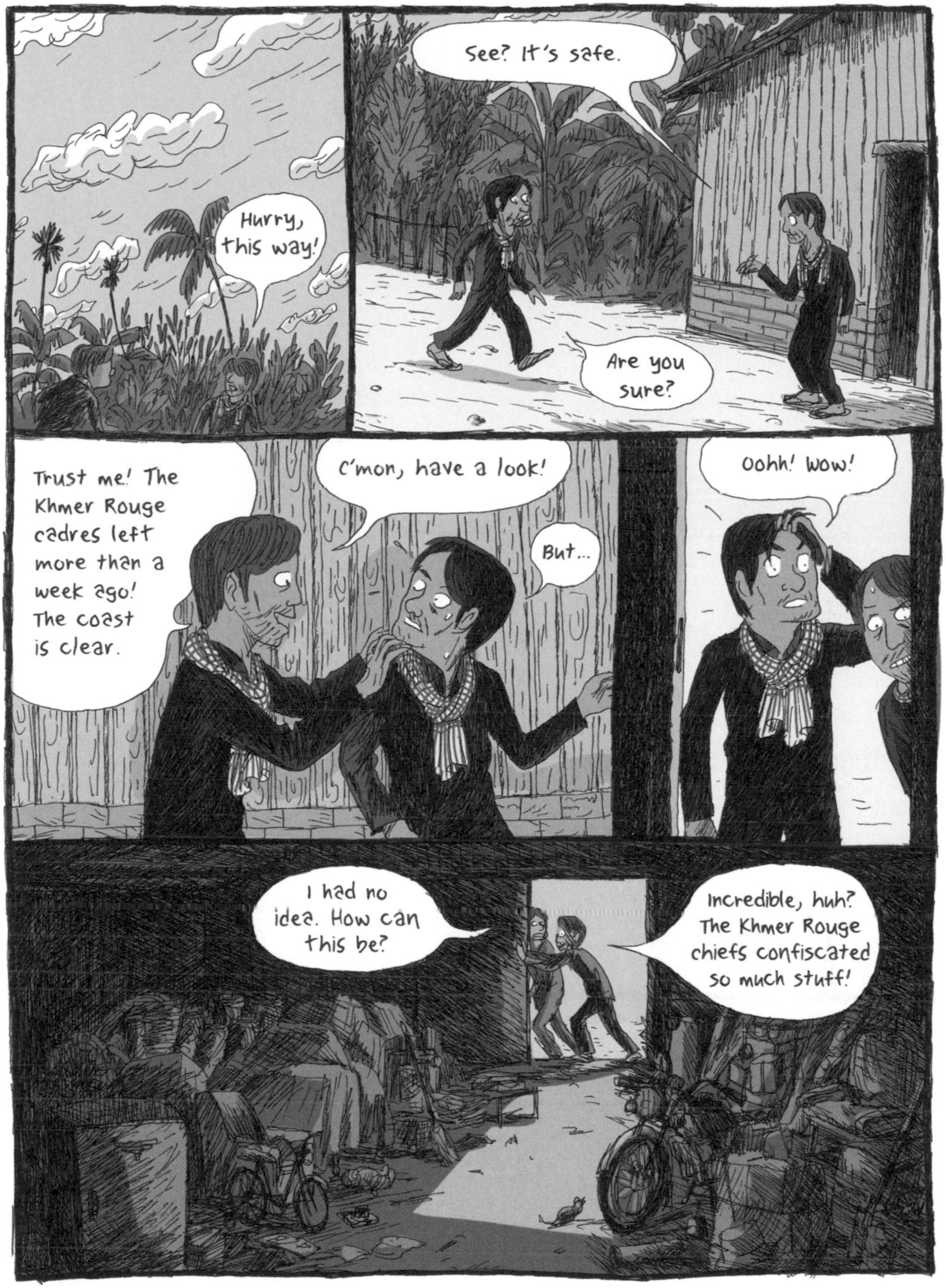
Hurry, this way!
See? It's safe.
Are you sure?
Trust me! The Khmer Rouge cadres left more than a week ago! The coast is clear.
C'mon, have a look!
But...
Oohh! Wow!
I had no idea. How can this be?
Incredible, huh? The Khmer Rouge chiefs confiscated so much stuff!

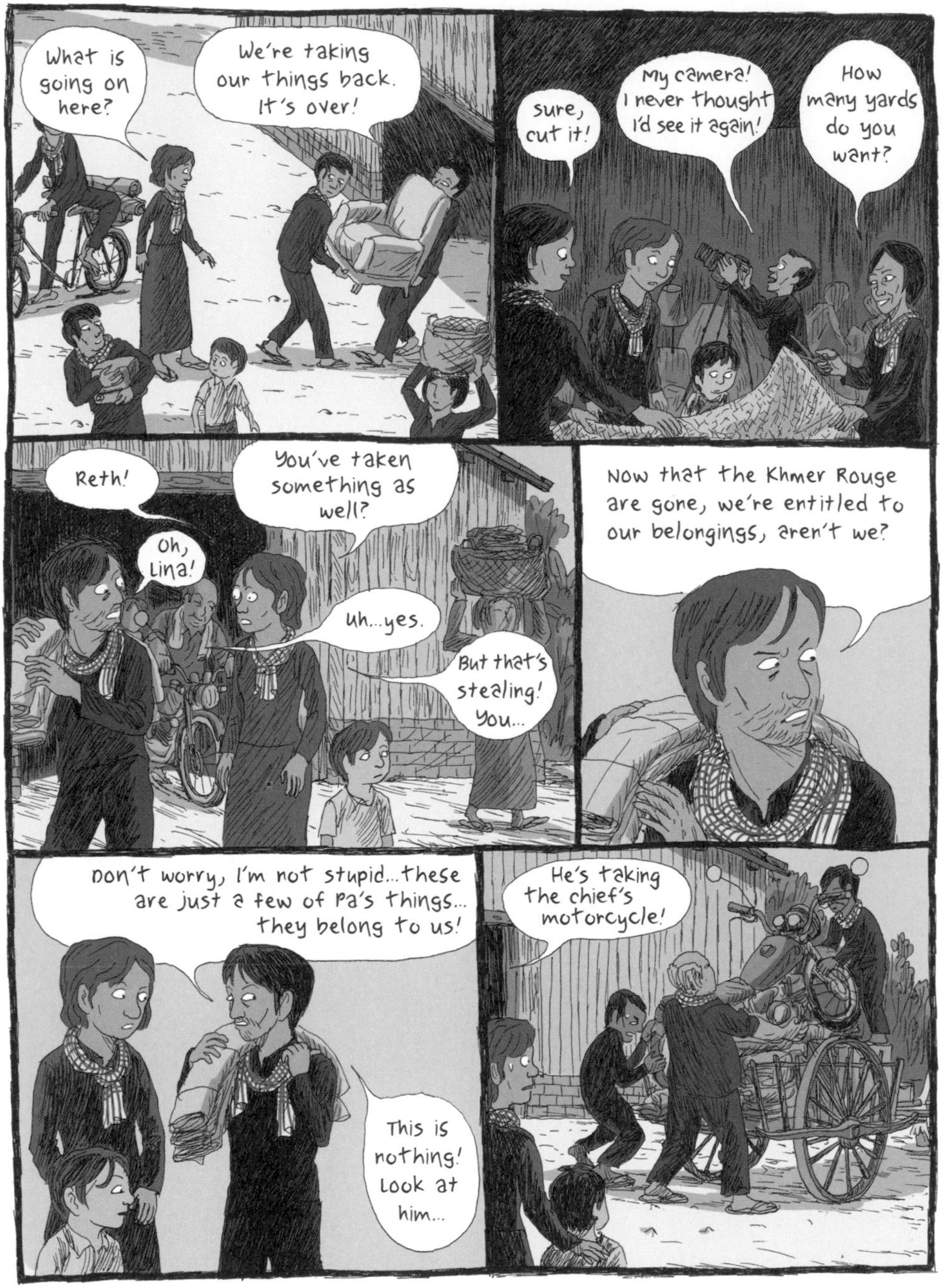
What is going on here?
We're taking our things back. It's over!
Sure, cut it!
My camera! I never thought I'd see it again!
How many yards do you want?
Reth!
You've taken something as well?
Oh, Lina!
Uh...yes.
But that's stealing! You...
Now that the Khmer Rouge are gone, we're entitled to our belongings, aren't we?
Don't worry, I'm not stupid...these are just a few of Pa's things... they belong to us!
This is nothing! Look at him...
He's taking the chief's motorcycle!

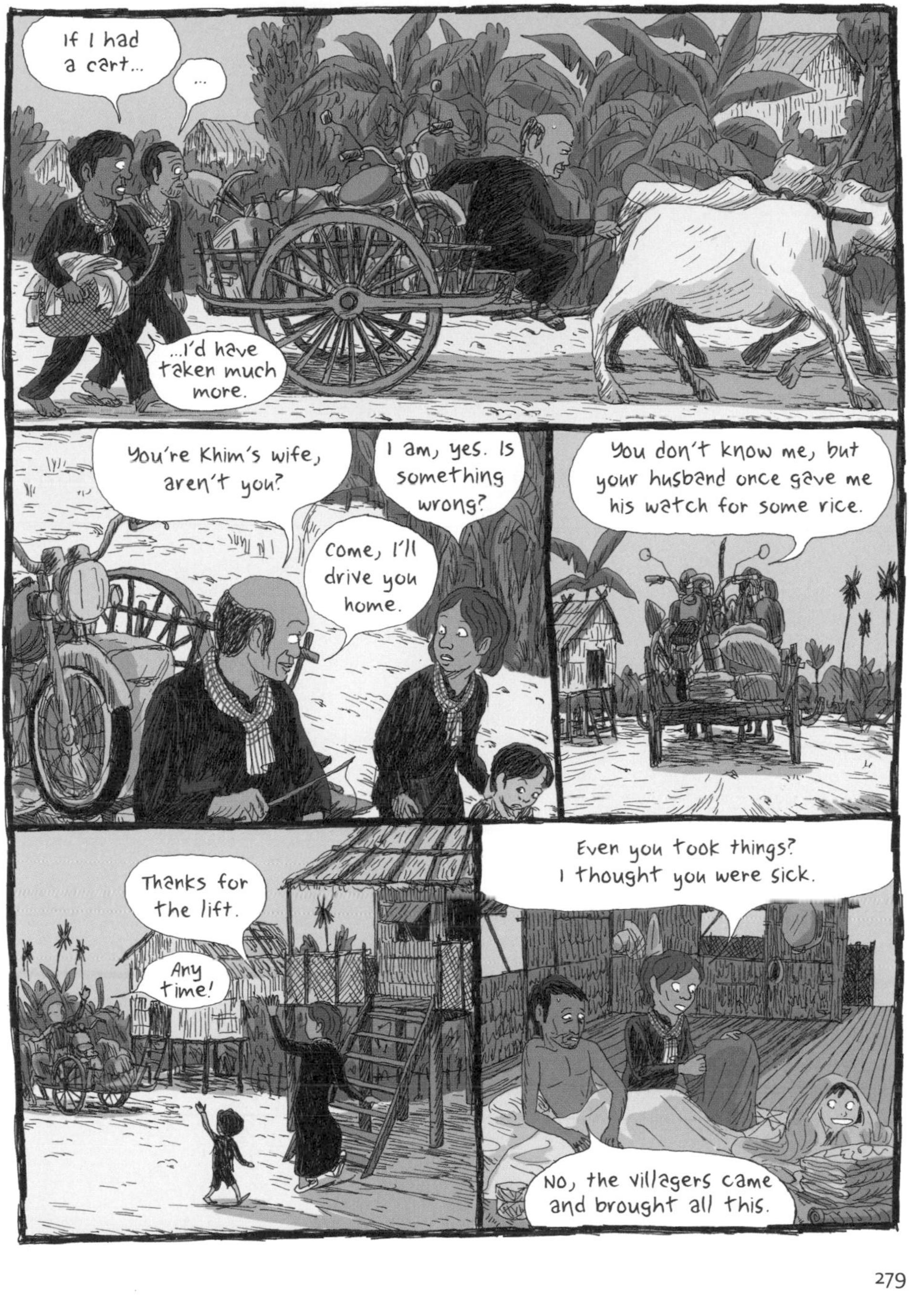
If I had a cart...
...
...I'd have taken much more.
You're Khim's wife, aren't you?
I am, yes. Is something wrong?
Come, I'll drive you home.
You don't know me, but your husband once gave me his watch for some rice.
Thanks for the lift.
Any time!
Even you took things? I thought you were sick.
No, the villagers came and brought all this.

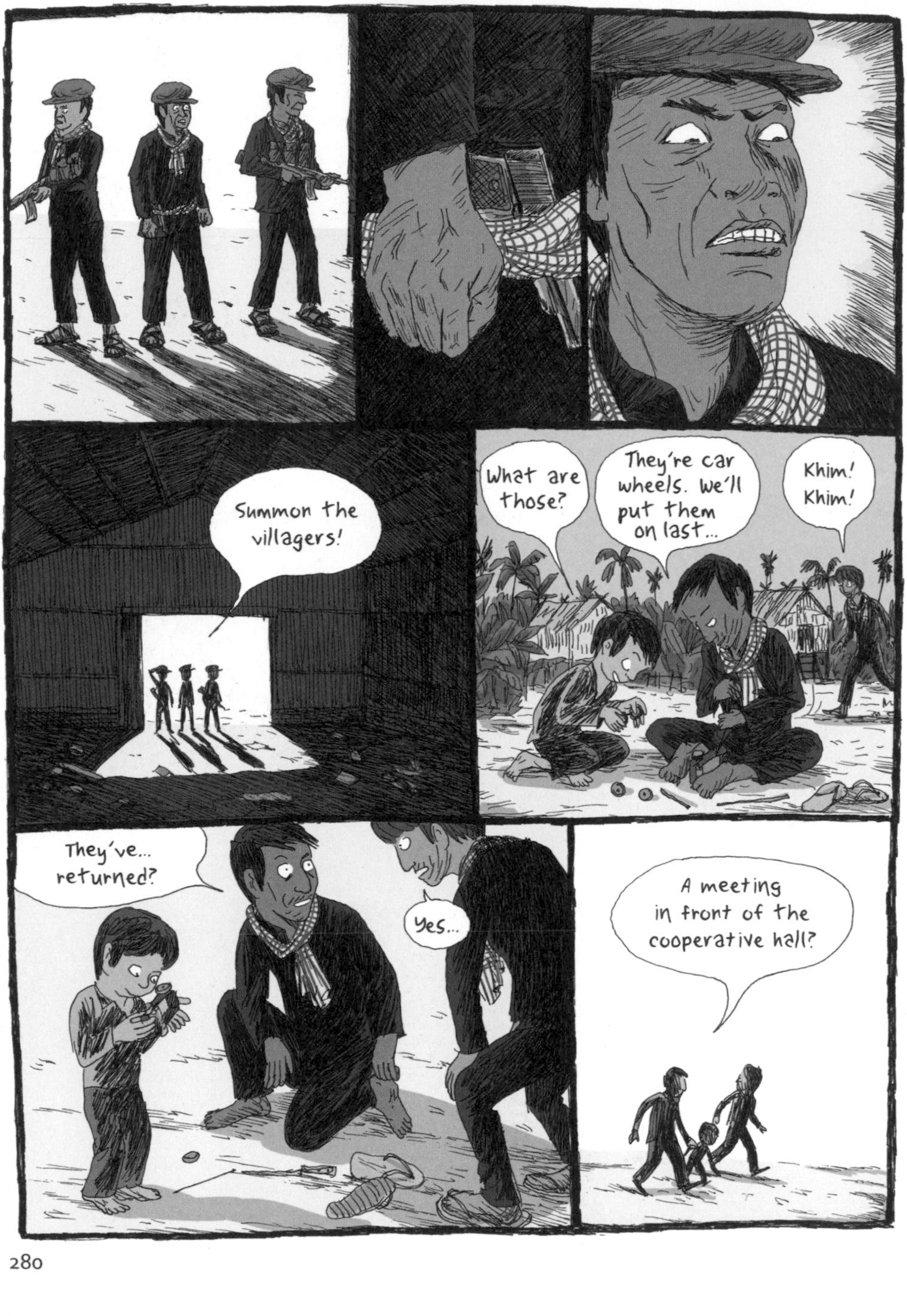
Summon the villagers!
What are those?
They're car wheels. We'll put them on last...
Khim! Khim!
They've... returned?
Yes...
A meeting in front of the cooperative hall?

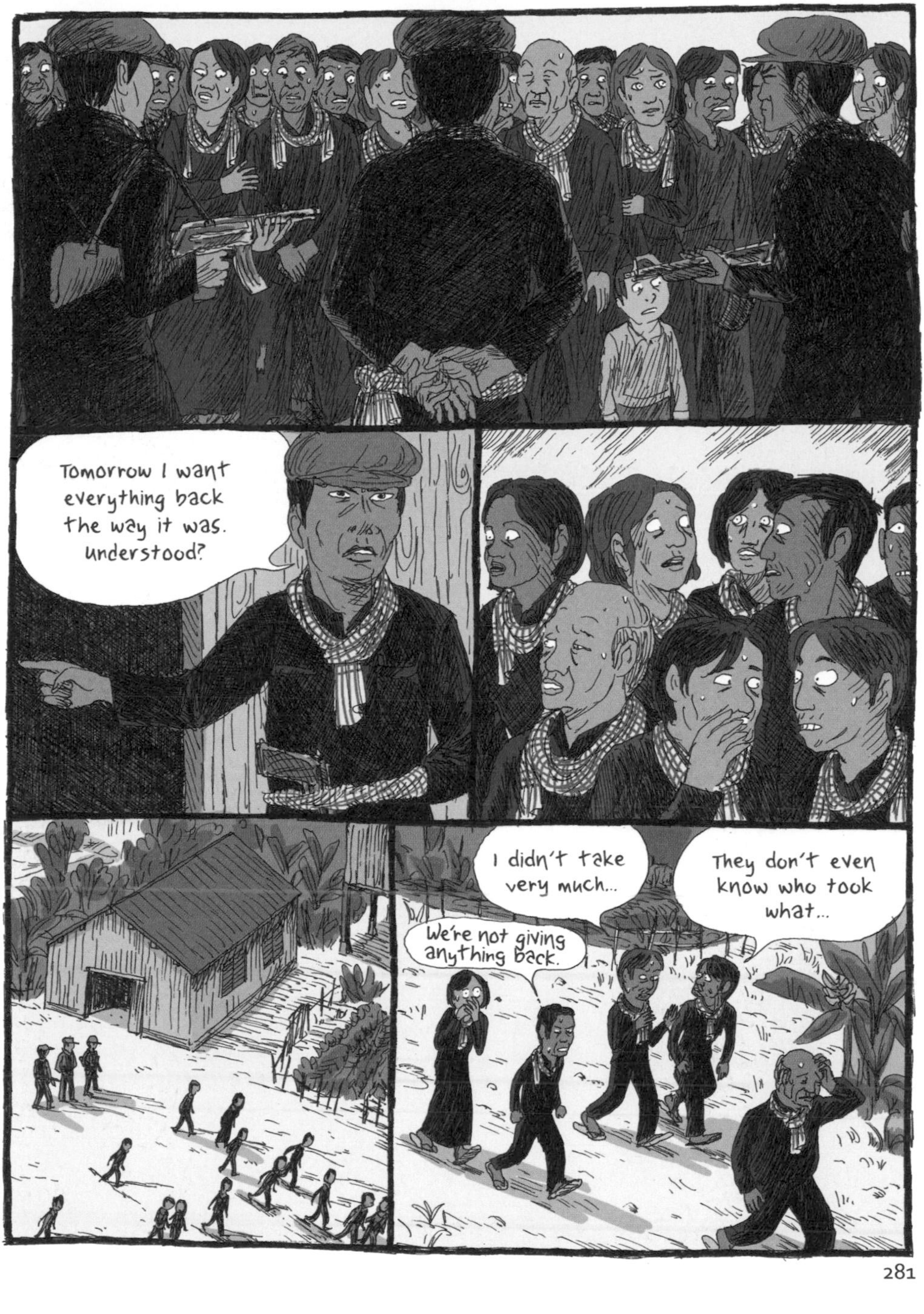
Tomorrow I want everything back the way it was. Understood?
I didn't take very much...
We're not giving anything back.
They don't even know who took what...

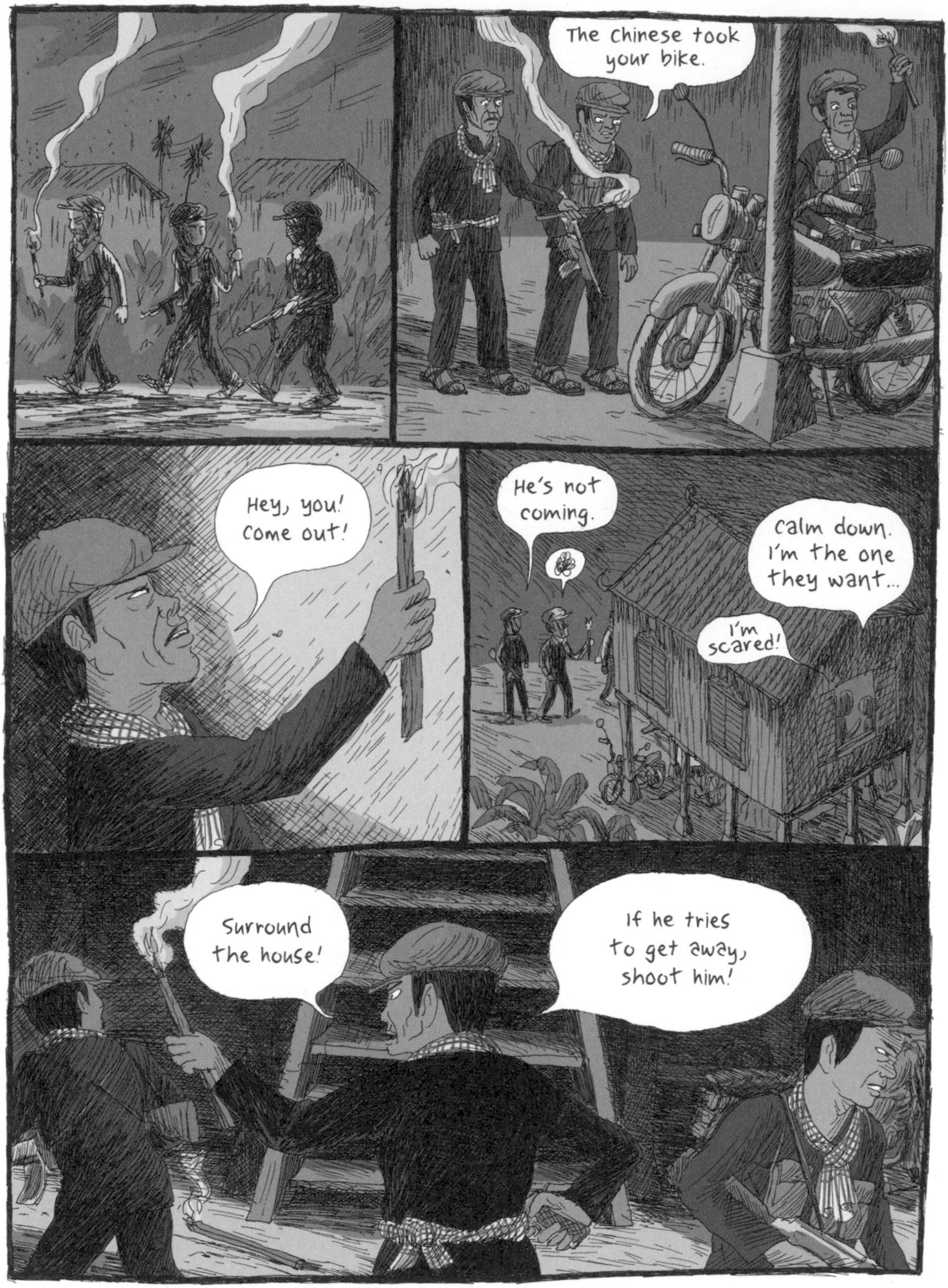
The Chinese took your bike.
Hey, you! Come out!
He's not coming.
Calm down. I'm the one they want...
I'm scared!
Surround the house!
If he tries to get away, shoot him!

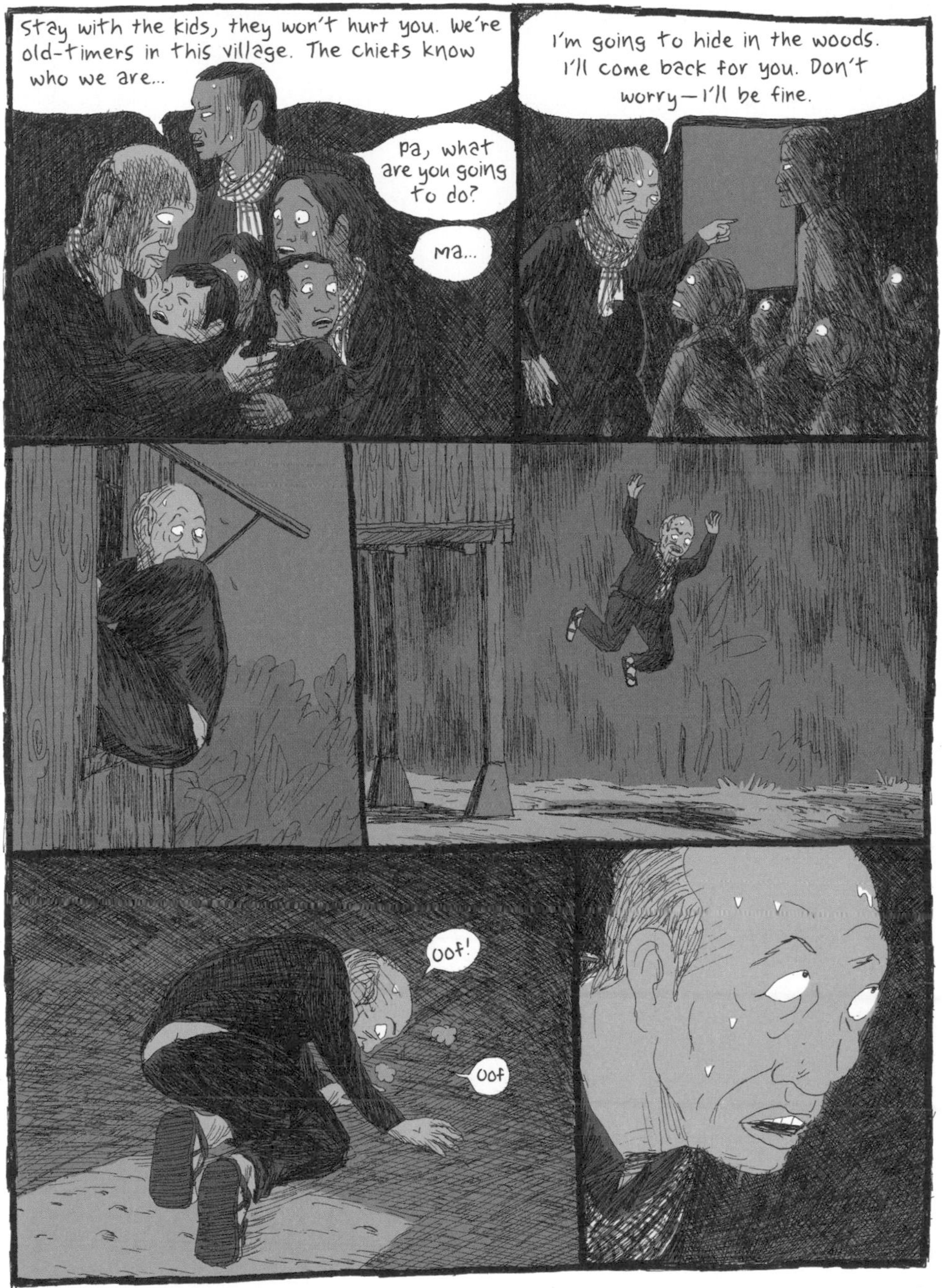
Stay with the kids, they won't hurt you. We're old-timers in this village. The chiefs know who we are...
Pa, what are you going to do?
Ma...
I'm going to hide in the woods. I'll come back for you. Don't worry—I'll be fine.
Oof!
Oof

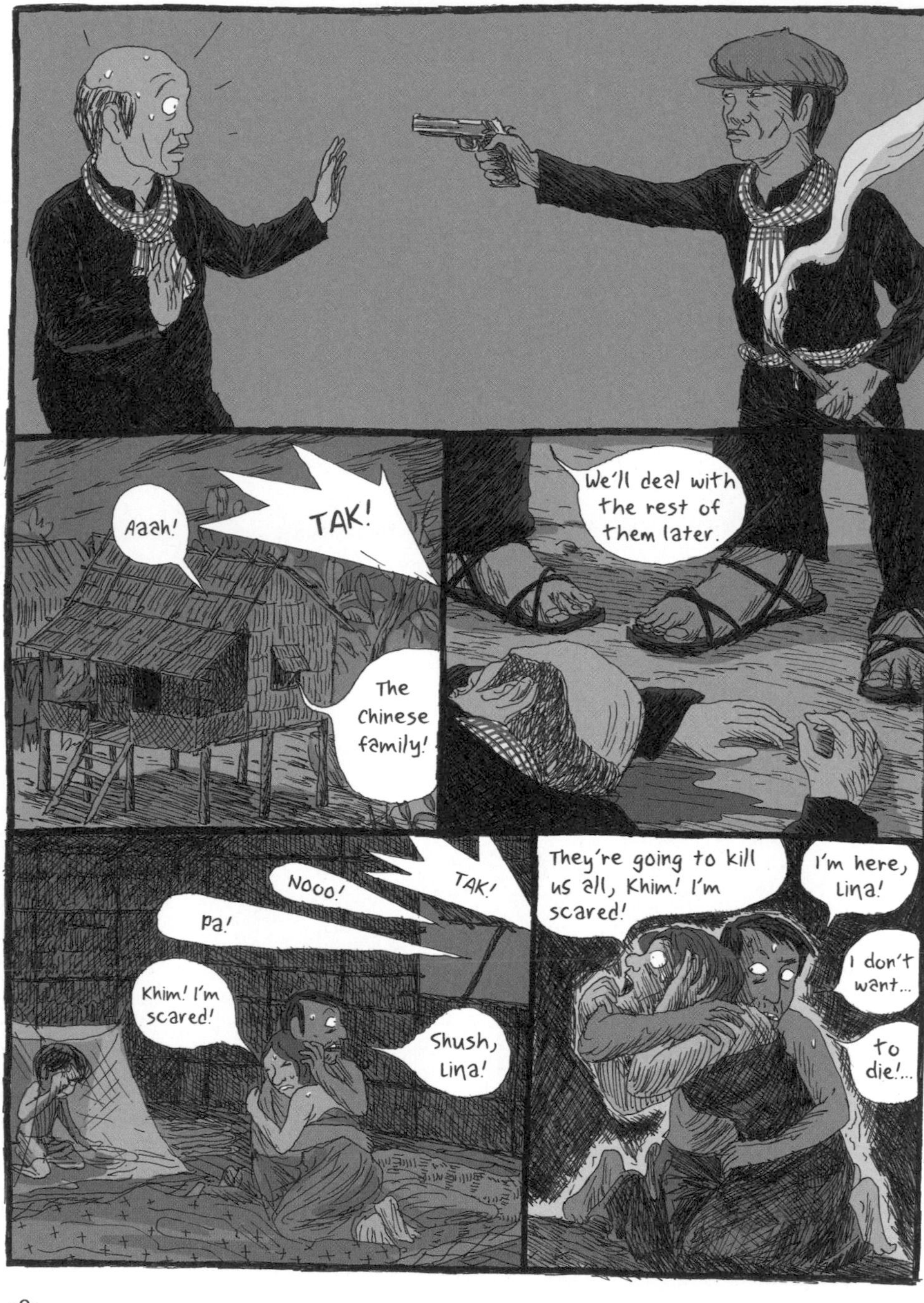
Aaah!
TAK!
The Chinese family!
We'll deal with the rest of them later.
Nooo!
TAK!
Pa!
Khim! I'm scared!
Shush, Lina!
They're going to kill us all, Khim! I'm scared!
I'm here, Lina!
I don't want...
to die!...

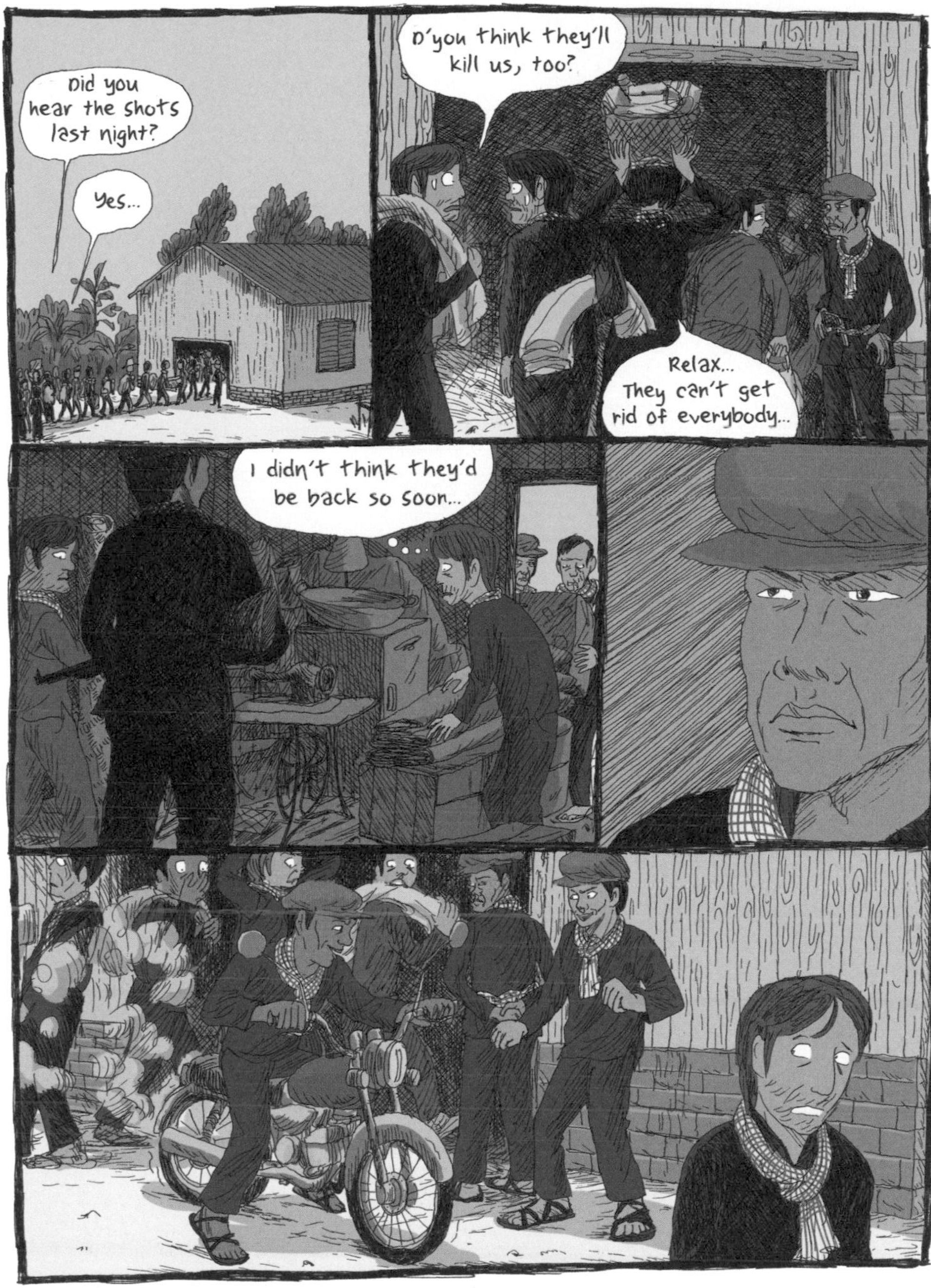
Did you hear the shots last night?
Yes...
D'you think they'll kill us, too?
Relax... They can't get rid of everybody...
I didn't think they'd be back so soon...

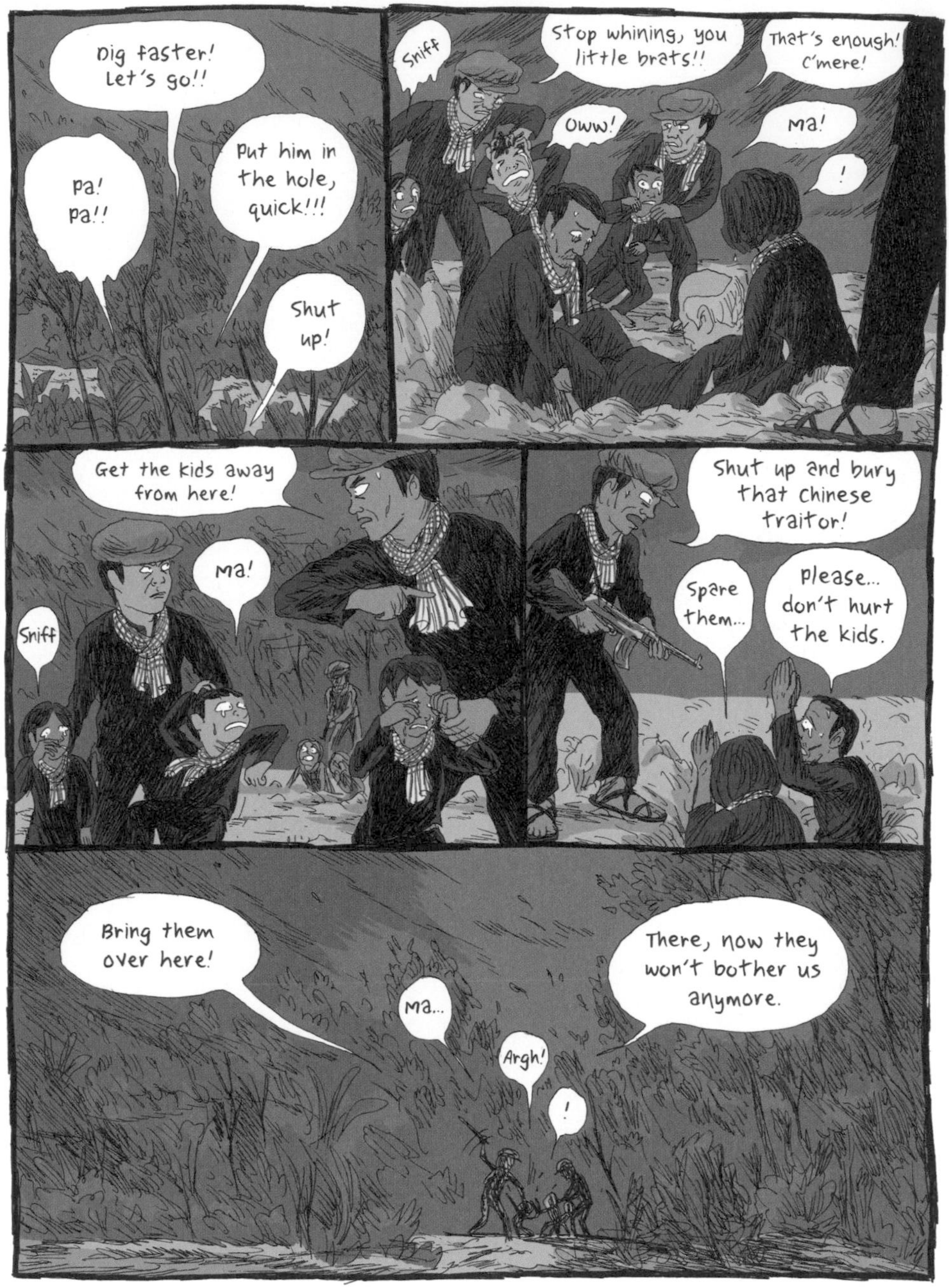
Dig faster! Let's go!!
Pa! Pa!!
Put him in the hole, quick!!!
Shut up!
Sniff
Stop whining, you little brats!!
That's enough! C'mere!
Oww!
Ma!
!
Get the kids away from here!
Sniff
Ma!
Shut up and bury that Chinese traitor!
Spare them...
Please... don't hurt the kids.
Bring them over here!
Ma...
Argh!
!
There, now they won't bother us anymore.

chapter 17

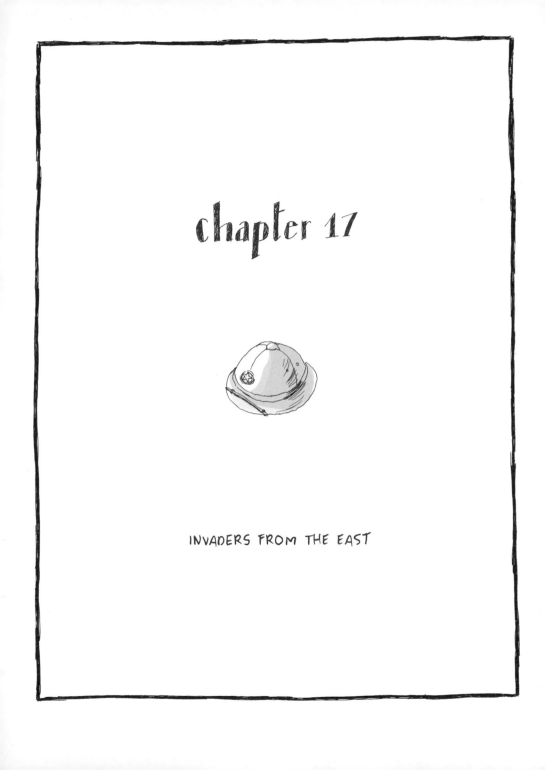

INVADERS FROM THE EAST

THE VIETNAMESE INVASION

In 1978, escalating border clashes led to a breakdown in diplomatic relations between Democratic Kampuchea and Vietnam. Alarmed by Khmer Rouge advances into strategic regions, the Vietnamese decided to intervene. Conditions within Cambodia were dire: repeated purges had ravaged the Eastern Zone, hardening the opposition of some 10,000 Khmer Rouge soldiers to Angkar's draconian policies. When Vietnam's 120,000 troops invaded in December, they were able to occupy Cambodia without any difficulty.

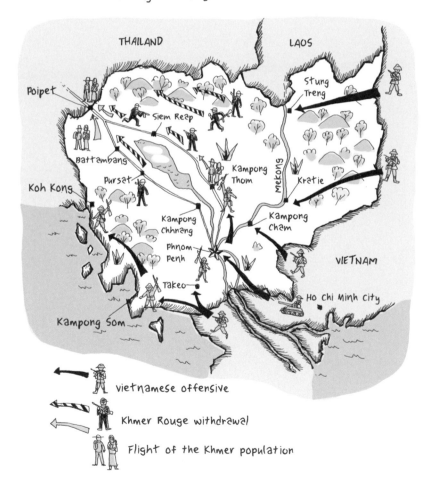

THAILAND

LAOS

Poipet

Stung Treng

Siem Reap

Battambang

Pursat

Koh Kong

Kampong Thom

Mekong

Kratie

Kampong Chhnang

Kampong Cham

Phnom Penh

VIETNAM

Takeo

Ho Chi Minh City

Kampong Som

Vietnamese offensive

Khmer Rouge withdrawal

Flight of the Khmer population

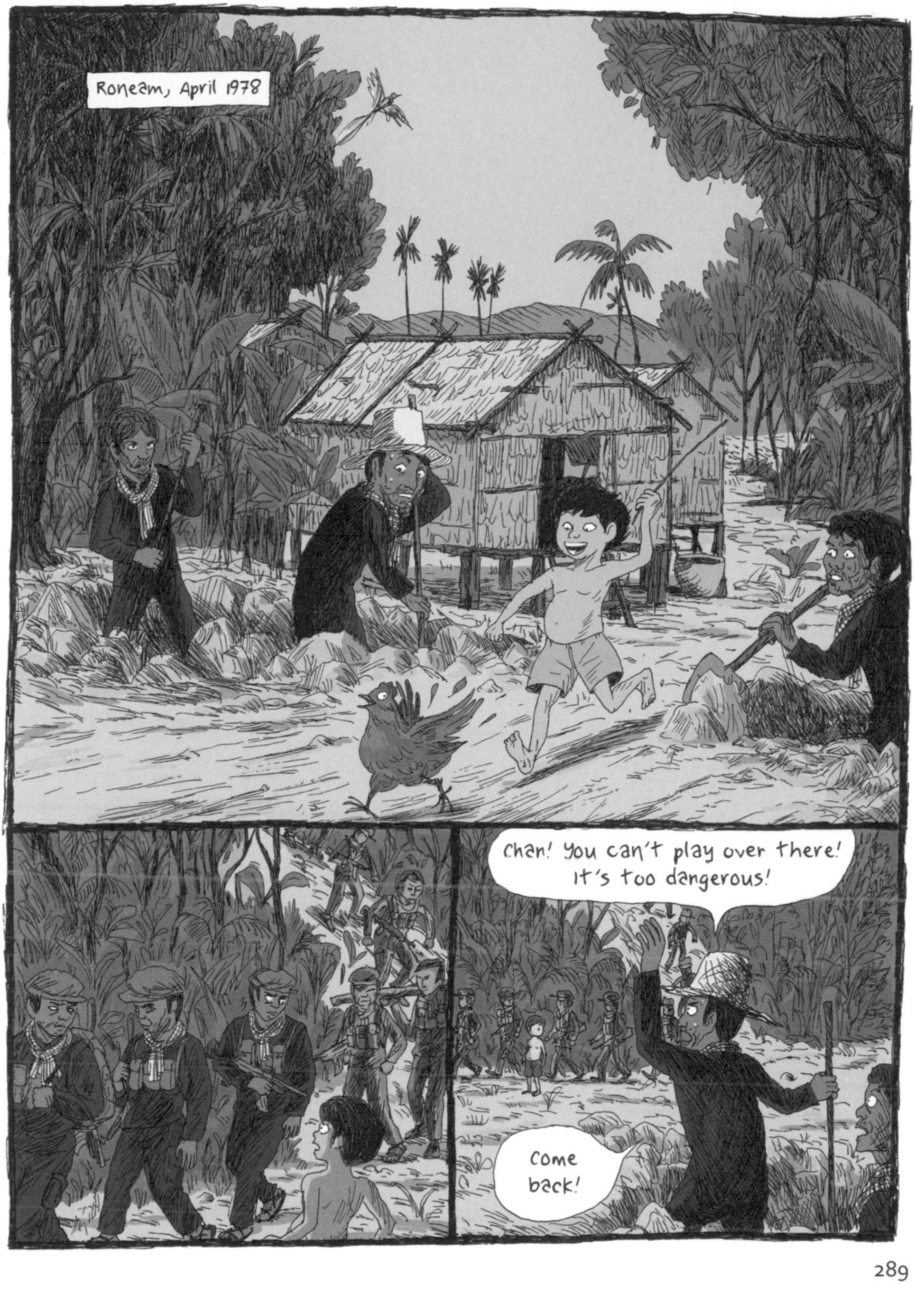
Roneam, April 1978
Chan! You can't play over there! It's too dangerous!
Come back!

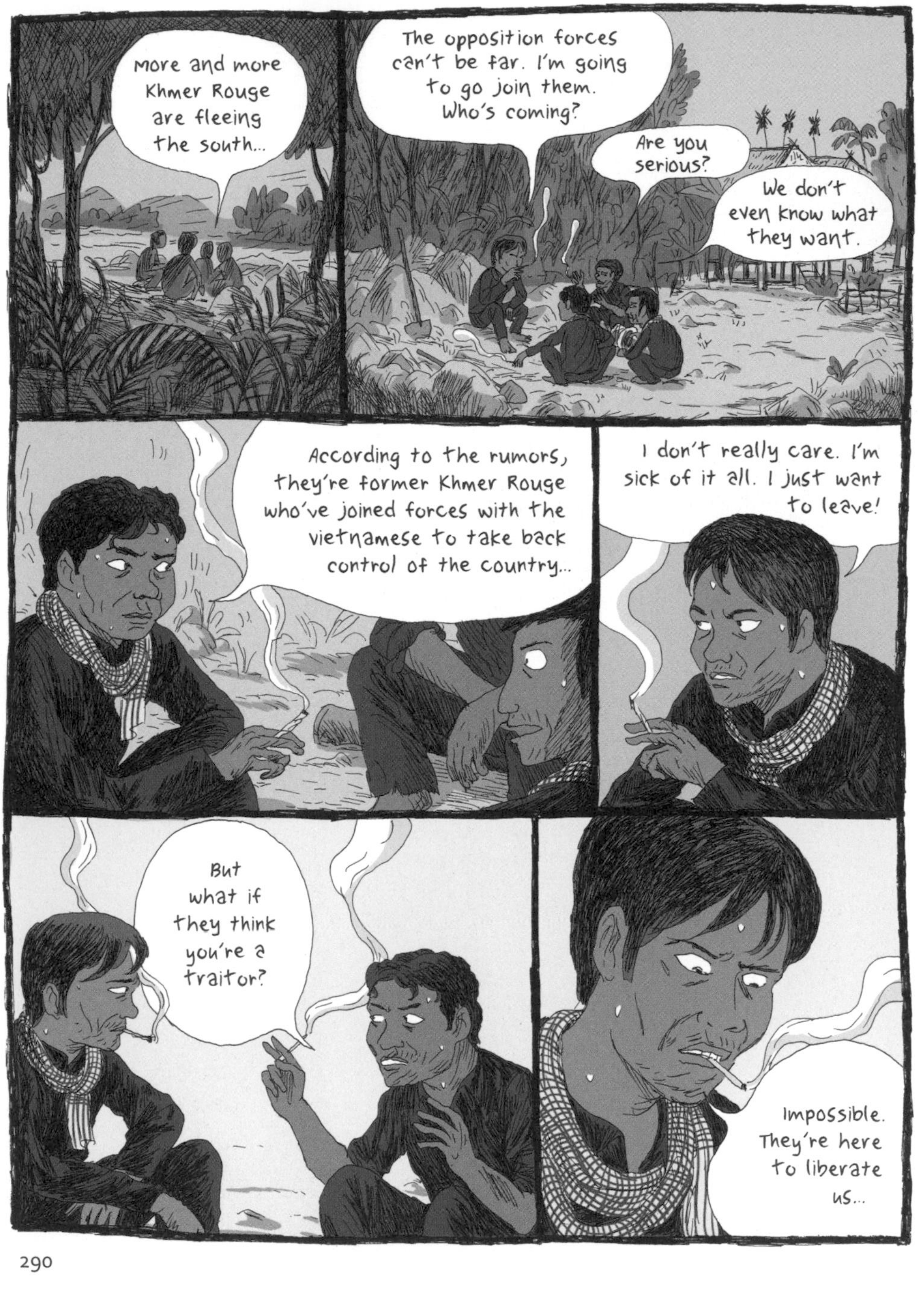
More and more Khmer Rouge are fleeing the south...
The opposition forces can't be far. I'm going to go join them. Who's coming?
Are you serious?
We don't even know what they want.
According to the rumors, they're former Khmer Rouge who've joined forces with the vietnamese to take back control of the country...
I don't really care. I'm sick of it all. I just want to leave!
But what if they think you're a traitor?
Impossible. They're here to liberate us...

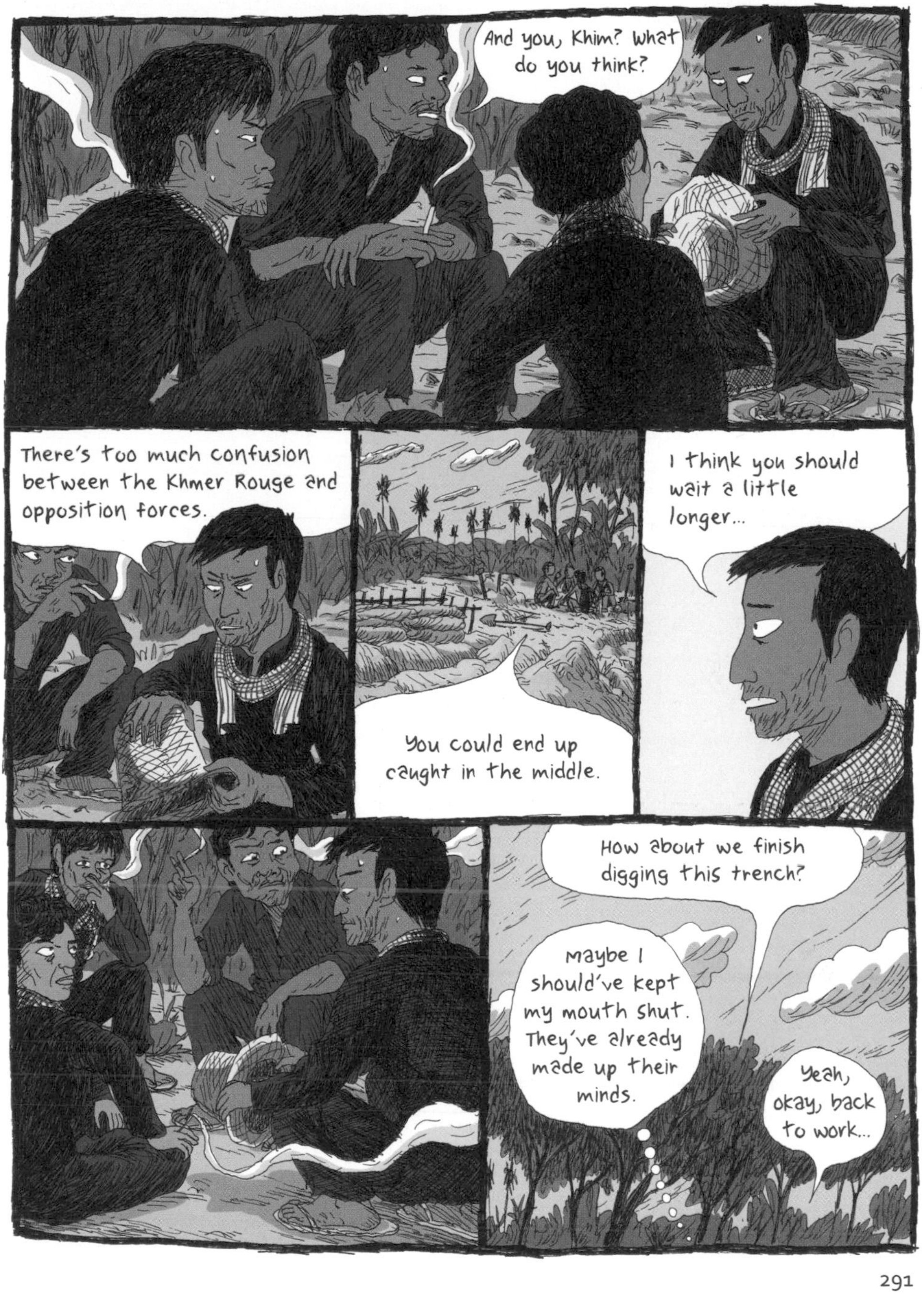
And you, Khim? What do you think?
There's too much confusion between the Khmer Rouge and opposition forces.
You could end up caught in the middle.
I think you should wait a little longer...
How about we finish digging this trench?
Maybe I should've kept my mouth shut. They've already made up their minds.
Yeah, okay, back to work...

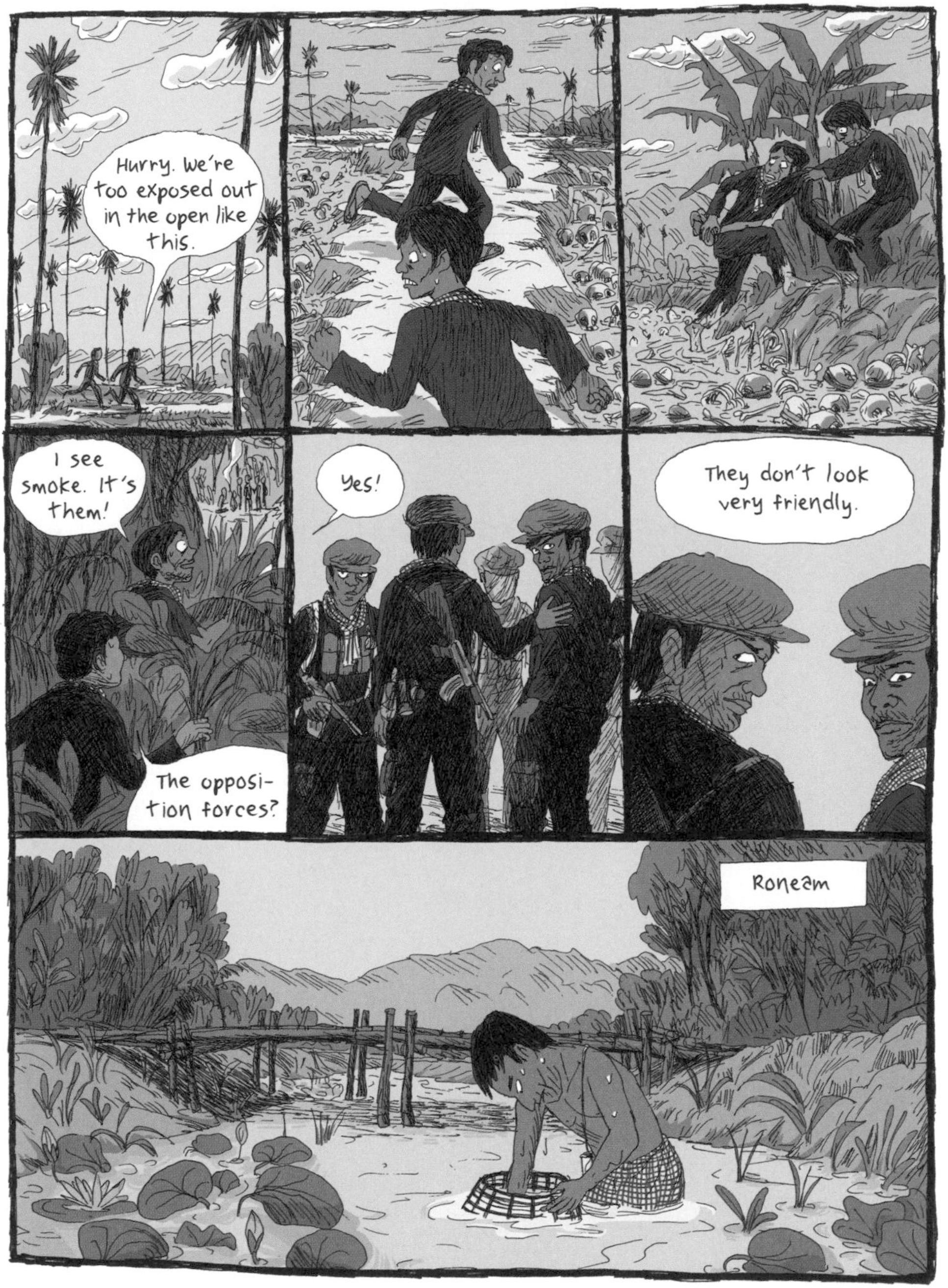

Hurry. We're too exposed out in the open like this.
I see smoke. It's them!
The opposition forces?
Yes!
They don't look very friendly.
Roneam

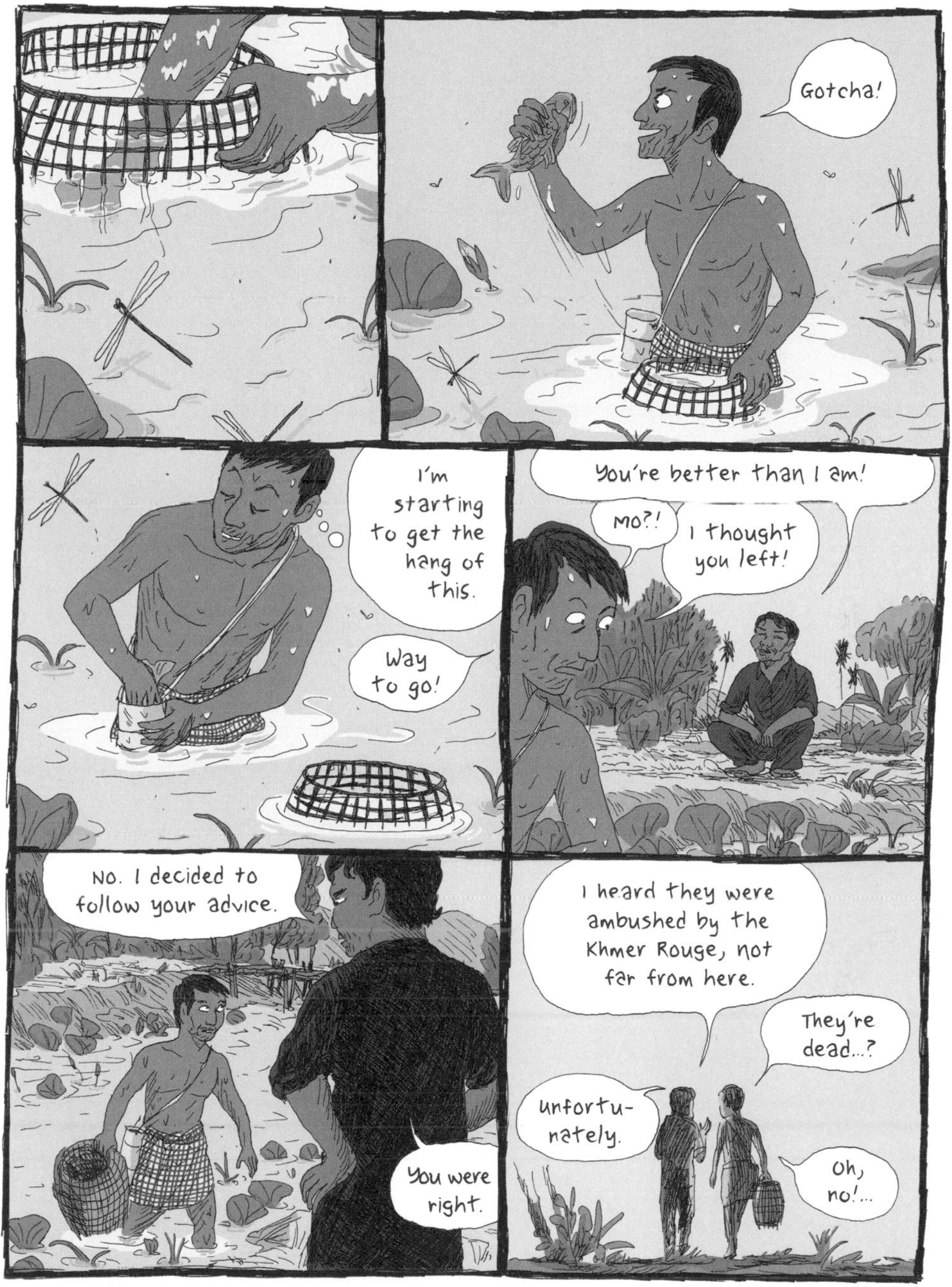
Gotcha!
I'm starting to get the hang of this.
Way to go!
You're better than I am!
Mo?!
I thought you left!
No. I decided to follow your advice.
You were right.
I heard they were ambushed by the Khmer Rouge, not far from here.
They're dead...?
Unfortu-nately.
Oh, no!...

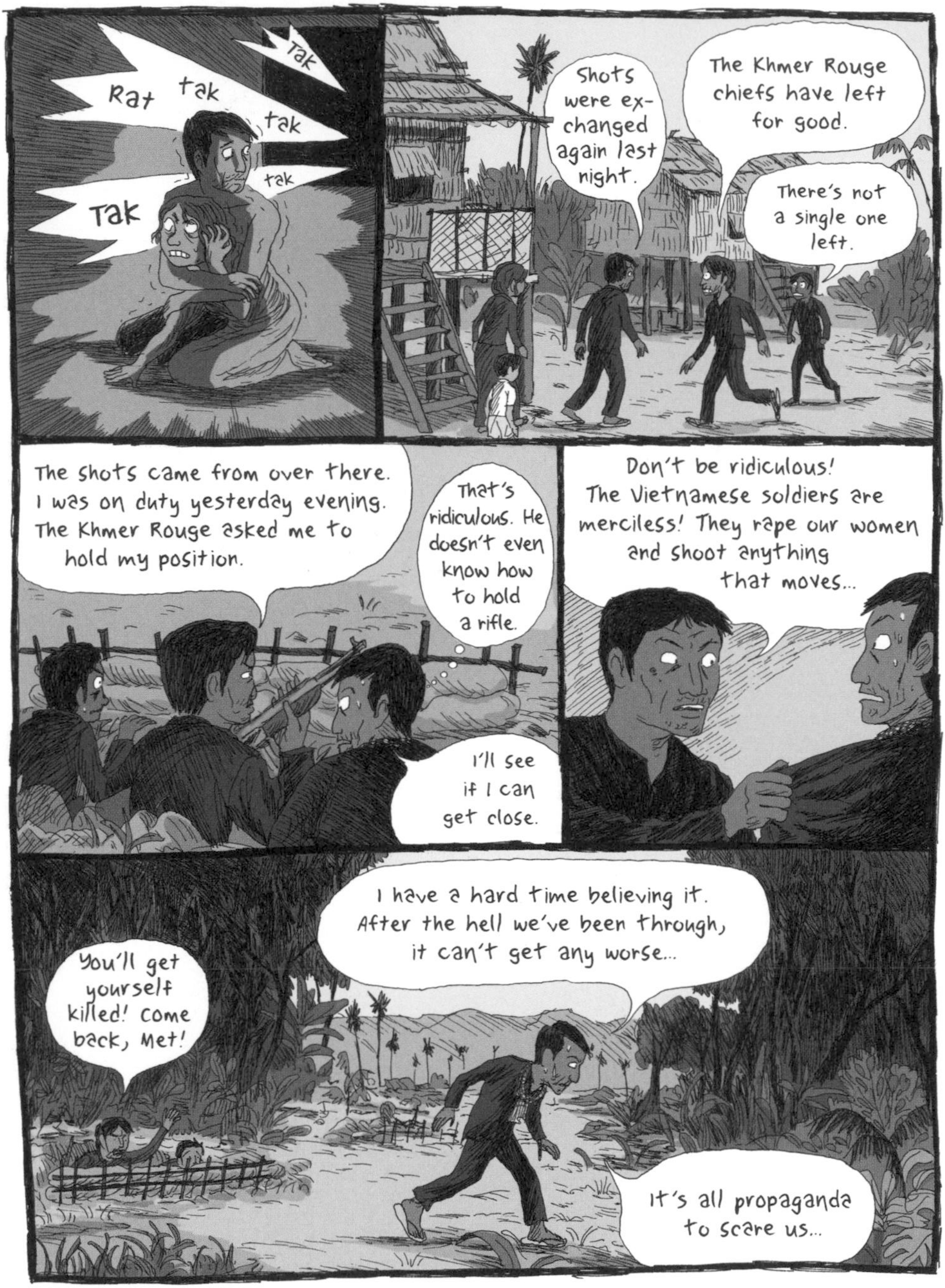
Rat tak tak tak
Tak
Tak
Shots were exchanged again last night.
The Khmer Rouge chiefs have left for good.
There's not a single one left.
The shots came from over there. I was on duty yesterday evening. The Khmer Rouge asked me to hold my position.
That's ridiculous. He doesn't even know how to hold a rifle.
I'll see if I can get close.
Don't be ridiculous! The Vietnamese soldiers are merciless! They rape our women and shoot anything that moves...
I have a hard time believing it. After the hell we've been through, it can't get any worse...
You'll get yourself killed! Come back, Met!
It's all propaganda to scare us...

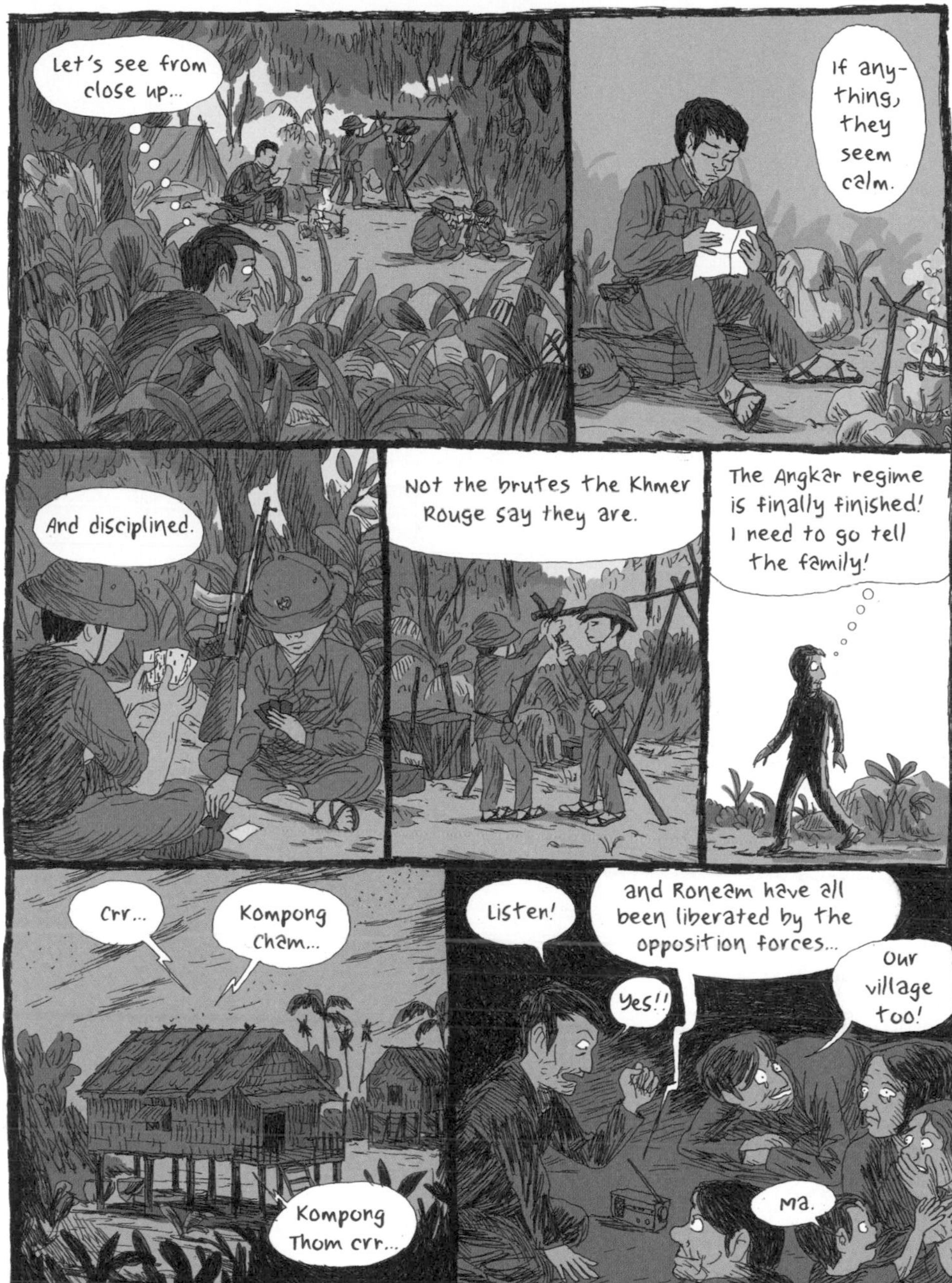

Let's see from close up...
If anything, they seem calm.
And disciplined.
Not the brutes the Khmer Rouge say they are.
The Angkar regime is finally finished! I need to go tell the family!
Crr...
Kompong Cham...
Kompong Thom crr...
Listen!
and Roneam have all been liberated by the opposition forces...
Yes!!
Our village too!
Ma.

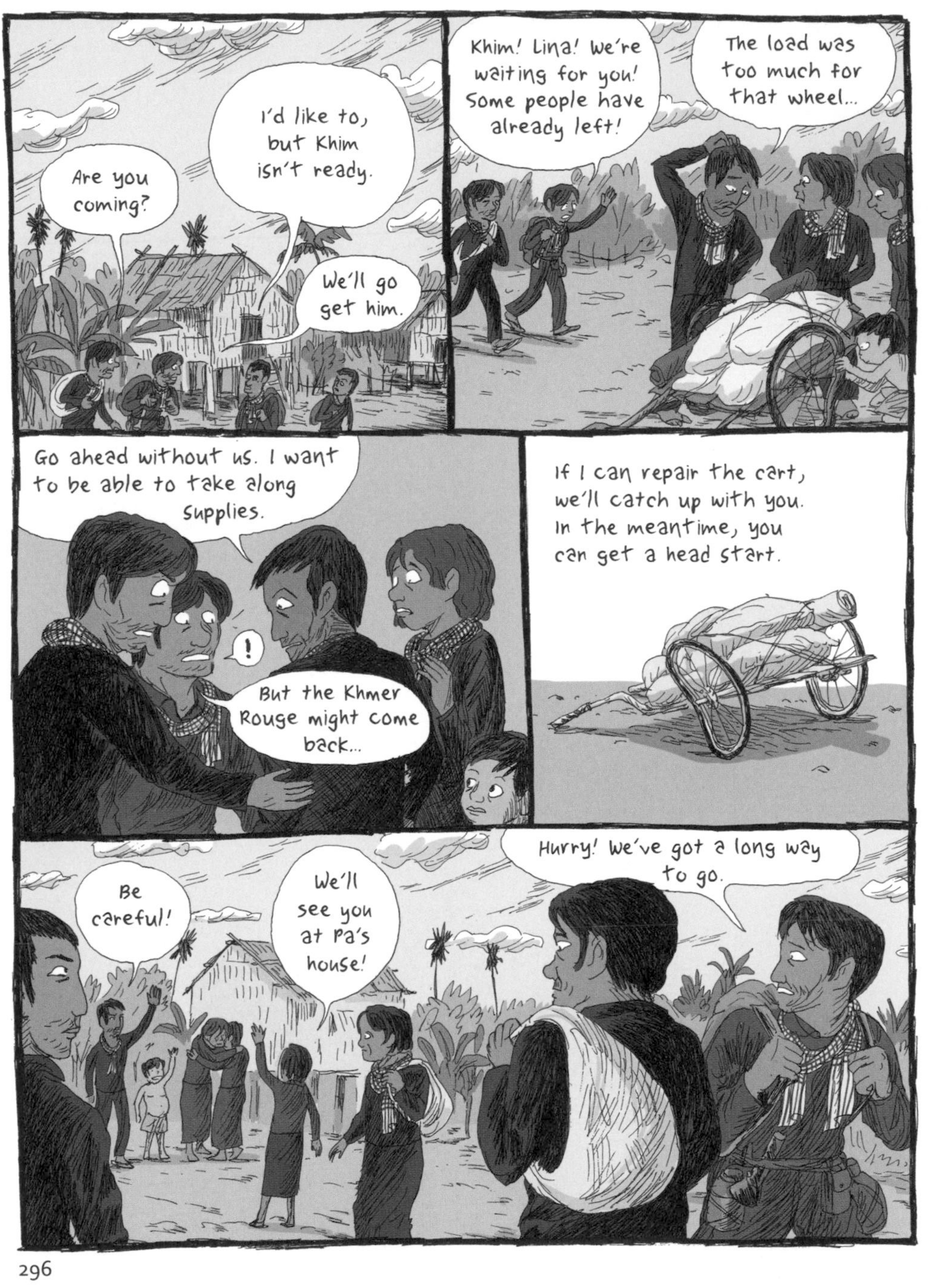
Are you coming?
I'd like to, but Khim isn't ready.
We'll go get him.
Khim! Lina! We're waiting for you! Some people have already left!
The load was too much for that wheel...
Go ahead without us. I want to be able to take along supplies.
!
But the Khmer Rouge might come back...
If I can repair the cart, we'll catch up with you. In the meantime, you can get a head start.
Be careful!
We'll see you at Pa's house!
Hurry! We've got a long way to go.

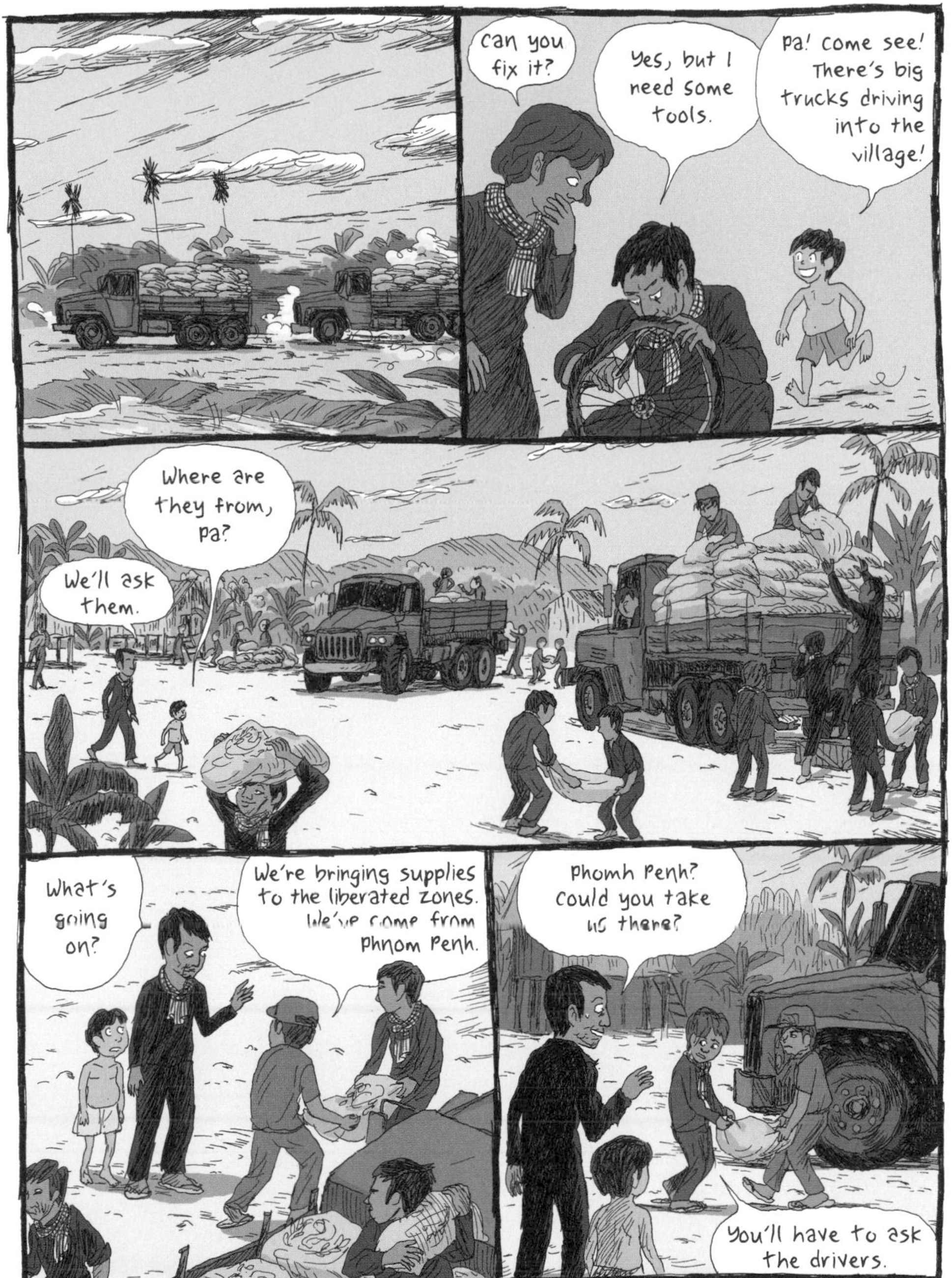
Can you fix it?
Yes, but I need some tools.
Pa! Come see! There's big trucks driving into the village!
Where are they from, Pa?
We'll ask them.
What's going on?
We're bringing supplies to the liberated zones. We've come from Phnom Penh.
Phomh Penh? Could you take us there?
You'll have to ask the drivers.

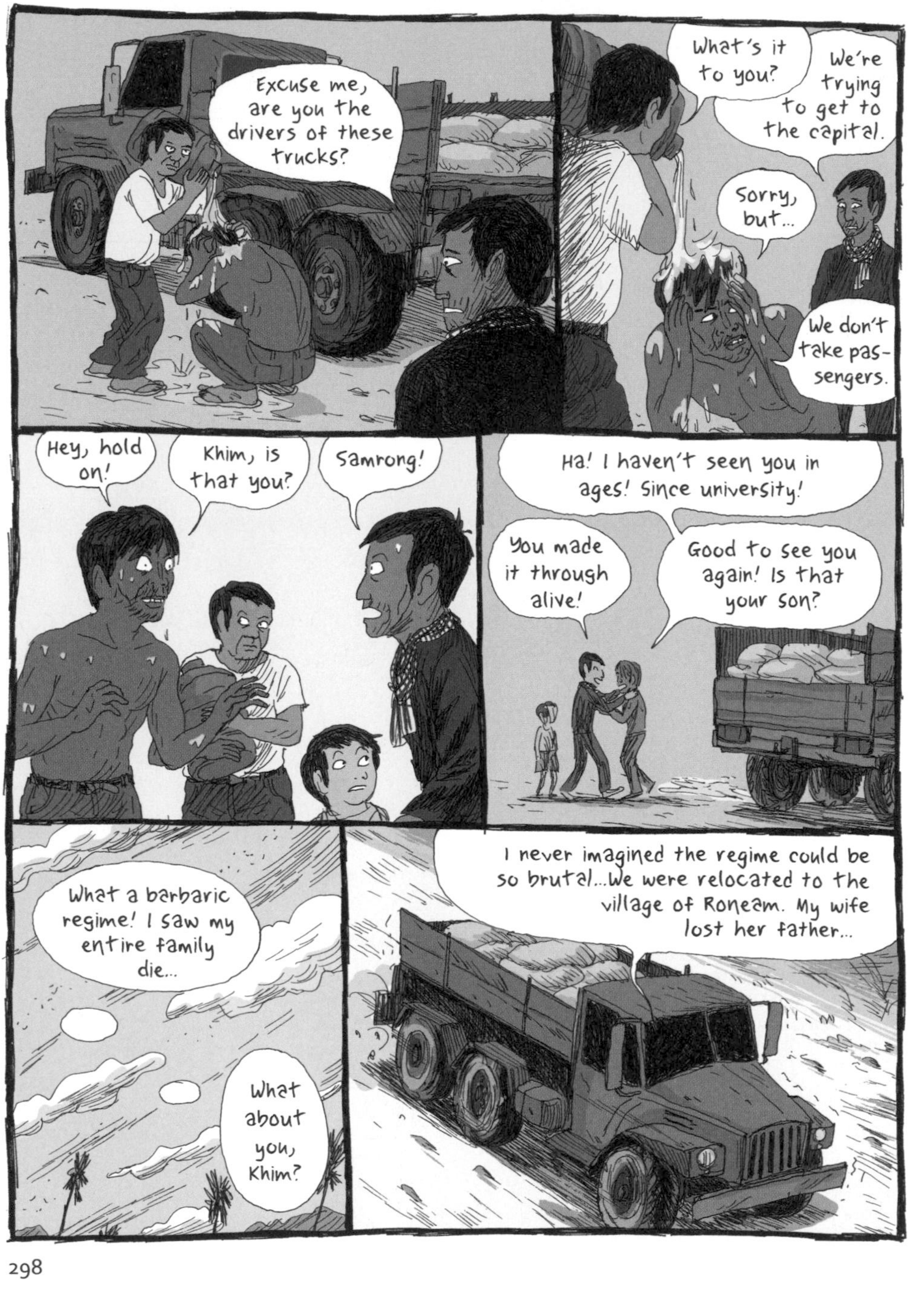
Excuse me, are you the drivers of these trucks?
What's it to you?
We're trying to get to the capital.
Sorry, but...
We don't take passengers.
Hey, hold on!
Khim, is that you?
Samrong!
Ha! I haven't seen you in ages! Since university!
You made it through alive!
Good to see you again! Is that your son?
What a barbaric regime! I saw my entire family die...
What about you, Khim?
I never imagined the regime could be so brutal...We were relocated to the village of Roneam. My wife lost her father...

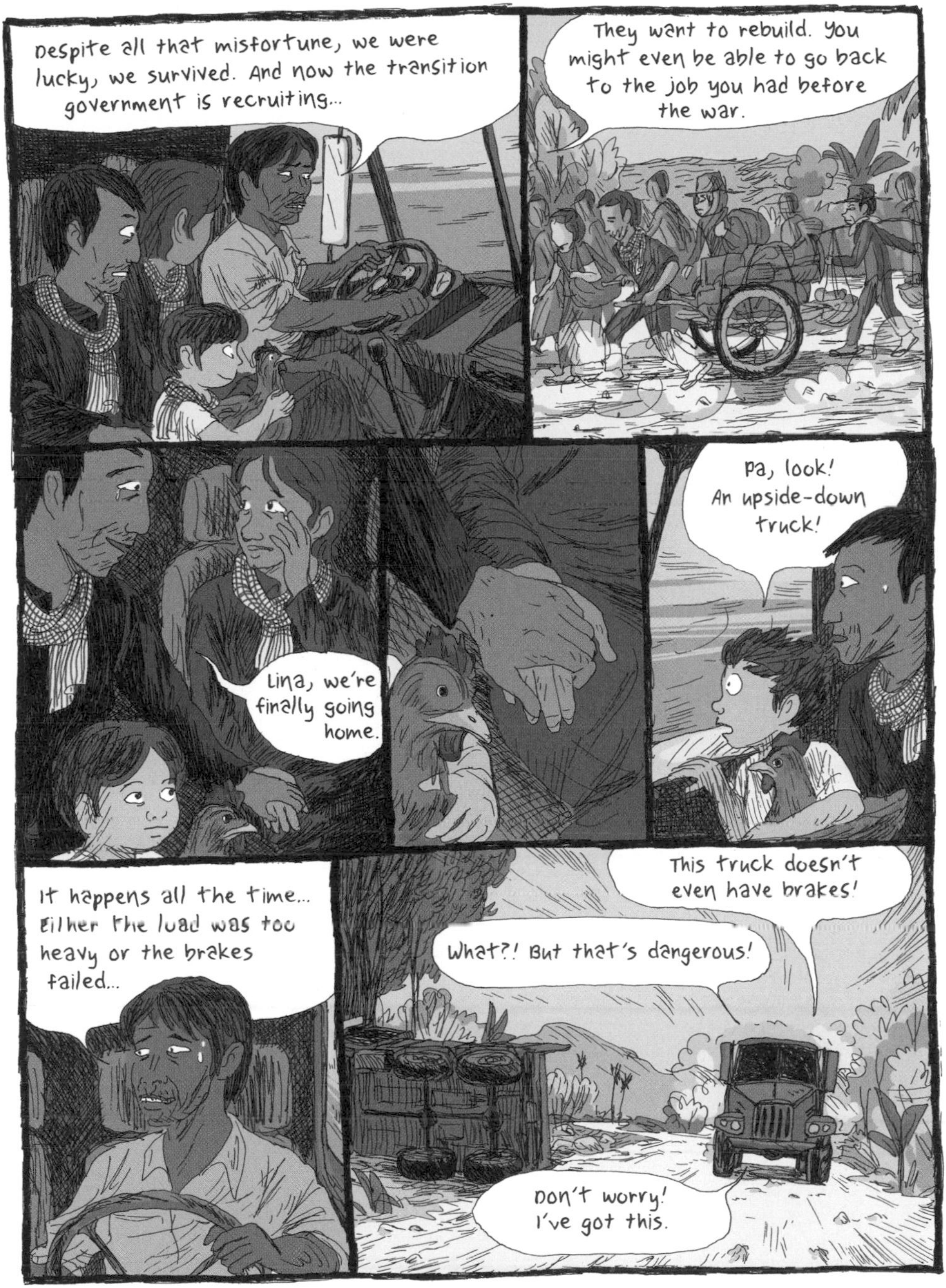
Despite all that misfortune, we were lucky, we survived. And now the transition government is recruiting...
They want to rebuild. You might even be able to go back to the job you had before the war.
Lina, we're finally going home.
Pa, look! An upside-down truck!
It happens all the time... Either the load was too heavy or the brakes failed...
This truck doesn't even have brakes!
What?! But that's dangerous!
Don't worry! I've got this.

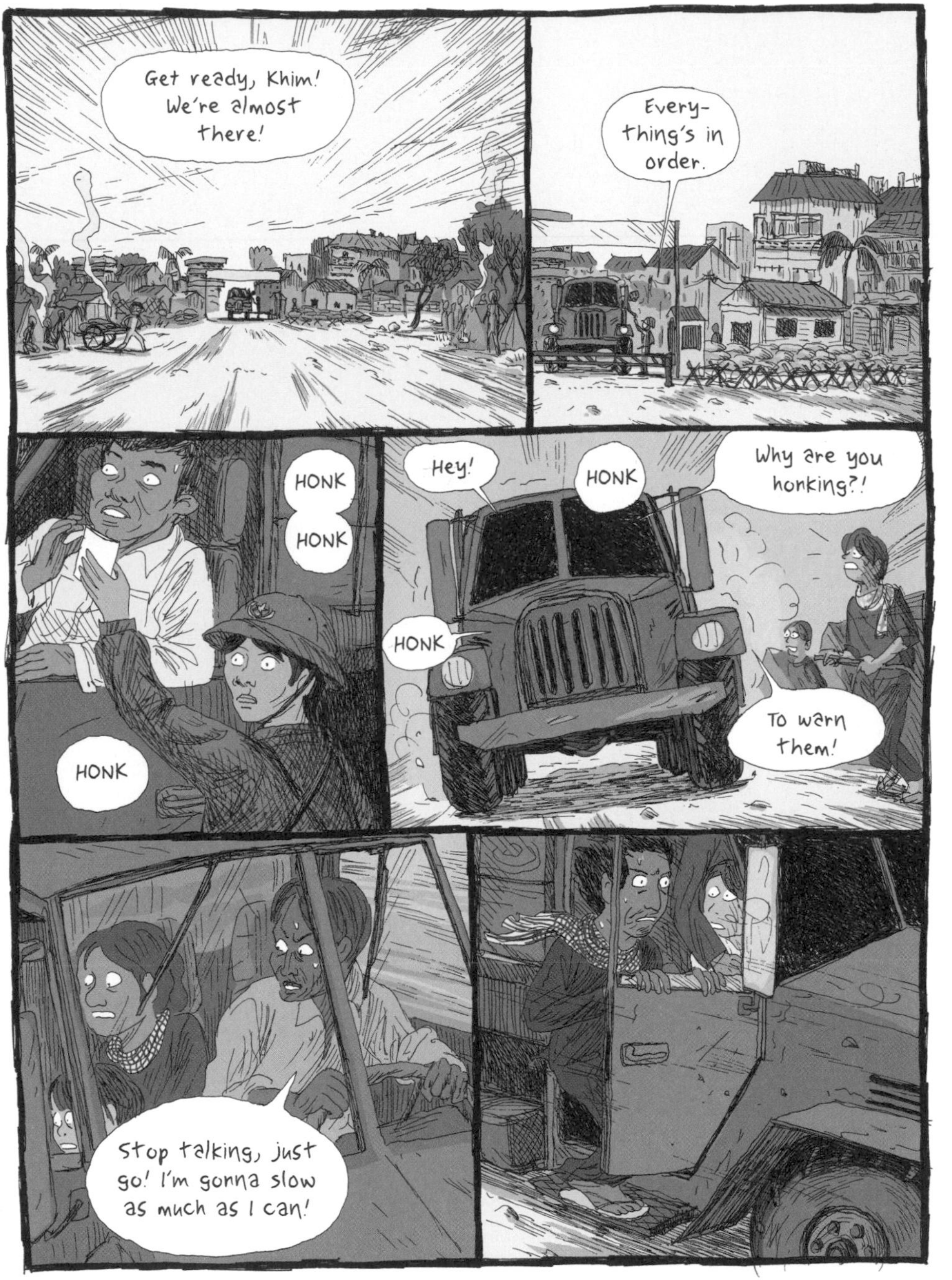
Get ready, Khim! We're almost there!
Every-thing's in order.
HONK
HONK
HONK
Hey!
HONK
Why are you honking?!
HONK
To warn them!
Stop talking, just go! I'm gonna slow as much as I can!

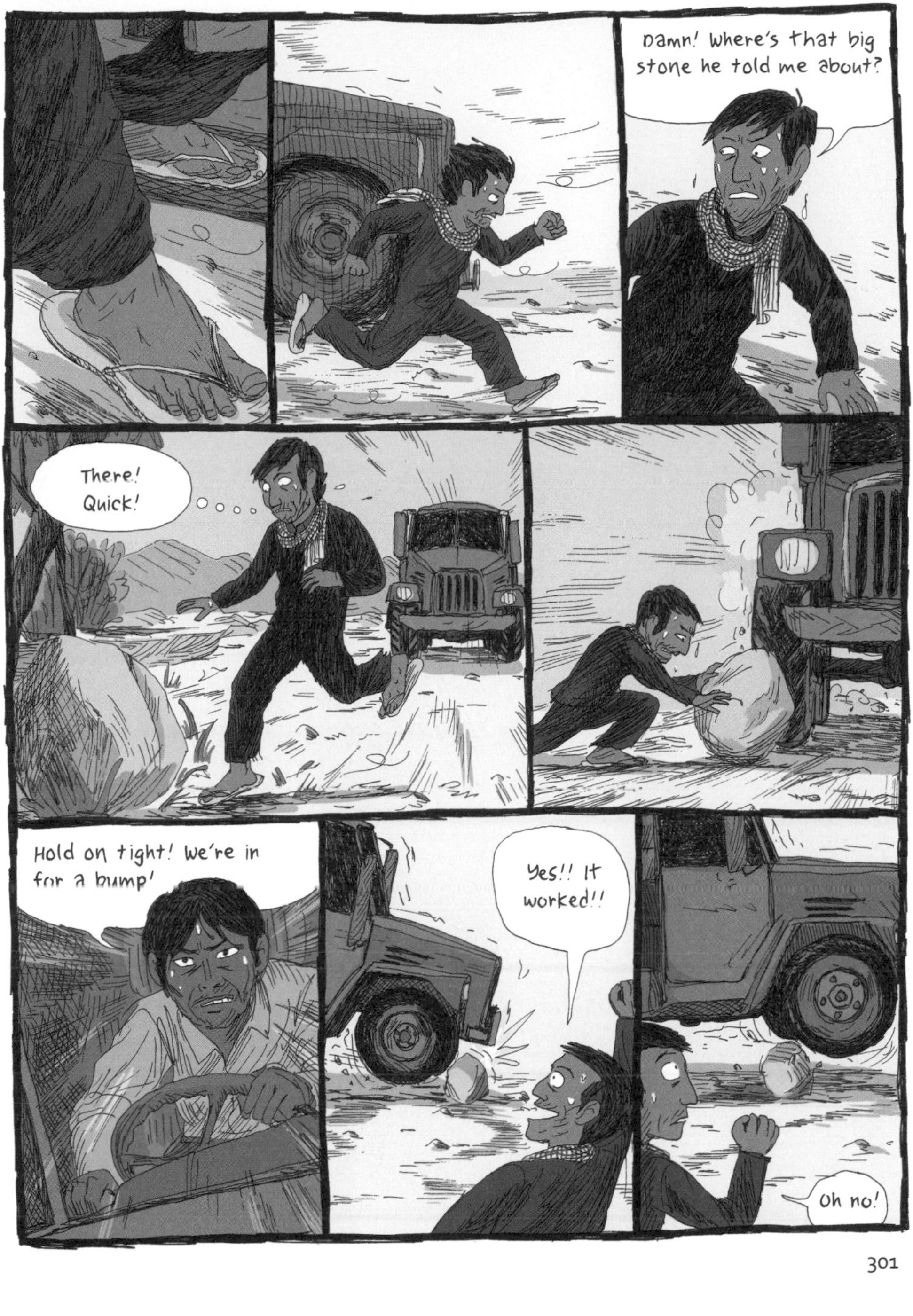
Damn! Where's that big stone he told me about?
There! Quick!
Hold on tight! We're in for a bump!
Yes!! It worked!!
Oh no!

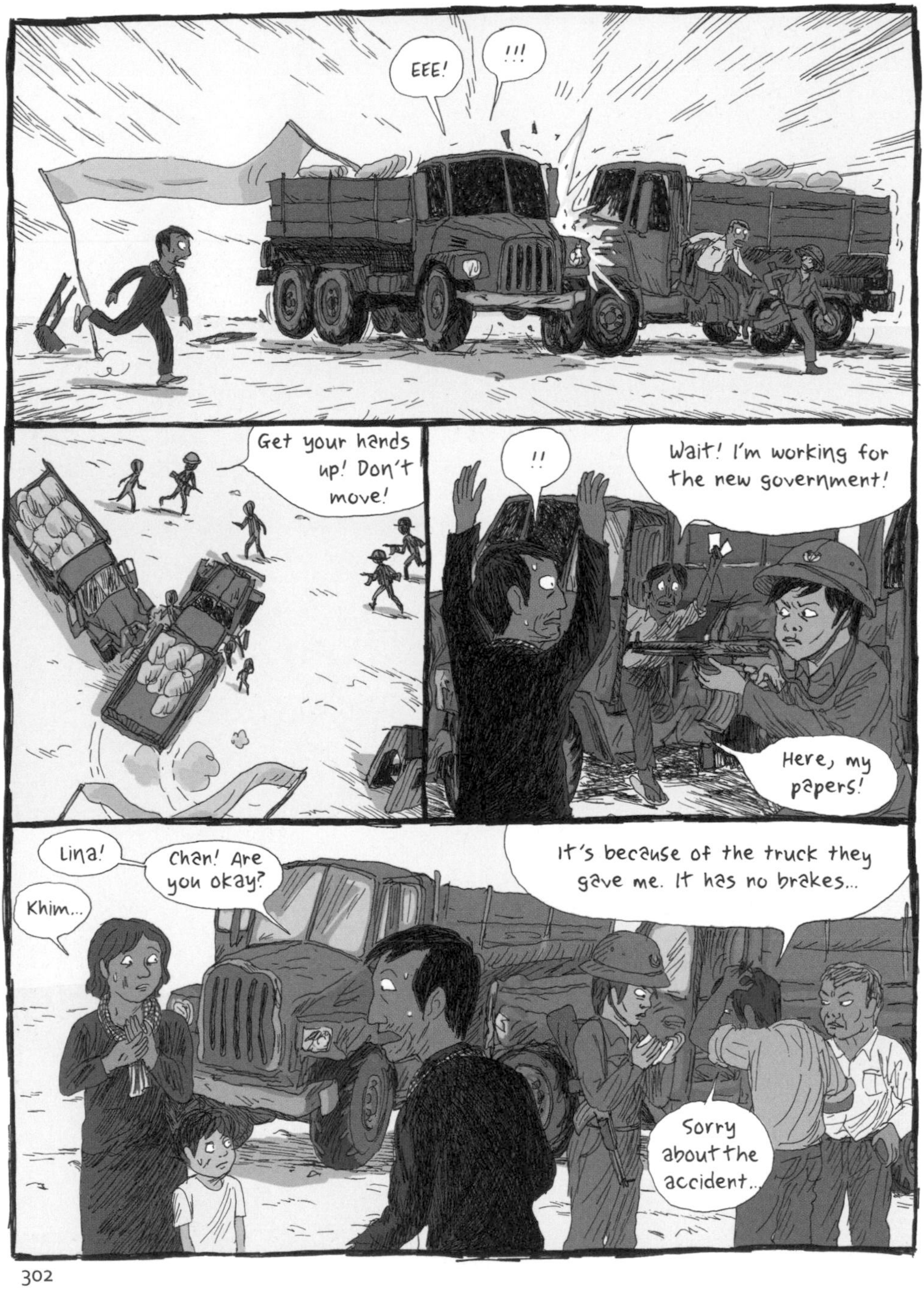
EEE!
!!!
Get your hands up! Don't move!
!!
Wait! I'm working for the new government!
Here, my papers!
Lina!
Chan! Are you okay?
Khim...
It's because of the truck they gave me. It has no brakes...
Sorry about the accident...

chapter 18

LIFE RESUMES

A POPULATION IN MOURNING

In 2007, 19,733 communal graves were inventoried in Cambodia.
Some 150 new graves are found every year.

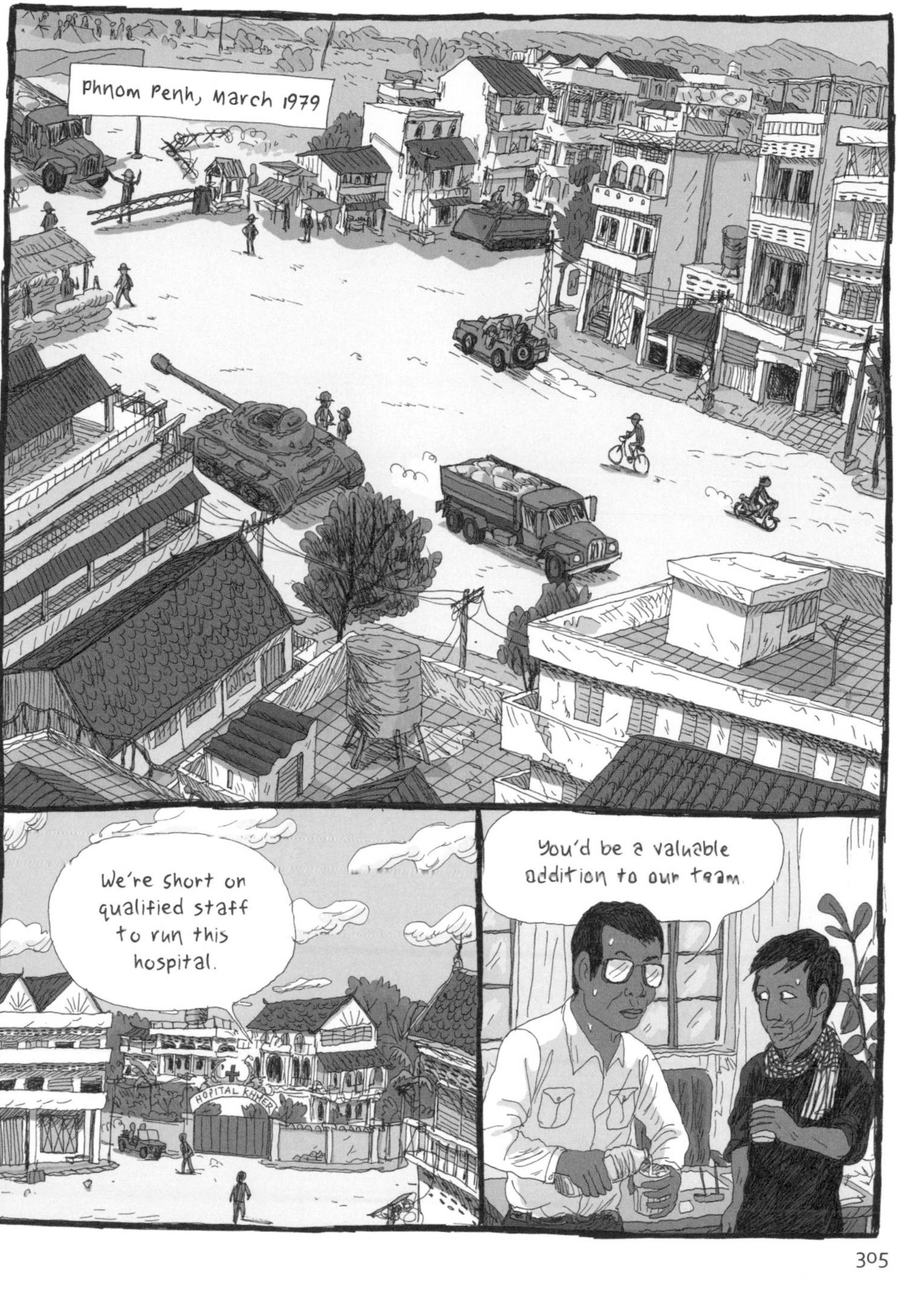
Phnom Penh, March 1979
We're short on qualified staff to run this hospital.
HOPITAL KHMER
You'd be a valuable addition to our team.

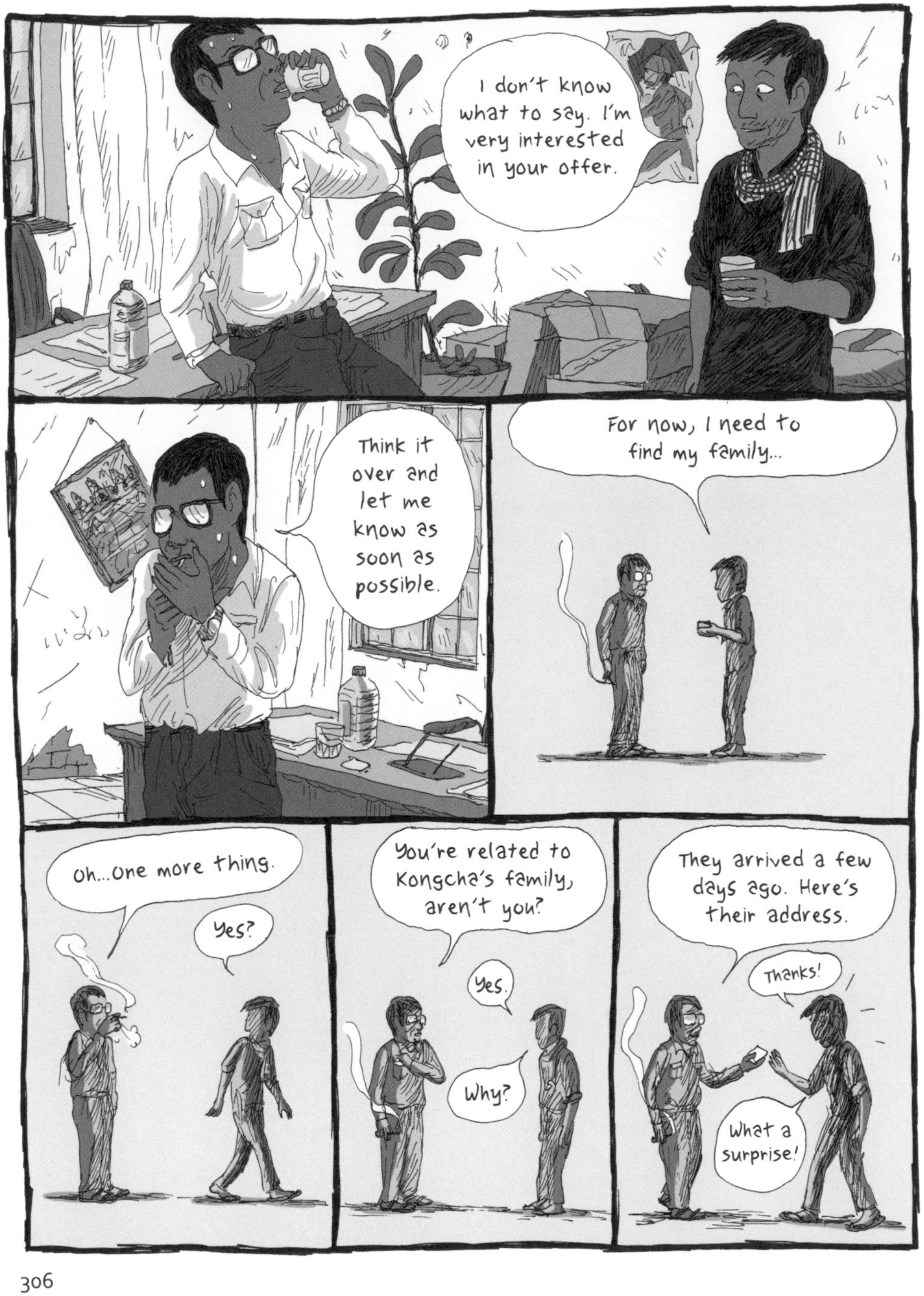
I don't know what to say. I'm very interested in your offer.
Think it over and let me know as soon as possible.
For now, I need to find my family...
Oh...One more thing.
Yes?
You're related to Kongcha's family, aren't you?
Yes.
Why?
They arrived a few days ago. Here's their address.
Thanks!
What a surprise!

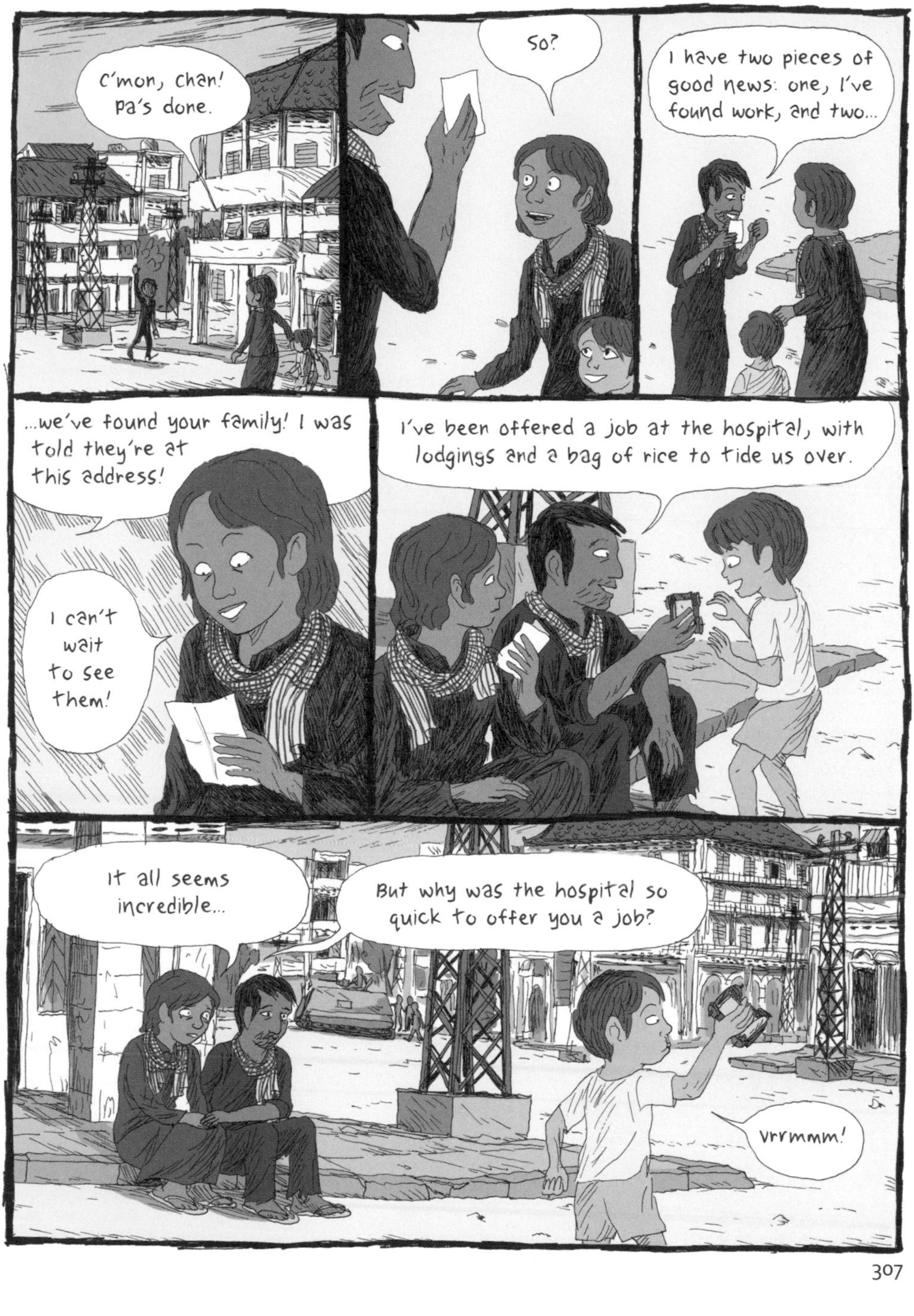
C'mon, Chan! Pa's done.
So?
I have two pieces of good news: one, I've found work, and two...
...we've found your family! I was told they're at this address!
I can't wait to see them!
I've been offered a job at the hospital, with lodgings and a bag of rice to tide us over.
It all seems incredible...
But why was the hospital so quick to offer you a job?
vrrmmm!

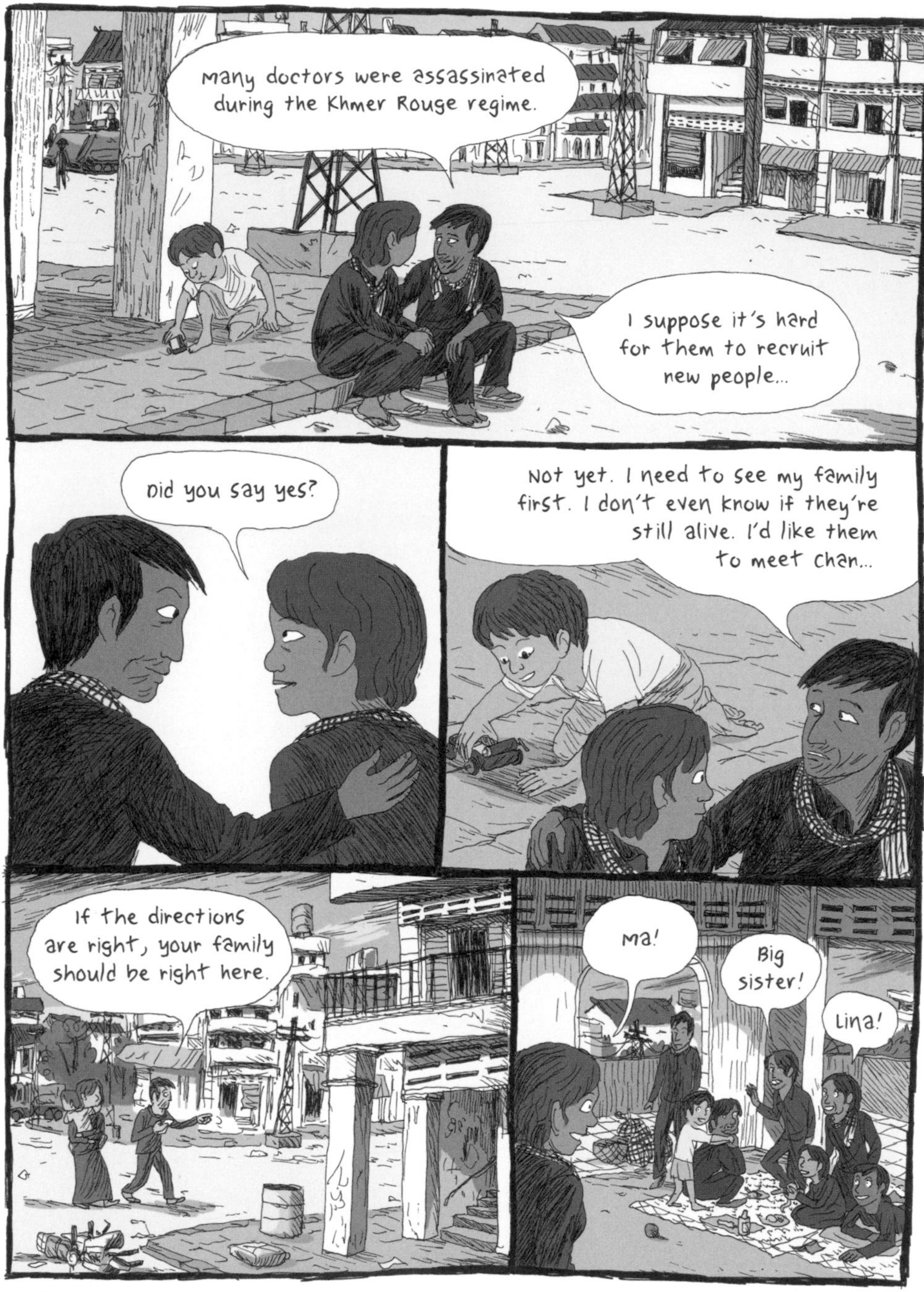

Many doctors were assassinated during the Khmer Rouge regime.
I suppose it's hard for them to recruit new people...
Did you say yes?
Not yet. I need to see my family first. I don't even know if they're still alive. I'd like them to meet Chan...
If the directions are right, your family should be right here.
Ma!
Big sister!
Lina!

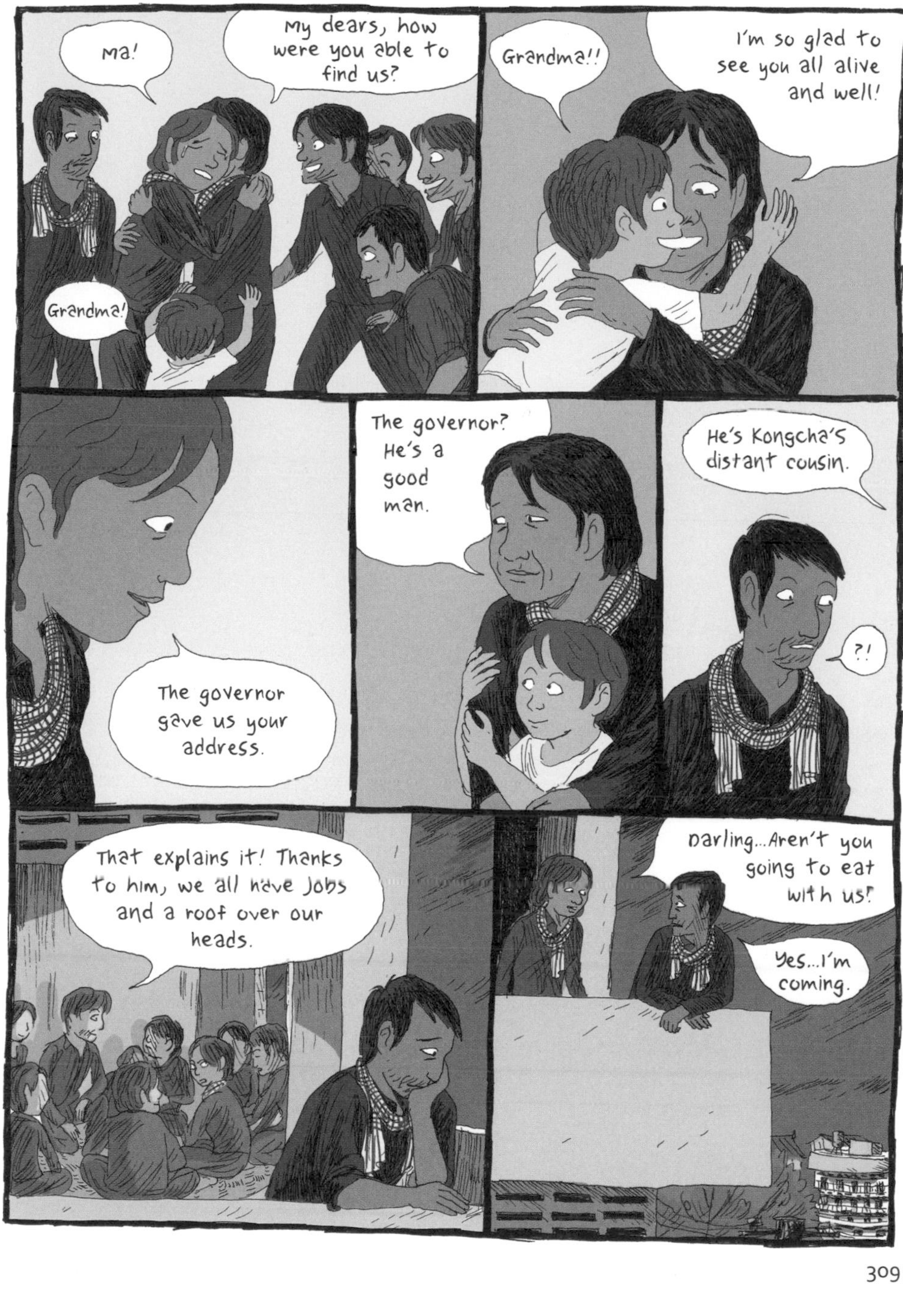
Ma!
My dears, how were you able to find us?
Grandma!
Grandma!!
I'm so glad to see you all alive and well!
The governor gave us your address.
The governor? He's a good man.
He's Kongcha's distant cousin.
?!
That explains it! Thanks to him, we all have jobs and a roof over our heads.
Darling... Aren't you going to eat with us?
Yes... I'm coming.

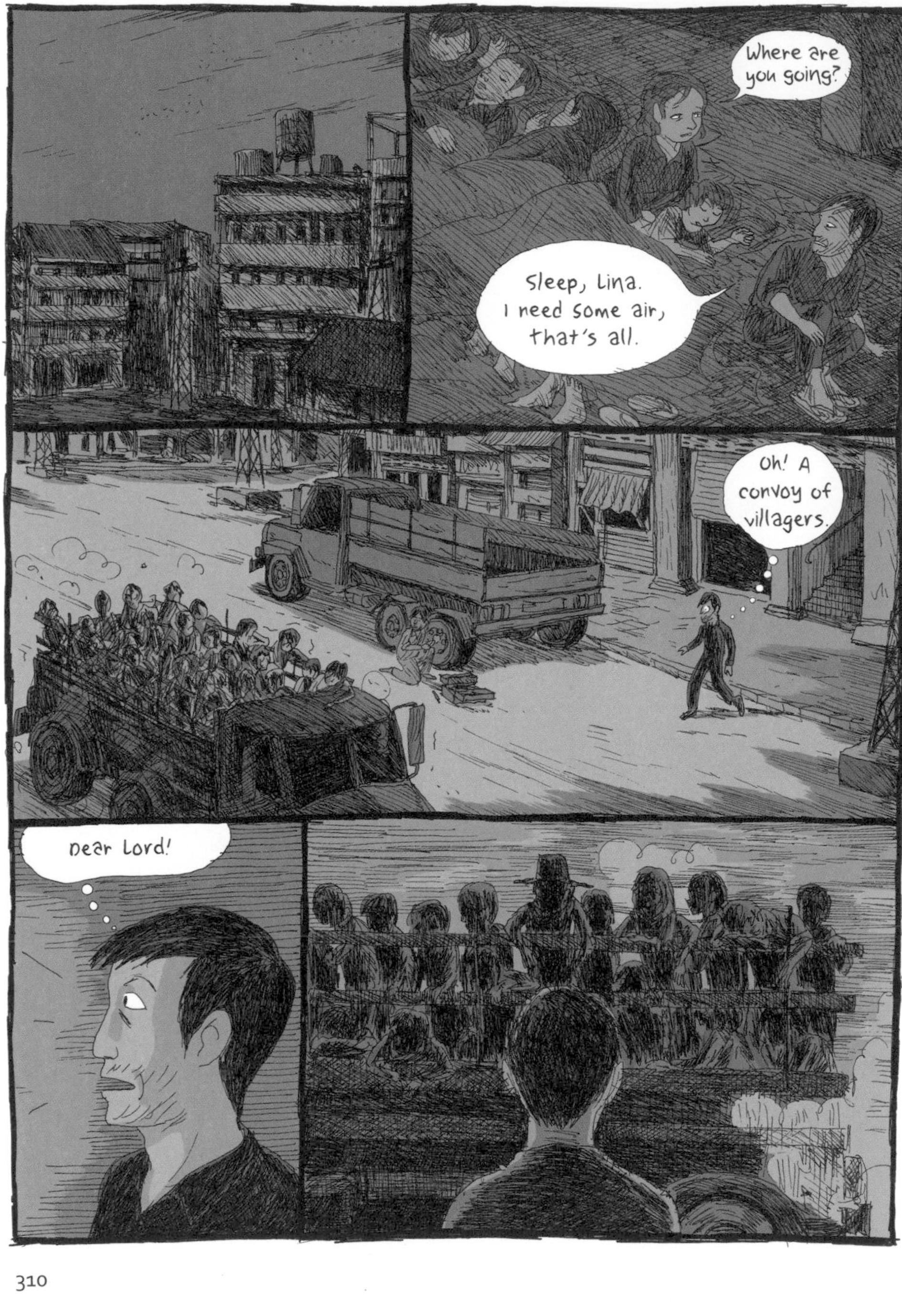
Where are you going?
Sleep, Lina. I need some air, that's all.
Oh! A convoy of villagers.
Dear Lord!

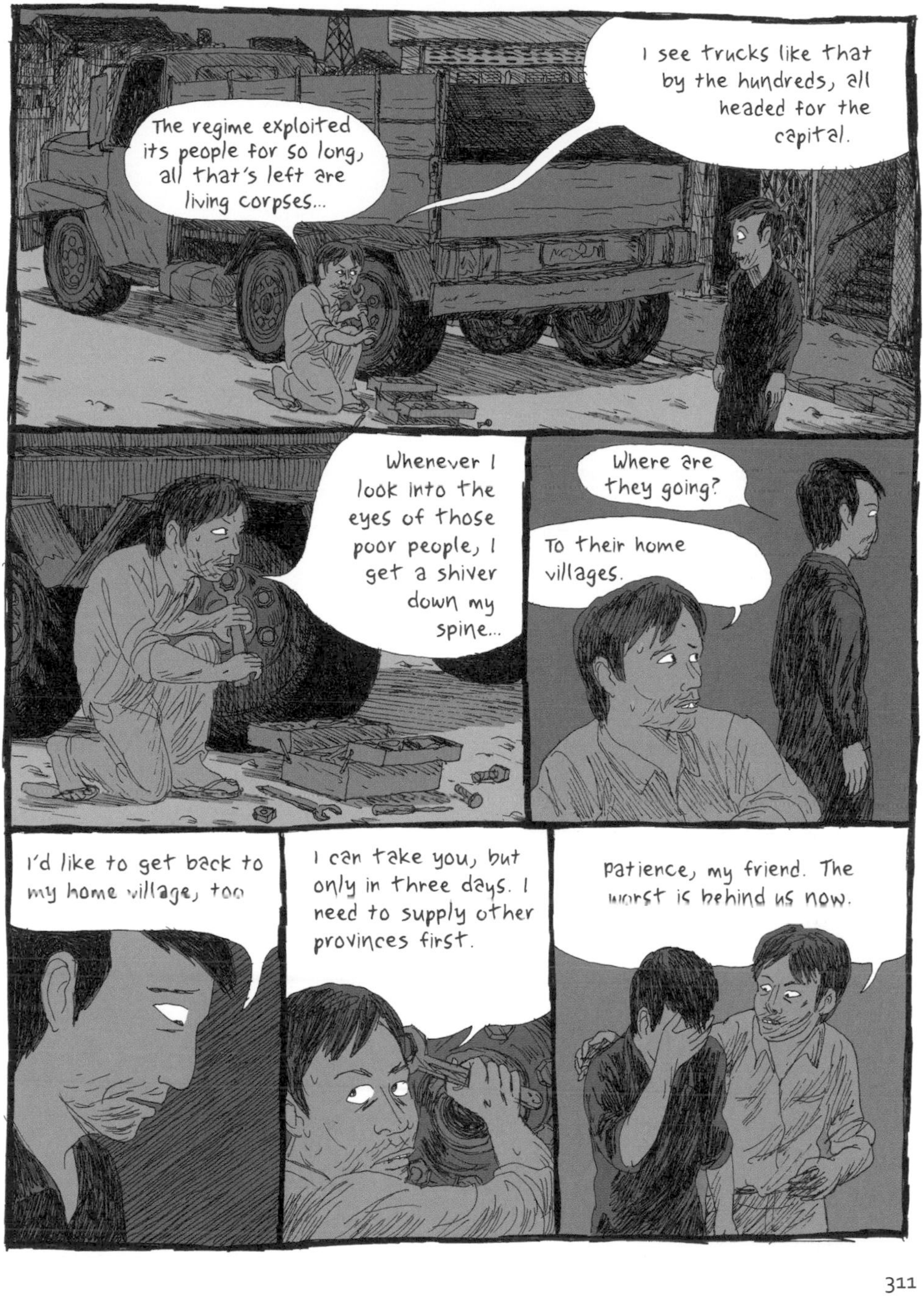
The regime exploited its people for so long, all that's left are living corpses...
I see trucks like that by the hundreds, all headed for the capital.
Whenever I look into the eyes of those poor people, I get a shiver down my spine...
Where are they going?
To their home villages.
I'd like to get back to my home village, too
I can take you, but only in three days. I need to supply other provinces first.
Patience, my friend. The worst is behind us now.

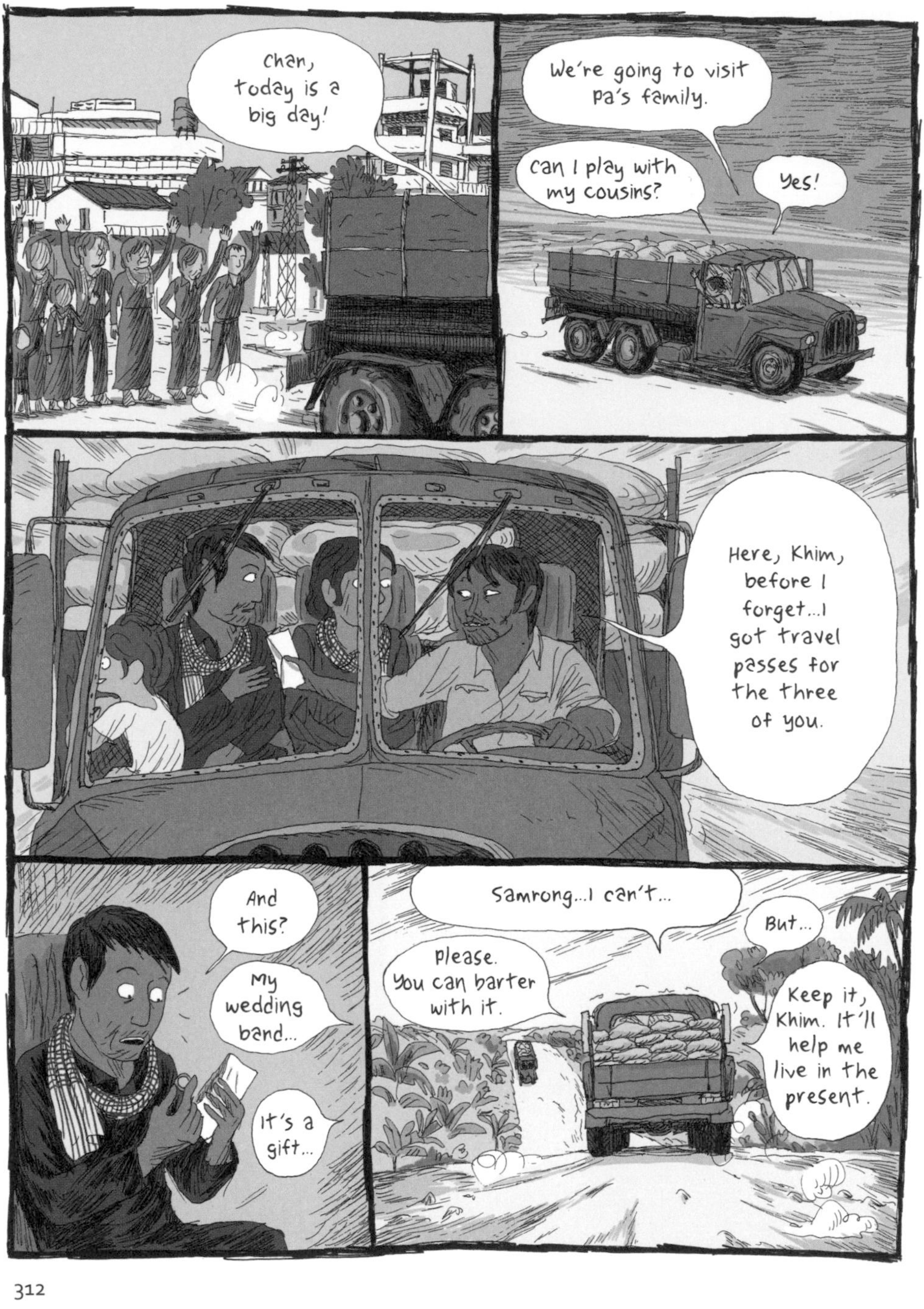
Chan, today is a big day!
We're going to visit Pa's family.
Can I play with my cousins?
Yes!
Here, Khim, before I forget...I got travel passes for the three of you.
And this?
My wedding band...
It's a gift...
Samrong...I can't...
Please. You can barter with it.
But...
Keep it, Khim. It'll help me live in the present.

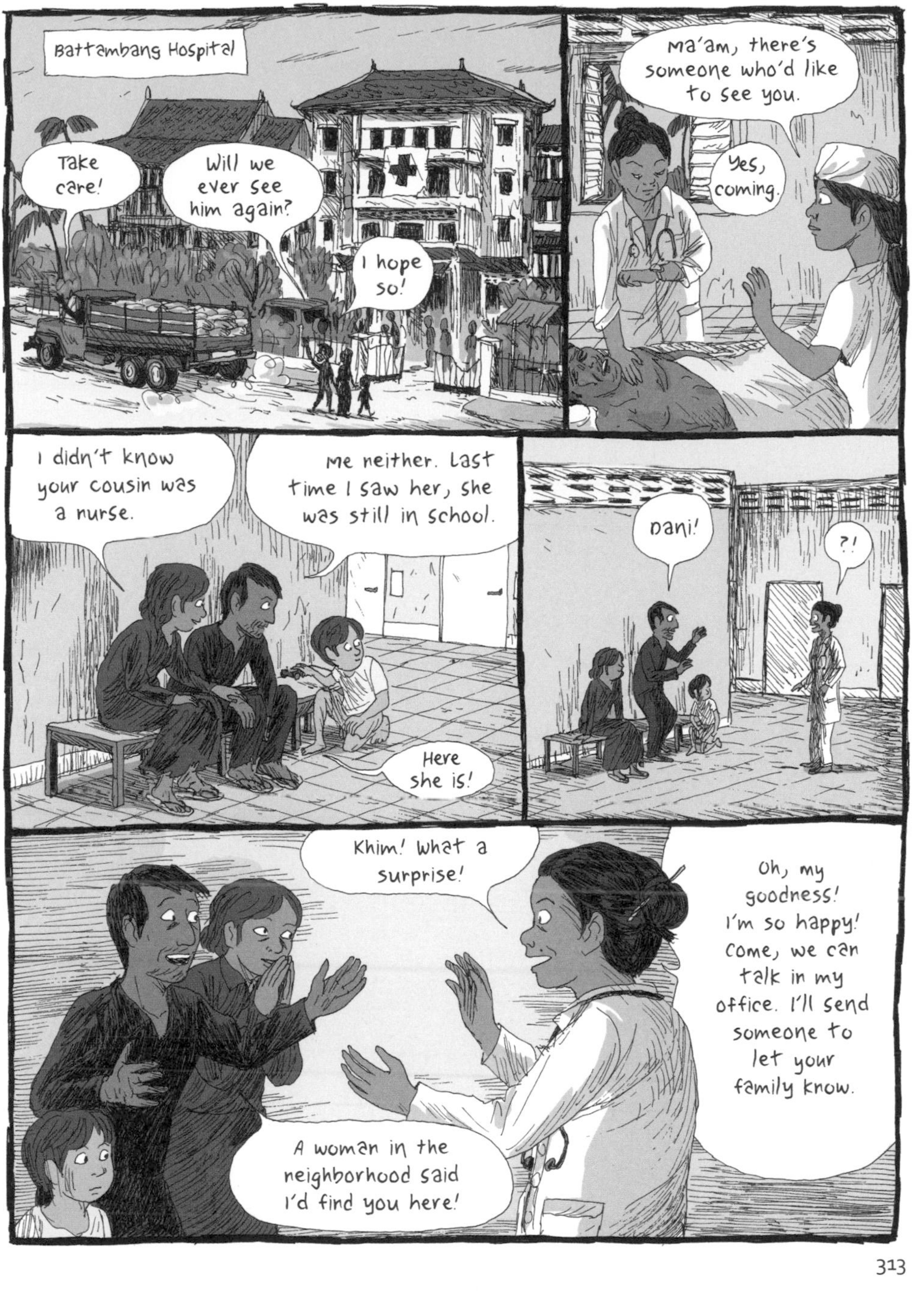
Battambang Hospital
Take care!
Will we ever see him again?
I hope so!
Ma'am, there's someone who'd like to see you.
Yes, coming.
I didn't know your cousin was a nurse.
Me neither. Last time I saw her, she was still in school.
Here she is!
Dani!
?!
Khim! What a surprise!
A woman in the neighborhood said I'd find you here!
Oh, my goodness! I'm so happy! Come, we can talk in my office. I'll send someone to let your family know.

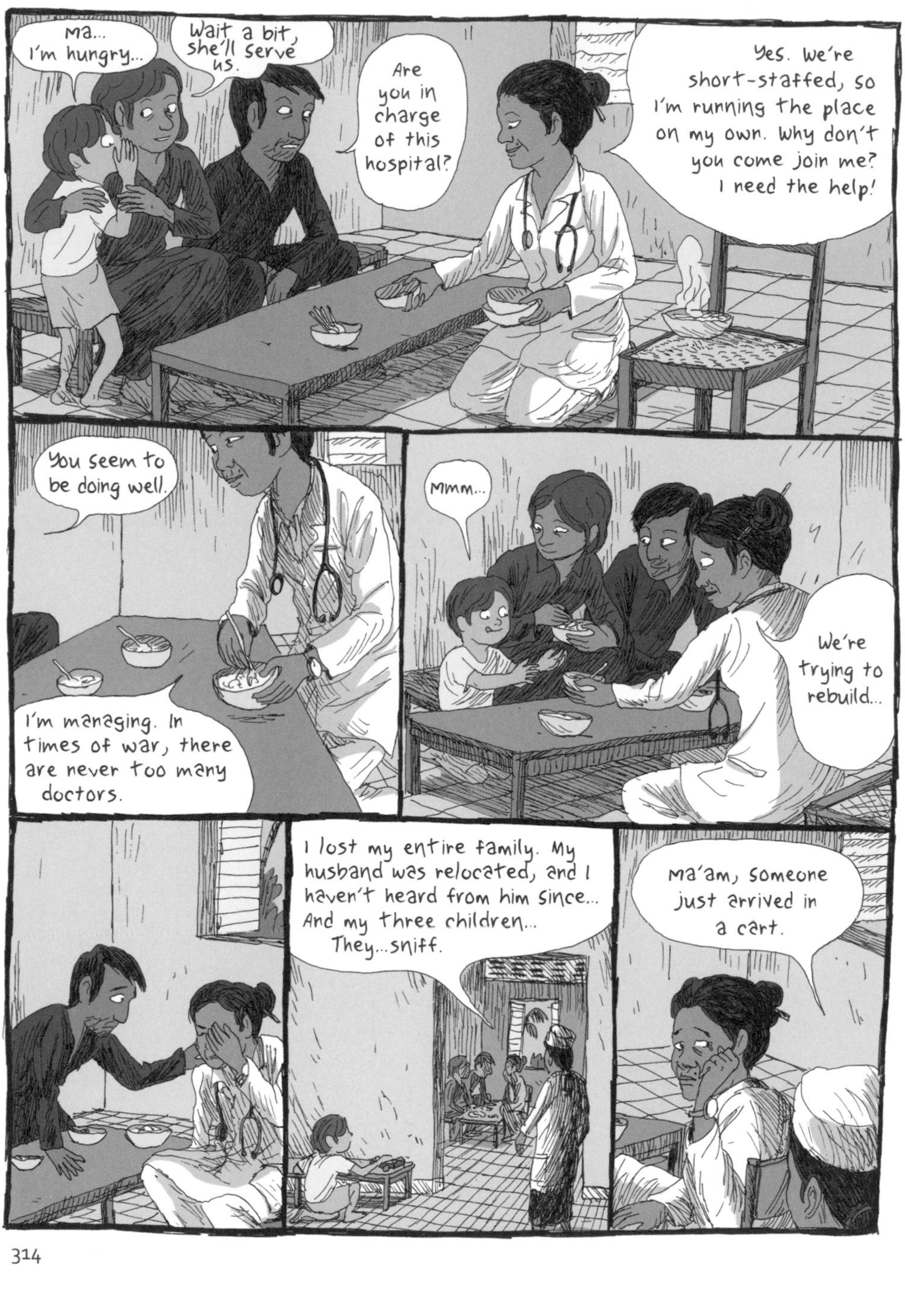
Ma... I'm hungry...
Wait a bit, she'll serve us.
Are you in charge of this hospital?
Yes. We're short-staffed, so I'm running the place on my own. Why don't you come join me? I need the help!
You seem to be doing well.
I'm managing. In times of war, there are never too many doctors.
Mmm...
We're trying to rebuild...
I lost my entire family. My husband was relocated, and I haven't heard from him since... And my three children... They...sniff.
Ma'am, someone just arrived in a cart.

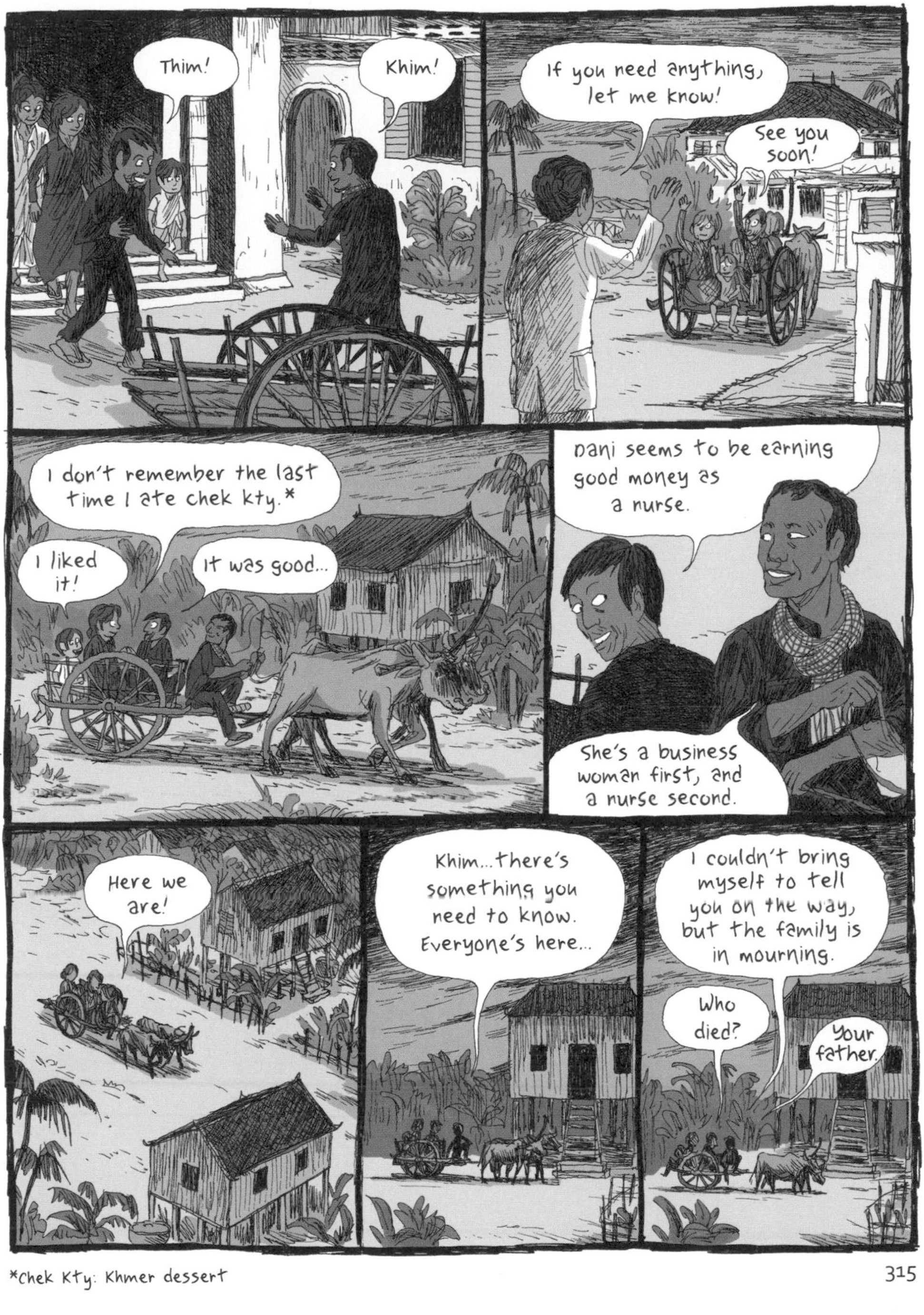
Thim!
Khim!
If you need anything, let me know!
See you soon!
I don't remember the last time I ate chek kty.*
I liked it!
It was good...
Dani seems to be earning good money as a nurse.
She's a business woman first, and a nurse second.
Here we are!
Khim... there's something you need to know. Everyone's here...
I couldn't bring myself to tell you on the way, but the family is in mourning.
Who died?
Your father.

*Chek Kty: Khmer dessert

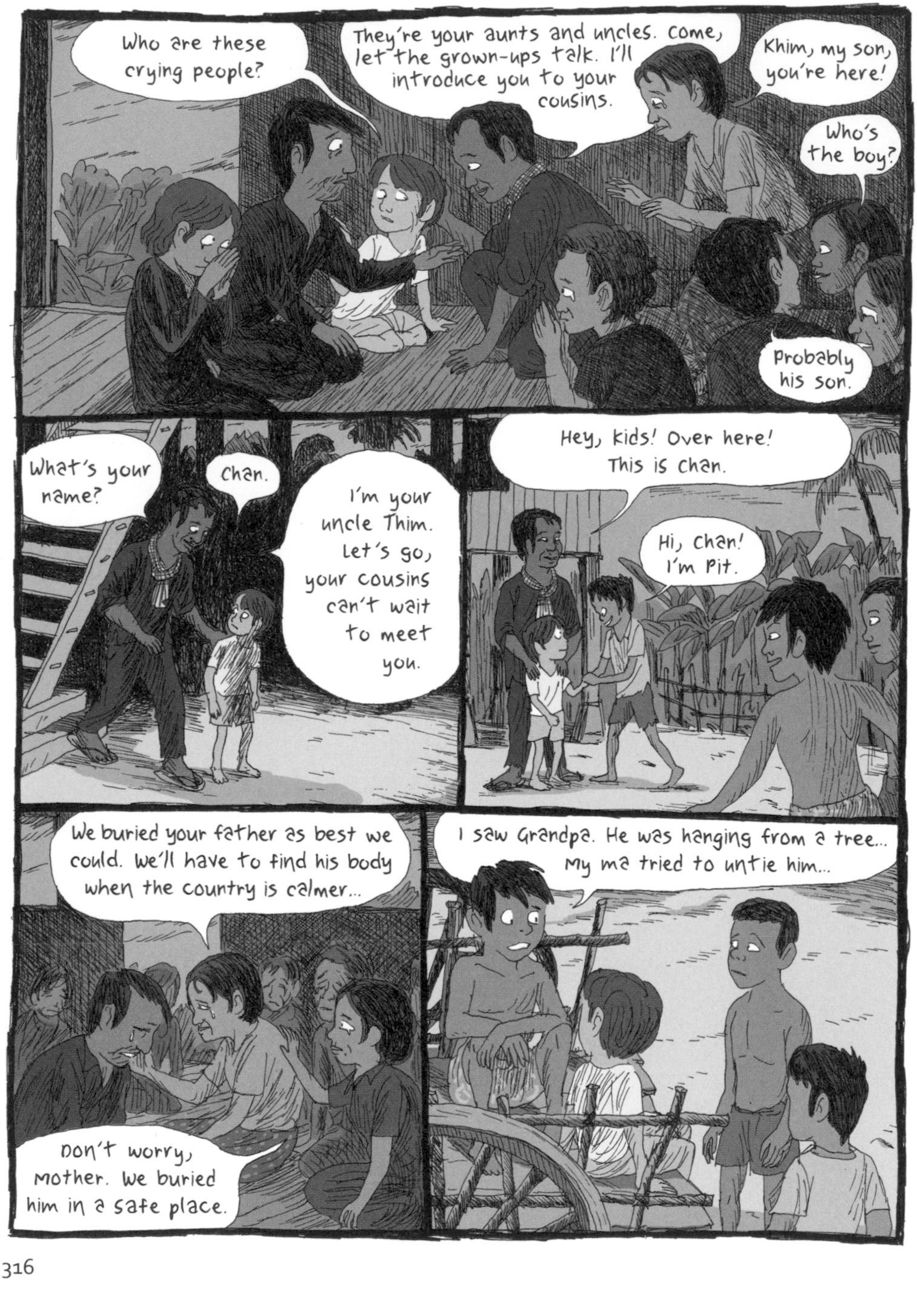
Who are these crying people?
They're your aunts and uncles. Come, let the grown-ups talk. I'll introduce you to your cousins.
Khim, my son, you're here!
Who's the boy?
Probably his son.
What's your name?
Chan.
I'm your uncle Thim. Let's go, your cousins can't wait to meet you.
Hey, kids! Over here! This is Chan.
Hi, Chan! I'm Pit.
We buried your father as best we could. We'll have to find his body when the country is calmer...
Don't worry, mother. We buried him in a safe place.
I saw Grandpa. He was hanging from a tree... My ma tried to untie him...

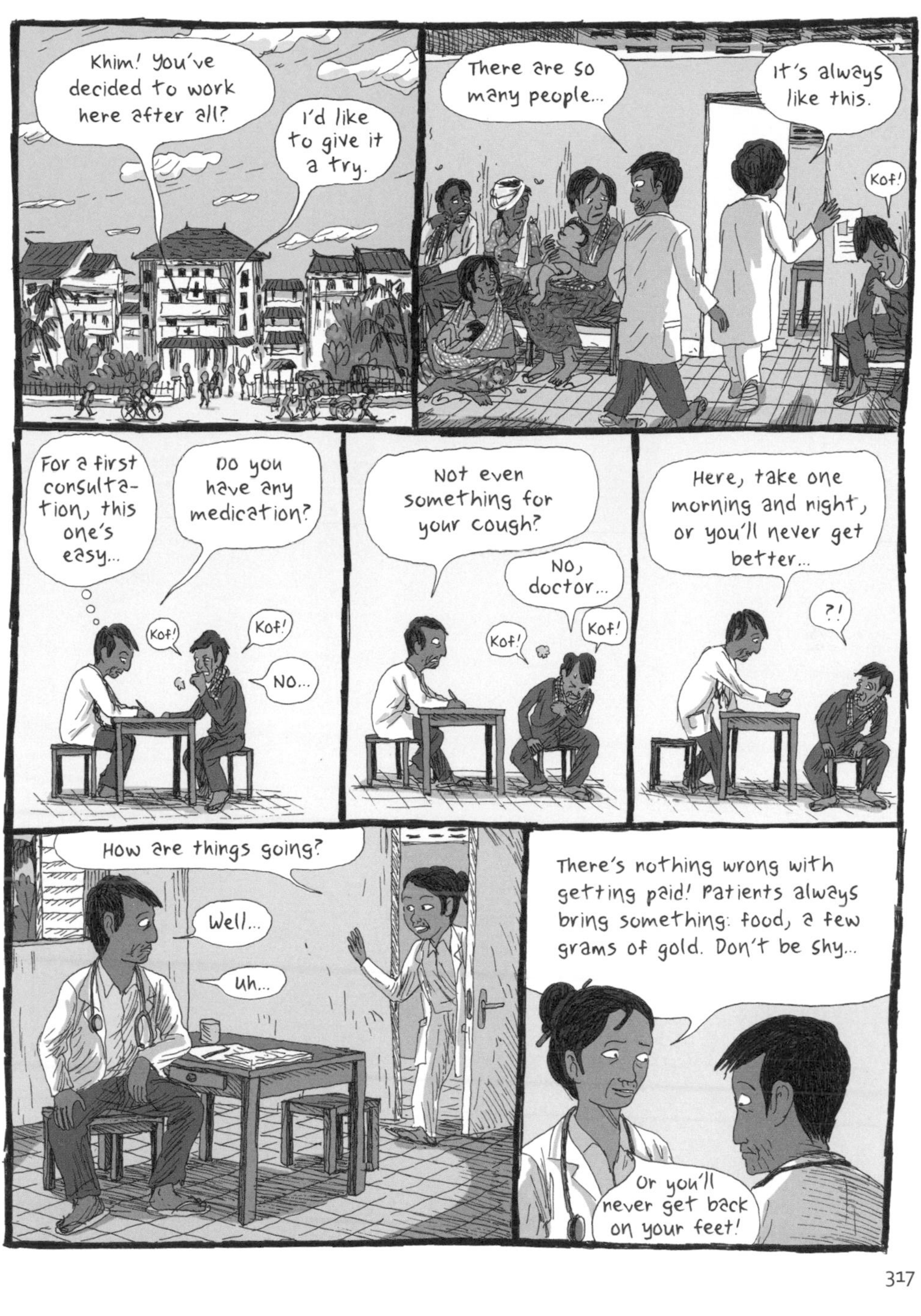
Khim! You've decided to work here after all?
I'd like to give it a try.
There are so many people...
It's always like this.
Kof!
For a first consulta-tion, this one's easy...
Do you have any medication?
Kof!
Kof!
No...
Not even something for your cough?
No, doctor...
Kof!
Kof!
Here, take one morning and night, or you'll never get better...
?!
How are things going?
Well...
Uh...
There's nothing wrong with getting paid! Patients always bring something: food, a few grams of gold. Don't be shy...
Or you'll never get back on your feet!

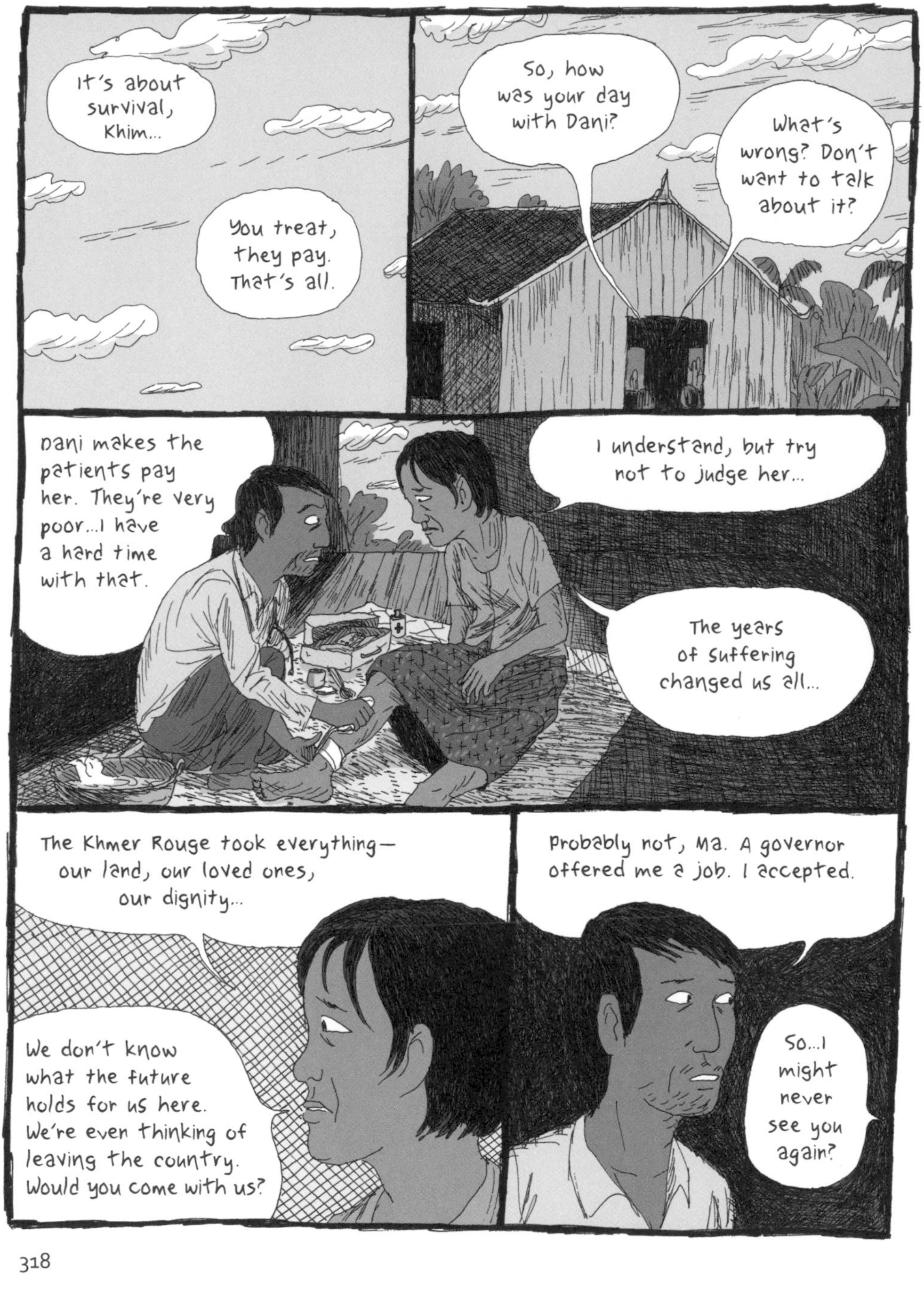
It's about survival, Khim...
You treat, they pay. That's all.
So, how was your day with Dani?
What's wrong? Don't want to talk about it?
Dani makes the patients pay her. They're very poor... I have a hard time with that.
I understand, but try not to judge her...
The years of suffering changed us all...
The Khmer Rouge took everything— our land, our loved ones, our dignity...
We don't know what the future holds for us here. We're even thinking of leaving the country. Would you come with us?
Probably not, Ma. A governor offered me a job. I accepted.
So... I might never see you again?

chapter 19

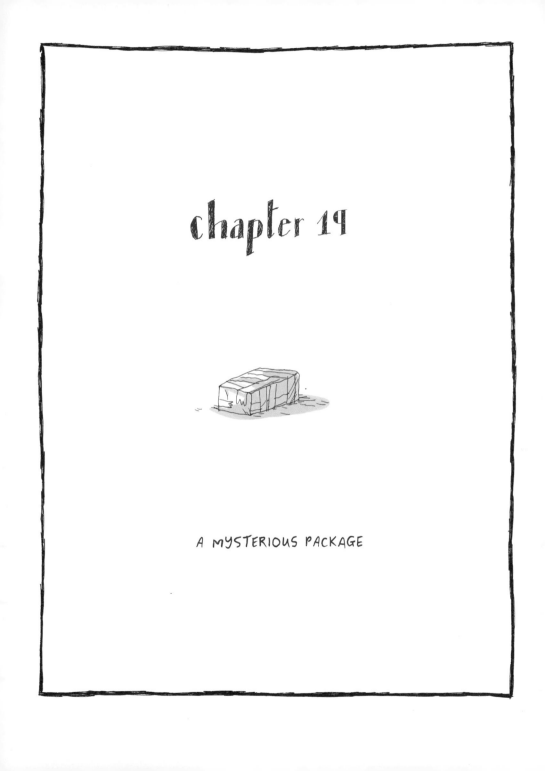

A MYSTERIOUS PACKAGE

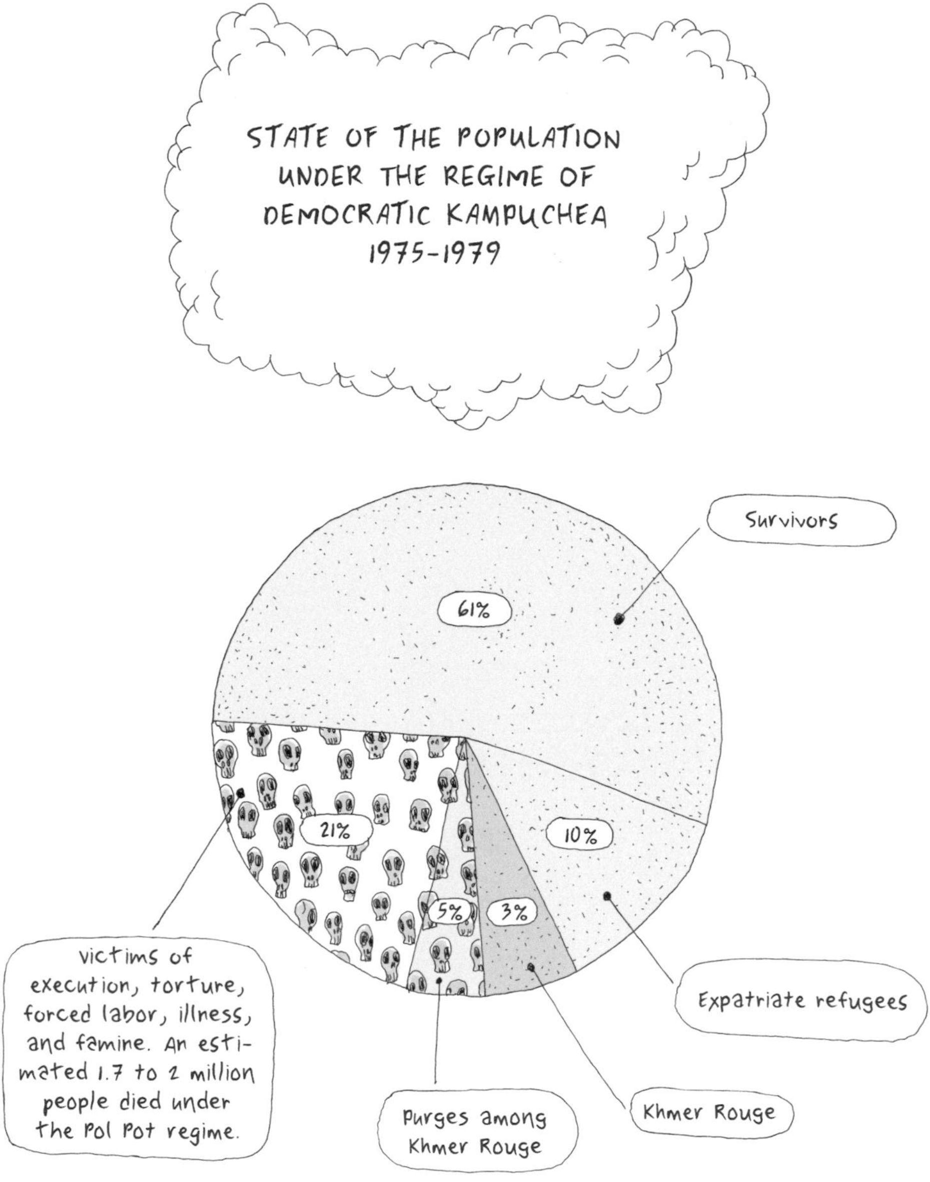
STATE OF THE POPULATION UNDER THE REGIME OF DEMOCRATIC KAMPUCHEA 1975-1979
61%
Survivors
21%
victims of execution, torture, forced labor, illness, and famine. An estimated 1.7 to 2 million people died under the Pol Pot regime.
5%
Purges among Khmer Rouge
3%
Khmer Rouge
10%
Expatriate refugees

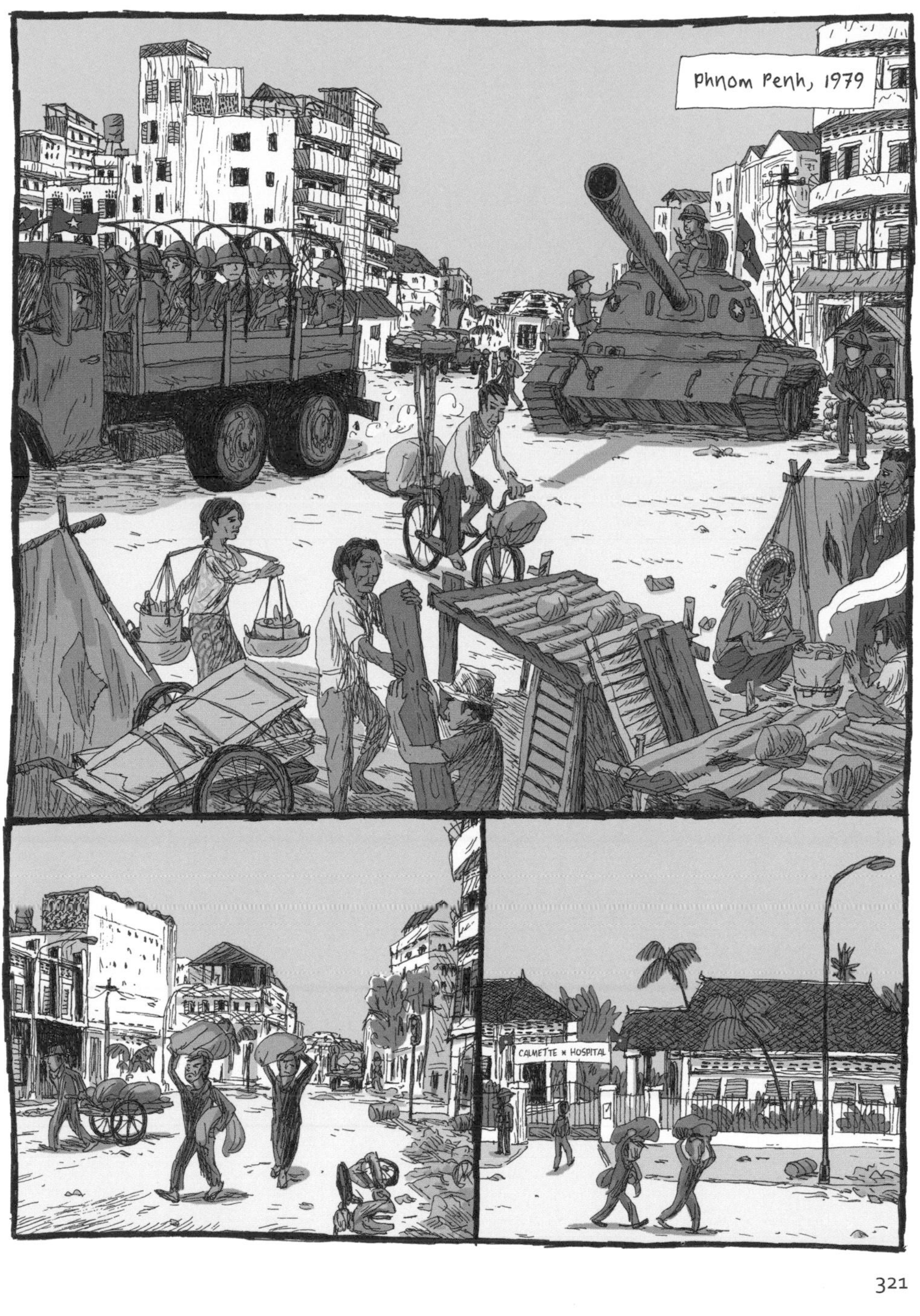
Phnom Penh, 1979
CALMETTE HOSPITAL

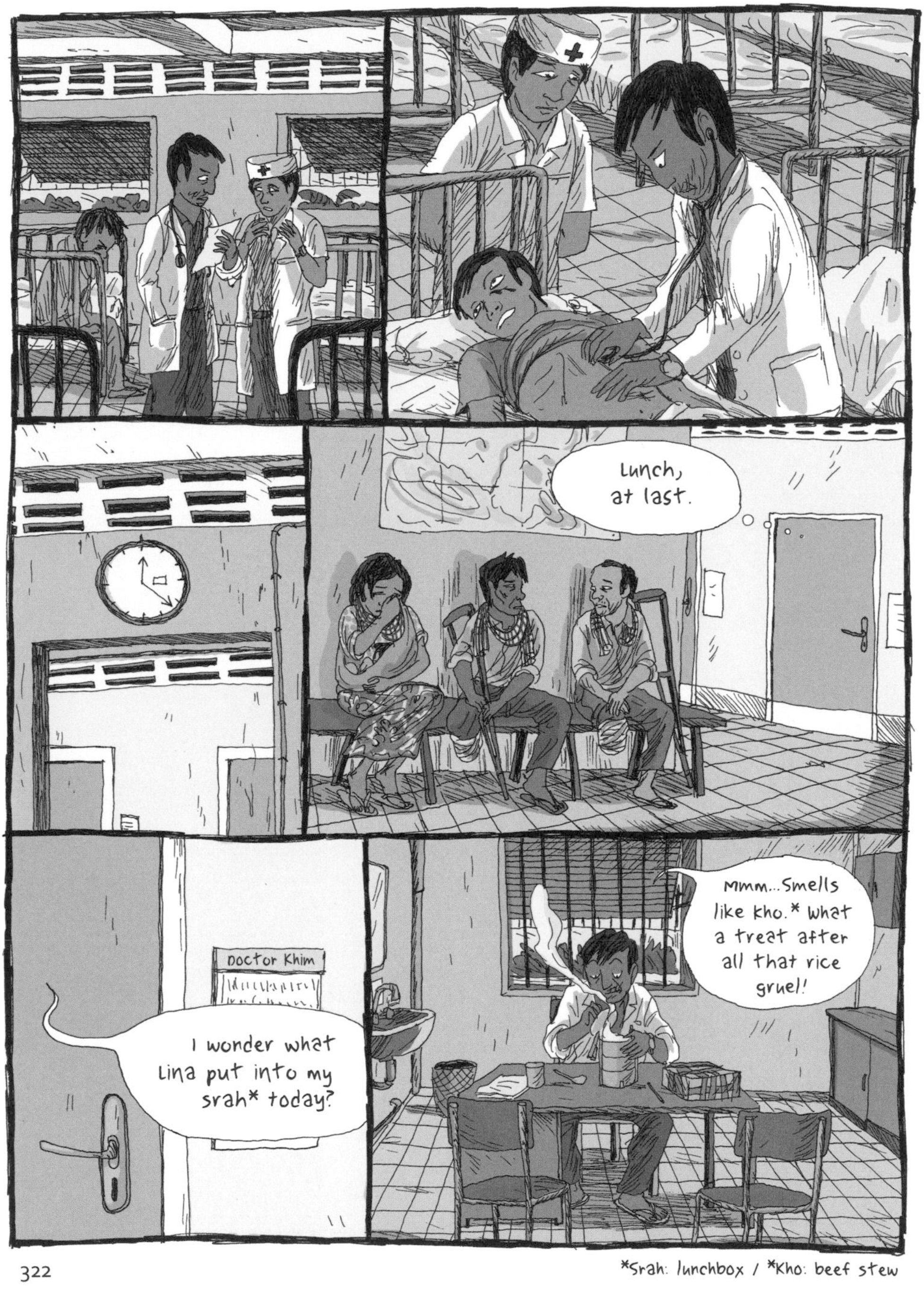
Lunch, at last.
Doctor Khim
I wonder what Lina put into my srah* today?
Mmm...Smells like kho.* What a treat after all that rice gruel!

*Srah: lunchbox / *Kho: beef stew

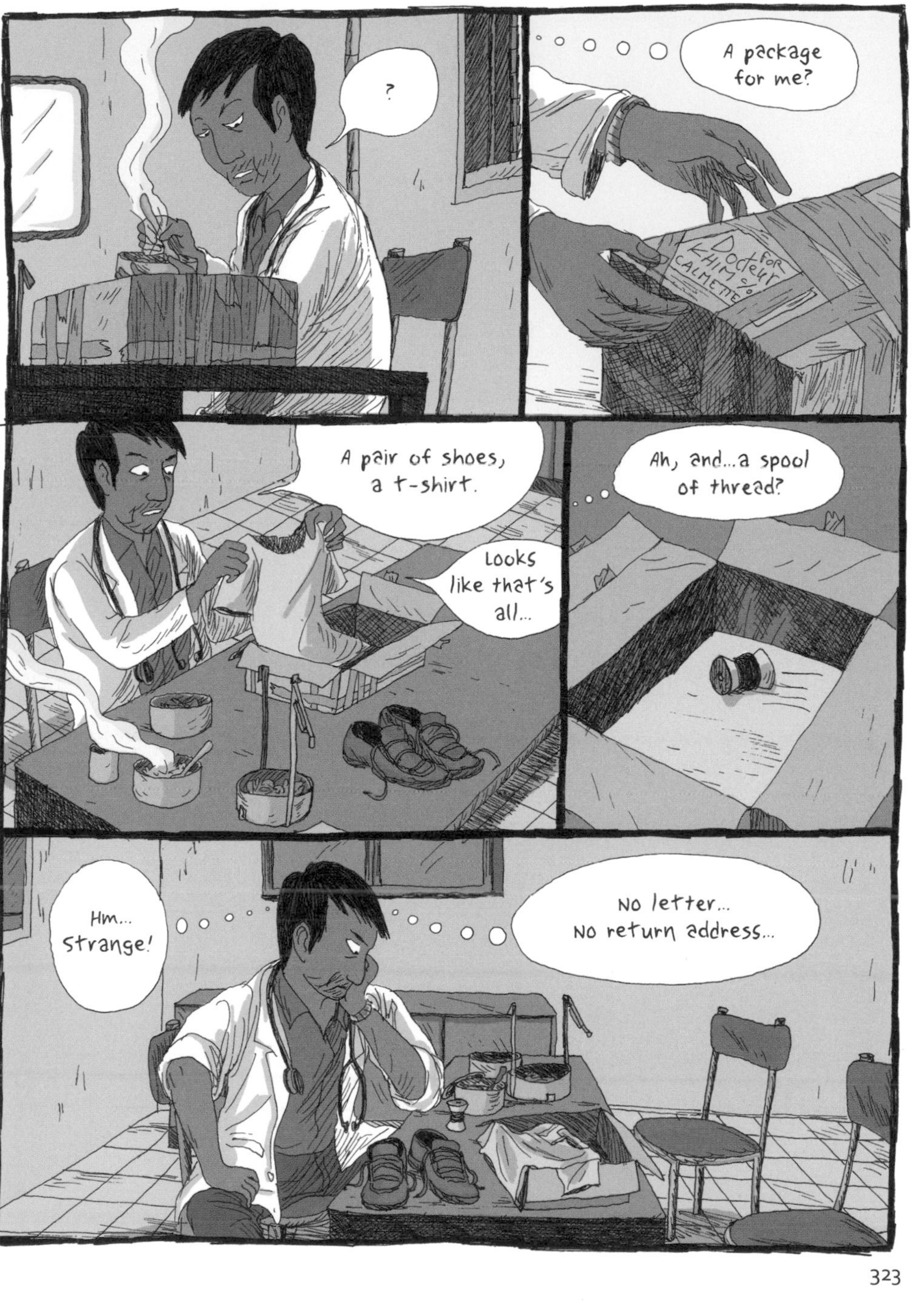
?
A package for me?
FOR Docteur KHIM CALMETTE
A pair of shoes, a t-shirt.
Looks like that's all...
Ah, and...a spool of thread?
Hm... Strange!
No letter... No return address...

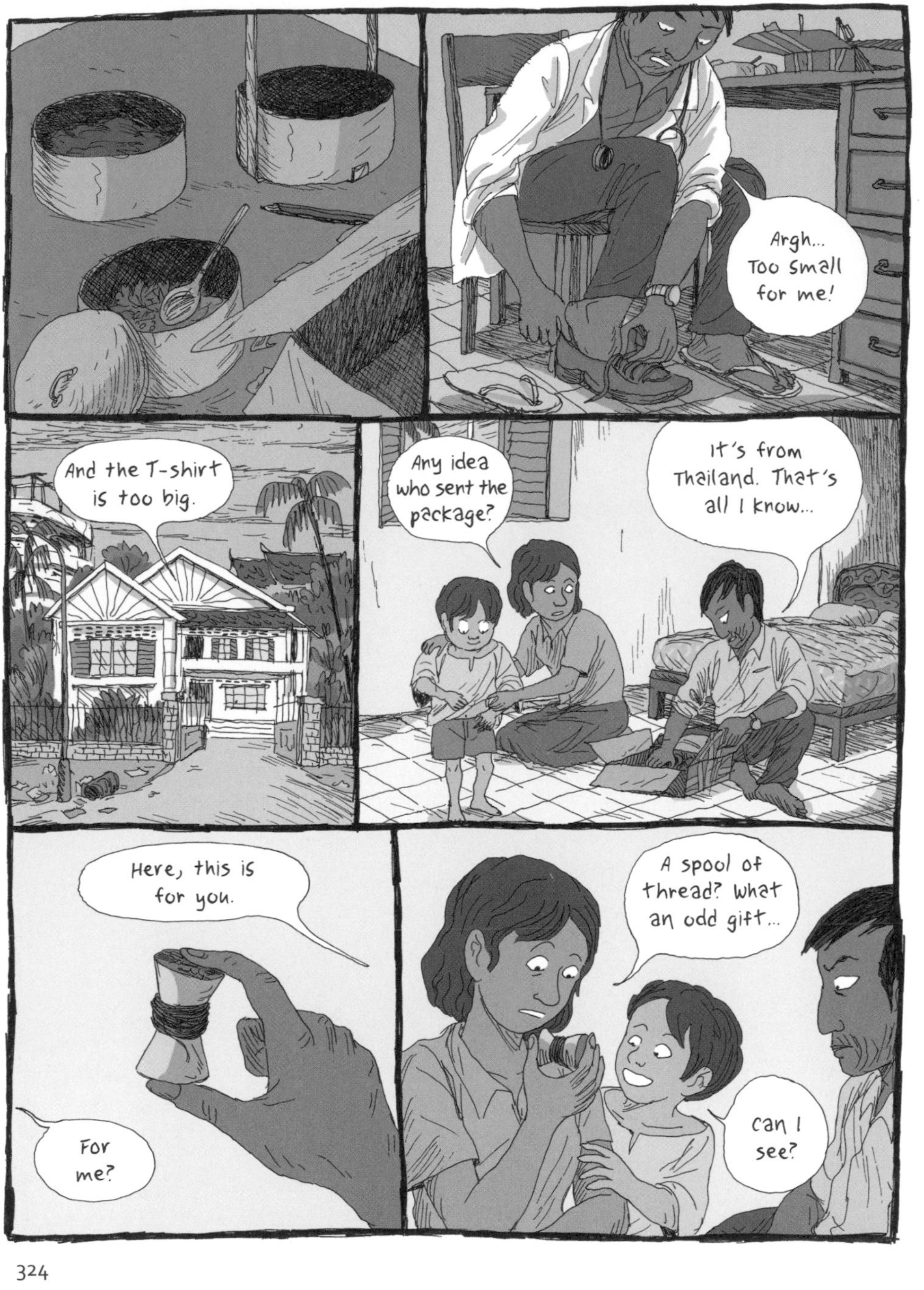
Argh... Too small for me!
And the T-shirt is too big.
Any idea who sent the package?
It's from Thailand. That's all I know...
Here, this is for you.
For me?
A spool of thread? What an odd gift...
Can I see?

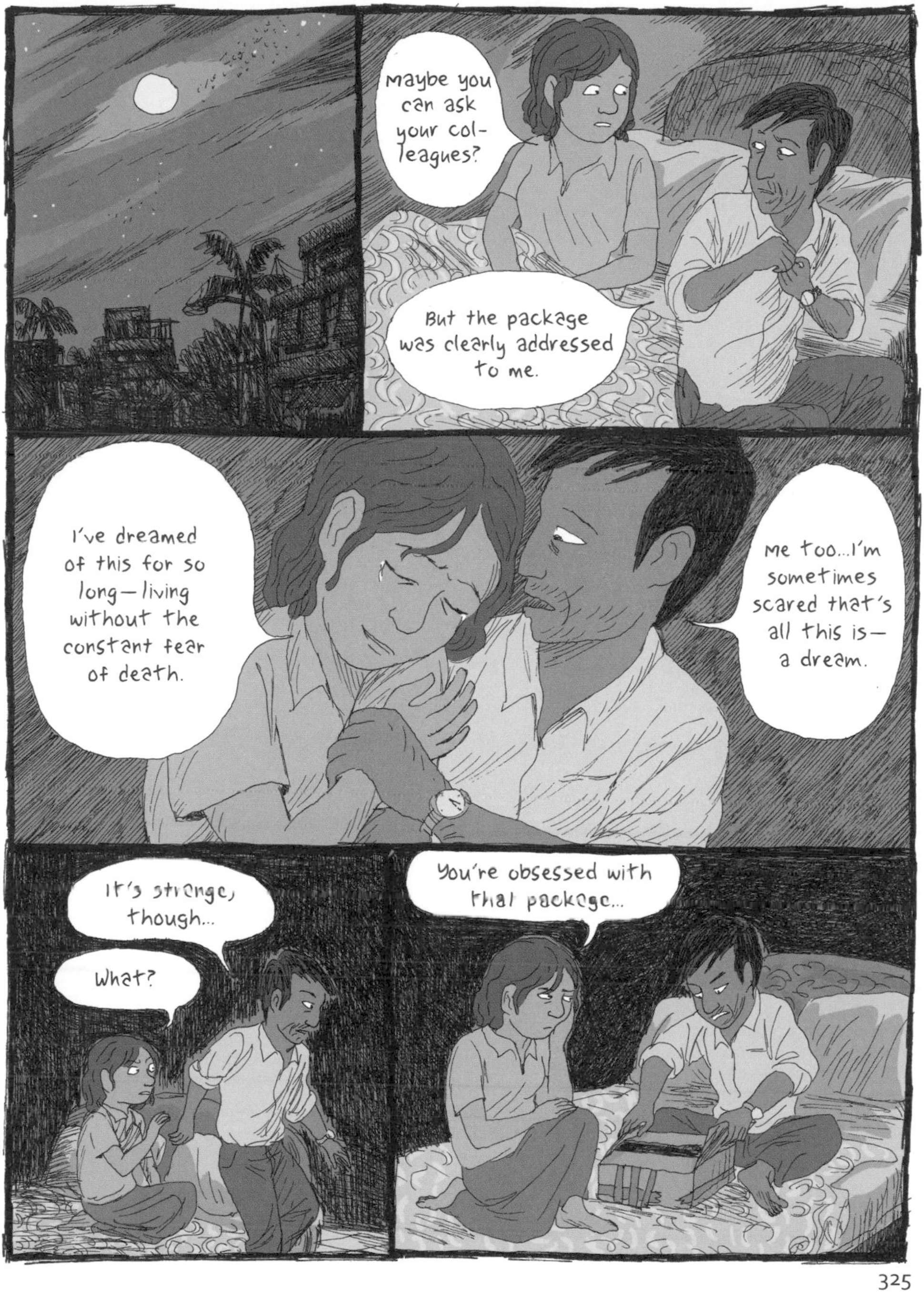
Maybe you can ask your col-leagues?
But the package was clearly addressed to me.
I've dreamed of this for so long—living without the constant fear of death.
Me too...I'm sometimes scared that's all this is—a dream.
It's strange, though...
What?
You're obsessed with that package...

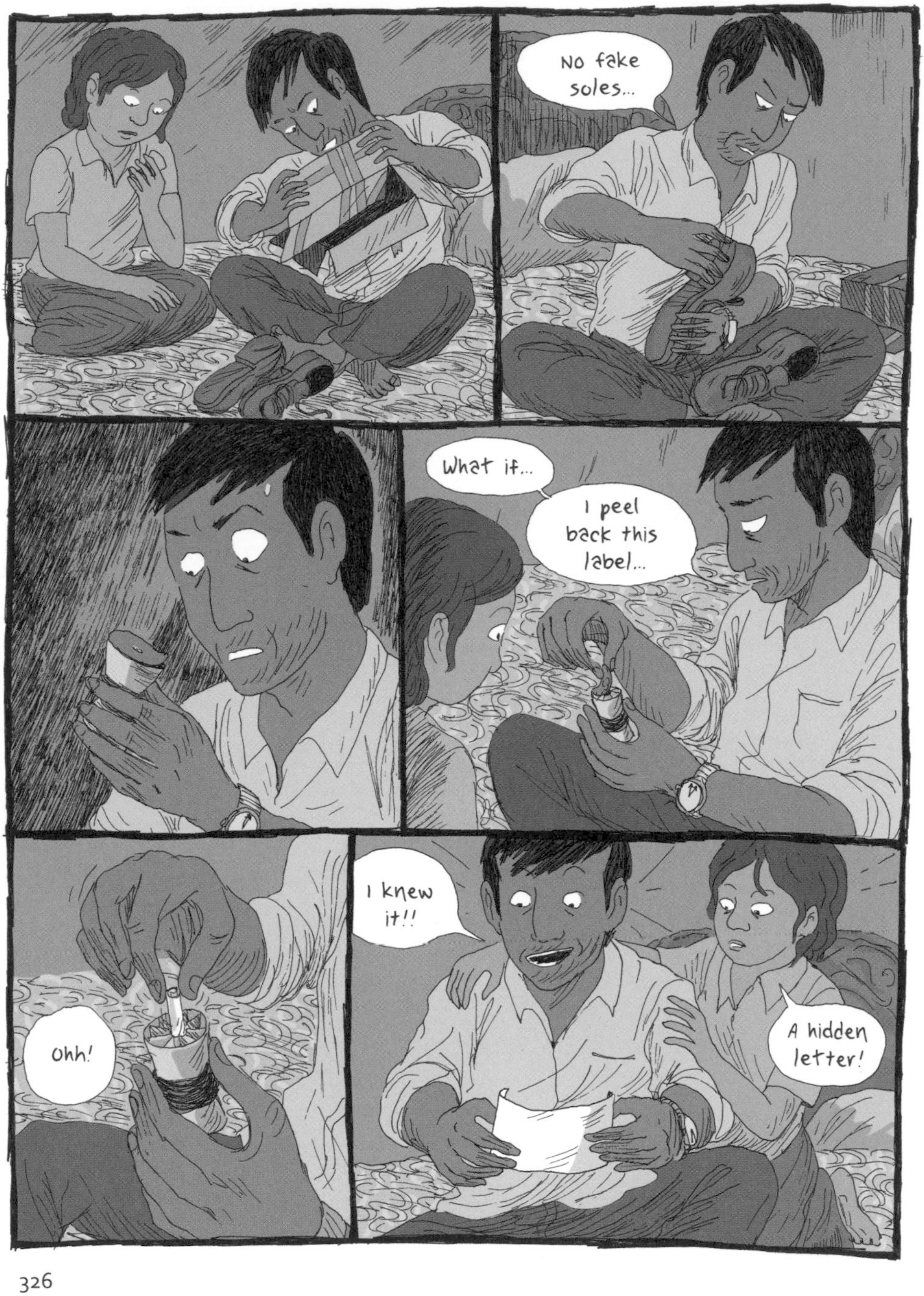
No fake soles...
What if...
I peel back this label...
Ohh!
I knew it!!
A hidden letter!

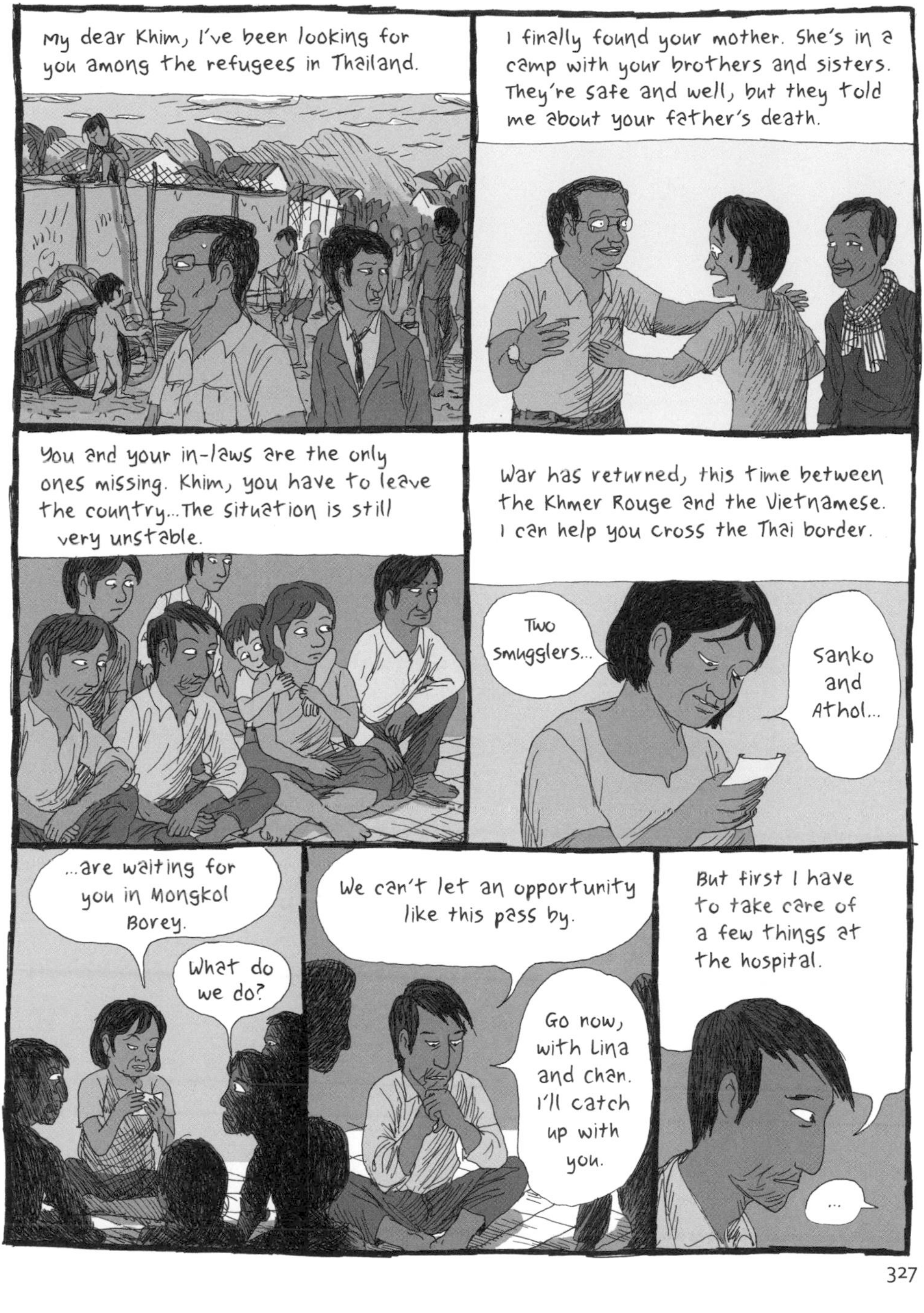
My dear Khim, I've been looking for you among the refugees in Thailand.
I finally found your mother. She's in a camp with your brothers and sisters. They're safe and well, but they told me about your father's death.
You and your in-laws are the only ones missing. Khim, you have to leave the country...The situation is still very unstable.
War has returned, this time between the Khmer Rouge and the Vietnamese. I can help you cross the Thai border.
Two smugglers...
Sanko and Athol...
...are waiting for you in Mongkol Borey.
What do we do?
We can't let an opportunity like this pass by.
Go now, with Lina and Chan. I'll catch up with you.
But first I have to take care of a few things at the hospital.
...

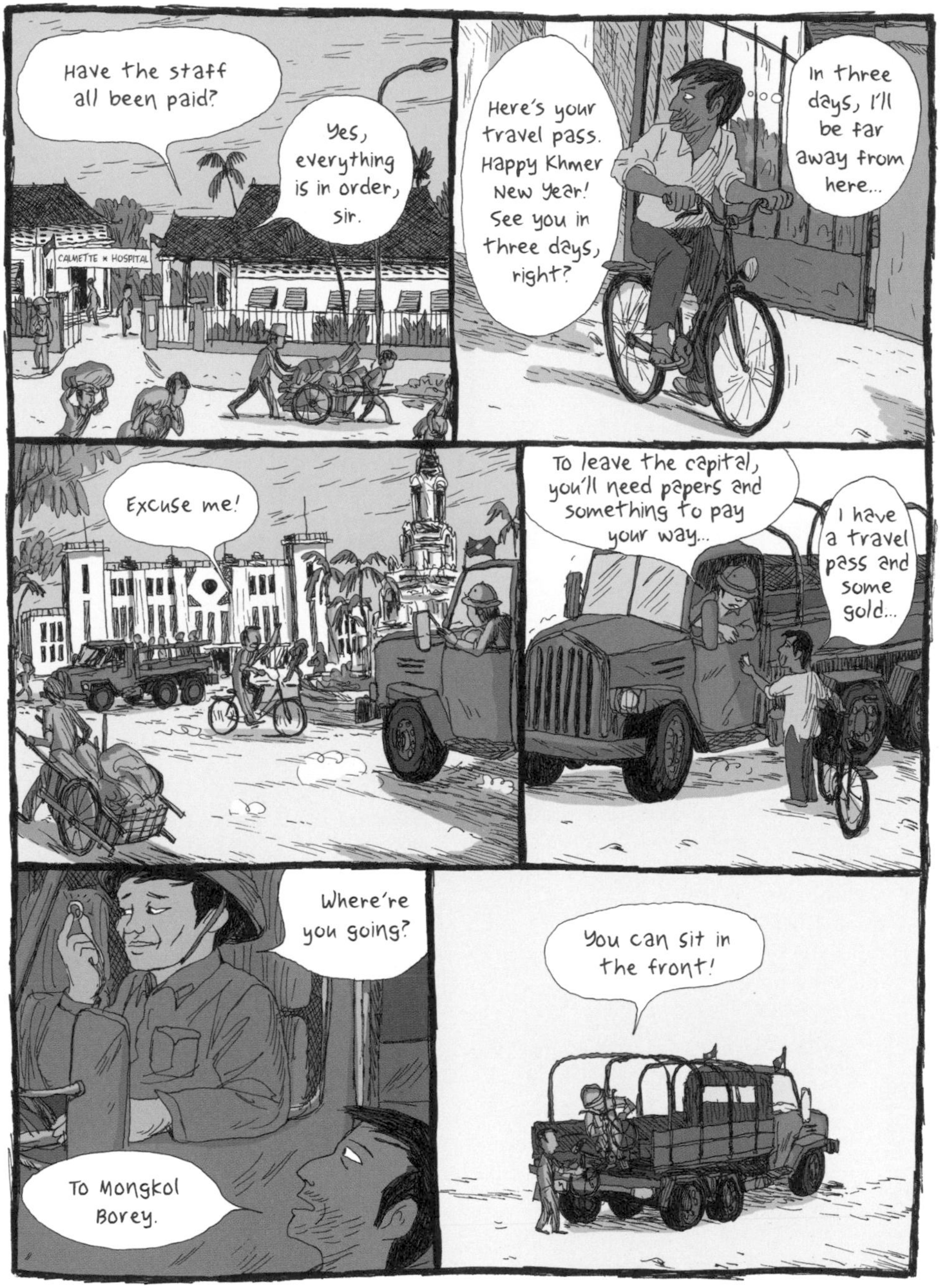
Have the staff all been paid?
Yes, everything is in order, sir.
CALMETTE HOSPITAL
Here's your travel pass. Happy Khmer New Year! See you in three days, right?
In three days, I'll be far away from here...
Excuse me!
To leave the capital, you'll need papers and something to pay your way...
I have a travel pass and some gold...
Where're you going?
To Mongkol Borey.
You can sit in the front!

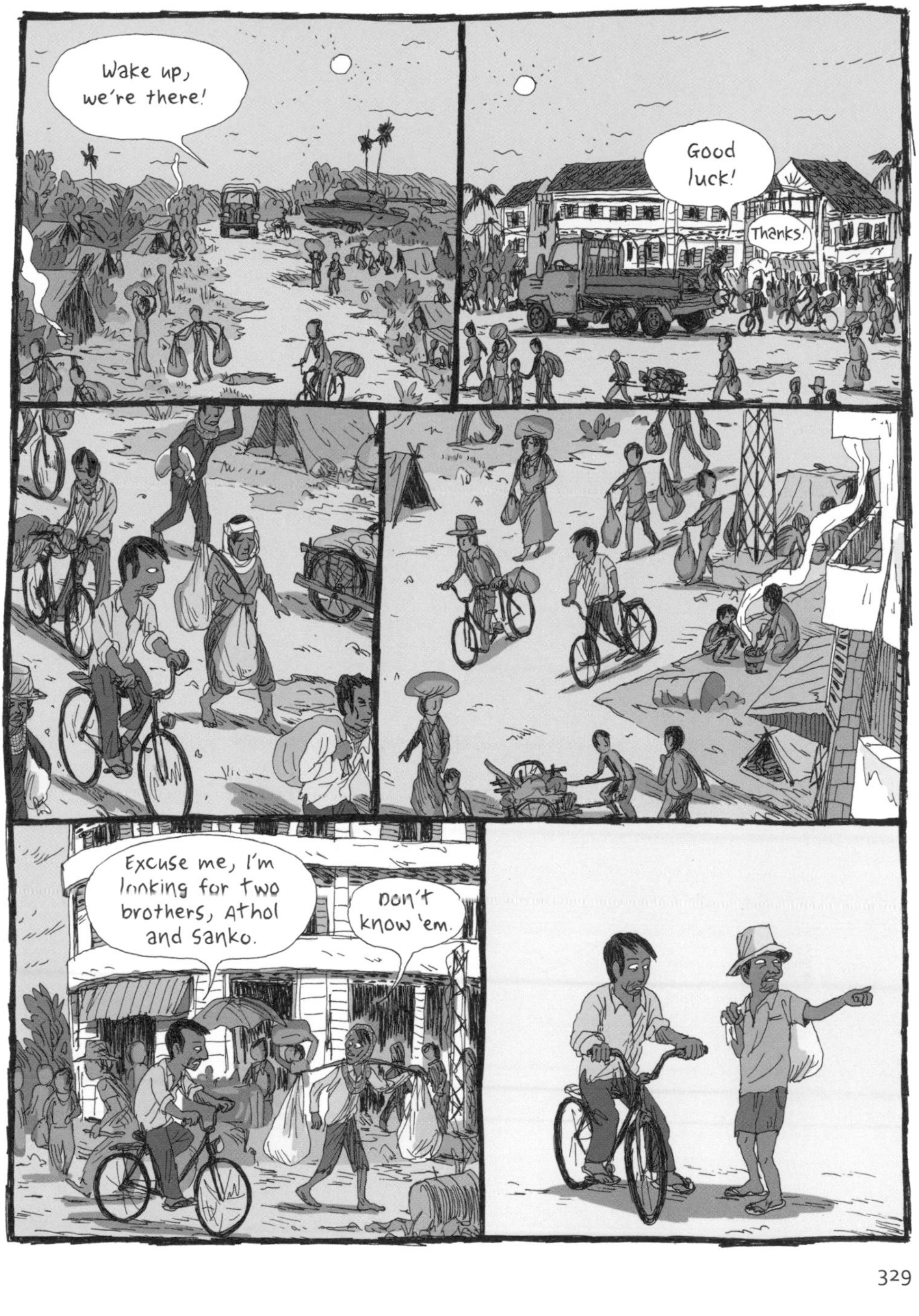
Wake up, we're there!
Good luck!
Thanks!
Excuse me, I'm looking for two brothers, Athol and Sanko.
Don't know 'em.

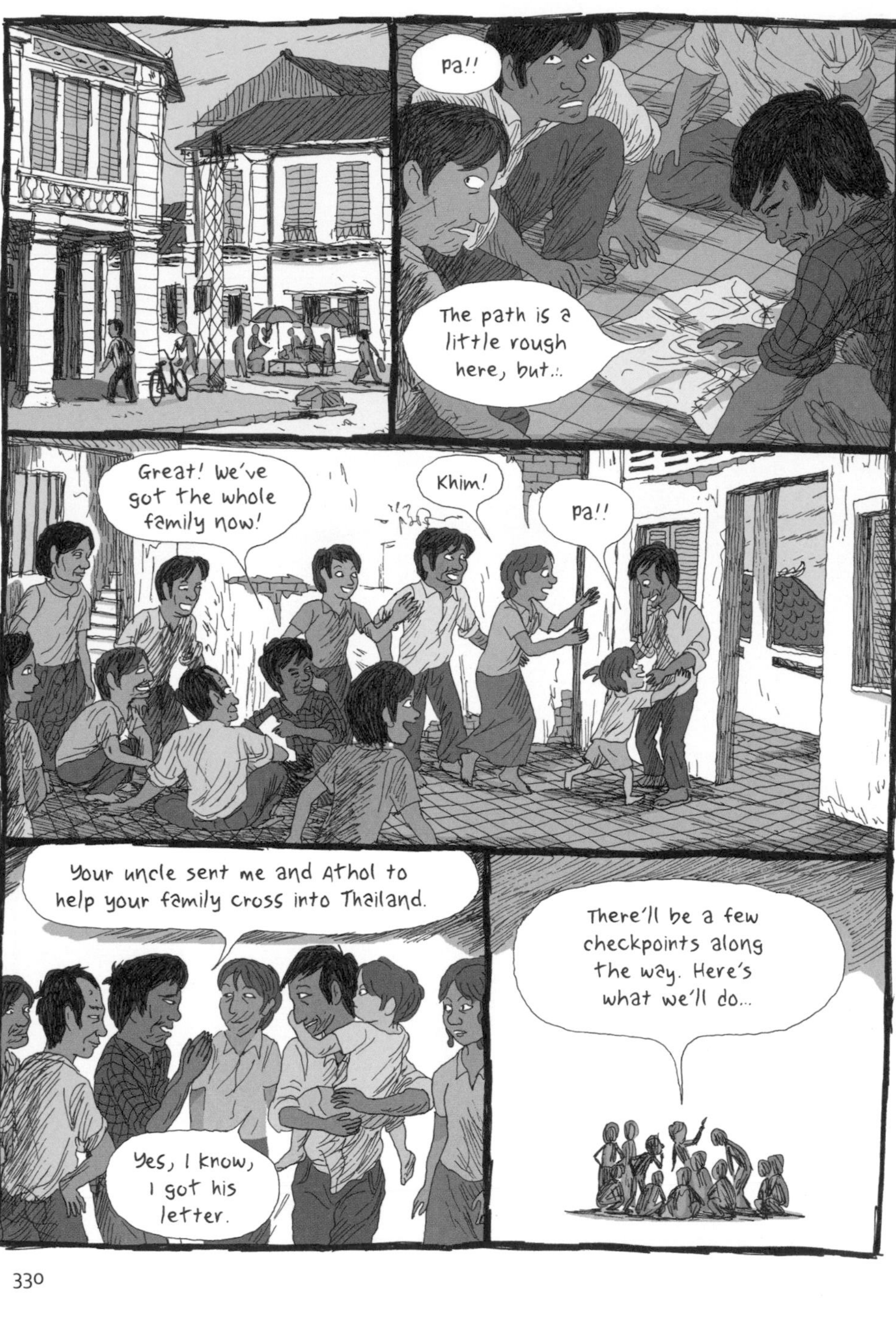
Pa!!
The path is a little rough here, but...
Great! We've got the whole family now!
Khim!
Pa!!
Your uncle sent me and Athol to help your family cross into Thailand.
Yes, I know, I got his letter.
There'll be a few checkpoints along the way. Here's what we'll do...

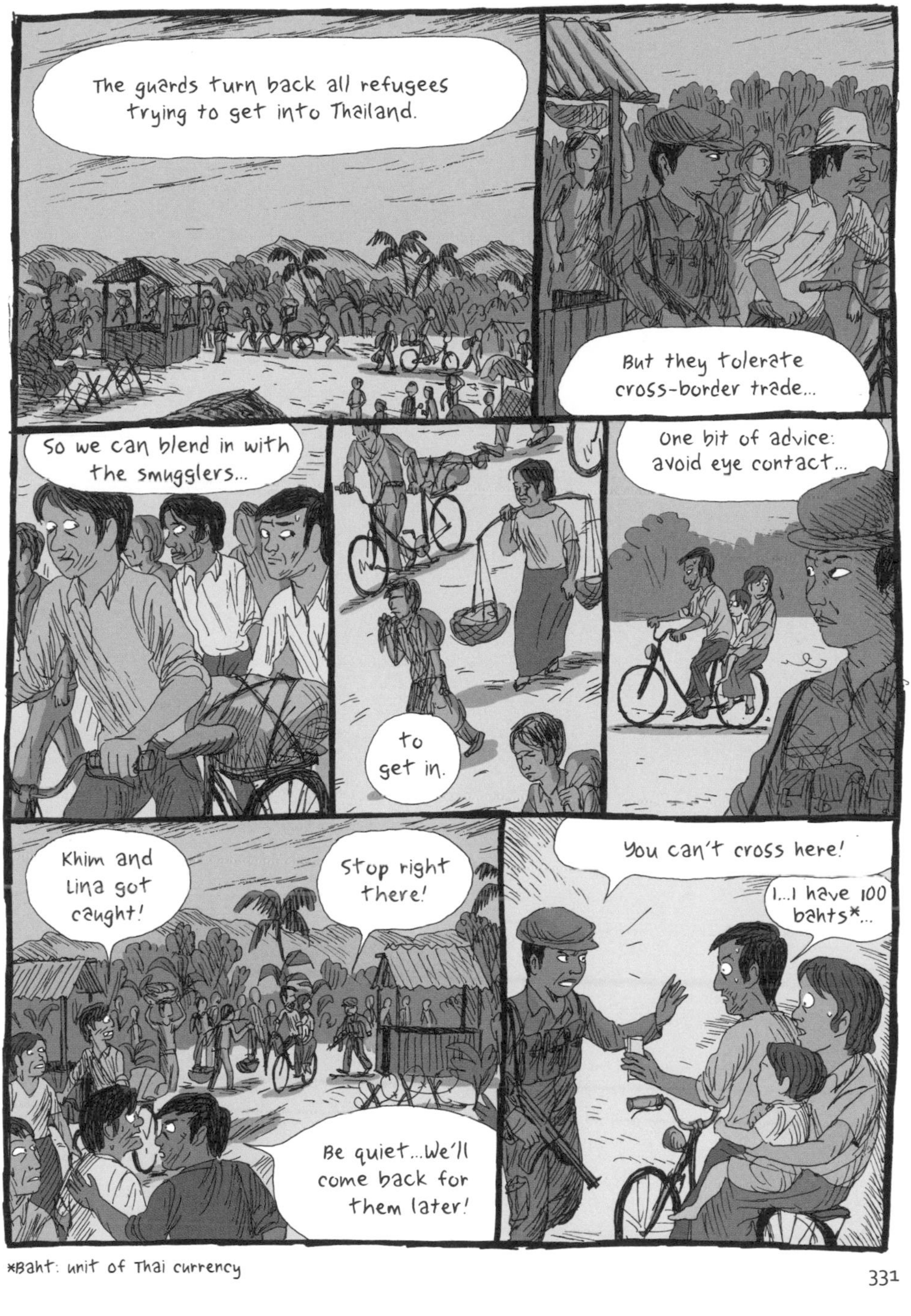
The guards turn back all refugees trying to get into Thailand.
But they tolerate cross-border trade...
So we can blend in with the smugglers...
to get in.
One bit of advice: avoid eye contact...
Khim and Lina got caught!
Stop right there!
Be quiet...We'll come back for them later!
You can't cross here!
I...I have 100 bahts*...

*Baht: unit of Thai currency

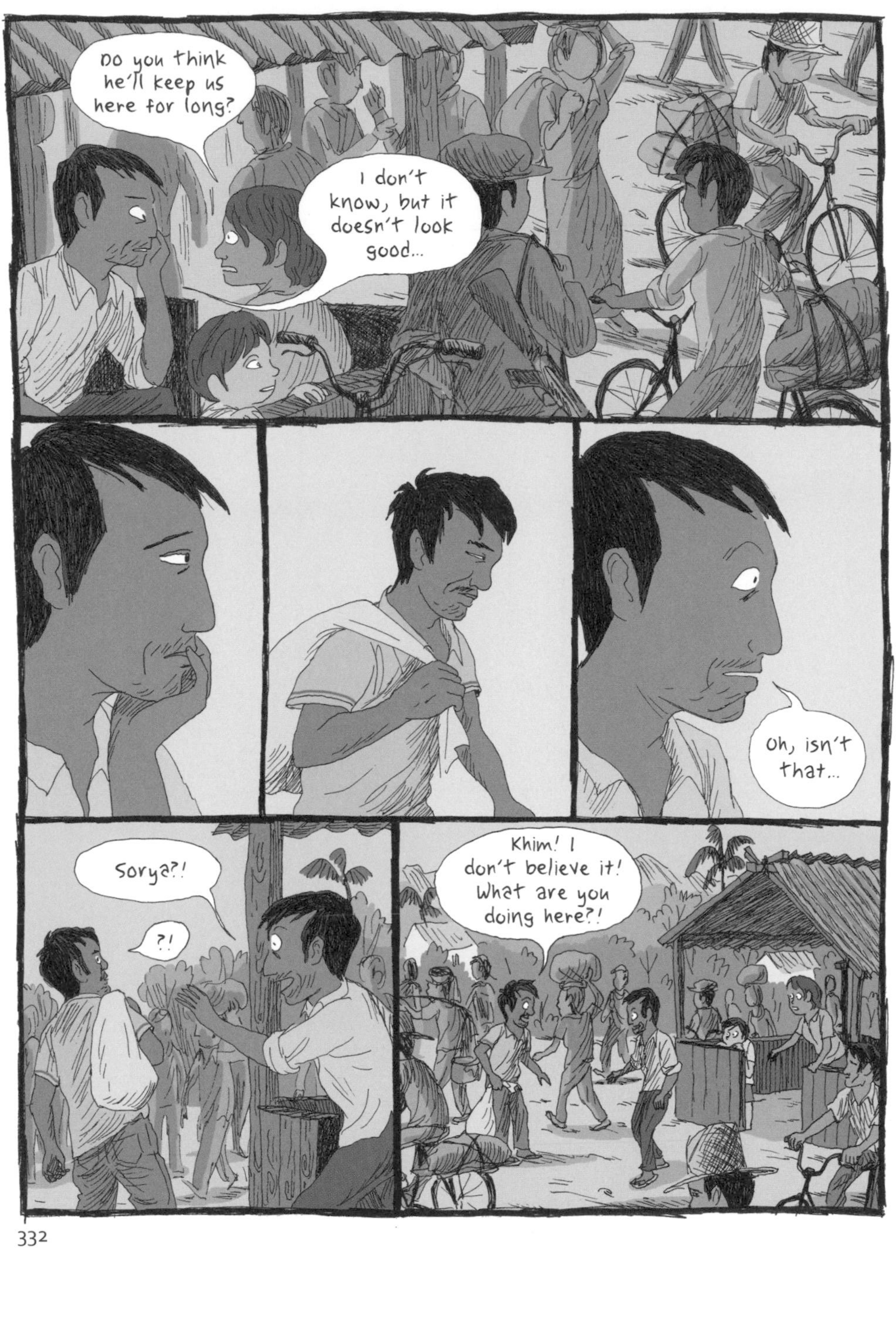
Do you think he'll keep us here for long?
I don't know, but it doesn't look good...
Oh, isn't that...
Sorya?!
?!
Khim! I don't believe it! What are you doing here?!

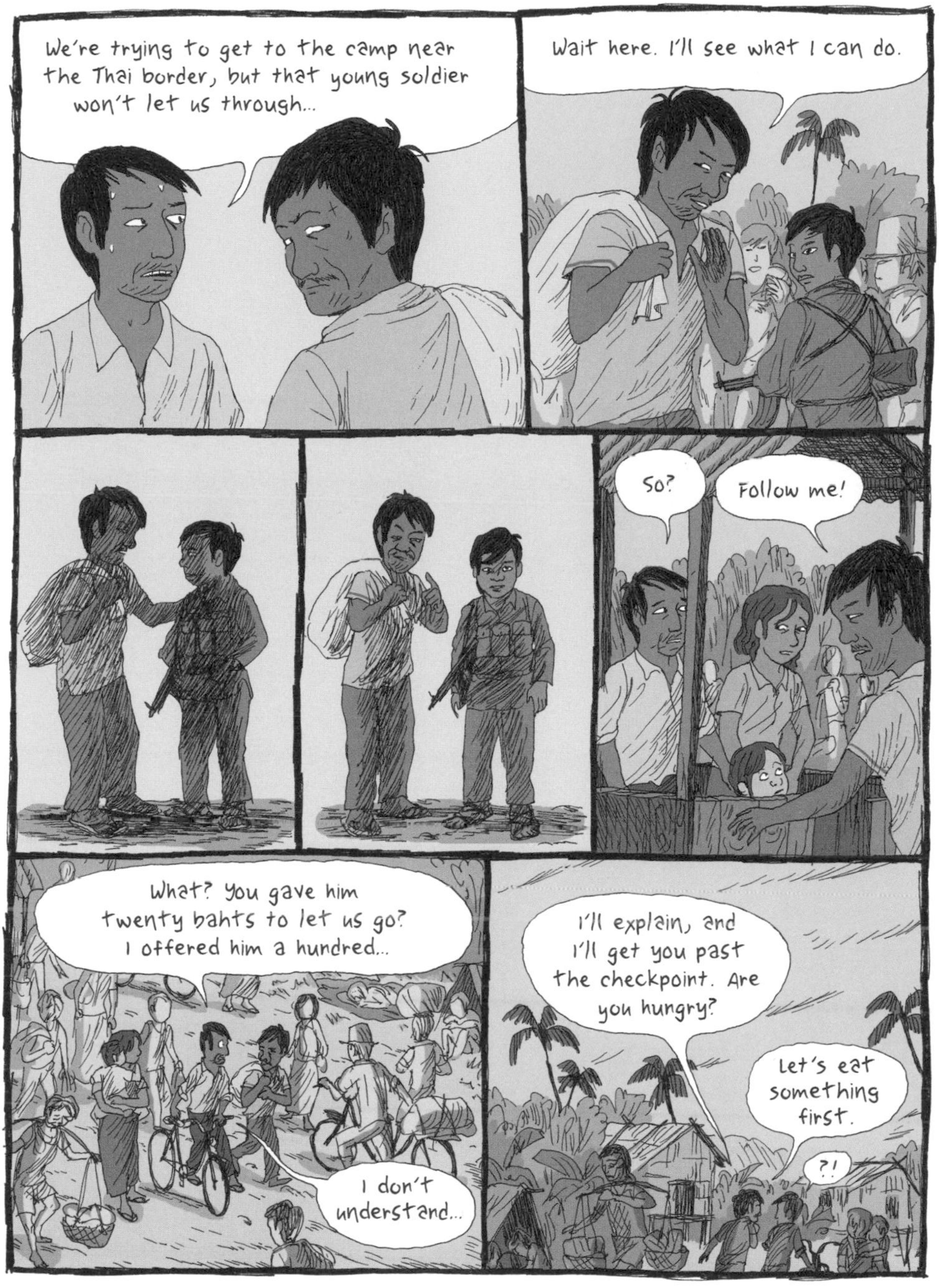
We're trying to get to the camp near the Thai border, but that young soldier won't let us through...
Wait here. I'll see what I can do.
So?
Follow me!
What? You gave him twenty bahts to let us go? I offered him a hundred...
I don't understand...
I'll explain, and I'll get you past the checkpoint. Are you hungry?
Let's eat something first.
?!

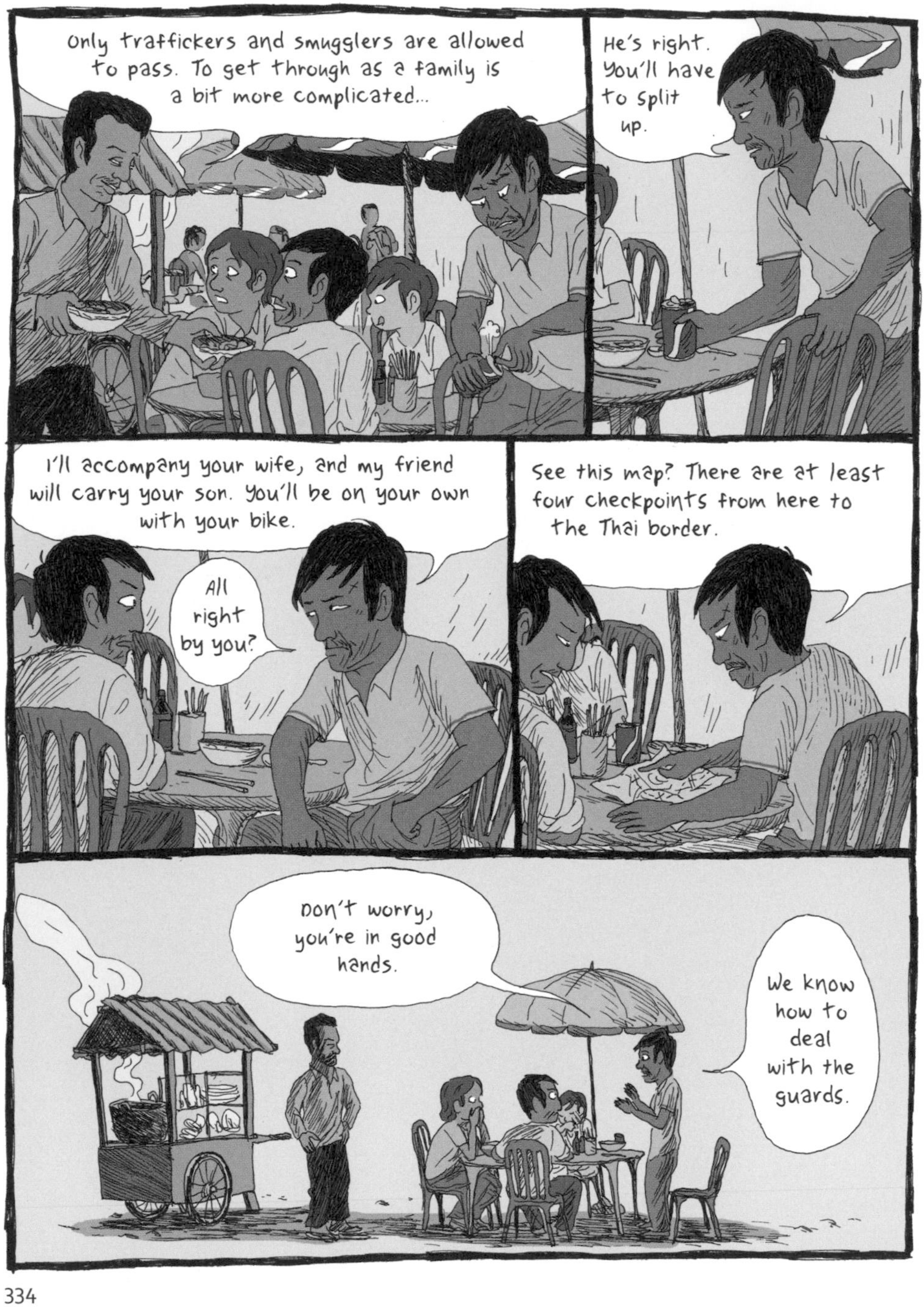
Only traffickers and smugglers are allowed to pass. To get through as a family is a bit more complicated...
He's right. You'll have to split up.
I'll accompany your wife, and my friend will carry your son. You'll be on your own with your bike.
All right by you?
See this map? There are at least four checkpoints from here to the Thai border.
Don't worry, you're in good hands.
We know how to deal with the guards.

chapter 20

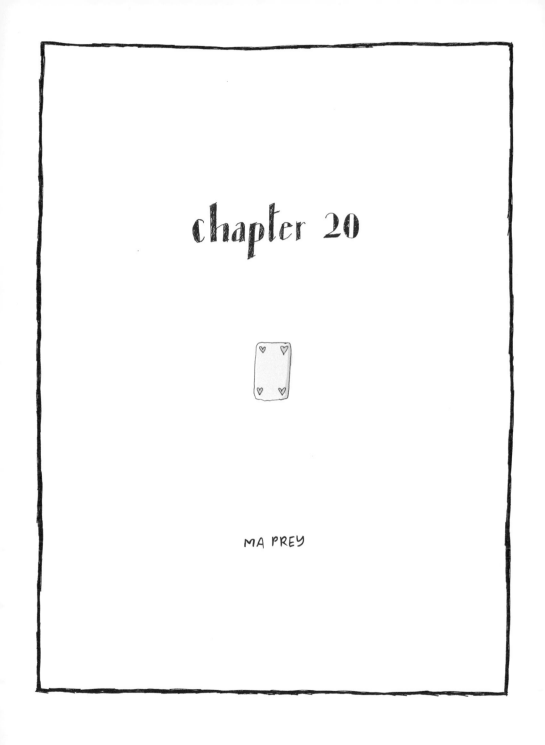

MA PREY

GUIDE MAP TO THE KHAO I DANG REFUGEE CAMP

Khao I Dang camp
N
S
Check-points
Phnom Chat: Camp con-trolled by the Khmer Rouge
3km
6km
3km
4km
4km
Check-point
1km
WOODS
RICE PADDY
Check-point
THAI BORDER
Nong Samet:
Camp (Camp 007) controlled by the Khmer People's National Liberation Front (FNLPK)

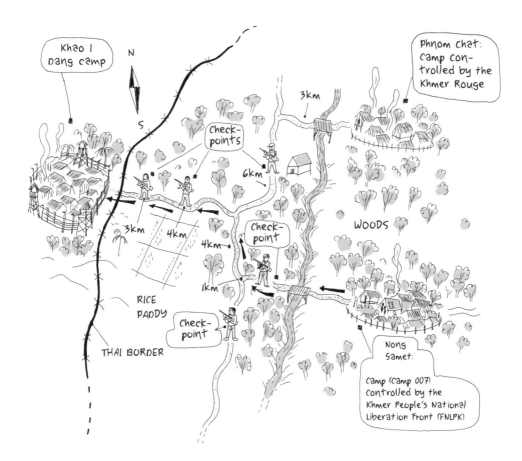

The Vietnamese occupation scattered the Khmer Rouge army. For many Cambodians who had suffered under the Pol Pot regime, the resulting chaos was an opportunity to flee the country.

Refugee camps were set up along the Thai border, awaiting humanitarian aid and a return to calm. The camps were often under the control of armed groups with very different political objectives.

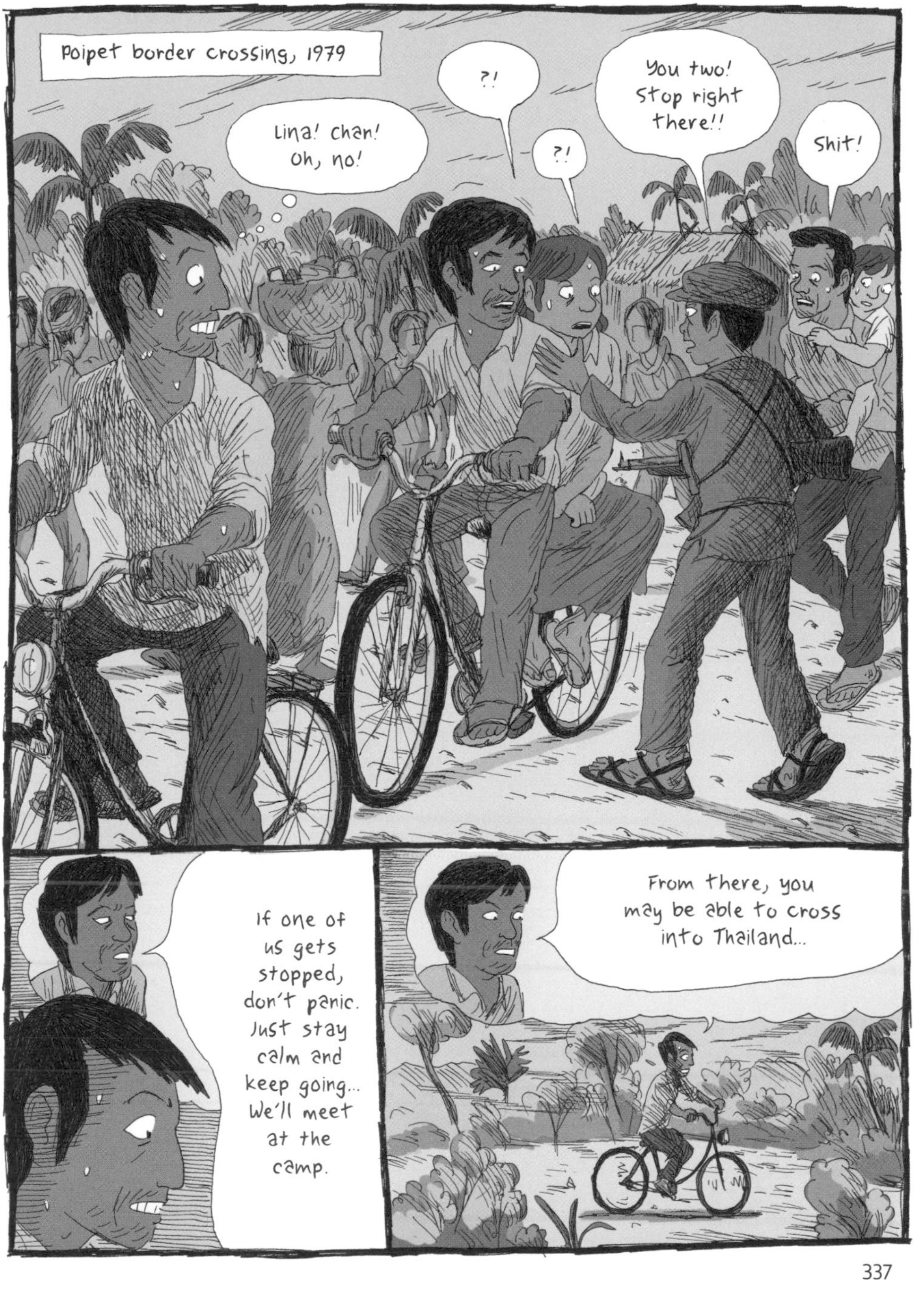
Poipet border crossing, 1979
Lina! Chan! Oh, no!
?!
?!
You two! Stop right there!!
Shit!
If one of us gets stopped, don't panic. Just stay calm and keep going... We'll meet at the camp.
From there, you may be able to cross into Thailand...

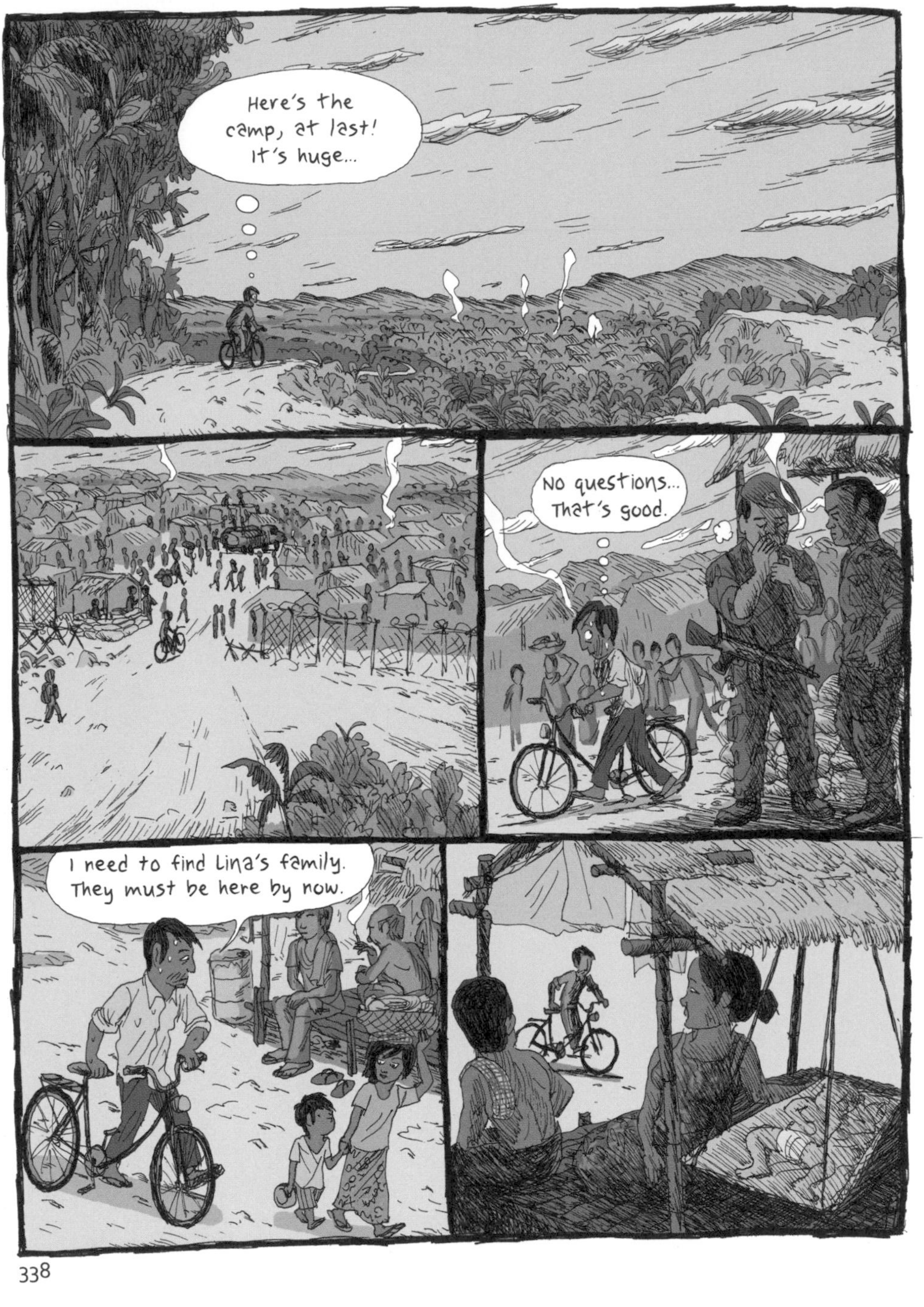
Here's the camp, at last! It's huge...
No questions... That's good.
I need to find Lina's family. They must be here by now.

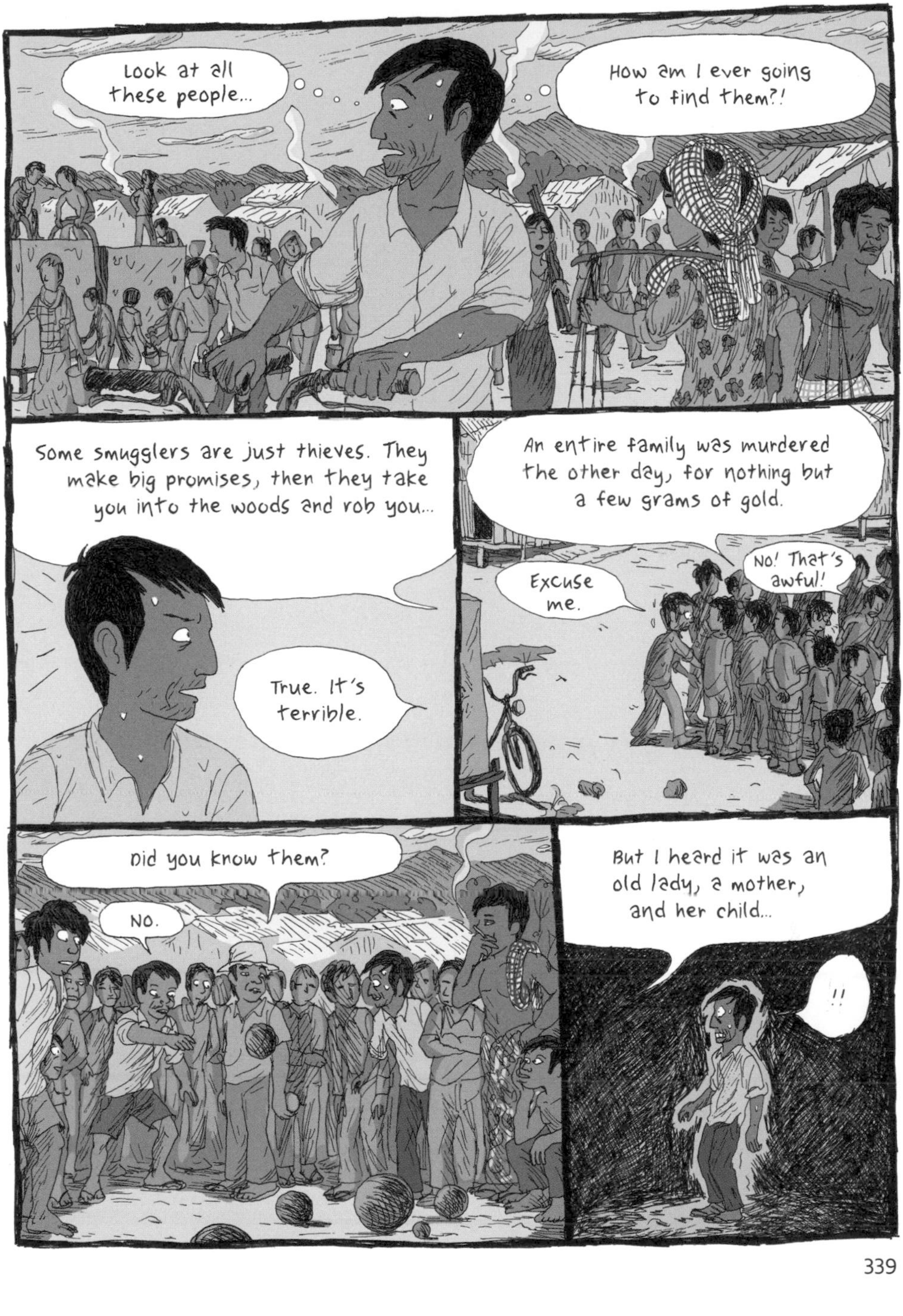
Look at all these people...
How am I ever going to find them?!
Some smugglers are just thieves. They make big promises, then they take you into the woods and rob you...
True. It's terrible.
An entire family was murdered the other day, for nothing but a few grams of gold.
Excuse me.
No! That's awful!
Did you know them?
No.
But I heard it was an old lady, a mother, and her child...
!!

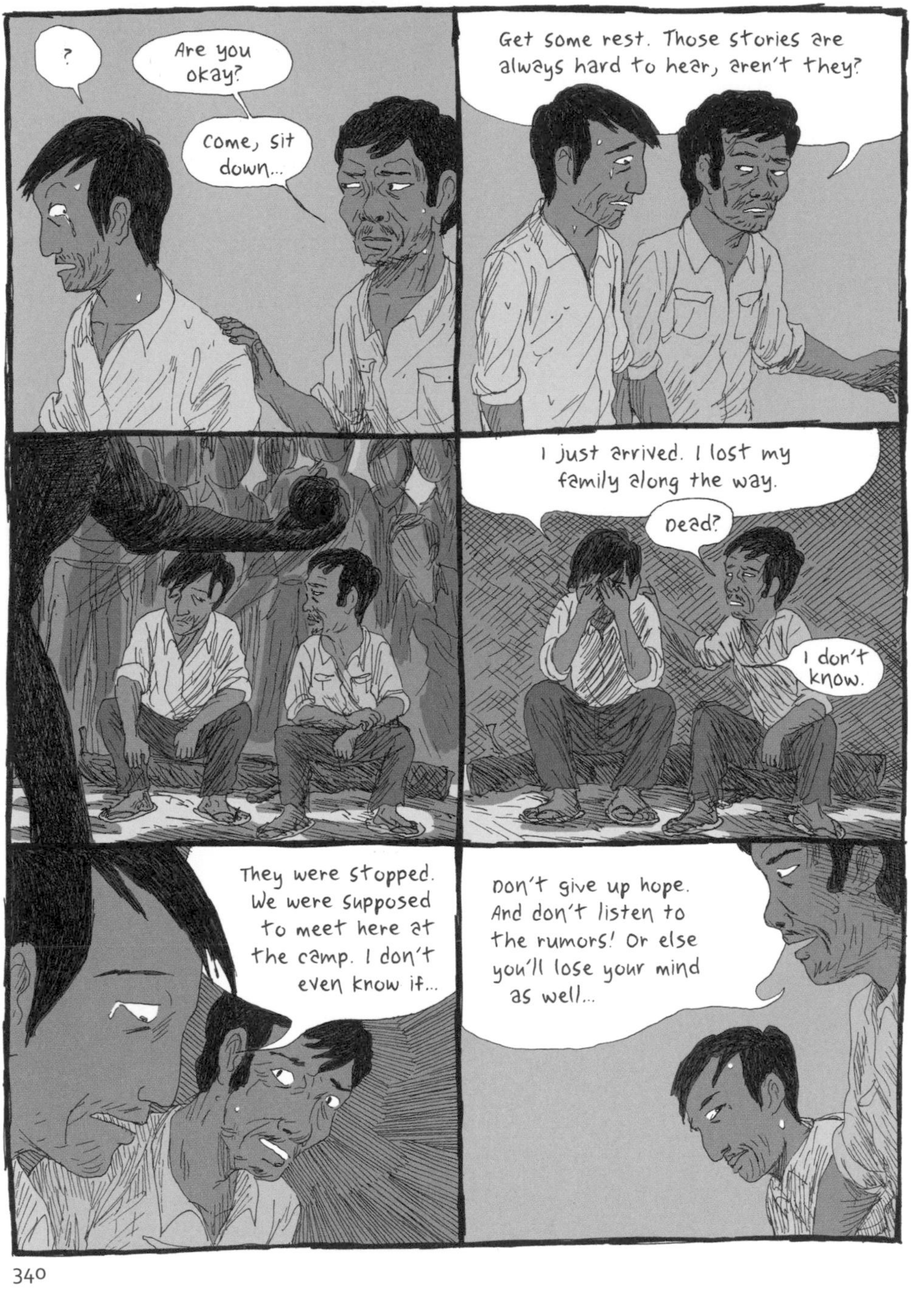
?
Are you okay?
Come, sit down...
Get some rest. Those stories are always hard to hear, aren't they?
I just arrived. I lost my family along the way.
Dead?
I don't know.
They were stopped. We were supposed to meet here at the camp. I don't even know if...
Don't give up hope. And don't listen to the rumors! Or else you'll lose your mind as well...

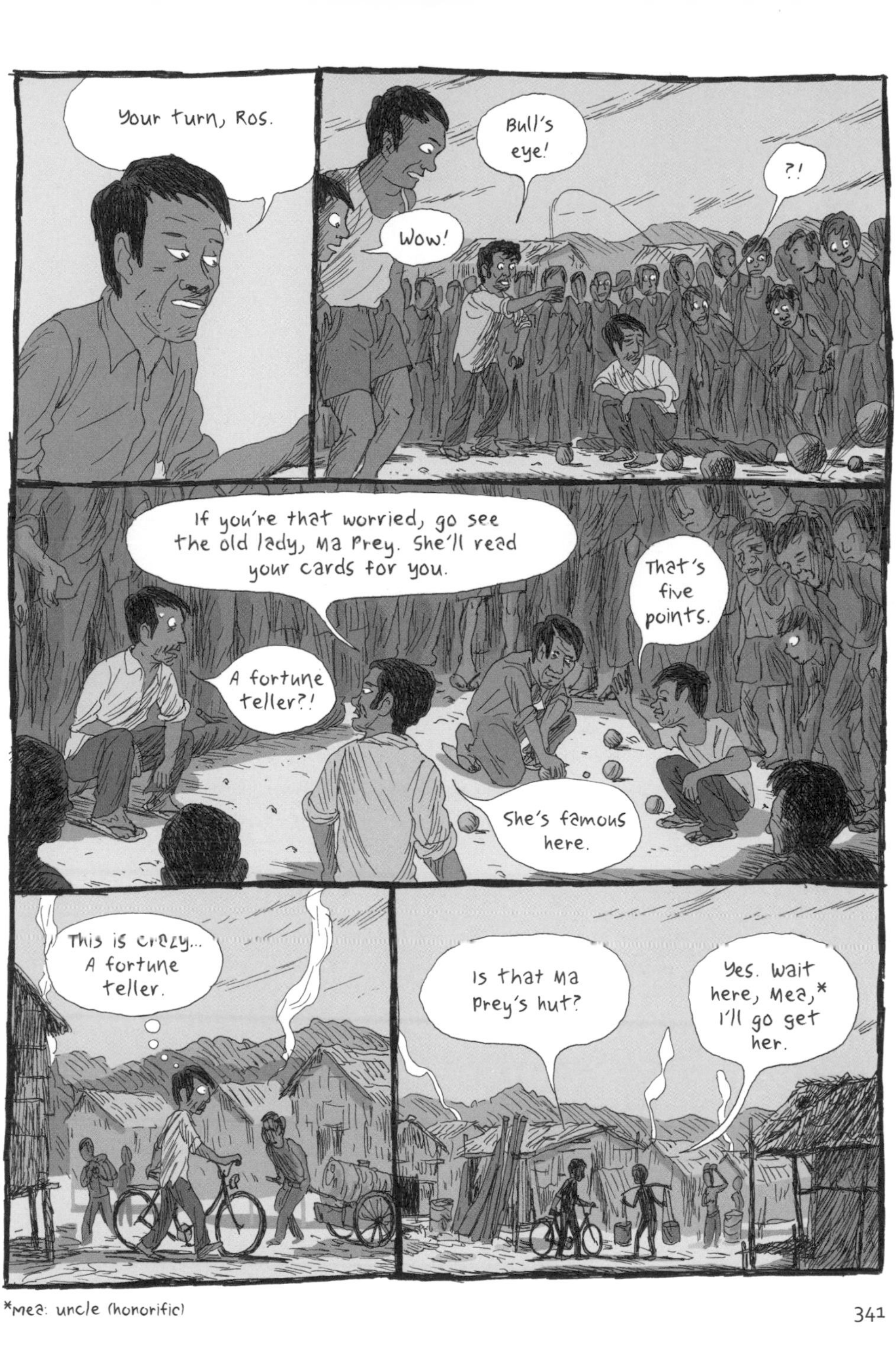
Your turn, Ros.
Bull's eye!
Wow!
?!
If you're that worried, go see the old lady, Ma Prey. She'll read your cards for you.
A fortune teller?!
That's five points.
She's famous here.
This is crazy... A fortune teller.
Is that Ma Prey's hut?
Yes. Wait here, Mea,* I'll go get her.

*Mea: uncle (honorific)

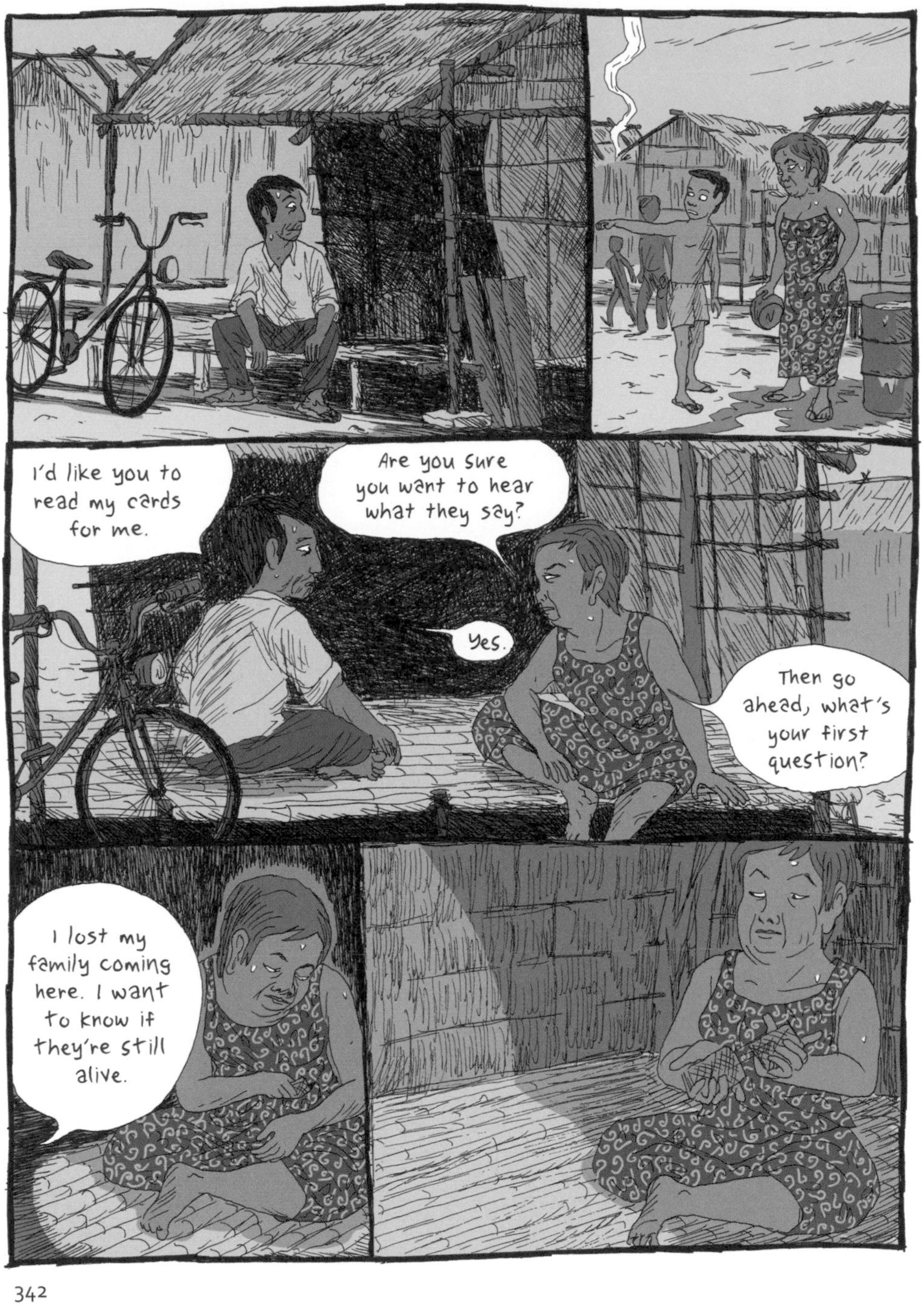
I'd like you to read my cards for me.
Are you sure you want to hear what they say?
Yes.
Then go ahead, what's your first question?
I lost my family coming here. I want to know if they're still alive.

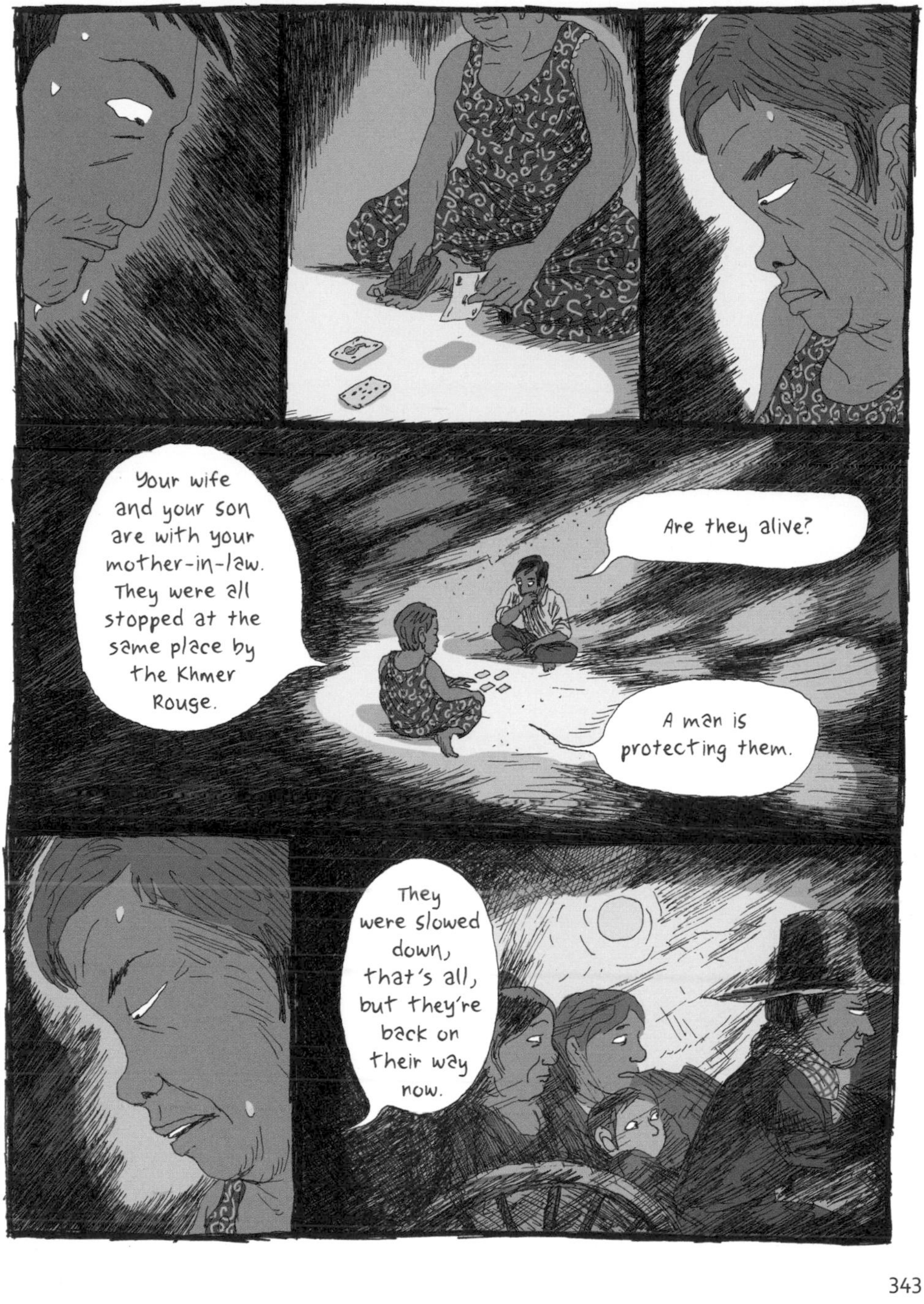
Your wife and your son are with your mother-in-law. They were all stopped at the same place by the Khmer Rouge.
Are they alive?
A man is protecting them.
They were slowed down, that's all, but they're back on their way now.

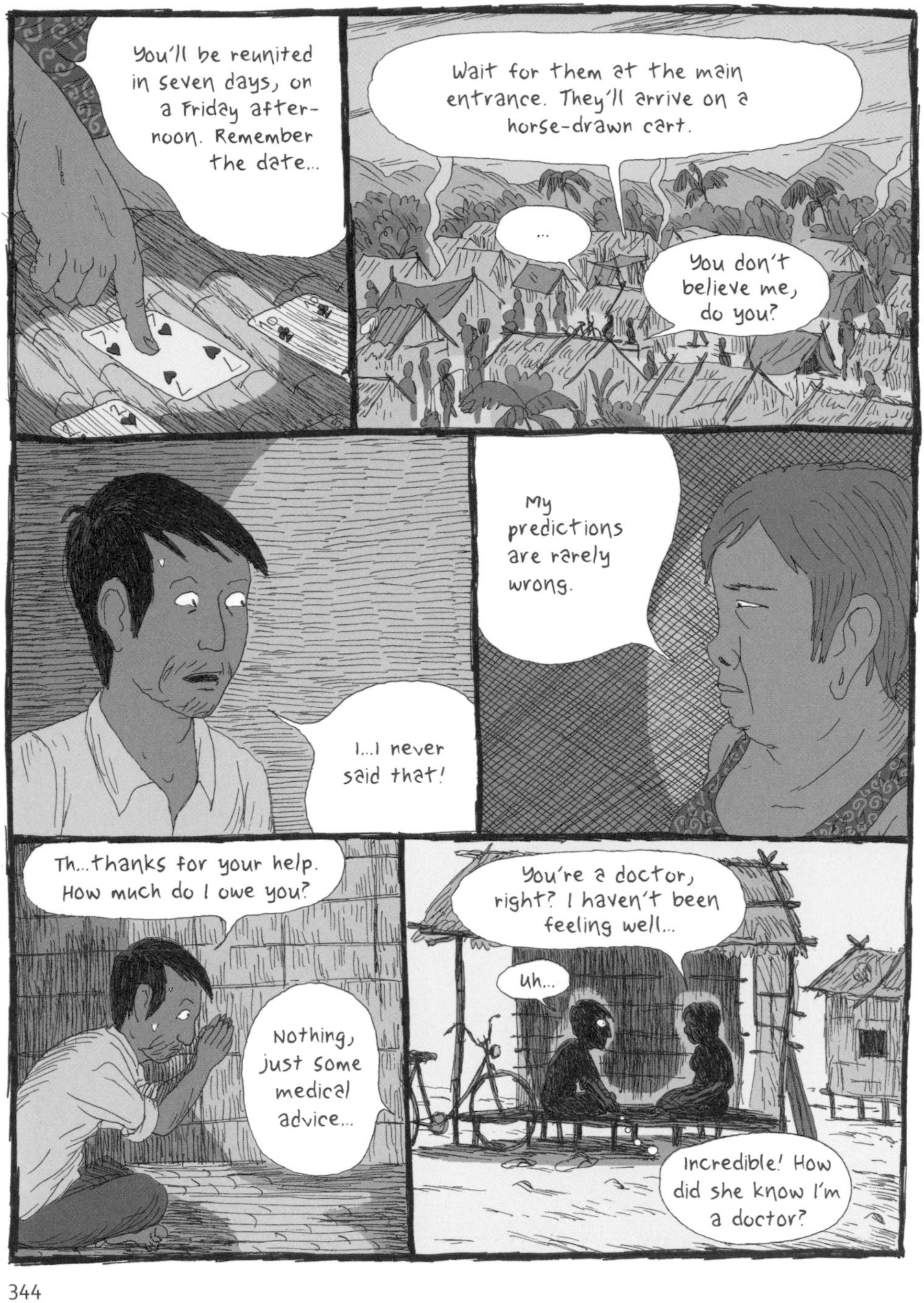
You'll be reunited in seven days, on a Friday afternoon. Remember the date...
Wait for them at the main entrance. They'll arrive on a horse-drawn cart.
...
You don't believe me, do you?
I...I never said that!
My predictions are rarely wrong.
Th...thanks for your help. How much do I owe you?
Nothing, just some medical advice...
You're a doctor, right? I haven't been feeling well...
Uh...
Incredible! How did she know I'm a doctor?

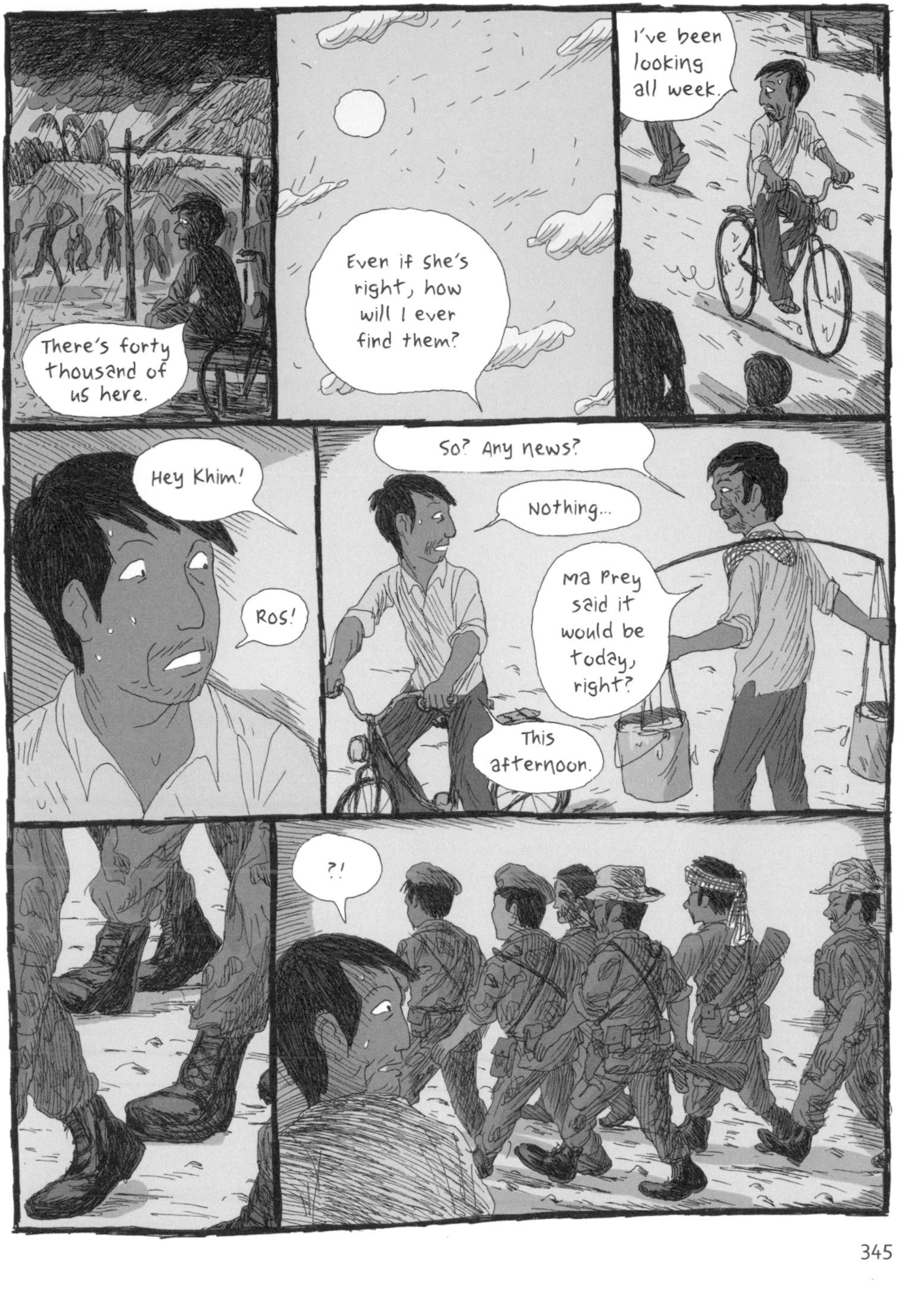
There's forty thousand of us here.
Even if she's right, how will I ever find them?
I've been looking all week.
Hey Khim!
Ros!
So? Any news?
Nothing...
Ma Prey said it would be today, right?
This afternoon.
?!

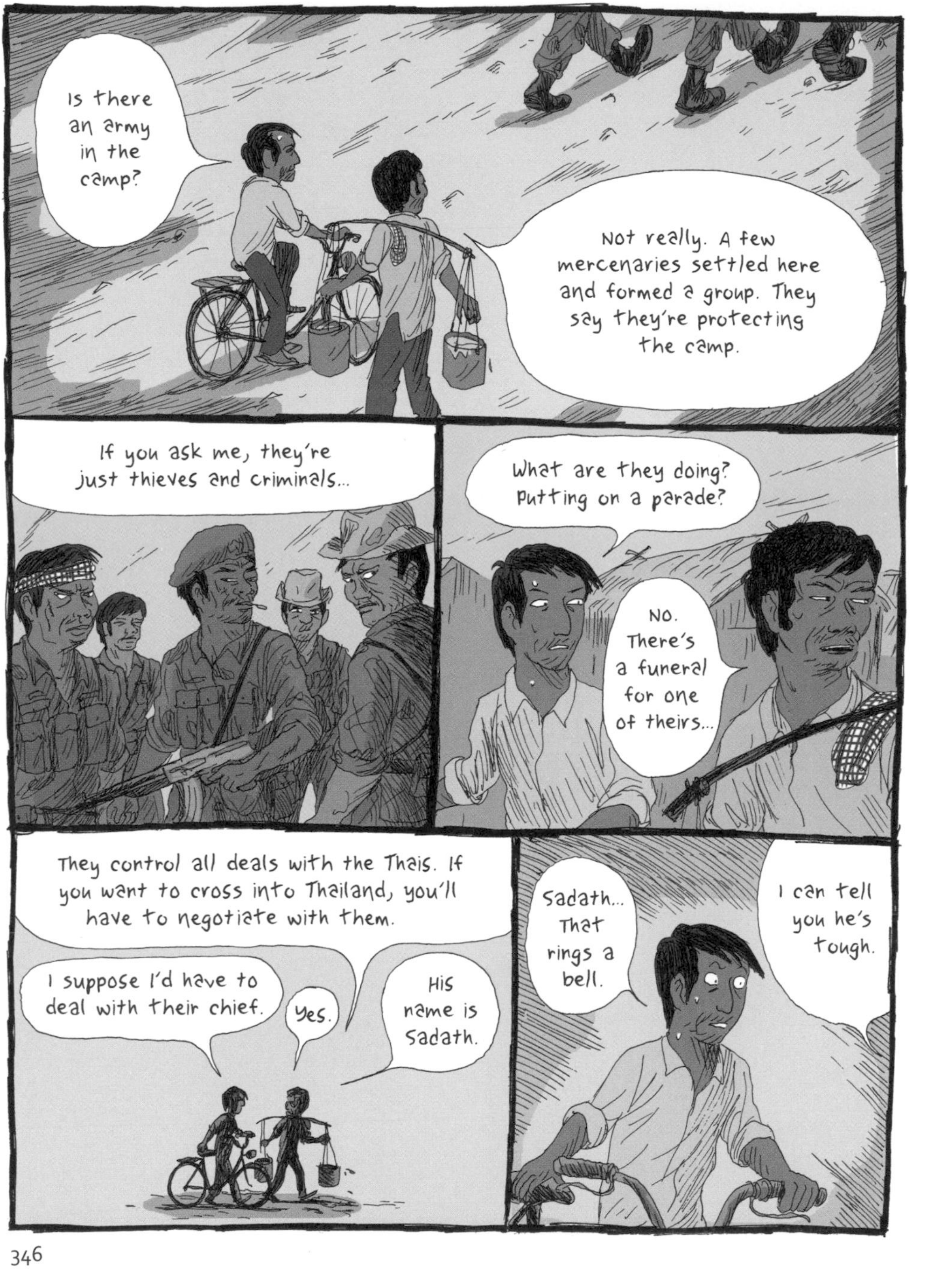
Is there an army in the camp?
Not really. A few mercenaries settled here and formed a group. They say they're protecting the camp.
If you ask me, they're just thieves and criminals...
What are they doing? Putting on a parade?
No. There's a funeral for one of theirs...
They control all deals with the Thais. If you want to cross into Thailand, you'll have to negotiate with them.
I suppose I'd have to deal with their chief.
Yes.
His name is Sadath.
Sadath... That rings a bell.
I can tell you he's tough.

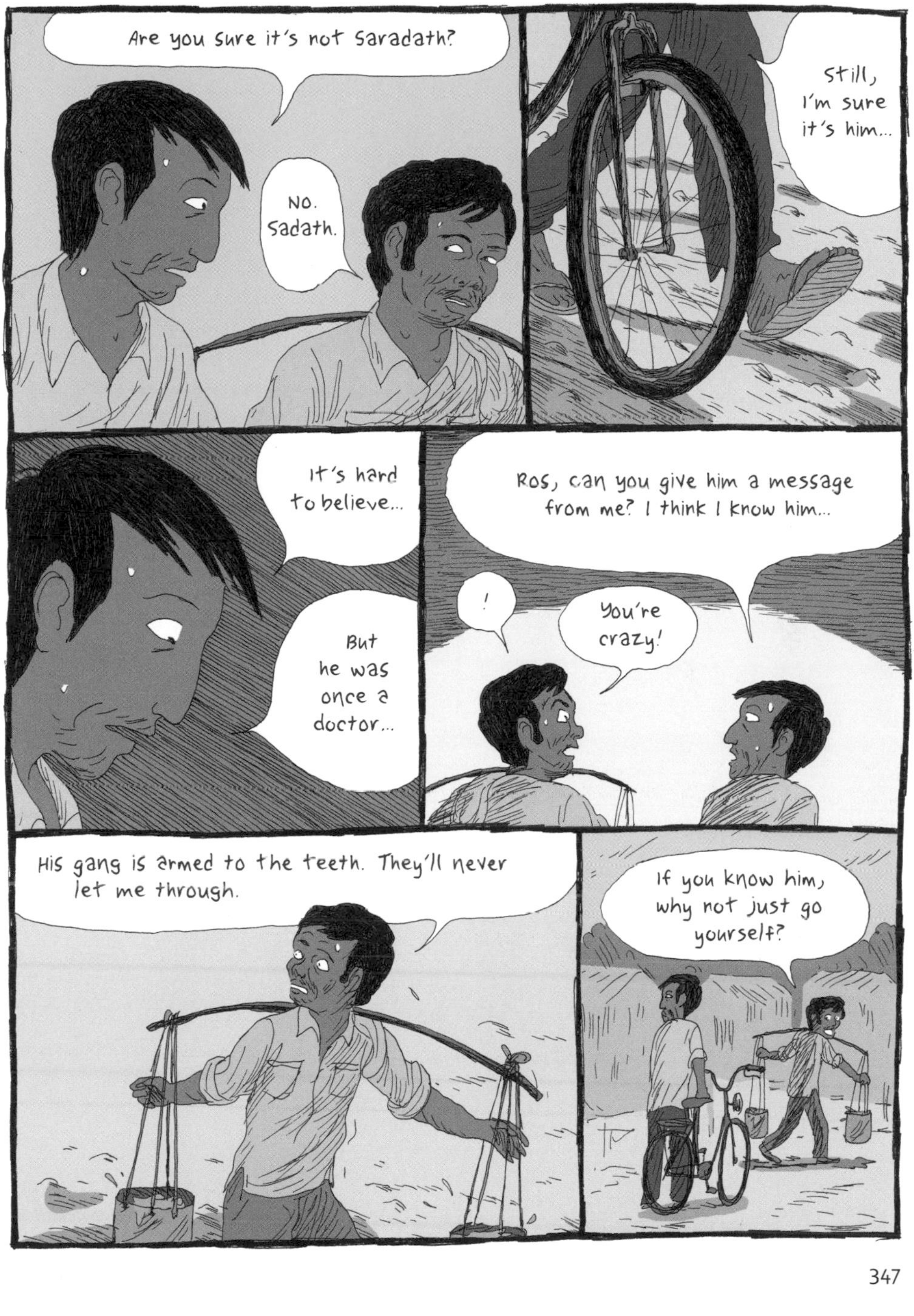
Are you sure it's not Saradath?
No. Sadath.
Still, I'm sure it's him...
It's hard to believe...
But he was once a doctor...
Ros, can you give him a message from me? I think I know him...
!
You're crazy!
His gang is armed to the teeth. They'll never let me through.
If you know him, why not just go yourself?

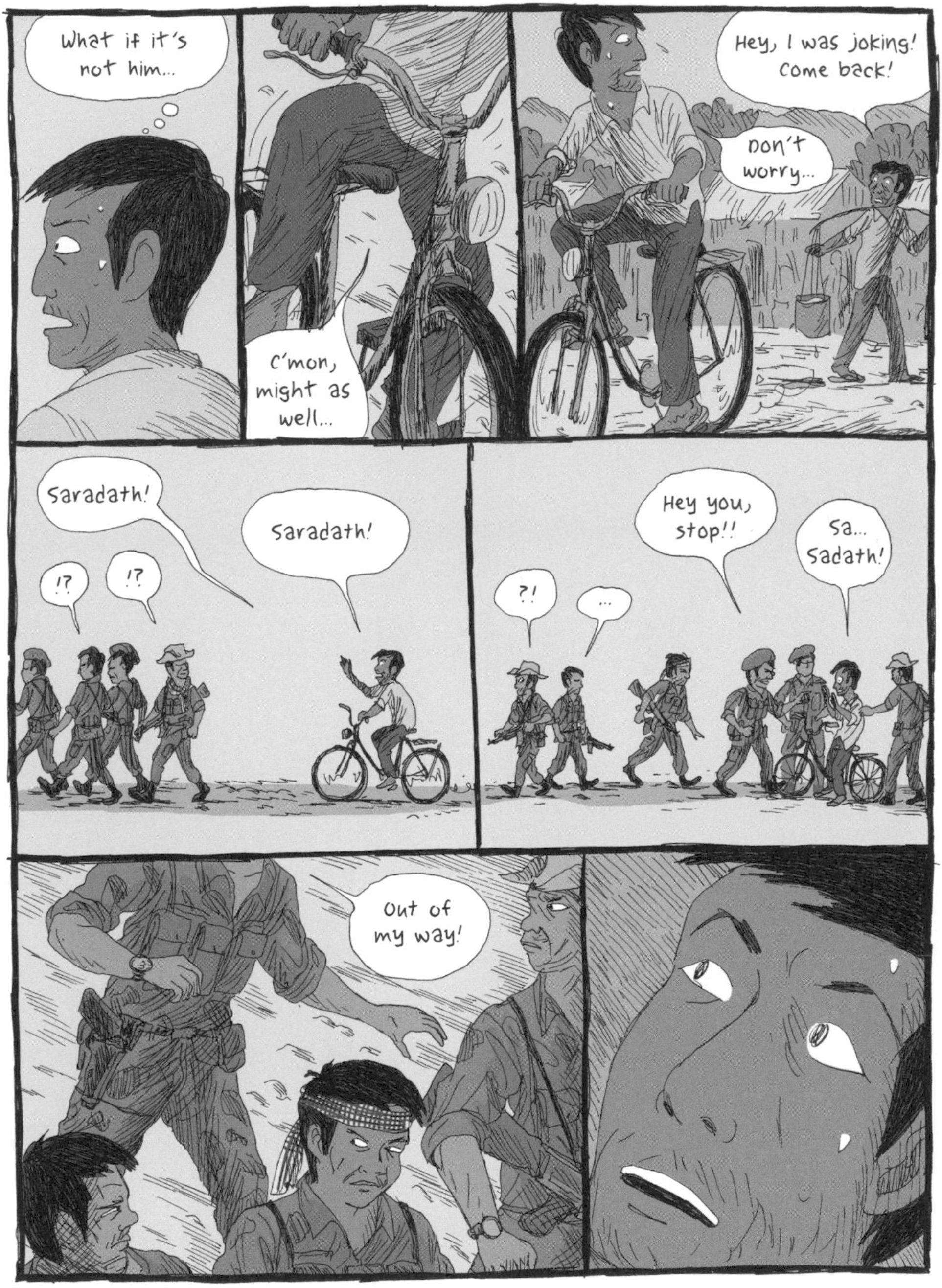
What if it's not him...
C'mon, might as well...
Hey, I was joking! Come back!
Don't worry...
Saradath!
!?
!?
Saradath!
?!
...
Hey you, stop!!
Sa... Sadath!
Out of my way!

chapter 21

SADATH, THE MERCENARY

WHAT YOU NEED TO KNOW TO GET TO THE KHAO I DANG CAMP...

Beware of landmines

Keep an eye out for snakes and spiders

Know the woods

Expect to cross a river

Bring a map and a flashlight

Avoid Thai soldiers

Enlist the help of a smuggler

Have cash on hand for checkpoints and the smuggler

Avoid the Khmer Rouge

Beware of thieves, traffickers, and mercenaries

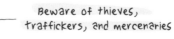

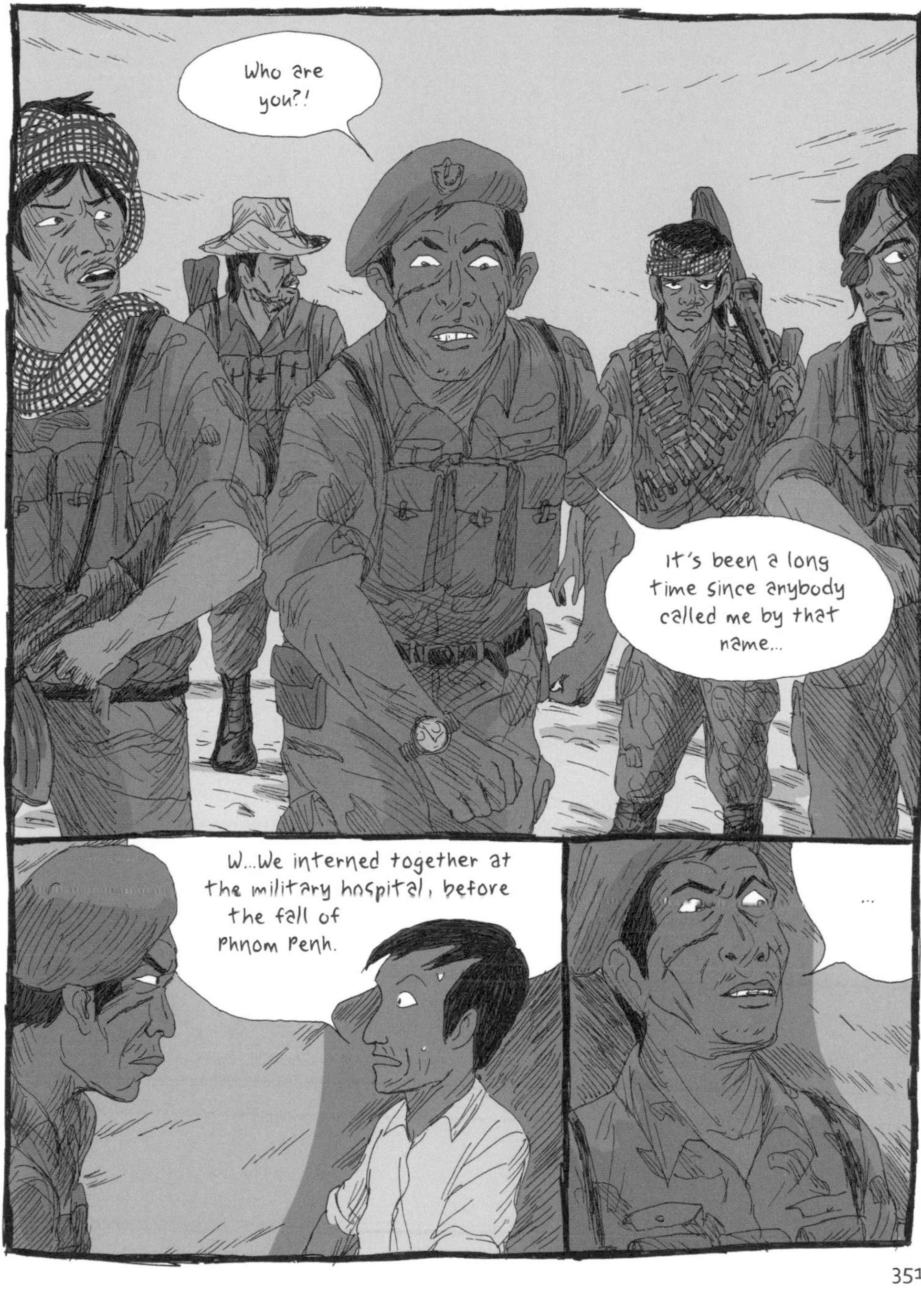
Who are you?!
It's been a long time since anybody called me by that name...
W...We interned together at the military hospital, before the fall of Phnom Penh.
...

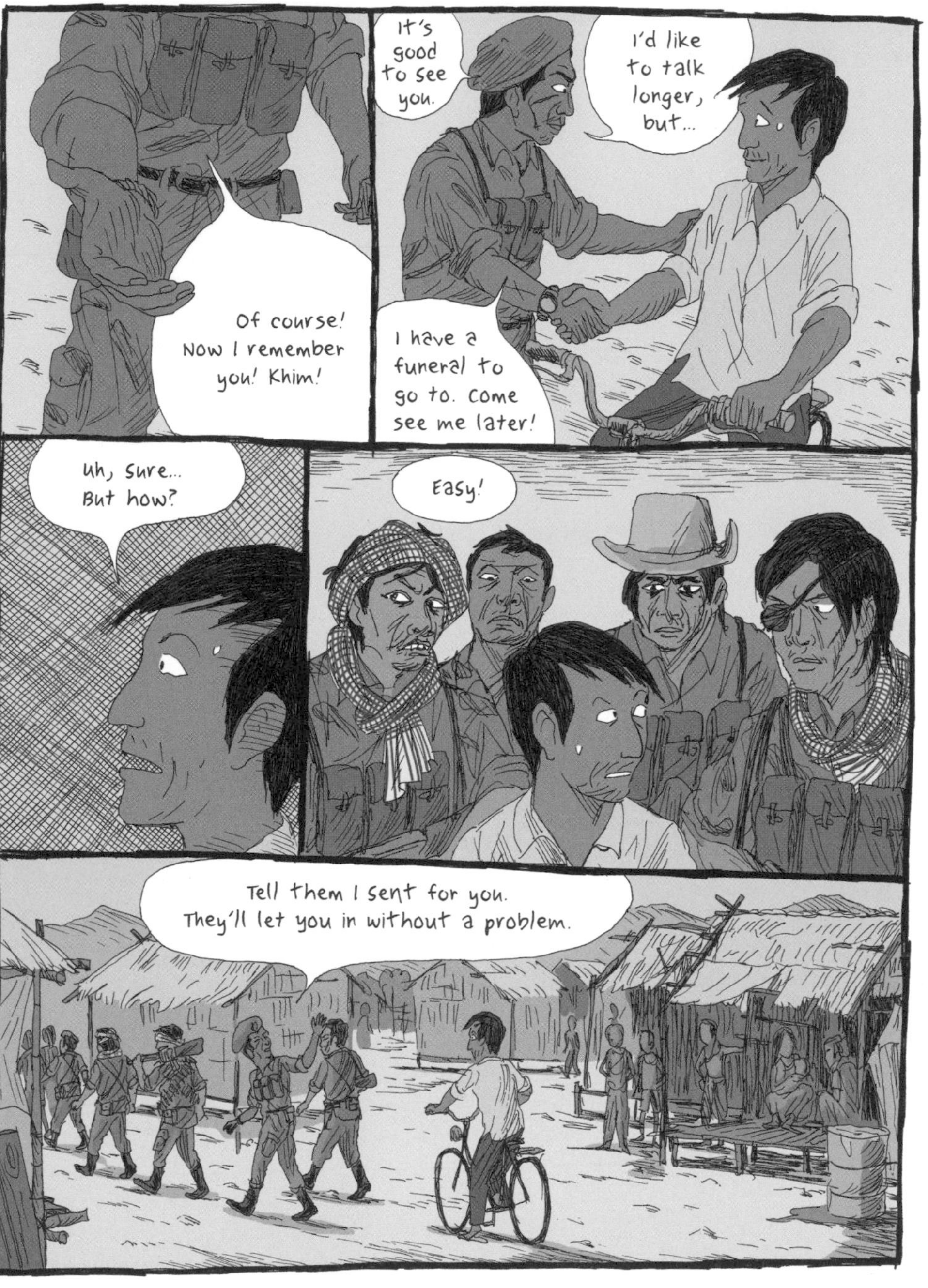
Of course! Now I remember you! Khim!
It's good to see you.
I'd like to talk longer, but...
I have a funeral to go to. Come see me later!
Uh, sure... But how?
Easy!
Tell them I sent for you. They'll let you in without a problem.

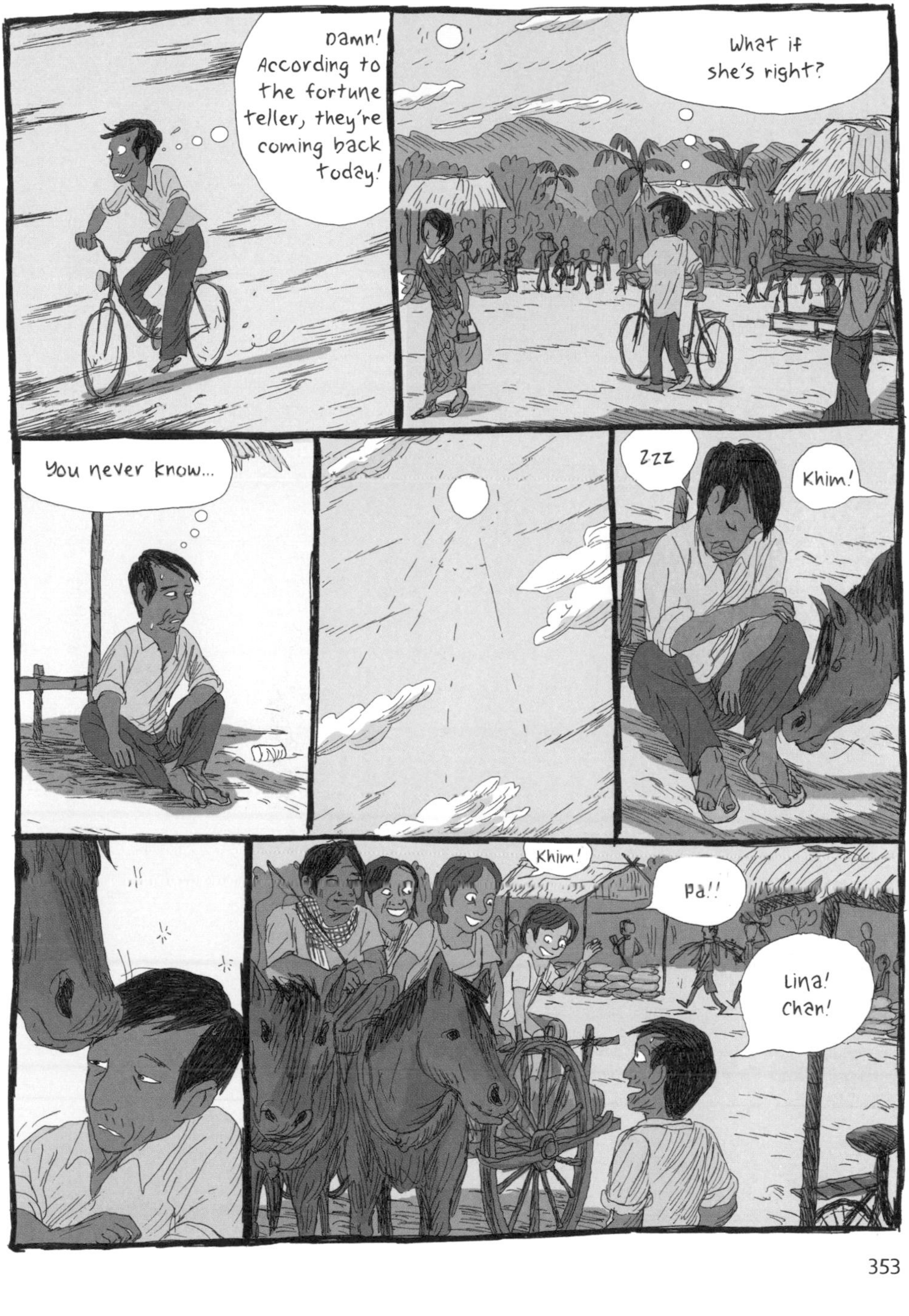
Damn! According to the fortune teller, they're coming back today!
What if she's right?
You never know...
Zzz
Khim!
Khim!
Pa!!
Lina! Chan!

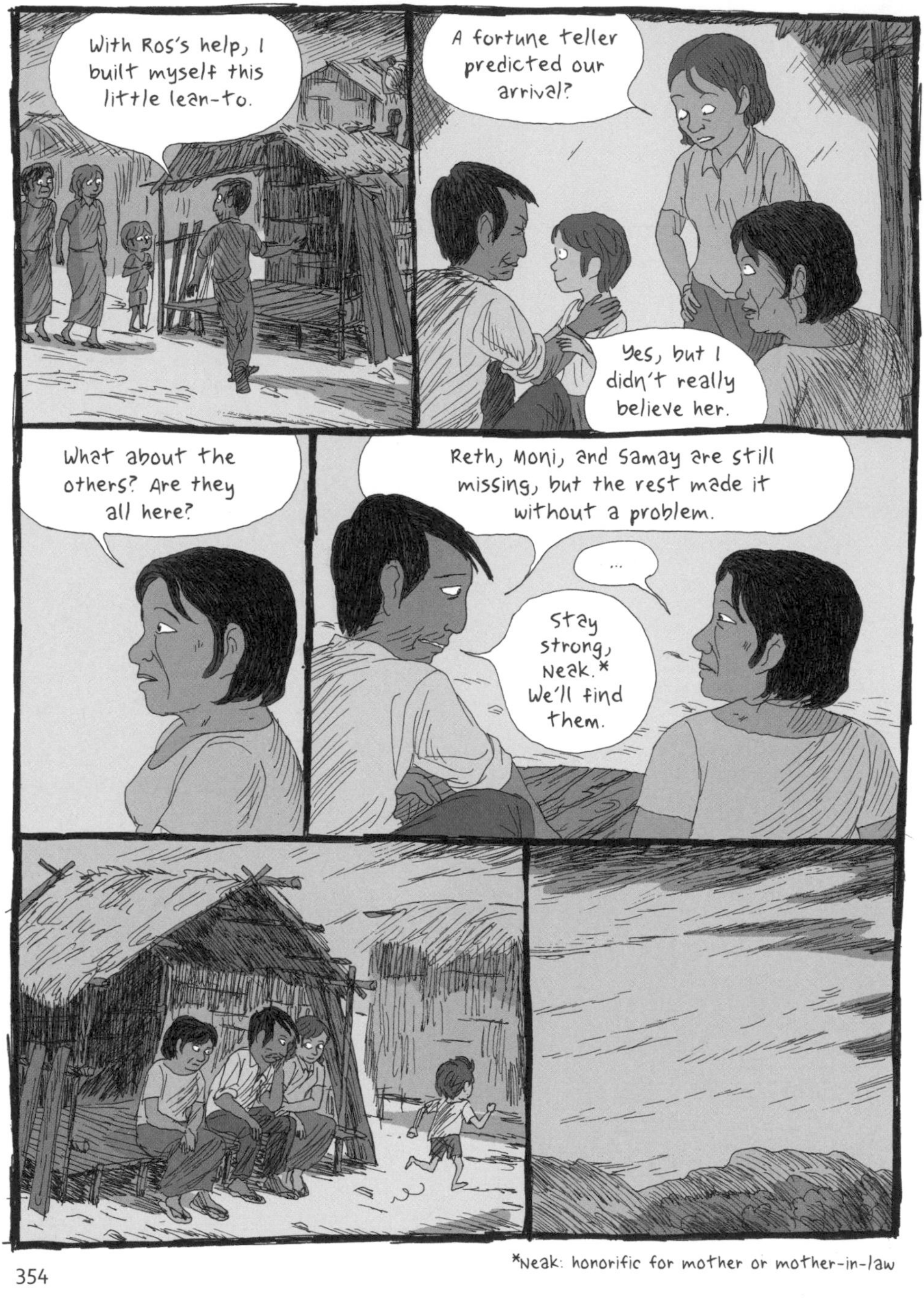
With Ros's help, I built myself this little lean-to.
A fortune teller predicted our arrival?
Yes, but I didn't really believe her.
What about the others? Are they all here?
Reth, Moni, and Samay are still missing, but the rest made it without a problem.
...
Stay strong, Neak.* We'll find them.

*Neak: honorific for mother or mother-in-law

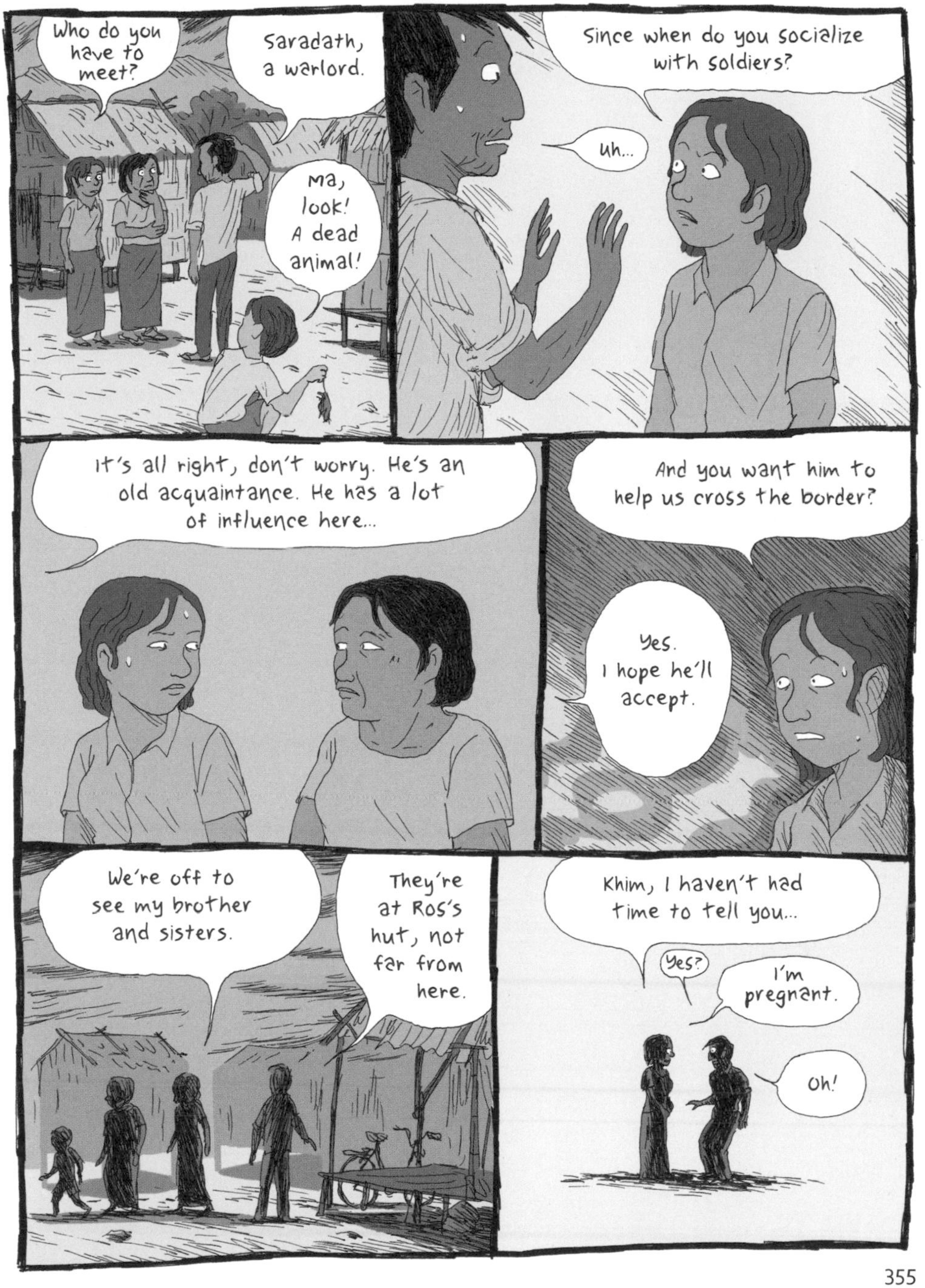

Who do you have to meet?
Saradath, a warlord.
Ma, look! A dead animal!
Since when do you socialize with soldiers?
Uh...
It's all right, don't worry. He's an old acquaintance. He has a lot of influence here...
And you want him to help us cross the border?
Yes. I hope he'll accept.
We're off to see my brother and sisters.
They're at Ros's hut, not far from here.
Khim, I haven't had time to tell you...
Yes?
I'm pregnant.
Oh!

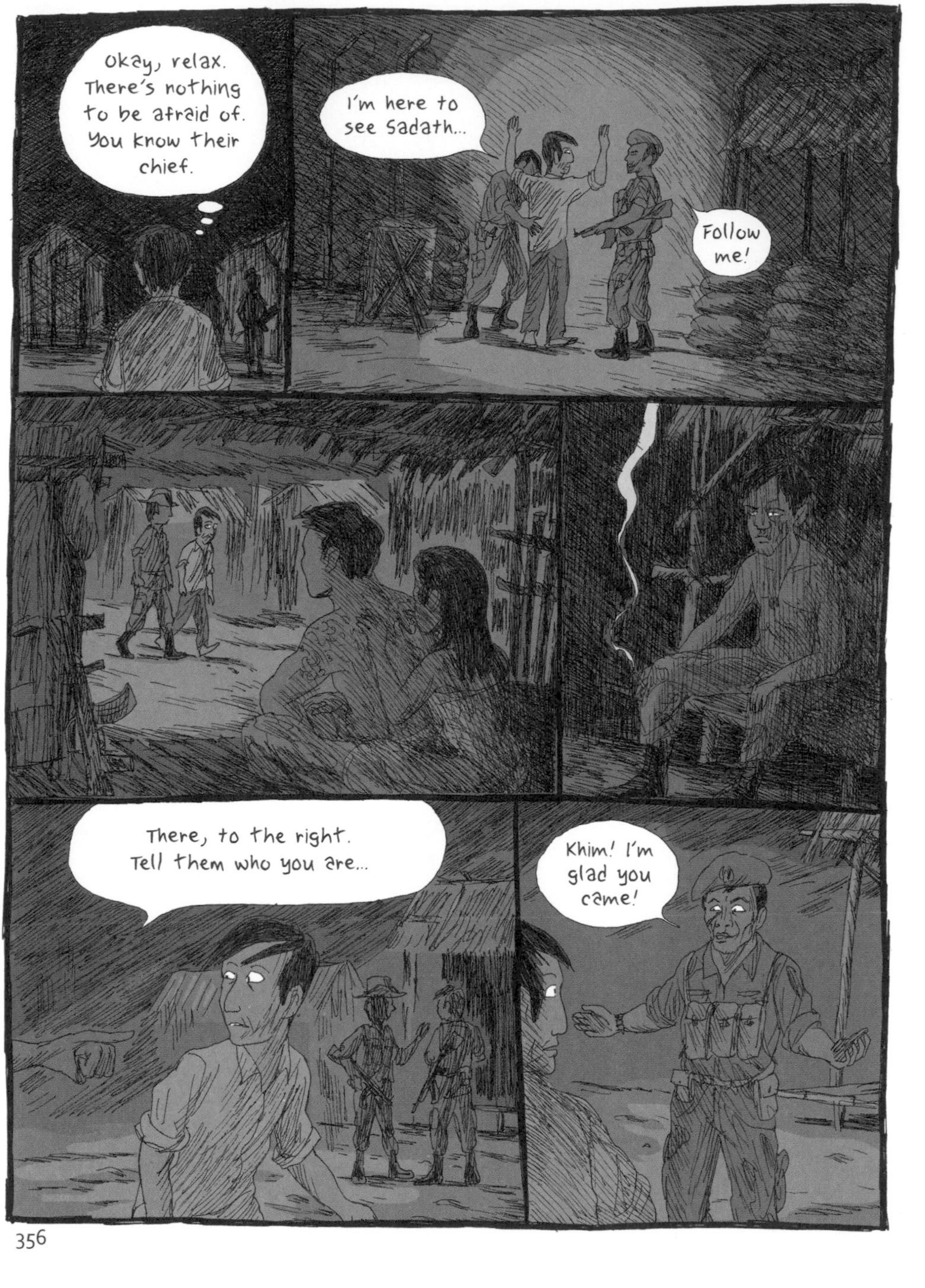
Okay, relax. There's nothing to be afraid of. You know their chief.
I'm here to see Sadath...
Follow me!
There, to the right. Tell them who you are...
Khim! I'm glad you came!

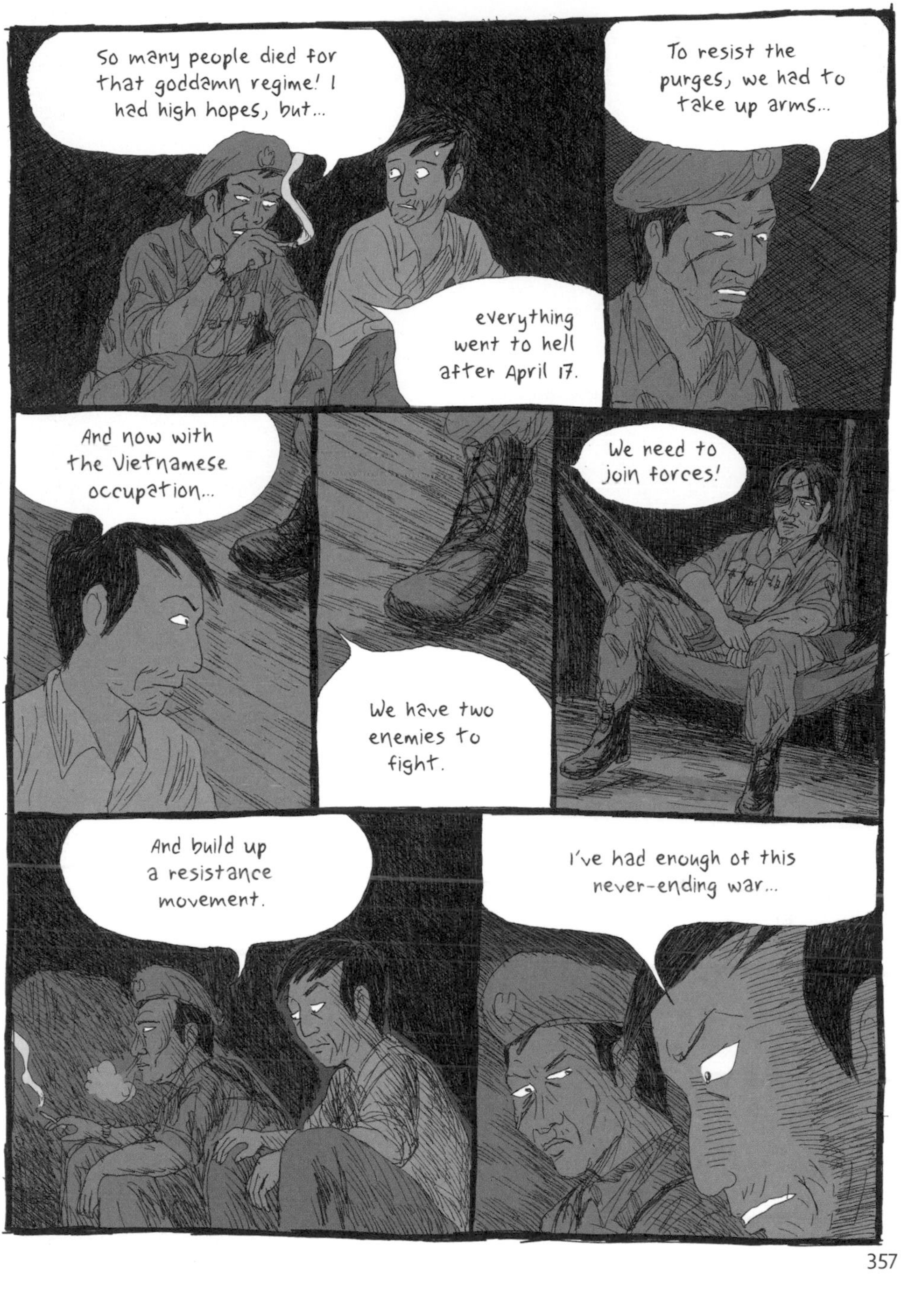
So many people died for that goddamn regime! I had high hopes, but...
everything went to hell after April 17.
To resist the purges, we had to take up arms...
And now with the Vietnamese occupation...
We have two enemies to fight.
We need to join forces!
And build up a resistance movement.
I've had enough of this never-ending war...

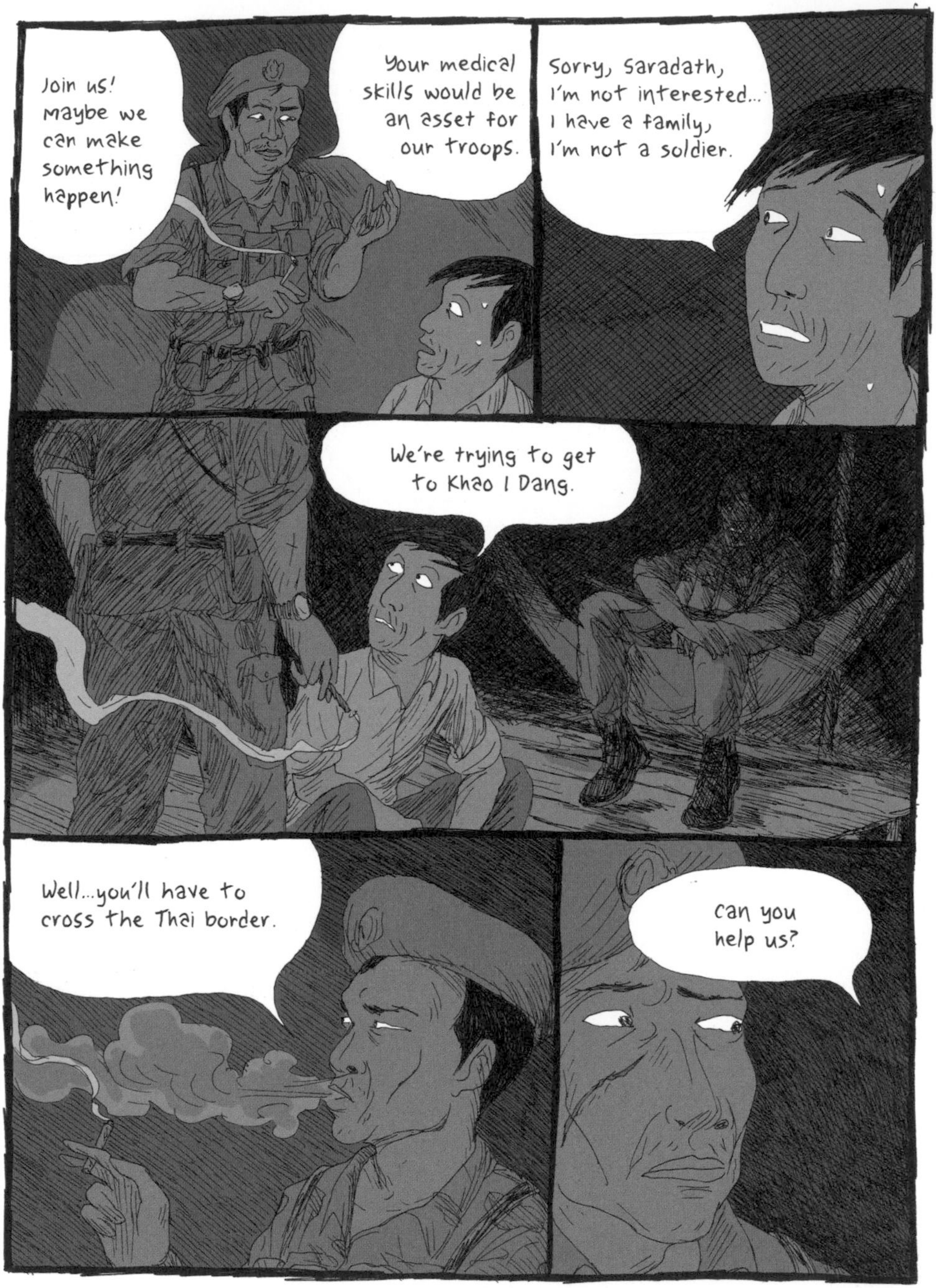
Join us! Maybe we can make something happen!
Your medical skills would be an asset for our troops.
Sorry, Saradath, I'm not interested... I have a family, I'm not a soldier.
We're trying to get to Khao I Dang.
Well...you'll have to cross the Thai border.
Can you help us?

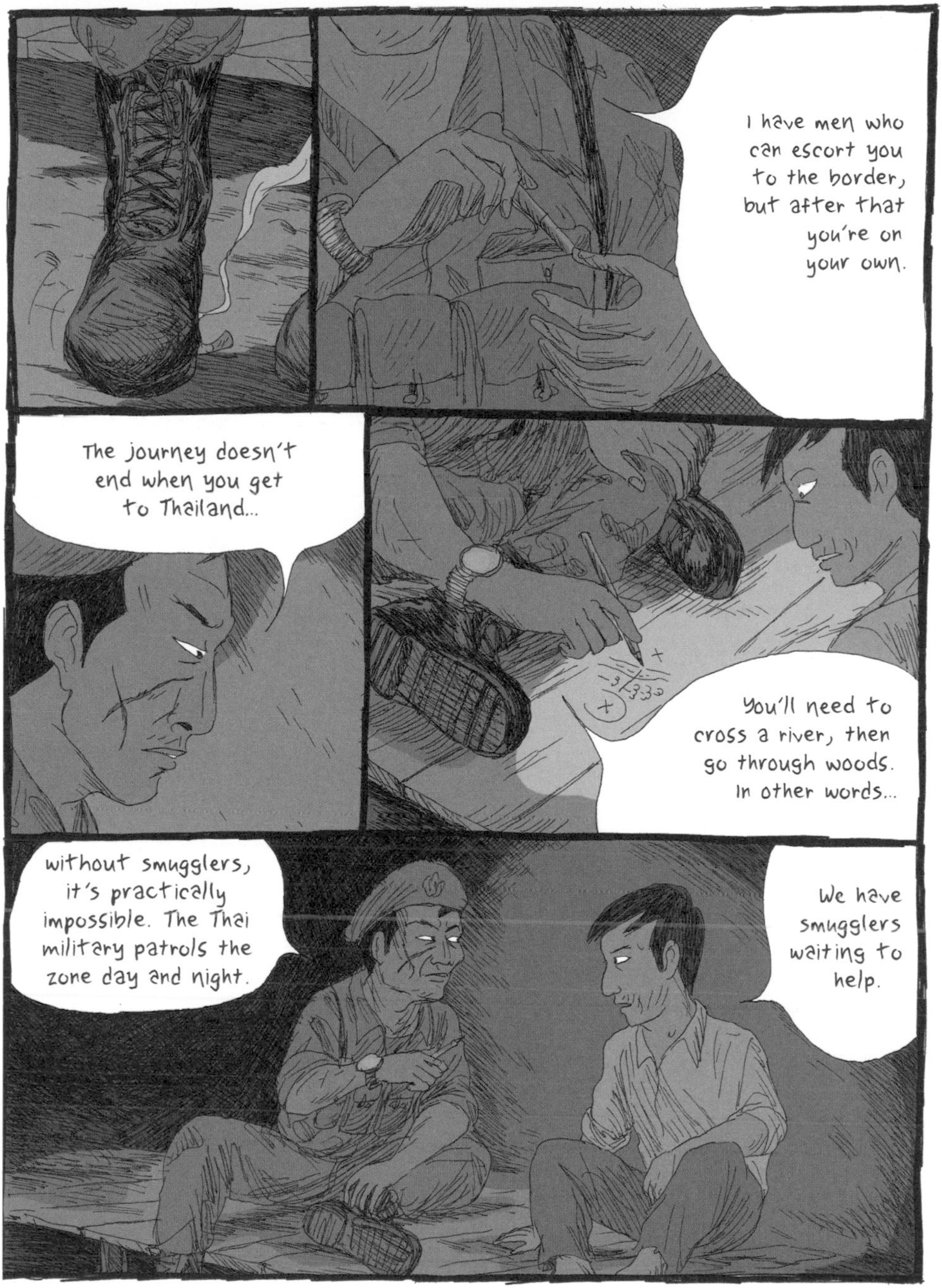
I have men who can escort you to the border, but after that you're on your own.
The journey doesn't end when you get to Thailand...
You'll need to cross a river, then go through woods. In other words...
without smugglers, it's practically impossible. The Thai military patrols the zone day and night.
We have smugglers waiting to help.

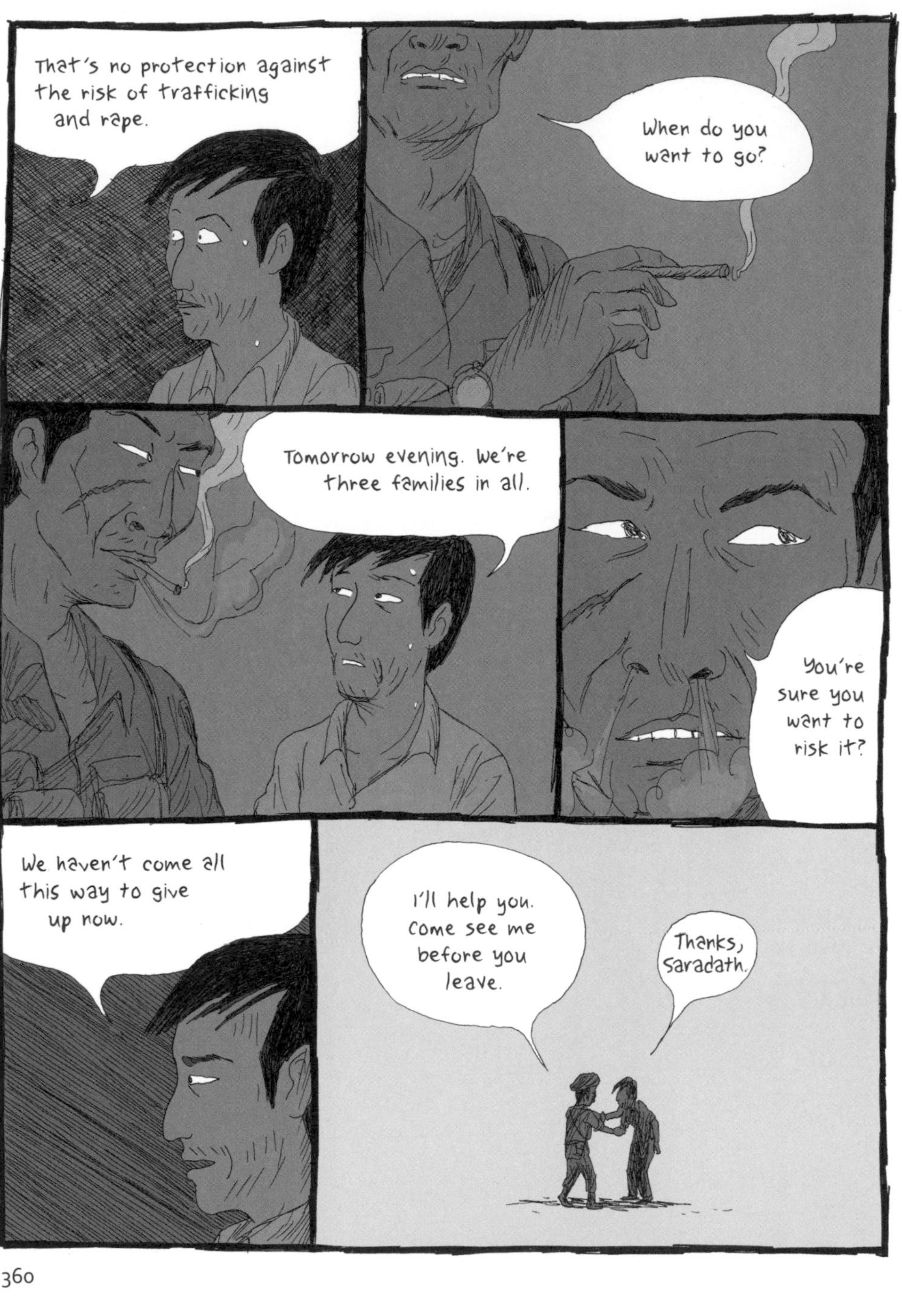
That's no protection against the risk of trafficking and rape.
When do you want to go?
Tomorrow evening. We're three families in all.
You're sure you want to risk it?
We haven't come all this way to give up now.
I'll help you. Come see me before you leave.
Thanks, Saradath.

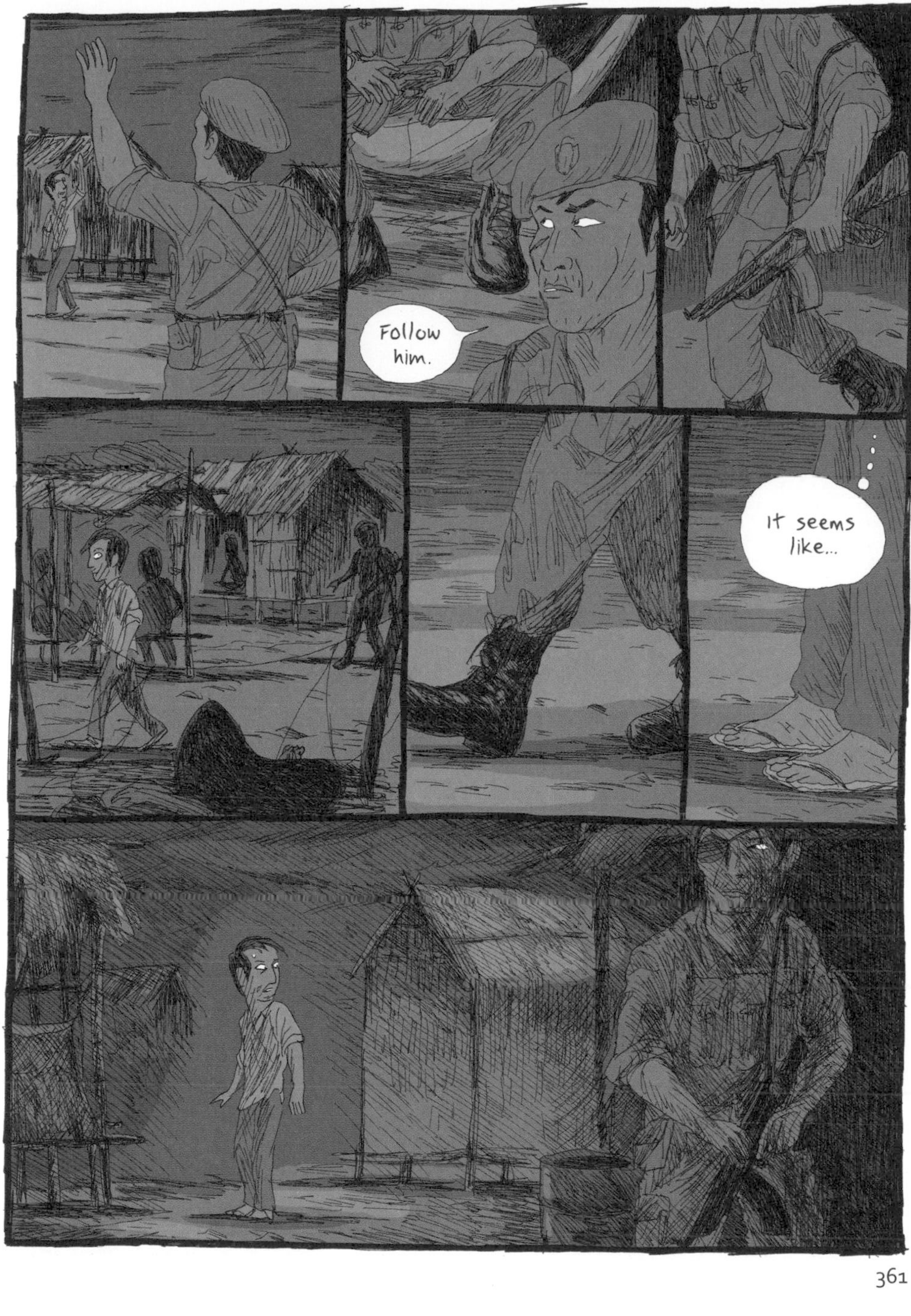
Follow him.
It seems like...

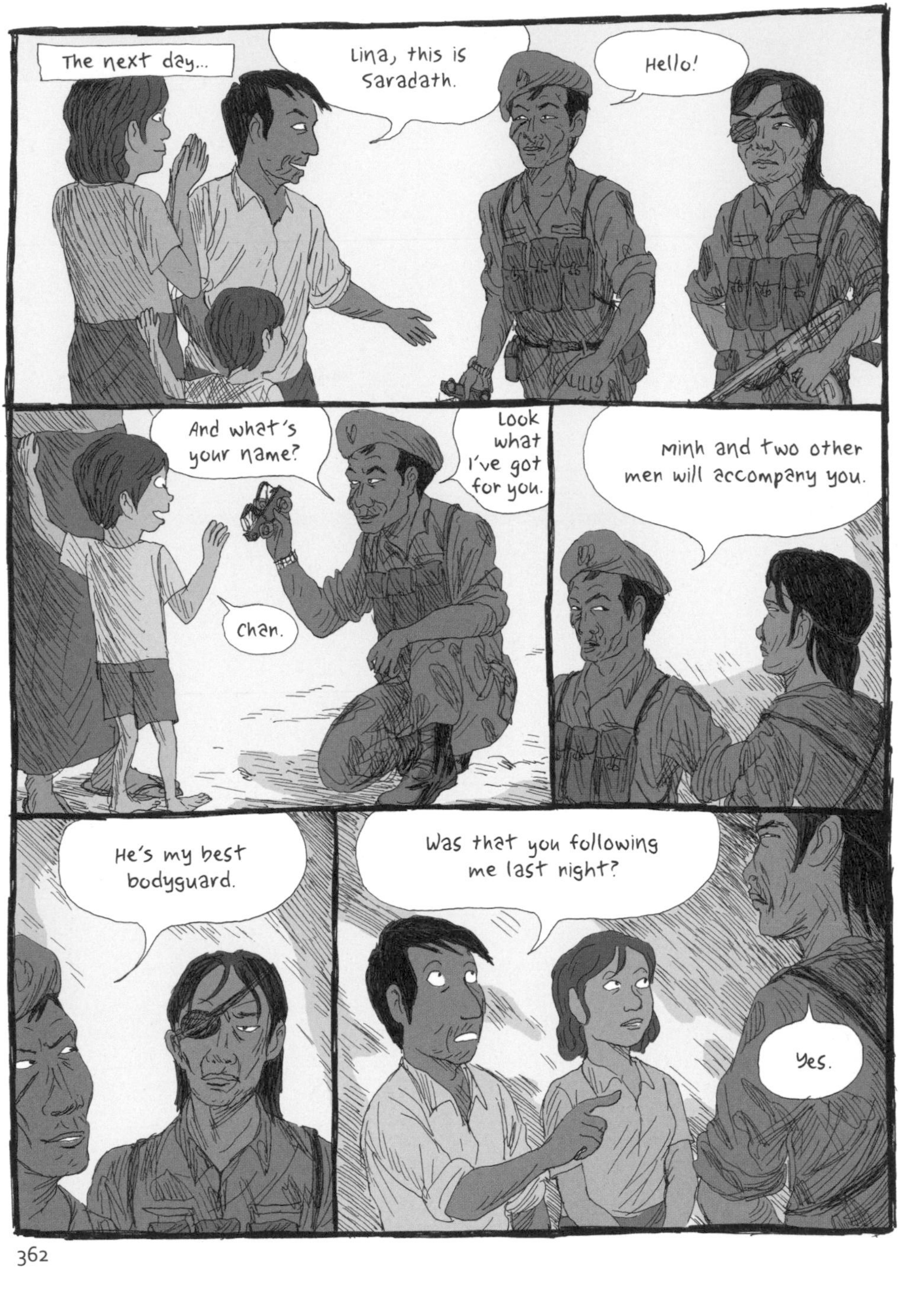
The next day...
Lina, this is Saradath.
Hello!
And what's your name?
Look what I've got for you.
Chan.
Minh and two other men will accompany you.
He's my best bodyguard.
Was that you following me last night?
Yes.

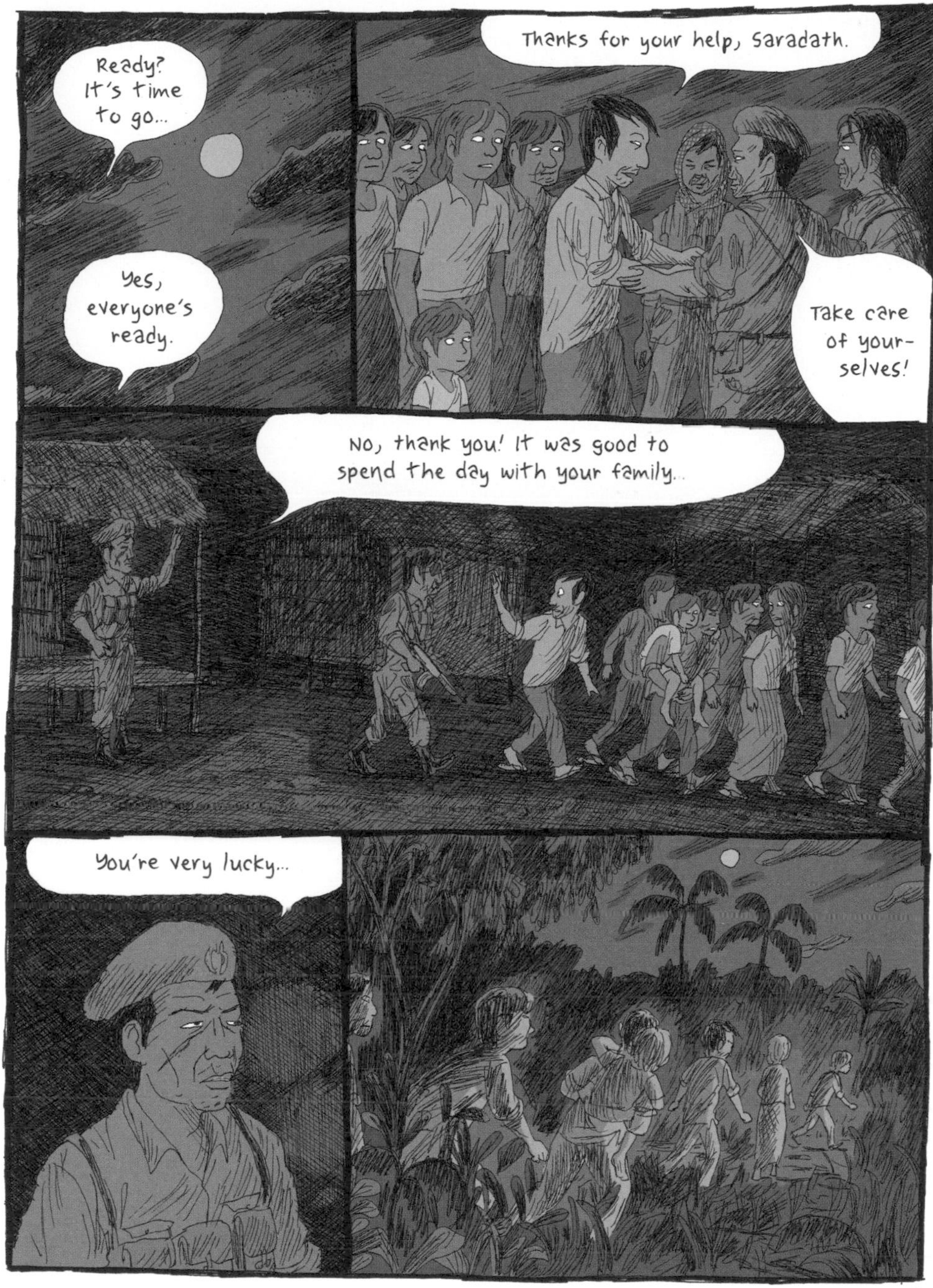
Ready? It's time to go...
Yes, everyone's ready.
Thanks for your help, Saradath.
Take care of your-selves!
No, thank you! It was good to spend the day with your family...
You're very lucky...

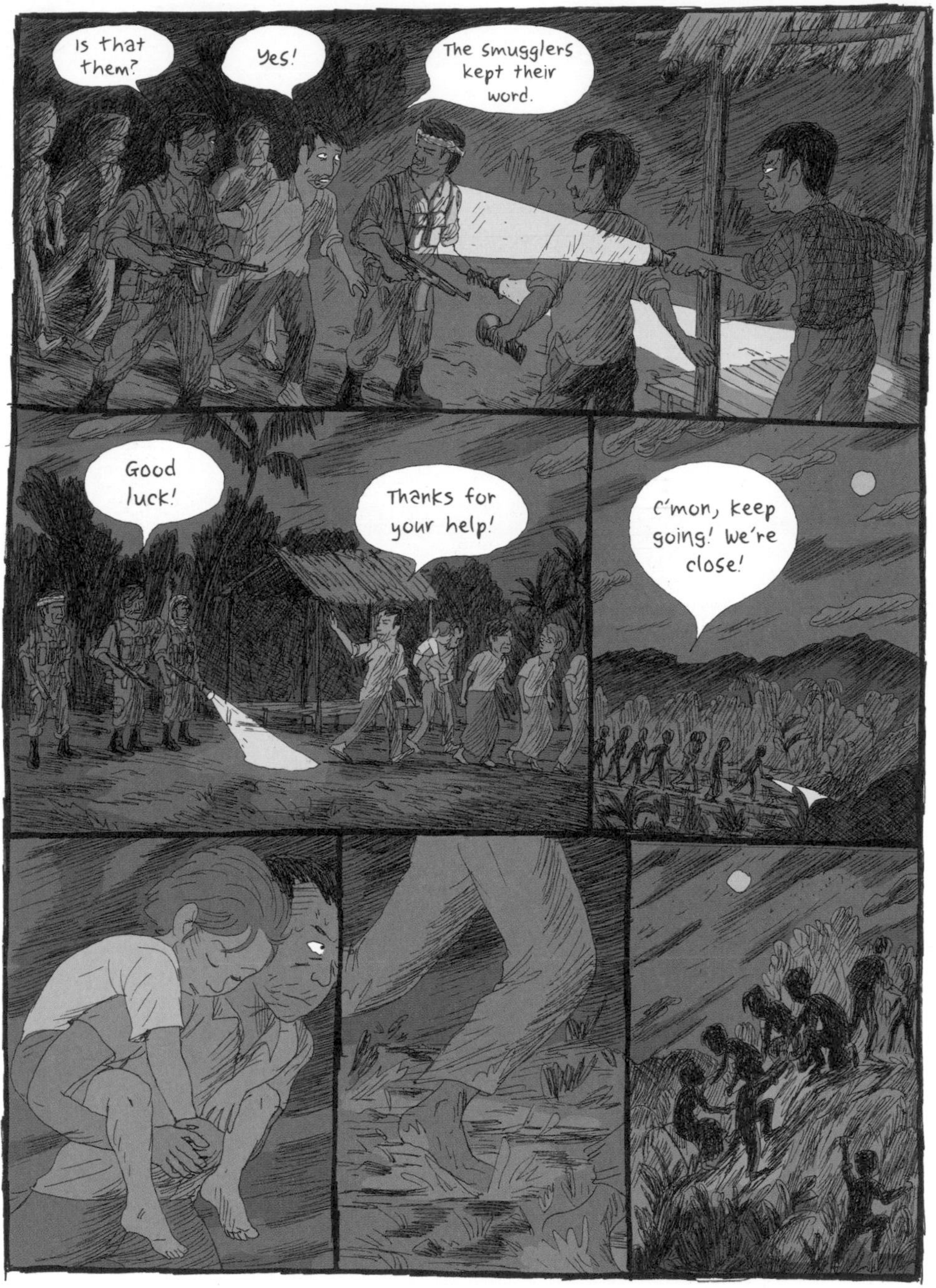
Is that them?
Yes!
The smugglers kept their word.
Good luck!
Thanks for your help!
C'mon, keep going! We're close!

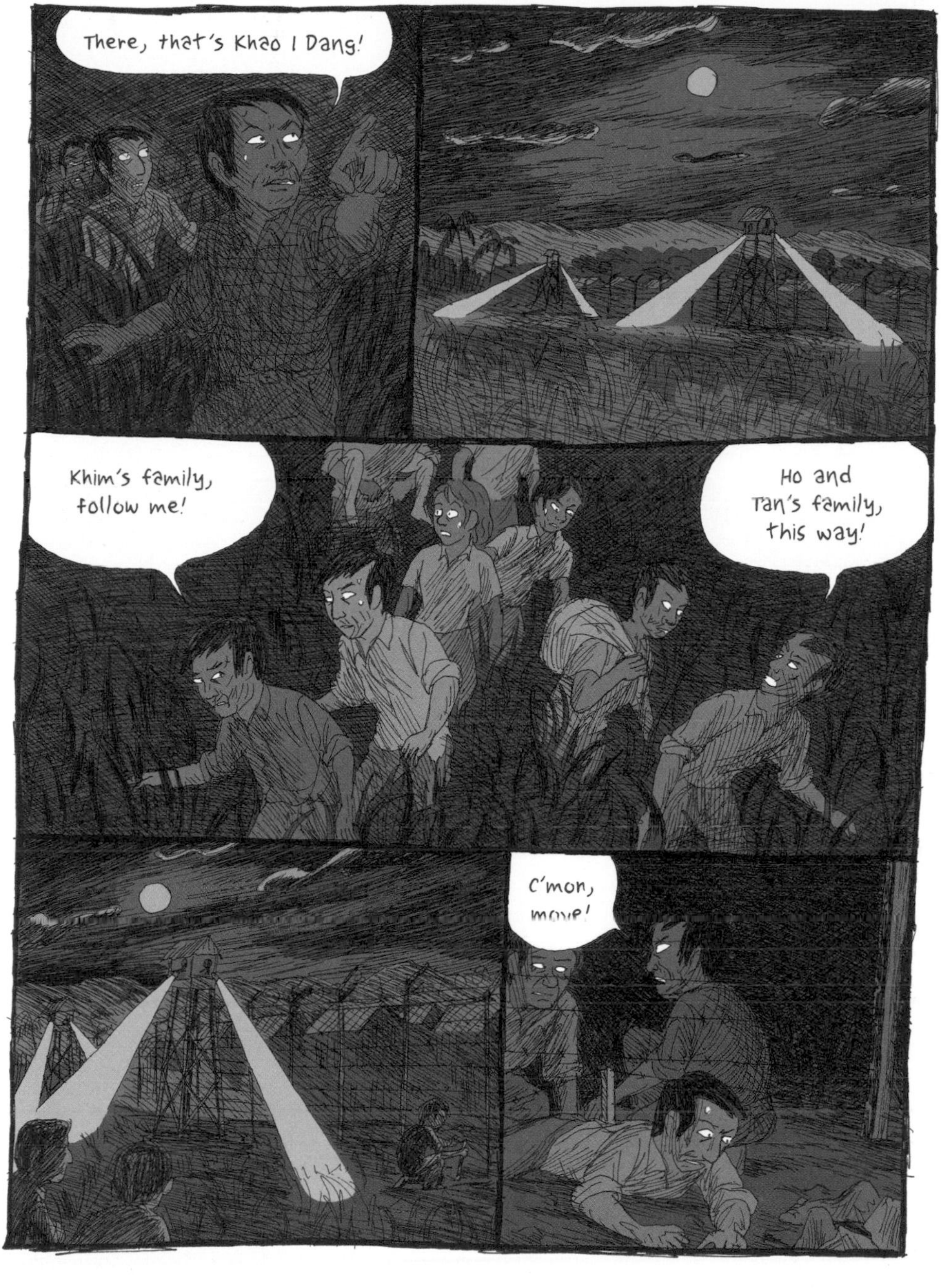
There, that's Khao I Dang!
Khim's family, follow me!
Ho and Tan's family, this way!
C'mon, move!

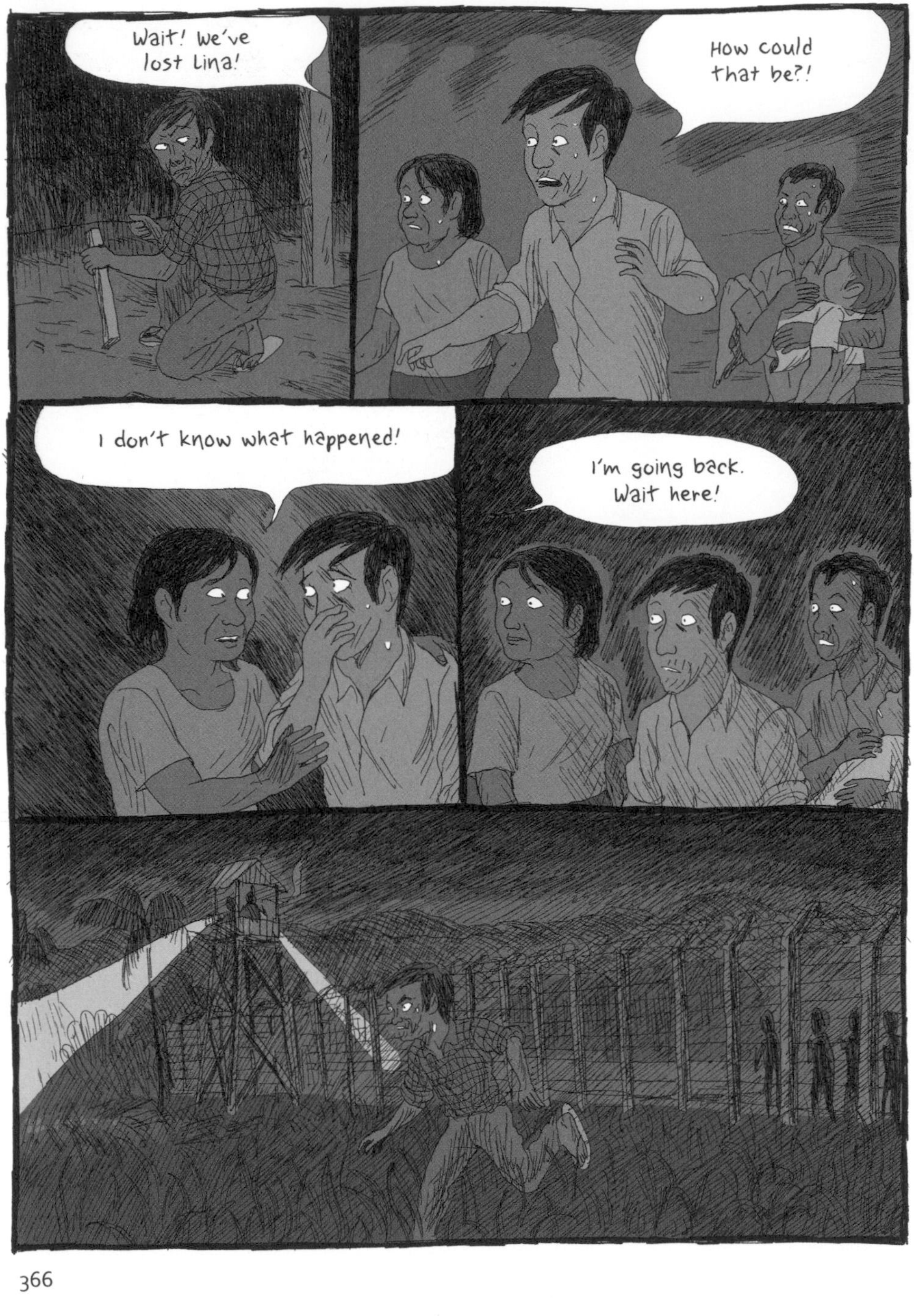
Wait! We've lost Lina!
How could that be?!
I don't know what happened!
I'm going back. Wait here!

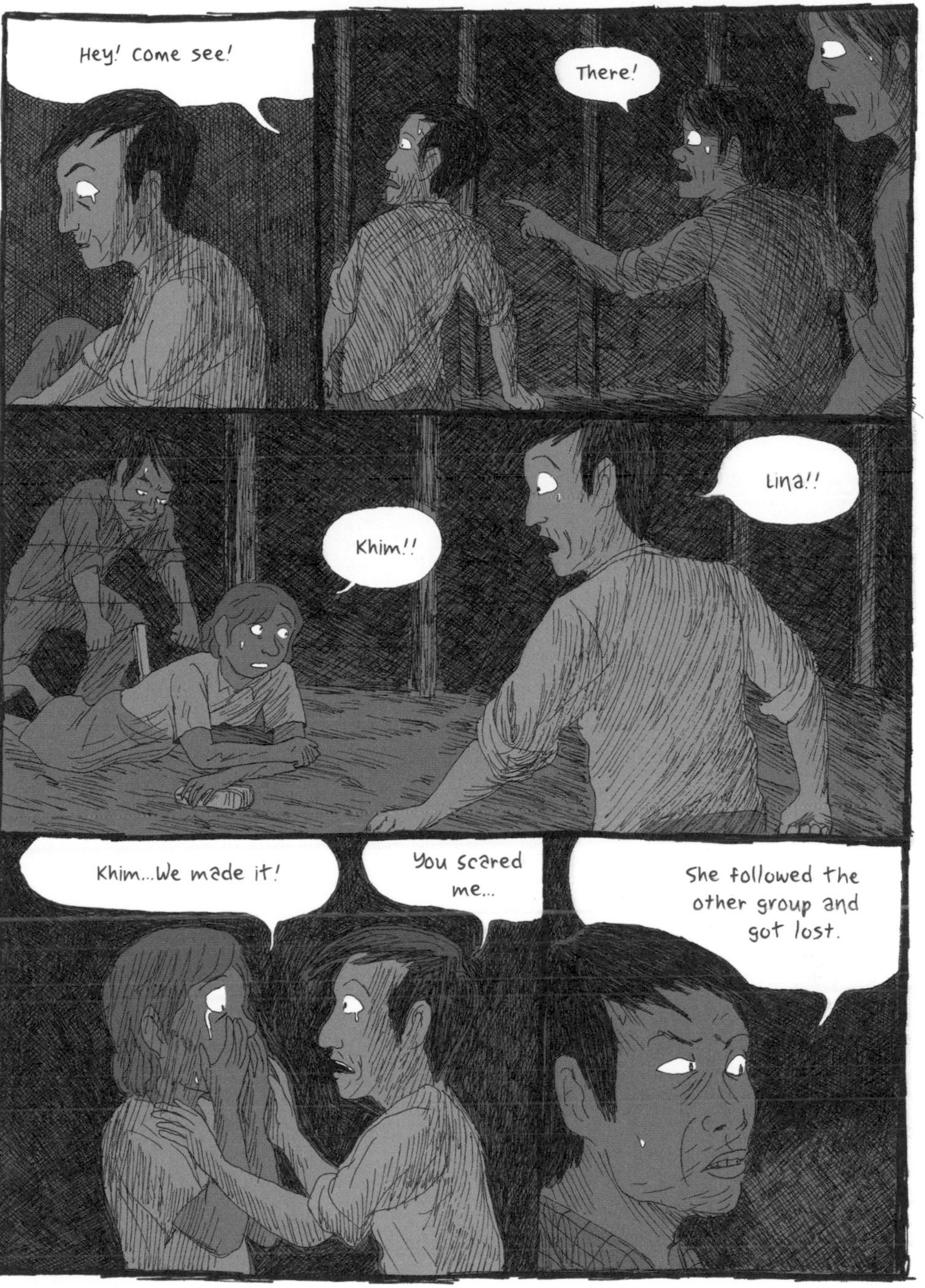
Hey! Come see!
There!
Lina!!
Khim!!
Khim...We made it!
You scared me...
She followed the other group and got lost.

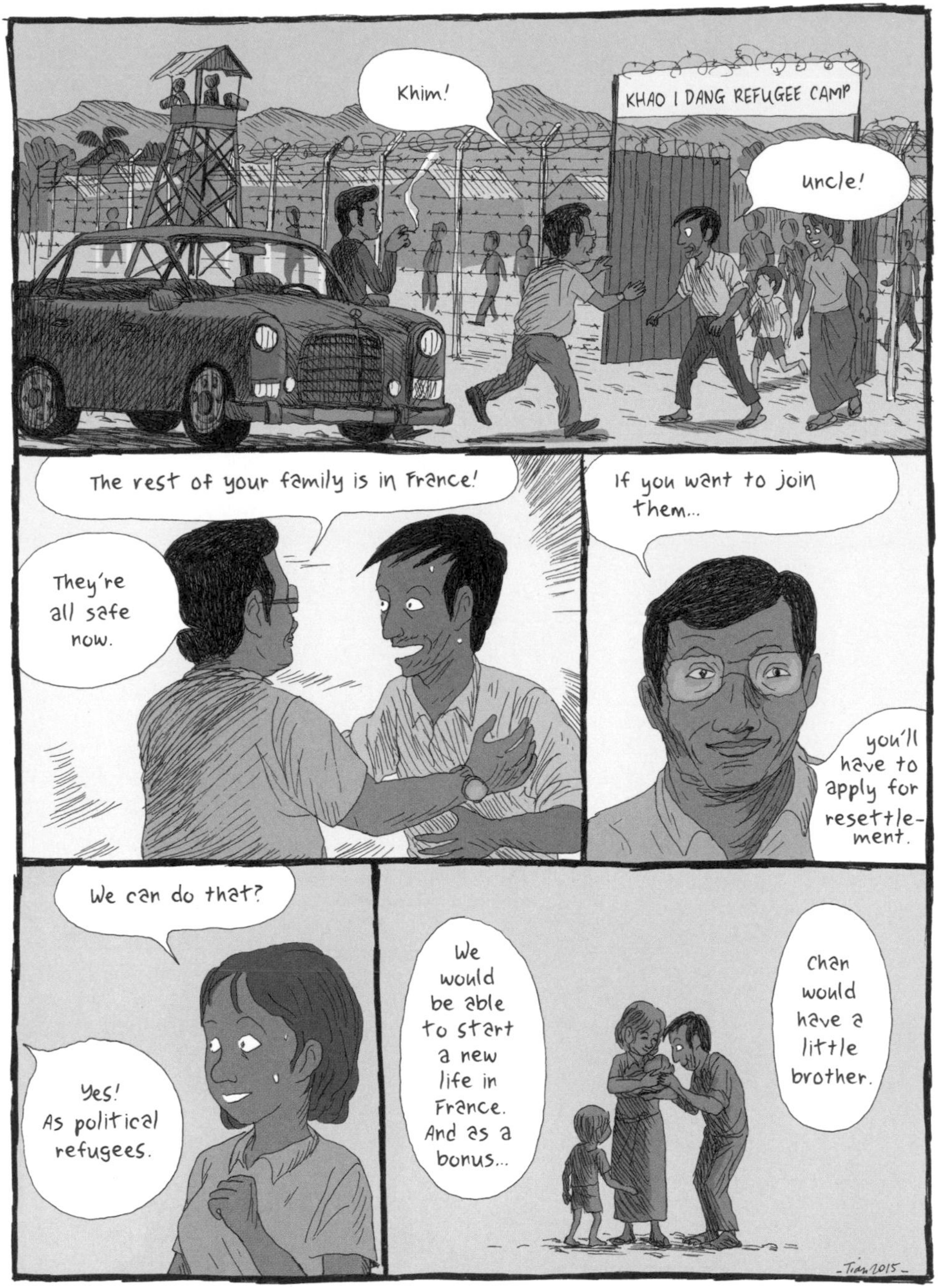
KHAO I DANG REFUGEE CAMP
Khim!
Uncle!
The rest of your family is in France!
They're all safe now.
If you want to join them...
you'll have to apply for resettlement.
We can do that?
Yes! As political refugees.
We would be able to start a new life in France. And as a bonus...
Chan would have a little brother.
-Tian 2015-

A New
Beginning
—
1980
and
beyond

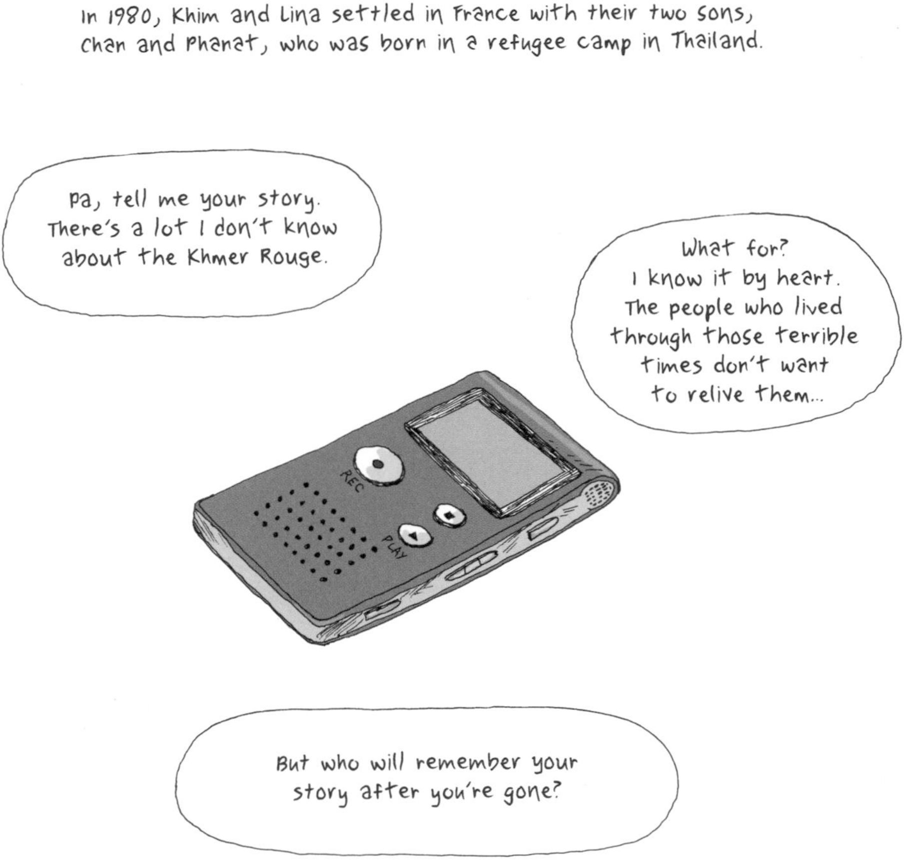
In 1980, Khim and Lina settled in France with their two sons, Chan and Phanat, who was born in a refugee camp in Thailand.
Pa, tell me your story. There's a lot I don't know about the Khmer Rouge.
What for? I know it by heart. The people who lived through those terrible times don't want to relive them...
REC
PLAY
But who will remember your story after you're gone?

Lina remains scarred by the events of the Khmer Rouge regime. France gave her a new life, but the past often catches up with her. To chase away her nightmares, she listens to Khmer songs that bring back happy memories of her teenage years, when she was a fan of Sin Sisamuth, "The King" of Khmer pop.

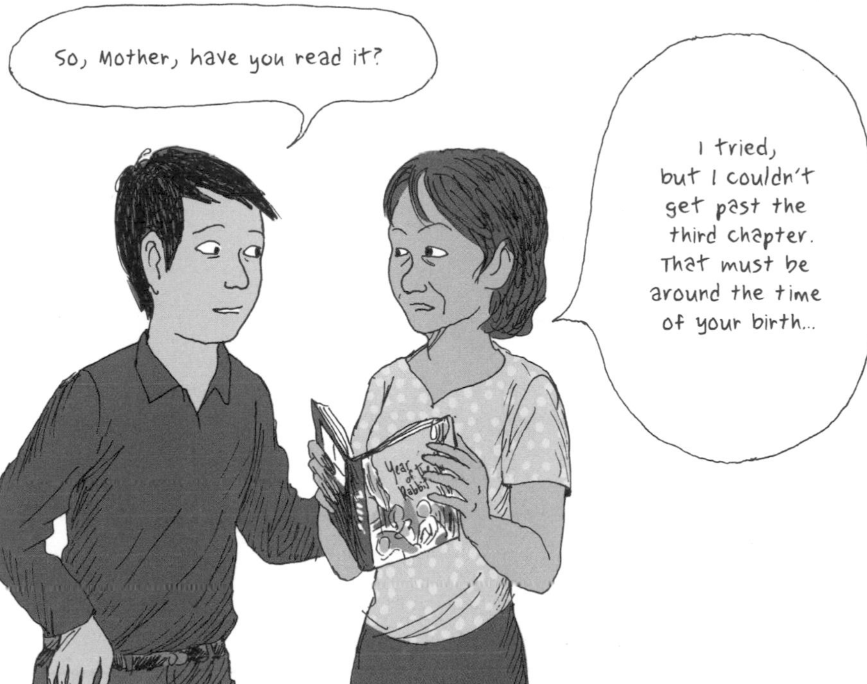
So, Mother, have you read it?
I tried, but I couldn't get past the third chapter. That must be around the time of your birth...
Year of the Rabbit

Vanny lives in France with Koliane and Samay. She hasn't been back to Cambodia since 1980. She misses her home country, and was glad to hear that her story has been told in a comic.

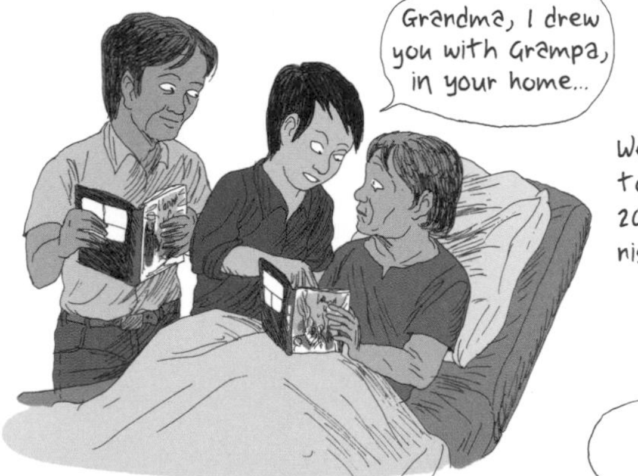
Grandma, I drew you with Grampa, in your home...

Weakened by old age, she went to live with Koliane and Samy in 2014. They trade shifts day and night to care for her.

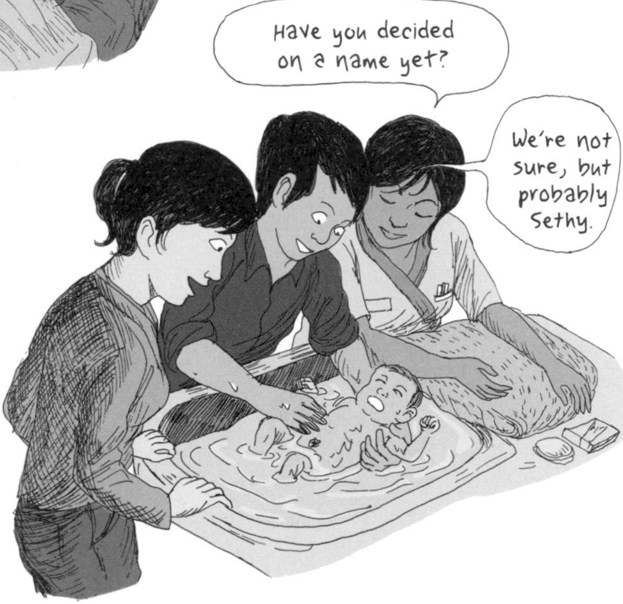
Have you decided on a name yet?
We're not sure, but probably Sethy.

Already as a young girl, Koliane knew that she wanted to work with children. Because of the war, her life took a different path, but after 1980, she was able to go back to school. Today, she works in a maternity clinic in France. And as luck would have it, she was able to be on hand for the birth of Chan's son.

Moni and Chenda settled in Montreal, where they live happily with their three children and their grandchildren. The loss of her loved ones was so painful to Chenda that she doesn't want to hear about Cambodia anymore. To put it out of her mind, she listens to country music and lives like a Canadian. Chan has visited them a few times.

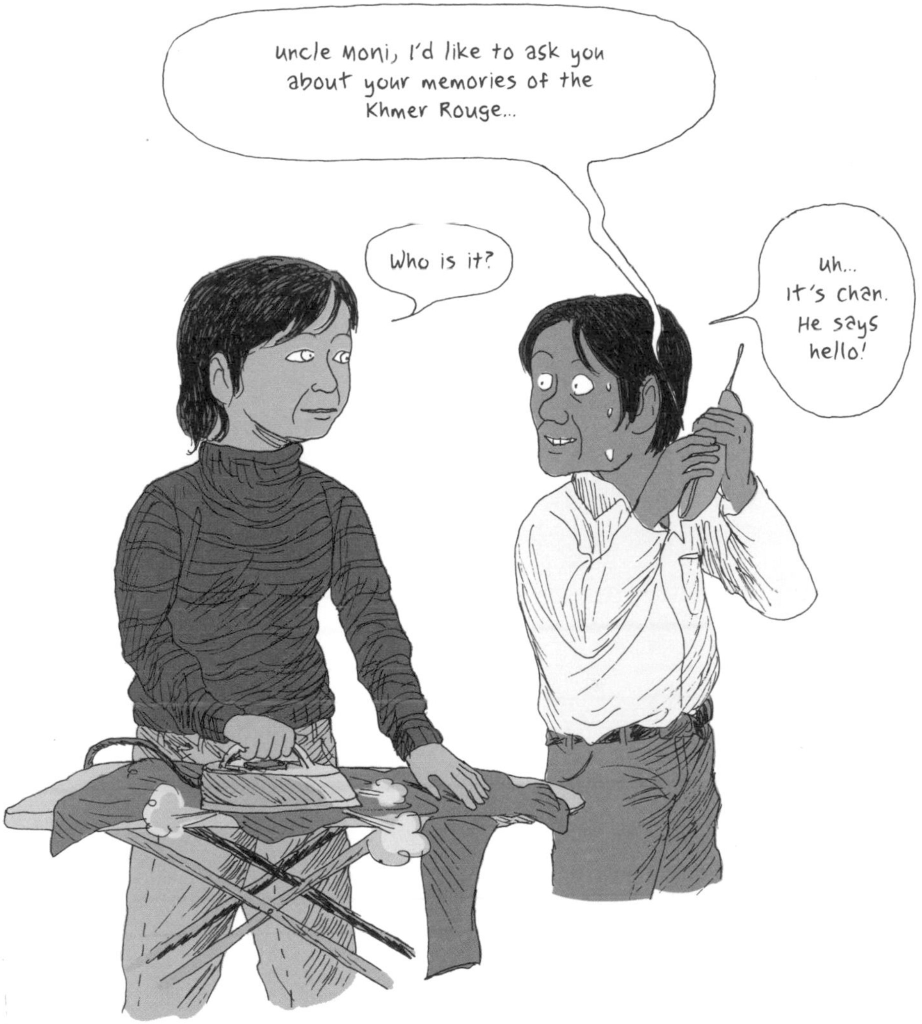
Uncle Moni, I'd like to ask you about your memories of the Khmer Rouge...
Who is it?
Uh... It's Chan. He says hello!

Reth lives in Paris with his wife and children. In 2015, he returned to Cambodia for the first time, to try to come to terms with his painful past. It was an emotional visit. In Phnom Penh, he visited his family home, now converted into a restaurant by its new owners.

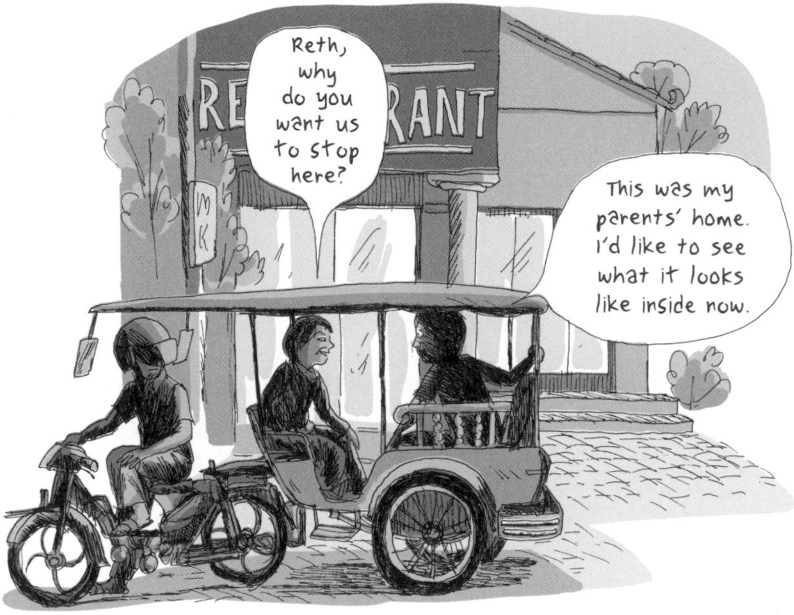
Reth, why do you want us to stop here?
This was my parents' home. I'd like to see what it looks like inside now.

Sokha immigrated to Canada. Since 1980, he has lived in Montreal, where he married and has three children.

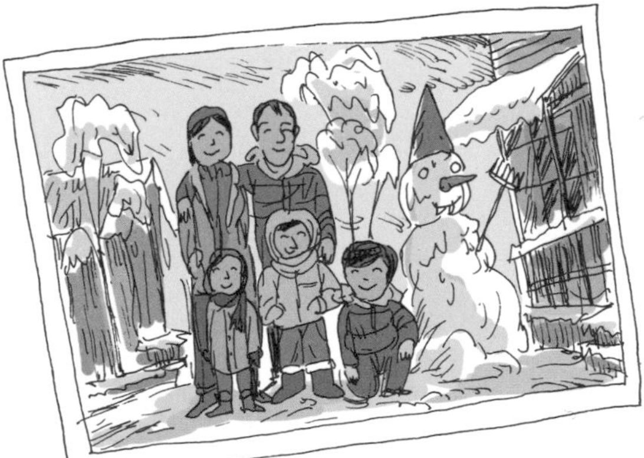

Phara went back to university to become a pharmacist.
She lives in Switzerland with her husband and their daughter.

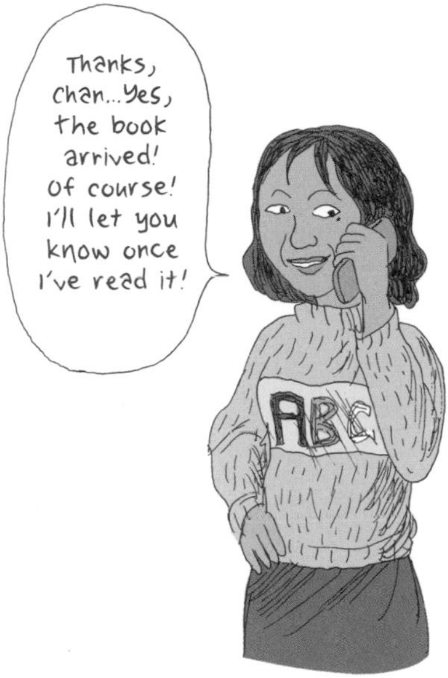
Thanks, Chan... Yes, the book arrived! Of course! I'll let you know once I've read it!
ABC

Chan often tells his son about Cambodia.

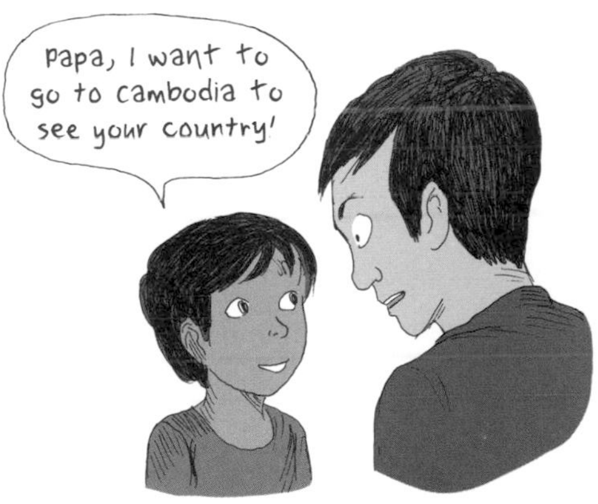
Papa, I want to go to Cambodia to see your country!

Cambodia still bears the scars of three decades of war and violence, from the Lon Nol coup in 1970 through the Khmer Rouge genocide of 1975-79 and the Vietnamese occupation that followed. But the country has opened up since the 1990s, especially to tourism, and has experienced tremendous economic growth.

In 2009, a United Nations-backed tribunal was established to prosecute those accused of mass atrocities. Though the process was complex, costly, and long, senior Khmer Rouge leaders were at last found guilty of crimes against humanity and sentenced to life in prison.

Although inequality is increasing and social injustices remain, Cambodia remains true to its reputation as "the land of smiles."

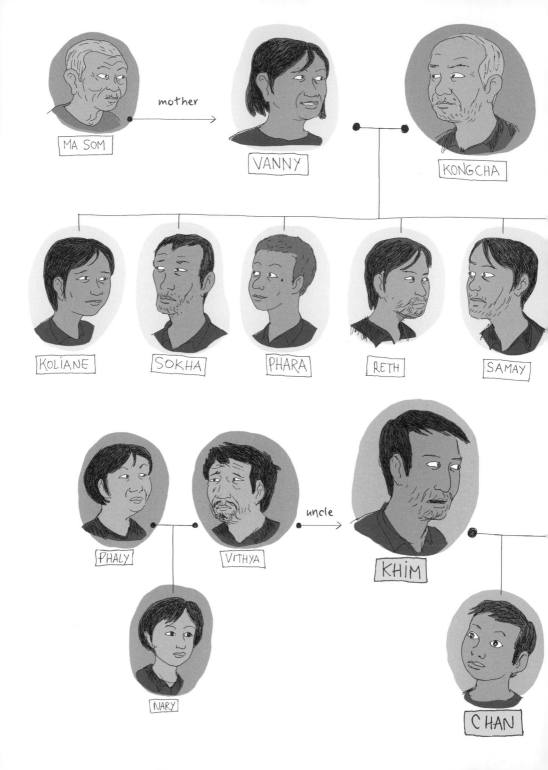

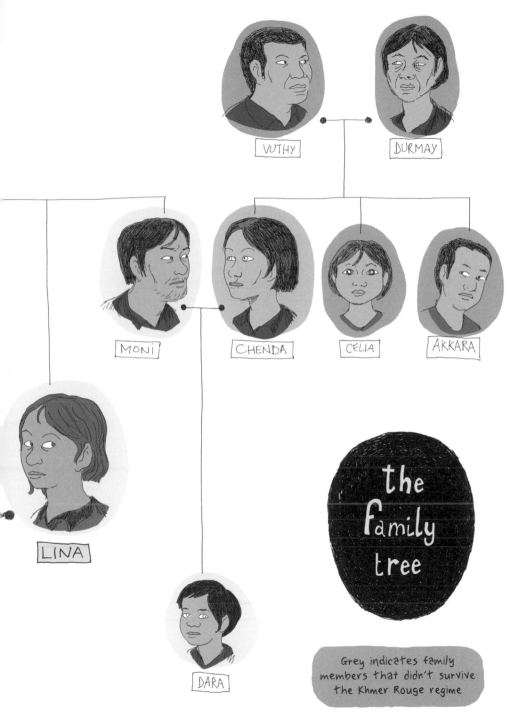

VUTHY

DURMAY

MONI

CHENDA

CELIA

AKKARA

LINA

DARA

the family tree

Grey indicates family members that didn't survive the Khmer Rouge regime

Tian Veasna was born in Cambodia in 1975, three days after the Khmer Rouge came to power. He moved to France with his parents in 1980, where he graduated from Strasbourg's École des Arts Décoratifs in 2001. That year, he also returned to Cambodia for the first time, offering drawing classes as part of a United Nations humanitarian project. Since then Veasna has worked in publishing, taught visual art, and cofounded the workshop and gallery space Le Bocal, which specializes in illustration and graphic art. Veasna's desire to recount what his family lived through in 1975 led him to return to Cambodia frequently and record the memories of his family members. Those stories became *Year of the Rabbit*, his first book. Veasna lives in France.